The
Nuclear
Almanac

NORTH   100 METERS

July 16, 1945: The view from above, 28 hours after
Trinity—the first nuclear explosion on earth, Alamogordo, New Mexico.

The Nuclear Almanac

Confronting the Atom in War and Peace

Compiled and Edited by Faculty Members at the Massachusetts Institute of Technology

Editor Jack Dennis

Contributing Authors

Daryl E. Bohning	Anthony Nero
Henry Steele Commager	Nan Randall
Thérèse Dennis	Alfred Romer
Bernard Feld	Alice Kimball Smith
H. Jack Geiger	Pamela Solo
G. Allen Greb	Gordon Thompson
Mike Jendrzejczyk	Kosta Tsipis
John Lamperti	Paul F. Walker
Kai Lee	Paul C. Warnke
Philip Morrison	Herbert F. York
Alan Nelson	Charles Zimmermann

853211

ADDISON-WESLEY PUBLISHING COMPANY
Reading, Massachusetts • Menlo Park, California
London • Amsterdam • Don Mills, Ontario • Sydney

MEDFORD SENIOR HIGH LIBRARY/MEDIA CENTER
MEDFORD SCHOOL DIST. 549C

Library of Congress Cataloging in Publication Data

Main entry under title:

The Nuclear almanac.

   Includes bibliographical references and index.
   1. Atomic weapons.   2. Atomic warfare.   3. Atomic
energy.   I. Massachusetts Institute of Technology.
UG1282.A8N9 1982   355′.0217   82-20596
ISBN 0-201-05331-4
ISBN 0-201-05332-1 (pbk.)

ISBN 0-201-05332-1 (pbk.)
     0-201-05331-4

ABCDEFGHIJ-DO-8987654

Design by Mike Fender
Drawings by Kenneth J. Wilson

The threat of nuclear war has moved us, the MIT Faculty Coalition for Disarmament, to prepare this *Almanac* for those who wish to find in a single volume a factual account of the discovery, development, and use of nuclear energy, and a critical evaluation of policy issues raised by nuclear armaments and nuclear power. We hope that when this knowledge is readily accessible, public opinion will be better informed and public policy more responsible and wise.

Contents

Boxes, Tables, and Illustrations

Acknowledgments

The Editorial Board wishes to acknowledge with sincere thanks the many minds and hands that worked to put *The Nuclear Almanac* together. Many of the authors helped by reviewing other chapters of the book; in addition, reviews were done by Albert Carnesale, Roger Fisher, Richard Lester, Frank Long, Everett Mendelsohn, George Rathjens, and Jack Ruina. We wish to thank the Union of Concerned Scientists, the Physicians for Social Responsibility, and the NARMIC Project of the American Friends Service Committee for making information available from their libraries and files. Anne Rubin deserves special mention for her many hours of work on correspondence and assistance to the Editorial Board. Others helped individual authors by supplying or locating material and helping in the preparation of their chapters: Mary Lee Benner, Garry D. Brewer, E. William Golglazier, David Goodman, Harold L. James, Daniel Kevin, Marilyn King, Terry R. Lash, Howard Morland, Frederic A. Morris, K. J. Notz, Gorden H. Orians, Rebekah Ray, Gene I. Rochlin, Cyril Smith, Randall F. Smith, Arlene Winer, Gene L. Woodruff.

The
Nuclear
Almanac

The Future Is Ours

Professor Henry Steele Commager has for forty years been counted among the most productive historians of Americans. His essay challenges us to put the common interests and concerns of all peoples ahead of national loyalties in our world of nuclear-armed confrontation.

I

MODERN NATIONALISM and modern science emerged on the stage of history some three centuries ago and still provide the latitude and longitude of the world in which we life. The science ushered in by Francis Bacon, Johannes Kepler, and Isaac Newton, and their affluent successors, opened up a new universe of nature and formulated a philosophy that could comprehend it. It provided, impartially, instruments both for progress and for ruin, made possible the beneficent exploitation of natural resources and their ruthless destruction, and encouraged an increase in global population that seemed to require wars and epidemics to satisfy the Malthusian logic. At the same time it appeared to point the way to the solution of the problems that it created.

Like the new science, nationalism, too, emerged out of the Renaissance and the Refor-

mation; it speedily associated itself with religion and launched a century of religious and imperialist wars. Not until the American and French Revolutions did it assume its modern character. It has to its credit immense practical, political, administrative, and cultural achievements. But for two centuries it has found its most characteristic expression in imperialism, aggrandizement, conquest, and war; in racism and the exploitation of backward peoples by the strong; and in the cultivation of ideologies more often malign than benign.

In the uneasy alliance between modern nationalism and science, it was, increasingly, nationalism that held the upper hand. That had not always been true. The leaders of the Enlightenment almost everywhere in the Western world assumed the priority of the claims of science: thus David Hume, who championed an interna-

Henry Steele Commager

Commager is a distinguished historian at Amherst College.

1

tional, not a national, commerce and "prayed for the commerce of Germany, Spain, Italy, and even France"; thus Joseph Banks, who for forty-one years as president of the Royal Society of London was sponsor and guardian of science and scientists everywhere; thus the polymath Joseph Priestley, who combined science and religion, contributed to history and philosophy, and unhesitatingly placed the claims of science and philosophy ahead of those of his own nationalism. So, too, in France that goodly host of Enlightenment philosophers inspired by Montesquieu; led by Voltaire, Diderot, and d'Alembert; abetted by members of the Church like Raynal and the fantastic Cloots; allying themselves with the new generation of Turgot and Condorcet; formed the most powerful phalanx of *philosophes* in the eighteenth-century world. Thus in Germany, Lessing and Humboldt, Wieland and Ebeling, and above all Goethe thought of themselves as cosmopolites—not as Germans, but as natural philosophers.

What is perhaps most instructive is that the leaders of the first people to "bring forth a new nation," the Americans, were no less loyal to Enlightenment than to national ideas: indeed, of most of them—Benjamin Franklin and Thomas Jefferson, Richard Rush and Joel Barlow, the naturalized Albert Gallatin and the expatriate Benjamin Thompson, Count Rumford—it could be said that they were, in Tom Paine's famous phrase, "citizens of the world."

Clearly, in the eyes of the natural philosophers there was no incompatibility between cosmopolitanism and nationalism. Their philosophy and their vision encompassed both. And what a vision it was! Except in the realm of science there had been nothing like it before, and except in the realm of science there has been nothing as exhilarating since. People's minds were enraptured by the concept of a universe whose manifestations were governed by cosmic laws, laws that controlled alike the wheeling of the stars and the ebb and flow of the tides, the

operations of government, law, arts, letters, and even morals—for did not Immanuel Kant's categorical imperatives have the force of law? Philosophers, and rulers too, were inspired by the conviction that reason and wisdom could somehow come to know those laws and conform to them and thus bring the conduct of people into harmony with the great forces of nature (and, if you will, of nature's God). Such a philosophy admitted no conflict between the claims of the world of morals and of secular affairs.

It was an era when the new United States, speaking through Dr. Franklin, and France, through Jacques Necker, decreed immunity for Captain Cook and his men engaged in the exploration of the Pacific because "they were common friends of mankind." It was an age when Jean Jacques Rousseau could pay tribute to "those great cosmopolitan minds that make light of the barriers assigned to sunder nation from nation, and . . . embrace all mankind within the scope of their benevolence"; and when George III could appoint the American Benjamin West as Royal painter and encourage West to welcome to his atelier a stream of American students whose paintings celebrated American victories over the British. It was a day when Napoleon could, at the request of Joseph Banks of the Royal Society, intervene to free the great scientist Dolomieu from imprisonment in Naples and, a few years later—at the height of the war between France and England—grant immunity from military assault to the city of Göttingen because it was the home of the great classical scholar, Christian Heyne. It was an era when the French Institute could confer, in 1808, its gold medal on Sir Humphry Davy, and a few years later, but while the war still raged, Davy could cross the Channel and accept the medal to the plaudits of all the great scientists of France. "Some people," wrote Sir Humphry, "say I ought not to accept this prize, but if the two countries, or governments, are at war the men of science are not." That note sounded and resounded all through the Enlightenment, even in its Napoleonic twilight. Dr. Edward Jenner, discoverer of the smallpox vaccine, stated most succinctly the philosophy that animated the philosophers: "The scientists," he said, "are never at war. Peace must always preside in those bosoms whose object is the augmentation of human happiness." A century and a half later Albert Einstein made the same point with characteristic conciseness: "Politics are for the moment; an equation is for eternity."

Much of this was the expression of the philosophy of highly gifted individuals; much of it, too, was an institutionalized expression of enlightened governmental policy.

How illuminating the history of the Royal Society of London, founded in 1642 by Charles II, and under the auspices of the most distinguished of natural philosophers, Isaac Newton, and the most distinguished of moral philosophers, John Locke, and embracing in its membership men of arts and letters, as well as men of science. Christopher Wren, who doubled as Savilian Professor of Astronomy at Oxford, and architect of St. Paul's Cathedral, drafted its charter:

> The way to so happy a government [he wrote] we are sensible, is in no manner more facilitated than by the promoting of useful arts which, upon mature inspection, are found to be the basis of civil communities and free government, and which gather multitudes, by an *orpheus charm* into cities, and connect them in companies . . . [The Royal Society, therefore, was to meet weekly] and orderly to confer about the hidden causes of things with a design, by their labors in the disquisition of nature, to prove themselves real benefactors to mankind."

The American Philosophical Society, formally launched in 1769, contained a similar admonition:

> Whereas nations truly civilized will never wage war with the arts and sciences, and the common interests of humanity, the Society should retain

cordial relations with learned societies everywhere in the world, regardless of politics and war.

The same spirit presided (though somewhat anxiously) over the foundation of the Smithsonian Institution in Washington and had inspired James Smithson's original gift of his entire fortune to found "an institution for the increase and diffusion of knowledge among men," and it also inspired John Quincy Adams's long and gallant effort to assure that such an institution would indeed fulfill its benign purpose.

The bequest, Adams's bill made clear, "is for the benefit of mankind. The Government of the United States is merely a trustee to carry out the design of the testator." In his address on the significance of that bequest, Adams observed that "the responsibility of the Nation for the faithful application of the funds is great before the world of mankind in this and in all future ages."

Some of the Enlightenment philosophers had already gone so far as to propose learned academies not merely to advance knowledge but to guide the destinies of nations. This was the essence of Condorcet's plan in *The New Atlantis*. Almost at the end of his life, Condorcet proposed the creation of an international society of natural philosophers, whose members would be devoted not to practical investigations but to pure research, sponsored by the crowned heads and supported by contributions from government, the aristocracy, and the business and commercial community. Condorcet was persuaded that all the scientists would be animated "by a passion for truth" and that enlightened monarchs, conscious of what such a society can contribute to the "happiness of the human species" would follow its recommendations. All this assumed that "a basic union of the scientists in a universal republic of science" would eschew all merely national or religious loyalties and devote its talents only to the progress of mankind.

It was, in short, a prevision of the work of

some of the more effective of the independent agencies of the United Nations.

The philosophy that animated Lessing and Turgot and Condorcet and their followers was the Platonic concept of a republic where philosophers were kings. Certainly in their day the attempt by kings to be philosophers had proved a bitter failure: Frederick the Great, Catherine the Great, the Emperor Joseph, Gustavus III—all put the claims of their thrones ahead of the claims of humanity. Alone in the United States it was the philosophers, natural and moral alike, who were in fact chosen by the people themselves to guide the affairs of the state and society: Dr. Franklin, who was president of Pennsylvania, founder of the University of Pennsylvania, and representative of America to the world of science; Jefferson, who was governor of the Old Dominion, represented the nation abroad, and presided over the national government for twenty-four years—eight as president of the United States and the other sixteen as elder statesman—and who also served as president of the American Philosophical Society, founded the Library of Congress, and created the University of Virginia, which was dedicated to "the illimitable freedom of the human mind." John Adams drafted the constitution of Massachusetts and was president of the United States and president and founder of the American Academy of Arts and Sciences; and Adams's son, John Quincy, another president of the United States, was the true founder of the Smithsonian Institution. All this was in the lifetime of the Revolutionary generation. The principle of the superiority of the claims of science over those of nationalism or politics was as much a part of the American tradition as the principle of the supremacy of the Constitution and the Bill of Rights over mere legislative or executive conduct. This was never more felicitously stated than by the then Governor Jefferson in his letter to David Rittenhouse, written in 1778, in the midst of the war for independence:

Your time for two years past has been principally employed in the civil government of your country. Tho' I have been aware of the authority our cause would acquire with the world from its being known that yourself and Dr. Francklin [sic] were zealous friends to it, and am myself duly impressed with a sense of the arduousness of government and the obligation those are under who are able to conduct it, yet I am also satisfied there is an order of geniuses above that obligation and therefore exempted from it. Nobody can conceive that nature ever intended to throw away a Newton upon the occupations of a crown. It would have been a prodigality for which even the conduct of providence might have been arraigned had he been by birth annexed to what was so far below him. Cooperating with nature in her ordinary economy, we should dispose of and employ the geniuses of men according to their several orders and degrees. I doubt not there are in our country many persons equal to the task of conducting government. You should consider that the world has but one Ryttenhouse [sic], and that it never had one before.

II

With the triumph of nationalism in the nineteenth and twentieth centuries, most of this came to an end. There were gestures toward peace and internationalism: the creation of the Hague Tribunals, the establishment by Alfred Nobel of a prize for peace, the creation by Andrew Carnegie of the Endowment for Peace. The Wilsonian crusade for a League of Nations provided a glimmering of hope, but the failure of the United States to join the league and the exclusion of Russia condemned that organization to futility. There were faint echoes of the Enlightenment concern for the preservation of civilization in World War II: the Luftwaffe spared Oxford and Cambridge; the Allied Air Forces did not bomb Heidelberg or Göttingen (but did destroy the museum city of Dresden); and, thanks to the intercession of Secretary of War Henry L. Stimson, the U.S. Air Force spared the temple city of Kyoto. Even if our current statesmen might be that enlightened, which is doubtful, it is inconceivable that modern nuclear warfare can be that selective.

Yet we can no more blame the idea, or the institution, of nationalism for the threats that glare upon us than we can blame science or technology. Nationalism, like science, is what man makes of it. The nationalism that is now sweeping the world—150 nations, no less, many of them at sword's point; and some with fingers on the atomic button—is of Western making. The architects of the Enlightenment, and of nationalism, sought to reconcile the claims of science and of nationalism by bringing both under the rule of Law and of Reason. In this hope they were frustrated. In the hands of Western man, these two prodigious forces proved almost irreconcilable—which is not surprising. Science is by its nature universal, harmonious, and indivisible; nationalism—particular, parochial, and divisive. Ideally the world of science makes for unity and harmony and for a collective assault on the problems that confront man; nationalism, in response to almost irresistible pressures of economics, race, and religion, as implacable as the laws of Newton, made for rivalry, conflict, and the exacerbation of the problems that threaten man and nature.

For over two centuries, civilization has been plagued by this paradox of its commitment to a science that is by its nature orderly, rational, and impersonal, and a political nationalism that is irrational, disorderly, subjective, and wasteful of intellectual and material resources, in futile strife. In our own time this paradox has spread to every quarter of the globe; it is one of the supreme ironies of history that the revolt of the peoples of Asia and Africa and the Third World generally against the European world has been carried through with those weapons of nationalism, science, and technology which were invented by the West. What is even more ominous is that modern nationalism increasingly

associates itself with ideologies as fanatical as those that rationalized the Inquisition and launched the religious wars of the seventeenth century: witness the Holocaust, the bitter wars that tore India apart, the ceaseless strife in the Middle East, the racial and imperial strife in much of Africa; witness even our own conduct in Vietnam and Cambodia. The genius that, since Newton, has enabled man to penetrate to the secrets of life and of the universe now enables him to realize the apocalyptic vision when the great globe itself shall dissolve and leave not a rack behind.

III

There is, to be sure, another dimension to this whole problem of divided loyalties, and it would be simplistic not to recognize how elusive and immeasurable this dimension is. It is all very well for the scientist to say, with Tom Paine, that "my country is the world and my religion is to do good," but suppose the scientist is confronted with a crisis that he or she believes portends nothing but evil and threatens all humankind? Should scientists have held aloof in 1940 when the fate of civilization was threatened by Nazi barbarism which reached its consummation in the Holocaust? Both Niels Bohr and Einstein were "citizens of the world," ultimately loyal not just to one nation but to science and civilization. Were they right to warn President Roosevelt of the threat of Nazi production of the atomic weapon, or should they have held aloof? Confronted with the moral problem of a Nazi-dominated Europe, scores of the most distinguished German and Italian scientists chose not to cooperate with the Hitler and Mussolini regimes but, like Werner Heisenberg, retired from their laboratories or, like Fermi and Bohr, took refuge in neutral or even in "enemy" countries. History, we may safely conclude, has justified their refusal to embrace the Stephen Decatur maxim (still popular in our own country): "My country, in her intercourse with foreign nations, may she always be right, but my country, right or wrong."

The moral dilemma that confronted the distinguished body of nuclear scientists who were responsible for the Manhattan Project was as intractable as that which had confronted German and Italian scientists. How moving, now, to ponder Robert Oppenheimer's recollection of Bohr's "high hopes that the outcome would be good, and that in this the role of objectivity, friendliness, cooperation incarnate in science, would play a helpful part." All this, Oppenheimer added, "was something we wished very much to believe."

Like Condorcet, although without his naiveté, many of the nuclear scientists hoped, if not to occupy the seats of power, at least to reach the seats of power with counsel and guidance. Bohr did reach Winston Churchill, who rejected without a moment's hesitation Bohr's misgivings about the use of the atomic weapon and, what is more, asked President Roosevelt to have him watched! Leo Szilard was unable to reach President Truman or even Secretary Stimson but was fobbed off to Secretary Byrnes who had no more grasp of science than he had of statesmanship. In vain the leading scientists of the Manhattan Project and Los Alamos counseled caution, prudence, humanity; in vain they urged a peaceful demonstration of the awesome power of the bomb before it was used against any cities; in vain they urged delay on a second bomb. A month before Hiroshima, Szilard and fifty-six associates on the Manhattan Project sent a letter to President Truman protesting, on moral grounds, dropping an atomic bomb on Japanese cities. General Leslie R. Groves saw to it that it never reached the President. Even as the Japanese cabinet was discussing terms of surrender, the Air Force was instructed to destroy Nagasaki.

Nor were Szilard and Fermi any more successful in their recommendations for an international committee of atomic scientists to advise on the future of nuclear weapons—just such a committee as Condorcet had proposed. As Alice Smith tells us,

> Hundreds of (scientists), once the war ended, espoused the cause of international control to prevent further destructive application of atomic energy. No such collective recognition of responsibility was apparent among the statesmen, administrators, military personnel, engineers, industrialists, and construction workers.

President Truman's precipitate decisions to drop two atomic bombs on Japan and then to push ahead with the hydrogen bomb program may have been the most fateful in history, for their consequences—unlike those of earlier fateful decisions—are quite literally global in embrace and may prove ultimate.

But it was not just the decision of President Truman, supported by Churchill, to use the ultimate weapon that was reckless. The responsibility was far more widely diffused, far more irresponsibly shared. An international agreement, concluded when the United States held all the trump cards, might still have prevented the nuclear race; so, too, a show of modesty rather than arrogance: Szilard warned that the Soviet Union would have the bomb within five years, but the military mind was certain that God or history would grant the United States a monopoly for at least fifteen years! The responsibility for our ever-growing obsession with the cold war and the nuclear race must rest on the whole political and military leadership in the United States and Russia—in both countries, a leadership that speedily became the prisoner of its own illusions and delusions, and still is. Once the two great superpowers committed themselves irretrievably to the cold war, the emergence of the military-industrial-financial-commercial-labor-communications-religious-scientific-university complex became inevitable. Like some irresistible magnet, that cold war brought together all the most powerful economic and political interests in both the super-powers, and substantial segments of the scientific and intellectual communities as well. What is more, in both nations it endowed this alliance with moral sanctions. No wonder that, without a countervailing moral force, it proved irresistible.

In all this we see once again what George Meredith saw so clearly:

No villains need be.
Passions spin the plot. We are betrayed
By what is false within.

That can fairly be said for those responsible for the bomb. It cannot be said of those responsible for the thirty-year cold war.

Henry Steele Commager
Amherst, Massachusetts
August 1981

Minutes to Midnight

CONSCIENCE OF THE INTERNATIONAL SCIENTIFIC COMMUNITY

The "doomsday clock" appears monthly on the cover of the *Bulletin of the Atomic Scientists*. The clock is a symbolic warning of the lateness of the hour as humankind confronts (or fails to confront) the urgent problems of our times. The minute hand, never far from midnight, has moved ten times since the founding of the magazine at the end of World War II.

1947
7 MINUTES TO MIDNIGHT

The clock makes its first appearance on the *Bulletin* cover as a symbol of nuclear doomsday hovering over humankind.

1963
12 MINUTES TO MIDNIGHT

Signing of the Partial Test Ban Treaty, halting nuclear tests in the atmosphere, further eases international tensions.

1949
3 MINUTES TO MIDNIGHT

The Soviet Union explodes its first atomic bomb, intensifying the nuclear arms race.

1968
7 MINUTES TO MIDNIGHT

The nuclear weapons club now stands at five, with France, China, Britain, the U.S., and U.S.S.R.

1953
2 MINUTES TO MIDNIGHT

Development of the hydrogen bomb by the United States and the Soviet Union adds a new dimension to the nuclear threat.

1969
10 MINUTES TO MIDNIGHT

Ratification of the Nuclear Non-Proliferation Treaty begins hope that the atomic arms may be contained.

1972
12 MINUTES TO MIDNIGHT

Strategic Arms Limitation Talks (SALT) lead to first nuclear arms control agreement between U.S. and U.S.S.R.

1980
7 MINUTES TO MIDNIGHT

The danger of nuclear war increases; irrationality of national and international actions.

1974
9 MINUTES TO MIDNIGHT

SALT fails to make progress; the arms race intensifies; India joins the nuclear weapons club; the nuclear safety problem grows.

1981
4 MINUTES TO MIDNIGHT

Nuclear war officially declared "thinkable." U.S. and U.S.S.R. deploy nuclear war-fighting weapons.

Monticello—Jefferson's home—atop a hill overlooking the city of Charlottesville.

Charlottesville:
A Fictional Account

There is no experience of large-scale nuclear war. In this evocative piece, adapted from a research report prepared for the Office of Technology Assessment of the United States Congress, a novelist pictures what might happen. Her theme is not the awful scenes of physical damage, but the effects on an old and beautiful city which is fortunate enough to escape all the warheads. Yet their destructive power echoes loudly, and daily life is transformed and perilous even in that haven.

MOST DID NOT SEE the attacks on Richmond and on Washington as they huddled in their shelters. But the sky to the east and north of Charlottesville glowed brilliant in the noonday sun. At first no one knew how extensive the damage was.

Communication nationwide was interrupted as the Earth's atmosphere shivered with the assault of explosions. Each town, city, village, or farm was an island, forced to suffer its selected fate of death or salvation alone. (Some time later it was learned that more than 4,000 megatons had destroyed military and industrial targets, killing close to 100 million people in the United States. The U.S. counterattack on the Soviet Union had had a similar, devastating effect. Destruction ranged from the large industrial centers on the coasts and Great Lakes to small farming communities that had the misfortune to be close to the great missile silos and military bases.)

Areas of the country such as the northeast corridor were reduced to a swath of burning rubble from north of Boston to south of Norfolk. Still, there were some sections of the nation that were spared the direct effects of blast and fire. Inland in Virginia, only the town of Radford, west of Roanoke, received a direct hit. The farming and orchard land of the rural counties were not targets.

Charlottesville, the small but elegant center of learning, culture, and trade in central Virginia, was not hit either. This monument to the mind and manner of Jefferson retained its status as a kind of genteel sanctuary, momentarily immune to the disaster that had leveled the cities of the nation.

Two and one-half hours after the warnings had sounded, the nuclear engineering staff from the University of Virginia picked up the first fallout. Starting at a moderate level of about 40 rems an hour—a cumulative dose of 450 rems received in a one-week period would be fatal to one-half of those exposed—the intensity rose to 50 rems before starting the decline to a level of about four-tenths of a rem per hour after two

Nan Randall

Randall is a novelist and has worked as a consultant to the Office of Technology Assessment, U.S. Congress.

weeks. (The total dose in the first four days was 2,000 rems, which killed those who refused to believe shelter was necessary and increased the risk of eventually dying of cancer for those who were properly sheltered.) For the immediate period, it was essential to stay as protected as possible.

For several days, Charlottesville remained immobile, suspended in time. It was unclear just what had happened or would happen. The President had been able to deliver a message of encouragement, which was carried by those emergency radio stations that could broadcast. As the atmosphere had cleared, radio station WCHV was able to transmit sporadically on its backup transmitter and emergency generator in the basement. However, the message from the President posed more questions than it answered— the damage assessment was incomplete. Nevertheless, he said that there was a tentative cease fire.

In the first days of sheltering, only those with some particular expertise had much to do. Nuclear engineers and technicians from the university were able to monitor radiation in the shelters they occupied, and CB radios broadcast results to other shelters. The doctors were busy attempting to treat physical and psychological ailments—the symptoms of radiation sickness, flu, and acute anxiety being unnervingly similar—while the police and government officials attempted to keep order. The rest waited.

Not all of the shelters had enough food and other necessities. Most shelters had no toilets. The use of trash cans for human waste was an imperfect system, and several days into the shelter period the atmosphere was often oppressive. Because many suffered from diarrhea—the result either of anxiety, flu, or radiation sickness— the absence of toilet facilities was especially trying.

Shelter life was bearable in the beginning. Communications by CB radio allowed some shelters to communicate with one another, to locate missing family members and friends. A genuine altruism or community spirit of cooperation was present in almost all the shelters— though some of them were fairly primitive. Even those refugees who were crowded into halls and basements with the local residents were welcomed. Parents watched out for one another's children or shared scarce baby food. Most people willingly accepted direction from whomever took charge. Among the majority of the shelter residents, the out-of-town refugees being an exception, there was a sense of relief, a sense that they had been among the lucky ones of this world. They had survived.

THREE DAYS AFTER the attacks, a large influx of refugees poured into Charlottesville, many of them suffering with the early symptoms of radiation sickness. They had been caught poorly sheltered or too close to the nuclear targets. A few showed the effects of blast and fire, bringing home to Charlottesville tangible evidence of the war's destruction. Some refugees had driven, while others had hitchhiked or even walked to reach what they hoped was safety and medical help. On the way, many were forced to abandon those who were too weak to continue.

The hospitals were completely overwhelmed. Up to now, the hospitals had managed to treat the ill with some modicum of order. The hospitals themselves were fallout shelters of a kind; patients' beds had been moved to interior corridors for fallout protection; emergency surgery was feasible with the emergency generators; hospital staff slept in the most protected areas. Some borderline cases in intensive care were released to nature's devices while any elective medical procedures were eliminated. Still, hospitals were able to cope, even with the increasing number of common ailments caused by the shelter crowding.

Suddenly, this changed. Fallout levels were too high for anyone to be out in the open for any length of time, but the people came anyway. The carefully laid plans of the University of Virginia Emergency Room, devised for the pos-

Jefferson designed the University of Virginia with the vision of promoting a world unity transcending national boundaries.

sibility of peacetime accidents, were hurriedly modified. No longer was the careful showering and decontaminating of victims possible with the single shower and uncertain water pressure. Instead, patients were stripped of their clothes and issued hospital gowns. With no time for studied decision, doctors segregated the very sick from the moderately sick—the latter to be treated, the former given medication and allowed to die.

Nevertheless, the day came when the hospitals were full. The University Hospital, Martha Jefferson Hospital, the Blue Ridge Sanatorium, and the others were forced to lock their doors to protect those patients they had already accepted.

After being turned away, the sick had no specific destination. Many still clustered around the middle of town near the two major hospitals, taking up residence in the houses abandoned by local residents several days before. With minimal protection from fallout and no medical treatment for other trauma, many died, their bodies left unburied for several weeks.

The combined populations of Charlottesville and Albemarle County rose to 150,000 in the seven days after the nuclear attack. Slowly, hostility and resentment wedged a gap between residents and refugees who attempted to join the group shelters. The refugees, still in a daze from their experience, believed that they had priority rights after all they had suffered. The local residents viewed the outsiders as a threat to their own survival, particularly as the extent of the war damage was becoming evident.

For the first week or so after the nuclear attacks, authorities had few options. Simple survival was the priority, the elements of which included food and water distribution, fallout protection, and retention of some civil order. Government was ad hoc, with the leadership of the city and county naturally cooperating along with the different police forces. City and county authorities were becoming painfully aware that they were not set up to "go it alone" without any outside help. Even were the weather suitable for planting, Charlottesville was no longer an agricultural center. There wasn't enough energy to process any food that might be grown. Where would people get clothes and building materials and medicines and spare parts for the cars and buses? The very complexity of American society—its technological marvels and high standard of living—could well prove to be a barrier to the reconstruction of any one part.

The radioactivity level continued to drop, and it was "safe" to go outdoors. However, the resulting doses, though too low to cause immediate illness or death, posed a long-term health hazard. The authorities, recognizing that everybody would receive many times the prewar "safe dose," tried to reduce the hazards by urging people to stay inside as much as possible when not picking up food rations at the distribution centers.

THREE WEEKS AFTER the nuclear attack, almost all the Charlottesville and Albemarle County residents had returned to their homes. Those few whose homes had been occupied by squatters or destroyed by fire easily found some alternate housing with the government's help.

This left the refugees. Though the drop in fallout intensity allowed the refugees to move out of basements and interior halls, they still were forced to live a version of camp life. They spent their endless, empty hours waiting in lines for food, for a chance to use the bathrooms—which at least functioned now—or for a chance to talk to authorities. Information from the outside was still sketchy, and for the refugees, this uncertainty added to their already high level of anxiety.

The city manager and the emergency government attempted to solve the refugee housing problem by billeting refugees in private homes. At first they asked for volunteers but got few. The authorities then announced that any house with fewer than two people per room would be assigned a refugee family. Resistance to this order was strong, and, particularly in the outlying areas where it was hard to check, outright defiance was common. Families would pretend to comply and then simply force the refugees out as soon as the authorities had left. The refugees would struggle back to town or take up residence in barns or garages.

By now, the emergency government recognized that the need for food was going to be acute. Without power for refrigeration, much food had spoiled; stocks of nonperishable foods were mostly exhausted. As the shortages became clear, the price of food skyrocketed. Many people refused money for food, preferring to barter. Food and fuel were the most valuable

commodities, with shoes and coats high on the list as well.

For some time, the relatively few surviving farm animals had been gradually and mysteriously disappearing. The farmers concluded that "those damned city folks" were stealing them for food, although some of the local residents were also making midnight forays on the livestock. Farmers themselves slaughtered animals they had planned to fatten for the future. They couldn't spare the feed grain, and they needed food now.

ALTHOUGH THE CITY government had relatively frequent contact, mostly by radio, with the federal and state governments, the citizens had to rely on the occasional presidential message that was broadcast on WCHV. Three weeks after the attacks, the President made a major address to reassure the people. He announced that the cease-fire was still holding. Describing the damage that the country had suffered, the President noted that, even with the loss of over 100 million lives, "We still have reserves, both material and spiritual, unlike any nation on earth." He asked for patience and for prayers.

Charlottesville was still on its own. Residents hunted game as the last of the food stocks disappeared, but the fallout had killed most animals that were in the open. A number of people managed to fill their gas tanks with contraband gasoline and set out to forage in the mountains to the west.

Three and one-half weeks after the attack, an old propeller-driven cargo plane landed at the Charlottesville Airport with a supply of flour, powdered milk, and vegetable oil. The emergency airlift was supposed to supply Charlottesville with food for a week or two. However, the officials who had calculated the allotment had overlooked the refugees. Charlottesville's population was some three times the normal. (No one was absolutely sure because the refugees moved around from camp to camp.)

The first deaths from radiation had occurred

ten days after the attacks, and the number grew steadily. By now, it was not uncommon to see mass funerals several times a day. The terminally ill were not cared for by the hospitals—there were too many, and there was nothing that could be done for them anyway—so it was up to their families to do what they could. Fortunately there were still ample supplies of morphine, and it was rumored that college students had donated marijuana. The city set aside several locations on the outskirts of town for mass graves.

In addition to those with terminal radiation sickness, there were those with nonfatal cases and those who showed some symptoms. Often it was impossible for doctors to quickly identify those with flu or psychosomatic radiation symptoms. The number of patients crowding the emergency rooms did not slacken off. The refugees, crowded together, passed a variety of common disorders, from colds to diarrhea, back and forth. Several public health experts worried that an outbreak of measles or even polio could come in the late spring. "So far, we have been lucky not to have a major epidemic of typhus or cholera," a doctor observed to his colleagues.

The supply of drugs on hand at the hospitals was dwindling fast. Although penicillin could be manufactured fairly easily in the laboratories at the university, many other drugs were not so simple to make, even with talent and ingenuity. (The penicillin had to be administered with large veterinary hypodermics, as the homemade mix was too coarse for the small disposable hypos that most doctors stocked. There was a considerable shortage of needles.) Other medications were in such short supply that many patients with chronic illnesses such as heart disease, kidney and respiratory problems, hypertension, and diabetes died within a few weeks.

FOOD RIOTS broke out four and one-half weeks after the attacks—precipitated by the first large shipment of grain. Three large tractor-trailers had pulled into the parking lot of the Citizens Commonwealth Building quite unexpectedly, the word of their arrival somehow misplaced between the Agriculture Department dispatchers and the local authorities. The trucks were greeted with cheers until the residents of Charlottesville discovered that they had been shipped raw grain rather than flour. The drivers were taken by surprise when empty cans and bottles showered them, and one driver jumped in his cab and departed. (The official explanation, delivered some time later, was that processed food was going to those areas where the bulk of the population was sick or injured. It was also assumed that Charlottesville had some livestock reserves.)

With only a fraction of the population knowing what to do with raw grain, a number of angry citizens broke open the sacks and scattered wheat through the parking lot. They in turn were set upon by those who wanted to conserve as much as possible. The local public safety forces waded into the melee with night sticks and tear gas.

Everyone blamed everyone else for the incident, but the fragile glue that had held public order together began to unstick.

From this time on, it was almost impossible for the local authorities, not to mention the state and federal governments, to convince everyone they were getting a fair share. People in one section of town would watch suspiciously as delivery trucks passed them by and headed somewhere else. The poor and rich distrusted each other, and everyone distrusted the refugees as "outsiders."

One day, quite without warning, the city manager was informed that one-half of his fuel stores were to be confiscated by the federal government for the military and for the reconstruction effort. After it was clear that there was no way to stop the government from taking the fuel, the city manager suggested that unmarked tank trucks, well guarded, pick up the stocks at night. He was aware of the effect this action would have on the morale of the population.

Transportation was already difficult for the elderly and those who lived in the rural areas. A sporadic bus service ran from one end of town to the other once a day, and an occasional school bus made a sortie out into the suburbs. Bicycles were prized and sometimes fought over. With even less fuel, the bus service would be cut in half.

By now, barter was clearly established as the preferred means of trade. For a time, the government had paid for commandeered foodstuff and resources with checks and promissory notes, but no one wanted them any more. The local banks had opened for a few days, only to find all their savers lined up to withdraw everything. They closed down. Stores either never opened or shut down quickly when they were overrun. (Many stores had been looted in the second week after the attack, when the fallout intensity had dropped.) A few people hoarded money, but most thought money worthless.

Serpentine walls grace the gardens of the university.

Workers in the small industries in the Charlottesville area saw no point in turning up for work if all they could get was paper money. They preferred to spend the time hunting for food and fuel. If barter was a highly inefficient way to do business—it's hard to make change for a side of beef—still, it was preferable to using worthless currency.

SPRING CHANGED a lot of things. A new optimism surfaced as everyone looked forward to planting, to good weather and warmth. At the university, agronomists studied the best crops to plant in the Charlottesville area. No one was certain what effect the nuclear explosions had had on the ozone layer. If indeed the ozone was severely damaged, more ultraviolet rays could reach the crops and perhaps burn them. This effect would be more pronounced on delicate crops such as peas and beans. Instead it was suggested that people be encouraged to plant potatoes and soybeans, and whatever limited fertilizer became available would go to farmers who followed the government guidelines.

Many people were unable to return to their former jobs. In many cases, their employers never reopened for business, their goods and services being irrelevant in the postattack society. For some, it was relatively easy to adapt. Electronics experts set up CB and shortwave radio repair shops. Cottage industries—sandal and clothing manufacturing from recycled materials, soap and candle making—sprang up in many homes. Some workers were able to acquire new, relevant skills quickly. Others had to make do with menial jobs—burying the dead, cleaning the streets, assisting carpenters and bricklayers—that required little skill.

WINTER WAS HARDER than anyone had expected. There were few additional deaths that could be directly attributed to the nuclear blast effects or the radiation; however, a large percentage of the surviving population was weakened. Lack of medicines, lack of adequate food and reasonable shelter, plus the lingering physical and psychological effects, meant that many were unable to work effectively, even if work was available. An epidemic of flu raged through the cities of the east where refugees were huddled in camps. Many died, especially children and old people. Although vaccine for this particular, common strain of flu had been developed, the stocks had been destroyed in the attacks.

In the northern sections of the country, food supplies were inadequate and poorly distributed. The average diet—day in, day out—consisted of unleavened bread and potatoes, where there was enough of these. As animal herds, both domestic and wild, had been decimated by fallout and indiscriminate hunting, the only available meat came from dogs, cats, and rats—those animals whose living habits protected them from fallout. Dietary deficiency diseases appeared.

Growing children were the first to notice the lack of replacement clothes—particularly leather shoes. Coats and blankets were highly prized in the cold climates.

A YEAR AFTER the nuclear attack, the people were growing hostile to the imposition of strict governmental controls over their lives—what they could or could not buy, or eat, where they could travel, and so on. In certain rural sections, such as Nelson County, south of Charlottesville, farmers had barricaded themselves off, ignored government orders, and occasionally, it was rumored, took potshots at government agents.

Attempts to conscript the able-bodied to rebuild the damaged areas often failed miserably. Many simply walked off the job and returned to their families. Since there were no adequate records remaining of the prewar population, and no records at all of war deaths, the government found it impossible to track down offenders. (Criminals in medium-security and light-security detention facilities had simply evaporated into the population.)

Medical problems were still acute. Drug supplies were almost exhausted, but the weakened population remained more susceptible to disease. The birthrate had fallen drastically nine months after the attacks, partly because of the radiation which produced temporary sterilization—but there had also been a rise in miscarriages, stillbirths, and abnormalities. Infant mortality soared. Experts worried that an unprecedented increase in cancer, particularly in children, could be expected in several years. And there was still the possibility of some devastating epidemic such as cholera running unchecked through the population. The Blue Ridge Sanatorium in Charlottesville, which had seen few tuberculosis patients in the last years before the attacks, was making plans to convert back to specializing in the disease. TB was making a comeback.

The nation's economy was in shambles. The bulk of the oil-refining capacity had been knocked out, and only a few facilities were functioning again. The small oil wells around the country that were situated away from target areas produced more oil than the refineries could handle—and it was only a fraction of the need. Coal mining, mostly by the time-honored pick-and-shovel method (as strip mining required heavy equipment), was the only industry that could be called booming. (There was a major migration to the mining areas by the unemployed.) Agriculture, of course, was a major undertaking for much of the population. However, yields from the farms were considerably below what had been hoped for. The lack of pesticides and fertilizer cut heavily into crop productivity and there was concern about a major insect invasion next summer.

Part One

The Story of Nuclear Weapons

Trinity test base camp. Ten miles from the desert tower where the first atomic explosion was set off, this was the headquarters and living area of the team that made the test.

1. Manhattan Proj
The Atomic Bomb

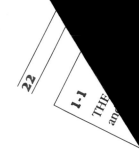

Alice Kimball Smith lived at Los Alamos during the war and served as assistant editor of the Bulletin of the Atomic Scientists *from 1946 to 1948. A professional historian, she is recognized as a leading chronicler of scientists' efforts to counter the threat to world peace posed by nuclear weapons.*

This chapter outlines the course of bomb development in the United States and describes how certain scientists tried to help political leaders to understand the revolutionary impact that the release of atomic energy would have upon international relations, and to decide within that context whether atomic bombs should be used against Japan.

I—BUILDING THE BOMB

THE NUCLEAR FISSION of uranium was discovered late in 1938 in the Berlin laboratories of Otto Hahn and Fritz Strassmann. The theoretical interpretation of fission was soon formulated by physicists Lise Meitner and Otto Frisch, and the news was brought to the United States by Niels Bohr on January 16, 1939. Ten days later Bohr and Enrico Fermi, a recent arrival from Rome via Nobel Prize ceremonies in Stockholm, talked about this epoch-making development at the Fifth Washington Conference on Theoretical Physics. Word quickly spread to laboratories across the country, giving fresh impetus to ongoing experiments in physics and chemistry and opening new avenues of theoretical speculation. Papers relating to fission soon appeared in a dozen countries. At Columbia University in New York City, Fermi and Leo Szilard measured the release and absorption of neutrons in uranium and made a preliminary report of results in July. In September, Bohr and John A. Wheeler at Princeton University published what has been described as the classic analysis of the fission phenomenon.

In France, Frederic Joliot-Curie and his associates confirmed experimentally the Meitner-Frisch interpretation of fission and then tried to produce a chain reaction in natural uranium using a water moderator. At the University of Birmingham, England, Rudolf Peierls was determining the critical mass of fissile material needed for a chain reaction. The work of French and British scientists would play an important role in atomic bomb development.

Given the challenge and excitement inherent in the discovery of fission, it is probable that scientists would have worked with equal intensity had there been no threat or actuality of war in 1939. At various times, and with varying degrees of apprehension, individuals admitted that fuller understanding of nuclear reactions could lead to a weapon of unprecedented power. Ger-

Alice Kimball Smith

Smith is a historian of the scientists' entry into the atomic age.

THE EINSTEIN LETTER

FOLLOWING PASSAGE from "Brighter than a Thousand Suns" by Robert Jungk tells of Alexander Sachs's meeting with President Franklin D. Roosevelt. Dr. Sachs began:

"All I want to do is to tell you a story. During the Napoleonic wars a young American inventor came to the French Emperor and offered to build a fleet of steamships with the help of which Napoleon could, in spite of the uncertain weather, land in England. Ships without sails? This seemed to the great Corsican so impossible that he sent Fulton away. In the opinion of the English historian Lord Acton, this is an example of how England was saved by the shortsightedness of an adversary. Had Napoleon shown more imagination and humility at that time, the history of the nineteenth century would have taken a very different course."

After Sachs finished speaking, the President remained silent for several minutes. Then he wrote something on a scrap of paper and handed it to the servant who had been waiting at table. The latter soon returned with a parcel which, at Roosevelt's order, he began slowly to unwrap. It contained a bottle of old French brandy of Napoleon's time, which the Roosevelt family had possessed for many years. The President, still maintaining a significant silence, told the man to fill two glasses. Then he raised his own, nodded to Sachs and drank to him.

Next he remarked: "Alex, what you are after is to see that the Nazis don't blow us up?"

"Precisely."

It was only then that Roosevelt called in his attache, General "Pa" Watson, and addressed him—pointing to the documents Sachs had brought—in words which have since become famous:

"Pa, this requires action!"

> Albert Einstein
> Old Grove Rd.
> Nassau Point
> Peconic, Long Island
> August 2nd, 1939

F. D. Roosevelt
President of the United States
White House
Washington, D.C.

Sir:

Some recent work by E. Fermi and L. Szilard, which has been communicated to me in manuscript, leads me to expect that the element uranium may be turned into a new and important source of energy in the immediate future. Certain aspects of the situation which has arisen seem to call for watchfulness and, if necessary, quick action on the part of the Administration. I believe therefore that it is my duty to bring to your attention the following facts and recommendations:

In the course of the last four months it has been made probable—through the work of Joliot in France as well as Fermi and Szilard in America—that it may become possible to set up a nuclear chain reaction in a large mass of uranium by which vast amounts of power and large quantities of new radium-like elements would be generated. Now it appears almost certain that this could be achieved in the immediate future.

This new phenomenon would also lead to the construction of bombs, and it is conceivable—

though much less certain—that extremely powerful bombs of a new type may thus be constructed. A single bomb of this type, carried by boat and exploded in a port, might very well destroy the whole port together with some of the surrounding territory. However, such bombs might very well prove to be too heavy for transportation by air.

The United States has only very poor ores of uranium in moderate quantities. There is some good ore in Canada and the former Czechoslovakia, while the most important source of uranium is the Belgian Congo.

In view of this situation you may think it desirable to have some permanent contact maintained between the Administration and the group of physicists working on chain reactions in America. One possible way of achieving this might be for you to entrust with this task a person who has your confidence and who could perhaps serve in an inofficial capacity. His task might comprise the following:

a) to approach Government Departments, keep them informed of the further development, and put forward recommendations for Government action, giving particular attention to the problem of securing a supply of uranium ore for the United States,

b) to speed up the experimental work, which is at present being carried on within the limits of the budgets of University laboratories, by providing funds, if such funds be required, through his contacts with private persons who are willing to make contributions for this cause, and perhaps also by obtaining the co-operation of industrial laboratories which have the necessary equipment.

I understand that Germany has actually stopped the sale of uranium from the Czechoslovakian mines which she has taken over. That she should have taken such early action might perhaps be understood on the ground that the son of the German Under-Secretary of State, von Weizsäcker, is attached to the Kaiser-Wilhelm-Institut in Berlin where some of the American work on uranium is now being repeated.

Yours very truly,

A. Einstein

man scientists shared the theoretical knowledge, and German industry commanded the requisite technology to develop such a weapon. Evidence, inconclusive but alarming, indicated that this effort was under way.

The fragments of information had the most immediate and powerful effect upon refugee scientists from countries controlled or threatened by Hitler. On March 16, 1939, at the urging of Szilard and Eugene Wigner of Princeton, Fermi told army and navy officials in Washington about the Columbia experiments, explaining that a chain reaction in uranium might have military application. The response was polite but noncommittal. Szilard was sure that Fermi had understated the likelihood of chain reaction.

"We both wanted to be conservative," Szilard recalled, "but Fermi thought that the conservative thing was to play down the possibility that this may happen, and I thought the conservative thing was to assume that it would happen and take all necessary precautions."[1] A chain reaction was no less possible in Berlin than in New York.

A Bomb by Committee

Several other abortive efforts to interest government officials convinced Szilard that he must get the message directly to the president. Intermediaries would be needed. Szilard and Wigner persuaded Albert Einstein to sign a letter requesting action on an urgent matter which the president's friend, economist Alexander Sachs, would discuss with him, and Szilard prepared a memorandum on the applications of nuclear research and the threat of a German bomb. The Sachs interview was delayed by the outbreak of war in Europe, but after talking with Sachs on October 11, President Franklin D. Roosevelt immediately authorized the National Academy of Sciences to appoint an Advisory Committee on Uranium to coordinate fission research and decide whether atomic bombs could be developed for use in the current war.

Chaired by Lyman J. Briggs, director of the National Bureau of Standards, the Committee on Uranium met promptly, but implementation of its mandate was slow. The minimal progress achieved in the next year and a half is usually attributed to Briggs's conservatism and to bureaucratic suspicion of foreign scientists who were indeed excluded for a time in 1940 from participation in the committee's work. But British historian Margaret Gowing has noted that scientists in America at this period still thought of their research in terms of pure science and did not press the government for the financial commitment needed for a quick answer to the feasibility of a bomb. It should also be remembered that scientists approaching middle age in 1940 belonged to a generation disillusioned by the aftermath of World War I. They did not readily accept war as the way to settle international tensions or easily think of themselves as weaponeers.

As fighting in Europe intensified in the spring of 1940, mobilization of American science picked up momentum; Vannevar Bush, director of the Carnegie Institution of Washington, became head of a new National Defense Research Committee (NDRC), and under its auspices he reorganized the Committee on Uranium. Progress was made on several fronts, but it was not yet clear whether the objective should be an explosive bomb, a radiation bomb, or power for submarines; nor was there agreement on the best method of separating from natural uranium

its isotope 235, which was recognized as the material most readily fissionable with slow neutrons.

British scientists were confronting the same problems though with a greater sense of urgency and also of frustration. Mobilization for defense precluded a major atomic project in Britain, and while all agreed in the wisdom of placing the project in the United States, British scientists were dismayed to find themselves without access to American research results. The issue was not fully resolved until the autumn of 1943, when several dozen British workers were assigned to appropriate parts of the Manhattan Project; but in April 1941, through a cautious exchange of reports, the American Committee on Uranium learned that Peierls and Frisch had completed theoretical calculations showing that relatively pure uranium-235 could be used to construct a bomb small enough to be delivered by airplane. This news further stimulated studies of separation processes. At Columbia, Fermi and Szilard continued working toward a chain reaction using natural uranium in a graphite pile. Others were experimenting with heavy water and beryllium as moderators to slow neutrons and increase the probability of their capture. Meanwhile, Glenn T. Seaborg and his team at the University of California at Berkeley demonstrated that the newly discovered element 94, named plutonium, was also subject to fission with slow neutrons—more readily than U-235. The idea began to take hold that plutonium might be produced in a chain-reacting pile starting with natural uranium.

The Advisory Committee on Uranium seemed unable to decide which route to follow. Bush was finding that the NDRC did not have authority to coordinate its research with that of other agencies or to compete for funds and scarce materials. Influential scientists were increasingly impatient with the uranium committee. Among the critics were three Nobel laureates: Harold C. Urey, working on separation by centrifuge at Columbia; Ernest O. Lawrence, who was using the Berkeley cyclotron magnet in attempts to separate U-235 by the electromagnetic process; and Arthur H. Compton, University of Chicago physicist and, after April 1941, chairman of a National Academy of Sciences uranium review committee. Bush did not always take kindly to criticism, but in this case it spurred him to obtain Roosevelt's authorization to superimpose on the NDRC a more powerful Office of Scientific Research and Development (OSRD), with himself as director, to coordinate all war-related research. Harvard University president James B. Conant replaced Bush as chairman of NDRC and also became his deputy at OSRD. Urey, Lawrence, and Compton were leaders of a reorganized uranium committee, the S-1 Section of OSRD.

The First Chain Reaction

During the early months of 1942 the S-1 Section wrestled with interrelated problems rendered more pressing by America's entry into the war: the direction and progress of German atomic research; whether the United States, however great the investment of money, personnel, and materials, could achieve a bomb in time to affect the outcome of the war; and which of the yet unproven methods of obtaining fissionable materials would produce the largest amounts in the shortest time. New research results constantly changed the specifications. In December 1941 the S-1 Section executive committee had made Compton responsible for theoretical studies and experimental work relating to plutonium and bomb design. Compton promptly organized the Metallurgical Laboratory, or Met Lab, at the University of Chicago and began bringing individuals and entire projects from Princeton, Illinois, and eventually Berkeley.

Between March and June 1942, the staff grew from 45 to 1,250. It was further augmented with the transfer from Columbia of Fermi, Szilard, and their associates, who worked on the design of the uranium-graphite pile to be erected in the autumn under the stands of Chicago's Stagg Field. Aware of the radiation hazards associated with much of this work, Compton set up a health division at the Met Lab in July 1942. The biophysicists, physicians, and biologists who did research at Chicago and later at other project sites became pioneers in a crucially important new field. Among numerous significant advances that took place in Compton's expanding domain during 1942 was the conclusion reached by theorists that fission would occur in a smaller critical mass of U-235 than previously estimated.

Meanwhile, Lawrence's enthusiastic reports on prospects for electromagnetic separation of U-235 helped the S-1 Section to narrow the

1-2 FERMI AT THE BLACKBOARD

"To me it was as entrancing to watch and listen to Fermi's masterly development and exposition of this evolving theory as it was to watch and listen to Pablo Casals. . . . Casals always seemed to me to be above the details of fingers, strings and bowing. . . . Fermi seemed also to be above the details of the theory he was explaining; he saw beyond the symbolism to its basic structure and harmony, but he also had each note and semiquaver well in hand." (Philip M. Morse, *In at the Beginnings: A Physicist's Life*)

choices among methods. In May 1942 it recommended concentrating on two separation
processes—gaseous diffusion and electromagnetic—and on a chain reaction in a uranium-
graphite pile to produce plutonium. Inadequate
supplies of sufficiently pure uranium metal and
of graphite slowed preparations for Fermi's definitive experiment, but the achievement of a
self-sustaining chain reaction on December 2,
1942—a scientific landmark quite apart from its
importance to the war—made it feasible to proceed with a large pile for plutonium production.

General Groves and the Manhattan Project

These successive scientific and technical
breakthroughs were necessary preliminaries to
the major operations of the Manhattan Project—
the separation plants at Oak Ridge, Tennessee; the piles for production of plutonium at
Hanford, Washington; and the laboratory for the
design and production of the first nuclear weapons at Los Alamos, New Mexico. But the exigen-
cies of war demanded the utmost speed, and
during 1942, reorganization, research, and plans
for expanded facilities proceeded together,
though not always at an even pace. Months of
skirmishing over contracts and procurement,
even with OSRD's expanded powers, convinced
Bush that no civilian agency could command
the resources to design, construct, and operate
the required installations, and it was at his urging that in August 1942 the U.S. Army set up the
Manhattan Project (officially the Manhattan Engineer District) to negotiate contracts with industrial firms and supervise construction, procurement, and security. On September 23,
General Leslie R. Groves became its commanding officer. As one of a three-member Military
Policy Committee, Bush shared administrative
authority with representatives of army and navy.
Conant, as his alternate, continued to supervise
research and, eventually, bomb design and
production.

Groves moved with a decisiveness that aston-

ished all observers. Within a matter of days he
confirmed the selection of Oak Ridge as the site
for the separation plants, visited Chicago and
Berkeley, and sized up key staff members and the
progress they were making. Like Bush and Conant, Groves realized that plant construction
could not wait until engineers had designed
every pump and valve and scientists had analyzed all their data. He knew that experienced
engineers would need to revise plans evolved in
laboratories. Stone and Webster Engineering
Corporation, selected the previous June as the
project contractor, could not possibly do all the
construction, for by December it was clear that
this would include not only the Oak Ridge
plants but piles to produce plutonium, the laboratory at Los Alamos, and new housing for

1-3   GENERAL GROVES

General Leslie R. Groves, military commander of the
Manhattan District, U.S. Army Corps of Engineers,
1942–46. He had been the construction engineer responsible for building the Pentagon.

thousands of workers at sites in isolated and sparsely settled areas. Groves also began negotiations with industrial firms that already employed the chemists, engineers, and metallurgists needed to supervise plant operation. Bush's hope was realized. The uranium project, conceived and nurtured with scientific deliberation, was quickly transformed by military organization and priorities.

Materials for Fission—Oak Ridge and Hanford

Groves's first major task was construction at Oak Ridge. Of the four plants built there during the war, two were started immediately. The plant for separation of U-235 by the electromagnetic method (Y-12) was built by Stone and Webster and operated by an Eastman Kodak subsidiary, Tennessee Eastman. The huge gaseous diffusion complex (K-25) with its own power plant was built by Kellex, a specially formed division of the M. W. Kellogg Company, and operated by the Union Carbide and Carbon Corporation. Construction and operation of both Y-12 and K-25 were plagued by serious problems, and when production finally began it was found that they could run most efficiently by turning over the moderately enriched U-235 from K-25 to Y-12 for final enrichment. To speed up the process still further, a small thermal diffusion separation plant (S-50) was later attached to the K-25 power house so that K-25 might begin with slightly enriched material. In June 1944, minute quantities of U-235, sufficient for neutron capture experiments, began arriving at Los Alamos.

At the fourth Oak Ridge installation, known as Clinton Labs (X-10), were laboratories for research on the chemical separation of plutonium from the highly radioactive spent fuel elements removed from a pile, and a small pilot production plant. Even before the successful chain reaction of December 1942, Compton and Groves had agreed that a larger pile to produce plutonium should be built in an uncongested area

and had persuaded the E. I. du Pont de Nemours Company, with its staff of expert chemists, to undertake construction. Du Pont found the available space at Oak Ridge too constricted for the large pile but adequate for the laboratories and pilot plant. These were built at Oak Ridge in the spring of 1943. Compton was placed in charge of their operation, and by summer, Seaborg, Charles Cooper, and others engaged in plutonium research moved from Chicago to Clinton Labs.

In January 1943, Groves and du Pont decided to locate the large plutonium production plant in southeastern Washington near Hanford on the Columbia River. Construction of Oak Ridge in wartime was a monument to the ingenuity and dedication of American industrial workers, and in some ways the obstacles faced at Hanford were even greater. Final plans called for three water-cooled piles six miles apart on the south bank of a bend in the river between Hanford and the downstream village of Richland, and four separation plants ten miles to the south. A construction camp at Hanford served immediate needs while a permanent residential community was being built at Richland. Recent warnings about radiation from the Met Lab's health division underlined the need for space, and the acquisition of nearly 500,000 acres in arid country laced with water rights was prolonged by legal wrangles. Shortages of materials were acute. Skilled workmanship was essential because repairs would be impossible, or at best hazardous, once the piles and plants were in operation. Construction was delayed while chemists at the Met Lab and Clinton decided exactly what processes were to be used in them. The first completed pile began to operate in September 1944, and on February 2, 1945, a shipment of plutonium nitrate arrived at Los Alamos to be transformed into metal for experimental purposes.

The Climax—Los Alamos

The operation of Clinton Labs at Oak Ridge, which Compton had reluctantly assumed in

March 1943, so greatly extended his already scattered command that he gradually reorganized it into the Metallurgical Project. New directors of the major research centers such as the Met Lab and Clinton were responsible to him. The study of fast-neutron reactions, an understanding of which was essential for bomb design, was still being carried out by physicists and chemists who were collecting and analyzing data in university and other laboratories. One such team had been working on fast fission at Berkeley with theoretical physicist Robert Oppenheimer since early 1939. In October 1941, in response to a wire from Lawrence saying "Oppenheimer has important new ideas," Compton invited Oppenheimer to a conference at which the principal topic was the amount of U-235 needed for a bomb. At the conference and in subsequent correspondence, Oppenheimer made such significant contributions that in May 1942, Compton placed him in charge of all fast-neutron research, with experimentalist John H. Manley of the Met Lab as his assistant.

During the summer of 1942, Oppenheimer and Manley visited laboratories, met occasionally, and wrote long letters, but as Manley later commented, it was no way to run a project. They were trying to coordinate experimental data with theoretical interpretations in order to calculate both the critical mass of material needed for fission and the efficiency of a weapon. Scientists in the various laboratories were using three different types of equipment to accelerate neutrons; they were bombarding a variety of substances; and they were using different counting devices to measure the results. These were reported as cross sections, that is, the probability that a given type of reaction, such as fission, will occur in a particular substance at some specified energy, but cross sections obtained under such diverse conditions were not reliable. Groves, Bush, and Conant agreed that the solution was a central laboratory for the design and construction of a bomb. By December 1942, Groves had selected Oppen-

heimer as its director, accountable directly to himself and Conant. A boys' school that occupied the two-mile-long Los Alamos mesa stretching eastward from the Jemez Mountains northwest of Santa Fe, New Mexico, received orders to vacate its buildings. Construction workers were rushed to the site to build laboratories and apartments. Oppenheimer spent the winter arranging the transfer of research teams, including his own at Berkeley, and recruiting additional staff. To those not already familiar with the Manhattan Project he offered the prospect of building a weapon that would end the war and research that would bring great benefits to a world at peace. In the dark days of 1943, these were persuasive arguments. In April some three dozen scientists attended a two-week conference at Los Alamos. Most were eminent in their fields; the younger ones soon would be. They listened to lectures summarizing experimental data and current theories, and they helped organize the laboratory in preparation for the hundreds of co-workers who would join them in the coming months. Wives and children soon arrived. Those who worked under Oppenheimer's leadership developed an esprit de corps unlike that in any other part of the project. Housing was marginal, shortages of water, electricity, and milk recurred, but families were together, colleagues were stimulating, and the surrounding mountains, canyons, and desert cast their spell over almost everyone.

As the end point of a long chain of project operations, the laboratory was a combination of esoteric scientific research, advanced design engineering, and down-to-earth production. To Los Alamos came the uranium and plutonium nitrates to be purified and turned into metal, shaped, and assembled with other components into something that would explode with unprecedented force. At first only minute amounts were available for carefully planned experiments. Production estimates gave Los Alamos about two years to design a weapon before bomb quantities were available, but design involved studying nuclear reactions, developing new instrumentation, devising new procedures, and eliminating impurities that might cause pre-detonation. From the beginning the staff worked with a sense of great urgency.

Trinity

For the first year the objective was a bomb in which a highly supercritical mass of either U-235 or plutonium would be assembled by using an almost conventional gun to shoot a subcritical projectile into a subcritical target, whereupon an "initiator," crushed by the impact, would emit a burst of neutrons to start fission at an exponential rate. But when it was learned that the plutonium isotope 239 coming from the Hanford pile also contained the isotope 240, which had a higher rate of spontaneous fission, it became clear that the gun method of assembly was too slow for a plutonium bomb.

Efforts to perfect the gun mechanism for use with uranium continued, but in the summer of 1944 the laboratory was drastically reorganized in order to develop the implosion method of bomb assembly in which a spherically converging explosive shock front was used to compress a solid sphere of low-density plutonium alloy to supercritical density at an extremely high rate. This required less plutonium than the gun method and somewhat relaxed the purity requirements but necessitated development of an entirely new technology using explosive lenses and multiple detonation devices of extreme precision. British scientists, who began arriving at Los Alamos in December 1943, made substantial contributions to the implosion work.

Bomb quantities of U-235 from Oak Ridge and plutonium-239 from Hanford arrived at about the same time in early summer 1945. The uranium went directly into the gun-type weapon. So great was the confidence in its design and reliability that it was used at Hiroshima without testing. The implosion principle was new and untried, so an elaborately instrumented trial of

a plutonium device, planned months in advance under the code name Trinity, was held near Alamogordo, New Mexico, on July 16, 1945. For this first atomic explosion every available gram of plutonium was collected from Los Alamos labs—where physical and chemical experiments to determine its properties were still under way—and was converted into metal for the core of the device. Soon after Trinity, enough plutonium arrived from Hanford for a second core around which the Nagasaki bomb would be assembled. A special air force team, already completing its training on Tinian in the Mariana Islands, was alerted to prepare for action in early August. Scientists from Los Alamos went to Tinian to assemble the bombs. The uranium bomb was dropped on Hiroshima on August 6, the plutonium bomb on Nagasaki on August 9.

II—PROPHETS VERSUS POLICY MAKERS: HIROSHIMA

"Any process started by men toward a special end," wrote Elting Morison in his biography of Henry L. Stimson, "tends, for reasons logical, biological, aesthetic or whatever they may be, to carry forward, if other things remain equal, to its climax. Each man fully engaged over four years of uncertainty and exertion in the actual making of the weapon was moved, without perhaps a full awareness, toward conclusion by the inertia developed in the human system."[2]

Scientists who worked on the bomb were peculiarly subject to this inertia, for developing a weapon to be used in defense of freedom was inextricably linked with their commitment to extend human knowledge and control of nature. They have often been reproached for not intervening more vigorously to disrupt the inertial process when the bomb was no longer a defensive weapon against Germany but an offensive weapon against Japan. Some still ask themselves why they did not do so. Time, which has so greatly eroded memories of the horrors and urgencies of war, has by no means settled this question, and now, when new recruits are join-

1-4   **THE FIRST ATOMIC BOMB**

The steel tower.

The intense efforts of the Manhattan Project under President Roosevelt culminated in the Trinity test at Alamogordo. The device assembled for the test shows neither its complexity nor its awesome power. Visible are the detonators of the implosion charge—they must fire with an accuracy of millionths of a second—with their connecting cables.

Upon first learning of the massive project, President Truman appointed James Conant and Vannevar Bush as scientist members of an "Interim Committee" to advise on atomic weapons policy, with the assistance of a Scientific Panel consisting of Arthur Compton, E. O. Lawrence, Enrico Fermi, and Robert Oppenheimer. With Conant and Bush among the observers, the device was detonated at 5:30 A.M. on a platform elevated above the desert sand. Philip Morrison, physicist and a former student of Oppenheimer, observed from a distance of 10 miles: "You felt the morning had come, although it was night, because your face felt the glow of this daylight—this desert sun in the midst of the night."

The first atomic bomb.

The first of radioactive clouds, 15 seconds after detonation.

Bush and Conant after Trinity.

1-5   THE FIRST NUCLEAR WEAPONS

ABOVE: Little Boy—the gun-assembly fission bomb using uranium-235, dropped on Hiroshima without prior testing on August 6, 1945.

BELOW: Fat Man—the implosion bomb using plutonium-239, dropped on Nagasaki after its prototype had been tested in New Mexico.

ing the veterans of efforts to de-escalate the nuclear arms race, it is appropriate to explain how earlier advocates of restraint and international cooperation tried to influence national policy and to see wherein they failed.

The Met Lab Looks Ahead

The common denominator in these wartime efforts—official, unofficial, individual, or collective—was recognition of the revolutionary impact of the release of atomic energy and the need to plan in advance for its control. Among working scientists on the Manhattan Project this concern was most evident at the Chicago Met Lab where it reached a climax in the so-called Franck report of June 1945, which urged that the Japanese government be given a demonstration of a nuclear explosion in an uninhabited area before bombs were used in combat.

Anxiety over the absence of postwar planning was first expressed at the Met Lab in 1943 by young academic scientists who learned through Du Pont employees awaiting transfer to Oak Ridge about the scale of the installations there and feared this meant a postwar commitment to private industry. By the summer of 1944, senior Met Lab people were also becoming restive as rumors spread that the laboratory might close because research directly related to bomb development had been moved to Oak Ridge or Los Alamos. Basic research would make possible the application of radioactivity to medicine, agriculture, and power, but a systematic study was needed, argued Met Lab leaders. So Compton appointed a committee chaired by industrial metallurgist Jay Jeffries, which in turn assigned topics to subcommittees, and the findings were embodied in a "Prospectus on Nucleonics," usually called the Jeffries report, which Compton forwarded to Washington on November 18, 1944.

The term *nucleonics* soon became obsolete, and the prospectus did not become a chart for

the atomic age. There were as yet too many imponderables. But two sections added to the original outline by Eugene Rabinowitch and Robert S. Mulliken, the committee secretary, were in fact an early draft of the Franck report: Work on the bomb must continue lest our strong hand be covered by a stronger, but in the long run we had two alternatives—to stop work on nucleonics and lose all potential benefits or to alert the public to the dangers and mobilize support for an international agreement to control atomic weapons. Until a control authority existed, only fear of retaliation would deter a nuclear attack. It was essential therefore to enlist the cooperation of our allies, particularly Russia, at an early stage.

The question of alerting the public had been raised a few months earlier in another Met Lab communication to Washington, which argued that the magnitude of the project made secrecy impossible and that the American people should be told immediately about the bomb's destructive potential to prepare them for its possible use by Germany and for the revolution in international relations which the bomb's mere existence would bring about.[3] It is interesting to note that over half of the twenty-two senior scientists who signed this radical challenge to prevailing policy did not actively support organized efforts to relax atomic secrecy after the war.

Control: Bipartite or International?

The strict compartmentalization of information upon which General Groves insisted prevented the Met Lab ferment from spreading to other laboratories; it also interfered with vertical communication. Although Compton conscientiously forwarded successive exhortations from Chicago to project administrators in Washington, he was authorized to return only vague assurances that adequate planning was taking place. It was not generally known that a Committee on Postwar Policy chaired by physicist

Richard C. Tolman was proposing a postwar domestic agency to support and coordinate atomic research and development by government, universities, and industry. In any case, the Tolman report addressed the international issue only in its assumption that the need to maintain military superiority would determine domestic policy.

More reassuring to Met Lab dissidents would have been the knowledge that for the past six months Bush and Conant had been deciding what they should say about international control when the time seemed ripe to discuss it with Secretary of War Stimson and President Roosevelt. Informal notes in OSRD files show that as early as April 1944, Conant was jotting down for Bush "some thoughts on international control of atomic energy." On September 30, 1944, they sent Stimson a long memorandum to use in talking with Roosevelt. It urged that control should be placed in the hands of an international agency after the war. Bush had learned to his dismay that an exclusive Anglo-American hegemony had been discussed by Churchill and Roosevelt at their recent meeting in Quebec, so the memo specifically cautioned against a bipartite arrangement that would provoke Russia to develop its own bomb. Security did not lie in secrecy; the U.S. advantage was temporary, and as soon as the first bomb was dropped the government should release basic scientific information and all but the manufacturing and military details of bomb production. The possibility of a hydrogen weapon made it useless to rely on a monopoly of uranium ore. Unprecedented danger demanded radical action, and if this was understood by the general public the weapons might never be used—exactly the message that was currently being attached to the "Prospectus on Nucleonics" in Chicago under the impression that it was not fully understood in Washington. Strongly influenced by Bush and Conant, Stimson became a firm supporter of the concept of international control, and before he retired in

September 1945, he had helped to make it a plank in U.S. atomic policy. Unfortunately, he was not around to oversee its implementation.

Bohr Pleads for Openness

Something else that the Chicago scientists did not know was that the world's most eminent living nuclear physicist, Niels Bohr, was waging a quiet campaign to promote immediate talks with Russia about the bomb. As a citizen of Nazi-occupied Denmark, Bohr was proceeding cautiously, and James Franck later said that in brief wartime visits with his old friend they did not discuss atomic politics. But Bohr's influence was strong at Los Alamos, where he arrived in December 1943 as a member of the British delegation. During this and subsequent visits Bohr talked frequently with Oppenheimer, and more guardedly with others, about his deep conviction that the atomic bomb would revolutionize international relations, that greater openness was essential, and that Churchill and Roosevelt should immediately tell Stalin about the project and enlist his cooperation instead of waiting until his suspicions were aroused. Years later, Oppenheimer recalled these talks with Bohr: "He made the enterprise, which often seemed so macabre, seem hopeful [as he spoke of his] high hope that the outcome would be good, and that in this, the role of objectivity, friendliness, cooperation incarnate in science would play a helpful part; all this was something we wished very much to believe."[4]

In April 1944 Bohr returned to England for a conference with Churchill. In London he found a letter from physicist Pyotr Kapitsa inviting him to Moscow and assuring him a welcome from other old friends. Bohr's discreet reply, checked with British security, looked forward to a reunion when conditions permitted, but the names Kapitsa mentioned conveyed a picture of Russian physicists engaged in the same quest as their counterparts in the West and further persuaded Bohr of the importance of what he had to say to the prime minister. The meeting, however, was a disaster. Churchill was intensely irritated by Bohr's low-voiced talk of openness, cooperation, and the international fraternity of science. The more Churchill blustered, the more inarticulate Bohr became. Greatly discouraged, he resumed the role of consultant at Los Alamos and prepared for a July meeting with Roosevelt. Misled by the president's suave manner, Bohr thought this interview a success, but when the two leaders met in Quebec in September they agreed to have Bohr watched. Bush intervened to prevent sterner measures; vague and visionary though Bohr might sound when talking anything but physics, he would never betray secrets to Russia.

A Demonstration Bomb?

The papers that Bohr later assembled to document his wartime crusade contain no evidence that he advocated not using the bomb against Japan. However, in their international control memo to Stimson, Bush and Conant raised the possibility of a "demonstration . . . over enemy territory, or in our own country, with subsequent notice to Japan that the materials would be used against the Japanese mainland unless surrender was forthcoming."[5] As technical uncertainties persisted, Bush and Conant ceased to consider a demonstration, but a similar proposal reached President Roosevelt in November through Sachs, bearer of the 1939 Einstein letter. Sachs suggested "a rehearsal demonstration" of the bomb before a body of internationally recognized scientists and representatives of religious faiths and outlined subsequent steps that might induce Japan to surrender.[6] It is possible that word of Sachs's proposal reached Chicago via his friend Szilard, who may, in fact, have been its originator.

The idea that atomic bombing of Japan might be avoided by a nonmilitary demonstration became a common topic of discussion at the Met Lab in the early weeks of 1945. The context was the adverse effect that use without warning would have upon the postwar international climate. Press and radio reports of atrocities committed by Japanese troops on the one hand and reports of the U.S. firebombing of Japanese cities on the other made it difficult to support a humanitarian argument against use, but the international one assumed critical importance with the realization that most of the statesmen meeting in San Francisco in April to plan the United Nations Organization did not know about the bomb. (Only after Stimson received the Bush-Conant international control memo the previous September had he decided to let the U.S. secretary of state in on the secret.) Young scientists at the Met Lab held seminars to discuss alternatives to military use of the bomb and the terms of a possible international control agreement.

1-6 SZILARD MAKES A POINT
Physicist and a native of Hungary, Leo Szilard foresaw clearly the political implications of nuclear energy and acted forcefully in the cause of world peace, both before and after World War II.

Szilard and Franck Take Action

When later asked to account for their preoccupation with issues that were scarcely raised at Oak Ridge or Los Alamos until the war ended, Chicago scientists cited the relaxation of pressure at the Met Lab just when it was most intense at other places. They also stressed the seminal influence of Franck and Szilard. Some responded most warmly to Franck's gentle suasion, impressed by the keen intellect and moral integrity that lay behind it. Others were stimulated by the flow of ideas from Szilard's mercurial brain and the ingenious logic with which he supported them. Having started their young disciples—and older colleagues too—on the road to self-education, Franck and Szilard took independent initiatives in the spring of 1945.

Szilard drew up a memorandum addressed to President Roosevelt about the adverse effect that the very existence of atomic weapons would have upon the position of the United States—the inevitable expiration of its monopoly and the vulnerability of its cities to surprise attack. He urged that eminent scientists engaged in work on the weapon be allowed to convey their views about control to those responsible for making policy.[7] Szilard was negotiating an appointment when the president died on April 12. Truman, whose sudden elevation gave him much to learn, including the very existence of the Manhattan Project, proved inaccessible, and Szilard had to settle for an interview on May 28 with James F. Byrnes, Truman's personal advisor and, after July, his secretary of state. Szilard considered Byrnes too ill-informed to grasp the thrust of his memorandum; Byrnes was antagonized by Szilard's presumption in suggesting that he and other scientists should discuss its contents with the cabinet.

It is no secret that Szilard's penchant for independent wheeling and dealing worried and angered project administrators. James Franck, a man of very different temperament, preferred to work within the system. He later explained the background of his characteristically more modest undertaking. Three years earlier, when Compton asked him to head the chemistry section at the Met Lab, Franck agreed on one condition: that if the time came to use the bomb and it had not been developed elsewhere, he might present his views on its use to someone at the highest level of decision making. "I did not always agree with Compton," Franck recalled, "but he was an honest man and a gentleman."[8] In early April, Compton told Franck that he would arrange a meeting for him in Washington.

Accordingly Franck proceeded to incorporate in a memorandum the ideas currently being discussed at the Met Lab. Natural eloquence made Franck an effective speaker in English, but he did not write it with ease, so he turned for help to his colleague Eugene Rabinowitch. Warnings about international implications of atomic energy, which Rabinowitch had put into the final chapters of the nucleonics report five months earlier, were now tailored to the plea that statesmen recognize the obsolescence of traditional competition between nations. Whoever held the pen, the words had the authentic Franckian ring: Scientists had willingly obeyed rules about secrecy so long as the inconvenience was personal, but "these regulations become intolerable if a conflict is brought about between our conscience as citizens and human beings and our loyalty to the oath of secrecy. . . . How is it possible that the statesmen are not informed that the aspect of the world and its future is entirely changed . . . and how is it possible that the men who know these facts are prevented from informing the statesmen about the situation?"[9] Franck did not comment on the use of the bomb in Japan. On or about April 21, Compton accompanied Franck to Washington with his memorandum, but the highest official available to receive it was Secretary of Commerce Henry A. Wallace, whose influence had long been minimal.

A copy reached Bush's office, but Bush himself was busy preparing Stimson to give President Truman his first full briefing on the Manhattan Project. The memorandum that Stimson used for his talk with Truman on April 25 contained most of the points made by Franck and showed no less understanding of the awesome challenge presented by the bomb. Had they known this, Chicago scientists could no longer have complained about what was being said at the highest level. But Franck, as respected and trusted as any scientist on the project, returned to Chicago without this assurance.

Early in May, Stimson appointed a War Department Interim Committee on Atomic Energy and made it responsible for statements to be issued after bombs were dropped, for drafting legislation for domestic control, and for making recommendations relating to international control. Stimson was chairman and his assistant, George L. Harrison, was deputy chairman. The other members were James F. Byrnes as Truman's personal representative; Ralph A. Bard, undersecretary of the navy; William L. Clayton, assistant secretary of state; Vannevar Bush and James B. Conant as director and deputy director of OSRD; and Karl T. Compton, chief of OSRD's Office of Field Services. Three meetings were devoted to briefing Bard, Byrnes, and Clayton and to outlining the committee's functions. On the advice of Bush and Conant, an advisory panel of four project scientists was appointed: Arthur Compton, Enrico Fermi, Ernest Lawrence, and Robert Oppenheimer. (Oppenheimer's reputed comment: "Now we are in for trouble!") By May 31 the committee was ready to consult them. Its three scientist members and the four on the panel took an active part in the morning's discussion of questions on Stimson's carefully planned agenda. They stressed the brief duration of a U.S. monopoly, the possibility of a thermonuclear bomb, and the need to restock the reservoir of basic knowledge that had made possible the development of radar, the proximity fuse, and the atomic bomb.

Use of the bomb was not on the agenda, but during lunch Arthur Compton mentioned inter-

est at the Met Lab in a nonmilitary demonstration. The minutes of the afternoon session note that this possibility was raised, and dismissed, as part of a discussion under the heading "Effect of bombing on the Japanese and their will to fight."[10] No one spoke on behalf of a demonstration. Before adjournment the panel was asked to submit recommendations for domestic control. The panel was not present the following day, June 1, when the Interim Committee voted unanimously that the bomb should be used against Japan as soon as possible, and without prior warning, on a combined military-civilian target, the choice of which should be left to the secretary of war. (Three weeks later Bard revoked his affirmative vote on the grounds that use of such a weapon without warning was inconsistent with the position of the United States as a great humanitarian nation, and shortly resigned as undersecretary of the navy.)

The Franck Report and the Panel

Panel members had been authorized to tell their colleagues that the Interim Committee existed "to deal specifically with the problems of control, organization, legislation, and publicity." In Chicago on June 3, Compton conveyed this information to Met Lab leaders. He would be going to a panel meeting later in the month and would present to it proposals that were ready by June 14. Some of those present were primarily interested in research, production, controls, the organization of an atomic authority, and public education, and before the meeting broke up, committees were appointed in these five areas. Their conclusions were eventually combined in a single report and forwarded to the Interim Committee in mid-July. The Interim Committee had not solicited advice about how the bomb was to be used, but Compton knew how strongly some of his colleagues felt on this issue and readily concurred in a request to appoint a Met Lab committee on social and political implications with Franck as chairman. The other

1-7   **THE FRANCK REPORT**

Excerpts from a Report to the Secretary of War
June 11, 1945

Preamble

... The scientists on this Project do not presume to speak authoritatively on problems of national and international policy. However, we found ourselves, by the force of events during the last five years, in the position of a small group of citizens cognizant of a grave danger for the safety of this country as well as for the future of all the other nations, of which the rest of mankind is unaware. We therefore feel it our duty to urge that the political problems, arising from the mastering of nuclear power, be recognized in all their gravity, and that appropriate steps be taken for their study and the preparation of necessary decisions. ...

In the past, science has often been able to provide new methods of protection against new weapons of aggression it made possible, but it cannot promise such efficient protection against the destructive use of nuclear power. This protection can come only from the political organization of the world. Among all the arguments calling for an efficient international organization for peace, the existence of nuclear weapons is the most compelling one. *In the absence of an international authority which would make all resort to force in international conflicts impossible, nations could still be diverted from a path which must lead to total mutual destruction, by a specific international agreement barring a nuclear armaments race.* ...

Summary

The development of nuclear power not only constitutes an important addition to the technological and military power of the United States, but also creates grave political and economic problems for the future of this country.

Nuclear bombs cannot possibly remain a "secret weapon" at the exclusive disposal of this country for more than a few years. The scientific facts on which their construction is based are well known to scientists of other countries. Unless an effective international control of nuclear explosives is instituted, a race for nuclear armaments is certain to ensue following the first revelation of our possession of nuclear weapons to the world. Within ten years other countries may have nuclear bombs, each of which, weighing less than a ton, could destroy an urban area of more than ten square miles. In the war to which such an armaments race is likely to lead, the United States, with its agglomeration of population and industry in comparatively few metropolitan districts, will be at a disadvantage compared to nations whose population and industry are scattered over large areas.

We believe that these considerations make the use of nuclear bombs for an early unannounced attack against Japan inadvisable. If the United States were to be the first to release this new means of indiscriminate destruction upon mankind, she would sacrifice public support throughout the world, precipitate the race for armaments, and prejudice the possibility of reaching an international agreement on the future control of such weapons.

Much more favorable conditions for the eventual achievement of such an agreement could be created if nuclear bombs were first revealed to the world by a demonstration in an appropriately selected uninhabited area.

In case chances for the establishment of an effective international control of nuclear weapons should have to be considered slight at the present time, then not only the use of these weapons against Japan, but even their early demonstration, may be contrary to the interests of this country. A postponement of such a demonstration will have in this case the advantage of delaying the beginning of the nuclear armaments race as long as possible. If, during the time gained, ample support can be made available for further development of the field in this country, the postponement will substantially increase the lead which we have established during the present war, and our position in an armament race or in any later attempt at international agreement would thus be strengthened.

On the other hand, if no adequate public support for the development of nucleonics will be available without a demonstration, the postponement of the latter may be deemed inadvisable, because enough information might leak out to cause other nations to start the armament race, in which we would then be at a disadvantage. There is also the possibility that the distrust of other nations may be aroused if they know that we are conducting a development under cover of secrecy, and that this will make it more difficult eventually to reach an agreement with them.

If the government should decide in favor of an early demonstration of nuclear weapons, it will then have the possibility of taking into account the public opinion of this country and of the other nations before deciding whether these weapons should be used in the war against Japan. In this way, other nations may assume a share of responsibility for such a fateful decision.

To sum up, we urge that the use of nuclear bombs in this war be considered as a problem of long-range national policy rather than of military expediency, and that this policy be directed primarily to the achievement of an agreement permitting an effective international control of the means of nuclear warfare.

The vital importance of such a control for our country is obvious from the fact that the only effective alternative method of protecting this country appears to be a dispersal of our major cities and essential industries.

J. FRANCK, CHAIRMAN
D. J. HUGHES
J. J. NICKSON
E. RABINOWITCH
G. T. SEABORG
J. C. STEARNS
L. SZILARD

members were Donald Hughes, J. J. Nickson, Eugene Rabinowitch, Glenn Seaborg, Joyce C. Stearns, and Leo Szilard. The group already knew what it wanted to say. Drawing upon the 1944 "Prospectus on Nucleonics" and Franck's April 1945 memorandum, Rabinowitch produced a statement urging a nonmilitary demonstration to the Japanese which all members were willing to sign, and Franck—again with Compton's help—left for Washington on June 11 with "A Report to the Secretary of War," which he deposited the next day with Stimson's assistant, George Harrison.

Evidently Compton did not wish to take this document, now known as the Franck report, to the panel without this intermediate step, but when it met at Los Alamos on the weekend of June 15–16 he was surely not surprised to receive a call from Harrison asking the panel to review the feasibility of a demonstration so that the Interim Committee might have the benefit of its opinion when it considered the Franck report.

There seems no doubt that the panel took this request seriously. Apparently Lawrence, often portrayed as a hardliner, was the last to abandon the idea of a demonstration. But in mid-June there was no bomb. Parts were still being tested and calculations refined. The test a month hence would involve a device, not an assembled weapon. There was as yet no assurance that a stray neutron, initiating a premature reaction, would not produce a feeble explosion—a dud that would only fortify Japan's will to resist. The panel's succinct report of June 16, drafted by Oppenheimer, made three points: (1) Russia, France, and China, as well as Britain, should be advised that atomic weapons might be ready for use in the present war and asked to suggest ways in which this development could contribute to improved international relations; (2) The opinions of their scientific colleagues on the initial use of these weapons ranged from "a purely technical demonstration to . . . the military ap-

plication best designed to induce surrender.... We find ourselves closer to these latter views; we can propose no technical demonstration likely to bring an end to the war; (3) It is true that we are among the few citizens who have had occasion to give thoughtful consideration to these problems during the past few years. We have, however, no claim to special competence in solving the political, social, and military problems which are presented by the advent of atomic power."[11]

On June 21, the Interim Committee confirmed its earlier decision to use the bomb without warning but, at the urging of Bush and Conant, recommended that Truman should tell Stalin about the new weapon during the forthcoming July conference in Potsdam, Germany.

Szilard's Petition: The Moral Issue

The Franck report had concentrated on political issues. "We were all deeply moved by moral considerations," Rabinowitch later explained, "but we did not think that in the necessarily amoral climate in which wartime decisions are made these would be effective." Szilard wanted the record to show scientists' concern with the moral issue. A petition to the president, dated July 17, 1945, urged that the United States should not use atomic bombs unless Japan fully understood the terms to be imposed and still refused to surrender; the final decision should rest upon moral considerations.[12] The petition with sixty-eight signatures reached Washington after the president left for Potsdam. Franck and Rabinowitch did not sign lest the petition weaken the force of the Franck report by going over the head of the secretary of war to the president. Szilard got a copy to Clinton Labs where it produced much discussion but found few signers, whereas an indigenous petition, asking simply that before the weapon was used its powers should be adequately described and demonstrated, elicited many signatures—recollections of the number ranged from two or three dozen to several hundred—but the document was confiscated by security because it revealed the state of progress on the bomb.

About July 1 an early draft of Szilard's petition reached Los Alamos in the pocket of a Met Lab visitor, but Oppenheimer refused permission to circulate it, knowing that security would act if he did not. He had discouraged an earlier move to discuss "the impact of the gadget," at a meeting convened by physicist Robert R. Wilson as well as a more recent one to talk about postwar employment, with the argument that scientists should concentrate on completing the bomb. However, Oppenheimer made no attempt to stop the flood of talk that swept the mesa after the July 16 test. In fact, he freely shared the hope engendered by his conversations with Bohr that so terrible a weapon must inevitably revolutionize international relations. Recast in Oppenheimer's own inimitable phrases, the message became one of hope and—after Hiroshima and Nagasaki—of solace. At the same time, Oppenheimer's exposure via the Interim Committee and its panel to the complex military and political factors that were determining the prosecution of the war and the conclusion of peace made him doubtful that scientists possessed enough information to advocate specific policies.

Strategy Takes Over

A weapon that ended the war quickly would solve several problems that had troubled the architects of U.S. strategy since early 1945. It would avoid the invasion of the Japanese mainland, with untold loss of life on both sides, that seemed inevitable when the fire bombing of Japanese cities failed to break Japan's resistance. An early peace might also avoid Soviet intervention against Japan. Back in January the United States had welcomed a Russian promise to declare war on Japan within three months after Germany surrendered, but as Russia made Poland a satellite and adopted a generally expansionist policy

in Europe, its participation in a Far East settlement seemed undesirable.

Truman requested postponement of the opening of the Potsdam conference from July 1 to July 15 so that when he talked with Churchill and Stalin he would know the outcome of the Trinity test. A coded message received on the evening of July 16, then more complete reports, assured Truman and Stimson that a plutonium bomb and a uranium bomb would be ready for use in Japan soon after August 1, certainly by August 10. Churchill, with whom Truman shared the news, recorded his great relief at the removal of the "nightmare of invasion." On July 24, surrounded by both American and British advisors, who were increasingly mistrustful of Soviet intentions, Truman casually told Stalin that the United States had a new weapon "of unusual destructive force." Stalin replied that he hoped we would make good use of it against Japan. This perfunctory exchange was a far cry from the full disclosure to build mutual trust and cooperation as urged by Bohr, the Franck committee, and the panel. The same day, Truman ordered the War Department to alert air force crews to be ready to drop an atomic bomb on Japan as soon after August 3 as weather permitted.

As for Japan, Truman had adhered to Roosevelt's policy of unconditional surrender and ignored the advice of former Ambassador Joseph E. Grew to assure the Japanese that the institution of the emperor might be retained. The United States had long since broken the Japanese code, and the Potsdam negotiators knew that on July 13 the Japanese foreign minister had wired Japan's ambassador in Moscow that unconditional surrender was the only obstacle to peace. Apparently they did not know that for the past year antimilitarists, including the emperor himself, had been trying to steer Japan toward peace in the face of formidable opposition by the war party. On July 27, the United States, Britain, and (in absentia) China issued the Potsdam Proclamation calling upon Japan to avoid "prompt and utter destruction" by surrendering unconditionally. Japan was promised a responsible government established by the will of the people, but no reference was made to the emperor, and two days later the Japanese premier declared that Japan would continue to fight.

In view of this reply, no thought was given in Potsdam to countermanding orders to implement the threat of utter destruction, and the uranium bomb was dropped over Hiroshima on the morning of August 6. Two days later, when the Japanese ambassador called upon the Soviet foreign minister to ask assistance in peace negotiations, he learned that Russia had declared war on Japan. Within hours Soviet forces attacked the Japanese army occupying Manchuria. The bombing of Hiroshima, the nature of which Japanese scientists had scarcely had time to assess, plus the Russian declaration of war, strengthened the emperor's peace party, but time was needed to convince the opposition. Orders from Washington had proposed a five-day interval between the two bombs to give time for surrender but allowed the commander on Tinian some leeway. The weather forecast of August 8 gave one more day of clear skies, and on August 9 the implosion bomb devastated the port city of Nagasaki while the peace party in Tokyo was drafting acceptance of the Potsdam terms, providing the emperor's position was unchanged. After a final exchange of messages, war in the Pacific ended on August 14.

All accounts of the atomic bombings of Japan, whatever the bias of the author, have tended to emphasize the reactions of scientists. It is true that without them there would have been no bomb, but in a sense they brought this attention upon themselves by the missionary zeal with which hundreds of them, once the war ended, espoused the cause of international control to prevent further destructive applications of atomic energy. No such collective recognition of responsibility was apparent among the statesmen, administrators, military personnel, engineers, industrialists, and construction workers without whose contributions the Manhattan Project could not have been carried to a conclusion. Their reactions to Hiroshima merged in the wave of thanksgiving that swept the country with the coming of peace. But scientists, whatever their views on nuclear weapons, still wrestle with the problems which some among them addressed with such foresight before atomic bombs changed the world.

Suggested Readings

GOWING, MARGARET. *Britain and Atomic Energy, 1939–1945.* London: Macmillan and Co., 1964.

GROUEFF, STEPHANE. *Manhattan Project: The Untold Story of the Making of the Atomic Bomb.* Boston: Little, Brown, 1967.

HEWLETT, RICHARD G., AND OSCAR E. ANDERSON, JR. *The New World, 1939–1946.* University Park, Pa.: Pennsylvania State University Press, 1962.

SHERWIN, MARTIN J. *A World Destroyed: The Atomic Bomb and the Grand Alliance.* New York: Alfred A. Knopf, 1975.

SMITH, ALICE KIMBALL. *A Peril and a Hope: The Scientists' Movement in America, 1945–1947.* Chicago: University of Chicago Press, 1965.

SMITH, ALICE KIMBALL, AND CHARLES WEINER, EDS. *Robert Oppenheimer: Letters and Recollections.* Cambridge: Harvard University Press, 1980, Chap. 4 and 5.

Hiroshima and Nagasaki

Enola Gay, the B-29 aircraft that carried the atomic bomb to Hiroshima, at its base on Tinian in the Mariana Islands.

Mushroom cloud over Hiroshima.

Hiroshima's only ladder truck—4,000 feet from ground zero.

Refugees of the attack at the foot of Miyuki Bridge.

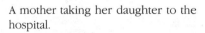
A mother taking her daughter to the hospital.

Medical treatments were given in the devastated Japan Red Cross Hospital.

A mile and a half from the center, in the Danbara neighborhood, rows of houses were shattered.

Disposal of the dead by the army. The smoke of cremation coiled up everywhere for more than a month.

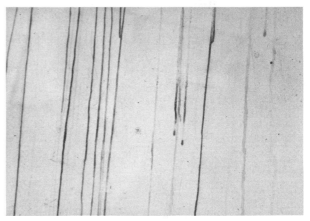

Black traces on a wall were left by a downpour of radioactive rain extending several miles northwest of the city.

"I THOUGHT MY LAST HOUR HAD COME . . ."

An eyewitness account of the atom bomb explosion at Hiroshima thirty-eight years ago, by Mrs. Futaba Kitayama, then aged thirty-three.

"IT WAS IN Hiroshima, that morning of August 6. I had joined a team of women who, like me, worked as volunteers in cutting firepaths against incendiary raids by demolishing whole rows of houses. My husband, because of a raid alert the previous night, had stayed at the *Chunichi (Central Japan Journal),* where he worked.

"Our group had passed the Tsurumi bridge, Indian-file, when there was an alert; an enemy plane appeared all alone, very high over our heads. Its silver wings shone brightly in the sun. A woman exclaimed, 'Oh, look—a parachute!' I turned toward where she was pointing, and just at that moment a shattering flash filled the whole sky.

"Was it the flash that came first, or the sound of the explosion, tearing up my insides? I don't remember. I was thrown to the ground, pinned to the earth, and immediately the world began to collapse around me, on my head, my shoulders. I couldn't see anything. It was completely dark. I thought my last hour had come. I thought of my three children, who had been evacuated to the country to be safe from the raids. I couldn't move; debris kept falling, beams and tiles piled up on top of me.

"Finally I did manage to crawl free. There was a terrible smell in the air. Thinking the bomb that hit us might have been a yellow phosphorus incendiary like those that had fallen on so many other cities, I rubbed my nose and mouth hard with a *tenugui* (a kind of towel) I had at my waist. To my horror, I found that the skin of my face had come off in the towel. Oh! The skin on my hands, on my arms, came off too. From elbow to fingertips, all the skin on my right arm had come loose and was hanging grotesquely. The skin of my left hand fell off too, the five fingers, like a glove.

"I found myself sitting on the ground, prostrate. Gradually I registered that all my companions had disappeared. What had happened to them? A frantic panic gripped me, I wanted to run, but where? Around me was just debris, wooden framing, beams and roofing tiles; there wasn't a single landmark left.

"And what had happened to the sky, so blue a moment ago? Now it was as black as night. Everything seemed vague and fuzzy. It was as though a cloud covered my eyes and I wondered if I had lost my senses. I finally saw the Tsurumi bridge and I ran headlong toward it, jumping over the piles of rubble. What I saw under the bridge then horrified me.

"People by the hundreds were flailing in the river. I couldn't tell if they were men or women; they were all in the same state: their faces were puffy and ashen, their hair tangled, they held their hands raised and, groaning with pain, threw themselves into the water. I had a violent impulse to do so myself, because of the pain burning through my whole body. But I can't swim and I held back.

"Past the bridge, I looked back to see

that the whole Hachobori district had suddenly caught fire, to my surprise, because I thought only the district I was in had been bombed. As I ran, I shouted my children's names. Where was I going? I have no idea, but I can still see the scenes of horror I glimpsed here and there on my way.

"A mother, her face and shoulders covered with blood, tried frantically to run into a burning house. A man held her back and she screamed, 'Let me go! Let me go! My son is burning in there!' She was like a mad demon. Under the Kojin bridge, which had half collapsed and had lost its heavy, reinforced-concrete parapets, I saw a lot of bodies floating in the water like dead dogs, almost naked, with their clothes in shreds. At the river's edge, near the bank, a woman lay on her back with her breasts ripped off, bathed in blood. How could such a frightful thing have happened? I thought of the scenes of the Buddhist hell my grandmother had described to me when I was little.

"I must have wandered for at least two hours before finding myself on the Eastern military parade ground. My burns were hurting me, but the pain was different from an ordinary burn. It was a dull pain that seemed somehow to come from outside my body. A kind of yellow pus oozed from my hands, and I thought that my face must also be horrible to see.

"Around me on the parade ground were a number of grade-school and secondary-school children, boys and girls, writhing in spasms of agony. Like me, they were members of the anti-air raid volunteer corps. I heard them crying 'Mama! Mama!' as though they'd gone crazy. They were so burned and bloody that looking at them was insupportable. I forced myself to do so just the

same, and I cried out in rage, 'Why? Why these children?' But there was no one to rage at and I could do nothing but watch them die, one after the other, vainly calling for their mothers.

"After lying almost unconscious for a long time on the parade ground, I started walking again. As far as I could see with my failing sight, everything was in flames, as far as the Hiroshima station and the Atago district. It seemed to me that my face was hardening little by little. I cautiously touched my hands to my cheeks. My face felt as though it had doubled in size. I could see less and less clearly. Was I going blind, then? After so much hardship, was I going to die? I kept on walking anyway and I reached a suburban area.

"In that district, farther removed from the center, I found my elder sister alive, with only slight injuries to the head and feet. She didn't recognize me at first, then she burst into tears. In a handcart, she wheeled me nearly three miles to the first-aid center at Yaga. It was night when we arrived. I later learned there was a pile of corpses and countless injured there. I spent two nights there, unconscious; my sister told me that in my delirium I kept repeating, 'My children! Take me to my children!'

"On August 8, I was carried on a stretcher to a train and transported to the home of relatives in the village of Kasumi. The village doctor said my case was hopeless. My children, recalled from their evacuation refuge, rushed to my side. I could no longer see them; I could recognize them only by smelling their good odor. On August 11, my husband joined us. The children wept with joy as they embraced him.

"Our happiness soon ended. My husband, who bore no trace of injury, died suddenly three days later, vomiting blood. We had been married sixteen years and now, because I was at the brink of death myself, I couldn't even rest his head as I should have on the pillow of the dead.

"I said to myself, 'My poor children, because of you I don't have the right to die!' And finally, by a miracle, I survived after I had again and again been given up for lost.

"My sight returned fairly quickly, and after twenty days I could dimly see my children's features. The burns on my face and hands did not heal so rapidly, and the wounds remained pulpy, like rotten tomatoes. It wasn't until December that I could walk again. When my bandages were removed in January, I knew that my face and hands would always be deformed. My left ear was half its original size. A streak of cheloma, a dark brown swelling as wide as my hand, runs from the side of my head across my mouth to my throat. My right hand is striped with a cheloma two inches wide from the wrist to the little finger. The five fingers on my left hand are now fused at the base...."

—*Translated from the French by William R. Byron*

Nagasaki also . . .

Within one mile, most buildings were destroyed and most people were either killed or seriously injured.

For many of the injured, little could be done but wait for death.

Cremation fires burned day and night.

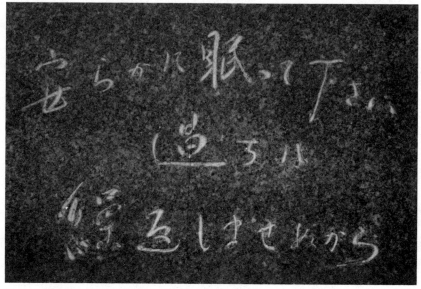

The memorial cenotaph. The inscription reads:

Let all souls here rest in peace,
for we shall not repeat the evil.

The *Mike* shot, October 31, 1952: The first true thermonuclear test, equal to about ten million tons of high explosive. The fireball removed the islet of Elugelab from the Enewetak Atoll. This view is from fifty miles away, two minutes after detonation. The mushroom cloud rose ten miles high.

2. The Superbomb

Herbert York, physicist and first director of Defense Research and Engineering under President Dwight Eisenhower, has seen at first hand the inner workings of that technical and political process he called the "race to oblivion." Dr. G. Allen Greb is his historian-collaborator at the University of California, San Diego, where both now work.

In this narrative, the authors recount just how it happened that the superbomb—the hydrogen or thermonuclear weapon—exploded into 1952 as a United States initiative. The story includes the wartime glimpse of the thermonuclear future, the early efforts at international control, and the rise in American effort spurred by the first Soviet atomic explosion in late 1949. The crucial decision by Truman, against the advice of many scientists, is a story of secret debate within the government and among its divided advisors. By 1952, the island of Elugelab had vanished in a full-scale thermonuclear explosion, an American first. By November 1955, the Soviets had followed with their own hydrogen bomb. The arms race was on.

AS EDWARD TELLER RECALLS, Enrico Fermi asked him in early 1942, "Now that we have a good prospect of developing an atomic bomb, couldn't such an explosion be used to start something similar to the reactions in the sun?"[1] Specifically, Fermi had in mind reactions between deuterons, the nuclei of a relatively rare but naturally occurring heavy form of hydrogen. As we now know, and as Fermi then speculated, at temperatures of the order of 100 million degrees centigrade, deuterons react explosively with each other in a process called fusion, ultimately producing helium and releasing huge amounts of energy. "After a few weeks of hard thought," Teller reports, "I decided that deuterium could not be ignited by atomic bombs. I reported my results to Fermi and proceeded to forget about it."[2]

The War Period

Shortly thereafter, J. Robert Oppenheimer gathered together a small group of theoretical physicists at Berkeley to discuss atomic bombs and to plan a program for the projected new weapons laboratory at Los Alamos, New Mexico. Teller's views by this time had shifted, and he and Emil Konopinski presented more optimistic calculations about the hydrogen bomb to the Oppenheimer group. All of them discussed the new weapon at length, along with many other questions concerning the uranium-fission bomb. During these conversations the idea of using tritium as well as deuterium to fuel a fusion reaction was first suggested.

Thus from the outset of the U.S. nuclear program, the exploration of the "superbomb" (as the hydrogen bomb came to be known) was

Herbert F. York
and G. Allen Greb

York was chancellor and is now a professor of physics and director of the Program in Science, Technology, and Public Affairs at the University of California, San Diego. Greb is a research historian with Professor York at UCSD.

among the original objectives of scientists. But because the development of fission bombs turned out to be more difficult than expected, the Los Alamos lab directed virtually its full attention to the fission weapon during World War II. Only a few persons, Teller among them, put in much effort on the super during the war period. When the war ended, most Los Alamos physicists, especially those with well-established reputations, left and returned to university life and basic research. Teller considered remaining but only if the laboratory gave the superbomb a high priority. When this did not happen, he too left Los Alamos to join the staff of the University of Chicago.

The Baruch Plan: International Control of the Atom?

For several technical reasons—the attention given to fission weapons, the difficulty and high cost of conducting actual thermonuclear experiments, and the ambiguous results of theoretical calculations—work on the superbomb continued at a slow pace during the 1946–1949 period, involving a relatively small number of persons. The full-time membership of the Los Alamos theoretical group, both mathematicians and physicists, dwindled to a few dozen people, and only a small portion of their time could be devoted exclusively to the study of the new weapon. During this time, moreover, growing numbers of atomic scientists became deeply concerned about unbridled nuclear weapons development and turned much of their attention to promoting the international control of atomic energy.

As we have seen, even before the end of World War II, some leaders of the Manhattan Project began to question the traditional "amoralism of science" and consider the implications of the weapons they had created. Typically they put special emphasis on avoiding a nuclear arms race with the Soviet Union. This had been a major theme of the Bohr memorandum, Franck report, and Szilard petition. After the war, these

and other concerned scientists continued and expanded their efforts. In cities and towns across the country, they preached on the subject of nuclear energy before PTAs, Rotary clubs, and sometimes even from church pulpits. Their message usually consisted of two parts: first, an explanation of how atomic energy "worked," and second, an attempt, often passionate and naive, to persuade the audience of the grave dangers inherent in the new discoveries. Scientists also established formal organizations to augment individual actions, including the Federation of American Scientists (FAS), led by William Higginbotham and Robert R. Wilson of Los Alamos, and the *Bulletin of the Atomic Scientists (BAS),* the self-proclaimed "conscience of the international scientific community" founded by Eugene Rabinowitch and Hyman H. Goldsmith of the Chicago Metallurgical Lab (Met Lab).

The atomic scientists' principal ideas about international control coalesced in one important document, the so-called Baruch plan of 1946. It was originally conceived by Oppenheimer and Isidor I. Rabi, modified by Atomic Energy Commission (AEC) Chairman David E. Lilienthal, and Secretary of State Dean Acheson, and presented before the United Nations by financier Bernard Baruch on June 14. Briefly, the proposal called for the creation of an international nuclear authority and a suitable system of safeguards after which the United States would be obliged to dismantle its atomic bombs. The Soviet reply, presented by Deputy Foreign Minister Andrei Gromyko, came only five days later. Because the United States enjoyed a nuclear monopoly, the Soviet Union called for the destruction of existing atomic arsenals before any discussion of inspection and control procedures took place. This difference, couched in thousands of different words on dozens of different occasions, blocked all progress toward any form of arms control or disarmament for a dozen years.

Later, during the height of cold-war tensions

fueled at home by Senator Joseph McCarthy's attacks on alleged communists in the government, acrimonious debate raged over whether the effort put into the hydrogen bomb (H-bomb) during the immediate 1946–49 postwar period was adequate or not. Teller, who steadfastly contended it was not, wrote in 1962 that if "the Los Alamos Laboratory had continued to function after Hiroshima with a full complement of such brilliant people as Oppenheimer, Fermi, and [Hans] Bethe, I am convinced that someone would have had the same idea much sooner—

and we would have had the hydrogen bomb in 1947 rather than in 1952."[3] Norris Bradbury, the laboratory director at the time, held the opposite view. In 1954 he reported:

> We would have spent time lashing about in a field in which we were not equipped to do adequate computational work. We would have spent time exploring with inadequate methods a system which was far from certain to be successful. . . . I cannot see how we could have reached our present objectives in a more rapid fashion . . . [than] the mechanism by which we went.[4]

2-1   **THE McCARTHY ERA**

AT THE OPENING of Haydn's opera "La Fedelta Premiata," a foreboding inscription near Diana's temple shapes the life of the community:

> Every year the monster shall have
> two faithful lovers;
> but if, in their place,
> facing that same death,
> a brave soul exposes itself
> you shall have peace, and the tears (of grief)
> shall cease.

In America during the 1950s, a similar sort of curse and monster overshadowed the populace, but instead of giving rise to a musical chairs comedy of lovers, as in the opera, a more nightmarish plot evolved. The rhetoric of Senator Joe McCarthy and others fueled a widespread fear of communism and communist sympathizers.

"I feel strongly about labeling products for what they are.

> Poison should be labelled as poison;
> treason should be labelled as treason;
> truth should be labelled as truth;
> lies should be labelled as lies."

Communist activities were vividly depicted as infiltrating the entire fabric of social life, with intent to undermine every-

thing from the highest government offices to the grade school classroom. Racism and bigotry contributed to the intensity of attacks against suspected citizens.

When the Soviet Union tested its first atomic bomb in 1949, years earlier than expected, anti-communist passions, coupled with a new fear of two-way nuclear war, escalated. A tangible explanation, or scapegoat was required, as California Representative Richard Nixon announced, "I feel the American people are also entitled to know the facts about the espionage ring which was responsible for turning over information on the atomic bomb to agents of the Russian government." Early in 1950 (shortly after Truman's decision to pursue H-bomb research), British physicist Klaus Fuchs' confession to providing Soviet agents with atomic bomb information set off a series of arrests, confessions, trials, and enflamed emotions that concluded with the execution of an American couple.

Public opinion, already agitated by such headlines as:

"War is Declared by North Korea" (June 25, 1950)

"Atom Bomb Shelter for City at Cost of $450,000,000 Urged" (August 6, 1950)

(Truman) "Warns Against Hysteria"
"Demands Registration of any Trained as
Spies" (August 9, 1950)

sensationalized the trial of "The United
States *versus* Julius Rosenberg, Ethel Rosenberg and Morton Sobell" as a tale of an
accomplished "atom spy" couple willing
to betray both family and country to provide the Soviet Union with (rudimentary)
knowledge of the most devastating weapon
yet used on the planet.

The principal witnesses for the prosecution were confessed accomplices—David
Greenglass, his wife Ruth, and Harry Gold
(legally, testimony of accomplices cannot
be taken as corroborating). The two men
shared a prison bunk for months before
the trial during which they had ample opportunity, allegedly under FBI pressure, to
adorn their story with names and details.
The plot was that David Greenglass, a machinist soldier in a Los Alamos lab during
the war, was requested by Julius Rosenberg of New York, using Ruth Greenglass
and Harry Gold as go-betweens, to supply
information on the atomic bomb for Soviet
contacts (a United States ally during World
War II, not an enemy). Ethel had conspired by typing David's handwritten reports. Throughout the trial, the Rosenbergs insisted upon their innocence, stating
that feuds resulting from the failure of a
family business embittered David against
them. They believed that David, when arrested by the FBI for uranium theft, had arranged to contrive a story in return for a
light sentence. The jury convicted the Rosenbergs, and the judge, holding them per-
sonally responsible for the deaths of 50,000
U.S. servicemen in the Korean war, gave
the maximum sentence of death.

Over the months following the trial,
protests against the injustice of the trial
and sentence were mounted in letter campaigns, speeches, and rallies, especially in
Europe. Dr. H. Urey, a scientist from the
Manhattan Project, telegraphed Eisenhower:

"The case against the Rosenbergs outrages
logic and justice . . . a man of Greenglass' capacity is wholly incapable of transmitting the
physics, chemistry, and mathematics of the
atom bomb to anyone."

Albert Einstein and others concurred in
Urey's request for clemency. The White
House received hundreds of thousands of
letters from around the world, including
messages from the Vatican, asking for an
executive change in the death sentence.
Eisenhower, discrediting the letters and
rallies as communist, and convinced of the
couple's "deliberate betrayal of the entire
nation," denied mercy.

Equipped with new evidence of discrep-
ancies in Greenglass' testimony and points
of law violated during their trial, the Rosenbergs appealed three times to the Supreme Court. The Court refused to hear
them, although Justice Hugo Black dis-
sented, writing just before their death:

"This Court has never reviewed this record
and has never affirmed the fairness of the trial
below . . . there may always be questions as to
whether these executions were legally and
rightfully carried out."

The Attorney General and the United
States warden had offered to grant clemency and preferential treatment such as
Greenglass had received if the Rosenbergs
confessed to espionage crimes at the last
minute. While the press reported "Mercy
for Couple Hinges on Their Talking," the
Rosenbergs were executed on June 19,
1953.

A Superbomb Seems Possible

The situation began to change by mid-1949. The small complement of scientists working on the problem had by then identified the main details of deuterium-deuterium and deuterium-tritium reactions and had come up with good estimates of the reaction rate as a function of temperature and density. They also had gained a good understanding of the mechanisms for heating and cooling a reacting mass of light elements. Their experiments had revealed that several different thermonuclear fuel combinations were possible: pure deuterium, deuterium plus varying amounts of tritium, and lithium deuteride. In addition, computing devices—such as the UNIVAC under development by Sperry-Rand in Philadelphia and the pioneer MANIAC developed by the Princeton mathematician John von Neumann—had advanced to the point where it became possible to make more definitive calculations about thermonuclear devices. In particular, groups at Los Alamos, the RAND corporation (under Richard Latter), and Princeton (Project Matterhorn-B, assembled and directed by John Wheeler) learned enough using the new electronic computers to be convinced that fission devices could be utilized to ignite small amounts of deuterium and tritium. Finally, work designed to produce further improvements and better understanding of fission bombs went forward and turned out to be an essential preliminary to the successful development of the hydrogen bomb. Several theorists outside Los Alamos, including Teller, thus found the prospects for further development of the super-bomb sufficiently attractive and promising that they joined the small group already working at the New Mexico facility under the direction of J. Carson Mark, the theoretical division leader.

Political Decision

At this still inchoate stage of research, a powerful political stimulus intervened to greatly expand and accelerate the thermonuclear program. On August 29, 1949, the first Soviet atomic explosion (dubbed "Joe 1" in the West) took place near Semipalatinsk in Siberia. This came on the heels of a series of major events—the Berlin blockade and Czechoslovakian coup of 1948, and the fall of China to Mao Tse-tung's forces in early 1949—which reinforced for most Americans the image of an aggressive, monolithic communism bent on ruling the world.

For policymakers one question took precedence: How should the United States respond? An intense, sharply focused, secret debate took place within government circles over the last half of 1949 to find an answer. After a short period of uncertainty, the debate came down to the single crucial issue of the hydrogen bomb. Was a program to develop such a super weapon the proper response to the Soviet threat? If so, how should the program be conducted? Participants in this momentous decision-making process were surprisingly few. They included the members of the AEC and the General Advisory Committee (GAC), which provided the parent commission with scientific and technical advice; the members of the Joint Committee on Atomic Energy (JCAE) in Congress; a few top Defense and State Department officials; and a small body of concerned scientists, mainly at the Berkeley and Los Alamos labs of the University of California.

The GAC Advice

In October 1949, soon after the Joe 1 test, the AEC called together the GAC to consider not only the question of a high-priority thermonuclear program but also other nuclear issues directly influencing U.S. defense and security. The Atomic Energy Act of 1946 had created the GAC to provide expert scientific advice on just such new programs and the management of U.S. nuclear energy policy in general. The committee at this time was composed of a particularly influential group of scientific-technical leaders, characterized most prominently by its chair-

man, J. Robert Oppenheimer, who had directed
the wartime development of the atomic bomb
at Los Alamos. The rest of the membership included James B. Conant, one of Franklin D. Roosevelt's chief scientific aides; Lee A. DuBridge,
wartime director of the M.I.T. Radiation Laboratory, Nobel laureates Enrico Fermi and Isidor
I. Rabi; Hartley Rowe and Cyril Stanley Smith,
formerly of Los Alamos; Glenn T. Seaborg, a
Berkeley chemist formerly at the Chicago Met
Lab; and Oliver E. Buckley, president of Bell
Telephone Laboratories.

After consulting with scientific, political, and
military experts and with the AEC commissioners, the GAC released its report on October 30,
1949. The report, which was not declassified
until 1974, concluded that the superbomb probably could be built but that an "all-out effort"
to do so "would be wrong at the present moment. . . ." Instead, the committee recommended
an expanded effort in many other phases of the

nuclear weapons program, including the development of new fission weapons for both tactical
and strategic purposes. The GAC members objected so adamantly to the superbomb precisely
because they believed it was an entirely new
class of weaponry that threatened to exacerbate
an already menacing technological competition
between the two nuclear powers. As summarized by Oppenheimer:

> We base our recommendation [against the super-
> bomb] on our belief that the extreme dangers to
> mankind inherent in the proposal wholly out-
> weigh any military advantage that could come
> from this development. Let it be clearly realized
> that this is a super weapon; it is in a totally differ-
> ent category from an atomic bomb.

> In determining not to proceed to develop the
> superbomb, we see a unique opportunity of pro-
> viding by example some limitations on the totality
> of war and thus of limiting the fear and arousing
> the hopes of mankind.[5]

2-2   "IN THE MATTER OF J. ROBERT OPPENHEIMER"

IN THE SUMMER of 1952, Oppenheimer
decided to end his service on the General
Advisory Committee of the Atomic Energy
Commission (AEC). In September he received a letter from President Truman that
stated, in part:

> As director of the Los Alamos Scientific Lab-
> oratory during World War II, and as chairman
> of the General Advisory Committee for the
> past six years, you have served your country
> long and well, and I am gratified by the
> knowledge that your wise counsel will con-
> tinue to be available to the Atomic Energy
> Commission on a consultant basis.

> I wish you every future success in your im-
> portant scientific endeavors.

It seemed that a unique public career
had come to an honorable conclusion. But
those were years of wild anticommunist
hysteria, encouraged by demagogues such
as Senator Joseph McCarthy. In April 1954,
only a year and a half after receiving Truman's laudatory letter, Oppenheimer was
in effect on trial, charged with being a "security risk" and, in the opinion of some of
his accusers, with being actively disloyal
to the United States.

Formally, the proceeding was not a trial
but an administrative hearing. Because of
charges against him, Oppenheimer's security clearance, which he still held only to
serve as an occasional AEC consultant, had

been summarily revoked. In the circumstances, taking no action might have seemed to admit some basis for the charges, and so Oppenheimer appealed for the restoration of his clearance.

Oppenheimer's judges were a panel of three men appointed by the AEC to hear this case. In a highly unusual step, the AEC also chose a prominent Washington lawyer to act as special prosecutor. The list of twenty-four charges presented by AEC General Manager Kenneth Nichols can be summarized under three headings: that Oppenheimer had a prewar record of left-wing beliefs and associations, that he had bent and broken security regulations while directing the atomic bomb project, and that

> it was further reported that in the autumn of 1949, and subsequently, you strongly opposed the development of the hydrogen bomb: (1) on moral grounds, (2) by claiming that it was not feasible, (3) by claiming that there were insufficient facilities and scientific personnel to carry on the development, and (4) that it was not politically desirable. It was further reported that even after it was determined, as a matter of national policy, to proceed with development of a hydrogen bomb, you continued to oppose the project and declined to cooperate fully in the project.

The first two charges, of course, were many years old and had several times been investigated, weighed, and found unimportant—when Oppenheimer's services were needed. Only the third charge was new.

Five scientists testified that they thought Oppenheimer *was* a security risk; the most prominent was Edward Teller, the rest were associates of Ernest Lawrence's group in California. Nineteen leading scientists and engineers testified in Oppenheimer's favor. As an example, here is an excerpt from the statement of Vannevar Bush, a leader in organizing American science for war:

> I had at the time of the Los Alamos appointment complete confidence in the loyalty, judgment, and integrity of Dr. Oppenheimer. I have certainly no reason to change that opinion in the meantime. I have had plenty of reason to confirm it, for I worked with him on many occasions on very difficult matters.... My faith has not in the slightest degree been shaken by that letter of General Nichols' or anything else.... But I think this board or no board should sit on a question in this country of whether a man should serve his country or not because he expressed strong opinions. If you want to try that case, you can try me. I have expressed strong opinions many times, and I intend to do so. They have been unpopular opinions at times. When a man is pilloried for doing that, this country is in a severe state."

In the context of the times, the results of the security hearings were predictable: the denial of Oppenheimer's clearance was upheld by a 2/1 vote of the special panel and later by a 4/1 vote of the AEC itself. (The panel, while judging Oppenheimer a security risk, did not confirm the charges of disloyalty.) The denial effectively excluded Oppenheimer from government service, and he "retired" to the directorship of the Institute for Advanced Study in Princeton, New Jersey.

Most of the scientific community never accepted the verdict as just or reasonable. In December 1963, President Lyndon Johnson presented Oppenheimer with the AEC's Enrico Fermi medal and award. This was widely seen as a kind of rehabilitation of Oppenheimer's reputation, although the "security risk" verdict was never officially reversed. Oppenheimer died of cancer in 1967.

Reaction: The AEC, Politicians, and Pro-Superbomb Scientists

The parent AEC split 3 to 2 on the recommendations of its committee. Not surprisingly, Lilienthal liked the report. A lawyer by training, Lilienthal had drafted major elements of the Baruch plan. He agreed with the GAC that the fission weapons program should be upgraded. He also believed that renunciation of the superbomb should be coupled with new proposals to control nuclear arms, what he called a "Plan, or Pact, for World Survival."[6] Commissioner Henry DeWolf Smyth, the one scientist on the AEC, and Commissioner Sumner Pike, a former Wall Street executive, also generally supported the Oppenheimer-GAC position.

Commissioners Lewis Strauss, another former financier with a philanthropic interest in science, and Gordon Dean took a contrary point of view. Strauss in particular made a concerted effort to push development of the super. He believed that the only possible response to the Soviet atomic test was for the United States to make its own "quantum" technological leap. "I believe it unwise to renounce, unilaterally, any weapon which an enemy can reasonably be expected to possess," he wrote President Truman on November 25, 1949. "I recommend that the President direct the Atomic Energy Commission to proceed with the development of the thermonuclear bomb, at highest priority. . . ."[7]

The pro-superbomb forces received powerful political support from Senator Brian McMahon, Democratic chairman of the influential JCAE, and William L. Borden, McMahon's staff chief. McMahon took a decidedly apocalyptic view of the problem, as did many others within the government. In November 1949, he wrote to Truman:

> If we let Russia get the super first, catastrophe becomes all but certain—whereas, if we get it first, there exists a chance of saving ourselves.[8]

McMahon and other like-minded politicians, such as Admiral Sidney Souers of the National Security Council, were influenced in their thinking by a triumvirate of nuclear physicists who, since the Soviet test, had been lobbying steadily in Washington for a crash thermonuclear program: Edward Teller, Ernest O. Lawrence, and Luis Alvarez.

Teller of course was the unquestioned champion of the thermonuclear cause, promoting the superbomb whenever and wherever he could from 1942 on. Lawrence and Alvarez, both of the prestigious University of California Radiation Laboratory (UCRL), joined this campaign because they, too, believed strongly in the scientific imperative: that scientists had a duty to pursue new knowledge and technology to their fullest. Together this group made good use of its extensive personal government connections, developed primarily during the war, to push the hydrogen bomb as the best U.S. reply to the Soviet nuclear test.

Military Opinion and Truman's Decision

The military, also in close contact with the Teller-Lawrence-Alvarez group, leaned heavily toward the civilian proponents of the super. The Military Liaison Committee, the services' direct link to the AEC, concluded in late 1949 that work should proceed because "possession of a thermonuclear weapon by the USSR without possession by the United States would be intolerable." The Joint Chiefs of Staff (JCS), although not overly enthusiastic about a crash program, took the position that the superbomb was a natural extension of existing weapons systems. They dismissed moral objections to the bomb, such as those voiced by the GAC, saying, "It is folly to argue whether one weapon is more immoral than another." According to David Rosenberg, who has made the closest study of the military's involvement in the early U.S. nuclear program, "It can be said that the JCS played a significant role in the policy-making process by offering Truman a historical context and a strategic justification for what was essentially a political decision."[9] This decision came on January 31, 1950, when Truman directed the AEC "to continue its work on all forms of atomic weapons, including the so-called hydrogen or superbomb."[10]

Public and congressional reaction to the decision in early 1950 was overwhelmingly favorable. "No Presidential announcement since Mr. Truman entered the White House seemed to strike such an instant and general chord of nonpartisan congressional support," the *New York Times* declared on February 1. The decision was in keeping with the broadly based belief that American nuclear supremacy must be maintained in the face of the communist menace. "The repeatedly expressed theme," the *Times* continued, "was that regardless of how dreadful the hydrogen weapon might be, Mr. Truman had no other course in view of the failure so far of negotiations for international control of atomic energy and of the 'atomic explosion' ... in the Soviet Union."[11]

The few caveats raised came mostly from informed scientists and some congressmen who objected to the supersecret nature of the H-bomb debate. Oppenheimer, Arthur H. Compton, Louis Ridenour, Bethe, and Robert Bacher, among others, complained in the pages of *Bulletin of the Atomic Scientists* and *Scientific American* that issues of such great consequence should receive a full public hearing. Oppenheimer eloquently stated that "wisdom itself cannot flourish, nor even truth be determined, without the give and take of debate or criticism."[12]

It is difficult to envision a scenario in which the President would have eschewed development of the superbomb even temporarily. The intensity of the cold war, the domestic political climate, and Truman's own distrust of the Soviets worked powerfully against such a course of action. Yet, in retrospect, it seems unfortunate that the government did not take the Oppenheimer-GAC-Lilienthal advice more seriously. The GAC report, it is now clear, made both accurate estimates of the technological situation and correct assessments regarding the risks involved. Unilateral restraint, as the authors pointed out, would not have jeopardized U.S. security and perhaps could have served to reverse the momentum of the nuclear arms race. Even in the event that the Soviet Union had gone ahead to develop and deploy the superbomb first, the United States could have effectively countered this threat with its large stockpile of fission bombs and the production of powerful new atomic weapons in the 500-kiloton range. Most probably, however, in this hypothetical world in which officials heeded the GAC advice, the United States still would have developed and deployed the superbomb ahead of the Soviet Union if diplomatic efforts to stop the weapon altogether had failed.

Technology Wins Out

In any case, Truman's announcement—and the sudden outbreak of the Korean conflict in June 1950—led to several concrete changes and results in the thermonuclear program. The Los Alamos lab, for example, expanded its theoretical division staff and accelerated research on the super. Several prominent scientists, among them Frederic DeHoffmann, Frank Hoyt, Burton Freeman, and Marshall Rosenbluth, joined Mark's group on a permanent basis. Others, such as Bethe, Fermi, Konopinski, von Neumann, and Richard Garwin, put in extensive part-time work as consultants. The UCRL group at Berkeley, the Naval Research Laboratory at Washington, and a new team at Princeton also initiated programs to augment the Los Alamos efforts.

The George Shot

Thus theoretical and experimental physicists, mathematicians, and engineers were brought together to concentrate on the basic problems of configuring a device, determining the properties of fissile materials at extremely high temperatures, and determining how to obtain diagnostic measurements of the thermonuclear process. After a year of feverish activity, they designed

2-3 THE SUPERBOMB PROGRAMS, 1949–55

When President Harry S. Truman announced on January 31, 1950, his decision to develop the H-bomb, he cited the need for national defense as the result of the first Soviet fission detonation of August 1949 (*Joe* 1) and the lack of a satisfactory plan for international control of atomic energy. Truman's decision was widely acclaimed in Congress and the press. Edward Teller, who was to be one of the chief architects of the superbomb, noted in anticipation of future work that "the scientist is not responsible for the laws of nature." Events thereafter were rapid and irreversible.

Chronology

Late 1949–50:   The Soviet Union and the United States initiate high-priority programs to develop the H-bomb.

February–April 1951:   Edward Teller and Stanislaw Ulam discover at Los Alamos, New Mexico, how to configure a device so that a relatively small fission explosion can ignite an arbitrarily large amount of thermonuclear fuel.

May 8 and 24, 1951:   The *George* and *Item* shots are successfully carried out at Enewetak: large fission explosions ignite small thermonuclear devices.

November 1, 1952:   The first true superbomb, a device configured to ignite a large thermonuclear explosion by means of a relatively small quantity of fissile material, is exploded at Enewetak. Known as the *Mike* test, the device yields the equivalent of 10 million tons of TNT, roughly 1,000 times the yields of the first atomic bombs.

November 15, 1952:   The United States also tests a very powerful fission bomb, code-named *King,* which represents a straightforward extension of fission weapon technology.

August 12, 1953:   The first Soviet explosion involving thermonuclear reactions takes place; probably smaller than the U.S. all-fission *King* device, it is only some ten times as big as the standard atomic bombs of the day. It is the first device anywhere to use lithium deuteride as a fuel and presumably could be converted to a practical weapon.

Spring 1954:   The United States successfully explodes six variants of the superbomb in Operation *Castle,* with yields up to 15 megatons. The first and most famous of these tests, code-named *Bravo,* is exploded on March 1, 1954, at Bikini Atoll. Its design, initiated before the *Mike* explosion, incorporates the Teller-Ulam configuration but uses the more practical lithium deuteride as its thermonuclear fuel. Its yield is 15 megatons, and it is readily adaptable for delivery by aircraft.

November 23, 1955:   The Soviets explode a bomb, some few megatons of yield, by "using a relatively small quantity of fissionable material . . . to produce [in Nikita Khrushchev's words] an explosion of several megatons." This device is evidently the first Soviet bomb to incorporate something like the Teller-Ulam configuration. It uses lithium deuteride as a fuel and is a true superbomb, comparable to the U.S. *Bravo* some 20 months earlier.

Conjectures

—All of the U.S. explosions from *George* to *Nectar,* except *Item,* are the U.S. reaction (or overreaction) to the Soviet *Joe 1* and the speculations about what would follow it. As a measure of the degree of overreaction, the number and power of this group may be compared with the actual 1953 and 1955 Soviet explosions charted.

—What might have happened if the United States had followed the advice of Robert Oppenheimer and the General Advisory Committee (GAC), and David Lilienthal and the majority of the Atomic Energy Commission (AEC) commissioners, and had not initiated a program to develop the superbomb in the spring of 1952? At best the invention of very large, relatively inexpensive superbombs would have been forestalled or, at least, substantially delayed until both Dwight D. Eisenhower and Khrushchev were in power. These two leaders were both more seriously interested in arms limitations agreements than their predecessors had been, and it is possible that they might have coped successfully with the superbomb. It was clearly worth striving for and was worth at least running some small risk.

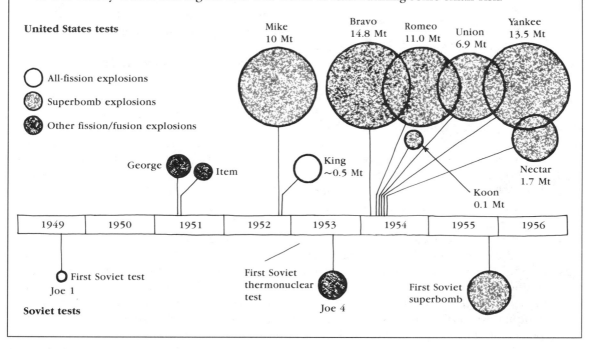

and tested a device which, while it was not a prototype of the long-sought superbomb, did produce the world's first small thermonuclear flame. Under the command of Air Force General Elwood R. Quesada, Joint Task Force 3 carried out this experiment on May 8, 1951, at Enewetak Atoll in the Marshall Islands. Part of the Greenhouse Series to study and verify thermonuclear principles, the George shot, as it was known, used a relatively large fission yield to ignite a small tritium-deuterium mixture. Data from this test proved to be particularly significant, playing the role, as Teller later described it, of a "pilot plant" in thermonuclear development.[13]

Operations IVY and CASTLE

The AEC soon after determined that further experiments on the superbomb should proceed in two separate stages or test series. The first, Operation IVY, confirmed the next step in the experimental sequence, that large thermonuclear reactions could be initiated with relatively small fission explosions using the so-called Teller-Ulam configuration. The initial explosion in this series, the *Mike* shot of November 1, 1952, had a yield of approximately ten megatons, or about one thousand times the power of the Hiroshima atomic bomb. The second series, Operation CASTLE, demonstrated that such a device could be developed into a practical military weapon. The AEC exploded the first bomb of Operation CASTLE on March 1, 1954. Codenamed *Bravo,* it had a yield of fifteen megatons and was followed by five similar tests and the development of still lighter, smaller, and more efficient weapons.

Other Consequences

The technological momentum generated in the quest for the superbomb produced two other results having a direct bearing on the arms race: (1) the creation of a second nuclear weapons laboratory at Livermore, California, and (2) a more rapid proliferation of the nu-

clear weapons arsenal. Prodded by Teller—who was dissatisfied with Bradbury's administration of Los Alamos—and Lawrence—who desired a more direct role for Berkeley scientists in nuclear affairs—the AEC approved the establishment of a new laboratory in 1952 in order to accelerate thermonuclear research. The Lawrence Livermore Laboratory, as it was called after Lawrence's death in 1958, was organized specifically to set up, in Teller's words, a situation of "friendly competition" with Los Alamos, and it did eventually result in a doubling of the American nuclear weapons effort.[14]

Besides their work on the superbomb, Los Alamos and Livermore scientists introduced other new designs and ideas—such as the booster concept—that helped increase both the size and especially the versatility of the U.S. fission stockpile. Boosting refers to a process whereby a synergistic interaction takes place between fission and fusion reactions which can appreciably increase the efficiency and output of the fissile material. As early as October 17, 1949, Truman, acting on a JCS recommendation, authorized a stepped-up production rate for fission bombs. Then in 1951–52, Project Vista extolled the possible tactical value of small-yield atomic weapons, noting in particular their potential in Western Europe where leaders for years had been urging the development of a nuclear capability to counteract the Soviet lead in conventional forces. Tactical Nuclear Weapons (TNWs) received added impetus from the U.S. Army, which "clearly wanted to have its own tactical nuclear combat support arm."[15] Many of the experts associated with Project Vista, Oppenheimer included, advocated more and better fission bombs and TNWs at least in part as an alternative to the development of the superbomb. Ironically, as it turned out, proponents of *both* types of weapons systems got their way, drawing upon the expanded resources and expertise of the two weapons laboratories.

Thus, despite the fears and protestations of a significant body of scientists, the technological momentum of the arms race continued unabated. Nurtured in the familiar atmosphere of Soviet-American distrust and apprehension, both superpowers continued their quest for more complex and more sophisticated nuclear arsenals. In each country, technological successes stimulated (and continued to stimulate) still greater technological efforts. Soviet physicists, for example, spurred on by their initial nuclear achievement of August 1949, and the development of the U.S. superbomb, developed and exploded their own hydrogen bomb in November 1955. It is with this legacy that scientists, decision makers, and others concerned about the dangers of nuclear weaponry and nuclear war must contend today.

Suggested Readings

HEWLETT, RICHARD G., AND FRANCIS DUNCAN. *Atomic Shield, 1947–1952,* vol. 2. *A History of the United States Atomic Energy Commission.* University Park, Pa.: Pennsylvania State University Press, 1969.

ROSENBERG, DAVID ALAN. "American Atomic Strategy and the Hydrogen Bomb Decision." *Journal of American History* 66 (1979): 62–87.

SCHILLING, WARNER R. "The H-Bomb Decision." *Political Science Quarterly* 76 (1961): 21–46.

TELLER, EDWARD, AND ALLEN BROWN. *The Legacy of Hiroshima.* Garden City, N.Y.: Doubleday, 1962.

YORK, HERBERT. *The Advisors: Oppenheimer, Teller and the Superbomb.* San Francisco: W. H. Freeman and Company, 1976.

The complex of plants and laboratories at Oak Ridge, Tennessee, is the symbol of U.S. government involvement in nuclear energy. At Oak Ridge there are a national research laboratory for the study of nuclear materials, processes, and phenomena; the Y-12 plant, where materials for nuclear weapons are fabricated; and one of the uranium enrichment plants for producing both reactor fuel and highly enriched uranium for weapons use.

3. Government and the Atom

United States involvement in the development of atomic weapons began with the famous Einstein letter of October 1939. After a slow start came the crash effort of the Manhattan Project. John Lamperti traces the growth of the organizations, both governmental and private, which over the years came to operate the network of facilities that design and manufacture nuclear warheads. The story includes the roles of the Atomic Energy Commission and its successors through the present Department of Energy.

For much of its workload, the Department of Energy, like its predecessors, rests heavily on its contractors, both business firms and not-for-profit labs of universities. The organization of the civilian nuclear power industry is also sketched, with comments on future trends.

This conjunction of an immense military establishment and a large arms industry is new in the American experience....

In the councils of government, we must guard against the acquisition of unwarranted influence, whether sought or unsought, by the military-industrial complex.

President Dwight D. Eisenhower
January 17, 1961

THE DISCOVERY OF nuclear fission led directly to a new weapon of unprecedented horror and, in time, to an extensive civilian industry as well. It also led to new institutions of government in the United States and to new types of interaction between government, private industry, science, and the universities. Today it is difficult to recall that major government involvement in scientific research and development has not always been part of our public life; above all, the technology of the atomic nucleus brought this about. This chapter will outline the changing arrangements with which the U.S. government has managed the development of nuclear weapons and energy.

The Beginnings

The U.S. government first really took note of nuclear physics on October 11, 1939. On this day the "Einstein letter," explaining the military possibilities of nuclear fission, was presented to President Franklin D. Roosevelt. Roosevelt appointed an Advisory Committee on Uranium to deal with the issue, and this committee made the first appropriation of money by transferring $6,000 from the army and navy budgets to purchase experimental materials.

A variety of ad hoc arrangements carried the nuclear work forward during the next two and a half years, slowly at first but with gathering momentum as the war developed. In August 1942, efforts to build the atomic bomb were organized under the U.S. Army Corps of Engineers into the Manhattan Project. A month later, General Leslie R. Groves became its commanding officer, and the project received top priorities

John Lamperti

Lamperti is a professor of mathematics at Dartmouth College and an experienced consultant on the nuclear industry.

This map shows how the operations of the Atomic Energy Commission in 1971 were spread across the country from coast to coast. If the facilities of AEC contractors were included, the map would be unreadable. Today's map of DOE facilities would look much the same.

for the resources it needed. The U.S. race for the bomb was on in earnest. This story is told briefly in Chapter 1 of this book.

One fundamental policy adopted by the Manhattan Project under General Groves has continued to characterize government nuclear work: the job was done by *contracting* with a selected few of the nation's largest and presumably best qualified corporations and universities. The Hanford Reservation was built and operated during the war by Du Pont. Tennessee Eastman Company (an Eastman Kodak subsidiary) and the University of Chicago were responsible for most of the work at Oak Ridge. Some thought was given to making Los Alamos a military laboratory, but this idea was rejected, and the Los Alamos laboratory was put under the management of the University of California. The pattern was established: contractors would perform the work for the government, in government-owned facilities sometimes built by the same contractors, under agreements that provided for payment of expenses plus a fee for services rendered. (Some of the wartime contractors waived the management fee temporarily.) This system of organization has proved extremely durable—unlike the military control under which the first plants and laboratories were developed.

Civilian Rule: The Atomic Energy Commission

In August 1945, the American public and Congress discovered the existence of the secret, $2.2 billion, government-owned empire in which the first nuclear weapons had been created. The future of this huge program immediately became controversial. Legislation to implement continuing military control was drafted with the help of the War Department and introduced in Congress in the fall of 1945. This measure, known as the May-Johnson Bill, soon encountered heavy opposition, and an alternative plan for civilian direction emerged from a special joint House and Senate committee chaired by Senator Brian McMahon. American scientists, organizing politically for the first time, played an important part in the struggle for civilian management of the atomic program.[1]

Congress decided for civilian control, and on August 1, 1946, President Harry S. Truman signed into law a bill from McMahon's committee which became the Atomic Energy Act of 1946. The act established a complete government monopoly over nearly all aspects of nuclear technology, including ownership of materials and facilities. Control was placed in the hands of a five-member civilian board called the Atomic Energy Commission (AEC); the commissioners and a general manager would be appointed by the President subject to Senate confirmation. The AEC's Division of Military Application was to manage the weapons work; other divisions included Production (of nuclear materials), Biology and Medicine, and Research. A Military Liaison Committee of six senior officers would express the military's interests, and a nine-member General Advisory Committee (GAC) of scientists was established to assist the commissioners, who would not necessarily have technical training.

The "McMahon Act," as the Atomic Energy Act was also known, also set up a permanent Joint Committee on Atomic Energy (JCAE), one of the few congressional committees to be established by law rather than by congressional rule. The JCAE had authority over all aspects of the atomic energy program except appropriations and was supposed to be kept "fully and currently informed" by the AEC. In addition, the act prohibited most forms of international cooperation in the nuclear field, required FBI clearances for everybody who was to work for the AEC or (in many cases) for one of its contractors, and provided the death penalty for disclosing restricted data "with intent to injure the United States."

The new commission took over the atomic program on January 1, 1947. The AEC's first chairman was David E. Lilienthal, who had directed the Tennessee Valley Authority (TVA) during the New Deal era. Lilienthal later wrote of his hopes that nuclear energy would lead to a far-reaching civilian industry to benefit the nation.[2] His actual service, however, was almost entirely devoted to revitalizing and enlarging the wartime facilities for producing nuclear bombs. During Lilienthal's term as AEC chairman (1947–50) and that of his successor Gordon Dean (1950–53), facilities at Los Alamos, Hanford, and Oak Ridge were restored and enlarged, important new ones were planned and constructed, and a great many new nuclear weapons were designed, built, and tested.

During the early years of the commission, especially the years after the first Soviet atomic test explosion in 1949, major steps were taken which together constituted a great escalation of the U.S. nuclear weapons effort. The most dramatic of these was the decision to build the "super" or H-bomb. The first superbomb was tested on November 1, 1952, at Enewetak Atoll, and it produced an explosion nearly 1,000 times more powerful than that which destroyed Hiroshima. But other developments were also of great importance. The Savannah River plant was built—"the biggest single construction job in history"[3]—in order to produce more plutonium and other materials for both fission and fusion bombs. The Rocky Flats plant near Denver and a new weapons lab at Livermore, California, were established; other facilities were expanded and upgraded (see Chapter 11). A United States uranium mining and milling industry was created and two more gas-diffusion uranium enrichment plants were planned and built (see Chapter 20). The variety of nuclear fission weapons multiplied; they became both larger, approaching the megaton range, and smaller, intended for "theater" or tactical use. Altogether, in a few years an awesome advance in destructive power was achieved.

"Atoms for Peace": The Atomic Energy Act of 1954

The Atomic Energy Act of 1946 went a long way to try to preserve a U.S. government monopoly on nuclear technology, but for many reasons this proved impossible. The Soviet bomb, the British nuclear program, and domestic pressures for a commercial nuclear technology all pushed the Republican administration of 1953 toward a changed policy. President Dwight D. Eisenhower's dramatic "Atoms for Peace" speech at the United Nations in December 1953, and the revised Atomic Energy Act of 1954, were the U.S. government's response to these forces.

The purpose of the 1954 act, which was a major rewrite of the original McMahon Act, was to open the door both for international nuclear cooperation and for the development of nuclear power by private industry in alliance with the AEC. Privately owned nuclear reactors would be licensed by the commission. The government would retain ownership of all nuclear fuel but would permit its use in private power stations. Bilateral agreements with other countries for the peaceful development of atomic energy were authorized. The 1954 act also contained liberalized patent and secrecy provisions.

The main issue in dispute during the debate on the revised act was the question of public versus private development of nuclear power, and the decision was made in favor of private industry. The AEC itself would not be permitted to enter the electricity supply business, so the vision of a nuclear-power TVA was rejected and replaced by one calling for private capital and initiative. According to one analyst: "The passage of the 1954 act truly represented the birth of a new era in atomic energy development. Its enactment brought the JCAE squarely into the middle of the AEC reactor program, where it has remained since."[4]

Although the 1954 revision made possible the growth of a civilian nuclear industry, it hardly had any effect on the development and manufacture of nuclear weapons by the AEC. Despite hopes that "atoms for peace" could mean turning swords into plowshares, the production of atomic "swords" continued with little change under the new law.

The Boom Years

After the 1954 revision of the Atomic Energy Act, the entire nuclear program, military and civilian, continued for twenty more years under essentially the same system of government control. The AEC encouraged the growth of uranium mining and milling, and the United States became the world's largest producer of yellowcake. The nuclear weapons stockpile continued to expand in both numbers and variety, and by the mid-sixties it had reached roughly the level (around 30,000 weapons) at which it would remain throughout the seventies. All the major nuclear warhead production facilities date back to the fifties. And with much help and prodding from the government, the nuclear power industry was born and began its rapid expansion which continued into the seventies.

In September 1954 at Shippingport, Pennsylvania, ground was broken for the nation's first nuclear power station. Although the Shippingport plant's electrical output was for civilian use, its origin was military. The reactor design was based on the naval power plants that Westinghouse had been building for nuclear submarines, and Admiral Hyman G. Rickover and his navy group were in charge of construction. A

3-2   NUCLEAR POWER: FROM SHIP TO SHORE

COMMERCIAL NUCLEAR POWER in the United States began with the naval reactors project headed by Captain (Admiral after 1953) Hyman Rickover. In 1950 Rickover's group, long active in development of the nuclear-propelled submarine, drafted a memorandum to the Joint Chiefs of Staff proposing development of a nuclear aircraft carrier. The Joint Chiefs of Staff responded in November 1951 with a formal requirement for the carrier reactor. Both the navy and the Atomic Energy Commission (AEC) then endorsed Rickover's choice of Westinghouse Corporation as the principal contractor for the project.

But in 1953 a new Republican administration took office in Washington. The Eisenhower administration was determined to cut the federal budget—and (in contrast to the present time) high-cost military projects were not excluded. The nuclear carrier reactor was an early victim of the economy drive.

Other issues clouded the picture, however. Commercial and political interest in nuclear *power* generation was growing, and some industry groups were seeking wider participation in the new technology. The old struggle between public and private power advocates was finding a new battleground in the nuclear field, with enthusiasts for public power pushing for a civilian demonstration project. The AEC felt itself under pressure from several directions, military and civilian.

By the end of 1953 these forces had resulted in a decision to build the nation's first nuclear power plant. It would be a scaled-up version of the discontinued carrier reactor, using a pressurized-water design similar to that being incorporated into the submarine *Nautilus*. Rickover and his navy group were to be in charge of the construction. A new contract was signed in October with Westinghouse, whose Bettis Laboratory would design and build the reactor itself and its primary coolant system. (Another contractor would provide the rest of the steam machinery and the generating equipment.) The project, though not the aircraft carrier itself, was saved.

Early in 1954 the Duquesne Light Company of Pittsburgh was chosen as the industrial partner, and Shippingport, Pennsylvania, was selected as the plant site. The reactor went critical for the first time on December 2, 1957—exactly fifteen years after the first chain reaction was achieved by Enrico Fermi's group at the University of Chicago. Electrical power generation began a few days later. The cost of Shippingport's sixty megawatts of electricity was some ten times higher than the prevailing rate, but the plant was technically successful. It contributed greatly to the public prestige of the Naval Reactors Branch and its chief as well as to the U.S. government's "Atoms for Peace" program, and it helped to secure the predominance of light-water reactors in the nuclear power boom which was soon to follow.

civilian firm would build, own, and operate the electrical generating equipment, but the nuclear reactor would remain the property of the AEC. The plant went into operation at the end of 1957 as a technically successful, but very expensive, demonstration project.

Revision of the Atomic Energy Act and the start of construction at Shippingport did not immediately result in large investments of private capital in nuclear power development. An important additional boost was provided in 1957 with the passage of the Price-Anderson amendment to the Atomic Energy Act. This measure put a ceiling on the possible liability of any nuclear power licensee in the event of an accident—one far below the possible costs; it also set up a system of federal government indemnity to supplement the limited private insurance that was available. The amendment removed a major obstacle to private nuclear power development, and it has been bitterly attacked by critics of the industry.[5] The Price-Anderson Act was extended by Congress in 1965 and again, in modified form, in 1975.

Electrical utilities soon began to build and operate their own nuclear plants. Five privately owned nuclear power reactors, all of the light-water type, were in operation by the end of 1962 and were capable of generating somewhat under 800 megawatts of electricity. Fourteen years later, sixty reactors with a total capacity of 43,000 megawatts were on line, and 146 more were under construction or on order. Power reactor sales throughout the nonsocialist world were dominated by two U.S. companies—Westinghouse and General Electric. The nuclear power boom had apparently matured and seemed to be here to stay.

In 1964 another change in the law further increased the role of the private sector. For the first time, utilities were permitted to own the nuclear fuel for their power reactors, and after 1970, private ownership was to become the norm for the industry. Privately owned uranium would be enriched for a fee in the U.S. gas-diffusion plants, for both domestic and foreign customers.

One major governmental change during this period cannot be found in the statute books: the congressional Joint Committee (JCAE) assumed a much more active role as developer and promoter of the multifaceted nuclear enterprise. In the process, the traditional separation of powers between the executive (the AEC) and the legislative (JCAE) branches of government was badly strained. Critics plausibly charged that when the committee opted to become a nuclear promoter, its assigned role as critical "watchdog" and guardian of the public interest was left vacant. Examples of its neglect include the public health dangers from the testing of nuclear weapons and the needless deaths of many of the early uranium miners.[6] Observers friendly to the JCAE and the AEC have described the situation as follows:

> The paternalism of the Joint Committee—its fatherly concern for the atomic energy program—has never been more clearly revealed than in the committee's response to criticism from environmentalists. Witnesses who appeared before the Joint Committee during hearings on the issues of thermal pollution and the hazards of power plant radiation were heard to complain that some JCAE members were unabashed advocates of nuclear power, whereas the witnesses had expected legislative objectivity.[7]

The JCAE also promoted a number of projects, such as the nuclear-powered airplane, which outside experts (and sometimes insiders, too) regarded as ill-conceived and undesirable.

During these years, the AEC continued to use industrial and university contractors to operate the facilities it owned, which included all the laboratories and plants for designing and making nuclear weapons, the facilities for producing nuclear materials such as plutonium and tritium, and the uranium-enrichment plants. The bulk of the AEC contracts continued to go to the same firms, many of them with involvements dating back to the Manhattan Project. The largest recipients have included Union Carbide, General Electric, Bendix, Sandia (a subsidiary of Western Electric and the American Telephone and Telegraph Company), Du Pont, the University of Chicago, and the University of California. Most of the contracts have been on a cost-plus-fee basis. In addition to the direct advantages to the company, holding such contracts gave firms the opportunity to develop nuclear expertise that could later be put to commercial use. In many cases the experience could be gained in no other way, since the technology was a secret government monopoly. For example, AEC-sponsored work on naval nuclear propulsion unquestionably gave General Electric and Westinghouse their early lead in power-reactor technology and helped the two become the giants of this field for the entire Western world.

Almost from the beginning, the AEC's operational work was managed through field and area offices. The system set up by the AEC's first general manager had its "Operations Offices" in New York, Chicago, Richland (in Washington, close to Hanford), Los Alamos, and Oak Ridge. The Los Alamos office, later moved to Albuquerque, was responsible for the actual manufacture of nuclear weapons. Subsequently, additional offices were added in Las Vegas (responsible for the Nevada Test Site), Idaho Falls, San Francisco, and Savannah River, while the New York office which had been responsible for uranium procurement was eventually closed. Area offices reporting to these Operations Offices are responsible for, and often located at, individual facilities.

In 1971 these field offices employed about 4,000 people, with another 2,000 in Washington, D.C. The AEC's regulatory side involved 2,000 more, four-fifths of them in the D.C. area. Most of the actual nuclear work was done by over 100,000 employees of the AEC's 200-odd contractors.

Reorganization: ERDA and the NRC

One source of trouble in the AEC's management of nuclear power was the unfortunate combination of the functions of regulator and promoter within one organization. Licensing nuclear power stations and supervising their operation demands a conservative, safety-first approach which can conflict with a promoter's zeal to entice new investment and to see the industry grow. As in the case of the JCAE, outsiders such as environmentalists, public-interest groups, or local governments often felt that their concerns did not receive an adequate hearing within an organization responsible for development.[8]

The Energy Reorganization Act of 1974 was in part a response to this problem. In this act the nonregulatory parts of the AEC—including weapons design and manufacture, production of nuclear materials, reactor design and development, and related physical research—were separated from the licensing and regulatory functions. The former became the responsibility of a new body called the Energy Research and Development Administration (ERDA), while the latter were reorganized into an independent agency called the Nuclear Regulatory Commission (NRC). ERDA was to be directed by a single administrator appointed by the President, while the NRC was composed of five appointed commissioners.

At the same time that Congress separated the regulatory functions of the AEC, it transferred into the new ERDA a number of nonnuclear federal energy programs so that it became a central agency for energy planning and development. The oil embargo and "energy crisis" of 1973 had made it clear that the era of cheap and plentiful fossil fuels could not last idefinitely and that planning and preparation for a transition to other sources was essential. ERDA was established in part to help meet this need, although about one-third of its budget was to be spent on nuclear weapons—an activity of doubtful help to our energy future.

Creating an independent regulatory body was widely seen as a constructive step, but there is some doubt as to how effective the change has

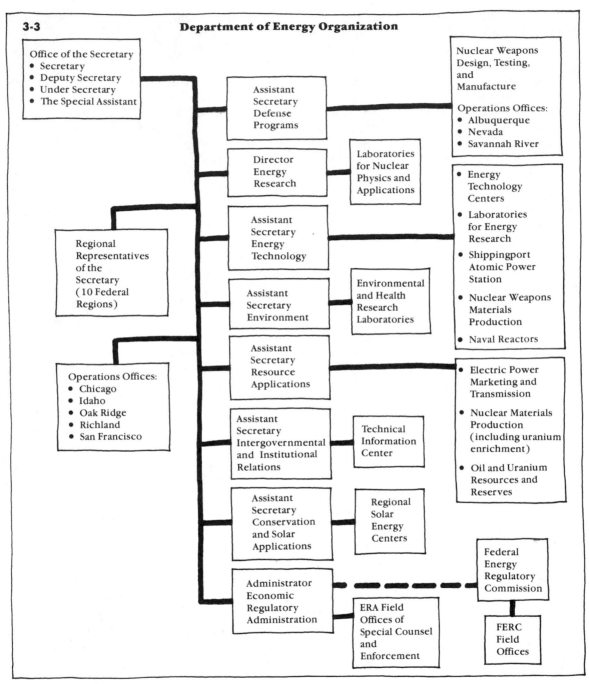

3-3   **Department of Energy Organization**

Office of the Secretary
- Secretary
- Deputy Secretary
- Under Secretary
- The Special Assistant

Assistant Secretary Defense Programs

Nuclear Weapons Design, Testing, and Manufacture

Operations Offices:
- Albuquerque
- Nevada
- Savannah River

Director Energy Research

Laboratories for Nuclear Physics and Applications

- Energy Technology Centers
- Laboratories for Energy Research
- Shippingport Atomic Power Station
- Nuclear Weapons Materials Production
- Naval Reactors

Assistant Secretary Energy Technology

Regional Representatives of the Secretary (10 Federal Regions)

Assistant Secretary Environment

Environmental and Health Research Laboratories

Assistant Secretary Resource Applications

- Electric Power Marketing and Transmission
- Nuclear Materials Production (including uranium enrichment)
- Oil and Uranium Resources and Reserves

Operations Offices:
- Chicago
- Idaho
- Oak Ridge
- Richland
- San Francisco

Assistant Secretary Intergovernmental and Institutional Relations

Technical Information Center

Assistant Secretary Conservation and Solar Applications

Regional Solar Energy Centers

Administrator Economic Regulatory Administration

Federal Energy Regulatory Commission

ERA Field Offices of Special Counsel and Enforcement

FERC Field Offices

This elaborate bureaucracy administers the ramified operations of the Department of Energy. The major activities are the production of nuclear materials and weapons, the strategic petroleum reserve, and research and regulation for the energy industry.

been. As one NRC commissioner recently commented, "I still think it [the NRC] is fundamentally geared to trying to nurture a growing industry."[9] The Kemeny Commission, created by President Jimmy Carter to investigate the accident at the Three Mile Island nuclear plant in March 1979, states in its report: "We find that the NRC is so preoccupied with the licensing of plants that it has not given primary consideration to overall safety issues." The report concludes that "with its present organization, staff and attitudes, the NRC is unable to fulfill its responsibility for providing an acceptable level of safety for nuclear power plants."[10]

The End of the Joint Committee

The Joint Committee on Atomic Energy (JCAE) was once considered the most powerful committee in Congress. It was created at a time when the new technology possessed glamour and prestige, and service on the JCAE was a sought-after plum. It was the only permanent joint committee ever to receive continuing authority to report legislation, and it usually reported identical bills to each chamber of Congress. If its bills were amended, the JCAE itself acted as the House-Senate conference committee and could restore the measures to their original form. The long tenure of some of the JCAE's early stalwarts, and its close relationship with the AEC (especially after 1958), added to its domination of nuclear-related legislation.

However, the JCAE did not long survive the end of the AEC. The committee's first major setbacks came in 1976. Most important was its inability to implement a Ford administration proposal that would have opened the uranium-enrichment step in the nuclear fuel cycle to private investment. Opponents defeated an attempt to have a veteran committee staffer appointed to the NRC. Retirements and electoral defeats left the JCAE weakened, and a caucus of House Democrats voted to strip it of most of its extraordinary legislative powers. At the opening of the Ninety-fifth Congress, the House voted

rules changes assigning nuclear concerns to five other committees, thus giving greatly increased access to outsiders. The Senate soon passed a similar measure, and it was then little surprise when the Joint Committee on Atomic Energy was abolished on August 7, 1977.

The Department of Energy

ERDA did not prove to be a long-lived organization. On August 4, 1977, President Carter signed a bill creating the Department of Energy (DOE) as the twelfth cabinet-level department in the executive branch of the federal government. The new department was charged with giving "... a clear direction and focus to America's energy future by providing the framework for carrying out a comprehensive, balanced national energy policy."[11] Despite the peaceful sound of this statement, the DOE has spent over one-third of its funds (excluding oil purchases for the Strategic Petroleum Reserve) for military activities, mostly nuclear bombs and warheads. The Reagan administration plans to increase these expenditures from about $3 billion to $5 billion per year.

At its creation, the DOE was entrusted with all the functions formerly assigned to ERDA, as well as those of the Federal Energy Administration and the Federal Power Commission. The DOE also took on certain energy-related functions of five other cabinet departments. It has continued to carry out most of the AEC/ERDA production and development functions through the already existing network of field offices and contractors. The NRC, which was not affected by the reorganization, retained the responsibility for licensing and supervising the civilian nuclear power industry.

The first secretary of the DOE was James Schlesinger. Schlesinger, who has a Ph.D. in economics from Harvard, previously served in government as chairman of the AEC, director of the CIA, and Secretary of Defense. This background suggests a military and nuclear bias for the new department, and the DOE's budget for fiscal

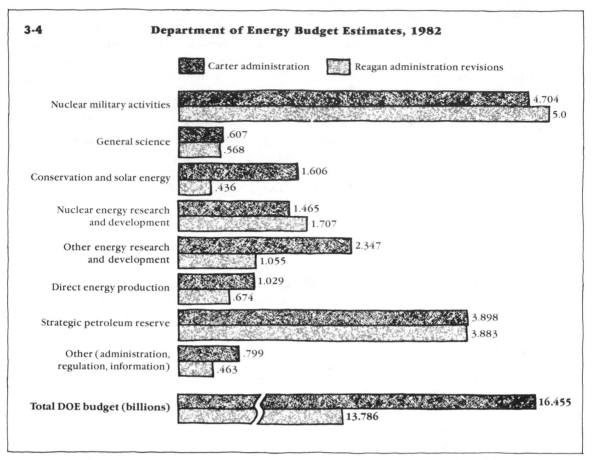

3-4   **Department of Energy Budget Estimates, 1982**

Carter administration   Reagan administration revisions

	Carter	Reagan
Nuclear military activities	4.704	5.0
General science	.607	.568
Conservation and solar energy	1.606	.436
Nuclear energy research and development	1.465	1.707
Other energy research and development	2.347	1.055
Direct energy production	1.029	.674
Strategic petroleum reserve	3.898	3.883
Other (administration, regulation, information)	.799	.463
Total DOE budget (billions)	16.455	13.786

Note that nuclear military activities and the strategic petroleum reserve account for 64 percent of President Reagan's budget. Portions of the budget categories "General Science" and "Nuclear Energy Research and Development" are also attributable to military activities. In comparison, the Department of Energy spent $15 billion in 1980, of which $3 billion was for military nuclear activities.

year 1978 confirms that these were the main priorities. Three programs dominate the figures: nuclear weapons, Energy Supply R & D (largely nuclear) plus uranium enrichment, and the Strategic Petroleum Reserve. Although many analysts believe that the most important energy resources to be developed in the near future are conservation and solar energy,[12] these areas account for a relatively small, and shrinking, fraction of the DOE's expenditures.

The legislation establishing the DOE provided for eight assistant secretaries, an Office of Energy Research, an Economic Regulatory Administration, an Energy Information Administration, and the Federal Energy Regulatory Commission (which deals only with nonnuclear matters). The DOE has roughly 20,000 employees—about 12,000 work in the field and the remainder work in the Washington, D.C., area.

The DOE, like its predecessors, carries out most of its program by contracting with private firms and universities, and its activities involve some 120,000 contractor employees. Many of the largest DOE contractors, including the top

3-5   SOME MAJOR U.S. NUCLEAR CONTRACTORS: THEN (1965) AND NOW (1980)

Contractor Name	Rank (1965)	Dollars in 1965 (millions)	Rank (1980)	Dollars in 1980 (millions)
University of California	—	at least $257	1	$902
Union Carbide	1	218	2	684
Sandia (Western Electric)	2	218	3	560
Westinghouse Electric	9	61	4	486
E. I. du Pont de Nemours	6	89	5	388
Bendix	4	100	6	295
Tennessee Valley Authority	—	—	7	293
AUA; University of Chicago	—	at least 79	8	283
Ohio Valley Electric Co.	—	—	9	264
EG&G	15	26	10	263
Rockwell International	8	62	11	242
General Electric	3	196	12	237
Associated Universities	—	at least 52	13	203
Reynolds Electrical and Engineering	5	97	16	153
Goodyear Atomic	7	63	20	90
Aerojet-General	10	44	Not listed among top eighty DOE contractors for 1980.	
Phillips Petroleum	11	40		
Dow Chemical	12	38		

In fiscal year 1980, a total of 11,494 contractors, including 243 colleges and universities, did business with the Department of Energy. The contracts totaled $9.474 billion.

four, are heavily engaged in nuclear weapons work, and many (but not all) of these firms are also large contractors with the Pentagon. Several large companies and the University of California have persisted for many years as major recipients of government contracts for nuclear weapons and energy work.

Concluding Remarks

We have examined a variety of arrangements that have been used to manage and develop nuclear technology in the United States. Underneath the complexity, some clear evolutionary trends can be described. The technology originated as a secret government-military monopoly during World War II, and many wished it to remain so after the war. But political and commercial pressures acted in a different direction, and civilian nuclear power was born. This industry has grown unevenly, with a boom period during the sixties and early seventies followed by a major slowdown. The scope of the private sector has also expanded and now includes most of the "front end" of the fuel cycle except for uranium enrichment. The government has not failed to nurture the nuclear power industry. Estimates of the dollar value of government support for nuclear energy vary widely, but all agree that the industry has enjoyed assistance worth tens of billions of dollars.[13]

The organization of nuclear weapons production still has much in common with the system that developed during the forties. The work is done in a network of labs and plants which are owned by the government but operated by contractors. This network, although much expanded, includes the major Manhattan Project facilities: Hanford, Oak Ridge, and Los Alamos. Many of the contractors, such as Du Pont, General Electric, and the University of California, have been deeply involved since the beginning. Government control is exercised through a chain of field offices which were set up under the AEC in the forties and which have been retained (and others added) by the AEC's successors. Additional major facilities have been added to the system, including the "national laboratories" (in addition to the weapons-development labs) which contribute to knowledge of nuclear physics and its applications, including nuclear power technology.

It was pointed out long ago that the relationships between government, the universities, science, and industry which have characterized nuclear technology were a new development in U.S. political life. "What we are trying to do," said David Lilienthal in 1950, "... is develop a new kind of set-up in American industrial affairs which is a hybrid of public and private."[14] Another commentator described the system as suggesting a "missing link between capitalism and socialism."[15] Although time and familiarity have dulled the sense that there is anything surprising or controversial about such a hybrid, nothing quite like it was around before the discovery of nuclear fission in 1938.

The future of the current government organization responsible for nuclear technology—the Department of Energy—is uncertain.[16] It seems highly likely, however, that many features of the present system, such as contractor operation of government-owned facilities, will persist even if there are changes at the top. The great corporations such as General Electric, Du Pont, Union Carbide, Westinghouse, and Bendix (among many others) will undoubtedly retain their commanding positions in the industry. The exchange of high-level personnel between industry and government is also likely to continue, as will the basic similarity of outlook between leaders within the industry and the government officials who supervise and regulate it.[17] Continued governmental tenderness toward nuclear power is probably to be expected, whether or not the DOE is replaced by some other form of organization.

It is wise to recall President Eisenhower's warning. The United States does have a "military-industrial complex" with great influence and power. Within its orbit, it is commonly assumed that the national interests of our country are closely identified with the well-being of the nuclear weapons complex and the nuclear power industry. It is essential that this assumption be questioned and that vital decisions about weapons and energy are made in the interest of the nation as a whole—and of the human race.

Suggested Readings

Allardice and Trapnell give in *The Atomic Energy Commission* an admiring account of the evolution of the nuclear industry and the government institutions associated with it, up to about 1973. *Light Water: How the Nuclear Dream Dissolved; Nuclear Power: Development and Management of a Technology;* and *The Menace of Atomic Energy* concentrate on the nuclear power industry; *Light Water* and *The Menace of Atomic Energy* are in quite different ways critical of it. York in *The Advisors: Oppenheimer, Teller and the Superbomb* describes the decision to proceed with a crash program for the hydrogen bomb, and also outlines the general development of both the U.S. and Soviet nuclear weapons programs. Metzger in *The Atomic Establishment* is severely critical of the Atomic Energy Commission and the Joint Committee, charging them with mismanagement and the coverup of major mistakes. In *Contracting for Atoms* Orlans focuses on the question of operation by contract, including a discussion of why that method was chosen and how it has worked. The DOE document, *DOE Research and Development and Field Facilities,* gives an extensive description of the offices, labs, and plants under the Department's control, and its annual reports (such as the *Secretary's Annual Report to Congress,* January 1981) help to form a picture of its current budget, operations, and policies. Finally, *Congressional Quarterly* is useful in describing legislation and changes in the congressional committee system.

ALLARDICE, CORBIN, AND EDWARD R. TRAPNELL. *The Atomic Energy Commission.* New York: Praeger, 1974.

BUPP, IRVIN, AND JEAN-CLAUDE DERIAN. *Light Water: How the Nuclear Dream Dissolved.* New York: Basic Books, 1978.

DAWSON, FRANK. *Nuclear Power: Development and Management of a Technology.* Seattle: University of Washington Press, 1976.

METZGER, H. PETER. *The Atomic Establishment.* New York: Simon and Schuster, 1972.

NADER, RALPH, AND JOHN ABBOTTS. *The Menace of Atomic Energy.* New York: W. W. Norton, 1977.

ORLANS, HAROLD. *Contracting for Atoms.* Washington, D.C.: The Brookings Institution, 1966.

U.S. Department of Energy. *Secretary's Annual Report to Congress,* January 1981.

U.S. Department of Energy. *DOE Research and Development and Field Facilities.* Washington, D.C., June 1979.

YORK, HERBERT. *The Advisors: Oppenheimer, Teller and the Superbomb.* San Francisco: W. H. Freeman, 1976.

Part Two

Nuclear Weapons Effects

The force of the blast wave from the Nagasaki bomb ripped the siding and roofing from these industrial buildings half a mile from ground zero. The smoke-stacks, because of their tubular structure, withstood the blast of about 8 pounds per square inch and the accompanying winds of around 200 miles per hour.

4. Blast, Heat, and Radiation

The prompt effects of a nuclear weapon explosion are predictable. They can be detailed with great precision based on the experience of tests, of prior use, and on the physics of radiation and shock wave behavior. The expanding fireball of a one-megaton bomb rises to form a mushroom cloud ten miles across and thirteen miles high. It gives rise to prompt effects of blast, fire, thermal radiation, nuclear radiation, and the delayed effects of fallout and ozone depletion. A one-megaton weapon releases about sixty times more total energy than the Hiroshima bomb, which caused 200,000 deaths.

THE DEVASTATING EFFECTS of a nuclear weapon explosion come from the blast and heat that radiate out from the point of detonation, and from the radioactive debris sucked into the mushroom cloud and carried downwind. It all starts with the fireball.

The Expanding Fireball

At the instant of detonation all the energy of a nuclear explosion is contained in a small superheated volume of nuclear debris, at conditions of pressure and temperature much like those in the center of the sun. In less than a thousandth of a second this fireball cools down to around 300,000°c. Simultaneously a powerful shock wave develops in the air, traveling beyond the fireball at supersonic speed. The energy of the explosion, originally largely in the form of high-energy X rays, transforms first into a brilliant flash of visible light and then into intense thermal radiation that can set fires for miles around. If the weapon detonates high above the ground, the radioactive remains of weapon material rise, with the fireball, high into the atmosphere and travel with the prevailing winds, spreading long-lived radioactive fallout around the earth. If the explosion is a ground-burst, the fireball vaporizes and carries a large volume of surface materials into the atmosphere. Radioactive nuclei of weapon debris attach to the dirt particles and return to earth downwind from the point of detonation as deadly fallout.

The fireball from explosion of a one-megaton nuclear weapon grows to more than a mile in diameter in seconds and rises into the atmosphere, forming a mushroom cloud ten miles across and extending to an altitude of 70,000 feet. The energy released in a nuclear explosion is so great that a special unit is needed to quantify it. When a one-megaton weapon explodes it releases energy equal to the amount released by exploding one million tons of TNT. This would fill a freight train 300 miles long. It is enough energy to transform about ten million tons of

Kosta Tsipis

Tsipis is a nuclear physicist who has devoted most of his recent research efforts to studies of the technological aspects of national and international security issues.

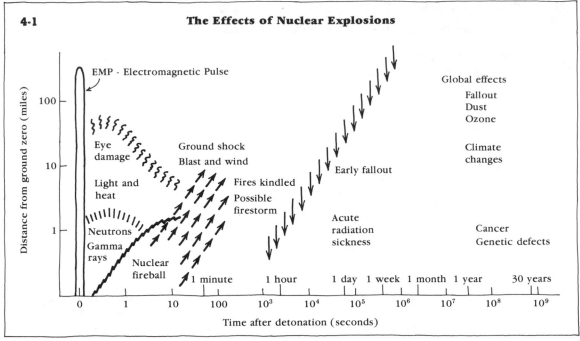

4-1 The Effects of Nuclear Explosions

Nuclear weapons effects are extensive in space and time. In addition to the blast and heat that cause the most severe immediate damage, and the radioactive fallout downwind from a surface burst, there are the electromagnetic pulse, which instantly disrupts electronic equipment perhaps hundreds of miles away, and potential genetic damage expressed in future generations of beings.

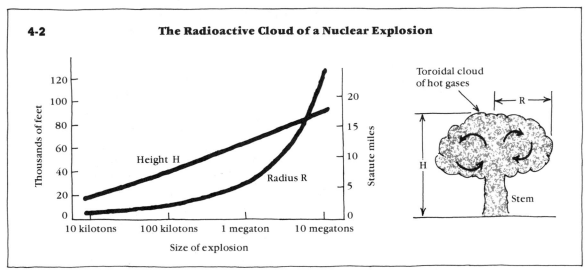

4-2 The Radioactive Cloud of a Nuclear Explosion

The mushroom cloud of a nuclear explosion reaches its full height in just a few minutes. Here the height and radius are estimated for 10 minutes after a surface or low-altitude burst.

water from ice into steam. It is the energy that would be released by burning about thirty million gallons of gasoline.

The sudden release of such an enormous amount of energy in a very small volume sets off many physical processes, some of catastrophic effect. We will consider the effects of a one-megaton ground burst and an airburst just high enough that the fireball never touches the ground. We begin with the effects of the prompt burst of nuclear radiation, which consists primarily of the gamma rays, X rays, and neutrons of the initial fireball, and the strong electromagnetic pulse that accompanies a nuclear explosion. Then come the effects of thermal radiation, and later on the mechanical effects—cratering and earth tremor together with the blast wave and the hurricane winds that follow. Finally, there are long-term effects: the radioactivity of the fallout which may last for weeks, the depletion of the ozone in the atmosphere from which recovery might take a decade. Although we consider these effects individually, the separation is artificial: in the real

world they all take place simultaneously, compounding the damage that each effect alone can cause.

What we know of the physical effects of nuclear explosions comes mainly from the extensive series of above-ground tests carried out by the United States, and from the experience of Hiroshima and Nagasaki, the only instances of wartime use of nuclear weapons. The arsenals of the world include nuclear weapons having yields ranging from under one kiloton for tactical weapons to twenty megatons or more for strategic warheads aimed at cities. Many of these weapons designs have been tested only by underground explosions; perhaps some models have never been tested.

Prompt Nuclear Radiation

An intense burst of neutrons and gamma rays is produced during the first few millionths of a second of a nuclear explosion. Although weakened by collisions with air molecules, this radiation is lethal to humans out to about 1.7 miles

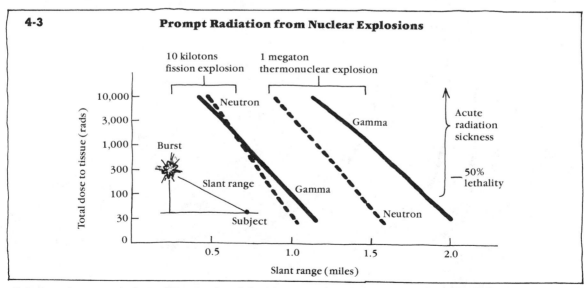

4-3   **Prompt Radiation from Nuclear Explosions**

All forms of ionizing radiation are produced, but the forms that travel far enough through air to have significant effects are gamma rays and neutrons. These are

produced in an instantaneous burst followed by a rapid decrease, so practically all prompt radiation occurs in less than one second.

from a one-megaton detonation. Within this distance, people closest to ground zero would be rendered unconscious within minutes. Farther away, unsheltered victims would die of radiation sickness in a few days or up to a month later, depending on the amount of radiation they had absorbed.

For all but the smallest nuclear weapons the prompt radiation is not the major lethal effect for humans. The radiation fluxes that can cause serious health problems and death occur at such close distances to the detonation that the effects of blast, overpressure, and thermal radiation are much more assuredly lethal than the ef-

fects of radiation. Exceptions to this are tactical weapons in the low kiloton range and especially the *neutron bomb,* known also as an *enhanced radiation weapon,* which is intended to give a lethal dose of radiation to soldiers shielded from blast and heat in tanks or other armored equipment.

Thermal Radiation

When a one-megaton weapon explodes, between 40 and 50 percent of the energy released is radiant energy in the form of light and heat; this energy travels with the speed of light, and most is absorbed by buildings, structures, peo-

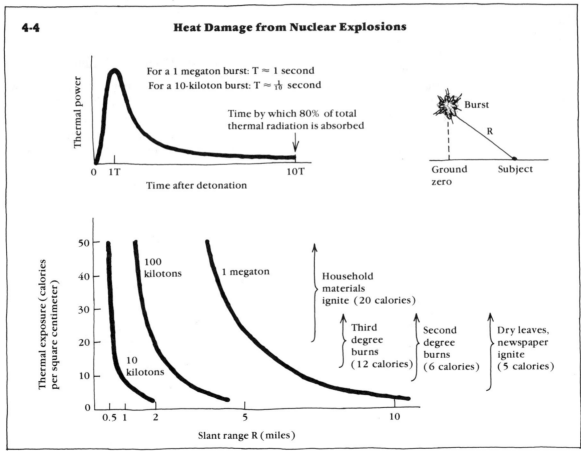

4-4   **Heat Damage from Nuclear Explosions**

The thermal effects come from an intense pulse of radiation that produces most of its effect in the first few seconds following detonation.

ple, and other living plants and animals within a second of the detonation. Even at a distance of 8.5 miles, materials such as newspaper, dry leaves, and twigs will ignite. Closer in, at 4.5 miles, the thermal radiation is sufficient to set bedding and curtains ablaze—even plywood. The exposed skin of people located out to nearly nine miles will suffer second-degree burns. Within 6.5 miles, exposed skin will suffer third-degree burns that destroy the tissue, leaving disfiguring scars.

The thermal effects of a nuclear explosion include more than the immediate flash burns. Fires are caused by thermal radiation from the weapon that ignites materials released by the blast wave: broken gas pipes, upturned stoves, ruptured gasoline tanks, and splintered wooden

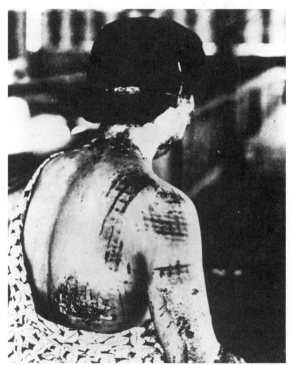

4-5 SKIN BURNS FROM THERMAL RADIATION
The skin of this Japanese bomb victim was burned in a pattern corresponding to the heat-absorbing dark-colored fabric of the kimono worn at the time of the explosion.

houses. The numerous fires that a nuclear weapon would thus initiate in a city could spread and coalesce into a mass-fire known as a *firestorm*—a single, very large fire that covers an extended area and expands by radiative heating to adjacent areas. A firestorm generates a column of rising hot gases that sucks in fresh air from the periphery of the fire causing winds of 100 miles per hour. Very high temperatures can be reached inside a firestorm, which burns until all combustible materials in the area are exhausted. Carbon dioxide formed by the firestorm tends to settle into cellars, basements, subway tunnels—asphyxiating those who may have sought shelter there.

A firestorm occurred following the Hiroshima attack, fueled by the light, combustible materials used in buildings. Apparently no firestorm occurred at Nagasaki. Extensive firestorms were ignited at Dresden and Tokyo during World War II by large incendiary air raids against these cities by the U.S. Air Force.

Electromagnetic Pulse and Induced Currents

The complete ionization of atoms within the fireball produces a separation of electric charge (negative electrons knocked away from positive nuclei). In turn the motion of the electrons generates a giant electromagnetic pulse, like that created by a bolt of lightning and evident as "static" on radio and television sets. The electromagnetic pulse of a nuclear blast, however, takes place about a thousand times faster than a lightning stroke, and it can be many tens of thousands of times stronger. The electric field of the pulse rises to many tens of thousands of volts per meter hundreds of miles away. This electromagnetic pulse reaches much farther than any other prompt effect of a nuclear detonation and can damage electrical and electronic equipment tens or hundreds of kilometers away. All unprotected devices such as radios and television transmitters and receivers, control circuits and devices, computers and

4-6   **Air Blast and Wind from Nuclear Explosions**

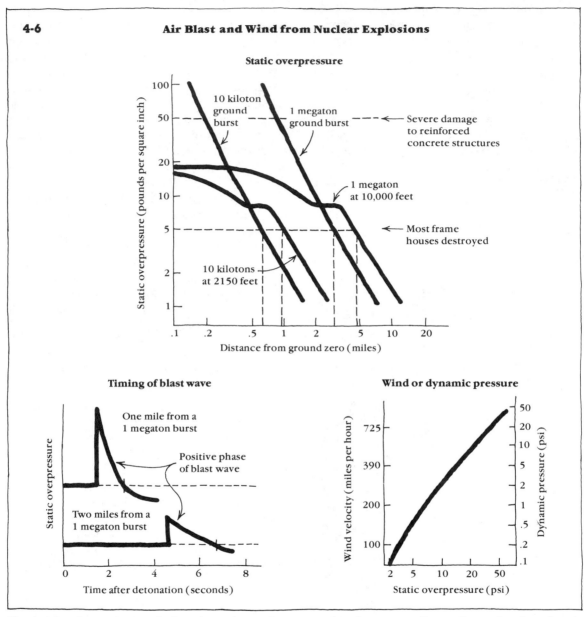

The height of a nuclear explosion above the surface has an important effect on the blast wave produced. For an airburst, the blast wave and its reflection from the ground combine to produce a higher overpressure than for a groundburst. For each value of static overpressure there is a corresponding dynamic pressure, first experienced as a fierce wind blowing outward from the explosion.

hospital equipment would be vulnerable. Such effects were seen after the high-altitude tests over Johnston Island in 1962. It is probable that several nuclear explosions high over the United States would disrupt the command and control communications network of the Defense Department and destroy the great majority of civilian electrical and electronic equipment.

Airblast Overpressure and Dynamic Pressure

By far the most destructive effect of a nuclear weapon on humans and the human habitat is the airblast caused by the explosion. A nuclear detonation in the air or on the ground creates a shock front of very high pressure that propagates outward from the point of detonation, crushing and sweeping everything in its path. Arrival of the overpressure shock wave at a point away from the explosion is experienced as a sudden and shattering blow followed by hurricane winds directed away from the target.

The high pressure inside the front that bears down on structures and living beings is known as "overpressure," since it is pressure above the normal atmospheric pressure of 14.7 pounds per square inch (psi), while the "dynamic pressure," caused by the winds trailing the rushing shock front, is experienced as a strong wind moving away from the explosion that pushes against every surface it encounters. Both overpressure and dynamic pressure diminish as the shock wave moves out from the point of detonation. The distance from the point of explosion to which a given overpressure will extend varies somewhat with the height of burst of the weapon above the ground.

An ordinary frame house will collapse at five pounds per square inch (psi) overpressure, which is exceeded out to 2.8 miles from a one-megaton explosion. Reinforced concrete structures will be crushed within the region of fifty to one hundred psi overpressure, which extends to about 0.6 miles from the point of detonation. However, a one-megaton weapon ex-

ploded at 10,000 feet will generate five psi overpressure out to 4.4 miles away from the point of detonation.

The gale-force wind that follows the shock wave is sufficient at 4.5 miles to hurl a standing human being against a wall with several times the force of gravity. It will cause glass shards, stones, metallic objects, anything shattered by the overpressure, to fly with velocities above one hundred miles per hour. Within five miles few people in the open or in ordinary buildings are likely to survive the overwhelming force of the blast. Trees will be uprooted and even heavy vehicles overturned. Many people inside will be crushed as buildings collapse or will be wounded by the debris. Even farther away, those in the open will be stuck and lacerated by flying debris.

Cratering and Ground Shock

When a nuclear weapon is exploded high enough—more than 2,000 feet for a one-megaton burst—its fireball does not touch the ground, and there is no appreciable removal of dirt into the ascending fireball. If, however, a weapon is exploded on the surface of the earth, as much as 10 or 15 percent of the released energy is coupled directly into the ground: it excavates a sizable crater and sends earthquake-like tremors through the ground. A one-megaton weapon exploded on the earth's surface will dig a crater about 200 meters in radius and 50 to 70 meters deep in ordinary soil. Most of the excavated material will be ejected to a distance about twice the radius of the crater, but a substantial amount will be vaporized or pulverized and lifted into the upper atmosphere by the rising fireball and updraft winds. This material attaches to radioactive nuclei of weapon debris and is the major source of lethal radioactive fallout downwind from a nuclear ground burst.

The shock wave in the ground has two sources: the mechanical impulse produced in reaction to the mass of soil ejected from the crater, and the ground shock induced by the air-

4-7   WEAPON EFFECTS ON A WOOD FRAME HOUSE

At the Nevada Test Site many civil structures were exposed to the fury of nuclear test explosions in 1953 and 1955. The accompanying photographs show what happens when a residence of typical frame construction takes the heat and blast about 0.7 mile from a 16-kiloton nuclear explosion. One second after detonation the radiant heat of the explosion (25 calories per square centimeter) produces a layer of black smoke; this disappears a second later. (The surface of the house did not ignite—it had been painted white to prevent ignition so that blast effects could be studied.) A second or two later the blast wave strikes with an overpressure of 5 pounds per square inch (psi).

Farther away, where the blast wave overpressure has diminished to 1.7 psi, a similar house was left standing, but its windows and doors were blown out and its joists and rafters were fractured. A house with brick veneer fared better at 1.7 psi, but one exposed to 5 psi was demolished.

Wood frame house before the test.

One second after the detonation.

The effects of the blast wave.

blast shock wave as it travels away from the point of detonation. This airblast-induced ground tremor travels for large distances with little attenuation and can cause structural damage in such things as missiles protected by concrete silos in the ground.

The amount of energy coupled to the ground by a nuclear weapon is comparable to that of an earthquake. For example, the energy released by the 1906 San Francisco earthquake has been estimated to be about 10^{16} joules, or roughly three times the energy released by a one-megaton weapon. But since only 10 to 15 percent of weapon energy is coupled to the ground, it would take a twenty-megaton weapon exploded on the ground to generate an earth tremor comparable to the San Francisco earthquake.

Fallout

The lingering radioactivity from a nuclear explosion is caused mainly by the mass of fission fragments generated by the fission of plutonium or uranium nuclei. These include radioactive isotopes with half lives ranging from tiny fractions of a second to many millions of years. These radioactive nuclei are lifted upward by the rising cloud and are carried by the prevailing wind and dispersed in the atmosphere before settling down to earth. One hour after the explosion the radioactivity from a one-megaton weapon is 10^{11} or 100 billion curies. (Each curie represents 31 billion emissions of an alpha or gamma ray, an electron, or a neutron each second.) As excited nuclei return to their normal state by emitting gamma rays or electrons, the fraction that remains radioactive becomes smaller with passing time. After a day, the activity is down to a billion curies and after a month a bit below 100 million.

How much this radioactivity affects the human population, their places of habitation and work, or their food supplies depends on many things, but the most important factor is the altitude of the weapon when detonated. If the fireball does not touch the ground, the vaporized weapon debris is lifted into the upper atmosphere. Because the particles of debris are very small, they descend very slowly and days or weeks may pass before they return to the surface, perhaps having circled the earth many times. The weapon debris is spread over a very large area and its diminished radioactivity will cause only a small increase in natural background radiation. Air bursts of nuclear weapons pose little hazard to people from radioactive

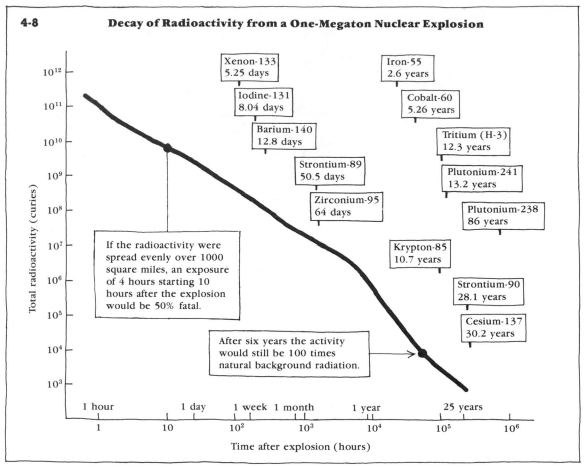

4-8   **Decay of Radioactivity from a One-Megaton Nuclear Explosion**

Xenon-133
5.25 days

Iodine-131
8.04 days

Barium-140
12.8 days

Strontium-89
50.5 days

Zirconium-95
64 days

Krypton-85
10.7 years

Iron-55
2.6 years

Cobalt-60
5.26 years

Tritium (H-3)
12.3 years

Plutonium-241
13.2 years

Plutonium-238
86 years

Strontium-90
28.1 years

Cesium-137
30.2 years

If the radioactivity were spread evenly over 1000 square miles, an exposure of 4 hours starting 10 hours after the explosion would be 50% fatal.

After six years the activity would still be 100 times natural background radiation.

Any fission explosion produces radioactive products in proportion to the fission yield. Much of this material falls back to the surface downwind from a ground-burst. The remainder circulates in the atmosphere and descends gradually over the ensuing months and years. Shown with their half lives are some of the radioactive isotopes present in the debris of nuclear explosions.

fallout unless a very large number of weapons are exploded in the atmosphere.

The situation is totally different if a nuclear weapon is exploded on or near the ground. Large quantities of dirt are vaporized, pulverized, or thrown into the air. Radioactive nuclei from the weapon debris attach themselves to these dirt particles as they are lifted by the updraft of the rising fireball. As the fireball cools, the vaporized material condenses and starts falling back to earth as black rain, or just small particles of dirt. Since the dirt particles are much larger than unattached particles of weapon debris from a mid-air explosion, they fall faster. The result is the contamination of large areas of land downwind from the point of detonation with varying levels of radioactivity. We know the lethal effects of radioactivity largely from the air bursts at Hiroshima and Nagasaki. A few days after absorbing 100 rems of radiation, a portion of the population exposed will suffer from radiation sickness—nausea, diarrhea, dehydration, increased sensitivity to infection, loss of hair, and other secondary symptoms. Larger exposures, ranging from 400 to 500 rem, result in death of about 50 percent or more of the exposed population from internal bleeding and dehydration. This level of radiation exposure causes destruction of the mucosa of the intestinal tract, and affected individuals literally pass their own insides. Exposures above 1,000 rem cause prompt and certain death within a few days. Almost instant disorientation and death occurs from exposures greater than 8,000 rem that destroy the central nervous system.

In general, the population would most probably have to be evacuated from areas that have been covered with enough radioactivity to cause accumulated doses of ten to fifty rem over a year. By this criterion, a single one-megaton weapon exploded on the ground will require evacuation of an area of 4,900 square miles for a week following detonation. A smaller area of 1,400 square miles closer to the detonation point must be evacuated for a month. Some time could be saved by large-scale bulldozing of the soil.

It is important to understand that the damaging effects of radioactivity are completely unknown to the victim until it is too late to repair the damage. There is no pain, no perception of danger—radioactive materials look, smell, and taste no different from uncontaminated materials. It will prove very difficult to keep people from entering areas having dangerous levels of radioactivity.

Ozone Depletion

Ozone, a special form of molecular oxygen, forms a thin layer ten to twenty miles up in the atmosphere where it absorbs a large fraction of the sun's ultraviolet radiation before it reaches earth. This is the radiation that causes skin burns (sunburn) and corneal damage to the eyes (snow blindness). Detonation of a nuclear weapon in the atmosphere generates a very large number of nitrogen oxide molecules: a one-megaton burst will create 10^{32} such molecules. Nitrogen oxides are known to combine with ozone and destroy it.

It is to be expected that if a substantial fraction of the ozone is depleted by nitrogen oxides, many of the diurnal vertebrates of the earth (except humans, who will probably wear protective glasses) may be blinded and die. The National Academy of Sciences estimates that 10,000 megatons of energy released by explosions of nuclear weapons would deplete as much as 80 percent of the ozone in the northern hemisphere and 30 to 40 percent in the southern hemisphere.[1] A depletion of 20 percent seems sufficient to cause blinding of unprotected animals on earth. The ozone layer would eventually re-form, but it could take five to ten years. During that time, the ecosystem on earth would have been greatly disturbed by the disappearance of thousands of diurnal species. (These estimates, however, are highly uncertain.)

Ozone depletion is a physical phenomenon that places an upper limit to the number of weapons that can be used in a nuclear war before the ecosystem of the earth collapses. There may be other effects of nuclear war (the changing of the local reflectivity of the ground, for example) that may have equally drastic effects at even smaller numbers of nuclear explosions. But we do not know about them and that is one of the dangers of nuclear war: we may perchance initiate a global catastrophe without realizing it.

Effects on Cities

The atomic bombs dropped on Hiroshima and Nagasaki had explosive yields of about sixteen kilotons and twenty-two kilotons, respectively. They were small weapons in comparison with those in the arsenals of the eighties. Nevertheless, the death toll was staggering: out of about 300,000 persons exposed in Hiroshima, between 130,000 and 150,000 people had died by December 1945, and the total, including delayed deaths by 1950, is estimated at 200,000.

4-9   **RADIOACTIVE FALLOUT FROM NUCLEAR EXPLOSIONS**

Radioactive material from a groundburst falls to earth in amounts that can be lethal for several days following detonation. Idealized, cigar-shaped fallout patterns have been computed under the assumptions of constant wind direction and velocity and stable weather conditions. The dose values on each contour are the exposure that would be acquired by a person who re-mains at the site forever. A separate figure shows the fraction of this dose that a person would receive according to how soon after the explosion the exposure begins and for how long it continues.

The idealized patterns give poor guidance about the actual pattern of fallout distribution to be expected in a nuclear attack. Local wind fluctuations and precipitation will produce vari-ations and hot spots. Some idea of an actual distribution of fallout can be obtained from the measurements taken after the Bravo test explosion in the Marshall Islands, March 1, 1954.

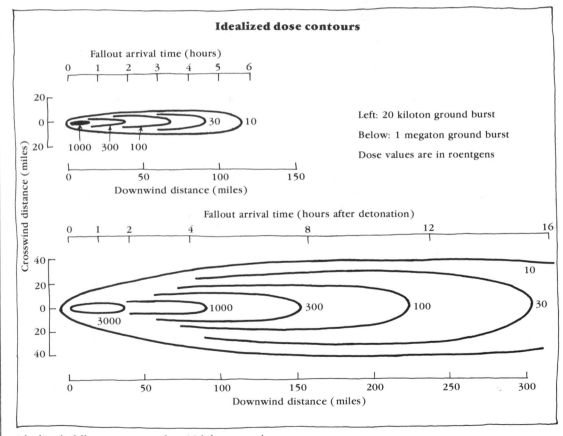

Idealized fallout patterns for 20-kiloton and one-megaton nuclear explosions occurring at ground level with a 20-mile-per-hour wind.

Fallout pattern shape

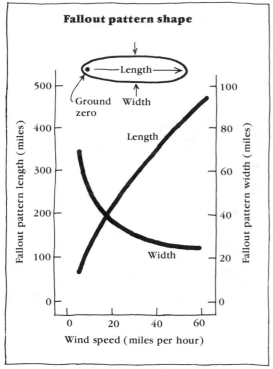

Curves giving length and width of the 100-rad contour computed for a one-megaton groundburst with various wind speeds.

Fraction of maximum dose

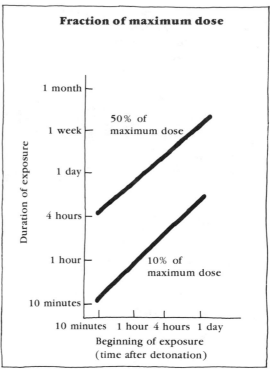

These curves show how the dose received by a subject depends on when exposure begins and how long it continues.

Estimated fallout contours for the Bravo test (15 megatons)

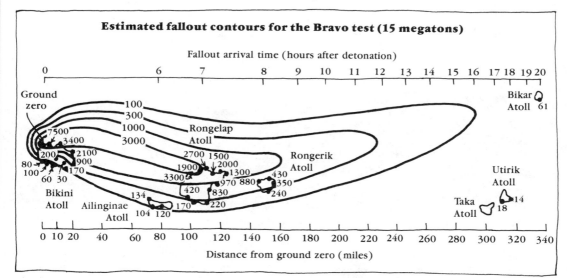

The labeled sites give accumulated doses in rads measured 96 hours after detonation.

The fatalities at Nagasaki were about half as many because that explosion was off target.[2] But a twenty-megaton explosion over New York City would destroy all buildings not only in Manhattan but also in the Bronx, Brooklyn, and Queens, and in Hoboken and Jersey City as well. Exposed people would receive second-degree burns out to twenty-five miles from the detonation. There would be between five and ten million casualties.

4-10 BAKER DAY: NUCLEAR EXPLOSIONS GO UNDERWATER

July 25, 1946: The second nuclear test explosion in the Marshall Islands. It was also the first underwater explosion—carried out to evaluate the effects of explosions in the sea on some seventy crewless ships anchored at various distances. An underwater blast wave travels about five times faster than in air, is briefer, but diminishes more slowly with distance. A 100-kiloton burst can produce an overpressure of 2,700 pounds per square inch at a distance of 3,000 feet.

Suggested Readings

The standard reference work on the effects of nuclear weapons is the volume edited by Glasstone and Dolan. Earlier editions were published in 1957 and 1962. The two other books cited below are largely based on the Glasstone and Dolan material. Numerous detailed studies of nuclear weapons effects, especially of blast effects and fallout, have been carried out under government contracts and reported through the U.S. Defense Nuclear Agency, Washington, D.C.

ADAMS, RUTH, AND SUSAN CULLEN, EDS. "The Final Epidemic." Chicago: Educational Foundation for Nuclear Science, 1981.

GLASSTONE, SAMUEL, AND PHILIP J. DOLAN. "The Effects of Nuclear Weapons." Washington, D.C.: U.S. Government Printing Office, 1977.

Report of the Secretary-General of the United Nations. "Nuclear Weapons." Boston: Autumn Press, 1980.

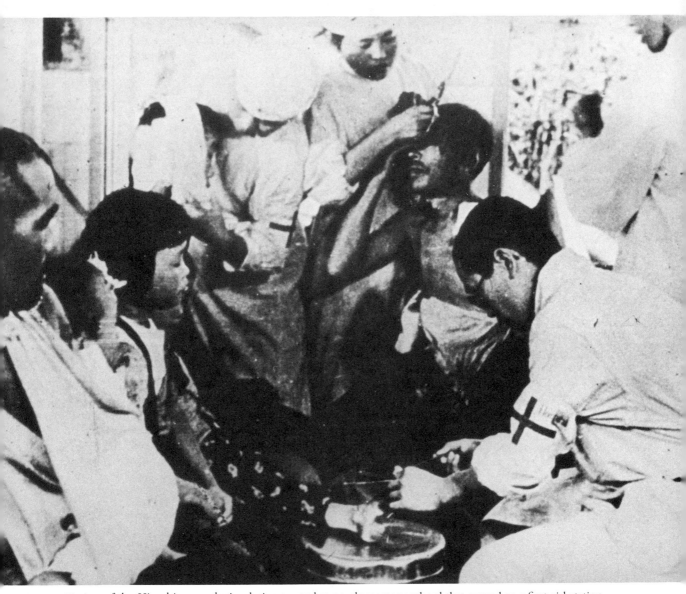

Victims of the Hiroshima explosion being treated at an elementary school that served as a first-aid station.

5. Medical Effects of a Nuclear Attack

Death and severe injury from blast, radiation, and heat are immediate effects of a nuclear attack. Protracted trauma and suffering, crowded fallout shelters, and the spread of infectious diseases are conditions that will confront the survivors. Medical, hospital, pharmaceutical, and nursing facilities will be virtually nonexistent. Food, water, and medicines will be scarce and contaminated if available at all, particularly in the remains of urban areas. The unprecedented trauma likely to follow an all-out nuclear exchange would be beyond contemplation, and certainly beyond the capacity of any remaining medical community to handle.

LANGUAGE IS NOT ADEQUATE to the task of describing the aggregate effects of a modern thermonuclear weapon on a human population. We may estimate the numbers of people killed and seriously injured, or describe the diverse processes by which bodies are crushed, skulls are fractured, flesh is burned, and tissue is radiated; nuclear strategists routinely make such calculations. Yet simply adding up these events and expressing the totals as "medical effects" fails to convey the magnitude of devastation and desolation that even a single nuclear warhead would create. A description of the "medical effects" of a full-scale exchange between nuclear superpowers risks missing the essential nature of the consequences: so profound a degree of damage to populations, their physical environments, the ecosphere—and, perhaps most important of all, to the social fabric on which human life uniquely depends—that the very nature of human existence, and the very meaning of "survival," would be changed.

Any attempt to describe and measure the medical effects—the human death and injury—caused by even a single moderately large nuclear weapon therefore creates a paradox. On the one hand, the nature and the magnitude of the immediate effects are, within reasonable limits of precision, specifiable. The calculations are straightforward and only moderately complex; indeed, over the past three decades, these effects have been described in detail in hundreds of scientific publications. On the other hand, despite this apparent specificity, the consequences are unfathomable, for we are attempting to describe and understand an event that is without precedent in human experience.

Hiroshima and Nagasaki will not serve as precedents. The weapons used on those cities were much smaller than the nuclear weapons of

Dr. Geiger, the Arthur C. Logan Professor of Community Medicine, City College, City University of New York, was co-author of the first major publication on the effects of a nuclear attack in the American medical literature and has remained concerned ever since that 1962 publication. He is a founding member of Physicians for Social Responsibility.

H. Jack Geiger, M.D.

today. Describing the effects of a single one-megaton weapon requires us to try to imagine eighty Hiroshima explosions at the same instant in one place. Since modern multiple-warhead weapons produce less energy or overkill near a single ground zero, the death and destruction produced by one new MX missile, carrying a total of six megatons in ten warheads, would equal the effect of a single 20-megaton weapon—or 1,600 Hiroshima explosions.

Hiroshima and Nagasaki, furthermore, were isolated and self-limited events occurring in an otherwise intact society. In the short term, their victims could be aided (and in the longer term, the cities themselves reconstructed) by help from outside. In any probable contemporary nuclear exchange, however, there will be no "outside" to rely on. We cannot safely assume that there will be unaffected major areas within reach of a targeted city, that resources could be mobilized effectively to help the stricken target, or that an effort to help would even be considered rational to undertake. In a population-targeted attack, every major population center may be effectively destroyed.[1]

Finally, at the time of Hiroshima, the world's total nuclear arsenal comprised two bombs. Today the two nuclear superpowers alone have more than 50,000 nuclear weapons of many sizes and types, with a wide variety of sophisticated delivery systems. The global stockpile represents a destructive potential that is literally beyond description.

The total number of deaths, and the number and types of injury from a nuclear attack, will vary with the total number of weapons, their size, their distribution, and the pattern of attack—airbursts, groundbursts, or both. Other important factors are the time of year, the day of the week, and the time of day (since commuter shifts into central cities during the working hours produce much higher concentrations of people at greatest risk than do residential distributions), and the amount, type, and adequacy of sheltering. Atmospheric conditions have a sig-

nificant effect, particularly with regard to burns and radioactive fallout, and so the presence or absence of clouds, fog, rain, and snow and the strength and direction of prevailing winds are important.

The causes of death and injury in nuclear war are blast, heat, and radiation. The medical aspects of an attack on a large city can be understood by considering the nature and impact of each force separately, and then their combined effect and the problems of survival. To be very specific we will suppose detonation of a one-megaton weapon on the heart of the target city.

Primary Blast Effects

Blast effects are produced by a huge shock wave created at the surface of the fireball in the first fraction of a second after a nuclear explosion. The shock travels as a wave of sudden increase in air pressure (static pressure) followed by high winds (dynamic pressure). *Primary blast effects*—the collapse of buildings, bridges, and other structures, and the crushing of humans within, below, or near them—are due to peak static overpressures. In the inner circle of destruction within 1.5 miles of the center of a one-megaton airburst, static overpressures will exceed twenty pounds per square inch (psi), sufficient to collapse and destroy even the strongest steel and reinforced concrete multistory office buildings. At four miles from ground zero, the static overpressure would be five psi, or over 180 tons of pressure on the wall of an average two-story home. Very high static overpressures on human bodies will produce internal hemorrhage and fatal impairment of the respiratory and circulatory systems, but the overwhelming medical consequences of primary blast effects will be due to the collapse and destruction of buildings and other physical structures: crushing injuries of the skull, chest, abdomen, and limbs; traumatic amputations; multiple compound fractures of bones; paralyzing lesions of the spinal cord; damage to internal organs, particularly the brain, liver, kidneys,

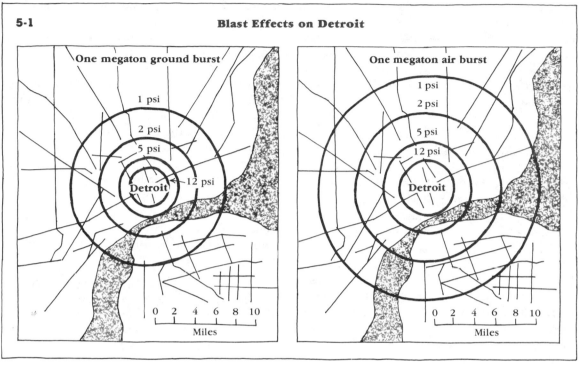

5-1 **Blast Effects on Detroit**

One megaton ground burst

1 psi
2 psi
5 psi
12 psi
Detroit

0 2 4 6 8 10
Miles

One megaton air burst

1 psi
2 psi
5 psi
12 psi
Detroit

0 2 4 6 8 10
Miles

This pair of maps shows the effect of burst height on the blast effects of a nuclear explosion. The circles are labeled with the blast overpressure in pounds per square inch (psi). At the optimum altitude of burst, the direct and ground-reflected blast waves combine to push the 5-psi circle more than a mile farther out. Inside the 5-psi circle, most buildings would be destroyed.

and spleen; rupture of the lungs and eardrums; multiple severe lacerations, hemorrhage, and shock.[2] Even rapid medical intervention would have little effect on traumatic injuries of this severity. Medical help of any sort will in fact be virtually nonexistent.

Secondary and tertiary blast effects are most simply described as flying objects and flying people, respectively, and are chiefly due to dynamic pressures—the winds of devastating velocity (exceeding 600 miles per hour near ground zero) that follow the shock wave.[3] The range of secondary and tertiary blast effects is much greater than that of primary blast effects, and therefore they are the major causes of blast-induced injury. Far beyond the area of totally collapsed buildings—as far away as thirteen miles from ground zero—people will be endangered by enormous numbers of flying missiles: bricks, pieces of masonry, steel, wood, and glass traveling at high speeds.[4] At a range of almost fifteen miles, many such objects will have an impact velocity sufficient to have a 50 percent chance of fracturing a human skull.[5] Secondary blast effects thus include fractures, penetrating wounds of the chest and abdomen, and serious lacerations. Even superficial small lacerations may be so numerous in a single victim, and so likely to cause subsequent infection, as to create a major medical problem.[6]

The human body is highly vulnerable to the direct effect of winds. As far as eight miles from ground zero, wind force is sufficient to hurl a 180-pound adult against a wall at several times the force of gravity. At six miles, winds of nearly 100 miles per hour are sufficient to blow workers out of typical modern office buildings.[7] These tertiary blast effects are serious—again, they include skull and other fractures, damage to internal organs, and hemorrhage—and may lead rapidly to death.[8]

Heat and Fire

When a nuclear weapon explodes, a great wave of *heat*, traveling at the speed of light, is emitted from the fireball. This enormous pulse of thermal radiation causes *direct effects:* flash burns of exposed skin. Such flash burns accounted for nearly one-third of the fatalities at Hiroshima. The severity of damage to human tissue is directly related to the amount of heat delivered to a given area in a given time; this is usually expressed as calories per square centimeter of body surface. In a one-megaton airburst at 2,000 feet, one of every two unshielded victims will suffer second-degree burns at a distance of 9.5 miles from ground zero, and third-degree burns at a distance of eight miles.[9] At distances up to five miles, shielding the skin itself is not necessarily protective, since spontaneous ignition of clothing will cause flame burns, with even more severe injury and a higher probability of death. Second-degree burns covering 30 percent of the body surface, and third-degree burns covering 25 percent of the body surface, will almost always lead to shock and prove fatal if untreated.[10]

The *indirect or incendiary effects* of a thermonuclear explosion—in a word, fires—will be among the greatest causes of injury and death. The heat flash is so intense that paper, dry trees, leaves and grass, debris and wood outside of buildings will burst into flames as far as ten miles away from the center of a one-megaton airburst. Within buildings, there will be spontaneous ignition of clothing, upholstery, bedding, carpets, papers, and fabrics, all likely to create self-sustaining and spreading fires in the wake of the gigantic thermal pulse that radiates from the explosion. To these innumerable fires must be added the blast-induced fires created by exploding boilers, overturned furnaces and stoves, broken gas mains, and downed power lines. Fires will directly ignite or spread to gasoline stations, fuel storage depots, large natural gas storage tanks, and industrial and chemical flammable stockpiles. Any stores of liquified natural gas would be an enormous additional hazard.[11]

Control or containment of these fires—hundreds of them per acre—would be virtually impossible. Water mains would be shattered and water pressure nonexistent. Streets would be impassable. Fire-fighting crews and equipment would be destroyed or disabled. If conditions were favorable to the attack, as one authority has noted:

... the many individual fires might consolidate into two types of mass fire: a firestorm or a conflagration. A firestorm is driven by a strong vertical updraft of heated air, which is replaced by cool air sucked in from the periphery of the fire. A conflagration is driven in addition by a strong ground wind that was present before the attack. Whereas a firestorm continues only as long as its centripetal winds do, a conflagration can continue as long as fuel is available. The consequence of a mass fire is total devastation within the affected area. The temperatures in a mass fire can exceed 1,000 degrees Celsius, a temperature higher than that necessary to melt glass and metal and to burn ordinarily fireproof materials.... After a nuclear attack, many people would be disabled, trapped in wrecked buildings or prevented from fleeing the city because the streets were blocked by debris or fire. If mass fires were to form ... the survivors among those who had escaped prompt incapacitation might be few. If mass fires were to begin in the Boston area, for example, the number of fatalities could be increased by 500,000.[12]

In any large city, a mass fire would cause a staggering increase in the numbers of burns, burns combined with other injuries, and burn-related fatalities. In a one-megaton airburst, the "lethal area"—the circle within which the entire population is counted as fatalities—is usu-

5-2 **CASUALTIES FROM A ONE-MEGATON ATTACK ON DETROIT**

Distance from Blast	Population in Zone	Blast Fatalities	Burn Casualties as a Percent of Persons Exposed to Fireball			
			HIGH VISIBILITY (10 MILES)		LOW VISIBILITY (2 MILES)	
0 to 1.7 miles	70,000	70,000				
1.7 to 2.7 miles	250,000	130,000	Deaths	100 %	Deaths	100 %
2.7 to 4.7 miles	400,000	20,000	Deaths	100 %	Injuries:	
					Severe	13 %
					Minor	87 %
4.7 to 7.5 miles	600,000	0	Deaths	43 %	Unharmed	100 %
			Injuries:			
			Severe	50 %		
			Minor	7 %		

Estimated blast and burn casualties for a hypothetical one-megaton ground detonation on Detroit. Note that the number of burn casualties from exposure to the fireball varies enormously with atmospheric conditions. If the attack occurred on a clear summer day, some 25 percent of the population might be exposed, resulting in 190,000 fatalities and 75,000 injuries.

ally drawn at the five psi overpressure line, with a radius of 4.3 miles from ground zero. In a mass conflagration the lethal area would be increased *five-fold*.

Mass fires, and especially firestorms, pose a threat in addition to their searing temperatures: the generation of large amounts of carbon dioxide and other toxic gases. Blast or fallout shelters would provide little protection. The survival of occupants of such a shelter would depend critically on the temperature and humidity inside the shelter. Moreover, unless there was an independent oxygen supply and a venting system for each shelter, toxic gases would be deadly to the occupants. Ordinary shelters, then, would become crematoria, in which occupants would be simultaneously burned and asphyxiated. In Hamburg during World War II, when a firestorm ignited by conventional bombs killed more than 100,000 people, only those inhabitants who had *left* their shelters before the firestorm began were able to survive.[13]

Radiation

Radiation effects, in contrast, are unique to nuclear weapons. They are the most complex and varied in their effects on individuals, populations, and the ecosphere. Radiation-induced injury and death in human beings is a function not only of the total amount of radioactive exposure but also of the type of radiation (alpha rays, beta rays, gamma rays, and neutrons), the rate at which it is delivered and the duration of exposure, the type of exposure (whole-body or partial), and the source in relation to the body (external radiation or internal radiation from inhaled or ingested radioactive particles). The threat posed by a given dose of radioactivity varies, furthermore, with the age and state of health of the victim. Finally, the radiation effects of nuclear weapons are both short-term and long-term. Nuclear weapons have long radioactive memories. For months or years after their initial effects have subsided, they may make large land areas unsafe for agriculture or habitation. Decades later, they may manifest themselves in increased rates of cancer. A generation later, genetic defects may appear.

The radiation from a nuclear explosion separates into (1) the *initial* burst, and (2) residual nuclear radiation—the subsequent radioactive decay of fission products occurring as *fallout*. Fallout, in turn, may be *early* or *long-term*, depending mainly on whether the explosion is a groundburst or an airburst.

The initial burst is composed of highly penetrating and dangerous gamma rays and neutrons, a radiation dose so intense as to be locally lethal—but very limited in range. At one mile from a one-megaton explosion (either airburst or groundburst), almost all of the population would be killed by initial-burst radioactivity even if shielded by twenty-four inches of concrete.[14] But this is precisely the population that is simultaneously being destroyed by blast and heat. The initial radioactive burst simply represents overkill. At only two miles, however, the radiation exposure from the initial burst drops to a relatively minor level.[15]

Early or local fallout is a consequence of groundbursts. Thousands of tons of soil, rock, concrete, and other material are melted or vaporized by the heat of the explosion and drawn up into the stem of the mushroom cloud to a height of some eight miles with the rising fireball. There, as the fireball cools, these particles serve as nuclei for the condensation of vaporized radioactive materials. The larger particles, carrying both short-lived and long-lived radionuclides, begin to descend within minutes and continue to descend to the ground for twenty-four to forty-eight hours, both on the blast-stricken and heat-stricken zones and over an area extending some hundreds of miles downwind, as local fallout. Smaller particles (some 20 percent of the total) are carried into the stratosphere with the mushroom cloud, travel with upper-level winds, and descend over months or years as *delayed or global fallout* of long-lived isotopes.

In airbursts, in contrast, there is relatively lit-tle early or local fallout, and most of the effect is delayed or global. Airbursts deliver a smaller radiation dose, over a longer period of time, to very large (global) populations; groundbursts deliver a heavy radiation exposure, rapidly, to a relatively smaller area and population. The key phrase here, however, is "relatively smaller"—for the area affected by fallout from even a single one-megaton groundburst may still be very large and contain millions of people. Such a groundburst on Detroit would, if the wind were blowing from the northwest, deposit lethal fallout on Cleveland and hazardous fallout as far away as Pittsburgh; with a wind from the southwest, fallout would extend deep into Canada.

For calculations like these, nuclear planners assume a symmetrical fallout pattern extending downwind, forming first a smooth ellipse and ultimately a cigar-shaped figure. But these shapes are the product of idealized wind patterns which do not exist in nature. In the real event, fallout patterns will be highly uncertain and irregular, with many unpredictable "hot spots" of intense radiation and other areas spared. Even the direction of fallout is unpredictable, since it depends on wind conditions at the time of the explosion. Each of these factors has medical consequences, for each one affects the number and location of people exposed to radiation, the intensity and danger of the exposure, and the duration of risk. Similarly, these variables and uncertainties will affect medical care. It will be difficult if not impossible to determine the radiation dose an individual has received, even though this is a critical factor in selecting patients for appropriate treatment.

But the final common pathways of radiation damage are the same, whether from the initial burst, from fallout exposure before shelter is reached, from low-level accumulation in shelters, or from later emergence into a radioactive environment. The biochemical processes within cells are disrupted, and cells and tissues are damaged or destroyed. The most actively dividing cells in the body, those with the highest

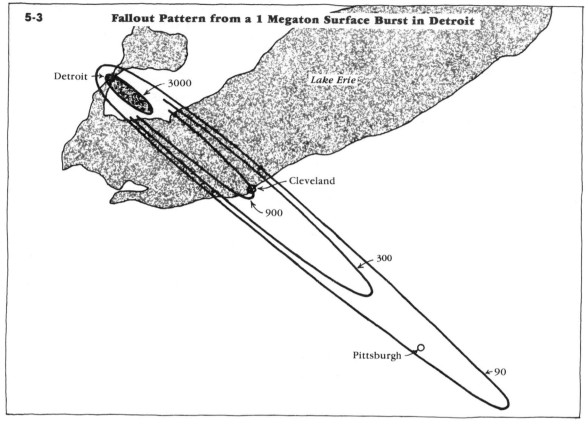

5-3 **Fallout Pattern from a 1 Megaton Surface Burst in Detroit**

The idealized pattern of fallout following a one-megaton surface burst in Detroit is shown for a uniform northwest wind of 15 miles per hour. The contours show the locations where the indicated radiation dose (in rems) would be received during seven days of exposure without shielding. A dose of 400 to 500 rems is roughly 50 percent lethal.

metabolic rates, are the most vulnerable. Thus the cells lining the gastrointestinal tract and in the bone marrow are particularly susceptible.

Acute Radiation Injury

Most medical estimates of risk are expressed in terms of the dose that is lethal to 50 percent of the population. An acute short-term exposure of about 450 rems would kill 50 percent of a healthy young adult population. Even much lower levels, however, would take the lives of many persons. A dose of about 225 rems would be lethal to the very young (infants and chil-

dren are the most likely victims of fallout radiation), the old, those with serious preexisting disease, and those with significant burn or blast injuries.

Long-term effects would be very different; levels of even 50 to 100 rems, which have limited acute effects, would significantly increase the later incidence of cancer and leukemia and double the spontaneous gene mutation rate in any population so exposed.

Whole-body doses of several thousand roentgens produce a central nervous system syndrome with inevitable death in hours or days, preceded by hyperexcitability, incoordination and staggering gait, difficulty in breathing, and intermittent stupor.

Doses of 1,500 roentgens may produce only a gastrointestinal syndrome before death, with nausea, vomiting, diarrhea, and destruction of the cells forming the lining of the gastrointestinal tract. Death usually occurs in the first week, but many of those exposed at this level would survive long enough to present major medical problems (inside or outside of shelters) in the postattack period.

Doses below 1,500 roentgens result in a gastrointestinal syndrome of later onset and somewhat lesser severity, so that victims survive long enough to develop other aspects of the radiation sickness syndrome. This syndrome is characterized by nausea, diarrhea, fatigue and weakness, delayed healing, and—most important—lowered resistance to infection because damaged bone marrow can no longer produce the cells that attack invading microorganisms or mediate immune responses. Marrow damage can also lead to anemia, failure of the blood-clotting mechanism, and hemorrhage. At these radiation dosages, deaths from infection will be most prevalent in the second and third weeks, and from bleeding disorders in the third to sixth weeks.

What is so striking about these responses is

5-4   INFLUENCE OF DURATION OF EXPOSURE

	Required Dose (rems)	
Effect	If Delivered Over One Week	If Delivered Over One Month
Threshold for radiation sickness	150	200
Five percent may die	250	350
Fifty percent may die	450	600

It does not matter much whether a dose of radiation is received as intense radiation for several hours or at a slower rate over several weeks. What matters is the total accumulated dose.

5-5   SHORT-TERM EFFECTS OF ACUTE RADIATION EXPOSURE

Acute Dose (roentgens)	Probable Effects
0 to 50	No obvious effects, except possible minor blood changes.
80 to 120	Vomiting and nausea for about one day in five to 10 percent of exposed persons; fatigue but no serious disability.
130 to 170	Vomiting and nausea for about one day, followed by other symptoms of radiation sickness in about 25 percent of persons; no deaths.
180 to 220	Vomiting and nausea for about one day, followed by other symptoms of radiation sickness in about 50 percent of persons; no deaths.
270 to 330	Vomiting and nausea in nearly all persons on first day, followed by other symptoms of radiation sickness; about 20 percent deaths within two to six weeks after exposure; survivors convalescent for about six months.
400 to 500	Vomiting and nausea in all persons on first day, followed by other symptoms of radiation sickness; about 50 percent deaths within one month; survivors convalescent for about six months.
550 to 750	Vomiting and nausea in all persons within four hours after exposure, followed by other symptoms of radiation sickness; up to 100 percent deaths; few survivors convalescent for six months.
1000	Vomiting and nausea in all persons within one to two hours; probably no survivors.
5000	Incapacitation almost immediately; all persons dead in one week.

A summary of the major features of radiation sickness showing the typical course of the sickness for different levels of exposure.

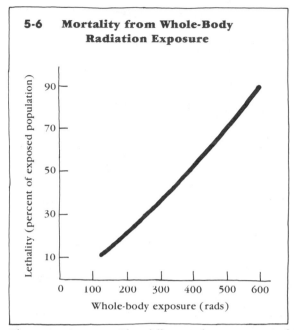

5-6 Mortality from Whole-Body Radiation Exposure

The curve is steep. The difference between survival without medical care and certain death is the difference between doses of 100 and 800 rads. It would be very difficult to identify the victims who should be treated.

their overlap. Persons who have been lethally irradiated, and who are doomed no matter what kind of medical help is provided, will have the same initial symptoms as those who have received sublethal doses and might be saved, or those who have a good chance of spontaneous recovery. Few if any survivors would know whether they had received 1,000 roentgens or only 100 roentgens. Physicians could only make guesses on the basis of early symptoms, using broad rules of thumb, in the absence of adequate laboratory facilities, trained technicians, or the ability to follow survivors systematically for several weeks. Geographic location would be little help. Given the irregularities of wind and weather mentioned above, two persons only five miles apart might receive hugely different doses. Yet the dose must be known to permit prediction of survival, degree of illness and incapacitation, and appropriate treatment.

It is on the basis of this guesswork that life-or-death decisions would be made for many victims as physicians attempted triage—the sorting of patients into groups: those who will certainly die, those who require intensive treatment, and those whose care can safely wait. Yet relatively small differences in radiation exposure would be critical, because the curve of mortality rises so steeply with increases in dose. For example, a dose of 200 rads to the bone marrow (corresponding to a 300-rem dose to the body surface) would cause only a 2 percent probability of death, while at 400 rads to the bone marrow the probability of death is 85 percent.

A crude guess could be made on the basis of the very early appearance of nausea and vomiting, which indicate exposure to a higher and more dangerous dose. But after a nuclear attack it is unlikely that people will remember when they had started vomiting, and the many other causes of nausea and vomiting (including psychogenic) will mask the usefulness of these symptoms as radiation indicators.

Initial symptoms aside, the *course* of illness in differently irradiated groups of victims has important implications for the postattack period and for medical care. *Lethally irradiated victims* will suffer early and continuous vomiting, followed rapidly by collapse, diarrhea, and fever. *Dangerously irradiated victims* will have early vomiting of short duration, followed by a period of apparent well-being. For one to three weeks there may be little evidence of injury other than fatigue. Then they will suffer diarrhea, bleeding into various organs, small hemorrhages under the skin, spontaneous bleeding from the mouth and intestinal tract, and loss of hair. Ulceration of the lips, mouth, and ultimately the entire gastrointestinal tract may develop. The decrease in the white cells of the blood and injury to other immune mechanisms of the body will allow overwhelming infections to develop.

Death from radiation sickness would be neither quick nor painless. Many victims will develop this course of illness *after* they are in shelters, having *already* been exposed to an external radiation dose from passing clouds of fallout, to an internal dose inhaled from fallout, or to an external dose from fallout activity deposited on the ground or on buildings.

One study of an attack on Washington, D.C., concluded that "in areas in and around a target subjected to multiple attack with high-yield surface burst weapons, contamination levels of 5,000 to 10,000 roentgens at one hour, and first week doses of 5,000 to 30,000 roentgens, are not unreasonable levels to consider . . . in planning recovery operations."[16] General life-saving operations (to say nothing of organized medical care) might not be possible in fallout areas until weeks after a nuclear attack.

Moderately irradiated victims, for whom survival is possible, may or may not have fleeting nausea on the first day. Within this group, too, the course of illness will vary with the dose. Some may have no further symptoms—although all will suffer greatly increased susceptibility to infection and impaired wound healing. Others will experience milder versions of the syndromes described above. The threshold for the development of radiation sickness is 170 to 200 rems in healthy adults.

In most victims, these radiation symptoms will be due chiefly to the highly penetrating forms of radiation—gamma rays and neutrons. But some who are exposed to fallout before they can find shelter, or who are forced to leave shelter while radioactivity is still high, will also suffer superficial burns, later skin lesions, and increased vulnerability to infection produced by so-called "soft" radiation, chiefly beta rays. These were experienced by Marshall Islanders and by the Japanese fishermen on a vessel in the huge contaminated area downwind from a test explosion on Bikini atoll in 1954. Such victims are heavily contaminated by radioactive particles and represent a threat to others. They would have to be hosed down, scrubbed, and shaved (all hair, including body hair, must be removed) before they could safely be admitted to shelters. In the probable chaos and panic of the immediate postattack period, such precautions are unlikely.

Survivors in a significant fallout area would have to remain in shelters for very substantial periods of time—two to four weeks in many instances. To leave a shelter even for an hour or two during this period (especially during the early days) would be to incur additional radiation damage. A person who had unknowingly already suffered a mild radiation exposure might leave shelter for an hour or two, return, and *then* begin to experience the full-blown syndrome of bone-marrow depression, gastrointestinal bleeding, and infection. The dose rate from local fallout decreases with time, so that at the end of two weeks it is only one-thousandth the dose rate at one hour, but even this reduction does not automatically indicate safety. If the initial level was very high, as it would be after a surface burst, then even after two weeks enough will be left to make it unsafe to stay in the open.[17]

As we noted earlier, the areas and the populations at risk of local fallout and in need of sheltering (whether or not it is available) may be very large. Patricia J. Lindop, a British radiobiologist, has noted that:

> With the idealized plume one can calculate the doses which may be received by persons from the local fallout for a bomb of given explosive power, and the area within which a person staying in the open would accumulate a certain dose. . . . If we take only the LD_{50} value [the dose that will kill 50 percent of a healthy adult population] then the area is more than 20,000 square kilometers for a ten-megaton bomb.
>
> For a known population density in the fallout area, the average exposure can be calculated. If the density were 100 people per square kilometer (the average for Europe), about two million people would receive a dose from which they would die within a few weeks, if they were exposed to the fallout in the open. All this from one bomb. Staying indoors will reduce the dose by a factor of

5-7   **MEDICAL RESOURCES FOR TREATMENT OF INJURY**

Type of Injury	Medical Conditions	Diagnostic and Treatment Needs
	TRAUMA:	
	Lung puncture	X ray, blood gas determination, oxygen, chest tube, intensive care unit (ICU), intravenous fluids.
	Broken bones	X ray, splints, tetanus toxoid, antibiotics, drugs for pain, orthopedic surgery, operating room, anesthesia.
	Lacerations	Soap, local anesthetic, sutures, tetanus toxoid.
Blast	Head injury	X ray, CAT-scan, ICU, neurosurgeon, neurologist, operating room, intravenous fluids, antibiotics.
	Hemorrhage	Intravenous fluids, whole blood, blood plasma, surgeons, operating room, clinical laboratory.
	Limb injuries, amputation	Vascular surgeon, neurosurgeon, orthopedic surgeon, X ray, operating room, anesthesia, antibiotics.
	Severe multiple injury, shock	Operating room, X ray, ICU, blood, intravenous fluids, clinical laboratory, respirator, antibiotics, advanced life support equipment.
	BURNS:	
	First degree	Drugs for pain.
	Second degree	Intravenous fluids, antibiotics, drugs for pain, clinical laboratory.
Heat	Third degree	Aseptic environment within hospital, operating room, surgeon, blood and plasma, intravenous fluids, topical and intravenous antibiotics, intensive nursing care.
	Smoke inhalation	Oxygen, blood gas determinations, X ray, antibiotics, respirator.

The sort of medical resources normally used in the treatment of the serious injuries to be expected in a nuclear attack. Few would be available.

three to five. A greater reduction will occur if people have, and have stayed in, shelters.[18]

Many of the short-lived fission products will have decayed significantly by three to six months, but residual radioactivity will remain for years. Large areas will be unsafe for habitation for long periods of time; how large, and for how long, depends on a decision as to the accumulated yearly dose it would be acceptable for an individual or a population to tolerate. The chief early hazard is the ingestion of radioisotopes such as iodine–131, which concentrates in the thyroid and causes decreased activity, benign nodules, or cancer. Again, the risk is greatest in children. The principal later hazards will come from such long-lived isotopes as cesium–

137 (half-life, thirty years) and strontium–90 (half-life, 27.7 years), though some contribution will be made by uranium and plutonium particles that have escaped fission.

Combined Injuries

We have separately reviewed the medical effects of blast (trauma and mechanical injury), heat (burns), and radiation. But in a real nuclear explosion, 25 to 50 percent of the immediate survivors may suffer *combined injuries*.[19] In every combination—blast and burn together, blast and radiation, burns and radiation, or all three—the death rate is increased, the time to death is shorter, and the frequency of complications is greater.[20] Two sublethal injuries in combination are likelier to be fatal. People with

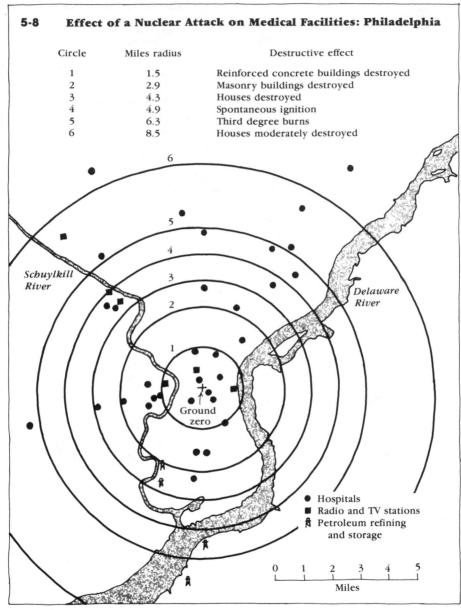

5-8   Effect of a Nuclear Attack on Medical Facilities: Philadelphia

Circle	Miles radius	Destructive effect
1	1.5	Reinforced concrete buildings destroyed
2	2.9	Masonry buildings destroyed
3	4.3	Houses destroyed
4	4.9	Spontaneous ignition
5	6.3	Third degree burns
6	8.5	Houses moderately destroyed

● Hospitals
■ Radio and TV stations
⚒ Petroleum refining
    and storage

The map shows the zones of destruction that would be produced by a one-megaton airburst exploded at 8,000 feet over City Hall, located at ground zero. Two other landmarks within the first circle are the Liberty Bell and the Philadelphia Museum of Art. The solid dots represent hospitals; the squares are newspapers and radio stations. The miniature oil rigs (two are shown near the bottom of the third circle) represent petroleum refining and storage facilities, which would be sites of major secondary explosions.

multiple small lacerations and a moderate radiation dose, neither of which by itself would ordinarily cause death, will be at grave risk. The
increased risk can be profound, especially for irradiated burn victims. One study shows that the
addition of 100 rads of external body radiation
to a standard burn injury increases mortality
eight-fold, and as little as twenty-five rads dou-
bles mortality.[21] In both burn and trauma cases,
where there are portals for the entry of bacteria,
radiation reduces resistance to infection. This is
a later complication, yet standard fatality estimates for nuclear explosions are limited to
deaths in the first thirty days. In the real event,
this figure will be increased enormously by later
deaths due to infection in wounded or burned
early survivors.

If the victims of serious trauma, burns, radiation injury, and combined injuries are to have
any hope of survival, they will require medical
care at the most complex and sophisticated
level, with highly skilled personnel and high-
technology equipment and facilities.

It is easier to comprehend these "medical effects" if we examine their distribution in a real
city under nuclear attack. Consider first the case
of a one-megaton airburst 8,000 feet over Philadelphia, with ground zero at City Hall. The circles on the map delineate the zones of
destruction.[22]

Within the *first* circle, which has a radius of
1.5 miles, all buildings will be destroyed or severely damaged, tunnels and subways will collapse, all but the strongest bridges will be down.
Winds will be in excess of 600 miles per hour.
Almost the entire population within this circle—
on a weekday during working hours, more than
a hundred thousand people—will be killed outright. In this area, all three mechanisms of death
and injury (blast, heat, and radiation) will be at
lethal strength.

In the *second* circle, which has a radius of 2.9
miles from ground zero, blast alone will kill 50
percent of the population, and winds will be
300 miles per hour. The heat will cause third-

degree flash burns to exposed skin and will
cause spontaneous ignition of clothing.

For the area within these first two circles, the
combined casualty figures will be: 90 percent
killed, 10 percent seriously injured.

The *third* circle, with a radius of 4.3 miles,
encompasses the area in which overpressure
will be at least five psi, and winds will reach 160
miles per hour. All unreinforced brick and
wood-frame houses will be destroyed, and
stronger structures severely damaged. Within
this circle, the heat will still be sufficient to give
third-degree flash burns to exposed skin and
produce spontaneous ignition of clothing. Even
without a firestorm or mass conflagration, this
circle represents the area of total fire burnout.
Within this circle, 50 percent of the population
will be killed, 35 percent seriously injured, and
15 percent only slightly injured or uninjured.

The *fourth* circle, with a radius of 4.9 miles
from ground zero, delimits the area within
which heat will exceed twenty-five calories per
square centimeter. Again, third-degree burns
and spontaneous ignition of clothing will be the
rule. At this distance, survivors with serious
burn injuries will begin to exceed those with
blast injuries, though 25 to 50 percent of those
still alive will have combined injuries.

The *fifth* circle has a radius of 6.3 miles from
ground zero. Although overpressures will be
down to three psi and winds to 100 miles an
hour, primary and secondary blast effects will
still be important causes of injury and death.
The heat will still be sufficient to cause third-degree burns.

In the *sixth* circle, with a radius of 8.5 miles,
secondary blast effects (flying missiles of brick,
steel, glass, etc.) will be predominant, causing
fractures, penetrating wounds, and lacerations.
The heat will be sufficient to cause second-degree burns.

In the total area encompassed by the last
three circles—beginning at 4.3 miles from
ground zero and extending to 8.5 miles from
ground zero in all directions—15 percent of the

5-9   **PROMPT DEATHS AND INJURIES FROM A NUCLEAR ATTACK
ON U.S. CITIES**

City	Census Population, 1970	Killed	Percent of Total Pop.	Injured	Percent of Total Pop.	Total Casualties	Percent of Total Pop.
Atlanta	1,298,000	363,000	28.0	350,000	27.0	713,000	54.9
Boston	2,884,000	695,000	24.1	735,000	25.5	1,430,000	49.6
Cleveland	1,890,000	572,000	30.3	380,000	20.1	952,000	50.4
Dallas	2,087,000	345,000	16.5	415,000	19.9	760,000	36.4
Kansas City	1,027,000	352,000	34.3	318,000	31.0	670,000	65.2
Los Angeles	8,664,000	2,033,000	23.5	2,172,000	25.1	4,205,000	48.5
Minneapolis	1,577,000	443,000	28.1	392,000	24.9	835,000	52.9
New York	16,323,000	1,667,000	10.2	2,838,000	17.4	4,505,000	27.6
San Francisco	3,613,000	624,000	17.3	306,000	8.5	930,000	25.7
Seattle	1,213,000	332,000	27.4	272,000	22.4	604,000	49.8

These figures show the devastation that would be wrought by a single one-megaton nuclear weapon exploded over an American city. The numbers of casualties were calculated by the U.S. Arms Control and Disarmament Agency using census data; they measure the effects of blast, heat, and prompt radiation, but not fallout. If the attack were to occur during working hours when "downtown" populations are much higher, or if a firestorm were to follow, the numbers of casualties would be much greater.

population will be killed, 40 percent seriously injured, and 45 percent only slightly injured or uninjured.

And even beyond this range, to a distance of more than thirteen miles, 2 percent of the population will be killed and 18 percent seriously injured. To a distance of thirty-five miles in all directions, if the day is clear, any persons who made a reflex glance at the fireball would risk retinal burning and some might be blinded.[23]

For the total Philadelphia metropolitan area, with a population of 4,557,000, this single one-megaton explosion and the resulting firestorm will kill 769,000 people, or 17 percent of the total, within thirty days; and it will seriously injure another 1,334,000, or 29 percent of the population. Total casualties will be in excess of 2,100,000, or 46 percent of the population.[24] Since many of the injured will die later on, the actual fatality figure will be still higher.

The same amount of death and destruction could be produced by only 320 kilotons, delivered as eight 40-kiloton warheads on a single MIRV missile. Although the total weapon yield is only one-third as large, less energy is "wasted" as overkill in the zones closest to ground zero, and the damage will be multicentric and distributed more widely.

In the event of a real population-targeted attack, of course, Philadelphia would be the target of a multiple-weapon strike totaling far more than one megaton. But even this artifically limited case underscores the fact that we would be dealing with an event beyond all precedent in human experience. Never have there been 1.3 million people seriously injured in one area in the space of a few hours.

Medical Resources

What medical resources will be available for this huge number of seriously injured victims?

Even superficial study shows that hospitals are concentrated in the inner circles of destruction. The total number of Philadelphia hospital *beds* within the first three circles is 7,091. All of them will be totally destroyed by direct bomb effects and fire. There are another 1,196 beds, not shown on the map, just across the Delaware river in the city of Camden, N.J.; these also would be totally destroyed.

Another 4,130 beds are located in the fourth, fifth, and sixth circles; to these must be added some 826 beds in Camden County, N.J., for a total of 4,956. Virtually all of these hospitals would be severely damaged or out of commission. Aside from blast, heat, and fire damage, which in many cases would be substantial, almost all of them will be without electric power and water pressure; their own generators—and almost all of the transistorized and other electronic equipment within their walls, including computers, cardiac monitors and the like—will have been destroyed by the electromagnetic pulse that follows the bomb's detonation and produces voltages as high as 1,000 volts per meter.

Thus, of the total of 19,933 beds serving the Philadelphia metropolitan region, 13,243 (or 66 percent) would be destroyed or rendered dysfunctional. The remaining 6,690 beds are located in the five-county area beyond the sixth circle, dozens of miles from the greatest concentrations of the injured. But at least 80 per cent of these beds would, in normal circumstances, already be occupied, leaving a grand total of 1,338 empty beds to serve Philadelphia's 1,334,000 seriously injured—almost precisely one bed for every 1,000 wounded victims, even assuming there was some effective system for transporting the wounded to these exurban resources.

Since physicians tend to be clustered in central-city areas where the fatality rates are highest, they will be killed and injured at rates substantially greater than those for the general population. A number of case studies suggest that the ratio of surviving, uninjured physicians to the number of seriously injured nuclear-attack victims will be somewhere between 1:350 and 1:1500.[25] If every surviving physician disregarded the risk of lethal radiation exposure, worked eighteen hours a day, saw each patient for only fifteen minutes—and all this assumes no expenditure of time in finding or reaching the injured—it would be five days to three weeks before every patient was seen for the first time for diagnosis and treatment. Obviously, hundreds of thousands would have died without even narcotics for the relief of their pain, without so much as first aid for their fractures, hemorrhages, burns, and infections.

On reflection, even this calculation is absurd. What could a physician equipped only with a black bag do for injuries of this severity and magnitude? The ruins of the buildings are lying in what is left of the streets; transportation is impossible; there are no emergency or rescue vehicles. There is no telephone or other communication system, no electric power, no reliable water supply. There are no emergency rooms, no operating rooms, no diagnostic or therapeutic equipment within reach. There are no blood banks left; drug stocks have been destroyed. In the case of a groundburst, at least, survivors huddled in any available shelter could not leave to rescue the wounded without risking dangerous or lethal radiation doses—and the probability of contaminating their shelters when they returned.

Medical care, in fact, serves most usefully as an illustration of the impossibility of any moderately complex activity in the postattack period. Even more than an undamaged physical infrastructure or a safe biological environment, such activities require high degrees of cooperation and an intact social structure. The deepest meaning of "survival," for humans, is social. The rupture of the social fabric by a nuclear attack may, in the long run, prove as damaging as any of the dreadful physical or biological effects. Certainly this will be the case for the millions of urban victims, dying slowly over a three-week period after an attack, suffering, unaided, because of the impossibility of cooperative effort to help them.

The consideration of limited cases—Detroit, Philadelphia, New York, or their counterparts in other nations—is neccssary to make some of the medical effects of nuclear attack comprehensible. But the true scope, magnitude, complexity, and duration of medical problems become clear only if we turn to a major nationwide attack. One such attack envisioned by U.S. civil defense planners and totaling 6,559 megatons, is aimed simultaneously at military targets, military-support targets (industrial, transportation, and logistic centers), other basic industries and facilities, and population concentrations of 50,000 persons or more. Some 4,000 megatons of the total will fall on urban areas and population centers. In moments after the attack, 86 million people—40 percent of the U.S. population—will be killed. Another 34 million, or 27 percent of the U.S. population, will be seriously injured. In the ensuing weeks or months, there will be 50 million additional fatalities, for a total of 133 million deaths; only about 60 million Americans will survive relatively uninjured and with limited radiation exposure.[26]

Abrams and Von Kaenel have recently examined this case in detail, with special attention to the problems that will occur *after* the immediate attack period, during the so-called "shelter," "survival," and "recovery" periods.[27]

Sheltering

During the shelter period, as Abrams and Von Kaenel point out, tens of thousands of people will be packed together in hugely crowded shelters that usually lack heating or cooling systems, adequate ventilation, water and food supplies, any system of sanitation, waste or sewage disposal, or facilities for food storage and cooking. An estimated 50 percent of the population will have had enough radiation exposure to lower resistance to infection; at least 23 million will have manifest radiation sickness. In high fallout areas—and it is assumed that one-third of the survivors are in regions with an initial radiation rate of 3,000 rems per hour—it will be five days or longer before shelter occupants can leave, even for one hour a day in search of food, water, other supplies, or medical help, without incurring significant additional radiation exposure.

Minimal water requirements for persons in a shelter would be one gallon a day for each individual. Many victims, however, will suffer severe dehydration as a result of protracted vomiting and diarrhea, and their requirements will be much higher. While healthy adults can probably withstand food deprivation during the shelter period, children and infants will be at risk of significant malnutrition. The high humidity and poor ventilation in shelters will facilitate the spread of microorganisms—and, indeed, it is difficult to imagine a setting that is more likely to result in epidemic outbreaks. Even an *uninjured* shelter population will include many persons with bronchitis and other respiratory infections; some will have tuberculosis (significant radiation exposure may convert inactive to active tuberculosis), and many others will have, or will develop, gastrointestinal infections. Morbidity and mortality will rise sharply as viral and bacterial pneumonia, streptococcal disease, gastrointestinal disease (further exacerbating the problems of vomiting and diarrhea), and hepatitis spread through shelter populations. Since persisting radiation levels may be significant for weeks, people may have to return to shelters to eat and sleep even after they are able to make brief forays to the outside, thus continuing the crowding, exposure, cross-infection, and other elements of the epidemic potential.

Survival

In the post-shelter survival period, when fallout has reached an "acceptable" level that allows survivors to emerge for longer times, the problems will change. Tens of thousands of still-surviving injured must be nursed. There will be millions of human and animal corpses to be buried or burned. Food will be an overwhelming concern; when survivors emerge from their shelters, most of the food stores in urban areas will have been destroyed. Other food supplies, particularly grain stored on farms and in small towns, are located precisely where population densities are lowest; since as much as 99 percent of the refinery industry will have been destroyed, there may be no fuel to transport the food to people. Locally food-rich regions may try to fight off any attempt to share their holdings.

In this setting, survival of the survivors may depend on clearing the land, planting the next crop, and reaping the next harvest. But throughout this period, the epidemic potential will continue and worsen, probably made more intense both by malnutrition (which lowers resistance to infection) and by the very large proportion of the population that has not been vaccinated against smallpox or immunized against cholera, typhoid, tetanus, poliomyelitis, measles, diphtheria, and the like. Since insects are far more resistant to radiation than humans, it is anticipated that cockroaches, mosquitoes, and flies—all the insect vectors of disease, in fact—will multiply unchecked in an environment that has no birds but has ample waste, untreated sewage, and human and animal corpses. Trillions of flies will breed in the dead bodies alone.

Disease problems in the survival period, then, may be heavily skewed toward infections. Particularly hazardous epidemics of tuberculosis and plague may occur (some authorities expect a 3 to 11 percent growth in the rat population), but outbreaks of influenza, amoebic dysentery, rabies, cholera, hepatitis, and bacterial dysentery are also likely. Abrams and Von Kaenel cite civil defense estimates of total deaths from acute communicable disease among survivors as high as 25 percent; one study concluded that it is possible that 12 percent of the survi-

vors may contract plague; in half of these, it would be fatal. All this is in addition to the *usual* incidence of coronary heart disease, stroke, diabetes, and the like, and *before* the appearance of an increased incidence of leukemia and cancer. A major consequence of this enormous burden of disease would be difficulty in maintaining the work of planting and harvesting crops, thus intensifying the cycle of malnutrition, decreased resistance, and epidemic outbreaks. As in underdeveloped areas of the world now, in times of famine, infant and childhood mortality would be particularly high.

Antibiotic supplies will be rapidly exhausted. Since the pharmaceutical industry will be almost totally destroyed in the hypothesized attack, there will be little chance of replacement. Diagnostic laboratories will be nonexistent in most areas. Vaccines and other immunizing agents will be unavailable; in any case, in a significantly radiated population, the incidence of pathological responses to immunization might be high.

Initially, according to civil defense estimates, there may be 79,000 surviving uninjured physicians to care for 34 million injured, a ratio of approximately 1:400. As large numbers of the seriously injured die, the ratio will drop. But if serious epidemics then develop, physicians also will become victims, just as the total number of sick people increases, further raising the injured-to-physician ratio.

For physicians and other health workers, all these scenarios will raise not only insurmountable practical burdens but also a series of unprecedented ethical dilemmas.[28] Shall the surviving physician in a shelter leave that shelter to try to treat the wounded, thus risking a radiation exposure that will incapacitate him or her in the future? Within the shelter or outside, how are health workers to accomplish triage, making life-or-death decisions on the basis of radiation exposure estimates that may be inaccurate by orders of magnitude? Shall the physician respond to demands for euthanasia from thousands of burn, trauma, or radiation victims who would realistically prefer an immediate death to a protracted and painful week of untreated fractures, continuing hemorrhage, and fulminating infection inevitably leading to the same end? Should antibiotics—or narcotics—be reserved only for those who have some prospect of survival, despite the pain suffered by others?

In the midst of this grotesque destruction of human beings and of the physical fabric of society, some observers have suggested yet another task for physicians. Patricia J. Lindop notes that:

> We must calculate—and I am sure that this has been done by every country preparing to defend itself in nuclear war—the optimum number of people to be allowed to survive. There must be enough in numbers and age distribution to work for recovery, but not so many as to swamp the severely restricted resources that may remain. As doctors, we need to know roughly how many survivors could be supported. But we are not only concerned about how many, we must consider the quality of survival. In the recovery period each survivor must be fit and well, otherwise he is a large drain on the rest.... What criteria would physicians use to decide the ... level at which an individual was not just expendable, but was an insupportable burden on limited resources? This is not a decision which we can abrogate to the health physicists.[29]

This suggestion, as poignantly as any, illustrates the ultimate destruction that nuclear war would accomplish—beyond the narrowly "medical," beyond the devastation of the physical environment, beyond the emotional desolation of shattered families and communities, beyond the endless contamination of the ecosphere, beyond even the rupture of the larger social fabric. In consequence of all of these, for those who survived, it would change the meaning of being human. For this, as for the medical effects, there is no cure; there is only prevention.

Suggested Readings

Glasstone and Dolan, the standard reference on effects of nuclear explosions, includes much material on the human injuries to be expected from use of nuclear weapons—injuries from blast, thermal radiation, and from fallout. The Office of Technology Assessment report extends the study of effects to national attacks on the United States, and indicates the scale of human damage to be expected in case of a counterforce attack directed at missile silos, military bases, and petroleum refineries, and that expected in an all-out nuclear war. *The Final Epidemic* gives a good presentation of the basic effects of nuclear weapons, but with more attention to the questions of medical care for the victims of nuclear war. *The Fallen Sky,* although published some years ago, remains a valid commentary on the medical consequences of nuclear war.

ADAMS, RUTH, AND SUSAN CULLEN, EDS. "The Final Epidemic." Chicago: Educational Foundation for Nuclear Science, 1981.

ARONOW, S., F. R. ERVIN, AND V. W. SIDEL, EDS. *The Fallen Sky: Medical Consequences of Thermonuclear War.* New York: Hill and Wang, 1963.

GLASSTONE, SAMUEL, AND PHILIP J. DOLAN. "The Effects of Nuclear Weapons." Washington, D.C.: U.S. Government Printing Office, 1977.

KATZ, ARTHUR M. *Life after Nuclear War.* Cambridge, Mass.: Ballinger, 1982.

Office of Technology Assessment, United States Congress. *The Effects of Nuclear War.* Washington, D.C.: U.S. Government Printing Office, 1979.

Nuremberg, Germany, after World War II. The aftermath of the heavy high-explosive and incendiary bombings of German cities illustrates the kind of social upheaval that could result from the explosion of just one high-yield weapon.

6. Global Environment and the Social Fabric after Nuclear War

Some environmental effects months after a massive exchange of nuclear warheads can be calculated roughly by extrapolation from nuclear test explosions and volcanic eruptions; other effects can only be estimated crudely. Radioactive fallout will increase the incidence of cancers of all kinds, dust may drastically reduce agricultural output because of climatic changes, and the ozone layer of the stratosphere might be severely reduced, causing a five- to ten-fold increase in the ultraviolet radiation reaching the earth's surface. How far such a change would disturb the biosphere may never be adequately determined.

The character of society after the millions of dead are buried—or abandoned—is difficult to predict. Physical and psychological trauma will persist, aggravated by severe shortages of food, water, fuel, medicines, and medical care. The accumulated culture of our species may not survive a full-scale nuclear war.

WHAT ARE THE EFFECTS of nuclear war that extend in time and space beyond destruction of target cities and decimation of targeted populations? Two distinct aspects on this question are: (A) the effects of nuclear war on the whole natural environment as habitat for biological species, including the remaining human population; and (B) the viability of the rent fabric of human society.

Environmental Effects

From direct experience we know some limits on the global effects of nuclear weapons detonations. Between 1945 and 1963, and to a limited extent thereafter, the nuclear powers conducted an unintended experiment bearing on this topic, for they set off test nuclear explosions in the open air, at the surface of the sea, undersea, and even at the edge of space, until the prohibition of such tests by the Partial Test Ban Treaty signed at Moscow in 1963. Up to the time of signing, there had been about 380 nuclear explosions that threw up material into the atmosphere. Since then, there have been perhaps sixty-five more, usually smaller ones. These tests have been performed at test sites around the world and therefore simulate the worldwide effects of nuclear attack.

Extrapolating from this experience to the consequences of nuclear war is difficult for several reasons. We do not know much about the design features of the various weapons deto-

Philip Morrison
Jack Dennis

Morrison, Institute Professor at M.I.T., was a physicist-participant in the first test and first combat use of the atomic bomb. Dennis, professor of computer science at M.I.T., is the editor of this volume.

nated, whose contributions to fallout vary with the details of their makeup; at present, all we have to go on are estimates by various expert groups of the total energy yield of all test explosions open to the atmosphere—somewhere in the range of 350 to 530 megatons.

The more significant factor, however, is the size of this total, which is roughly equivalent to that of a small nuclear attack, not to a full-scale war between the superpowers. All-out nuclear war is now estimated to yield between twenty and thirty times the total release from all earlier tests in the open air. That there have been global effects from even the smaller amount is certain; we can be sure, for example, that many individuals worldwide have suffered the induction of a fatal tumor from the fallout, although we cannot say just who or how many they are. Nonetheless, we can take comfort from one fact: a small nuclear attack, though terrible for its targets, has no great effect worldwide. The question remains of all-out war; it is this awesome event that we shall examine for its worldwide environmental effects.

The major consequences are threefold, resulting from fallout, the production of dust, and the depletion of the ozone layer in the upper atmosphere.

Fallout   Fallout is the deposit of radioactive material on the ground from the debris of bomb and target sent into the heights within the rising fireball after the explosion. The finer the dust particles on which the radioactive atoms have lodged, the slower the rate of fallout. Much of the fission product, the chief type of radioactivity from the bomb, is deposited nearby, falling to the ground within hours at most. This defines the local fallout which forms the so-called plume, blown downwind like the plume of smoke from an industrial chimney. But here we are concerned with fallout after months of time, not just a few hours.

The fireball of a surface burst rises as the familiar mushroom cloud, the stem bearing dust

from the ground and carrying the bomb debris itself. Much depends on the height to which the fireball rises. This is a function both of the atmospheric temperature structure and the weapon yield. Yields above one megaton heat sufficient air that the cloud of debris penetrates the stratosphere, even in tropical latitudes where this stable atmospheric layer lies more than ten miles high. Once the material is in the stratosphere its removal is slow. At this height there are no usual processes of rain or snow; the eventual removal requires first a slow mixing of the high air mass aloft into the lower unstable levels of the atmosphere, where precipitation is commonplace. In time, most of the radioactive material is brought down with the rain falling from the clouds. This tends to increase the fallout just where agriculture is most favorable. It should be noted that the air of the two hemispheres mixes still more slowly than the air above with that below. It is not easy for air at high level to cross the equator. The general result is that the upper air of the northern atmosphere—assumed to be the site of most explosions—will retain about two-thirds of the material placed there; only a third will ever pass to the south, even after a delay. Fallout levels are thus typically estimated to be about one-third as high south of the equator as they are north of it, allowing for the additional delay.[1] By scaling up the observed worldwide fallout from known tests, we arrive at a fairly reliable rate for worldwide fallout, once the size of weapons used is accounted for. Since the stratospheric winds are relatively steady and simple, blowing generally westward along the parallels of latitude, the fallout tends to occur along the same latitude belt as the explosion site itself. It slowly spreads, however, north and south after many months, but points all around the world at a given latitude are reached within a matter of a month or so. This pattern has been directly observed during the years after the large-scale tests.

Applying the rough factor of 25 to the worldwide measured deposition of the main radioactivity remaining over months of decay, that of the isotope strontium-90, the estimates agree that the surface contamination would amount to about 1 curie/km². Other isotopes are of significance, especially the plutonium, which contributes an internal lung dose from alpha particles in addition to the external and internal dose from the beta and gamma rays of the other isotopes of importance. The best study estimates the cumulative human dose over twenty or thirty years as "about 4 rem in the northern atmosphere and 1.25 in the southern to populations not exposed to early fallout." This amounts to a doubling of the typical natural background dose (about 0.1 rem/year) to the whole population of the Northern Hemisphere over the years.[2] Such a modest but widespread effect can be expected to increase the incidence of malignancies of all kinds by a noticeable amount. Admitting that the complex medical questions involved are very roughly understood, the experts estimate under a 2 percent increase in spontaneous cancer deaths over a generation. This effect would not be easy to detect, even though it corresponds to some thirty to forty deaths per year per million persons exposed on a continuous basis over a generation and more. Even these cancer deaths, totalling 150,000 people per year worldwide, are not easy to detect against an overall death rate among nearly 4 billion people of some 75 million per year, many from the same malignant conditions.[3] There are of course still more protracted genetic effects, built in to appear in future generations. These too bear more or less the same relationship to the spontaneous incidence of birth defects. While the matter is surely grave, it is necessary to conclude that the overall effects of the fallout from the terrible strike foreseen is not so important as the clear social and economic consequences of the essential destruction of one or both of the two most powerful societies on earth, the superpower targets. It is worth adding as a footnote that geography here is more important than diplomacy: neighbor states to the target powers, even if they are neutral and uninvolved, will suffer heavily. The worldwide effects are delayed and reduced, but the side effects of an all-out Soviet strike on the United States will be a fallout disaster in Canada across the border, with the serious risk of approximately a million Canadian deaths. In the same way, the downwind neighbors of the Soviet Union, farther away to be sure, are likely to be heavy sufferers from a big U.S. strike against the Soviet Union. China, as well as Japan, will undergo heavy damage even with precautions not now widely taken. This is of course a conclusion drawn under the assumption that not one single warhead explodes within the territory of either state.

Dust The second major worldwide effect is the lifting of dust particles up to the stratosphere by the explosions. This dust has most of the radioactive effects we have described, but it has others as well. The most evident consequence of dust in the upper air is the effect on the incoming sunlight. We know of this phenomenon, unlike the radioactive effects, not from the bomb tests so much as from the natural explosions of volcanos. In the 1880s the eruption of Krakatoa, west of Java, filled the world's air—both north and south, for the volcano is close to the equator—with its dust and ash. For a few years the phenomena of colorful sunset skies, even of blue and green moons, were noted everywhere. A few seasons of cooler weather were experienced, though this effect is at the margin of measurement, about 1°F on the average. In 1815 a similar eruption east of Java is held to have produced a major climatic disturbance in the Atlantic region, halfway around the world. It was the worst crop year in Europe and the United States for which we have good data. In much of New England for example, there was no single month without frost; upland grain harvests were minimal. Near famine was the result. In a couple of years the effect had run its course.

The studies of thermonuclear groundbursts suggest that such a detonation can be expected to place into the upper air from 1,000 to 10,000 tons of fine particles—aerosols—per megaton of yield. The estimate is made from the known volumes of surface craters and a judgment as to the fraction of material that is finely enough divided to remain aloft for years. It appears that the large-scale attack would result in some 10^7 to 10^8 tons of fine dust ejected into the upper air. The Krakatoa eruption seems to have contributed about this same amount, say 50 million tons of fine dust. (Larger particles and material within the lower atmosphere are not of importance for these estimates). It appears, then, that a noticeable but neither a major nor a long-lasting effect worldwide on climate is to be expected. Again this would be of local importance for crops raised especially in marginal situations, perhaps less important than the large effects on the two great agricultural systems close to the explosions. Recently the voluminous smoke of the worldwide industrial and forest conflagrations caused by a major nuclear attack has been estimated to have even more serious climatic consequences than the dust of the explosions.

Ozone It is well known that biologically damaging ultraviolet light, with wavelengths between about 310 nanometers and 290 nanometers, is copiously emitted by the sun. These rays are not penetrating; their effects are at the skin surface, though often important. Skin cancer, snow blindness (a sunburn of the outer layers of the eye), sunburn of exposed skin, and increased vitamin D production are effects known in humans and other animals. Plants are also affected; various agricultural crops, more the broad-leaved ones like peas, beans, or tomatoes, tend to lose chlorophyll and grow less well. Most of this radiation, however, does not reach the lower atmosphere because of a photochemical reaction in the thin air of the stratosphere and above; as a result of this photochemical re-

action, the substance ozone is formed, which absorbs the radiation in question. The ozone layer, as it is called, is in a state of dynamic equilibrium, which massive detonation of nuclear weaponry will surely disrupt, although the extent of the disturbance is uncertain.

What is sure is that the strongly heated air of a thermonuclear fireball undergoes chemical reactions that produce some amount of the several oxides of nitrogen. If these rise into the ozone layer, they may act to reduce the ozone that is present, thus allowing more of the biologically active ultraviolet rays to pass to the surface of the earth. Early estimates suggested that the full-scale explosions we are considering would send enough of the active nitrogen compounds into the upper air to reduce the ozone content very appreciably for a matter of several years before natural elimination of the new materials. But the chemistry is complex. With a great deal of uncertainty, estimates were offered that the ozone might be reduced by as much as 30 to 70 percent in the Northern Hemisphere, rather less in the Southern Hemisphere. This effect would increase the exposure of the living forms of the earth to this radiation by a factor of five or ten times.

The damaging effects of such a change—which plunges the ecosystems of the northern latitudes suddenly into the tropical ultraviolet regime—cannot be reliably estimated, since there has been no persuasive effort to work out such effects for the ecosystem as a whole. It is thought that ozone losses from such unlikely natural events as great asteroid collisions or supernova explosions have had overall effects on many forms of life, perhaps even important extinctions during the long history of evolution. All one can say is that while the estimated effects do not greatly exceed in magnitude the natural range of variation over the earth as a whole, they clearly threaten the carefully adapted temperate systems of living forms. No one can deny that the risk is real, though it has not been given quantitative estimate. Recently observed variations in chemical content of the high air have not led to the most extreme effects on ozone, which could not be excluded only some years back. The atmosphere appears to have its own stability. The recent United Nations expert report merely says: ". . . the full biological implications of an increased ultraviolet radiation to ecosystems at various latitudes are not known."[4] It appears that the estimates made a few years ago which we cited above—a 30 to 70 percent depletion in ozone—are on the high side. Such a big effect would be likely only if most of the yield was released through multimegaton weapons, or in high-altitude explosions. Indeed, it would seem that an international tendency to deploy only weapons with fractional megaton yield (those smaller fireballs don't usually rise into the stratosphere) would relieve this possible hazard without much effect on nuclear war itself.

The Social Fabric

After a nuclear attack, the immediate effects will all be over in one or two months. The fires will have burnt out. Most of the myriads of victims of blast injury and burns will either have died or at least partially recovered. Those suffering acute radiation sickness from direct radiation or from intense early fallout will either be dead or able to survive for years.

Outside the ruins, immediate problems of survival will concern controlling infection, providing water supply and sanitary services, reestablishing some kind of communications, and avoiding needless deaths from inadvertent exposure to fallout radiation in many contaminated areas.

The loss of housing would be immense since many survivors would be from areas where homes had been destroyed by blast and fire. A communal life-style would be thrust upon the surviving refugees of urban areas. Masses of people will attempt to escape from target areas both before and after an attack; the number of refugees from all urban areas might reach 50 to 100 million persons, an unprecedented number.

How will the economic and social structure of an attacked country survive? History provides us with little useful guidance. The yield of the bombs dropped on Japan was tiny in comparison with the megatons now carried by intercontinental missiles. More important, these were attacks on a single city by a single weapon—not the near-simultaneous destruction of many cities in a massive attack.

In the case of Hiroshima, electricity was restored in some less-damaged areas on the day following the attack, train service to the city was resumed on the next day, certain streetcar lines were operating on the third day, and telephone communications were restored in some sections within ten days. This rapid recovery of some basic services was made possible by the availability of human and material resources from unstricken areas.

In World War II, German cities, in particular, were subject to repeated massive bombing raids. Yet the interval between attacks provided an opportunity for conscious or unconscious adjustment to conditions. People improvised and experimented; they achieved a semblance of normal life between the repeated shocks, making it possible to better cope with each successive blow. Even so, the social, political, and economic effects of strategic bombing in World War II were severe. After the war, the revival of the damaged cities was accomplished with large infusions of U.S. capital through the Marshall Plan and with assistance from other outside sources. With the explosion of many strategic warheads against cities, the suddenness and extent of the devastation would be so great that neither the single-weapon attacks on Hiroshima and Nagasaki nor the protracted strategic bombing of Germany and Japan in World War II provide a basis for estimating the consequences. Within an attacked area the change from a normal to a devastated environment will be abrupt and all-encompassing.[5] Life after nuclear war would certainly be very different for the survivors. The banking system and currency would be in desperate disarray. The commodities in demand would be those essential for survival—food, water, shelter from the elements, and energy for space heating. Many industries, even if their plants survived, would find their starting materials absent, labor gone, products irrelevant to the postwar society. They would have to adapt or shut down. Those businesses providing basic materials from local resources would flourish, such as bakeries with stores of flour. Barter would become the usual way of transacting business. Many people would find their former jobs irrelevant. Those who were adaptive or had a variety of skills could readily find productive work, but people who were narrowly trained or had limited skill would be forced into menial work to subsist. In regions where resources were very scarce these people would perish or become dependent on others. Many would become outlaws, preying on the successful survivors.

In the United States there is a very efficient but complex and widespread national food distribution system. Following a major nuclear attack, a considerable area of farmland would be unusable for at least several seasons because of fallout. The scarcity of energy would lead to a scarcity of fertilizer which would further reduce farm productivity for prewar crops, especially wheat. While the nationwide railroad system would be workable, given some fuel, getting grain to the decimated population would be a problem of local distribution and fair division of the supplies. How would the farmers be paid for their grain? If urban areas and their residents are destroyed, the large fraction of the population living in suburban areas and in the countryside would turn to locally grown produce. Obtaining adequate protein would be a serious problem for many people incapable of growing the appropriate crops. Fresh milk, depending on a rapid local delivery system, would be a scarce and expensive commodity; maybe powdered milk could be produced.

Much food from farms would be contaminated with fission products from fallout—strontium-90 and cesium-137. Since the health danger is the ill-defined, long-term increase in the incidence of cancer, many people would prefer to accept the risk rather than starve.

Severe local food shortages—even winter famine, especially in northern regions—are likely to occur. Conflicts are sure to arise between the central government attempting to send relief to areas of famine and the residents of local regions trying, in a diminished economy, to provide for their own. Such conflicts were seen on a smaller scale, even in the less-damaged states of World War II.

The fullest attack postulated would not destroy all sources of energy; a fraction of the electric power plants would survive and some petroleum refining capacity. On the other hand, the cities and the manufacturing industries are large consumers of energy, and their destruction would remove much demand for energy. A large portion of all motor vehicles would probably be destroyed. Commuting to the city would largely disappear. Air conditioning and office lighting would be irrelevant. People would hang clothes outside to dry. The problem would be to manage the distribution of the remaining energy resources to the points of need. The major energy requirement for survival would be for home and apartment heating in severe winter regions; from New York to Denver and beyond, there would be much space heating using wood. The electric grid would be important and relatively easy to restore to, say, one-tenth to one-fourth its former capacity—more might not be necessary for the dwindled, immobilized, only semi-industrialized nation that remains.

Our modern, industrial society has become far more interdependent since World War II. If all large urban areas were struck in one attack, it is possible that the entire technical capacity to produce some high-technology products—lasers, for example—would be lost. Perhaps more crucial to survival, many stocks of replacement parts required to repair and maintain machinery and equipment would be wiped out, forcing cannibalization of some equipment to keep the rest in operation. Much sophisticated equipment—medical equipment, electronic apparatus, and computer-based systems—would more or less quickly fall out of use. The skills to maintain and operate it would be forgotten and not soon recovered.

A large portion of universities, professional personnel, and research laboratories are concentrated in the urban areas of the United States. The most extensive collections of written human knowledge are in the libraries of our great cities and universities. A large part of this knowledge and expertise would be lost in a nuclear attack on the cities. Of course, if just one major city or center of learning were spared, the knowledge could be recovered and redistributed—if it were seen to be relevant. If the destruction were so great that most technical products of our society fell out of use, and knowledge of them were not transmitted to succeeding generations, it is possible that the knowledge would not be regained.

It is questionable whether the federal government would survive a massive nuclear attack. At some level of damage, the remaining population would be so poor, and central government services so irrelevant to their lives, that support for past major functions of the central government (such as maintaining military superiority or providing a massive welfare system at high tax cost) would vanish.

Very likely new regional systems of governance would form based on common economic interests and the existence of strong leadership. In some areas, banditry and lawlessness would reign instead.

Conclusions

There is no doubt that the international catastrophe of large-scale nuclear war would be of unmatched damage to the target states and to their near neighbors, worse than any famine, war, or pestilence yet witnessed. No mere local events, like volcanos, floods, or earthquakes, compare at all with its continental scope, or its foreseeable 100 or 200 million deaths. For the physical effects on the world as a whole, it seems prudent to say that another factor of 10 beyond a 10-thousand megaton exchange would imply very damaging worldwide effects indeed to the human species and to its environment, not excluding the near-extinction of our kind. On the present yield scale, we are at risk of the unknown. We have no prudent safety factors left for events that have so universal an impact. No other such danger to public health has ever come so close to the foreseeable margin. At the same time it is not possible to point to sure worldwide disaster from a great-power nuclear exchange on present scale, though indeed there would be intense suffering everywhere, eventual deaths by the tens of millions, and above all, a desperate gamble for our entire species.

Suggested Readings

Perhaps sensitive fiction, rather than the estimates of experts, is the best of resources to examine this awful future. One might read again the fictional account at the opening of this volume: Charlottesville, a survivor city, unbombed but caught up in the national disaster.

The article by Barnaby is the best available portrayal of a possible nuclear war based on an assessment of superpower strengths and policies. The National Academy of Sciences Report is the most detailed expert study of the physical aspects of global weapons effects. It is technical and came a bit early to draw full conclusions, but it has valuable summaries. The Office of Technology Assessment Report contains a study of many levels of attack, with a summary and assessment of all long-range effects in Chapter 5; this is the most up-to-date account. It is brief and less technical than the 1975 study but is well founded; it treats both U.S. and Soviet circumstances. The Stockholm International Peace Research Institute (SIPRI) book is a comprehensive survey of its topic, but it does not address the world-wide effects at all. It treats the environmental effects region by region and concerns itself more with conventional than with nuclear warfare. However, it does offer useful data on nuclear tests, leakage, and the like. The United Nations report is broad in perspective, but weapons effects are the topic of just one chapter; it also covers weapons arsenals, strategies, and efforts at control. The book by Griffiths and Polanyi is an anthology of papers on avoiding nuclear war and contains a very good chapter by J. Carson Mark on the consequences of nuclear war at a variety of scales. It is especially good as a summary of local effects but barely touches the global consequences. The books by Katz and by Schell aim far beyond the merely physical-biological effects; Schell is philosophical in emphasis.

BARNABY, FRANK, ET AL. "Reference Scenario: How a Nuclear War Might Be Fought." *Ambio* 11 (1982): 94–99.

GRIFFITHS, FRANKLIN, AND JOHN POLANYI, EDS. *The Dangers of Nuclear War*. Toronto: University of Toronto Press, 1979.

KATZ, ARTHUR M. *Life after Nuclear War*. Cambridge, Mass.: Ballinger, 1982.

Long-Term Worldwide Effects of Multiple Nuclear Weapons Detonations. Washington, D.C.: National Academy of Sciences, 1975.

Office of Technology Assessment, United States Congress. *The Effects of Nuclear War*. Washington, D.C.: U.S. Government Printing Office, 1979.

Report of the Secretary-General of the United Nations. *Nuclear Weapons*. Brookline, Mass.: Autumn Press, 1980.

SCHELL, JONATHAN. *The Fate of the Earth*. New York: Knopf, 1982.

Stockholm International Peace Research Institute. "Military Impact on the Human Environment," *Warfare in a Fragile World*. London: Taylor and Francis Ltd., 1980.

Part Three
Nuclear War

An Air-Launched Cruise Missile (ALCM) dropped from a B-52 bomber, perhaps to carry a nuclear warhead 1,000 miles to strike within a few hundred feet of a chosen target.

7. A Primer of Nuclear Warfare

Philip Morrison and Paul Walker worked together on a comprehensive 1979 volume on nuclear and conventional warfare. Here, they outline the basic ideas and terms that underlie discussion of the weapons and doctrines of nuclear war, especially between the superpowers. They discuss and distinguish various types of nuclear weapons, the methods employed to bring them to their targets, and the nature of those targets. They discuss tactical and strategic weapons, soft and hard targets, first and second strikes, deterrence and counterforce plans, all-out and limited war, and the history of the nuclear arms race.

AFTER THIRTY-FIVE YEARS and enormous human effort, a complicated system of weapons, delivery systems, and electronic systems of command and control has been built—all brought about by a large, joint enterprise of government, universities, and industry for the sole purpose of suppressing the possibility that similar systems of destruction might ever be used. What are these systems? And what is the nature of the strategic confrontation between the United States and the Soviet Union? We shall answer these questions, but first some spelling out of useful words and phrases is necessary.

The Jargon of Nuclear Weapons

Nuclear weapons derive their explosive energy from actual transmutation of elements, not from mere chemical rearrangements of atoms. In a *fission* reaction, atoms of a heavy element—uranium or plutonium—change, or transmute, into lighter elements—generally a whole series of atoms like barium or strontium. The primitive weapons that devastated Hiroshima and Nagasaki were fission bombs. In *fusion,* by contrast, two light nuclei—certain isotopes of hydrogen or lithium—combine to form other nuclei. In most modern weapons, a fission reaction is the trigger, providing the extreme heat necessary to initiate a fusion reaction, which forms the major explosion. These weapons are called *thermonuclear weapons* due to the extreme thermal energies they require.[1]

A nuclear weapon is often mounted on a large carrier such as a rocket or a bomb, and in this case it is called a *nuclear warhead.* The warhead includes various protective and control devices. Indeed, carriers designed for dual purposes can be fitted with a choice of nuclear or chemical explosive warheads, while others provide a selection of nuclear explosive sizes to be

Philip Morrison
Paul Walker

Morrison is an Institute Professor at M.I.T. Walker is a political scientist and national security consultant with Klein Walker Associates.

"dialed" in before launch. But in context one may describe the nuclear weapon simply as the warhead.

The heart of the matter is the enormous energy available from the nuclear changes, for the deeper-lying nuclear forces are much greater than the chemical ones. The energy release from nuclear explosive is measurable in ordinary energy units, such as the calorie, used in food-energy measurements, or the kilowatt-hour, a familiar measurement in metered electrical energy. But because this nuclear energy is released with enormous suddenness and explosive speed, it has many physical effects that are not associated with the burning of fuel or the glow of a lamp. This has led to the introduction of a special unit for describing the energy release in nuclear explosions.

A nuclear weapon is rated by its yield of energy, expressed in terms of the weight of a familiar World War I chemical, TNT (or trinitrotoluene), that would release the same amount of energy. Here is the unparalleled feature of all nuclear weapons:

> The fission of only one kilogram of nuclear fission explosive releases the same energy as the chemical explosion of 17,000 tons of TNT.

One kilogram (2.2 pounds) is approximately the weight of a large book; 17,000 tons of TNT are a mid-sized shipload. Fusion explosive is more variable because various fuel mixes are used, but its energy yield is even higher.

> The fusion of one kilogram of thermonuclear explosive releases the same energy as the chemical explosion of some 50,000 to 100,000 tons of TNT.

It should be noted that the most powerful manmade explosion ever made with chemical explosive amounts to a couple of thousand tons, usually the result of the accidental explosion of a shipload of conventional munitions, as in Halifax during WWI, or in Texas City after WWII. But the limit of nuclear weapons at the low-yield end of their range is also measured in thousands of tons of TNT and is about the same as the high-energy limit of conventional explosions!

Such comparisons are based on a rounded figure for the energy release of TNT: one kilocalorie per gram. This number enables the conversion of yield data into more ordinary energy units. Thus, a kilogram of TNT provides 1,000 kilocalories of energy release; a metric ton releases a million kilocalories. It should be clear that precision is not to be expected; yield data for nuclear explosions are not precisely measurable. The ton can be interpreted as the metric ton (or tonne) of 1,000 kilograms or as the short ton of 2,000 pounds; the difference in this context is academic.

The effects of nuclear weapons have been discussed in some detail in Chapter 4 of this volume.[2] Here we will summarize the situation briefly in the context of the use of weapons. Our main point is the dominant effect of distance from the explosion center, for the energy in all its forms yielded by the weapon spreads out and dilutes with distance, at a rate that depends upon many variables. This dilution clearly has one general effect: near the center there is always overkill from a military viewpoint, for at the very heart of the fireball or even a small nuclear weapon, the target is overdestroyed. Indeed, even solid steel, rock, and concrete are vaporized along with the material of the weapon itself in the fierce heat, which is not unlike the center of a star. Obviously the damage is overdone; no target, building, machine, ship, or whatever, needs to be vaporized to lose its utility. It would be enough to break it up into pieces the size of a pea. Vaporization uses much more energy than is needed for destruction.

Thus a high-yield explosion will vaporize the center and reach out miles beyond to damage a target by blast or heat. However, for heat, blast, prompt radiation, and shock effects on targets, the overdamage falls off so strongly with distance that a given weapon's yield will do more total damage when divided up into several smaller explosions spaced out over the area than in one fierce blast at the center. This blast phenomenon is the basis for what is called fractionation—the present tendency for nuclear weapons to be multiple in number and smaller for a given total yield or weight of weapon—to make more economical use of the energy rather than the most severe overdamage as caused by one large warhead.

Fractionation was first carried out in modern missiles by the use of Multiple Reentry Vehicles (MRV). The acronym MRV represents the use of several smaller warheads in one missile, much as a shotgun spreads the charge into small pellets instead of one bullet. Even more remarkable, the newer technology of missile aim-guidance (in present jargon) allows the designer to use Multiple Independently-targetable Reentry Vehicles (MIRVs). Here not only is the energy fractionated, but each separate small warhead can be aimed to strike a particular target, like aiming a few individually shot pellets. Since its introduction by the United States about 1970, MIRV has become important technology, as will be explained below.[3]

Technology is now reaching still further toward Maneuverable Reentry Vehicles (MARVs). MARVs will not only be well-aimed and multiple but each one will eventually have some degree of terminal, or final, homing guidance built in so that as it approaches the target, it can make a last-minute maneuver to avoid a defensive interceptor and improve its final aim. It will use the stars, or satellite signals, for mid-course orientation, or sense the target and ground below. The *miss distance* at intercontinental range may become as little as thirty meters or less.

The most long-distance effect of nuclear weapons is fallout, radioactive substances made within the nuclear explosion that fall to ground level and contaminate the surface of the earth and the air at low altitudes. This effect can be worldwide, although the drift of the material in the upper-air winds carrying it around the world is slow, taking months perhaps. Most fall-

out descends closer to the target area over hours and days, making a long plume of pathogenic effects downwind from ground zero. Roughly, the overall effect of fallout—which damages living organisms, humans, plants, and animals, not structures—is proportional to the total yield of the weapons. Its effects extend farthest in space and time; the effects are invisible and are not prompt, but they are extremely damaging to life and the environment.[4]

The next most extensive effect of a nuclear explosion is on ordinary civil structures—cities, factories, railroad yards, airports, and so on. This is a complex effect; nearby it tends to include the effect of *blast* and pressure in crushing and blowing over structures as well as *radiation*; farther away, it includes the terrible bursts of *heat, light,* and consequent fires. Again roughly speaking, these are rather immediate effects, occurring in a matter of minutes or hours.

The area of physical damage is less than proportional to the energy yield.

For example, the damage of a one-megaton weapon against civil targets is not twenty-five times larger than that of a forty-kiloton weapon, though the energy release—and roughly the

7-1   Weapon Damage Equivalents

Eight explosions of 40 kilotons each are equal in area of damage to one explosion of 1000 kilotons or 1 megaton.

High-yield warheads, such as those of the U.S. Titan II missiles and many Soviet missiles, overdamage and even vaporize the center of the target, thereby wasting energy. Several smaller warheads are more effective. The area of severe damage increases by about 60 percent for each doubling of weapon yield.

overall fallout—is twenty-five times greater. The area of damage to civil targets is only about eight times larger. This is only a useful rule of thumb; it is a tendency, not a firm result, for it depends on complex details of the layout of cities and their buildings.

Finally we look at the case of military targets—strongpoints—which, in general, are costly, underground, steel-and-concrete structures built to house people and systems deemed essential to protect against nuclear attack. No such protection is complete; even a mountain will not protect against a bomb that is sufficiently large and strikes close enough to the target. But there is clearly some protection in such a structure.

The jargon currently in use includes the terms hard targets and soft targets. A hard target is "hardened" by its physical strength. A missile center and silos holding the missile, its controls, and controllers deep underground are the best known hard targets. Others include various command bunkers such as those provided for high officials around Washington and the underground headquarters of the Strategic Air Command (SAC) in Omaha; also included are communication centers, warehouses for the storage of nuclear weapons, and structures such as the great concrete pens in which some Soviet submarines are kept. Ordinary structures—houses, factories, office buildings, airports, and especially aircraft in their big, light hangars—are all soft targets. Sometimes an ordinary building such as the well-built Pentagon is rather soft, but deep below it are specialized hard bunkers, for the protection of a small number of those who occupy the building against direct nuclear attack.

The quantitative criteria for hardness are as follows: Ordinary houses will collapse when a pressure wave of five pounds per square inch crosses them rapidly. A person in the open is more resistant than a house but is not likely to survive an overpressure twice that large. A buried missile silo of steel and concrete is built to withstand 100 or 200 times such pressures. Ab-

solute confidence in the hardened structure is not possible, for it may have weaknesses unforeseen by the designers, and a full-scale nuclear test cannot be carried out on every structure. Other effects of nuclear explosions, such as radiation, heat, and strong electrical pulses which can damage electronics gear, must also be considered. A strong electrical pulse accompanies a nuclear explosion and can damage unprotected electronic gear connected to long lines or high antennas even hundreds of miles distant. Thus hardening is of necessity extended to such effects; a radio link is hardened not only by building its transmitters in bunkerlike structures but also by designing features to protect its equipment from the other effects.

A direct hit is deadly. Any structure within the deep crater made by an explosion of a bomb on the surface of the ground turns to vapor and debris. In a nuclear war against strongpoints there is a kind of cannon-versus-armor race, unusual in the whole sweep of nuclear war, though of course typical for less energetic weapons. It is a contest between the hardening of the target and the accuracy of the incoming warhead. The ordinary warheads of missiles and bombers today will destroy strongpoints if they are exploded close by, within a few hundred yards of a very hard shelter. A rather complicated estimate can be made of the chance that a weapon of specified yield with a prescribed expected error in aim—the radius of the circle within which half the shots at a target point are expected to fall, which is called the Circular Error Probable (CEP)—will destroy a strongpoint. These are called lethality estimates. Aiming accuracy is much more important than yield in an attack against strongpoints. In conventional calculations, given a weapon of some yield and some expected miss distance (CEP) against a hard target, an increase in yield by a factor of ten is less effective than a reduction of the expected error (improving the CEP) by a factor of just above two. The practical limit of hardening (the theoretical ability to withstand overpres-

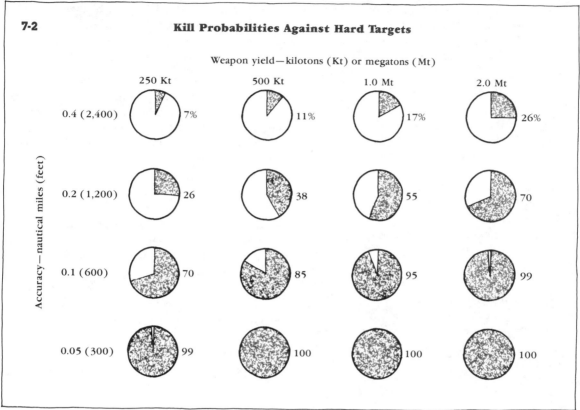

7-2   Kill Probabilities Against Hard Targets

Weapon yield—kilotons (Kt) or megatons (Mt)

	250 Kt	500 Kt	1.0 Mt	2.0 Mt
0.4 (2,400)	7%	11%	17%	26%
0.2 (1,200)	26	38	55	70
0.1 (600)	70	85	95	99
0.05 (300)	99	100	100	100

Accuracy—nautical miles (feet)

Getting closer to a target is much more effective than using bigger nuclear warheads, particularly for hardened targets such as missile silos. These kill probabilities are for targets designed to withstand 2,000 pounds per square inch of blast wave overpressure.

Doubling the yield improves the kill probability, but doubling the accuracy does much better. Additional factors such as missile reliability are not considered in these estimates.

sures of 2,000 to 3,000 pounds per square inch) is now more or less common practice for ICBM silos.[5]

Of course, two or more warheads could be dispatched against a single hard target, but this is difficult. They must be spaced out in time; if a second warhead comes to the same spot within five or ten minutes after the first nuclear warhead explodes, it is quite apt to be damaged in flight by the flying debris, heat radiation, and other effects of the first explosion. This has been given the curious name of *fratricide,* the killing of a "brother" warhead. But if time is allowed to avoid fratricide, the missile in the sur-

viving target can perhaps be fired off. So the ordinary reckoning does not allow for more than one or perhaps two warheads against one silo.

The result of all this can be expressed as the proposition that neither yield nor area damage measures the effect of attack against strongpoints. The crude measure is simply the number of warheads available to strike strongpoints. This has to be weighed by their accuracy and yield in a more elaborate calculation, whose reliability is somewhat suspect. It is not as easy to know accuracies and yields and effective hardness as it is to count the launchers of warheads and the warheads they can carry.

The size and weight of nuclear weapons depends both on their design details and on the overall energy they yield. The oldest devices, those used over Hiroshima and Nagasaki, provided low kiloton yields but weighed four to five tons each, like large conventional bombs. The weight of the nuclear explosive was a very small percentage of the total weight: in each the fission explosive weighed only some ten kilograms. The rest of the weight was in structural materials, the protective casing, and in the mechanisms needed to produce an explosive supercritical mass from the fission explosive provided. In the case of the Hiroshima bomb—which used the uranium fission isotope, U-235—the weight was largely that of a cannonlike assembly device, with steel tubing and a heavy target. In the Nagasaki bomb, much of the weight was that of the chemical high explosive which exploded symmetrically upon the plutonium fission charge present. Most of the weight of the weapons built today is also apt to be in structural materials, in the electronics used for firing and control, and in the conventional chemical explosive always needed to trigger the nuclear explosion.

The lightest nuclear weapons—such as the "Davy Crockett" infantry weapon once held in U.S. Army arsenals—weigh about a hundred pounds. The heaviest are several tons or more; the maximum explosion yield ever recorded, a Soviet test of nearly sixty megatons, required a ton of fusion explosive alone. There is good reason to believe that most modern weapons range between a low-yield weapon in the kiloton range with a physical weight of about a quarter of a ton, up to high-yield weapons in the many megaton range, each with a physical weight of about one or two tons.[6] It is clear that there must be some minimum weight devoted to the mechanisms required; the weight of added nuclear explosive to gain higher yield is often not very important compared with the other mechanical devices required. A weapon with only a hundred pounds of fission and fusion explosive can yield a megaton or two of explosive energy, and it is not likely in fact to ever detonate all the nucleaar explosive in place; some is wasted.

Hitting the Target

The development of nuclear explosives and the way to use them was the task for the fifties. In the sixties, the technology of delivery of the weapons to the intended target rapidly developed. The seventies have seen the perfection of these technologies in the direction of very large numbers of weapons, with more and more accurate and varied techniques for delivery.

The first use of these weapons—and still the dominant intended use—was in *strategic war,* the continuation of warfare from the air behind the lines, far from any battlefield where armed forces confronted each other. Strategic war refers to an attack deep into the homelands of the engaged nations, and is particularly relevant to warfare between the superpowers, the United States and the Soviet Union, two lands that are across the North Polar ice cap from one another. Such a war is *intercontinental.*

The means by which weapons are brought to their targets are called, in the jargon, the means of *delivery.* In the present situation there are two sorts of delivery at long range: *aircraft* and *missiles.*

Strategic War by Aircraft

Each long-range bomber can deliver nuclear weapons by flying near the target to drop the bombs. This is the style celebrated in the film *Dr. Strangelove* and is still an important delivery system. A large manned jet airplane can carry and drop a dozen or more bombs, for its load capacity is many tens of tons. But as missile technology improved, it became clear that many airplanes—whether high- or low-flying craft—could be shot down as they neared their targets. Since the early sixties, the bombers have included Short-Range Attack Missiles (SRAMs), unmanned missiles with nuclear warheads and a modest range up to around a hundred miles. So armed, the aircraft need not

7-3   **NUCLEAR WAR TERMS AND DEFINITIONS**

These ten definitions are basic to nuclear war, weapons, and strategy; there are hundreds more. The interested reader is referred to the Joint Chiefs of Staff, *Dictionary of Military and Associated Terms*.

Deterrence: Preventing someone from attacking by threatening unacceptable destruction in response, thereby "deterring" war.

First Strike: Hitting the enemy before he hits you; oftentimes called "preemptive" strike.

Flexible Response: Being able to respond to attack in a variety of ways over various time frames; being able to strike targets "flexibly."

Limited War: Less than all-out warfare, involving all nuclear forces on both sides of battle; use of a "limited" number of weapons.

Mutual Assured Destruction: The situation when opposing sides can both destroy each other in second strikes; both thereby mutually assure destruction on the other, theoretically deterring war. Oftentimes called "MAD."

Proliferation: The spread of nuclear weapons, either internationally or within a country's arsenal; the former is called "horizontal" proliferation, the latter "vertical" proliferation.

Second Strike: Hitting the enemy after he hits you; oftentimes called a "retaliatory" strike.

Stability: The situation where there is no incentive for either side to launch a nuclear war; if some incentive exists, the situation is called "unstable."

Strategic: Weapons or war which involves the homelands of the antagonists, namely, the Soviet Union and the United States.

Tactical: Weapons or war which does not involve the homelands of the superpowers, for example "tactical" nuclear war in Europe.

directly approach a well-defended city or a military base; it can launch its missiles from afar, having carried them most of the way across an ocean. These missiles can be air-breathing, powered by engines that take oxygen from the air, like small, unmanned aircraft. Or they can have their energy source and oxygen entirely within, like the rockets that traverse outer space. Both kinds are used; the air-breathing robot aircraft are often called *cruise missiles,* though recently the term has been used more often to describe the newer versions with longer range—a thousand and more miles. Ships and submarines can also launch cruise missiles of long range. But

current short-range missiles launched by ships or submarines cannot threaten the interior of national territory far from the sea and are perhaps still less than strategic. (One notes here the tendency to erase distinctions typical of the technology of this epoch. Aircraft nowadays are becoming a form of missile launcher, although they are rarely described by this term.)[7]

Strategic War by Ballistic Missiles

A missile that travels most of its way out of the atmosphere, up in the vacuum of space orbit, does not need to burn fuel for the major portion of its trip. This is termed a *ballistic mis-*

7-4   **AIRBORNE NUCLEAR WAR**

The B-52 jet bomber in flight.

Soviet Bear turboprop (TU-95) aircraft accompanied by a U.S. F-15.

Air-Launched Cruise Missile (ALCM).

Air-launched cruise missiles deployed on a B-52 aircraft.

Aircraft have always had a major role in U.S. strategic forces. Starting in the late fifties, long-range B-52 jet bombers were on constant alert, carrying multimegaton nuclear bombs. Their role diminished somewhat as intercontinental missiles took over much of the deterrent role in the sixties. Modern technology, however, has given the airplane a new role: carrying twenty or thirty cruise missiles to within a wide striking distance of strategic targets. Cruise missiles—miniature robot jet aircraft—can guide themselves the final 1,000 miles to a target by following an internal map of the terrain to be crossed.

Although the Soviet Union has not emphasized bombers, several varieties of air-launched cruise missiles, larger and of shorter range than the new U.S. models, are in the arsenals of both countries.

7-5   **THE TITAN INTERCONTINENTAL MISSILE**

Titan missile in its Kansas silo.

Titan missile launch at Vandenberg Air Force Base, California.

Following the Atlas and Titan I, the Titan II was the third model of ICBM to be deployed as part of the U.S. strategic forces. The Titan II was the first ICBM to use liquid fuel and oxidizer that could be stored in the missile, making it ready for immediate launch, and the first that could be fired from its stored position in a protective silo. The Titan II has been operational at fifty-four sites in Arkansas, Nebraska, and Arizona beginning in 1963. Accidents have destroyed two missiles and put their silos out of operation.

These out-of-date missiles are proposed for decommission, but they account for at least one-third of the destructive yield of U.S. land-based missiles and are thought to be too valuable as a bargaining asset to dismantle without an equivalent Soviet concession.

sile: it simply falls down back through the atmosphere at meteorite speed to strike a target above or on the ground. These space-age weapons orbit full intercontinental distances within about thirty minutes. They can cruise regardless of weather or darkness to deliver their deadly load close to a target anywhere on earth. Nowadays many of them are fitted with a multiplicity of nuclear warheads that are arranged to be sent off by the coasting vehicle in the right direction and at the right instant to strike a prescribed target below: one missile can deliver ten or more nuclear warheads, each individually aimed, along ballistic trajectories.

Ballistic missiles, which travel in looping orbits, can be launched in different ways. The Cape Canaveral style—launching from a fixed tower above ground—was the first used. But a missile at such a launch point could be easily destroyed by an adversary warhead that came in first; it was too soft. So the most familiar launching scheme was developed: the underground vertical missile silo. Silos are hardened to different degrees against a weapon burst at some distance. There are thousands of buried silos across the Great Plains of the United States and the wide steppes of the Soviet Union. These land-based missiles are called Intercontinental Ballistic Missiles, or ICBMs.

ICBMs could be carried and launched from ships or large aircraft, and one such scheme was tested by the U.S. Air Force in 1974, but it has not yet led to any system in operation.

The most remarkable launchers of ballistic missiles are submarines. Submarine-Launched Ballistic Missiles (SLBMs) make up a large part of all modern missile forces. The large submarines that carry the nuclear missiles—usually one to two dozen missiles per sub—are doubly nuclear, for they are fitted with nuclear-powered propulsion. Nuclear electrical power is perfectly adapted to submarine propulsion: it is free from any need for oxygen, and is so compact that a single charge of nuclear fuel easily lasts for many months or even years of submerged cruising. Such nuclear-propelled submarines need not carry missiles with explosive nuclear warheads; indeed, there are more non-missile-launching, nuclear-driven subs than there are nuclear subs equipped with launch tubes for ballistic missiles. SLBMs could also be carried by diesel-driven subs; some older Soviet submarines, now obsolete, were of this type.

There are important differences between the various types of launchers. The fixed silo is targetable—that is, photographic and other instruments carried by aircraft or satellites can record the fixed position of the silo. The silo can then be placed on the list of targets at which warheads can be precisely aimed. It remains survivable, that is, it remains likely to be able to function after a nearby nuclear explosion, only if it is hard enough to escape disabling damage at the miss distance expected. As accuracy improves, ICBM silos become less and less survivable, despite hardening with more steel, cement, and better shock mounts. The submarine missile system was introduced by the United States in the early sixties. The subs remain underwater for two-month-long cruises; they may be anywhere within a large area of ocean and can, in a matter of minutes, launch their missiles at specific inland targets thousands of miles away. The SLBM launcher is not targetable because it has proved very hard to locate the fast, silent sub hidden in the opaque seas; and it is highly survivable because it is not easy to damage by a salvo of missiles thrown into the wide oceans without close knowledge of where the sub is situated. Of course, the submarine must know its own position in order to direct its missiles to the fixed targets on land; although this is not as easy as it is for a land-based fixed launcher, it can be done. As well, it is difficult to transmit orders to submerged subs, and their confirmation is even more limited.

Only mobile launchers, either aircraft already in the air (called alert aircraft) or submarines at sea (at any time some must be in port for routine maintenance), can claim to be nontargetable. Soviet submarines are sometimes sheltered in heavy concrete pens in port to improve their survivability since many of them spend most of the time in port. Various schemes of moving land-based launchers have been suggested to reduce the targetability of fixed ICBMs; the United States is engaged in developing one version, system MX, which may shuffle missiles either among many hardened shelters, spaced a mile or two apart on land, or in many aircraft—sorts of pea-in-the-shell-type schemes. In this way the opponent must make every shelter or aircraft a

7-6   NUCLEAR WAR LAUNCHED FROM THE SEA

Missile tubes of the USS *Sam Rayburn*.

Soviet *Yankee* class nuclear-powered ballistic missile submarine under way.

Underwater firing of a Polaris A-3 missile, the first SLBM armed with multiple warheads.

The submerged nuclear-propelled submarine forms a nearly ideal launching platform for strategic missiles, for it is nearly impossible to detect, track, and target. The missiles are held in vertical tubes from which they are blown by compressed gas, to ignite and blast off once they reach the ocean surface. The first successful underwater test launch of a Polaris missile occurred from the USS *George Washington* in July 1960. Since then the United States has progressed through several generations of Submarine-Launched Ballistic Missiles (SLBM), as has the Soviet Union. Most U.S. missile submarines carry Poseidon missiles, but twelve have been converted to carry Trident missiles, and new Trident submarines are under construction.

target; the shelters would be very numerous, some two dozen per active missile. However, this scheme depends on sustained deception; if the opponent develops some means of recognizing from afar—say, by surveillance satellite—which shelter holds the real missile and which are the decoys hauled around in the system, its value would end. The submarines seem much better concealed, though in this case also, concealment by the deep waters will perhaps some day become incomplete. (It is not unimportant to note that the U.S. land-based ICBMs are a weapon of the U.S. Air Force; if land-based missiles were ever abandoned by the United States, the air force would lose an important mission, even though the country retained better missiles, more safely, in the same numbers at sea. The SLBMs at sea are, of course, by invariable custom part of the U.S. Navy.)[8]

Tactical Nuclear Weapons

Since the fifties there has been a rapid growth in nuclear weapons that are not intended for intercontinental war or for strategic use far behind the lines of battle or frontier. These nuclear weapons—called Tactical Nuclear Weapons (TNWs)—are instead part of the battlefield itself, intended for use by land, sea, and air. They are meant for a single "theater of war," not for a distant homeland. A great many of them are found in Europe, for it is in this theater of potential war that the United States and the Soviet Union confront each other, each with their allies. The United States already has 6,000 tactical nuclear weapons in Europe. (A cynical remark, not so far from the truth, is that a tactical nuclear weapon is one that explodes in Germany.)[9]

Some tactical nuclear weapons are intended for use in specialized air and sea combat. For example, U.S. fighter-interceptor aircraft intended to engage hostile planes entering U.S. air space (not an expected form of combat in the missile age) have available to them short-range rockets—air-to-air missiles with nuclear warheads which have several miles range—to home on

their flying targets. Nearly 2,000 of these nuclear Falcons are on hand, each with a nuclear warhead yield in the few kiloton range. Similarly, the United States has several score of nuclear-driven submarines that are meant to attack enemy subs, not send off SLBMs. These carry the complex weapon Subroc, which is launched through a torpedo tube while the sub is submerged, drives itself to the surface, and takes off as a short-range rocket, flying through the air a few dozen miles. At the right point, the nuclear warhead then separates and is driven down again into the sea to explode deep below at a preset depth, acting there as a nuclear depth charge. The United States also has nuclear torpedos and nuclear sea mines, and Asroc, a shipborne antisubmarine rocket with an optional nuclear depth charge, rather like Subroc.[10]

Other nuclear weapons are carried by attack and bomber aircraft and are intended for use against surface targets by land or sea. Some of these aircraft can fly at high speed for a thousand miles or more, far behind the usual zone of combat. Such devices—which include air-to-surface missiles—tend to blur the distinction between tactical and strategic nuclear weapons; that is, they are capable of hitting the Soviet homeland. The same can be said of the medium-range ballistic missiles—such as the Soviet SS-20 and the planned U.S. Pershing II—whose nuclear warheads can be sent in looping orbits to distances in the thousand-mile range. Then there are nuclear artillery shells for the heavy artillery, with short ranges of only ten or twenty miles; nuclear demolition land mines, whose craters could close an important river crossing, mountain pass, or highway; and nuclear bombs for various types of aircraft, both land-based and carrier-based. Many guns, planes, and submarines are rated as dual-capable, meaning they have the option of using either missiles with ordinary chemical explosive or with nuclear warheads.

Nearly all these tactical weapons have nuclear warheads with yields of at least a kiloton; most

7-7   **NUCLEAR WAR UNDER THE SEA**

Among the weapons in the U.S. nuclear arsenal are two antisubmarine missiles that
carry nuclear depth charges. The Asroc
missile is ship-launched, whereas the Subroc can be fired from the torpedo tubes of
a submarine. The Subroc travels to the surface, where it, like the Asroc, flies to the
vicinity of its target, perhaps some miles
distant. At that point the depth charge is
dropped into the sea to detonate at a preset depth. The navy's Tomahawk cruise
missile is under development as a successor to these weapons.

Launch of an Asroc missile from the destroyer USS
Paul F. Foster.

Test explosion of a nuclear depth charge delivered by an Asroc missile in May 1962,
before the nuclear test ban treaty entered into force.

7-8   **TACTICAL NUCLEAR WEAPONS**

Large artillery pieces such as this 155-mm how-itzer can lob conventional high-explosive or kilo-ton nuclear shells some 10 or 15 miles.

The U.S. nuclear weapons deployed in Europe for tactical use have many forms and are continually being improved in range and accuracy. They include artillery pieces, fighter-bomber aircraft, and ballistic missiles; long-range Ground-Launched Cruise Missiles (GLCM) are soon to be deployed. The Lance and Pershing Ia ballistic missile systems are already present in Europe in large numbers. The Soviet Union has also deployed a variety of similar weapons, but it is not clear whether any Soviet tactical nuclear-armed weapons are stationed outside the Soviet Union.

Launch of a Lance missile at the White Sands Missile Range, New Mexico.

Test firing of a Pershing II missile at the White Sands, New Mexico, missile range, May 1978.

Modern Tomahawk missile breaking the surface.

The U.S. Pershing II mobile missile, which has a much greater range than the Pershing Ia, is scheduled for deployment starting in 1983. It can reach Moscow with accuracy just six minutes after firing from its planned base sites along the West German frontier. The Tomahawk cruise missile is designed for launching from the sea to attack airfields, harbors, and missile bases with a nuclear warhead, or ships and other targets with high explosive. The Short-Range Attack Missile (SRAM) can strike with a nuclear warhead 100 miles from the launching aircraft.

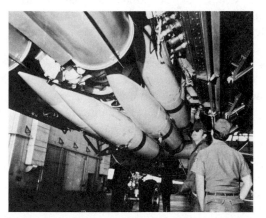

Short-Range Attack Missiles (SRAM) on a B-52.

of them can yield tens and hundreds of kilotons, and some surpass a megaton of explosive yield. The Soviet Union has similar weapons. It is not difficult to accept the unofficial estimates that the United States has some 20,000 to 25,000 tactical nuclear weapons worldwide on its ships, planes, and subs, and in its magazines. Their use in any important way would cause large-scale disaster in so populous a theater of war as Europe and would likely escalate the situation to strategic war.

It is also the case that a number of SLBMs— possibly 400 warheads—carried at sea on U.S. strategic missile submarines have been made available to targets chosen by the NATO military head, the supreme allied commander in Europe (an American officer by tradition). Thus the difference between strategic and tactical weapons has dwindled away. The new, fast, long-range Soviet jet bomber which NATO calls Backfire is intended for use against ocean shipping, it appears; but it also seems capable of longer runs, perhaps even of one-way overseas missions against the continental United States. Here, too, there is at least a potential blur of the sharp boundary between strategic and tactical nuclear weapons.

The Strategic Arms Race

The whole extraordinary arsenal outlined above has steadily grown since the first use of nuclear weapons in Japan in 1945. A sketch of this growth is revealing; it is this dynamic, perhaps even more than the terrible potential of what is presently in place, that is so full of foreboding.

In August 1949, the first nuclear explosion outside of U.S. control was carried out by the Soviet Union. By that time the United States had hundreds of atomic bombs, which were all gravity bombs to be dropped over enemy targets by a succession of heavy, long-range, propeller-driven bombers of the U.S. Strategic Air Command. Faster jet bombers began to be included in the

SAC squadrons in 1951. One Soviet countermove was to begin to build some long-range bombers of its own, but these have never become very numerous. Their main tactic was defensive: large numbers of short-range, fast interceptor aircraft, mainly MIGs, were deployed in the Soviet Union beginning in the mid-fifties. By the early sixties these were supplemented by thousands of antiaircraft, chemical-explosive missile launchers of short range (used against our B-52 bombers over Hanoi in the seventies). The first ICBMs were tested on both sides in the late fifties.

By the time of the Cuban missile crisis, in the fall of 1962, the American nuclear forces had the same pattern as they have today—the triad of missile launchers on land, undersea, and in the air. The United States held some 600 long-range bombers and almost 1,000 medium-range bombers, 300 ICBMs, and more than 100 SLBMs in 7 nuclear-powered submarines. At that time the Soviet Union had 100 long-range bombers, 1,400 medium-range jets, and at most a couple of dozen ICBMs. The curves of growth are clear. The United States took a big lead in ICBMs in the early sixties; by 1969 the Soviet Union had caught up and gone somewhat beyond. The United States built up its undersea forces to a very big lead in 1968; by now the Soviet Union has caught up and gone somewhat beyond in numbers of undersea launchers. The big U.S. lead in intercontinental bombers remains.

In the seventies the United States led still another race: a rapid buildup of its arsenal of nuclear warheads. It developed and installed many multiple-warhead MIRV missiles and added airborne missiles onto its bombers. This U.S. numerical lead remains strong today; but once again, the Soviet Union is hard at work catching up.

This perpetually increasing spiral—in the physical damage potential of the weapons systems, in their speed and complexity, with no clear steady change in relative position between

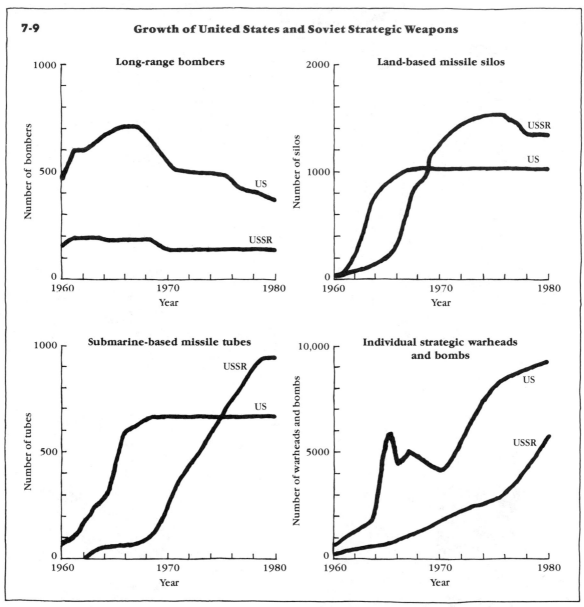

7-9   **Growth of United States and Soviet Strategic Weapons**

These four graphs illustrate the kind of nuclear marathon being run since 1960 by the United States and the Soviet Union. The United States has largely set the pace, continuing its lead in numbers of bombers and nuclear warheads; the Soviet Union has been a strong competitor and now leads the United States in numbers of land-based and submarine-based missile launchers. Both parties have more than enough.

7-10   THE PRACTICE OF MIRV

Minuteman III in its silo.

Simultaneous launch of two Minuteman missiles from Vandenberg Air Force Base.

Minuteman III warheads and nose cone.

A major change in prospects for strategic arms control came in the late sixties with the introduction of MIRV—Multiple Independently Targetable Reentry Vehicles. With MIRV, one missile can carry destruction to two or more targets within its "footprint," the large land area over which warheads can be delivered by one missile.

In each Minuteman III missile, three warheads are carried on a bus equipped with small rocket motors that permit it to adjust its trajectory to send each warhead toward a separate target. More recent missiles—Poseidon, Trident, and MX—are designed to carry eight to fourteen independently targetable warheads. To improve the probability that a target is destroyed, a pair of warheads from two missiles may be delivered to each of a set of targets, a procedure known as "cross targeting."

Test flight of six unarmed reentry vehicles from two Minuteman missiles, streaking to targets at Kwajalein Atoll in the Pacific.

the two superpowers—is the essence of the arms race. Few observers will claim that either power is more secure than it was in 1950; we who write these pages can only comment that it has become much less secure. The three past decades without nuclear war prove that a pru-

dent inhibition against its terrible destructiveness is so far found in the leaders on both sides. But if history shows anything, it is that events can sweep away prudence without clear intent for mutual destruction on either side. The curves must, some day, level off and start to descend, or the future will record unprecedented disaster. The only doubt one can have about disaster is when it will occur. How much time is left for the arrival of restraint or agreement?

Money is not the chief cost of this deadly spiral, though it costs tens of billions of dollars annually. Perhaps the important point to remember is that this fatal technology actually threatens such extensive damage at unexpectedly low cost. The total cost of offensive strategic forces today is about $15 billion a year (in fiscal year 1981 dollars) for the United States and an estimate of about $15 billion to $18 billion a year for the Soviet Union (including a costly air defense.) This is only 7 percent of the total U.S. military budget. The easiest way to understand this point is to recognize that only 100,000 military personnel are required to serve the strategic forces of the United States, out of a total of 2 million or more under arms. Clearly, these are forces with high capital costs and low demand in labor.[11]

In the Soviet Union, the strategic defensive forces—long in place as counters to the bombers of SAC—are at least as costly as all their offensive nuclear forces. The United States, on the other hand—not much concerned with the relatively minor Soviet air threat for the past fifteen years or more—has not maintained any substantial defensive forces against airborne or missile-carried strategic warheads. U.S. defensive forces are about an eighth as costly as our offensive forces and use about the same fraction of our total strategic forces. This is the clearest disparity between U.S. and Soviet preparations for nuclear war, but it is not a real disadvantage; our military planners simply do not view Soviet bombers as an important and credible threat.

Before we consider the details of present preparations and plans for nuclear war, we draw one conclusion: there is no winner in the arms race. Once there are thousands, or perhaps even hundreds of thousands, of powerful warheads, the ingenious stratagems, which we will outline below, outrun all human meaning. The destruc-

tion is too great; relative calamity no longer has weight. Careful counts and comparison are pertinent only before nuclear war, when some human perceptions might be affected. Afterwards there will be no heart for such grim accounting. The essential equivalence, in the jargon of the times, is an equivalence in disaster. Thus the race we have sketched has become less than accurately estimable in terms of damage.

The Strategies of Destruction

The simplest goal for such terrible arsenals is the threatened destruction of the enemy cities and resources, with a major portion of their people. Such a stance is called *countervalue.* Like all strategic war, it aims at vulnerable human lives and properties—values—behind the frontier. In the fifties, when the United States held a near-monopoly of deliverable nuclear weapons, the catchphrase for a countervalue attack was *massive retaliation.* Once the sixties came and the Soviet Union held a similar power to destroy us, this threat lost credibility, for only in desperation would we attack in the knowledge that a nuclear countervalue response would wreak a very heavy toll on our cities in return.[12]

In the presence of such forces, then, the strategy tended to resemble the mutual recognition that the cities on each side were hostages for the tolerable behavior of the adversary state. Absent any plausible defense—and none has yet appeared, neither some kind of broadly safe city shelter (civil defense) nor some way to knock down most inflying missiles (by Antiballistic Missiles, ABMs)—this stance, cruel as it is, seems most reasonable. It is called MAD—Mutual Assured Destruction. Some estimate of the potential kind of damage is found in Figure 7-13. This is the situation of *mutual deterrence,* "two scorpions in a bottle."

As the states continued to build their weapons, especially with the advent of multiple warheads on individual missiles, there was more discussion of *counterforce*—an attack against the nuclear weapons and military forces of the adversary rather than against life and property. Here the scorpion could strike in such a way that its sting would eliminate, or at least reduce, the toxic force of the sting it must expect in return. Forces that are arranged for use in counterforce—because they are swift to arrive and accurate enough to destroy hardened targets—are sure to threaten the deterrent stance, for they open the possibility that, if they are used, retaliation would not come. But they have one certain weakness: if counterforce is not used first, it will be chiefly destroyed by a *first strike* from the other side. On this line of argument, there is disproportionate gain from striking first. If this is true, then the danger is clearly greater; in time of crisis, the impulse will be to start the spiral, for the one who gets in the first blow will gain advantage. This situation is called *instability*. Any weapon or tactic that suggests that each side might realize an advantage from starting the exchange is said to be destabilizing. For example, unlike submarines which, hidden safely underseas, can well wait out the first strike from an adversary, visible, well-mapped, stationary silos are increasingly less stable than the subs, especially in these days of multiple warheads when only a portion of the missile strength would be needed to destroy most adversary silos.

On the other hand, these merely logical arguments are not the whole story. Counterforce is a risky procedure, adventurous in the extreme. The strike can hardly be tested in advance. It may all work, but there may be some error in the maps or whatever is involved in destroying the enemy silos far overseas and buried deep in the ground. Are they perhaps stronger than your estimates? Even more likely, the adversary will not wait to fire a missile until it is clear that you are attacking, because your warheads are exploding all around the missile fields, so-called Launch Under Attack (LUA). Your adversary can choose to fire upon detection of your own firing, which is called Launch

On Warning (LOW). But the warning is the product of an elaborate and largely untested system, a far-flung net of radars and satellites, whose notice of an all-out incoming strike is less than convincing, if one has to bet survival upon it.

Such scenarios feather out into bizarre judgments of "he knows that I know that he intends to fire tomorrow, so he may fire tonight instead—maybe I must fire now!" And this is all computerized. So far, heads of state have resisted such gambles. It is plain that a reasoning and prudent adversary is better than any new weapons system; it is worth emphasizing one's own visibly sober calculations. New and hair-trigger systems that purport to gain some logical advantage are hardly worth the uncertainty they can induce in one's opponent. Once an opponent fires mistakenly in force, both the scorpions are likely to be fatally stung, and in them, the population and hopes of a hemisphere.

If it were not for the inhibitions that clearly override these thin logical games, the future would be gloomy indeed. It does not seem that there is any other stance save to act with caution, avoid building systems that suggest counterforce capabilities, and let the opponent know that the retaliation is sure and strong but that one will not open battle. In such a climate the weapons might in time come to be held unusable, as in fact they are.

In 1980 the newspapers carried stories that the United States now plans explicitly to deal in counterforce and countercommand, seeking to aim its missiles at the leadership bunkers and control links of the other side. The matter became public via a quasi-official leak of the so-called Presidential Directive 59 (PD-59). (Directive PD-58 essentially provided for better bunkers for our own leaders, a logical complement to PD-59, if not very welcome to taxpayers and dwellers in soft structures.) Indeed, the stance had been signaled by various U.S. officials even since 1979; its publication was more a new symbol than a new decision. We learned that there are 40,000 targets for our 9,200 warheads listed in our plans, about half of them Soviet military targets; 15,000 economic and industrial targets (people and production); 2,000 leadership targets; and 3,000 counterforce opportunities.[13] The implication is clear: we hope to manage a controlled escalation of our attack, with a rich choice of alternatives. Of course we hope it will be limited, only a little way up the escalator—we hope. We hope also that the leaders we might kill are not the only ones who can limit Soviet response and negotiate an end to the nuclear exchanges. The game is full of such deadly paradoxes.

It is difficult to believe that elegant and measured stratagems will rule the day during the uncertainties of a terrible nuclear attack, with death for millions. Very likely there is some small number of warheads that a state will resent but will not counter by a desperate and little-controlled retaliation with all it has. This number might be at the level of hundreds of targets, or less. Speculation about further nuclear exchanges seems to belong to another world of scholastic elegances. With leaders dead, orders confused or absent, missiles threatened within minutes, millions likely to die in the radioactive fallout footprints . . . what will the missile crews do, by land, air, or sea?

The safest course seems to be to hold the line strong against nuclear weapons; against a nuclear-armed enemy, they can only be used for the deterrence of nuclear weapons use. This understanding implies hidden forces—weapons safe against surprise attack, slow and sure to respond.

The Less Extravagant Disasters

Any nuclear weapon exploded near people or property is a disaster. But there are circumstances in which one or a few such events might occur, and no more. These are often the subject of discussion, even of imaginative fiction: an accidental explosion caused by some human or machine failure in the routine transport or storage of a weapon; an accidental launch of some mis-

sile with an active warhead; similar acts by a lunatic or a terrorist group with access to one or a few weapons, instead of the large arsenal of the state. All of these events are possible, and some are very plausible indeed given the passage of enough time. Many accidents—*broken arrows,* in military jargon—have occurred, such as crashes of planes carrying nuclear bombs, missile fuel explosions in silos, and so on, but no known case of subsequent nuclear explosion.[14] The weapons are designed to prevent such unintended explosions. Attempts at bribery of military personnel who hold nuclear weapons is an old rumor in Europe; agents of one or another would-be nuclear power are blamed. So far they have apparently not succeeded. Finally, the clever novelists have considered the initiation of a great nuclear war between two heavily armed powers by the deliberate "catalytic" intervention of a third smaller power, which deceptively explodes one or a few weapons so timed and placed as to throw blame on the expected opponent, in some time of crisis.

All these events might occur; but it is useful to point out that the stakes here are very high indeed. A great power is not likely to initiate a large-scale attack unless it intends to do so, and the single, unintended stray missile or the first strike by one weapon is not apt to be answered by a huge salvo. The party in danger is certain to make known its plight, and the best assurance of its honesty will be the absence of corroborative signs of many more missiles and aircraft soon to come. The "hot line" between leaders is worth its cost. Single errors, tragic as they may be, will probably not grow to a cataclysm. It is intent, arising perhaps from misunderstanding and misperception, that we have most to fear, rather than accident or deception. This is not to deny that a single, unofficial bomb might some day threaten a city, but even such a melodrama is not in scale with the terrible events we are constrained to consider here. But one must always remember that even the slightest probability of any nuclear cataclysm must be diminished.

Limited Nuclear War

Military theorists are constantly trying to find effective use for nuclear weapons. We have considered two types of targets: civilian populations and enemy nuclear forces. This is no place to elaborate on limited nuclear war theories, for they seem less than plausible. Yet it is possible that nuclear weapons could be used in limited numbers to enforce some political demand, perhaps most likely in the face of a losing conventional military engagement. Such selective use— the number and type of targets limited by intention and probably by public avowal—is certainly full of risk. One major source of risk is the fact that even careful, limited attack spreads heavy damage to nearby civilian populations. The most recent study by the Office of Technology Assessment (OTA) of the U.S. Congress in 1979 showed this plainly. The study considered attacks by only ten launchers, with MIRV, amounting to seventy or eighty warheads in all. Both events (the Soviet attack on the United States and the counterpart U.S. attack on the Soviet Union) are limited to destruction of the vulnerable, essential, and costly petroleum refineries in each country. Both attacks succeed; the capacity is reduced sharply, to a third of its initial value at once, requiring years for rebuilding. But in each case there are many fatalities: 4 million Americans die, mostly within a month of the attack; the Russian losses are less, "only" a million or so, for our weapons are smaller, and their refineries are farther from centers of population. Millions more are injured on both sides. Years pass before economic recovery. Thus we have described a limited war, carried out to inflect economic damage, "without any effort to minimize or to maximize human casualties."[15]

It is simply unclear that such an attack would not draw a response in kind as a minimum. What would be gained by its initiation?

Counterforce and Damage Limitation

The same scheme can be extended to reduce the nuclear and overall military capabilities of the adversary power. Here too the matter is complicated. A modest counterforce attack leaves the opposing power with heavy residual power and a strong desire to use it. Such an attack does not greatly limit the damage the stricken power can inflict, for most of its weapons remain intact. In order to limit damage to oneself, or to end the nuclear threat from the other, a heavy attack must be made. Indeed, without the ability to find the submarines and the bombers which may be airborne or sent off at once, no such attack is good enough. An attack against all ICBMs, or against those plus the sub and air bases, is a big attack indeed. The OTA studies show that such an attack on the United States would have quite uncertain consequences, depending on the weather, the details of the weapons used, and the degree of shelter protection. A prudent estimate seems to run about 10 million dead, or about half that with ample warning and some crisis education and planning. "An attack during or just before harvest could result in the loss of the whole crop ... by preventing farmers from harvesting" in the air of the radioactive Great Plains.

In such conditions as these studies consider, the idea of using one's forces to limit damage in the case of a conflict seen as inevitable, by striking first, has not much to say for it. "Use them or lose them," is the flippant basis for such an action. But, in a "limited" or other nuclear strike, the damage is cruelly heavy, beyond the examples of history.[16]

All-Out War

There is not much more to be said; the studies are quite in agreement. The nuclear weapons each side possesses seem to ensure many tens of millions dead, up to a hundred million or more on each side. Soviet fatalities might be slightly lower than American, due mainly to the lower population density and higher weapons yields there. But each power would face a grim future, unprecedented since the Black Death.

The details of nuclear weapons effects are

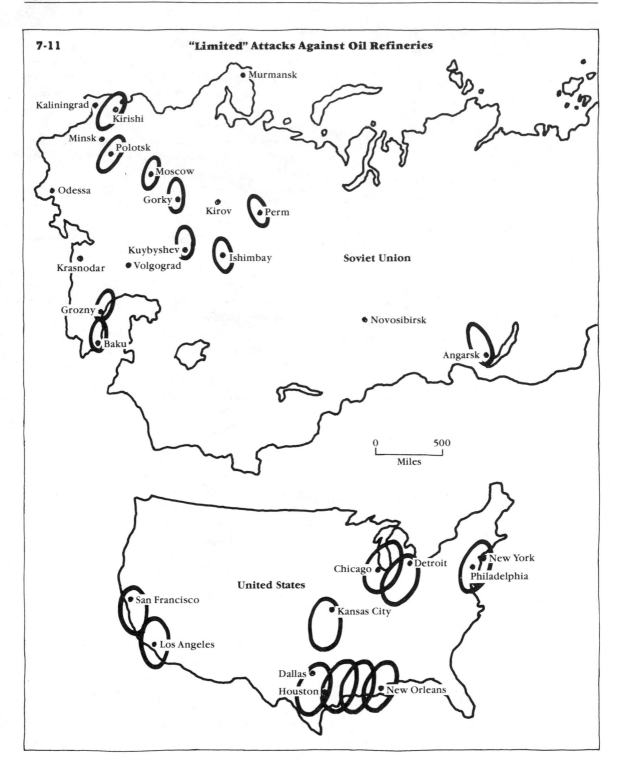

7-11   **"Limited" Attacks Against Oil Refineries**

7-12   **Fallout from an Attack on U.S. Strategic Forces**

0   500
    Miles

▩ 50% fatalities
▨ 15% fatalities
▦ Increased incidence of cancer

An attack on present U.S. strategic weapon bases, using a one-megaton warhead against each bomber base, submarine base, and missile silo, not only would damage the military targets but would kill some 20 million citizens and spread dangerous amounts of fallout over 50 percent of U.S. land area. Typical winds are assumed blowing from west to east, although the weather could produce a wide variety of fallout patterns.

outlined in an earlier chapter. The plain facts suggest that this danger is the greatest risk ever faced by human beings and their societies; the reluctance to face this conclusion is the greatest weakness of government leaders worldwide for three decades. They have shown the necessary restraint against the use of the weapons but have not been willing to accept the eventual consequences: the possession of growing capabilities is by now in itself a terrible danger.

Worldwide Effects of Nuclear War

The large-scale use of nuclear weapons is not a possibility only for the superpowers. The other member states of the Nuclear Club cannot go beyond the level of a percent or so of the

OPPOSITE:

Even so-called limited nuclear attacks—limited only in the sense of using relatively small numbers of nuclear weapons—offer massive devastation for any country. An attack by the United States on ten Soviet oil refineries, accounting for almost three-fourths of Soviet refining capacity, would promptly kill over one million people. A Soviet attack against ten U.S. refineries, using perhaps 2 percent of total Soviet nuclear megatonnage, would kill more than 5 million citizens.

7-13   EFFECTS OF A MAJOR NUCLEAR WAR

Immediate Effects

United States and Soviet Union	Deaths from blast and burns: 20–160 million

Middle-term Effects

Enormous economic disruption. If immediate deaths are in the low range, more tens of millions may die because the economy is unable to support them. Unprecedented psychological trauma.

Long-term Effects

	Cancer Deaths (millions)	Cases of Genetic Damage (millions)
United States	10	15
Soviet Union	20	20
Other countries	15	20

Over 100 million Americans, Soviets, and others would be killed or seriously injured in a major nuclear war between the superpowers. There would be an additional 100 million subsequent casualties from latent cancers and genetic defects.

overall strike capabilities of the United States or the Soviet Union, which is of course serious enough. But worldwide effects are likely to depend upon warheads by the thousands.[17]

There is no doubt that the drifting radioactive fallout from such high total yields will have serious effects beyond the frontiers of the target states. There will be heavy fallout downwind in China and Japan, or in Canada and Western Europe, and it will eventually cover the whole earth. Studies show that millions of casualties can be expected, mostly from the invisible hazard of cancer and genetic defects—the insidious and pervasive death from radiation exposure—rather than prompt death from the blast and fury of explosions. The spread of this warfare to neutrals and the uninvolved is certainly without precedent.

What is perhaps worse is the unknown effect upon the worldwide environment of these many man-made radioactive, volcano-type explosions. We simply do not know enough about the effects on the atmosphere, sea, and the living forms on land and sea to be sure of what will happen. Irreversible effects are possible, though they do not seem likely. (No safety factor can be estimated for such uncertainties; evidently they represent a great gamble with public health. It appears probable that an increase in the arsenals by another factor of ten would broadly endanger human survival. Perhaps this is the limit the powers will finally obey.) The most evident effect appears to be upon the ozone layer high in the stratosphere. The nitrogen oxides that are generated by high-yield explosions, especially if carried to high altitudes, would deplete the ozone layer by an important fraction if there are thousands of explosions of one-megaton yield. The case is marginal for the present size of the stockpiles, though the conclusion is far from firm. It is what we do not know that can hurt.

The social consequences of so novel and deep a trauma are best left to the imaginative writer. Social science today can hardly extrapolate to so great and sudden a disaster.

7-14   WAR WITH TACTICAL NUCLEAR WEAPONS: THE CASE OF EUROPE

STRATEGIC WAR is the attack at intercontinental distances with transoceanic weapons. But the big powers maintain thousands of nuclear weapons for use in or at least near the battlefield, rather than back in their respective homelands. These are known as tactical or theater nuclear weapons. The theater of war which is most open to planned tactical warfare of this sort is, of course, Europe. Although the events of a war with tactical nuclear weapons are too complex to anticipate, the following is an account of what the consequences might be:

At present, the most obvious danger of an extensive use of tactical or theater nuclear weapons would exist if there were a superpower conflict in Europe. Here there are large, diversified, and militarily integrated nuclear arsenals that could be used for extensive theater employment.

If such a war should occur, the probability is that it could not be kept at theater level. On the contrary, a crisis which had escalated beyond the use of a few theater nuclear weapons could be in imminent danger of reaching the level of "strategic exchange," owing to the magnitude of political objectives which by necessity would underlie a conflict of such tension. In particular, this could be the case if an extensive theater nuclear war should turn out to be of considerable disadvantage to one of the two sides.

In the situation being considered, both sides have mobilized and deployed forces in the range of fifty to one hundred divisions each, and these and their supporting tactical air forces have been issued nuclear munitions. It is assumed that the priority targets would be the adversary's nuclear delivery systems in the theater—field artillery, rocket and guided missile units, and air bases. Thus, the exchange would basically be a duel between the opposing nuclear systems. In addition, armoured units and command posts would be targeted and rear-area targets other than army forces and air bases would not be ex-

cluded *per se*. They would be less important to the outcome of a nuclear campaign of short duration, but might still add appreciably to the number of casualties.

The weaponry available to the two sides is somewhat asymmetrical. To reflect this, the average yield of weapons for battlefield targets might be one kiloton on one side and five kilotons on the other. It is further assumed that command and communication centers, air bases and other rear-area targets would be attacked with missiles equipped with 100 kiloton warheads.

The ensuing civilian casualties would depend on the distribution of people in targeted areas. The worst case would occur when the shots from both sides were distributed without any regard to civilian settlements in the battle area. The consequences would be less severe if one or both of the belligerents deliberately tried to avoid hitting these settlements.

The casualties would be caused by blast effects, thermal radiation and fire, radioactive fallout, and combinations of these. One could expect that virtually all of those with severe injuries would die, as adequate medical treatment would not be available.

The major damage to civilian society would be caused by the 100 kiloton weapons. The targets for these weapons would not as a rule be located within urban areas and would presumably be surrounded by an uninhabited safety zone. A population density of 300 persons per square kilometer is assumed, bearing in mind that the population density in large European cities is about ten times higher. Under this assumption, each of the 100 kiloton weapons might kill or injure about 25,000 civilians, giving a total of up to five million casualties as the immediate effect of this nuclear war. This would hold only if the weapons were properly aimed, however. Each missile going astray and hitting an urban area instead of the intended target would add another quarter million casualties to the total.

Fallout from the large weapons would constitute a more serious problem, as each explosion would release a much larger amount of radioactivity. A larger portion of the explosions might also be surface bursts, and the population density in the fallout areas would be higher. If half of these explosions were surface bursts, a total of about 0.7 million people could be expected to receive radiation doses causing death within a month, even if it were assumed that they made reasonable efforts to stay in shelters.

In addition to high dose effects, there would be a number of late somatic and genetic injuries caused primarily by the fallout from surface bursts. These would occur over a period of some decades after the war. The number of late cancers, including leukemia, could be about 400,000 in the countries where the explosions took place. These would mainly be caused by the 100 kiloton explosions, with perhaps some 10,000 cases originating in the fallout from the lower-yield weapons or from initial radiation among those who survived the direct effects of an explosion.

In the above scenario the total delivered yield of 23.5 megatons is a small fraction of the destructive power available to the superpowers; the individual weapon yields are all far below those common in strategic weapons, and restriction to military targets has been assumed. Although the plausibility of the scenario may be doubted, it is a conservative estimate of the possible effects of nuclear war-fighting. The important point is that civilian casualties could hardly be reduced below a certain, very high level, given the collateral effects of nuclear attacks against the enemy's air force and other long-range systems. In addition to the civilian casualties, large military forces would be virtually obliterated. But the civilian casualties would outnumber the military ones by more than twelve to one.

Persons Dead and Severely Injured in a Hypothetical Theater Nuclear War

Category of Casualty	200 Large Weapons (100 Kt. each)	1,500 Low-Yield Weapons (1 to 5 Kt. each)
Civilian		
Prompt Blast and Burn Injuries	5,000,000	100,000 to 1,000,000
Acute Radiation Sickness	700,000	20,000 to 50,000
Delayed Radiation (cancer)	400,000	10,000
Total	6 to 7 million persons	
Military		
Total from all Causes	400,000 persons	

Suggested Readings

The history of development of strategic nuclear delivery systems and their deployment is covered by Norman Polmar through the introduction of MIRVs. The Enthoven and Smith book is a good account of the early analytic appraisal of proposed weapon systems, including the balance of bomber and missile forces, and the effectiveness of ballistic missile defense. See especially Chapter 5, "Nuclear Strategy and Forces," and Chapter 6, "Yardsticks of Sufficiency." The Greenwood book is an analysis of the impact of MIRVs. Chapters 6 through 8 of *The Price of Defense* describe the U.S. and Soviet strategic forces and argue the case for U.S. reliance on its ballistic missile submarine fleet as a sufficient strategic deterrent force.

Articles on nuclear war doctrine and strategy appear often in the pages of *Foreign Affairs* and *Foreign Policy.* The papers by Keeny and Panofsky and by Gray and Payne are pieces on opposite sides of the controversy over "limited" nuclear war. The Aldridge book is a critique of nuclear war-fighting doctrine by a participant in advanced missile development, and the Zuckerman volume is an analysis of the arms race by a former science advisor to the British government.

The European theater is where international tension is thought most apt to lead to a nuclear holocaust. Much information on the tactical nuclear weapons that would be used in Europe, on levels of armament, and on tactical strategy and doctrine may be found in the SIPRI volume, *Tactical Nuclear Weapons: European Perspectives,* and in the paper by Metzger and Doty. Chapter 2 of the Calder book contrasts NATO and Soviet strategy and envisions how conflict in Europe would lead to nuclear war.

The disparity of US. military arsenals with its realistic economic and security objectives is addressed by *The Price of Defense* and by the book by James Fallows.

The effects of nuclear explosions and the consequences of nuclear war are covered in the basic volume by Glasstone and Dolan, the Office of Technology Assessment (OTA) report, and, in a more popular format, the United Nations report, *Nuclear Weapons.*

ALDRIDGE, ROBERT C. *The Counterforce Syndrome: A Guide to U.S. Nuclear Weapons and Strategic Doctrine.* Washington, D.C.: Institute for Policy Studies, 1978.

BOSTON STUDY GROUP. *Winding Down: The Price of Defense.* New York: Times Books, 1979; New York: Freeman, 1982.

CALDER, NIGEL. *Nuclear Nightmares: An Investigation into Possible Wars.* New York: Viking, 1979.

ENTHOVEN, ALAIN C., and K. WAYNE SMITH. *How Much Is Enough? Shaping the Defense Program 1961–1969.* New York: Harper and Row, 1971, especially Chapters 5 and 6.

FALLOWS, JAMES. *National Defense.* New York: Random House, 1981.

GLADSTONE, SAMUEL, and PHILIP J. DOLAN, EDS. *The Effects of Nuclear Weapons,* 3rd ed. Washington, D.C.: U.S. Government Printing Office, 1977.

GRAY, COLIN S., and KEITH PAYNE. "Victory Is Possible." *Foreign Policy* 39 (Summer 1980): 14–27.

GREENWOOD, TED. *Making the MIRV: A Study of Defense Decision Making.* Cambridge, Mass.: Ballinger, 1975.

KEENY, SPURGEON M. JR., and WOLFGANG K. H. PANOFSKY. "MAD Versus NUTS." *Foreign Affairs* 60: no. 2 (Winter 1981/1982), pp. 287–304.

METZGER, ROBERT, and PAUL DOTY. "Arms Control Enters the Gray Area." *International Security* 3: no. 3 (Winter 1978/1979), pp. 17–52.

OFFICE OF TECHNOLOGY ASSESSMENT, U.S. CONGRESS. *The Effects of Nuclear War.* Washington, D.C.: U.S. Government Printing Office, 1979.

POLMAR NORMAN. *Strategic Weapons: An Introduction.* New York: Crane, Russak, 1975.

STOCKHOLM INTERNATIONAL PEACE RESEARCH INSTITUTE (SIPRI). *Tactical Nuclear Weapons: European Perspectives.* London: Taylor and Francis, 1978.

UNITED NATIONS. *Nuclear Weapons: Report of the Secretary-General.* Brookline Mass.: Autumn Press, 1981.

ZUCKERMAN, SOLLY. *Nuclear Illusion and Reality.* New York: Viking Press, 1982.

World Nuclear Arsenals

The nuclear arsenals are fairly well known in broad outline, though important details such as accuracy and reliability are surmised rather than based on definite knowledge. Much of what we know about Soviet weapons, for example, derives from official releases by U.S. sources. It is probable that the figures presented here are a sound basis for thought and action, but they are not beyond question. This estimate of the strategic forces of the nuclear powers is for late 1982 and is based on information publicly available in January 1983.

Conjecture suggests that several other states possess nuclear weapons either in place or within a short time of completion. China, which has tested a number of missiles and nuclear warheads, is said to be slowly developing submarine-launched missiles as well. In 1980 they claimed to have one nuclear-propelled submarine under test. China has some jet bombers as well. India has tested a single nuclear explosive device and has some fifty light bombers of intermediate range that could deliver nuclear weapons. Israel and the Republic of South Africa are rumored to possess nuclear weapons; so far none have been openly tested. South

WORLD STRATEGIC NUCLEAR FORCES

WORLD STRATEGIC FORCES SUMMARY

	Land-Based Missiles		Submarine-Launched Missiles		Airborne Weapons	
	Launchers	Equivalent Yield (megatons)	Launchers	Equivalent Yield (megatons)	Aircraft	Equivalent Yield (megatons)
United States	1,052	1,479	600	950	316	1,827
Soviet Union	1,398	4,629	969	810	150	300
Great Britain			64	66		
France			80	80		
China	4	12				

The summary above shows the strategic balance, giving the total estimated megatonnage of nuclear weapon systems capable of striking at intercontinental range. A breakdown by weapon system type is given in the tables on the next two pages. The equivalent megatonnage of a warhead is calculated by the formula $Y^{2/3}$, where Y is the energy yield in megatons. Thus an eight-megaton warhead is equivalent in destructive power to just four one-megaton weapons. The quantities of launchers are fairly certain, but the multiplicity of warheads and their yield are difficult to verify from public sources. For example, we do not know how many Poseidon missiles are equipped with ten warheads rather than the maximum complement of fourteen; nor do we know how many of the Soviet missiles are loaded with the various warhead configurations that have been tested. For the purpose of the summary we have estimated how the deployed missiles are divided among the different warhead configurations.

UNITED STATES STRATEGIC FORCES

Weapon Type	Launchers (number)	Warheads (number × yield)	Total Yield (megatons)	Equivalent Yield (megatons)
Land-Based Missiles				
Titan II	52	1 × 9 Mt	468	225
Minuteman II	450	1 × 1.5 Mt	675	590
Minuteman III	300	3 × 335 Kt	302	434
	250	3 × 170 Kt	128	230
Totals	1,052	2,152	1,573	1,479
Submarine-Launched Missiles				
Polaris A-3	80	3 × 200 Kt	48	82
Poseidon C-3	304	12 × 50 Kt	182	496
Trident C-4	216	8 × 100 Kt	173	372
Totals	600	5,616	403	950
Weapons Carried by B-52 Aircraft				
SRAM	1,250 warheads	200 Kt	250	427
Bombs	1,400 bombs	1 Mt	1,400	1,400
Totals	316 aircraft	2,650	1,650	1,827

SOVIET STRATEGIC FORCES

Weapon Type	Launchers (number)	Warheads (number × yield)	Total Yield (megatons)	Equivalent Yield (megatons)
Land-based Missiles				
SS-11	550	1 × 1 Mt	550	550
	20	3 × 200 Kt	12	21
SS-13	60	1 × 750 Kt	45	50
SS-17	10	1 × 6 Mt	60	33
	140	4 × 750 Kt	420	462
SS-18	231	1 × 20 Mt	4,620	1,702
	77	8 × 900 Kt	554	574
SS-19	300	6 × 550 Kt	990	1,208
	10	1 × 5 Mt	50	29
Totals	1,398	3,897	7,301	4,629
Submarine-launched Missiles				
SS-N-5	57	1 × 1.5 Mt	86	75
SS-N-6	112	1 × 1 Mt	112	112
	288	2 × 200 Kt	115	197
SS-N-8	292	1 × 1 Mt	292	292
SS-N-17	12	1 × 1 Mt	12	12
SS-N-18	208	1 × 450 Kt	94	122
Totals	969	1,257	711	810
Aircraft with Bombs				
TU-95 (Bear)	105	2 × 1 Mt	210	210
MYA-4 (Bison)	45	2 × 1 Mt	90	90
Totals	150	300	300	300

OTHER STRATEGIC FORCES

Weapon Type	Launchers (number)	Warheads (number × yield)	Total Yield (megatons)	Equivalent Yield (megatons)
British submarine-launched missiles:				
Polaris A-3	64	3 × 200 Kt	38	66
French submarine-launched missiles:				
MSBS M-20	80	1 × 1 Mt	80	80
Chinese land-based missiles:				
CSS-3	4	1 × 5 Mt	20	12

Africa has a dozen light bombers; Israel has none but holds many very effective fighter-bombers of modest range but high speed.

For the near future, we estimate what the strategic forces of the superpowers will be in 1985. On the U.S. side, 165 of the B-52 aircraft will be modified so that they can carry twenty cruise missiles (ALCM) apiece. The last Polaris missiles will be retired, their part in the deterrent triad being taken over by new and old submarines armed with a total of 240 Trident I missiles (SLBM), each carrying eight independently targetable warheads. Deployment of the MX, planned to come later, would add 100 high-accuracy missiles with ten warheads apiece to the U.S. arsenal.

On the Soviet side, many older long-range missiles (SS-13 and some SS-11) will be replaced by newer types (SS-17, SS-18, and SS-19), which have four to eight warheads each. The Soviet strategic submarine fleet will be strengthened with more missiles carrying multiple warheads.

On each side the total number of launchers is expected to show little growth by 1985—to 2,180 for the United States and 2,438 for the Soviet Union. Yet the numbers of warheads—some 14,000 for the United States and 9,000 for the Soviet Union—give the United States a 50 percent increase, and the Soviets 30 percent, in the ability of each country to destroy prime targets in the other.

Estimating numbers of launchers can be done with considerable confidence on the basis of satellite surveillance and observations of military maneuvers and testing programs. Estimating numbers of warheads is more difficult: one generally assumes that each type of launcher is armed with the largest number of warheads it is known to carry. Particularly in the case of aircraft, the weapon loading must be thought of as optional, since the choice of weapon carried is not built in as firmly as it is in missiles.

These remarks apply even more forcefully to the tactical nuclear weapons deployed for use in a war in Europe. Even the numbers of launchers—aircraft, short-range missiles, and artillery pieces—are hard to determine because they are mobile and easily concealed. Moreover, most types may be armed with either conventional or nuclear explosives; the actual level of nuclear armament is not publicly known.

EUROPEAN THEATER NUCLEAR FORCES

North Atlantic Treaty Organization			Warsaw Pact Countries		
Delivery System	*Warheads*	*Number*	*Delivery System*	*Warheads*	*Number*
Long-Range Ballistic Missiles					
Poseidon (US)	10–14	48	SS-20 (SU)	3	315
Polaris (GB)	1	64	SS-5 (SU)	1	16
Medium-Range Aircraft					
Vulcan (GB)	2	48	Backfire (SU)	4	100
F-111 (US)	2	156	Badger (SU)	2	310
Mirage IV (France)	1	34	Blinder (SU)	2	125
			Fencer (SU)	2	550
Medium-Range Ballistic Missiles					
MSBS (France)	1	80	SS-4 (SU)	1	275
SSBS (France)	1	18	SS-N-5 (SU)	1	57
Short-Range Aircraft					
Carrier: A-6, A-7 (US)	1	68	Various fighter-bombers (SU, GDR, Poland, Czechoslovakia, Hungary)	1	1,550
Buccaneer (GB)	2	50			
F-104 (Belgium, Greece, Italy, Netherlands, Turkey, FRG)	1	290			
F-4 (US, FRG, Greece, Turkey)	1	424			
F-16 (US, Belgium)	1	68			
Jaguar (GB, France)	1	117			
Mirage III (France)	1	30			
Short-Range Delivery Systems					
Pershing Ia (US, FRG)	1	180	SS-12 (SU)	1	70
Lance (US, FRG, Belgium, GB, Italy)	1	97	Scud B (all Warsaw Pact countries)	1	143
Honest John (Greece, Turkey)	1	90	SS-23, Scud A, and Frog 7 (all Warsaw Pact countries)	1	460
Pluton (France)	1	42			
Howitzers (155 mm and 203 mm) (US)	1	452	Howitzers		(?)

Nuclear-capable weapon systems known to be available to NATO and Warsaw Pact forces for possible use in a European conflict. For each type of system we show the number of warheads carried by one missile or aircraft and an estimate of the number of systems deployed in the European theater. Outside of classified information, tactical nuclear weapon inventories are not known in full detail. The numbers vary with system retirement, updating, and replacement, and many nuclear-capable aircraft may carry nuclear or conventional armament. It is estimated that NATO forces have some 6,000 to 7,000 nuclear warheads, all under U.S., British, or French control. In addition to these weapons, the United States has nuclear-capable aircraft that could be sent as reinforcements. Although most Warsaw Pact countries possess nuclear-capable weapon systems of modest range, it is believed that the Soviet Union retains control of the nuclear warheads, about 4,000 in all.

United States Silo-Based Ballistic Missiles

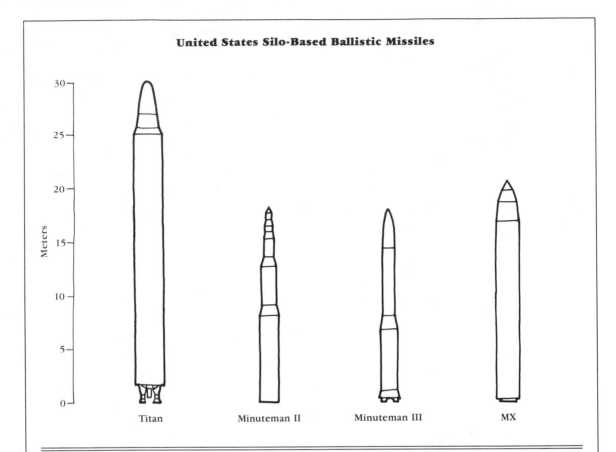

Name	Range (Nautical Miles)	Warhead(s)	Year of Initial Operational Capability	Number Operational
Tital II	8,100	9 Mt	1963	52
Minuteman II	6,100	1–2 Mt	1965	450
Minuteman III	7,000	3 × 170–355 Kt	1970	550
MX (basing mode unknown)	6,000	10 × (?)	1986–87	——

The United States possesses the most sophisticated and accurate missiles in the world. Soviet land-based strategic missiles are much larger and heavier than their U.S. counterparts of equivalent range. Their warheads are of higher yield to make up for the lesser accuracy of their guidance systems. Warhead configurations and estimates of range and yield vary among public sources of information. Thus the data listed should not be taken as fully reliable. Approximate missile range is given in nautical miles; one nautical mile is about 6,076 feet or 1.15 miles.

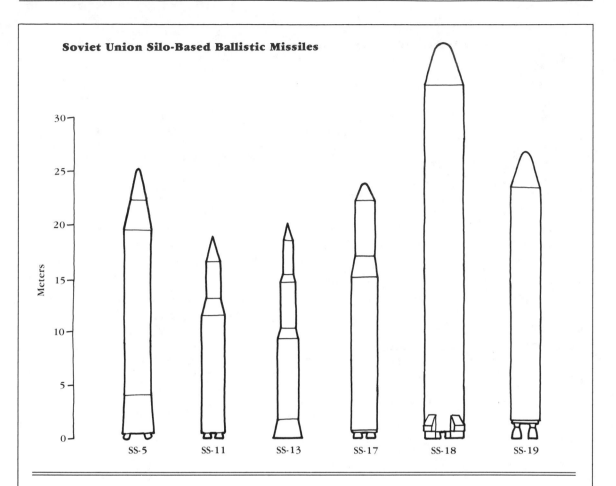

Soviet Union Silo-Based Ballistic Missiles

Name	Range (Nautical Miles)	Warhead(s)	Year of Initial Operational Capability	Number Operational
SS-5 (Skean)	1,900	1 Mt	1961	about 35
SS-11 (Sego)	5,700	1–2 Mt or 3 × 100–300 Kt	1966	about 500
SS-13 (Savage)	4,900	1 Mt	1968	about 60 sites known
SS-17	5,700	6 Mt or 4–6 × 200–600 Kt	1975	about 150
SS-18	5,700	10–30 Mt or 8–10 × 2 Mt	1974	308 (SALT)
SS-19	7,000	5 Mt or 6 × 200–600 Kt	1974	250 or more

United States and Soviet Submarine-Launched Ballistic Missiles

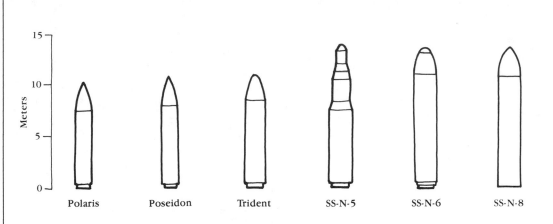

Name	Range (Nautical Miles)	Warhead(s)	Year of Initial Operational Capability	Number Operational
UNITED STATES				
Polaris A-3	2,500	1 Mt or 3 × 200 Kt	1960	1,400 built
Poseidon C-3	2,800 2,200	10 × 50 Kt 14 × 50 Kt	1971	about 300
Trident C-4	2,600	8 × 100 Kt	1981	about 200 planned
SOVIET UNION				
SS-N-5 (Serb)	860	1–2 Mt	1964	limited
SS-N-6 (Sawfly)	1,300– 1,600	1–2 Mt or 2–3 × 200 Kt	1968	about 400
SS-N-8	4,000	1–2 Mt or 3 × 200 Kt	1972	about 300

As is the case for land-based missiles, Soviet sea-launched missiles are larger and heavier than the U.S. weapons. Although undergoing retirement in the U.S. Navy, Polaris missiles remain operational in the strategic forces of Great Britain. The French ballistic missile forces are quite advanced for a country of modest size and a late start in the arms race. The Chinese missiles are less up-to-date; they are deployed as a deterrent to Soviet forces.

French and Chinese Ballistic Missiles

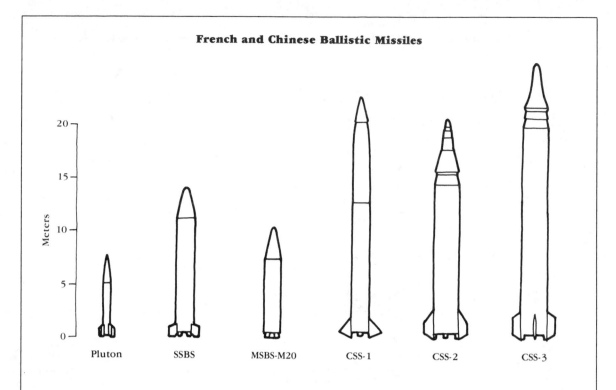

Name	Range (Nautical Miles)	Warhead	Year of Initial Operational Capability	Number Operational
FRANCE				
Pluton (land-mobile)	65	25 Kt, 15 Kt	1974	42
SSBS-S3 (silo-based)	1,800	1–2 Mt	1980	18
MSBS-M20 (submarine-based)	1,800	1 Mt	1977	80
CHINA				
CSS-1 (land-based)	about 600	20 Kt	about 1970	about 50
CSS-2 (land-based)	about 2,000		1971	about 70
CSS-3 (silo-based)	about 3,700	2–10 Mt	1975–80	a few

United States Land-Mobile Ballistic Missiles

Soviet Union Anti-Ballistic Missile (Land-Based)

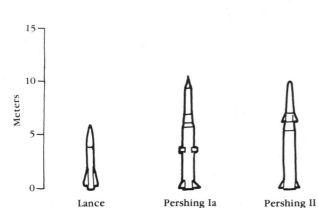

Name	Range (Nautical Miles)	Warhead(s)	Year of Initial Operational Capability	Number Operational
United States Land-Mobile Ballistic Missiles				
Lance	65	50 Kt	1972	hundreds
Pershing Ia	400	400 Kt or 40–60 Kt	1969	about 200
Pershing II	1,000	10–20 Kt	1984	In production
Soviet Union Anti-Ballistic Missile (Land-Based)				
Galosh (Defense of Moscow)	160	2–3 Mt	1968	64 launchers

ABOVE AND OPPOSITE:

Both superpowers and France have deployed nuclear-armed missiles on mobile launchers in the European theater. From sites in the Soviet Union the SS-20s threaten targets in much of Western Europe. From their planned sites along the eastern border of West Germany, Pershing II missiles could reach Moscow in six minutes, enormously increasing the tension of the European confrontation. Some Frog and Scud short-range missiles have been placed in Soviet satellite countries.

Sixty-four Galosh missiles are deployed to defend Moscow against ballistic missile attack. The outline is conjectured, as the uncased missiles have not been seen by Western observers.

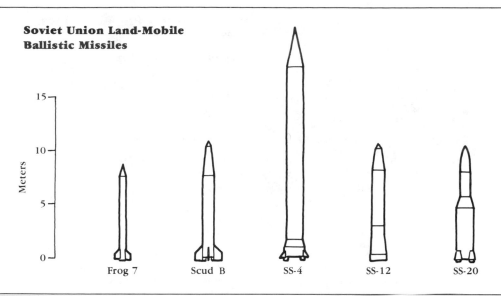

Soviet Union Land-Mobile Ballistic Missiles

	Range	Warhead(s)	Year	Number
United States Land-Mobile Ballistic Missiles				
Frog 7	32	200 Kt	1967 (shown)	about 70
Scud B	155	(?) Kt	1962 (seen)	hundreds
SS-4 (Sandal)	970	1 Mt	1961 (seen)	about 60
SS-12 (Scaleboard)	430	200 Kt	1967 (reported)	about 70
SS-20	3,000–4,000	50 Kt or 3 × 600 Kt	1978 (deployed)	300–400

WORLD NUCLEAR NAVIES

The world's first nuclear ship, the U.S. submarine *Nautilus,* went to sea in January 1955. It has been called "the first true submarine" because its nuclear power reactor gave it the ability to operate fully submerged at higher speeds than conventionally powered subs and for much longer periods of time. Allied with the Submarine-Launched Ballistic Missile (SLBM), the nuclear submarine became the basis for the least vulnerable strategic weapons system available to a modern military power.

Nuclear submarines are not easy to detect and may ply the seas without surfacing for many months. In 1960 a U.S. submarine circumnavigated the globe underwater in eighty-three days, surfacing only to allow an ill seaman to debark. The USS *George Washington,* the first submarine to launch a ballistic missile, traveled 100,000 miles in four and a half years before stopping for refueling of her nuclear reactor. Modern nuclear submarines are expected to steam 400,000 miles before refueling. Any one of

The USS *Nautilus,* the first ship propelled by nuclear power, made the first transit from the Pacific to the Atlantic, passing under the polar ice cap.

Nuclear-Propelled Ships	
Country and Ship Type	*Number of Ships*
United States	
Ballistic missile submarines	31
Attack submarines	86
Aircraft carriers	3
Guided missile cruisers	9
Research ship	1
Soviet Union	
Ballistic missile submarines	71
Guided missile submarines	52
Fleet submarines	50
Battle cruiser	1
Ice breakers	3
Great Britain	
Ballistic missile submarines	4
Fleet submarines	9
France	
Ballistic missile submarines	6
Fleet submarine	1
China	
Submarine (possible)	1

these missile submarines could, by itself, inflict awesome destruction on a target country, devastating its major cities and killing many millions of people.

In addition to the strategic missile submarines, the U.S. and Soviet navies include many submarines, both nuclear- and diesel-powered, with the mission of attacking enemy surface ships, and of tracking and destroying opposing submarines.

Since 1955, many nuclear-powered surface ships have been built, mainly naval cruisers and aircraft carriers. The first such vessel was the Soviet icebreaker *Lenin,* commissioned in 1959, which helps keep the northern seas open. Now the Soviet navy has added the nuclear-powered bat-

tle cruiser *Kirov,* and the newest U.S. aircraft carriers are designed to go a million miles or thirteen years without refueling. The high speed of these ships and their relative independence of port facilities make them valuable for intervention in far parts of the world.

These naval ships are nuclear in two senses: they carry nuclear reactors for propulsion, and they carry guided missiles and aircraft armed with nuclear warheads, bombs, and rockets for use against submarines, ships, and land targets.

OPPOSITE:

Some of the guided missile systems known to carry nuclear warheads. Most of these are dual-capable, meaning they are able to deliver either a nuclear or a conventional warhead. We do not know the extent to which the deployed systems

are equipped with nuclear warheads. The list is not complete. The U.S. cruise missiles (GLCM, SLCM, and ALCM) nearing deployment are small, long-range weapons that will be difficult to control through arms agreements.

Non-Ballistic Missiles with Nuclear Warhead Capability

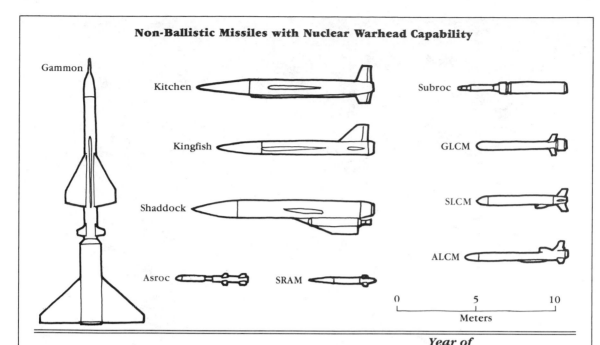

Name	Mission	Range (Nautical Miles)	Warhead	Year of Initial Operational Capability	Number Operational
SOVIET UNION					
Gammon	Surface-air	135	(?)	about 1967	many
Kitchen	Air-surface	up to 450	200 Kt	before 1967	about 200
Kingfish	Air-surface	up to 380	200 Kt	about 1976	about 100
Shaddock	Sea-surface	up to 450	200–800 Kt	before 1962	about 300
UNITED STATES					
Asroc	Air-undersea	6	nuclear depth charge	1961	hundreds
SRAM	Air-surface	85	200 Kt	1972	1500
Subroc	Sea-undersea	30	nuclear depth charge	1965	hundreds
GLCM	Land-surface	1,300	200 Kt (est)	1983	——
SLCM (Tomahawk)	Sea-undersea-surface	1,300	200 Kt	1984	——
ALCM	Air-surface	1,300	200 Kt	1982	some

PAVE PAWS Radar in Massachusetts, a system used to detect sea-launched ballistic missiles. (The acronym stands for Precision Acquisition of Vehicle Entry, Phased-Array Warning System.) In this type of large and powerful radar, many small, stationary antennas are electronically controlled to aim the beam over a wide arc of ocean.

8. The Control of Nuclear Warfare

Here the focus is on the long and complicated network of arrangements and communication links by which the superpower leaders can put nuclear weapons into action—or withhold them. These are questions of nuclear command, control, communications, and intelligence.

WHEN NAPOLEON COMMANDED his battalions from a hilltop, he could see most of the battlefield, and the riders who brought urgent news had only to gallop toward him at a faster pace than the foot soldier could march. But nuclear war—especially strategic nuclear war—is not like this. The battlefield is worldwide; the targets lie across the seas over a whole continent, and the forces under single command stretch from the Marianas Trench to the North Sea and beyond. The weapons travel at orbital speeds between continents in minutes, and while there are thousands of weapons, even a few can cause large-scale disaster. It is no wonder that the task of control is difficult. The U.S. military jargon for this task is C^3, which represents command, control, and communications. We will use the term *control* to stand for this complex of purposes.

Modern technology, especially telecommunications, must be pressed into service to meet the need of controlling modern warfare and managing nuclear deterrence. Indeed, the systems are examples of the most complex and modern technology: telecommunications satellites in orbit, remote sensing, cryptographic schemes, aircraft, radio, and computers, all coordinated by elaborate and far-flung systems. All this must function well, without grave error, always alert, yet never truly tested under the conditions of terrible physical damage that portions of the system will receive in the real event of nuclear war.[1]

The Planned Performance

Many people are aware of the more dramatic side of the plan. The underground war rooms lie deep below Washington, or in Omaha or Colorado. The rooms are always staffed and a stream of reports from far away, summarized and condensed, we expect, flow to them over many interwoven wire links and are displayed on a big screen. Special phones and teletypes

Philip Morrison
Paul Walker

Morrison is an Institute Professor at M.I.T. Walker is a political scientist with Klein Walker Associates.

8-1   **Ballistic Missile Warning and Attack Assessment Systems**

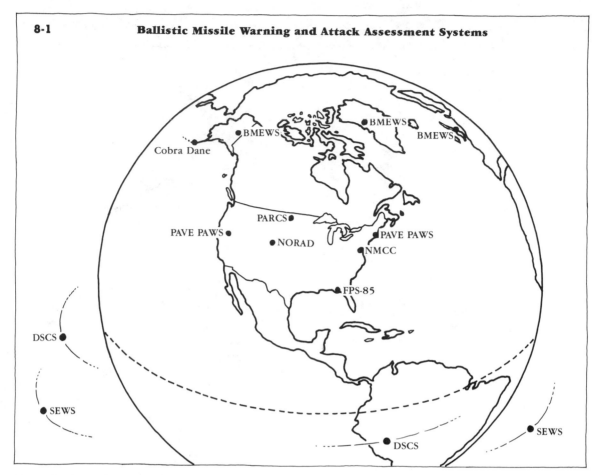

BMEWS: Clear, Alaska; Thule, Greenland; Fylingdales, England. Ballistic Missile Early Warning System. Stations using powerful phased array radars to detect and characterize a long-range missile attack.

FPS-85: Elgin Air Force Base, Florida; and

PAVE PAWS: Beale Air Force Base, California; Otis Air Force Base, Massachusetts. Phased array radar stations designed to detect and warn of attack by missiles launched from the Pacific, the Atlantic, or the Gulf of Mexico.

PARCS: Grand Forks, North Dakota. Perimeter Acquisition Radar Attack Characterization System. A radar station designed to track multiple reentry vehicles and project their targets.

Cobra Dane: Missile detection and attack characterization radar station also used to monitor Soviet ICBM tests.

SEWS: Satellite Early Warning System. Three satellites in stationary orbit around the equator provide detection of missiles in the boost phase of their launch.

NORAD: Cheyenne Mountain, Colorado. North American Air Defense Command, where information characterizing an attack is collected and a decision on an appropriate response is made.

NMCC: The Pentagon, Washington, D.C. National Military Command Center. A hardened command site where the National Command Authority (NCA) will reside in time of stress. An Alternate National Military Command Center (ANMCC) at an undisclosed location and a National Emergency Airborne Command Post (NEACP) are maintained in case the NMCC is lost.

DSCS: Defense Satellite Communications System. Satellites that provide one of the redundant communication links between the NMCC, radar sites, and missile launching platforms.

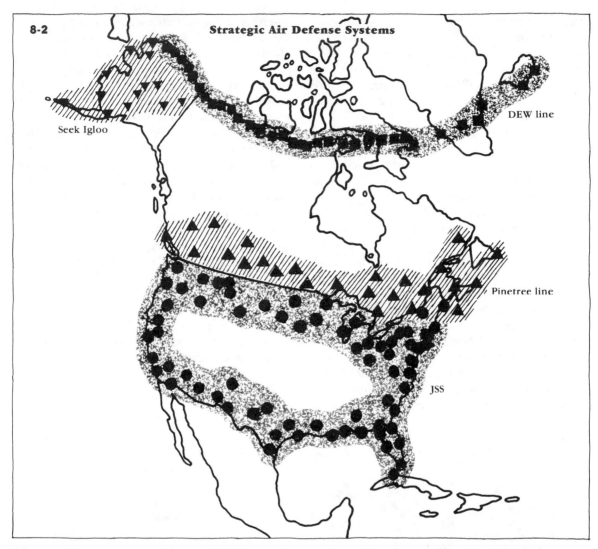

8-2   **Strategic Air Defense Systems**

Seek Igloo

DEW line

Pinetree line

JSS

Strategic defense systems to detect and track approaching Soviet bombers or their nuclear-armed, long-range cruise missiles stretch across northern Canada, through Alaska, and around the periphery of the United States. The air force is upgrading the radar coverage to close gaps that might enable low-flying aircraft to penetrate the air defense zone.

DEW: Distant Early Warning line. A chain of more than thirty radar stations stretching across northern

Alaska and Canada, established in 1952–56.

Pinetree: A chain of radar stations just north of the United States–Canada border. It was built in the same period as the DEW line and is jointly operated by the United States Air Force and Canada.

Seek Igloo: Radar stations of the Alaska Air Defense Command, United States Air Force.

JSS: Joint Surveillance System. Radar stations operated by the United States Air Force and the Federal Aviation Administration.

link these centers to airbases, silos, submarines, and the many other involved command posts worldwide. No simple, detailed description is possible; in fact, there is likely to be more relevant information still kept secret than for most other activities, but we can offer a general account of the plan.

Surveillance of the continental missile fields of the adversary—the Soviet Union—and of the oceans is perpetual. A set of three satellites in equatorial orbit, tens of thousands of miles up, watch steadily for signs of missile launch from land or sea. Imagine they have detected the powerful infrared emissions from the rocket jets of hot gas which propel missiles into orbit. These must flame for several minutes and are more powerful than almost any other heat source. They are counted, timed, and roughly located as they rise above the clouds into the vacuum of space. Several large, ground radar sets in Alaska and North Dakota and along the U.S. coasts keep steady watch for any high-rising missiles sent up much closer to the United States than along the Trans-Siberian railway, perhaps from Soviet missile submarines prowling the Atlantic or Pacific. As the most distant warheads rise still higher into orbit, special radars—their antennae as big as tall office buildings—

8-3 AWACS SURVEILLANCE AIRCRAFT
Advanced Warning and Control System: U.S. airborne radar station to detect enemy aircraft and to control the interception battle.

catch the echo of their own incessant pulses reflected from the fast-moving warheads as they climb beyond the bulge of the earth. These Ballistic Missile Early Warning radars (BMEWs) are situated in England, Greenland, and Alaska. Radars based in the continental United States confirm BMEWs ten minutes later.

By now the detection has been signaled from satellites and radar stations to the headquarters, and a variety of parallel networks carry the data to the computer screens. The duty officers and their crews check, confirm, notify, consider, and recheck. The data is compared with the information relayed by other special ground-based space detection systems which constantly count and check all orbiting space objects. These are confirmed: new objects in orbit. So far some ten minutes have elapsed.

Now the news must be distributed, and the authorities are told; indeed, some high-ranking officers are always present. The scores of missile centers and airbases are ordered, over a complex net of land lines and radio, to make ready—many nuclear bombers are always on the alert, and in times of crisis, many would actually be aloft on long, looping voyages. Special radio stations, located in Maine, Washington State, and Western Australia, are brought into prearranged contact. Their very powerful, extremely long-wave signals can be picked up deep beneath salt water anywhere on earth, and they speak to the distant subs which are more difficult to reach. New systems for communication with subsurface vessels by lasers on satellites are also under development. There are also a couple of less powerful U.S. backup stations. Another multiple satellite network is ready to pick up the dreadful sign of actual nuclear explosions; the fireballs of such explosions create light flashes of a strength and kind otherwise unseen. Other ground-based devices are ready to detect nuclear explosions in many points in U.S. territory and to report their signals to the centers. The American president is always in direct contact with this whole system through constant radio link via the officers who always ac-

8-4   **SELECTED FALSE NUCLEAR ALERTS**

These five "false alerts" of nuclear attack illustrate the potential seriousness of proposed "launch-on-warning" policies under which the United States would launch nuclear missiles upon warning that enemy missiles had been launched. In 1979 and the first half of 1980 there were 3,703 "routine missile display conferences," low-level false alerts. A few, such as those below, are sufficiently serious to come within minutes of launching nuclear war.

October 3, 1979: A radar designed to detect submarine-launched ballistic missiles picked up a low-orbit rocket body that was close to decay and generated a false launch and impact report.

November 9, 1979: The central NORAD computer system indicated a mass attack by incoming missiles as a result of an "inadvertent introduction of simulated data" into the computer.

March 15, 1980: A false warning of major nuclear attack was generated by one

of four Soviet submarine-launched ballistic missiles being tested during troop training exercises in the Kuril islands north of Japan.

June 3, 1980: A false warning of major nuclear attack was generated by a "bad chip in a communications processor computer."

June 6, 1980: The same warning was repeated when the June 3 incident was simulated during investigation of the computer problem.

company him (carrying radio codes and devices nicknamed the "football").

The Soviet Union operates a surprisingly similar structure, with high detection satellites, early-warning radars, and coastal radars of long range. They provide many redundant links for their signal network as well, largely by satellite. Recently they have come to use communication satellites in geosynchronous orbit, but in the past, and still of value to their system, they have used sets of many dozens of small, low-orbit satellites (about 100 miles high), which are put to use one after another as they come by in a long parade in circular orbit or strung out along an elliptical orbit deep in space. The geosynchronous orbit is less suited to the northerly position of many Soviet military bases than to the mid-latitude U.S. military bases.

The Pathologies of Control

Malfunction and Error Malfunctions and

human error must be expected in so complex and widespread a system. The satellites, for example, change station slowly and are replaced from time to time; their detectors require routine test and recalibration. This is part of everyday operations in peacetime. Indeed, we have learned within the last year or two that the built-in, twice-a-week routines are not enough to clear up all ambiguities. The indications of attack are then taken to the experienced personnel for decision after consultation. A few times a year even this is not enough, and senior officers must become involved. A couple of times during June 1980 an error compounded the matter, and incorrect alarms were passed on to activate the early steps of a full alert. The official 1981 statement of the Secretary of Defense says that "at no time did the alert go beyond the initial, precautionary phase"; it was ended at once by the duty officers. The spurious signals arose in one faulty computer "chip." "There is no chance," the secretary claims, "that any irreversible action would be taken based on ambiguous computer information."[2] Other conclusions are certainly possible.

Although false alerts have often been resolved in a few minutes, not much longer is needed for enemy nuclear warheads to land on target. Most importantly, in times of crisis, cool heads will be needed to prevent false alerts from becoming real.

By an agreement of 1963, brought up to date by another agreement in 1971, two satellite links connect a series of teleprinters in the United States and the Soviet Union for direct communication between leaderships (multiple terminals, in both English and Russian) in times of urgent need—the "Hot Line." There is a landline backup via London and Helsinki. This linkage system is routinely tested and is always staffed, giving a second chance in case of any really serious error.

There is some risk of a machine-caused failure or the error of a subordinate, but it seems to us that this risk is not large. A greater risk seems to be centered in misjudgments by the leaders who control the whole of the complex system, not a mere portion of it. Political and personal miscalculations seem far more risky than the fallible chip, against which many human minds in the control complex are prepared to take action.

Another peacetime hazard relevant here is the accidental explosion of a nuclear weapon as the result of an accident in flight or something similar. Many such incidents, "broken arrows," occur routinely; so far no unplanned nuclear explosion has taken place, though several bombs have been shattered in airplane crashes (in the United States, Spain, and Greenland), warheads have been lost in submarine mishaps, and some seventy-five military and civilian personnel have been killed.[3] Prudent design against such accidental explosion is again strongly motivated among all concerned. Even such an accident, locally tragic, is not likely to ignite a widespread

conflict; the "hot line" would be busy with urgent guarantees between superpowers. Again there remains residual risk.

The diversion or theft of a nuclear weapon from the huge inventory is of course a possibility. The magazines are well-guarded as a whole. Use of a weapon generally requires correct dialing of a combination lock or some equivalent task. The weapons are often arranged so that repeated errors in such a procedure, or other forms of tampering, disables the device by a small explosion within which would require skilled repair. Similar devices—double-key arrangements, for example, or electronics requiring the input of an up-to-date code—are fitted to prevent unauthorized use even by authorized officers, especially in the case of theater nuclear weapons, whose custody is shared between special U.S. and allied NATO forces. Two keys held by two officers, spaced more than an arm's length apart, are said to be required for arming any one missile silo, and similar cooperation is required aloft and at sea. Such schemes are somewhat reassuring, although they are less than perfect. Again, the experience has been satisfactory so far. Reports that certain governments have offered large sums for diversion of a usable nuclear weapon by some military person with access to the stocks, especially in the large U.S. installations in Europe, are so numerous and long-standing as to gain some credibility.

In Las Vegas, Nevada, the U.S. Department of Energy maintains equipment and air transport for a standing team of experts who are able to search for and evaluate any concealed nuclear devices and will respond to extortionate threats that might be so supported. Several threats of this kind have been acted upon, though no genuine event is known. This takes into account the response to the possibility of amateur construction as well as diversion of a professional nuclear device from military custody. The U.S. Air Force has similar teams, frequently called upon, that are able to respond to bomber crashes, missile silo fires, and the like.

Enemy Action There are three distinct threats to the control chain of nuclear forces that can be undertaken by an adversary. The first is physical attack on the installations of control, which include the deep underground shelters of the authoritative headquarters, as in Washington, Omaha, and Colorado Springs, and the physical apparatus of linkage—the satellites, radio masts, land lines, radar dishes, and so on. The latter are generally required to be out more or less in the open; they are often large installations, soft, vulnerable, and easy to damage, even to sabotage. The second threat is the electronic generation of interfering signals matched to the link under attack, or matched even more generally. This is called jamming, and it may well extend to false signals meant to deceive. Radio and microwave links are more susceptible than wire-borne signals, but wire nets, unless they are very redundant, are more open to physical damage. Finally, a nuclear explosion at very high altitude generates an Electromagnetic Pulse (EMP), a kind of synthetic lightning static, which is so powerful that it can damage radio and radar receivers (and even power-line equipment) over a distance of hundreds of miles, unless they have been specially protected against such effects.

These threats are well recognized. They have given rise to a redundant system of links, and a multiple set of alternative headquarters, some of which are always airborne and ready to relay weak ground instructions from emergency portable link systems, if the ground-based commanders still exist; they are even ready to exercise surrogate command, if the leadership has been caught in some direct hit or has lost all linkages. Both sides maintain such a system, which is, naturally, highly secret and not very well known to the public. A couple of examples may suffice to illustrate the schemes one can expect. The long-wave radio stations, whose antennae resemble large television or radio broadcast equipment and which carry the firing orders for the submarines at sea, are vulnerable even to nonnuclear forms of attack. As a backup, the United States operates a small fleet of propeller-driven aircraft—the TACAMO ("take charge and move out") squadrons of the U.S. Navy—to carry orders to the ballistic missile submarines should the main link be broken. At least one such plane is now operating at all times over the Atlantic, and a similar Pacific TACAMO watch is under order; a 1983 total of eighteen aircraft with transmitters and long-trailing antennae is planned. In the same vein, hidden among the thousand silos of our ICBMs are a number of missiles whose warheads have been replaced by satellite relay radio transmitters. If, for example, our satellites were attacked, these rockets would be fired and would replace the usual satellites, plus the spares kept in orbit, by an emergency system that is capable, at least for a little while, of relaying any weak orders from headquarters or alternate flying command posts below.

It does not require much imagination to conclude that there are likely to be other last-ditch schemes for sending at least some messages to submarines, planes, and silos once the main links are cut. Research into maintaining redundant command and communications (C³) facilities, especially under wartime conditions, has included launching many Remotely Piloted Vehicles (RPVs) as communication relays, to be utilized perhaps by roving command vans around the nation's highways. Since such redundancy in communications is much less expensive than the forces it might control, it seems plausible that the links can keep pace with the weapons. On the other hand, complicated, subtle orders cannot be expected to travel very well and quickly along a surviving network, heavily damaged after substantial nuclear attack. The experts speak of "degrading" the control schemes by nuclear attacks. It appears much surer that a command chain would survive and be able to utter some urgent final word. So, the combatant that tries a first strike is likely to have the only chance at subtleties of command. But by the same logic, it is most likely to induce a response that will bring down all that remains of the adversary forces, without much delicacy of choice—the wounded scorpion still has the toxic tail-sweep left. This truth seems to be stronger than the elaborate games of those who calculate strategic balance by a set of imagined exchanges, with the explicit assumption of the absence of any degradation of control.

The Shift of Strategy

Long ago, during the time America had a near-monopoly of nuclear weapons, John Foster Dulles warned of our massive retaliation at places and by means of our own choosing. The hint was broad: nuclear war could follow conventional attack on the United States or our allies. When the superpowers both began to hold large numbers of missiles, the view shifted. Deterrence became the aim, based on a plan to hold mutual hostage of the cities—the values—of the adversary. But at least since 1974, with the availability of many warheads following the U.S. development of the MIRV weapons, the planners began trying more seriously to use their very large stocks of warheads to attack various point targets—the missile forces, the submarine bases, and the command centers of the other side. Conventional forces, especially their headquarters, may be targeted as well, along with weapons warehouses and the like. Most of these targets are "harder," more protected, than cities.

This trend was given formal existence in the United States by the two presidential directives of the summer of 1980: P.D. 58 and P.D. 59. These directives have been officially discussed but have never been published in detail. We are told that P.D. 58 shapes the continuity of U.S. leadership after attack, presumably by fixing alternate commands and providing various protective means for the leaders. The flying command posts are certainly one form of this. P.D. 59 defines a complex policy of counterforce targeting against the Soviet systems, including flexible use of the missiles, especially of the new MX system—whose missiles will have a combi-

nation of yield and accuracy that greatly threatens hard targets. The Soviet silo-based SS-18 and SS-19 ICBMS seem similar in this respect; but the relatively invulnerable U.S. submarine force carries most American nuclear warheads, whereas the targetable Soviet ICBM force holds the great bulk of theirs.[4]

All this intricacy is dangerous in that it tends to support notions of nuclear war-fighting. Such exchanges might be limited if they remain confined to a handful of weapons; but they seem sure to bring down the whole house if they include, as the forces now permit, the use of many hundreds of missiles in a counterforce strike from either side. Such a strike would mean the death of 10 to 20 million civilians, apart from any military damage. It seems likely that control would be weakened, with the net result being a fatal escalation with little likelihood of reasoned and controlled war termination short of mutual holocaust. To launch such a counterforce scheme seems the height of adventurism. Never tested, such a large attack must be carefully planned and timed, worldwide; and it is possible that, as the missiles fly in, the opposition will simply launch all it has, using the grim slogan of "use 'em or lose 'em." Meanwhile, the claim of the U.S. Air Force that the new proposed MX missile is invulnerable because of its mobility is weakened by the circumstance that the missiles are powerful as first-strike counterforce weapons and many will likely be silo-based and actually immobile. The other side can now begin to fear this first strike of which we are so fearful, as indicated in American reports of the "Soviet threat."

The only path to long-range security in this awful morass is better control (now the less prominent portion of nuclear forces but worth much investment) and a return to nuclear weapon levels, types, and doctrines that promise a wide margin against nuclear war—a real deterrent, not a slowly rising scheme of missile duels.

The trend of the eighties is strongly in the

other direction, toward more deadly weapons and dangerous doctrines for nuclear war-fighting, though the air of unreality in all the plans and calculations offers much hope that real decisions are not very likely to follow these apocalyptic paths. Perhaps the plans are mainly for internal and diplomatic purposes, for if they ever turn from show to earnest, they threaten our very survival more than any other issue in this troubled time. The novelist Kurt Vonnegut remarked that you must be very careful who you pretend to be, for you are in danger of living up to the pretense. The Soviet and American nuclear powers are pretending to be terrible indeed.

Suggested Readings

Command, control, and communications in nuclear warfare have not received much discussion in the public literature, although considerable information may be inferred from the programs of professional technical conferences where research and development by contractors is reported. Brief discussions appear in the U.S. Defense Department *Annual Report,* and news items and articles occasionally in the pages of *Aviation Week and Space Technology.*

The October 1982 issue of *IEEE Spectrum* is devoted to military technology and includes a section on command and control. The topic is also covered briefly in Chapter 13 of *The Price of Defense.* The dangers of command and communications failure are dramatized in Chapter 4 of the Calder book.

BOSTON STUDY GROUP. *Winding Down: The Price of Defense.* New York: Times Books, 1979; New York: Freeman, 1982.

CALDER, NIGEL. *Nuclear Nightmares: An Investigation into Possible Wars.* New York: Viking, 1979.

IEEE Spectrum, October 1982, pp. 53–90.

Land-based test launch of the Trident SLBM. Two new submarines, the *Ohio* and the *Michigan,* carry these missiles in twenty-four launching tubes. The missiles have replaced Poseidon missiles on some older submarines.

9. Future Technologies for Nuclear War Fighting

*Here a look is taken into the near future, to see what is expected of technology yet
to come: the neutron bomb, anti-satellite weapons, and new means to attack
nuclear weapons or their launchers on land, under the sea, and from space.*

FORTY YEARS in the making, nuclear weapons
have progressed far from the relatively crude
gravity bombs of Hiroshima and Nagasaki. Today a large nuclear arms industry thrives in both
the United States and the Soviet Union, with
considerably smaller ones in Britain, France, and
China. India has built at least one bomb, and
several other countries may be on the verge of
building a few bombs. The United States alone
devotes over $30 billion annually to both nu-
clear and nonnuclear weapons procurement
and another $20 billion to weapons research
and development; of these amounts, some $5
to $10 billion annually buys nuclear arms and
another $3 to $5 billion funds the relevant
research.

Three laboratories—Los Alamos, Sandia, and
Lawrence-Livermore—provide much of the research and development for nuclear warheads;
a much larger, nationally dispersed industry de-

signs and builds the many related components,
such as missiles, submarines, bombers, and
many individual parts. This important industry,
described more fully in Chapter 11, has caused
a number of significant advancements in nuclear
technologies.

The warheads are most important, for they ultimately kill or destroy a target, although they
rely on sophisticated aiming and propulsion devices to fly them to intended destinations. The
1945 "Fat Man" and "Little Boy" bombs used in
Japan were large—over ten feet long and weighing about 9,000 pounds each. Their nuclear fission devices provided about 15 kilotons of nuclear explosive power, sufficient to kill over
100,000 people each.[1]

These two revolutionary weapons, striking in
their power and destructiveness, were nonetheless crude in at least three basic ways: weapon
size and weight limited each bomber to carry-

Philip Morrison
Paul Walker

Morrison is an Institute Professor at M.I.T. Walker is a political
scientist with Klein Walker Associates.

ing one weapon; explosive yield was small relative to present nuclear weapons; and good accuracy was lacking.

Nuclear technology, now more miniaturized and sophisticated, provides more "punch per pound"—*yield-to-weight* in military jargon—

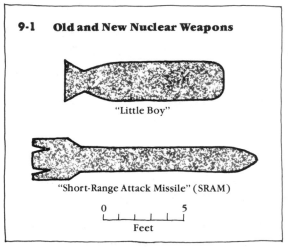

9-1   Old and New Nuclear Weapons

"Little Boy"

"Short-Range Attack Missile" (SRAM)

Nuclear weapons have progressed far in sophistication and deadliness since 1945. The top sketch is of Little Boy, the bomb dropped on Hiroshima in 1945. The lower silhouette is of the Short-Range Attack Missile (SRAM), a stand-off weapon carried on B-52 bombers. The SRAM is four feet longer but has less than a quarter of the weight. Little Boy weighed almost 700 pounds per kiloton of nuclear explosive, whereas SRAM weighs 11 pounds per kiloton, an improvement (over twenty-seven years) in yield to weight by a factor of 63. Today's B-52 can carry 20 SRAMs—some four megatons, or more than 300 times the B-29 package; the B-1 bomber will carry 32 SRAMs—some 500 times the 1945 load. And now SRAM is itself obsolete: the Air-Launched Cruise Missile (ALCM) is here, with much greater range and accuracy.

Name	Date Deployed	Weight (lbs.)	Length (ft.)	Range (mi.)	Yield (Kt)
Little Boy	1945	9,000	10	gravity drop	13
SRAM	1972	2,230	14	100	200
ALCM	1982	3,000	21	1,500	200

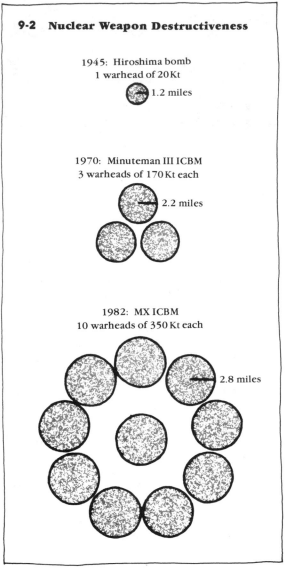

9-2   Nuclear Weapon Destructiveness

1945: Hiroshima bomb
1 warhead of 20 Kt

1.2 miles

1970: Minuteman III ICBM
3 warheads of 170 Kt each

2.2 miles

1982: MX ICBM
10 warheads of 350 Kt each

2.8 miles

The destructiveness of nuclear weapons increases with larger yields and through use of multiple warheads. Each circle indicates the area subjected to three pounds per square inch overpressure. The Hiroshima bomb produced three pounds overpressure over an area of four square miles. Produced some twenty-five years later, one Minuteman III can destroy over ten times that area; the new MX with ten warheads can destroy over fifty times the Hiroshima area.

than earlier weapons. The Hiroshima bomb weighed 600 pounds for each kiloton of explosive power. New nuclear bombs, for example, delivered to target by B-52 long-range bombers, weigh only 1,000 pounds but will explode with the energy of 200 kilotons of TNT; they weigh only five pounds for each kiloton.[2]

This technological evolution has allowed weapons to be more destructive. From the 1970 Minuteman III warhead with triple MIRVs to the 1980s Missile Experimental (MX), the potential for destruction has expanded by a factor of six. If one also considers that the number of nuclear weapons has risen to some 30,000 in the United States and 20,000 in the Soviet Union today, the cumulative potential for destructiveness in the nuclear arsenals has expanded far beyond that needed to destroy both countries.

Improved inertial guidance systems, better mapping techniques, and more precise aircraft and missile delivery systems are all affording much higher accuracy in new nuclear weapons. The accuracy of early weapons—gravity bombs dropped from aircraft—depended on the skills of the bomber crew; the Nagasaki weapon, for example, was perhaps a mile off target. When intercontinental missiles were first developed to deliver nuclear warheads faster over long ranges, accuracy was measured in nautical miles rather than meters. The U.S. Titan missile, carrying some ten megatons or more of nuclear explosive, is no more accurate than about 3,000 feet—this is its Circular Error Probable (CEP), or the radius within which its warhead will land 50 percent of the time. The mid-1960s Minuteman II missile improved upon this with a CEP of about 1,800 feet. The newest warheads on Minuteman III will have an accuracy of 600 to 1,000 feet, and future generational missiles will even surpass this, being accurate within the length of a football field (300 feet) over a 7,000 mile flight. Submarine-launched missiles are slightly less accurate, because they are launched while the sub is submerged and its exact posi-

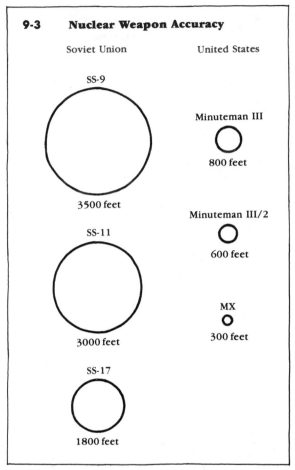

9-3   Nuclear Weapon Accuracy

Soviet Union   United States

SS-9

3500 feet

Minuteman III

800 feet

SS-11

3000 feet

Minuteman III/2

600 feet

MX

300 feet

SS-17

1800 feet

Each succeeding generation of nuclear delivery system comes closer to the bull's-eye. The older Soviet SS-9 ICBM, for example, was reported to have an accuracy of some 3,500 feet. The new U.S. MX is planned to hit within 300 feet of its target. Note that U.S. missiles have always been more accurate than their Soviet counterparts, at least based on inferences from the monitoring of test ranges.

tion is therefore uncertain, but the second generation of Trident missiles is expected to be as accurate as the MX.[3]

Larger yields, improved accuracy, and larger numbers of multiple-warhead missiles all combine to give the United States and the Soviet Union a higher kill probability against protected

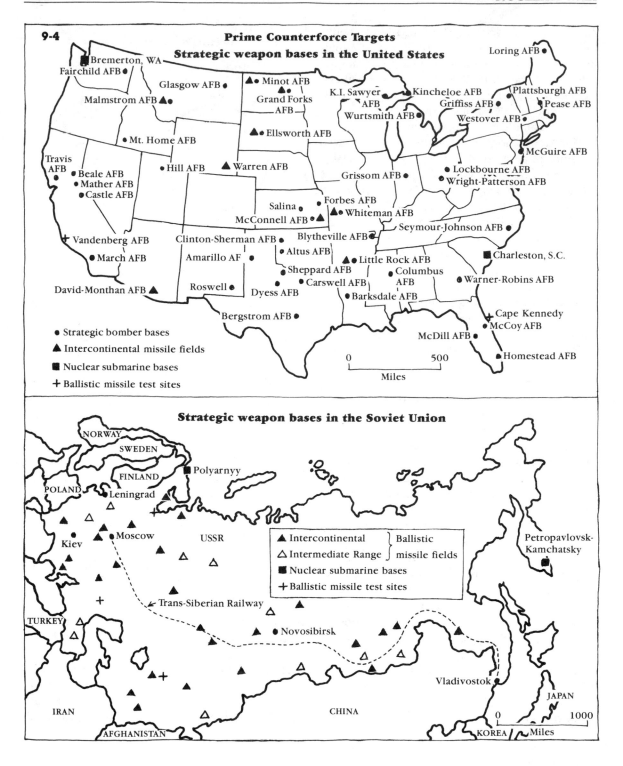

9-4

Prime Counterforce Targets
Strategic weapon bases in the United States

Bremerton, WA
Fairchild AFB
Glasgow AFB
Malmstrom AFB
Minot AFB
Grand Forks AFB
K.I. Sawyer AFB
Kincheloe AFB
Loring AFB
Plattsburgh AFB
Griffiss AFB
Pease AFB
Wurtsmith AFB
Westover AFB
Mt. Home AFB
Ellsworth AFB
McGuire AFB
Travis AFB
Beale AFB
Mather AFB
Castle AFB
Hill AFB
Warren AFB
Grissom AFB
Lockbourne AFB
Wright-Patterson AFB
Salina
Forbes AFB
Whiteman AFB
McConnell AFB
Seymour-Johnson AFB
Vandenberg AFB
Clinton-Sherman AFB
Blytheville AFB
March AFB
Altus AFB
Little Rock AFB
Charleston, S.C.
Amarillo AF
Sheppard AFB
Columbus AFB
Warner-Robins AFB
David-Monthan AFB
Roswell
Carswell AFB
Dyess AFB
Barksdale AFB
Bergstrom AFB
Cape Kennedy
McCoy AFB
McDill AFB
Homestead AFB

• Strategic bomber bases
▲ Intercontinental missile fields
■ Nuclear submarine bases
+ Ballistic missile test sites

0   500
Miles

Strategic weapon bases in the Soviet Union

NORWAY
SWEDEN
FINLAND
POLAND
Polyarnyy
Leningrad
Kiev
Moscow
USSR
Petropavlovsk-Kamchatsky
Trans-Siberian Railway
TURKEY
Novosibirsk
IRAN
AFGHANISTAN
Vladivostok
JAPAN
CHINA
KOREA

▲ Intercontinental ⎤ Ballistic
△ Intermediate Range ⎦ missile fields
■ Nuclear submarine bases
+ Ballistic missile test sites

0   1000
Miles

targets. No longer is the buried concrete silo, holding its ready nuclear missile, invulnerable to attack. Cities and other nonprotected targets have always been highly vulnerable to attack, but the newest American MX and Soviet SS-18 are claimed to have a 90 percent chance or more of knocking out protected strategic targets. This development drives much of the planning for a mobile missile, one that can shift its position to confuse the targeteer. (It should be noted that these estimates of kill are complex theoretical conclusions based on many incompletely tested assumptions.)

The United States began testing the Advanced Maneuvering Reentry Vehicle (AMARV)—the next step in accuracy development—in the South Pacific in December 1979. AMARV will provide a warhead with the ability to maneuver as it reenters the atmosphere, thus giving it still higher accuracy and the possibility of evading antimissile missiles fired against it. By the end of the century, it may very well be possible to place a nuclear warhead within a few feet of its intended target; this has led to speculation that it might be possible to destroy strategic targets in future wars with small nonnuclear warheads.

One major development in nuclear warheads is the "neutron bomb," or *enhanced radiation weapon*, presently under consideration by the United States and France for use in Europe. First tested by the United States in 1963 and reportedly also recently tested by the Soviet Union, the neutron bomb is designed to maximize neutron radiation and minimize blast damage. All nuclear explosions emit energy in forms of blast and shock, heat and light, and radiation; three-

OPPOSITE:

Prime targets—the strategic nuclear weapon bases—in the United States and the Soviet Union illustrate the widespread geography of target structures. Should either nation be struck by nuclear weapons, even in an unlikely "limited" way, much of the country would nevertheless be destroyed by blast, heat, shock, and the fallout drifting in an easterly direction.

quarters or more of the energy is usually in the first two forms, the remainder as "gamma rays" or neutron and other types of radiation. Enhanced radiation weapons are designed to maximize the neutron emissions, which are fatal to life over considerable ranges, but not as destructive to buildings as blast and heat. Thus, enhanced radiation weapons have been called "killer bombs" designed for battlefield use, where they would destroy soldiers and civilians but not much of the surrounding villages and environment. They have also been suggested for use as antimissile weapons, for they would limit the blast damage if used over one's own land against attacking warheads.[4]

With the recent advent of high accuracy and larger yields, the land-based silos have become somewhat vulnerable—up to 90 percent could theoretically be destroyed in a first-strike attack; this has goaded the United States to technologies for moving land-based missiles around, thus confusing Soviet nuclear war planners. Mobile missiles have existed for some time in tactical, battlefield systems, but only in the late 1970s have such designs been seriously considered for strategic, long-range forces. MX, for example, is designed to be air-or land-mobile; in one scheme, each missile would be shuttled among two dozen hardened, concrete shelters or garages. President Jimmy Carter's scheme included 200 missiles, each with ten nuclear warheads, to be shuttled on giant million-pound trucks among 4,600 shelters in Utah and Nevada; President Reagan has excluded this system from his MX basing plans. The Soviets, at least in theory, would have to strike all 4600 points to be assured of knocking out the whole land-based system.[5]

Nuclear-powered submarines are still the preferred mode of launching missiles and nuclear warheads. Both the United States and the Soviet Union are constructing newer, more powerful subs, which are larger both in displacement and in numbers of missiles than the first and second generation models. The new U.S. Trident sub-

**9-5   A NEW GENERATION OF
STRATEGIC AIRCRAFT**

Prototype of the B-1A penetrating supersonic jet bomber.
A newer version, the B-1B, is on production order for
the U.S. strategic forces.

marine, the first of twelve to enter the fleet
starting in 1981, displaces some 15,000 tons
submerged and is 560 feet long, almost twice
the displacement and one-third again longer
than its predecessor, Poseidon. Most striking is
the fact that it will carry twenty-four missiles,
each with at least ten warheads; both Poseidon
and Polaris carry sixteen missiles, each with
from three to fourteen warheads.

As costs of large submarines—with difficult
design goals of high speed and quietness—escalate, smaller submarines may be designed to
carry fewer missiles, either internally or encapsulated. In fact, one recently proposed launch
mode for MX is a relatively small, diesel sub
with encapsulated MX missiles attached to its
sides. Proposals have also been made for such
submersible missiles on platforms in lakes and
on ships on the high seas. For the foreseeable future, however, the deep-diving submarine with
subsurface-launched ballistic missiles remains
the most invulnerable and deadly nuclear system.[6]

Bombers, the air-based launchers of nuclear
warheads and nuclear bombs, have been in the
military inventories longest. The Soviets have
yet to build a long-range, highly capable nuclear
bomber; the Backfire, a shorter-range aircraft
designed to attack Europe and harass ships,

could be utilized at a longer range if fitted with
in-flight refueling devices and combined with a
fleet of tanker aircraft. The U.S. bomber fleet has
now declined to about 300, from as many as
600 in the mid-sixties, in recognition of the difficulty of successfully passing through air defenses. It was largely for this reason, as well as for
technical deficiencies in design, that the proposed B-1 bomber was rejected in the mid-
seventies. The current U.S. bomber, the B-52,
has been remodeled to carry nuclear Short-
Range Attack Missiles (SRAMs) and *cruise missiles,* nuclear-tipped weapons capable of flying
several hundred miles to their targets.

Such stand-off missiles have improved expected performance of the manned bomber and
will probably lead to development of successors
to the B-52 and the Backfire. The newest planes
will use "stealth" technology, a combination of
design and materials to minimize radar reflection by the aircraft, theoretically affording it a
better chance of penetrating antiaircraft defenses.

A major initiative in strategic war technologies has been *counterweapons*—Antiballistic
Missiles (ABMs, or BMD for Ballistic Missile Defense), laser and particle beams, antisubmarine
weapons, and a variety of other weapon designs,
such as antisatellite weapons to counter strategic attack. Both the United States and the Soviet Union planned and partially constructed
ABM systems ("Sentinel" and "Safeguard" for
the Americans, and "Tallin" and "Galosh" for
the Soviets) in the sixties, only to see them limited by the 1972 Strategic Arms Limitation
Treaty (SALT) and later partially or fully dismantled due to their ineffectiveness. Both countries
have maintained active research programs in
ballistic missile defense and may go on to
build limited systems—Low-altitude Air-Defense
(LOAD) systems—to help protect land-based
missiles, whether mobile or stationary.[7]

Antimissile missiles—designed to shoot a bullet with a bullet, so to speak—are still limited in
capability: they can be easily overwhelmed by a
large number of incoming warheads, their cen-
tralized radars are vulnerable to attack, and

9-6   **BALLISTIC MISSILE DEFENSE: EVOLVING TECHNOLOGY**

A Ballistic Missile Defense (BMD) system is intended to defend strategic targets—cities or missile launching sites—from attack by long-range nuclear missiles. The essential elements of a BMD system are means for detecting, recognizing, tracking, and destroying incoming missiles. Radar systems provide the means of detection, while computers and radars working together perform target recognition and tracking. The computers also command and guide intercepting missiles to attack and destroy offensive warheads.

Through the years since BMD systems were first proposed, there has been a continuing debate over the wisdom of their development and deployment. They are complex systems that perhaps can never be relied upon to function correctly; yet they would be called upon to operate with near perfection under severe conditions—an environment filled with the blast, heat, radiation, and electromagnetic pulse of multiple nuclear explosions, and a mixture of targets, decoys, and chaff. It is impossible to test a BMD system under conditions realistically approximating those that would exist when its effective operation would be required.

Two types of BMD system are considered: area defense and site defense. Area defense attempts to defend cities and civilian populations; it is difficult to prove effective and has been regarded as having a destabilizing effect on the strategic balance. In site defense, a BMD system is assigned to defend a particular missile or group of missiles. Site defense is easier since incoming missiles may be intercepted at close range. Site defense may have a stabilizing effect on the strategic balance since it protects the deterrent force.

A Selected Chronology

1954: The United States initiates an intense program of research into ballistic missile defense. The objectives: to defend the United States if possible, and to learn of the barriers an adversary could raise against U.S. offensive missiles. The air force "Wizard" and army "Nike-Zeus" Antiballistic Missile (ABM) programs are begun.

1966: The Soviet Union begins to build a "Galosh" ABM system with 64 missiles to defend Moscow.

1967: Secretary of Defense Robert McNamara announces decision to deploy a $5 billion "Sentinel" (ABM) system around seventeen U.S. cities, primarily for defending the U.S. population against possible limited nuclear attack by the Chinese in the mid-seventies.

1969: After intense protest and congressional debate, President Richard Nixon announces modification of the "Sentinel" into the $7 billion "Safeguard" system using "Spartan" and "Sprint" interceptor missiles, to be constructed at fourteen sites primarily to defend strategic missiles against limited Soviet nuclear attack. Malmstrom, Montana, and Grand Forks, North Dakota, are chosen as the first two sites.

1972: The SALT I ABM Treaty limits U.S. and Soviet ABM systems to 200 interceptors and 200 launchers, 100 each at two sites—the national capital, and one strategic missile site.

1974: A Protocol to the SALT Treaty further limits U.S. and Soviet ABMs to 100 interceptors and 100 launchers at no more than one site. Construction in progress at the Malmstrom site is stopped.

1974: Following completion of construction, the Safeguard installation at Grand Forks is operated for a brief period. (It was subsequently dismantled due to cost and technical ineffectiveness.)

1980: The Soviet Union dismantles 32 of its 64 defensive missiles surrounding Moscow, also due to perceived ineffectiveness.

1982: The U.S. fiscal year 1983 commitment to BMD activities is over $900 million, and that to space defense is over $200 million. Of particular interest in the United States is "LoAD," a Low-Altitude Defense system, designed to protect missile sites by intercepting warheads at less than 30,000 feet altitude. Active research and development continues in both the United States and the Soviet Union, carrying the arms race into space with exotic systems using missile-borne radars, satellites, lasers, and particle beams to detect, identify, and destroy enemy missiles, warheads, and military satellites.

their target acquisition capability is much less than optimal.

Researchers in laser and particle-beam weaponry have sought to overcome these obstacles by producing a weapon with multiple, quick-shot capability and instantaneous kill. Laser beams—intense, pencil-thin beams of light energy designed to burn through targets—might reach limited use within a decade or two, perhaps against cruise missiles at short range. However, their light beam is easily dispersed in opaque atmospheres—fog, clouds, smoke, mist, or rain—and can even be reflected by certain coverings on the target. The large size and sophisticated and delicate nature of lasers also preclude their practical use on battlefields today. Particle-beam weapons—intense beams of subatomic particles—have been promoted by weapons developers but are even farther from practical application.

One method of overcoming opaque atmospheres is to base the weapon in space; the United States and the Soviet Union are investigating use of lasers in satellites or space stations and shuttles, thus extending nuclear war into space: they propose to shoot down other satellites or even to destroy ballistic missiles as they rise above the atmosphere into space along their trajectory. Antisatellite weapons, including

the space-based lasers, still appear prohibitively expensive, large, and impractical for effective use. But countermeasures—using decoys, screens, and attacks on vulnerable orbiting stations—are clearly foreseeable.[8]

In 1968, the United States and the Soviet Union agreed to ban in the Outer Space Treaty all "weapons of mass destruction" from outer space. This agreement did not include weapons of "limited destruction," such as lasers and particle beams and nonnuclear explosives; but the later ABM Treaty rules out space-based ABM systems as a whole. The two countries have carried out preliminary talks—now in abeyance—on an Antisatellite Treaty (ASAT) to extend the ABM ban to such weapons used against satellites.[9]

The Soviets have tested an antisatellite satellite for several years now. It is designed to intercept a satellite at altitudes near 100 kilometers by orbiting alongside and self-destructing by nonnuclear means, destroying the enemy satellite with it. The United States has chosen to investigate a related but quite different antisatellite technology—a missile, launched from a high-flying aircraft, that would intercept a satellite from below rather than catching up to it in orbit. These two ASAT programs, if allowed to continue unchecked without agreed limits, might endanger all military satellites—weather, com-

9-7   SPACE SHUTTLE, A MILITARY PROGRAM?
Launching of the space shuttle *Columbia* from Cape Canaveral, Florida. The shuttle is a manned, reusable spacecraft; it blasts off into earth orbit assisted by powerful booster rockets and returns to earth by firing a braking rocket for reentry into the atmosphere, where it deploys wings for an aircraftlike landing. A major task for the space shuttle will be the launching of military satellites and some testing of military space systems.

munications, warning, reconnaissance—during this century.[10]

Counterweapon research and development also includes Antisubmarine Warfare (ASW), an effort to knock out sea-based missiles while still in their launch containers, that is, submarines. (This is not dissimilar in concept from seeking to knock out land-based missile silos.) The su-

perpowers are continuing to develop and deploy faster and more capable attack submarines armed with nuclear torpedoes designed to home on ballistic missile submarines. ASW capability is still primitive, however, due to the ability of submarines to hide in the vast reaches of the ocean depths. Improvements in satellite detection systems and sonar listening devices will enter antisubmarine warfare over the next twenty years but hardly to the crucial point whereby the sea-based leg of the nuclear triad becomes vulnerable to attack.[11]

Four important points stand out in any analysis of developing nuclear technologies. First are the extraordinary costs involved; Soviets and Americans are expending some $50 billion annually on nuclear weapons research and procurement. As systems grow in size and powerful destructiveness, so do their costs. The MX missile system may surpass $100 billion alone; one Trident submarine, $2 billion; and each new bomber, over $100 million. The Trident missile itself will cost $12 million each, and the air-launched cruise missile, $1.5 million. As nuclear weapons development progresses, and counter-weapons and counter-counterweapons become more complex, the nuclear arms race will become even more costly to all participants. The United States and the Soviet Union may expect to spend over $1 trillion on nuclear weapons systems—above and beyond the present 50,000 nuclear warheads—over the coming decade.[12]

Proliferation is an ongoing problem with all weaponry but is especially dangerous with nuclear weapons. As new weapons are produced and multiplied at sea, in the air, in space, or on land at home and abroad, security for them will become ever more pressing. Psychologically, the superpower nuclear-arsenal buildup sets an influential role model for nonnuclear countries to develop their own nuclear bombs. But, just as important, the number and diminishing physical size of nuclear weapons will make them subject to theft and diversion by subnational groups around the world.

9-8 THE MX MISSILE

The MX (Missile Experimental) is a new generation of ballistic missile with intercontinental range and accuracy substantially better than that of the Minuteman III. Its development is intended to overcome the assumed vulnerability of the U.S. Minuteman force to a possible first strike attempt by the Soviet Union. For this reason, the basing of the MX is planned to be some form of mobile carrier. The land-based scheme originally advocated involved an enormous construction program in Utah and Nevada, but this has been strongly opposed as expensive and disruptive of the environment. Other basing schemes under consideration include the use of small diesel submarines or aircraft as launchers of single multiwarhead missiles.

Environmental and socioeconomic costs to participants in nuclear weapons production will weigh heavily in future program planning, especially regarding land-based options for weapons deployment. Land-mobile missiles, if built by the United States and the Soviet Union, will demand large amounts of land and resources; in the case of the proposed MX missile, for example, upwards of 40,000 square miles of land would be crisscrossed by 8,500 miles of new roadway to handle the mobile weapons. A former pristine desert, ranching, and farming area would become a major military base, drastically changing the character of the states of Utah and Nevada should the Carter plan for MX ever be implemented. This experience will be repeated in less striking fashion in areas of bomber,

cruise missile, submarine, and antiballistic missile deployment. Nuclear arsenals, if further expanded, will become more visible and have more impact upon many more citizens.[13]

As nuclear arms improve in accuracy, flexibility of use, and destructiveness, nuclear warfighting may well become reality. Nuclear weapons have been primarily intended to deter war, never to be used; their use has always been judged suicidal for both the United States and the Soviet Union and perhaps for much of the rest of the world. Yet, technology races forward, unconstrained by arms control limits, and the limited utility of nuclear weaponry in "selective" or "limited" strikes will be seen by war planners as more plausible. Indeed, it already has.

The likelihood of nuclear explosion, accidental or intended, increases as arsenals are expanded in this decade. It is too difficult to foresee whether one or a few such explosions—in the Middle East, the Persian Gulf, Europe, or elsewhere—will necessarily escalate to an all-out holocaust. Only experience will tell; unfortunately, such experience may very well leave few individuals to chronicle the event. As weapon is targeted against weapon, as the numbers of these weapons escalate, and as more citizens dwell among proliferating nuclear arsenals, the gravity of the destruction becomes nightmarish to contemplate.

Suggested Readings

Significant technological developments and trends in weaponry are reported and analyzed in the *SIPRI Yearbooks*, in the annual reports of the International Institute for Strategic Studies, and in the pages of *Aviation Week and Space Technology*. The Department of Defense *Annual Reports* discuss future developments in brief, and the United Nations report includes a chapter on "Trends in the Technological Development of Nuclear-Weapon Systems."

The debate over the feasibility of ballistic missile defense attracted public attention when arguments on the Safeguard System were aired. The story is told in the Chayes and Wiesner book. A somewhat later analysis of the technical feasibility and cost of ballistic missile defense is given in the paper by Alexander in *Impact of New Technologies*. Two negative positions on the controversial MX missile are taken in the books by Scoville and by Gold, Paine, and Shields.

Scientific American publishes articles on advanced weapons technology from time to time, including skeptical views on the utility of weapons using particle beams (the article by Parmentola and Tsipis) or lasers (the paper by Tsipis).

Joel S. Wit provides a good introduction to antisubmarine warfare (ASW) in his *Scientific American* article. Another source on ASW is the SIPRI book.

ALEXANDER, B. "The Performance of Anti-Ballistic-Missile Systems." In B. T. Feld et al., eds., *Impact of New Technologies on the Arms Race*. Cambridge, Mass.: MIT Press, 1971.

CHAYES, ABRAHM, and JEROME B. WIESNER, eds. *ABM: An Evaluation of the Decision to Deploy an Antiballistic Missile System*. New York: Signet, 1969.

GOLD, DAVID, CHRISTOPHER PAINE, and GAIL SHIELDS. *Misguided eXpenditure: An Analysis of the Proposed MX Missile System*. New York: Council on Economic Priorities, 1981.

INTERNATIONAL INSTITUTE FOR STRATEGIC STUDIES. *Strategic Survey*. London: IISS, published annually.

PARMENTOLA, JOHN, and KOSTA TSIPIS. "Particle-Beam Weapons." *Scientific American*, April 1979, pp. 54–65.

SCOVILLE, HERBERT, JR. *MX: Prescription for Disaster*. Cambridge, Mass.: MIT Press, 1981.

STOCKHOLM INTERNATIONAL PEACE RESEARCH INSTITUTE (SIPRI). *World Armaments and Disarmament*. London: Taylor and Francis, published annually.

SIPRI. *Tactical and Strategic Antisubmarine Warfare*. Cambridge, Mass.: MIT Press, 1974.

TSIPIS, KOSTA. "Laser Weapons." *Scientific American* 245, no. 6 (December 1981), pp. 51–57.

UNITED NATIONS. *Nuclear Weapons: Report of the Secretary-General*. Brookline. Mass.: Autumn Press, 1981.

WIT, JOEL S. "Advances in Antisubmarine Warfare." *Scientific American*, February 1981, pp. 31–41.

Part Four
Nuclear Warheads

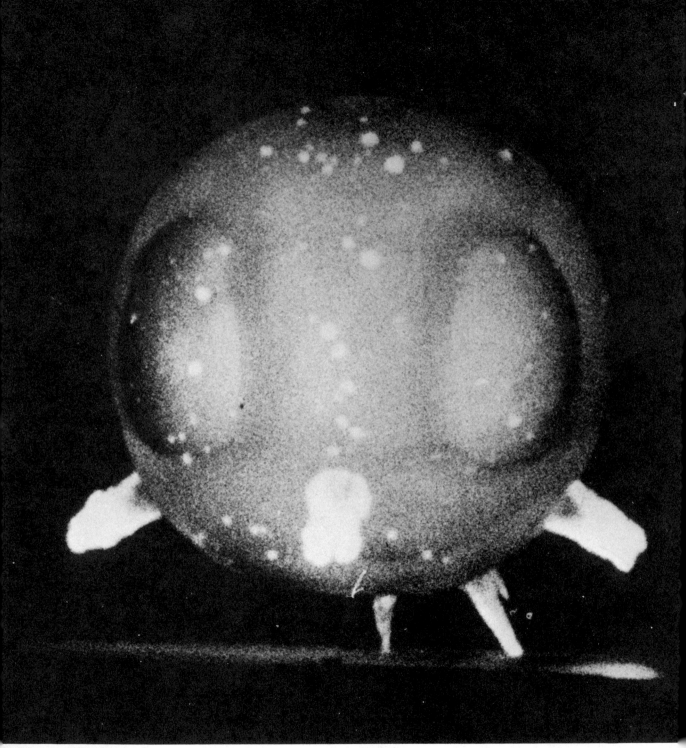

The fireball of a nuclear explosion, shortly after detonation. At this moment the fiery sphere of plasma is
the size of a house and is expanding at one-tenth the
speed of light.

10. The Physics of Nuclear Weapons

The secret of releasing the power of a nuclear weapon from so small a device was given us by modern physics. Understanding the fundamental properties of matter led to prediction of the chain reaction, in which one minute particle—a neutron—collides with the core or nucleus of an atom to release energy and two similar particles. The process continues, yielding a huge number of collisions, each of which releases energy trapped in the nucleus of an atom. This fission chain reaction creates enormous temperatures that can kindle the fusion of simple atoms such as hydrogen. The fusion process releases even greater amounts of energy than fission.

WHEN A NUCLEAR WEAPON explodes it releases an enormous amount of energy in the form of radiation, heat, and blast that shatters buildings and ignites fires over a large area. Where this energy orginates, by what mechanism it is released, and how this mechanism is built into warheads small enough to be delivered to a target by an airplane, a ballistic missile, or even a standard-size artillery shell, are the subjects of this chapter.

What Is a Nuclear Explosion?

At the instant of detonation the energy of a nuclear explosion is held in a small superheated volume of nuclear debris—the nuclear *fireball.* The temperature and pressure inside the fireball are those of the center of the sun. At a temperature of 10 to 100 million degrees centigrade, the electrons are stripped from all atoms—they are completely ionized. Since it is the electrons of atoms that absorb radiation, there is nothing to absorb the low-energy X rays generated by fission; they escape the fireball and heat up adjacent layers of undisturbed cool air. In the surrounding air, where atoms have attached electrons, the X rays are absorbed and heat the air to such a high temperature that it too is ionized and so becomes transparent. This allows the radiation to escape and heat up still more layers of air around the expanding fireball.

This process of expansion removes energy from the interior of the fireball, cooling it down uniformly. As its temperature decreases, the mean energy of radiation emitted by the fireball also decreases. The cooler radiation is more readily absorbed by the air and so cannot travel very far; growth of the fireball slows down. As the temperature of the fireball decreases so does the mean frequency of the radiation. From X rays it changes to visible light and then to thermal (infrared) radiation as the fireball expands and cools. After some fraction of a milli-

Kosta Tsipis

Tsipis is a nuclear physicist who has devoted most of his recent research efforts to studies of the technological aspects of national and international security issues.

10-1   FIREBALL—LATER STAGE

After one-sixtieth of a second, the blazing fireball is about 250 meters across.

second, the fireball temperature reaches about 300,000°C, and its speed of expansion falls to the speed of sound in air. At this point two things happen: First, a shock wave develops at the surface of the fireball and shock-heats the air around the fireball, producing an incandescent glow. At the same time the superheated weapon debris that were traveling inside the fireball with supersonic speed catch up with the original shock wave and contribute to the growth of the fireball by heating the as of yet unshocked air around it. Since hot air does not allow visible light to propagate through it, the fireball disappears from human sight until the gases around it have cooled enough for visible light to escape from the fireball. This period is called the "breakaway" point. The hiding of the fireball by shocked air causes the characteristic "double flash" of light that betrays a nuclear detonation in air. Monitoring satellites are programmed to detect nuclear weapons tests in the atmosphere by recognizing this signal.

So the sudden release of a very large amount of energy in a very small volume of space has several immediate effects: it produces intense X-ray, ultraviolet, visible, and infrared radiation; it yields very high pressures and a shock wave traveling supersonically from the point of detonation. In addition, the bomb debris and nearby atoms of matter are ionized by the X rays. These stripped nuclei are slower and stay behind while the much lighter electrons fly off in all directions, interacting with the radiation bath in which they find themselves, entering the ground underneath the explosion, or recombining with ions in collisions. The fission fragments—new atoms created by the splitting of plutonium (Pu-239) and uranium (U-235 and U-238) nuclei also nearly completely stripped of electrons— fly off, emitting gamma rays or neutrons and sticking to the vaporized particles of dirt that are lifted up by the ascending fireball.

Where does the enormous energy released in a nuclear explosion originate?

Energy from the Nucleus

In our usual conception of an atom, we imagine a tiny but massive nucleus surrounded by a cloud of whirling electrons. The electrons account for the chemical properties of the elements, and their interactions explain the release of chemical energy as in an explosion of TNT. The force that binds electrons as constituents of atoms is the *electromagnetic force*—the attraction of the negative electron for the positive nucleus and the repulsion of electrons from one another. In a nuclear reaction, the nucleus itself breaks up, and the energy released comes from the strong force that holds the nucleus together.

The nuclear force is about a thousand times stronger than the electromagnetic force, and the energy released during an interaction is proportional to the second power of the strength, so we must expect that the energy involved in a nuclear interaction should be about a million times the energy released in an electromagnetic interaction such as burning gasoline or exploding dynamite. Let's see if it turns out to be so.

There are two ways in which nuclear energy can be released in a nuclear explosion: A heavy nucleus of uranium or plutonium, after absorbing a neutron from outside, will split into smaller fragments and release energy—this is *fission*. In contrast, two light nuclei, isotopes of hydrogen, if brought together with sufficient force, will fuse into a single heavier nucleus and release energy—this is *fusion*.

The Fission Explosion

When a U-235 nucleus breaks up into two fragments, two or more neutrons are released, each having sufficient energy to split another uranium nucleus. This is the basis of the *chain reaction* that makes nuclear weapons possible. For all we know, this is a completely fortuitous circumstance. It could very well be that only one neutron is released for each fissioned ura-

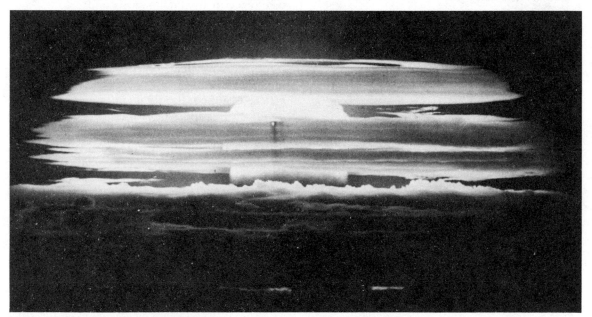

10-2 TEST EXPLOSION AT BIKINI

Cherokee, May 21, 1956. Fireball of a multimegaton weapon test, the first drop of a thermonuclear bomb from the air. The photograph was taken from an air- craft at an altitude of 12,000 feet, about 50 miles northwest of the test site.

10-3 Uncontrolled Fission Reaction

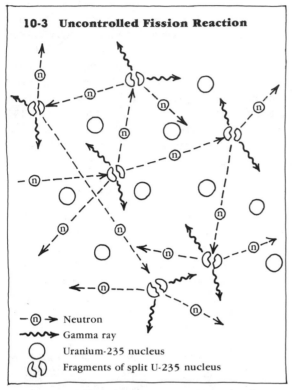

- (n) → Neutron
- ∿∿∿→ Gamma ray
- ◯ Uranium-235 nucleus
- ◖◗ Fragments of split U-235 nucleus

In an uncontrolled chain reaction, neutrons split uranium-235 nuclei, yielding fission fragments, gamma rays, and two or more neutrons which can multiply the number of nuclei split in each succeeding generation. Each generation takes just one-tenth of a billionth of a second.

nium nucleus, or it could be that neutrons released do not have enough energy to split uranium nuclei. But in fact, both in the case of U-235 and Pu-239, the neutrons produced during their fission can fission additional such nuclei.

Let us consider a sphere containing ten kilograms of U-235, which is about the size of the fission explosive used to trigger a modern nuclear weapon. This amount of uranium forms a sphere about ten centimeters in diameter. It contains about 2.5×10^{25} atoms of U-235.

Suppose one neutron enters the uranium sphere; it strikes a uranium nucleus, causing fission and release of two new energetic neutrons;

these cause two fissions, yielding four neutrons, and so on. Assuming this doubling process continues, in just eighty-five steps the number of fissioned nuclei would reach $2^{85} = 3.87 \times 10^{25}$, and there would be no atoms left to split.

How long does this take? Since the splitting of a U-235 nucleus is essentially instantaneous, the duration of one step is the time for a neutron to go from the uranium nucleus that generated it to the one it splits. On the average a neutron travels three centimeters (1.2 inches) in uranium before it hits a nucleus, and since it travels almost at the speed of light, it takes about one tenth of one nanosecond (or a tenth of one billionth of a second) to complete a step. So the entire process of fissioning ten kilograms of uranium takes about 8.5 nanoseconds! Moreover, the neutron population during this time is doubling each tenth of a nanosecond, following a geometric law of growth. Thus practically all of the fissions, and nearly all of the energy release, take place in the final nanosecond!

How much energy is released? The energy released in one fission event is about 200 million electron-volts (MeV), the energy gained by an electron in an electric accelerating field of 200 million volts. If every nucleus of the uranium sphere fissioned, the total energy released is the number of fissions times the energy released in each fission. Since in actuality only something like 1 percent of the fissile nuclei split in a real weapon, the total release is roughly 5.0×10^{25} MeV, which is 8.0×10^{12} joules of energy. This is the energy released by exploding about 2,000 tons of high explosive.

Can we compute the initial temperature of the fireball? A fundamental law of physics, Stephan's law, relates temperature T to energy density ε:

$$\varepsilon = \sigma T^4$$

where Stephan's constant has the value $\sigma = 7.6 \times 10^{-17}$ for the units of the formula. From the total energy and the volume of the sphere of fissioned uranium we find an energy density of roughly 10^{17} joules per cubic meter for a temperature of more than 130 million degrees!

Since the sphere has no time to expand in these eight nanoseconds, the pressure inside it has risen in proportion to the temperature to about 100 million atmospheres! These are the conditions in the center of the sun. Indeed, a nuclear detonation is a miniature sun that shines briefly on earth.

The Fusion Explosion

For two light nuclei to fuse, they must approach to within nuclear dimensions—about 5×10^{-13} centimeters. But nuclei contain protons that repel each other, and fusion can be achieved only if the nuclei have enough energy to surmount this repelling force. The energy required is proportional to the product of the numbers of protons in the two nuclei; it is least for the lightest element, hydrogen, a single proton in its nucleus. Besides ordinary hydrogen H-1 with atomic mass one, the hydrogen isotopes—deuterium (D or H-2) and tritium (T or H-3) with atomic masses two and three—are about as easy to fuse. The fusion reaction that yields the largest amount of energy is

$$D + T \rightarrow He\text{-}4 + n + 17.6 \text{ MeV}$$

in which a deuterium nucleus and a tritium nucleus combine to form a helium nucleus with the release of 17.6 MeV of energy and a neutron. This may seem small compared with the 200 MeV or so released in the fission of a uranium nucleus, but the mass of the reactants here is only 5 atomic mass units compared with 239 for uranium. So the energy released per unit mass is about four times that of a fission event. The single energetic neutron created in the fusion is essential to the thermonuclear warheads discussed below.

At room temperature and pressure, both deuterium and tritium are gases. To have enough material in a small enough space to produce a large explosion, the deuterium and tritium must be in liquid form. This requires bulky cryogenic

equipment to maintain temperatures close to absolute zero. There is another way, however, to package deuterium and tritium together: The substance lithium deuteride (LiD) is a solid at normal temperatures. If the lithium (atomic number three) in this compound is the isotope Li-6, it has the remarkable property that it can generate a tritium nucleus upon absorbing a neutron:

$$Li\text{-}6 + n \rightarrow He\text{-}4 + T + 4.6 \text{ MeV}$$

The tritium produced is free to fuse with the deuterium.

How can the conditions for fusion be produced? One needs a source of energy that will squeeze the deuterium and tritium nuclei together for a few millionths of a second until they fuse. In nuclear weapons this energy is provided by a fission explosion using at most ten kilograms of material, usually Pu-239. Once the fusion process has been started by the plutonium trigger, it is self-maintaining by virtue of its own energy release. Although fusion proceeds optimally at a billion degrees, it proceeds very fast even at the 10 to 100 million degree temperatures generated by the fissioning of plutonium.

Thermonuclear Bombs

It turns out that the neutrons released in the fusion of deuterium and tritium have an energy of 14 MeV—nearly three times the energy of the neutrons released in nuclear fission. This is enough energy to cause a U-238 nucleus to split, releasing another 200 MeV or so of additional energy. Therefore, the usual form of thermonuclear weapon incorporates a blanket of U-238 around it which produces by fission about half of the total yield of energy. Incidentally, the enhanced radiation weapon or "neutron bomb" is just like the thermonuclear weapon except it does not have the U-238 mantle around it, and the fast neutrons are released into the environment to perform their lethal function.

10-4   THE MATERIALS OF NUCLEAR DESTRUCTION

The basic materials of nuclear weapons are uranium-235 (U-235) and plutonium-239 (Pu-239), which have small critical masses—the amount of material which, when brought together, will produce a spontaneous, rapidly expanding chain reaction. Both materials are expensive to produce in present technology. Production of U-235 requires an elaborate separation plant to extract it from natural uranium, which contains only about 0.7 percent U-235. Plutonium-239 is obtained by a difficult and hazardous chemical separation from fuel rods of natural uranium which are made highly radioactive through exposure to neutrons in nuclear reactors.

Uranium-238 (U-238) is also used, but not as the fuel to start a nuclear explosion—the neutrons it releases in fission have insufficient energy to induce further fission. Yet the U-238 atom will split when struck by the high-energy neutrons released in the fusion of hydrogen, releasing the same amount of nuclear energy as the splitting of U-235.

Uranium-235, a basic fissionable material for nuclear weapons. Careful handling of U-235 is necessary to avoid accidental creation of a critical mass, which would result in intense radiation and a large release of thermal energy, but not a full-scale nuclear explosion.

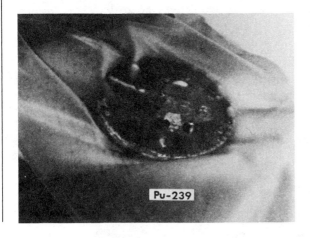

A button of plutonium-239. It must be kept in an inert atmosphere because it reacts spontaneously with air.

Sheet of uranium-238 emerging from the rolling mill at the Y-12 Plant, Oak Ridge, Tennessee. There is enough nuclear energy in the sheet to destroy several cities.

Let us see what materials are needed to make a one-megaton thermonuclear bomb, assuming the energy yield comes half from fusion and half from fission of the U-238 jacket. A 500-kiloton yield from the fission of U-238 requires the splitting of 7.25×10^{25} nuclei which amounts to some sixty kilograms of uranium. These fissions require an equal number of 14 MeV neutrons from the fusion process.

The other 500 kilotons of yield must come from fusion. Since each fusion event releases about 35 MeV, something like 3.7×10^{27} fusions are required. These fusions will produce an equal number of fast neutrons, five times the number that, if all were captured, would completely fission the U-238 blanket.

To fuel the fusion reaction, we need 3.7×10^{26} atoms each of deuterium and tritium—about a kilogram of deuterium and 1.8 kilo-grams of tritium. Both are available from 8.4 kilograms of lithium-6 deuteride, since neutron bombardment will convert the lithium into tritium.

How large should the plutonium trigger be? About 0.5 MeV of energy is needed to carry a deuterium nucleus and a tritium nucleus together with enough force to overcome the strong electrical forces and fuse. To produce 3.7×10^{26} fusions, a total energy of 2×10^{26} MeV is needed. This could be supplied by the complete fissioning of just one kilogram of plutonium. Actually, a nuclear warhead is designed so that once the fusion process starts, it becomes self-sustaining—energy released from the initial fusion events is channeled into fusing the remaining deuterium and tritium.

The fission-fusion-fission process of the thermonuclear weapon is completed in less than a

10-5   HOW NUCLEAR WEAPONS WORK

A fission bomb works by assembling a supercritical mass of fissionable material—uranium-235 or plutonium-239 in which a massive chain reaction occurs. This must be done very quickly or the initial energy release will blow the bomb apart before the chain reaction has gotten well started. Two methods have been used to assemble a supercritical mass. The gun mechanism was used in the uranium bomb exploded over Hiroshima: two subcritical pieces of uranium are brought together by an explosive charge inside a cylindrical tube much like the barrel of a gun. Although it was simple in concept, such bombs were cumbersome and heavy. In addition, the gun mechanism would not work in a plutonium bomb because sufficiently pure Pu-239 is nearly impossible to produce—plutonium-240 and other contaminants continually emit neutrons that would give a premature start to the chain reaction before full supercritical assembly was achieved. The solution to these difficulties is the implosion technique, now the preferred method. A sphere or shell of fissionable material is compressed by the focussed blast of surrounding chemical explosive. The pressure of some millions of pounds per square inch forces the fissionable material into a smaller volume, hence a higher density, increasing strongly the chance a neutron will split another nucleus before it escapes. The assembly becomes supercritical. A precisely timed burst from an electronic neutron source triggers a massive chain reaction ensuring

a high-yield nuclear explosion. The plutonium or uranium may be surrounded by a tamper, a shell of material—beryllium or uranium-238, for example—that "reflects" a portion of the neutrons escaping from the core. Use of a tamper significantly reduces the amount of fissionable material required to make a nuclear weapon.

A thermonuclear bomb uses a fission explosion to create the temperature and pressure required to ignite a fusion reaction in a mass of lithium deuteride. In a typical thermonuclear weapon, high-energy neutrons arising from the fusion reaction go on to split uranium-238 nuclei in a final surrounding mantle, adding to the destructive force of the explosion. In a "neutron bomb" the U-238 mantle is omitted, permitting the fast neutrons to escape into the surroundings.

A thermonuclear weapon is sufficiently complex that extensive testing would seem essential to develop a practical military weapon. Since the end of World War II digital computers have played an essential role in the design of nuclear weapons—solving the complex equations that describe the physical phenomena of a nuclear explosion and providing knowledge equivalent to that obtained from many test explosions. It all began with John von Neumann and the Institute for Advanced Studies (IAS) computer at Princeton. Now, the most powerful computers available are used at the Livermore and Los Alamos National Laboratories to develop designs of nuclear weapons.

OPPOSITE:

The gun principle used in the Hiroshima bomb; the implosion principle for detonating a fission bomb; the stages of a thermonuclear explosion.

Fission weapon: gun mechanism

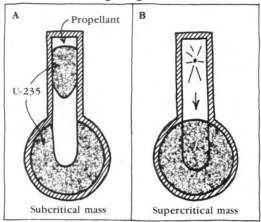

A — Propellant, U-235, Subcritical mass

B — Supercritical mass

Fission weapon: implosion technique

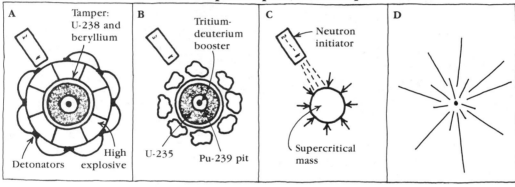

A — Tamper: U-238 and beryllium, Detonators, High explosive

B — Tritium-deuterium booster, U-235, Pu-239 pit

C — Neutron initiator, Supercritical mass

D

Thermonuclear weapon

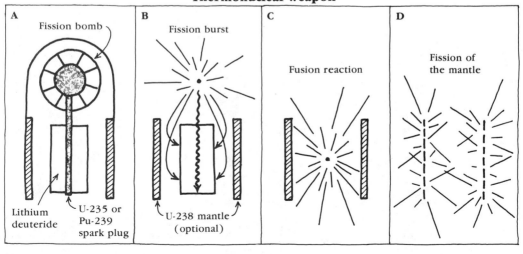

A — Fission bomb, Lithium deuteride, U-235 or Pu-239 spark plug

B — Fission burst, U-238 mantle (optional)

C — Fusion reaction

D — Fission of the mantle

millionth of a second, producing a seething, fu-
riously expanding mass of radioactive nuclear
fragments; newly created helium nuclei, all
stripped of their electrons, form a cloud of vaporized matter at a temperature of many tens of
millions of degrees—the nuclear fireball.

This description should give you a general
picture of the size and weight of nuclear
weapons: a one megaton weapon would weigh
at most a few hundred kilograms. Again, we see
the factor of one million between the energy released in electromagnetic and nuclear interactions. It takes a billion kilograms of TNT interacting electromagnetically to match the energy
released from a few hundred kilograms of matter interacting "strongly"! All this energy is released in the form of kinetic energy of bomb debris or in the form of radiation of one wavelength
or another. For a small weapon—one producing
one kiloton of released energy—90 percent of
its yield is in the kinetic energy of weapon debris, and the rest is in radiation. In explosions of
higher yield, the proportion of radiation is
higher. For yields above 200 kilotons, the released energy is about 95 percent radiation—
about half of which is converted into air-blast
and shock wave as the fireball expands in the
atmosphere.

Suggested Readings

Clearly there is little public information on the design of nuclear weapons. Yet the physical processes
involved are well understood and are treated in text-
books on nuclear physics. Explanations of the general
principles of nuclear weapons are given in Glasstone
and in the *Encyclopedia Americana*. The book by
Kosta Tsipis deals with the many areas where knowledge of physical phenomena is essential to understanding the nature and consequences of nuclear
war.

FOSTER, JOHN S., JR. "Nuclear Weapons," *Encyclopedia
    Americana*. Danbury, Conn.: Grolier, Inc., 1981,
    Vol. 20, pp. 518–528.

GLASSTONE, SAMUEL, AND PHILIP J. DOLAN. *The Effects of
    Nuclear Weapons*. Washington, D.C.: U.S. Govern-
    ment Printing Office, 1977. Chap. 1 and 2. (Earlier
    editions were published in 1957 and 1962.)

GLASSTONE, SAMUEL, AND R. LOVBERG. *Controlled Ther-
    monuclear Fusion*. Huntington, New York: R. Krie-
    ger, 1975.

TELLER, EDWARD. "Hydrogen Bomb," *Encyclopedia
    Americana*. Danbury, Conn.: Grolier, Inc., 1981,
    Vol. 14, pp. 654–656.

TSIPIS, KOSTA. *The Physics of Nuclear Warfare*. New
    York: Simon and Schuster, to be published.

The Rocky Flats weapons materials plant near Denver, Colorado, fabricates plutonium parts for nuclear weapons. The operation is risky; tight routine did not prevent a very costly fire in 1969.

11. Nuclear Weapons Manufacture

A major industry supported by American tax dollars has been developed to design and build the arsenals of nuclear weapons, and to mine and process the fission and fusion fuels they require. In this chapter we follow the entire sequence: we learn where nuclear weapons and their fuels are made, we see the extent of the physical plants needed for their manufacture, and we review the investment in high-technology and skilled workers, and the multibillion dollar annual operating costs.

"In the arts of life man invents nothing, but in the arts of death he outdoes Nature herself..."

Man and Superman, George Bernard Shaw

"Weapons development has entered the Baroque period: it does little, costs a lot and keeps a lot of people busy."

Herbert F. York (former director, Lawrence Livermore Laboratory) July 16, 1970

THE UNITED STATES has an arsenal of some 30,000 nuclear weapons.[1] Over the years, taking account of tests and, more importantly, retirement of obsolete weapons, the United States has produced far more than this number. Although we often think of these weapons abstractly in terms of the destruction they could cause, or even more abstractly as counters in a competition with the Soviet Union, the weapons are actual physical devices. They have shape, mass, and size—often surprisingly small.[2] They have to be *made*, by people working in a network of laboratories and plants stretching across the nation. These industrial facilities for making nuclear warheads are the subject of this chapter.

As explained in Chapter 3, responsibility for the design, testing, and manufacture of nuclear weapons is vested not in the Pentagon but in the Department of Energy (DOE). In recent years the DOE has spent roughly one-third of its budget for this purpose, and the amount is increasing. Before the governmental reorganization of 1974, another civilian agency, the Atomic Energy Commission (AEC), was in charge of the nuclear weapons program. This type of civilian control has not retarded nuclear weapons development. Paradoxical though it seems, knowledgeable people have suggested that these arrangements may actually have resulted in greater proliferation of weapons than would have taken place under military control.[3]

The DOE lists seven plants as its "weapons production complex." The seven are all government owned but are operated by private firms under contracts. The DOE's supervision of these

John Lamperti

Lamperti is a professor of mathematics at Dartmouth College.

11-1   PRINCIPAL PLANTS OF THE U.S. NUCLEAR WEAPONS INDUSTRY

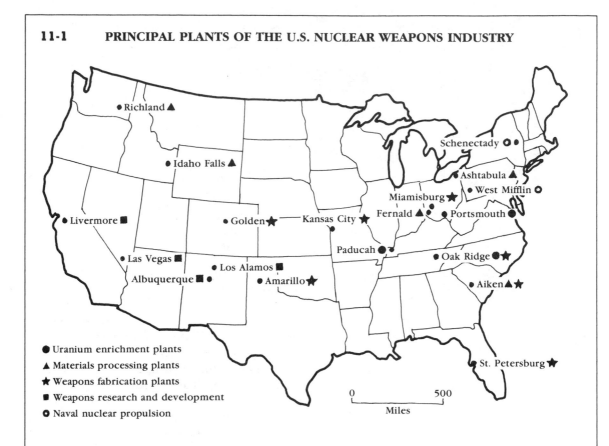

Uranium Enrichment Plants

Oak Ridge, Tenn. (Union Carbide); Paducah, Ky. (Union Carbide); and Portsmouth, Ohio (Goodyear Aerospace): These big plants concentrate the fissionable isotope uranium-235. They take in and produce the uranium as the fluid UF_6, uranium hexafluoride.

Materials Processing Plants

Ashtabula Feed Materials Plant, Ashtabula, Ohio (Reactive Metals) and Feed Materials Production Center, Fernald, Ohio (National Lead): These plants fabricate metal parts from depleted and low-enriched uranium for production reactors and for bomb parts.

Idaho Chemical Processing Plant, Idaho Falls, Ida. (Allied Chemicals): At Idaho Falls, unburned enriched uranium (mostly from submarines) is removed from used fuel rods and sent on for recycling.

Hanford Production Operations, Richland, Wash. (Rockwell Hanford and United Nuclear) and Savannah River Plant, Aiken, S.C. (E. I. DuPont): These large complexes make plutonium by chain reaction in uranium fuel rods and slugs, dump the waste part, and separate the plutonium from the fuel to send on for bomb parts. Savannah prepares deuterium as heavy water and also makes tritium by exposure of lithium in the reactor.

Weapons Fabrication Plants

Kansas City Plant, Kansas City, Mo. (Bendix): The Kansas City Plant makes many electronic and mechanical weapons components.

Mound Facility, Miamisburg, Ohio (Monsanto Research): Mound makes special small high-explosive components and radioisotope batteries for bombs. It uses plutonium-238 from Savannah River.

Savannah River Weapons Facility, Aiken, S.C. (E. I. DuPont) and Y-12 Plant, Oak Ridge, Tenn. (Union Carbide): Uranium and lithium deuteride parts are fabricated here.

Pinellas Plant, St. Petersburg, Fla. (General Electric): Pinellas makes neutron trigger tubes using tritium from Savannah River.

Rocky Flats Plant, Golden, Colo. (Rockwell International): Plutonium metal parts are fabricated here.

Pantex Plant, Amarillo, Tex. (Mason and Hangar-Silas Mason): Pantex fabricates larger high-explosive parts, assembles weapons from components, and recycles many older warheads.

Weapons Research and Development

Los Alamos National Laboratory, Los Alamos, N.Mex. (University of California); Lawrence Livermore National Laboratory, Livermore, Calif. (University of California); Sandia Laboratories, Albuquerque, N.Mex. (Western Electric); and Nevada Test Site, Las Vegas, Nev. (Reynolds Electrical and Engineering)

Naval Nuclear Propulsion

Bettis Atomic Power Laboratory, West Mifflin, Penn. (Westinghouse) and Knolls Atomic Power Laboratory, Schenectady, N.Y. (General Electric)

plants is delegated to its Albuquerque Operations Office, which in turn maintains area offices at the individual plant sites.

There is much more to the production of nuclear weapons. The DOE's Nevada Operations Office manages the Nevada Test Site, while the Albuquerque Operations Office and San Francisco Operations Office oversee the three major nuclear weapons laboratories at Albuquerque (Sandia Laboratory), Los Alamos, and Livermore, California. The production of nuclear materials for weapons and other uses is also part of the complex, as is the navy reactor program. Within the DOE the latter activities are not classified as 'defense,' but are organized under the assistant secretaries for "energy technology" (in the case of weapons materials and the navy program) and "resource applications" (enriching and fabricating nuclear fuel).

In this chapter we will take a "tour" of the most important facilities where nuclear weapons are planned and made. The tour will move from the completed weapons back to their design and testing; it begins where the bombs and warheads are assembled and sent on their way to be deployed. We will include the production of "special nuclear materials" for atomic explosives and take a brief look at the design and production of nuclear power reactors for the navy. The mining, milling, and enrichment of uranium are described in Chapter 20. Manufacturing of delivery systems such as aircraft and missiles is outside the scope of this report.

Putting It All Together: The Pantex Plant

The Pantex Ordnance plant, located twenty-three miles northeast of Amarillo, Texas, was built in 1942 to produce conventional bombs and shells for World War II. Temporarily deactivated after the war, Pantex was soon taken over by the AEC for nuclear weapons production. The plant has been operated for the AEC and its successors (now for the DOE) since 1956 by Mason and Hanger—Silas Mason Company. The plant site occupies over 10,000 acres.

In keeping with its historical role, Pantex makes chemical high-explosives—the explosive "lenses" whose implosion compresses a subcritical mass of fissile material to initiate an atomic explosion. The chemical explosive components for all U.S. nuclear warheads are made here and are added to the weapons during their final assembly, which is also done at Pantex using components shipped from the other plants in the DOE weapons-production network. Testing of chemical explosives, and nonexplosive testing of the newly completed weapons and others from the stockpile, is performed in Pantex's labs and on its ranges.

In addition to the flow of nuclear weapons *out* of the Pantex plant, surplus or outdated nuclear warheads and bombs are sent *to* Pantex for refurbishing or for disassembly in order to recycle the nuclear materials in the weapons. Such recycling is a large feature of the U.S. weapons program, for the total number of weapons in "service" has grown only modestly in the last two decades, despite production of many thousands of new ones. In both production and retirement, Pantex is the link between the weapons manufacturing complex and the actual deployment by the military forces.

Nuclear Components: Rocky Flats and Y-12

Nuclear fuel for the fission and fusion stages of nuclear warheads is fabricated into weapons components at two sites—the Rocky Flats plant near Denver, Colorado, and the Y-12 plant in Oak Ridge, Tennessee. Rocky Flats, occupying over 6,500 acres, is the second largest site (after Pantex) in the weapons-production complex. Rocky Flats and Y-12 are also by far the most expensive of these facilities, representing an in-

Design and Testing Facilities

Facility	Number of Employees	Operating Budget (fiscal year 1978)
Los Alamos	6,560	$288.1 million
Sandia	7,498	$398.9 million
Livermore	7,014	$303.6 million
Nevada Test Site	5,200	$257.6 million

Weapons Production Plants

Facility	Manpower (Employee-Years) Fiscal Year 1978	Budget (Millions)
Bendix, Kansas City (Missouri)	5,561	$194.7
Rockwell, Rocky Flats (Colorado)	2,986	96.0
Mason & Hangar, Pantex Plant (Amarillo, Texas)	1,858	46.5
Monsanto, Mound (Ohio)	1,705	59.4
General Electric, Pinellas (Florida)	1,233	42.2
Union Carbide, Y-12 (Oak Ridge, Tennessee)	4,911	161.7
Du Pont, Savannah River (South Carolina)	355	19.4
	18,609	$619.9

11-2 NUCLEAR WEAPONS EMPLOYMENT AND BUDGET

These two tables indicate the level of activity in the design, testing, and production of nuclear weapons by the United States. Here production includes only the fabrication of parts and their assembly into complete warheads; it does not include the sizable work forces engaged in the production of nuclear materials—enriched uranium, plutonium, tritium, and lithium deuteride—and in the naval reactor program. About 50 percent of the activity at the Y-12 Plant is for nonweapons purposes.

vestment of nearly $1 billion. Their combined operating budgets for fiscal year 1978 amounted to about $250 million. The functions of the two plants overlap to some extent, although each has special capabilities; together they perform a crucial stage in weapons manufacture.

The Y-12 plant was built in 1945 under the Manhattan Project to house the "Calutrons" which separated uranium-235 (U-235) from natural uranium by an electromagnetic process; most of the enriched uranium for the Hiroshima bomb came from Y-12. By the end of the war, gaseous diffusion was supplanting the Calutrons as the preferred method of enriching uranium, and in 1947 Y-12 was converted to a different role in weapons production.

Today, Y-12 fabricates uranium and lithium deuteride parts for all the hydrogen bombs (H-bombs) in the U.S. arsenal. Lithium deuteride is the principal fuel for nuclear fusion in the bomb. Uranium may be either highly enriched fissile material or "depleted uranium," almost entirely U-238. The latter is used for components such as "tampers" which compress other fuel during the explosion. However, the U-238 itself fissions during the third stage of a thermonuclear explosion to provide half or more of the energy, as well as most of the radioactive fission products. Facilities at the Y-12 plant include large metalworking equipment to deal with uranium, plus precision-machining facilities and the "dry rooms" necessary for work with highly water-sensitive lithium deuteride. Since 1947 the Y-12 plant has been operated for the U.S. government by the nuclear division of Union Carbide Company.

Rocky Flats was established in 1952 and operated by the Dow Chemical Company until 1975, at which time the contract was transferred to Atomics International, a division of Rockwell International. The primary mission of Rocky Flats is to fabricate plutonium into components for nuclear weapons. Nearly all U.S. weapons, whether thermonuclear or pure fission, use plutonium in their manufacture and in-

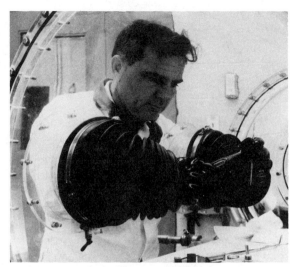

11-3 WORKMAN USING GLOVE BOX
The glove box is standard equipment for manipulation of substances such as plutonium that are to be kept out of contact with air. The box is filled with inert gas.

volve parts made at Rocky Flats. These parts include some or all of the fissile material for the primary stage and may also include the fission "spark plug" which assists the secondary, fusion stage of the explosion. A sophisticated technology is necessary for dealing with plutonium, its compounds, and alloys, and Rocky Flats is the home of most of these techniques. In addition, the plant has the capability for working with beryllium and uranium and for recovering plutonium from residues and wastes. Both Rocky Flats and Y-12 work closely with the nuclear-weapons laboratories in producing one-of-a-kind models for design and testing of new warheads.

The Rocky Flats plant has experienced numerous accidents which have released significant quantities of plutonium and other contaminants into the nearby environment. In 1957 and in 1969 there were major fires involving plutonium; the 1969 fire, which cost at least $45 million, was considered at that time the worst industrial fire in U.S. history. In 1974, plutonium particles were accidentally released into the atmosphere. Improper waste management has contributed to further contamination. Since the change of contractors in 1975 the health and safety record at Rocky Flats has improved, but a number of health authorities and many local citizens believe there is still much cause for concern.[4]

Tritium: Savannah River Weapons Facility

Deuterium and tritium are isotopes of hydrogen with one and two "extra" neutrons, respectively, in their atomic nuclei; normal hydrogen nuclei contain one proton and no neutrons. The fusion of deuterium and tritium nuclei is a key part of any thermonuclear explosion. Most of the tritium required for an H-bomb is actually created during the bomb's explosion by fissioning nuclei of the isotope lithium-6; thus the compound lithium-6 deuteride is the main fusion fuel in all such bombs and supplies both ingredients for the deuterium-tritium fusion reaction. However, small amounts of actual tritium are also required. A small fusion reaction takes place during the primary stage of the weapon's detonation and supplies fast neutrons which greatly increase the efficiency of the fission reaction. Some weapons that rely primarily on fission also use this principle in order to boost their yield.

All the tritium used in U.S. nuclear weapons is produced at the Savannah River plant. The method of production is similar to that for plutonium-239: "targets" containing lithium-6 are bombarded by neutrons in special "production reactors." After the irradiation some of the lithium atoms have fissioned, resulting in helium and tritium; the tritium can then be separated from the helium and lithium by chemical processes. All of this is done at Savannah River, and the Weapons Facility, only a small part of the entire plant, contains the separation equipment. The plant also has the capability for tritium loading of weapons components, as well as for unloading and reclaiming tritium from weapons being recycled or refurbished.

Since both tritium and plutonium-239 are produced in the same production reactors (using lithium and uranium targets, respectively), there is potentially a competition between the two for space in the reactors. Moreover, neutron bombs are said to require more tritium than other nuclear weapons. These considerations may help explain the "need" found by two recent studies for expanded plutonium production facilities to meet the expected demand for additional nuclear warheads during the eighties and nineties.[5]

More Bomb Components: Kansas City, Pinellas, and Mound

Parts for nuclear weapons are made in three more major plants under the supervision of the DOE's Albuquerque Operations Office. These plants make nonnuclear components that complement the fission and fusion-fuel parts produced at Rocky Flats and Y-12. All three are government owned and are operated for the DOE by major U.S. multinational corporations.

Since 1949 the Bendix Corporation has operated a plant in Kansas City, Missouri, where, the company says, "5900 employees make nonnuclear electronic, mechanical and electromechanical parts for nuclear weapons."[6] The electronics parts include radars, timers, high-energy power supplies, and telemetry units; mechanical parts include precision valves and coded locking devices. All these are essential for nuclear weapons, but the Kansas City plant also has a more exotic function: it manufactures a special high-density plastic foam that fills much of the space surrounding the package of fusion fuel in an H-bomb. Capability for making and forming these plastics is Bendix's most distinctive contribution to thermonuclear explosives.

In St. Petersburg, Florida, the Pinellas plant is operated for the DOE by the Neutron Devices Department of General Electric. According to the DOE, "The plant was built in 1956 for the purpose of development and production of neutron generators for nuclear weapons initiation."[7] This mission requires a variety of special

11-4 PRODUCTION REACTOR—SAVANNAH RIVER
Reactors like this one in South Carolina are the main sources of plutonium and tritium for U.S. weapons.

high-vacuum techniques which are unique to Pinellas. The plant's 1,300 employees and $42 million budget (1978) constitute only a small fraction of General Electric's nuclear weapons work, most of which is devoted to delivery systems rather than warheads.

Monsanto Company, the fourth largest chemical company in the United States, operates the Mound Facility in Miamisburg, Ohio, through its subsidiary Monsanto Research Company. The operation dates back to 1943 when Monsanto contracted with the Manhattan Project to study the element polonium and to use it to develop neutron initiators for the first atomic bombs. A permanent facility for this activity was completed in 1948. Today, Mound's major job is producing explosive components such as detonators and timers for nuclear weapons. Mound also makes isotopic heat sources using plutonium-238 for both weapons and nonweapons (such as space) applications. The facility recovers and purifies tritium from wastes and re-

cycled components, a capability described by the DOE as "an outgrowth of weapons production activities involving components containing tritium."[8] Mound also carries out research and testing in connection with many phases of nuclear weapons production.

Nuclear Materials:
The Savannah River Plant

On August 29, 1949, the Soviet Union conducted its first nuclear test explosion. The reaction of the United States to the loss of its nuclear monopoly was drastic; among other actions, it established a second nuclear weapons laboratory, began a crash program to build the hydrogen bomb (the "superbomb"), and greatly increased the production of nuclear weapons materials. The latter involved the construction of a major new production facility, the Savannah River Plant, in Aiken and Barnwell counties, South Carolina, some fifteen miles from Augusta, Georgia.

The Savannah River Plant was built by E.I. du Pont de Nemours Company for the AEC and has been operated by Du Pont ever since. The site occupies some 250,000 acres; several small towns and about 1,500 families had to be removed during its construction. Operations began late in 1952 with the start-up of a facility to extract "heavy water" (water containing deuterium instead of normal hydrogen) from the Savannah River. The first nuclear reactor was activated a few days before the end of 1953. By 1956 the basic plant was completed at a cost of over $1.1 billion.

Today, all the plutonium, deuterium, and tritium being produced for U.S. nuclear weapons comes from the Savannah River Plant. It has five production reactors—three are operating and two are in standby condition.[9] Both fuel and target elements for the reactors are made at Savannah River; the targets include both depleted uranium (with the U-235 removed) to be converted by neutron capture into plutonium-239, and lithium for the production of tritium. Two chemical separation plants extract plutonium from the irradiated uranium targets, while the tritium-containing lithium targets are sent to the Weapons Facility section of the plant for separation and processing. Savannah River's heavy-water extraction plant, the only one operating in the United States, produces all the deuterium needed for thermonuclear weapons and for the production reactors, which are heavy-water moderated, and sells its surplus to research laboratories and private industry.

The Savannah River Plant is also a major center for the storage and management of radioactive wastes (as well as a major producer of such waste). About one-fourth of the high-level liquid waste created by U.S. military nuclear production to date, mostly from chemical processes used in separating plutonium, is stored in steel tanks at the Savannah River site. Solid wastes are packaged and buried, and radioactive gases are filtered and released "in a controlled manner" into the environment.[10]

Approximately 7,500 people are employed at the plant, of whom about 1,300 are considered professionals, including 166 holders of doctorate degrees. Operating funds for the Savannah River Plant amounted to over $280 million in fiscal year 1978. DOE supervision of the plant (except the Weapons Facility) is exercised through the Savannah River Operations Office.

Hanford: The First Plutonium Plant

The Hanford Reservation, founded in 1943, produced the plutonium for the atomic bombs used at the Trinity test and at Nagasaki. The wartime project resulted in three plutonium production reactors, three separation plants, fuel fabrication facilities, and the first steel tanks of high-level, liquid radioactive wastes. Except for a much smaller pilot-project reactor at Oak Ridge, Hanford was the world's first plutonium factory. It was built and operated during the war by Du Pont and is located on some 570 square miles in southeastern Washington.

Today, Hanford apparently does not play a direct role in the production of nuclear warheads. Its only major operating reactor, N-reactor, is run with a dual purpose: plutonium production and electricity generation. N-reactor operates at 3,800 megawatts (thermal energy) and supplies sufficient steam to a Washington utility for generating 860 megawatts of electrical power. Hanford has five plants which the DOE says can "accomplish all phases of chemical separation, purification, and long-term production" of plutonium and other isotopes, including transuranics such as neptunium and americium.[11] Hanford's plutonium, however, is said to be of reactor grade, rather than weapons grade, and N-reactor's irradiated targets are being stockpiled for future processing.

Hanford's most important facility may be the one everyone regards with unease: its waste-storage tanks. High-level wastes from the chemical separation of plutonium have been stored there since 1943, and the total amounts to nearly three-fourths of the waste from U.S. military nuclear activities. This storage has caused considerable difficulties, and about 500,000 gallons of liquid waste have leaked into the earth.[12] Thirteen additional one-million-gallon tanks are under construction, at an estimated cost of nearly $50 million.

The Du Pont Company relinquished the Hanford contract soon after the end of World War II, and General Electric took over the management until 1964. At that point the contract was split into several parts which were awarded to a number of firms including the nonprofit Battelle Memorial Institute and subsidiaries of United Nuclear, Douglas Aircraft, and ITT. Today, Hanford's production operations are performed under contracts with United Nuclear Industries, which is responsible for fuel fabrication and reactor operation, and with a division of Rockwell International, which handles the chemical separation and waste management. These two firms, employing about 4,000 people at the Hanford site, received over $120 million in fiscal year 1978 for their services there.

The current program to increase production of nuclear weapons materials includes the restarting of one of the standby production reactors at Hanford. Beyond this, Hanford may be a leading contender for the site of a new reactor, if one is to be built.[13] Since the production reactors currently operating at Savannah River are expected to shut down before the end of this century, Hanford may have a chance to regain its one-time supremacy in the creation of plutonium for use in weapons of mass destruction.

Uranium: Idaho Falls, Fernald, and Ashtabula

Several more plants play important roles in supplying nuclear materials for weapons manufacture. Here we will pick up the trail of uranium at the point where Chapter 20 ends: the gas diffusion enrichment plants. As stated there, a small fraction of the uranium enriched at the three plants is raised to a high concentration (as much as 97 percent) of U-235. This material is not currently used *directly* in nuclear bombs, since a large stockpile of highly enriched uranium is already on hand; in addition, U-235 is recycled from weapons that are retired from active duty. Instead, the highly enriched uranium hexafluoride is sent to Erwin, Tennessee, where it is reduced to a solid uranium oxide in a plant owned by Nuclear Fuel Services, a Getty Oil subsidiary. From Tennessee the uranium goes either to a Babcock and Wilcox plant in Virginia or to a United Nuclear plant in Connecticut. At this stage it is formed into fuel rods for a naval propulsion reactor or for one of the many research and experimental reactors which need highly enriched fuel. The rods then are used at sea or serve their research function until enough fission products have accumulated to make them unfit for further use.

The used fuel, which still contains a large amount of U-235, is then sent to a major DOE facility—the Idaho National Engineering Laboratory (INEL) in Idaho Falls. This laboratory, formerly the National Reactor Test Station, has been the home of sixty-two experimental reactors, seventeen of which are still operating. The laboratory is operated for the DOE by two major contractors—EG & G Idaho and the Allied Chemical Corporation. The used fuel rods are taken to the Idaho Chemical Processing Plant within INEL, where the unburned uranium is chemically separated from the fission products. The recovered uranium, still highly enriched, is sent to Oak Ridge where it is reduced once more to metallic form in the Y-12 plant. The uranium then goes to the Savannah River Plant where it is again fabricated into fuel rods and used this time to drive the production reactors for making plutonium and tritium for thermonuclear warheads. The cycle—INEL, Oak Ridge, Savannah River—can be repeated many times.

Two more DOE facilities are part of the system of nuclear materials production. At Fernald, Ohio, the Feed Materials Production Center (FMPC) has been operated by National Lead of Ohio since its start in 1953. FMPC's tasks in-

11-5 LAWRENCE LIVERMORE NATIONAL LABORATORY

The second U.S. nuclear weapons laboratory. Most tactical warheads have been designed here; most stra- tegic weapons have been designed at the Los Alamos laboratory.

clude the chemical conversion of several ura- nium compounds into one another and into ura- nium metal, the forming of uranium from ingots into rods, and machining uranium components for use in plutonium production. FMPC is oper- ated in conjunction with an extrusion plant in Ashtabula, Ohio, which is owned by the private firm Reactive Metals. The extrusion plant con- tains one large and one small extrusion press (owned by the DOE) with which uranium metal ingots can be formed into tubes. Operating these two facilities costs about $20 million per year.

Both slightly enriched uranium and depleted uranium (the "tails" that remain when natural uranium has had most of its U-235 content re- moved) are shipped from the enrichment plants to Fernald. At FMPC both materials are trans- formed from the uranium hexafluoride form into metal and passed on to Ashtabula, where they are extruded into tubes. The tubes are then returned to Fernald for "finishing." The tubes of slightly enriched uranium go to Han- ford, where they are made into combined fuel and target elements for N-reactor. The depleted uranium tubes are sent to Savannah River, where they are transformed into target ele- ments for the production reactors, again for the production of plutonium-239 by neutron irra- diation in the reactors.

In addition, depleted uranium is itself a nu- clear bomb material, and supplies of this metal are sent from Fernald to Y-12 at Oak Ridge for the manufacture of bomb components. It is this uranium, fissioned by fast neutrons in the third stage of an H-bomb explosion, which supplies much of the power and most of the poisonous fission products the bomb produces.

Research, Design, and Testing: Los Alamos, Sandia, Livermore, and the Nevada Test Site

The world's first nuclear weapons were de- signed and built at the Los Alamos Laboratory during World War II. The laboratory was founded at the then-obscure site fifty-five miles north of

Albuquerque late in 1942 under the direction of J. Robert Oppenheimer. Using U-235 from Oak Ridge and plutonium from Hanford, it succeeded in building the bomb that was tested at "Trinity," as well as those used to destroy the Japanese cities of Hiroshima and Nagasaki, causing hundreds of thousands of casualties, mostly civilians.

After the end of the war, with the laboratory's mission apparently accomplished, consideration was briefly given to its closing. Instead, it was reorganized and renamed the Los Alamos Scientific Laboratory, and it took on primary responsibility for developing and testing an ever-expanding stockpile of weapons with a destructive capability unprecedented in human history.

At about the same time, some of the production functions first performed at Los Alamos were moved to Albuquerque, and in 1948 this branch was named Sandia Laboratory and given a more independent role in both development and manufacture of nuclear weapons. The building of other AEC production facilities gradually removed the manufacturing part of Sandia's mission, leaving as its primary job the development and testing of nonnuclear portions of nuclear weapons. According to the DOE, "Sandia's primary accomplishment is the existence of the national weapon stockpile . . . ."[14]

The reaction of the United States to the Soviet atomic bomb test in 1949 included, among many other things, the decision to establish a second general weapons-design laboratory, separate from Los Alamos. This laboratory was founded in 1952 at Livermore, California, some forty miles east of San Francisco; it was named after the inventor of the cyclotron, Ernest O. Lawrence, who was influential in starting the new lab. Since its first years, Lawrence Livermore Laboratory has been involved in all phases of nuclear weapons design and development, from high-yield H-bombs to compact tactical weapons and "neutron bombs" for delivery by short-range missiles or artillery. At present, nu-

clear weapons work accounts for about half of the laboratory's efforts, which also include research on the use of lasers for isotope separation and the possibility of obtaining usable energy from nuclear fusion.

Complementing the three weapons laboratories is the Nevada Test Site (NTS), established in December 1950, which is located about sixty-five miles northwest of Las Vegas. Covering some 800,000 acres, NTS was originally chosen as a site for atmospheric tests of nuclear weapons. Since the Partial Test Ban Treaty of 1963, however, more than 330 underground nuclear explosions have been conducted there; NTS also supervises off-site tests. Boring large holes, up to twelve feet in diameter and thousands of feet deep, and employing sophisticated instrumentation for measuring the effects of underground explosions are among NTS' special capabilities.

Since their founding, the Los Alamos and Livermore labs have been operated by the University of California.[15] Sandia was also operated by the University of California during its first year, but since 1949 Sandia has been a project of the Western Electric Company. NTS is operated by at least six contractors, with the largest contract (for "prime support") held by Reynolds Electrical and Engineering Company. NTS is administered by the DOE's Nevada Operations Office, Livermore by the San Francisco office, and both Sandia and Los Alamos by the Albuquerque office.

Naval Nuclear Propulsion: Bettis and Knolls

The Bettis and Knolls Atomic Power Laboratories (BAPL and KAPL, respectively) have been instrumental in the development of the U.S. nuclear navy. These two DOE-owned laboratories— operated by the two industrial giants in the nuclear-reactor field, Westinghouse and General Electric—have designed the power plants for all U.S. nuclear ships, from the time when navy nuclear propulsion was Captain (later Admiral)

Hyman G. Rickover's personal dream and obsession to the present. The experience gained through this work helped both companies to become the leading manufacturers of civilian nuclear power reactors for the Western world.

The main facility of BAPL is located about ten miles from Pittsburgh, Pennsylvania, and it was here that the power plant for the first nuclear ship, the *Nautilus,* was designed. Bettis also operates the Naval Reactors Facility at INEL, where the land-based prototype for the *Nautilus* reactor was built. The Shippingport (Pennsylvania) Atomic Power Station was another early Bettis project, and it has been run as an experimental facility as well as for power generation. (The Shippingport reactor was a direct outgrowth of development work originally intended for a nuclear aircraft carrier.[16]) All these reactors were of the pressurized-water type, using ordinary (light) water as coolant and moderator. Finally, BAPL developed the first reactor actually installed in a large surface ship, the nuclear cruiser *Long Beach,* as well as those for several classes of missile and attack submarines.

The story of the Knolls laboratory is quite similar. The main facility of KAPL is located near Schenectady, New York, the home of the General Electric Research Laboratories; KAPL also operates land-based prototypes of naval reactors at West Milton, N.Y., and at Windsor, Connecticut. KAPL's first navy project was a sodium-cooled reactor for the second nuclear ship, the submarine *Seawolf.* (This power plant had numerous problems and was replaced after about two years of operation. Light-water technology has been preferred for shipboard use since the middle fifties.) The large aircraft carriers of the *Nimitz* class and several nuclear-powered cruisers in the U.S. fleet use reactors developed by Knolls. As with Bettis and Westinghouse, the Knolls laboratory has been essential to General Electric's growth as a supplier of civilian power reactors. General Electric and Westinghouse have each built about one-third of the power reactors in the United States, and between them

they have sold all the nuclear power reactors exported from this country.

The Naval Reactors Program of the DOE, which includes BAPL and KAPL, is organized under the assistant secretary for energy technology. The operations of Bettis and Knolls are administered by the DOE's Pittsburgh and Schenectady Naval Reactors Offices, respectively. The contractors' work forces at Bettis and Knolls are about 3,300 and 2,930 people, while the DOE uses some 160 additional employees in carrying out its supervision. The operating budgets of the two laboratories in fiscal year 1978 were about $200 million and $160 million, respectively.

Concluding Remarks

The complex of plants and laboratories described in this chapter represent a major capital investment, and keeping them in operation costs well over $2 billion per year, with major increases in sight. However, this is only a small portion of the nuclear weapons costs, since delivery systems such as the Trident submarine and the MX missile are far more expensive. Many of the DOE's nuclear contractors are also major suppliers of other weapons, including nuclear delivery systems, to the Department of Defense (DOD). For example, General Electric, which operates only one plant in the DOE's weapons complex, ranked fourth with the DOD in 1979, holding over $2 billion worth of military contracts. Rockwell International, Bendix, and American Telephone and Telegraph are in similar positions.[17]

The United States has an awesome arsenal of nuclear weapons, produced by the complex we have examined. The invention and development of these weapons was a remarkable technical feat, one which has cost a high price in dollars, material resources, and human creative energy. Perhaps the last has been the greatest of these costs. A large part of the ingenuity and initiative that might have helped solve the problems of our society and create a better life for all of us has instead been expended on perfecting fantastic instruments of mass destruction.

The nuclear weapons complex does not merely respond passively to outside demands. Technical developments and improvements from within the system, such as the invention of MIRV and continual improvements in missile guidance and accuracy, have changed the nature of international relations. Many analysts believe that such progress, by bringing into question the precarious stability of the balance of terror between the superpowers, has seriously *diminished* our national security.

The laboratories and corporations in the weapons complex also form a powerful political force which may act directly to maintain the pace of the arms race. For example, the nuclear weapons laboratories have lobbied effectively against a treaty to ban all nuclear weapons tests, a measure that might help slow the rate of weapons development on all sides.[18] In this case, the self-interest of the labs has prevailed, at least temporarily, over the national security advantages that a mutual test ban with the Soviet Union would provide.

The prosperity and growth of the nuclear weapons complex is not synonymous with, and perhaps not even consistent with, the security and national interest of the United States. But it is clear that constructive change will not come from within. Veteran diplomat George Kennan, among many others, has pointed the way. "Statesmen on both sides," he has written, "should take their military establishments in hand and insist that these become the servants, not the masters and determinants, of political action. Both sides must learn to accept the fact that only in the reduction, not in the multiplication, of existing monstrous arsenals can the true security of any nation be found."[19]

Suggested Readings

Our principal source of information about the facilities for producing nuclear weapons is *DOE Research and Development and Field Facilities,* from the U.S. Department of Energy. Facts and figures concerning particular plants or laboratories that are not otherwise attributed can be found in this publication.

In addition, much information on the origin and development of the nuclear weapons industry up to 1952 can be found in the two-volume official history of the Atomic Energy Commission, *The New World, 1939–1946,* by Richard Hewlett and Oscar Anderson, Jr.; and *Atomic Shield, 1947–1952,* by Richard Hewlett and Francis Duncan. Ralph Lapp's *The Weapons Culture,* H. Peter Metzger's *The Atomic Establishment,* Roger Rapoport's *The Great American Bomb Machine,* and Herbert York's *Race to Oblivion* give insight into the further evolution of the system up to about 1970. The annual reports of the Department of Energy and its predecessors are useful resources. Finally, Morland's account in *The Secret That Exploded* and related publications such as *Born Secret* by A. DeVolpi and others help in understanding the situation as it exists today.

DeVolpi, A., et al. *Born Secret: The H-Bomb, The Progressive Case and National Security.* New York: Pergamon Press, 1981.

Hewlett, Richard G., and Oscar Anderson, Jr. *The New World, 1939–1946.* University Park, Pa.: Pennsylvania State University Press, 1962.

Hewlett, Richard G., and Francis Duncan. *Atomic Shield, 1947–1952.* University Park, Pa.: Pennsylvania State University Press, 1969.

Lapp, Ralph. *The Weapons Culture.* New York: W.W. Norton, 1968.

Metzger, H. Peter. *The Atomic Establishment.* New York: Simon and Schuster, 1972.

Morland, Howard. *The Secret That Exploded.* New York: Random House, 1981.

Rapoport, Roger. *The Great American Bomb Machine.* New York: Ballantine Books, 1971.

U.S. Department of Energy. *DOE Research and Development and Field Facilities.* Washington, D.C., 1979.

U.S. Department of Energy. *Secretary's Annual Report to Congress.* Washington, D.C. Published annually. The most recent report available was that for 1980, published in January 1981.

York, Herbert. *Race to Oblivion: A Participant's View of the Arms Race.* New York: Simon and Schuster, 1970.

Part Five
Consequences

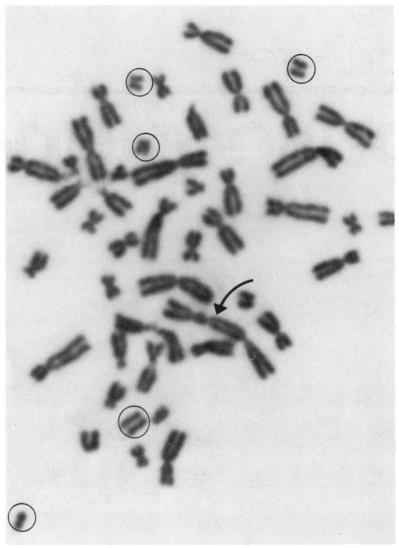

Human chromosomes from a lymphocyte cell that received an X-ray dose of about 300 rads within living tissue. The arrow points to a chromosome with three centromeres, and several chromosome fragments without centromeres are circled.

12. Biological Effects of Ionizing Radiation

While the damage done to living tissues by ionizing radiation—first from X rays and radium—became evident early in its use in medicine and experimental physics, the understanding of the mechanisms by which that damage is done is still primitive. Alan Nelson, who works in radiation biophysics, reviews here both the immediate and deferred biological effects of exposure to ionizing radiations. Their genetic consequences are also examined.

HIGH-ENERGY RAYS from X-ray machines and gamma rays and fast particles from atomic disintegrations will all penetrate the cells of living tissue to cause damage in varying degrees. The phenomena initiated by radiation in living tissue span an enormous scale of time—from the initial ionization that occurs instantly when a high-energy ray strikes matter to the human generations it may take for genetic damage to express itself. The effects of radiation begin with *ionization*—the knocking of electrons out of their orbits within atoms.

Ionization takes place within millionths of billionths of a second after the ray's arrival. The immediate consequences are chemical in nature: Ionization creates altered and often highly reactive chemicals that react with biological molecules to cause damage. These effects take place in times as short as a millionth of a second. Radiation sickness from large, acute radiation exposures shows up within minutes to weeks. Cancers and genetic effects show up years or generations later.

The effects of radiation on living tissue begin when the energetic particle or ray arrives at the surface of the tissue. What happens depends on the energy of the radiation, the nature of the tissue, and whether the radiation is a photon (X ray or gamma ray), a neutron, or a charged particle (beta particle, alpha particle, or other ion). Gamma rays and charged-particle radiation at low intensity have always been part of the human environment. The discovery and use of X rays for medical and industrial purposes added man-made radiation to the background of natural phenomena. In the nuclear age, our society has added the effects of fallout from nuclear explosions, emissions and waste from nuclear energy operations, and use of radioisotopes in medicine and industry.

Exposure of the biological tissues of people, plants, and animals to radiation can arise from

Alan Nelson

Nelson is an assistant professor of nuclear engineering and of health sciences, Harvard–M.I.T. Division of Health Sciences and Technology.

223

rays striking the individual from the outside, or from radioactive material absorbed into the body by eating or breathing. (The sources of radiation exposure are surveyed in Chapter 12.) Internal exposures to radiation raises very difficult questions since biological organisms process food and air very selectively, concentrating specific materials in particular tissues of the body.

Radiation Physics

The three major forms of radiation—photons, charged particles, and neutrons—lose energy by different physical mechanisms, so their interactions and depth of penetration in living tissue are significantly different.

Photons lose energy predominantly through interactions with atomic electrons in the atoms of matter. The photon may be totally absorbed by an atom, which soon ejects an energetic electron (a phenomenon known as the *photoelectric effect*), or the photon may collide, giving only some of its energy to the ejected electron and yielding a photon of lesser energy (a phenomenon known as the *Compton effect*). In the case of high-energy photons (gamma rays), a process known as *pair production* can occur in the dense nuclei of atoms. In pair production, the energy of the gamma ray is converted into matter—a positron and an electron which are ejected from the atomic nucleus. All of these interactions remove photons from the primary radiation, and the intensity of the radiation decreases with the depth of penetration in matter.

Charged particles such as beta particles and alpha particles interact very strongly with matter and are stopped rapidly in living tissue, leaving a path of dense ionization. This occurs because charged particles in radiation attract or repel the charged particles in matter (electrons and nuclei) and lose energy rapidly. Interestingly, the rate of energy loss increases as the particle slows down, creating the greatest ionization just at its maximum depth of penetration.

Neutrons interact only weakly with matter, the primary mechanism of energy loss being through collisions with the nuclei of atoms. This yields the same sort of decrease of intensity with distance as for photons, but the rate of decrease is very slow, and energetic neutrons have a good chance of passing through a human body. In its collisions, a fast neutron is likely to transfer enough energy to light nuclei to knock them out of molecules. Collisions with hydrogen nuclei (protons) are very likely, producing a recoil proton with sufficient energy to cause further ionization. Neutrons, especially those that have lost most of their energy, may be captured by the atomic nuclei in living tissue. The result is a transformed nucleus which is usually highly destructive.

Whatever form radiation takes, the predominant immediate effect is ionization—the removal of electrons from their orbits in atomic structure, leaving behind a net positive charge that can play havoc with molecular structure.

Protection against radiation may be accomplished through shielding. It is easy to shield against alpha and beta particles; less than an inch of most heavy solid materials will suffice. Gamma rays and X rays are more difficult to stop—they lose energy by interacting with elec-

OPPOSITE:

Penetrating radiation includes high-energy photons (X rays and gamma rays) and particles (alpha rays, beta rays, and neutrons). The graphs show how radiation intensity diminishes with distance of penetration in air and in living tissue. Photons and neutrons are the most penetrating but have a low rate of linear energy transfer (LET). X rays interact with matter principally by deflecting off atomic electrons, leaving behind ionized atoms. At gamma-ray energies a photon is very likely to interact within an atomic nucleus, producing two ionizing particles, an electron and a positron. Neutrons lose energy by colliding with nuclei, being deflected or absorbed; the recoiling nuclei become ionized. Fast-moving electrons (beta rays) interact strongly with the electronic structure of atoms. They are deflected in zigzag paths that terminate in relatively short distances. An energetic alpha particle is quickly brought to a halt in body tissue, leaving a short, dense path of ionized matter. Alpha and beta rays have a high rate of linear energy transfer.

12-1   **Penetration of Radiation in Air and Tissue**

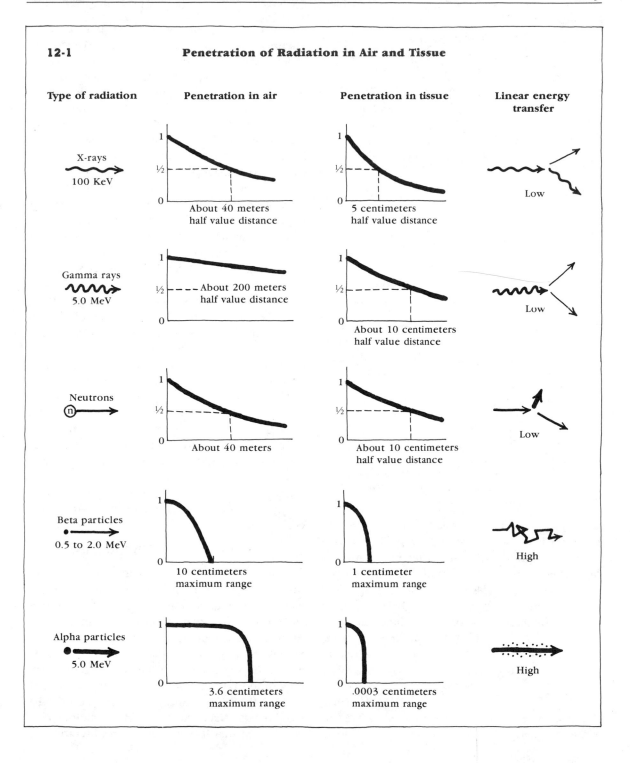

12-2 Radiolysis of Water

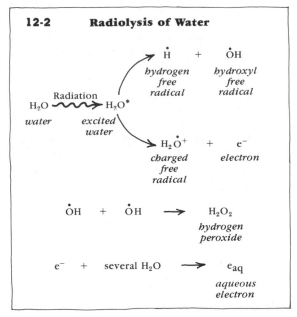

Radiation may directly affect protein molecules or molecules of nucleic acid in living tissue. But living tissue is mostly water; hence most of the direct effect of radiation is on water molecules, producing highly reactive *free radicals*. Although these species have short lifetimes, one product is hydrogen peroxide, a powerful oxidizing agent. It can damage chromosomes, membranes, enzymes, and other cell components at some distance from the site of ionization. Similarly, free electrons released by radiation may travel cellular distances, shielded by a group of water molecules, before causing biological damage.

trons in matter, but the rate of energy loss with distance is slow. Heavy materials are effective shields for photons because electron density is high. Neutrons, however, will penetrate deeply into dense materials; the most effective shield against neutrons consists of lighter materials such as hydrogen, boron, or carbon, but very thick walls are required. Luckily, free neutrons are extremely rare unless put into the environment as a result of human technological efforts.

Radiation Chemistry and Biochemistry

Once the energy of radiation is transferred to tissue through ionization, the subsequent effects are in the realm of chemistry. Highly reactive chemicals are created that cause damage to biomolecules—the enzymes, proteins, and genetic materials that form the structure and code information in all living tissues. Biological tissue is about 70 percent water, and thus the disruption of water molecules by radiation accounts for a large portion of biological damage caused by radiation. This is called *indirect action* because the damage to biomolecules is done not by radiation itself, but by active products of the irradiation of water. When radiation strikes water, the water molecules are split into several products which then attack other molecules even a considerable distance from the site of ionization. These secondary reactions can remove hydrogen atoms from molecules, leaving unstable molecular structures; they can cleave large molecules into pieces and can add bonds or hydroxyl groups to molecules. Virtually all biomolecules, including genetic material, are surrounded by water and are thus subject to attack by the radiation products of water.

The presence of oxygen in biological tissue generally increases its tissue sensitivity to radiation. Research has confirmed the generation of an extremely reactive compound called *super oxide* in irradiated materials containing oxygen. When super oxide is formed in biological material, it reacts rapidly and irreversibly to form organic peroxides which can alter or destroy local cellular functions.

Radiation Injury to Humans

When nuclear materials came into use, the Atomic Energy Commission sponsored research using experimental animals to explore the possible effects of radiation on people. In addition, unfortunate accidents that exposed some individuals to large, acute doses of radiation have added to knowledge of radiation injury. The most important source of data is the medical effects of the nuclear weapons exploded over Hiroshima and Nagasaki. These investigations have established that it is the rapidly proliferating tis-

12-3   **CURIES, ROENTGENS, RADS, AND REMS**

All kinds of radiation—X rays or gamma rays, alpha particles, beta particles, or neutrons—travel essentially straight paths except for their interactions with matter. Imagine rays emanating from a point source. The flux of particles at a distance from the source is described by the number of rays that pass through a unit area in one unit of time. For example, one milligram of radium will send about 24,000 alpha particles per second through each square centimeter of surface at a distance of ten centimeters.

The amount of radioactivity in material is measured in curies, a unit named for Marie Curie. One curie of radioactivity is 3×10^{10} disintegrations per second, the activity of one gram of radium. Inhaling or swallowing just one microcurie of a long-lived radioactive substance leads to 30,000 disintegrations per second inside the body.

The fundamental unit of radiation exposure is the roentgen, a unit suggested by Paul Villard in 1908 and still in use. It is named in honor of Wilhelm Roentgen, the discoverer of X rays.

One roentgen is the amount of X radiation or gamma radiation that liberates 2×10^9 electrons through ionization in a one-centimeter cube of air at standard conditions.

Radiation dose is described by giving the energy absorbed per unit volume of a specified material.

One rad is the amount of ionizing radiation that deposits 100 ergs of energy in each gram of exposed biological tissue.

One can calculate that one milligram of radium distributed through one liter of material will expose the material (water or living tissue) to a dose of about 8 rads per hour of alpha-particle radiation. The energies involved are so low that it would take a dose of 400,000 rads to raise the temperature of the material by one degree centigrade. Harmful doses of radiation are far smaller than those immediately felt by human senses.

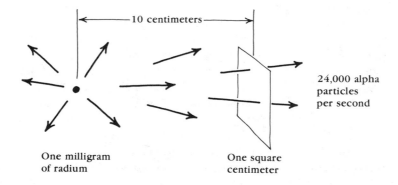

One milligram
of radium

One square
centimeter

24,000 alpha
particles
per second

10 centimeters

For X rays and gamma rays, one roentgen of absorption in air and one rad of dose to body tissue are roughly equivalent throughout the energy range from 0.3 to 3.0 million electron volts. This is the energy range of most gamma radiation from hazardous nuclides in fallout particles and nuclear waste. Thus for many purposes, roentgens and rads may be taken as equivalent.

Equal doses of different radiations may have different biological effects. The dose of fast neutrons to produce a cataract of the eye is perhaps one-eighth as much as the dose of X rays; thus it is said that the neutron radiation has a "relative biological effectiveness" of eight compared to X rays for this effect. For this reason, a second unit for radiation dose is in common use: the rem (for "roentgen equivalent, mammal"). To compute the dose in rems, one must sum the contributions of radiation components of different quality, weighting each component by its relative biological effectiveness. For example, the eight-rad dose from radium becomes an 80-rem dose since alpha particles are typically assigned a relative biological effectiveness of ten.

sues of the body that are most susceptible to radiation damage: the precursor cells of blood that multiply in the bone marrow; the cellular linings of the intestines; and the germ cells of the gonads. Damage to the bone marrow or the gut is the principal cause of death in cases of massive radiation exposure, although very large doses cause failure of the central nervous system. Radiation damage to the gonads may cause sterility but is generally not lethal to the victim. The skin is also a sensitive tissue because the body quickly builds new skin tissue in response to physical injury.

Following a high dose of radiation, symptoms show up in times ranging from minutes to a few weeks. If death does not come within three weeks, the victim is likely to recover. The effects show up as cell death in sensitive tissues: the gut and the bone marrow. The connection between ionization and cell death is not thoroughly understood, but cell death may be due to damage to the genetic material present in every cell.

A high level of radiation exposure would never be experienced except for the human effort to exploit nuclear energy. These exposures occur from nuclear explosions and accidental exposure to manufactured nuclear materials. At low dose levels there is no immediate effect—

no symptoms to warn the victim of danger. The damage may show up as cancer many years later, as birth defects to unborn fetuses, or as altered genes that will be expressed through many generations of progeny.

Acute Radiation Syndromes in Humans

Though great attention has been devoted to the effects of low doses of radiation on human health, it is also important to understand the effects of the large doses that millions of individuals might receive from a nuclear explosion. In the most acute exposures, the casualties are immediate and obvious; at intermediate levels, the consequence is radiation sickness.

Massive whole-body doses of radiation have been experienced in occupations that involve handling of radioactive materials, from willful acts such as nuclear bomb detonations, or from medical uses such as radiation treatment of leukemia. If the acute dose is of sufficient magnitude, the unfortunate individual will develop radiation sickness. The symptoms of radiation sickness fall into three characteristic categories known as the acute radiation syndromes. The bone marrow syndrome (BMS) and the gastrointestinal syndrome (GIS) result from severe damage to the bone marrow and gastrointestinal

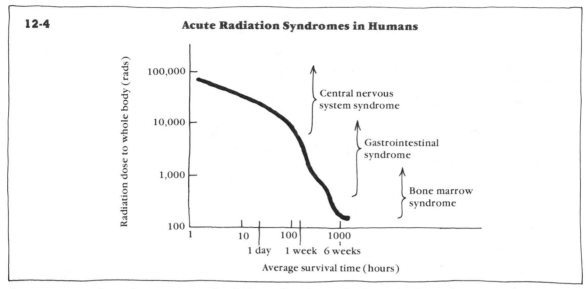

12-4   **Acute Radiation Syndromes in Humans**

A person exposed to a large amount of radiation will suffer acute radiation sickness. A very high dose causes destruction of the central nervous system; with lower doses, death results from damage to the intestines. The lowest fatal doses damage the bone marrow, causing loss of the white blood cells that fight infection.

tract, respectively. A third syndrome, observed for very high doses, results from damage to the central nervous system.[1]

Skin Compared to bone marrow or the gut, the skin is less sensitive to radiation damage. A dose of 1,000 rads will produce skin cancer in most subjects. Even at lesser doses some symptoms of radiation damage to the skin are manifest rather quickly. Skin erythema, or reddening of the skin, can appear in hours and is due to dilation of the capillary blood vessels. Higher doses cause desquamation (peeling or thinning of the skin) due to the inhibition of cell division in the Malpighian layer which normally supplies new skin cells. A later symptom of radiation skin damage is epilation, or hair loss, due to the destruction of hair follicles. If new hair grows, it is usually coarse, dry, and sometimes without color. At still higher doses, thousands of rads, the skin may blister and appear to be burned. If such a dose were received as a whole-body dose, the human patient would be unlikely to survive.

Bone Marrow Possibly the most radiosensitive organ of the body, bone marrow responds quickly to whole-body doses of a hundred rads or more. The bone marrow is a highly proliferative and complicated tissue. It supplies granulocytes, erythrocytes (red blood cells), platelets, and lymphocytes (white cells) to the circulatory system. These four product cells all seem to originate from a common stem cell called the colony forming unit (CFU). If CFUs are killed by radiation, the essential supply of blood cells will gradually disappear as old cells die away and are not replaced.

A whole-body radiation dose of 500 rads will do sufficient damage to the bone marrow to cause the *bone marrow syndrome*. The symptoms of this syndrome arise from the gradual depletion of various blood components. Within the first day or two after the radiation exposure the patient will feel nausea accompanied by vomiting. A sense of malaise often haunts the patient. Following this short period the patient often feels fine for a week or more; two to three weeks after exposure, however, serious symp-

12-5   THE BONE MARROW SYNDROME

Human blood contains several specialized types of cells derived from parent cells in the marrow of bones. Among these arc the red blood cells, necessary for taking up oxygen, and the platelets, which are necessary for wound healing. The white cells which pass through the lymph are needed for fighting infections. Each of the specialized cell types has its own typical lifetime in the body, ranging from less than a day for the white cells to four months for the red cells.

The specialized blood cells all derive from stem cells that proliferate within the bone marrow and are particularly sensitive to radiation damage. External whole-body exposure, or internal radiation exposure from ingested radionuclides, will cause damage to the bone marrow.

A whole-body radiation dose of a few hundred rads is sufficient to inactivate cell production in the bone marrow. Without production of new cells to replace those continually lost in the body, the concentration of vital blood components drops off in a manner determined by their life-

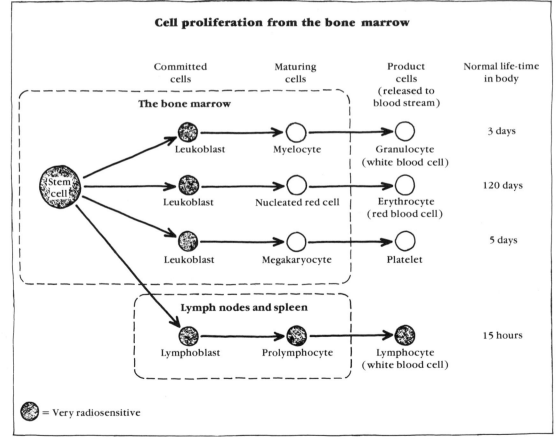

Cell proliferation from the bone marrow

Important cells in the blood are supplied from precursor cells formed in the bone marrow.

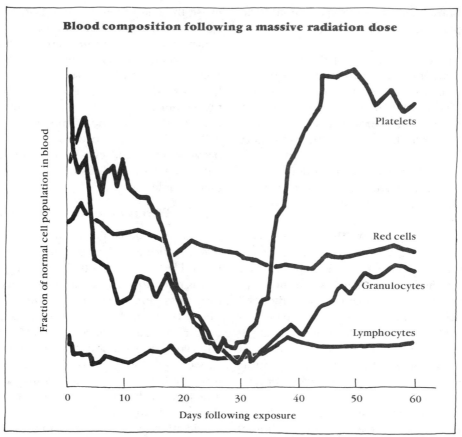

Blood composition following a massive radiation dose

Fraction of normal cell population in blood

Platelets

Red cells

Granulocytes

Lymphocytes

Days following exposure

On June 16, 1958, five persons received radiation doses of about 300 rads in a criticality accident at the Department of Energy Y-12 Plant at Oak Ridge, Tennessee. These curves show the course of blood composition with time, averaged for these five patients.

times and the ability of the marrow to recover partially from damage. The concentration of infection-fighting white cells (granulocytes and lymphocytes) reaches a nadir in about thirty days. If the victim survives past this critical time and escapes infection, recovery will usually follow.

toms set in. Small hemorrhages develop, and bleeding through body orifices commences due to platelet loss—this condition causes anemia. Disorientation and loss of equilibrium are common. Because the immune system is diminished by loss of lymphocytes and granulocytes, the blood may become infected (bacteremia). Death is possible by three to four weeks after the dose.

Treatment for bone marrow syndrome has occasionally been successful. The patient is isolated in a sterile room and transfused regularly with sterile whole blood. If the bone marrow does not show signs of recovery, a bone marrow transplant may be attempted.

Gut The mucosa or lining of the small intestine and duodenum is particularly sensitive to ionizing radiation. A close examination of the mucosa reveals the presence of many villi which are responsible for selective exchange of material between the gut and the circulatory system.

The lining cells of a villus are produced in the crypt of Lieberkuhn and begin moving toward the tip of the villus. As cells leave the crypt they mature, and when they reach the tip of the villus they are sloughed away. The lining cells are always regenerating and have a lifetime on the villus of three to four days. The crypt cells are the site of radiation sensitivity. When the crypt cells are inactivated by radiation, no further cell renewal occurs, and the villus eventually becomes denuded of lining cells. The denuded villus permits *E. coli* bacteria to enter and infect the blood. Hemorrhage and ulcerations appear in the gut and much body fluid drains through the intestine.

Whole-body radiation doses of 500 rads or greater will usually cause massive destruction of the gut, a condition known as the *gastrointestinal syndrome*. The first symptoms of this syndrome appear within three to five days after the dose. The victim will experience nausea, vomiting, loss of appetite (anorexia), and diarrhea of large volumes of fluid and blood. The symptoms have been compared to those of cholera and are treated similarly. Very few radiation victims have survived this disease. Even if the gut managed to recover, the patient would suffer from the bone marrow syndrome and probably die.

Neural Tissue When the whole-body radiation dose approaches thousands of rads, the central nervous system begins to collapse. Little is known about this radiation sickness, but one current theory is that extreme radiation doses cause the loss of nerve action potential by damage of the nerve cell membrane.

Symptoms of *central nervous system syndrome* appear within minutes and include disorientation, vomiting, irritability, hyperactivity, lack of reflex, convulsions, and possible coma. If the victim is conscious after the initial seizure, a sense of apathy and calmness may ensue. Finally, tremors set in, breathing is in gasps, blood pressure rises, and eyes may become deep red with hemorrhage. Death in a few hours is unavoidable.

Effects on Unborn Children

Organisms generally are most sensitive to radiation during embryonic development. Three main classes of effects have been observed: (1) retardation of growth, (2) congenital malformation, and (3) death *in utero* or at birth. The severity of the effect is dependent on dose, dose rate, and the stage of development of the embryo. Exposure of experimental animals to X rays can produce embryonic damage at doses as low as a few rads, but there is little evidence of an effect on the human embryo for doses lower than twenty-five rads.

Radiation effects on the unborn child may be profound if the dose is received during the sensitive period of embryo development. From week two through week nine after conception—the period of major organogenesis, when the relative timing of cell differentiation is crucial—the suppression of mitosis in rapidly dividing primordial cells can give rise to almost any imaginable malformation—teratogenesis, "monster genesis." The defects include skull and brain malformations, growth retardation, blindness, mongolism, and developmental deformities of most body parts.

Radiation exposure of the fetus can damage the central nervous sytem, causing a range of neurophysiological and behavioral abnormalities, such as mental retardation and coordination defects.

12-6   THE GASTROINTESTINAL SYNDROME

The lining of the intestines is particularly sensitive to ionizing radiation. This is because the villi that make up the walls of the gut are continually being renewed through proliferation of the lining cells (in sites called Crypts of Lieberkuhn). The pace of genetic activity is rapid and is easily upset by radiation exposure. After an exposure of 1,000 rads, the production of new lining cells is halted. In a few days the villi become denuded, leading to infection, hemorrhage, ulceration, and the symptoms of the gastrointestinal syndrome.

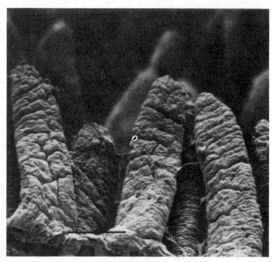

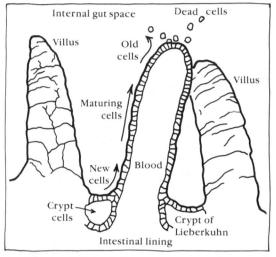

The villi of the normal intestine look like this—finger-like and erect. The subject is a mouse. The drawing shows how cells continuously formed in the Crypts of Lieberkuhn travel toward the tip of each villus to renew the intestinal lining. Surplus cells die and are sloughed off at the tip.

Other Somatic Effects

Little is known about the effects of protracted low-dose exposure of the gonads. Spermatocytes are relatively radio-resistant. Protracted exposures on the order of 100 rads impair fertility; doses in excess of 500 rads may cause sterility. Oocytes, on the other hand, are extremely sensitive to radiation. In studies on primates, 50 percent of the oocytes were killed with doses of five rads delivered during the sensitive period.

The evidence that radiation causes a nonspecific acceleration of aging is unclear. It may speed the onset of various diseases. For example, cataracts of the lens of the eye occur earlier in individuals exposed to radiation.

Physiological effects are also suspected, but with so many damaging agents in our environment, and the range of responses to them and to radiation in a large population, it is impossible to prove associations between radiation exposure and physiological abnormalities, especially at low dose levels. It is noteworthy, however, that many physiological disorders are caused by exposure to ozone and are thought to be related to hydroxyl formation, also a major product in tissues exposed to radiation.

Radiation Damage to DNA

Except for the egg and sperm cells, each biological cell of human tissue contains about five feet of genetic material—the double-stranded biomolecule known as DNA (deoxyribonucleic acid). The two strands are built from sugar-phosphate groups and organic base units known as nucleotides. Phosphate groups alternating with sugar (deoxyribose) molecules form the backbone with the organic bases out to the side. The strands are linked by hydrogen bonds between the bases and are twisted to form a spiral staircase—the well-known "double helix." The base pair in a "step" is either guanine and cytosine, or adenine and thymine. It is known that certain sequences of three bases—there are sixty-four possible combinations—code for the amino acids from which proteins are built.

Within each cell the DNA is organized into large linear structures, the *chromosomes*. Chromosomes in human cells are organized into twenty-three pairs, one chromosome of each pair derived from each parent. The genetic information coded in the chromosomes is divided into units called *genes;* each gene is made up of hundreds of bases—instructions written in the genetic code which specify some product or function.

Soon after the discovery of DNA it was realized that chromosomes and the genes they contain may be the most vulnerable site of radiation damage in cells. The passage of radiation through a cell can break molecular bonds within the cell's DNA. The damage is of three major types: single-strand breaks, double-strand breaks, and base damage. Single-strand breaks include all the variations of damage that result in the loss of continuity of one of the DNA strands, whether or not one or more bases are lost. With more extensive damage, the continuity of both strands can be lost, resulting in double-strand breaks.

Base damage occurs if the backbones of both strands remain intact and one or more bases is altered or lost.

Damage to DNA produces chromosome aberrations that are readily observed. During one portion of the cell life cycle—metaphase—chromosomes condense in the cell nucleus and can be seen clearly under a light microscope. Following irradiation of a cell, one can visually hunt for gross structural damage in the genetic material when the cell enters metaphase. And indeed, breaks and other structural aberrations in the chromosomes are found to correlate with radiation dose. Some commonly observed aberrations include chromosome deletions and rings.

Severe cases of chromosome aberrations usually interfere with cell division, and the cell becomes reproductively dead. If the cell is not reproductively dead, genetic aberrations may be passed to subsequent generations of cells. These inheritable chromosome aberrations, or any alteration of the base sequence, constitute *mutations*.

Cellular DNA repair mechanisms can mitigate the effects of radiation by excising a damaged section of one strand and replicating it using the other strand as a template. Thus the same dose delivered over a longer period of time produces less damage because there is time for DNA repair. Unfortunately, the repair mechanisms themselves can make mistakes and introduce further complications in the damaged DNA.

At low radiation doses, the number of genetic injuries increases nearly linearly with dose. However, with higher doses the increase in genetic injuries becomes quadratic or upward curving. That is, the response is *more than* proportionally greater, presumably because the biological repair system responsible for repairing DNA cannot function effectively at high levels of damage.[2]

The genetic effects of radiation can be classified as *hereditary* or *somatic*. For an effect to be hereditary, the cells of the gonads—the egg or sperm cells or their precursors—must be damaged. Mutations may then be passed on to children of the affected individual. If the damage is limited to the progeny of the affected cells and is confined to the organism in which it arose, the effect is somatic.

For somatic cells of the body, especially those that are dividing (mitotically active), DNA damage can transform the cell so that it no longer responds to the processes that maintain the organization and integrity of the organism. The cell may eventually proliferate without restraint, creating a cancer. Cancers rarely arise in germ cells, presumably because, except during their formation, mitosis does not occur.

Cancer

It is now well accepted that ionizing radiation causes cancer and that those tissues of the body in which cells are undergoing division are particularly sensitive to radiation. Almost invariably, tumors occur at the site of irradiation; thus the correlation between exposure to ionizing radiation and cancer is inescapable. The time that elapses between exposure and appearance of a cancer is called the latent period and ranges from a few years to as long as forty years.

A cancer or neoplasm is the uncontrolled growth and proliferation of a group of cells. The cells of a neoplasm can invade surrounding tissues or, if detached, form other neoplasms elsewhere in the body. Though most cancers arise in tissues—the intestines, the esophagus, the skin—that originate from a particular embryonic tissue (the epithelium), radiation is capable of inducing cancer in nearly all the tissues of the body.

The biochemical causes of cancer and the steps in its development are unknown, but two major steps have been identified: initiation and promotion. Initiation is the series of events leading to lesions in the DNA of a cell. Promotion includes processes in the transformed cell that undermine the regulatory control exerted by adjacent normal cells, as well as by hormonal, immunologic, and other influences.

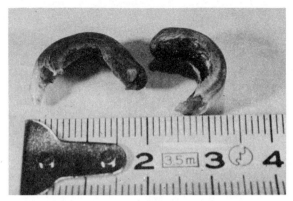

12-7 GENETIC DAMAGE FROM RADIATION
According to Japanese sources, these monstrous fingernails grew successively on the injured finger of a victim of the Hiroshima explosion. Rapidly growing tissues—the developing fetus in particular—are the most sensitive to radiation. The scale is in centimeters.

Both sex and age are important variables in estimating potential risks due to ionizing radiations. The risk of some kinds of cancer is greater after exposure *in utero* and in childhood than in adult life. Females of ages ten to twenty have the highest risk of radiation-induced breast cancer.

Conclusion

Though many of the biological effects of ionizing radiation are firmly established, their mechanisms are elusive and extremely difficult to ascertain. In particular, the enormous span of time between radiation exposure and its ultimate effect make this field of investigation one of the most difficult areas of scientific inquiry. But since we know the biological effects of ionizing radiation can induce mutations, cause disease, and be life-threatening, we should exercise extreme caution in applying this hazardous resource of modern technology.

Suggested Readings

ALPER, T. *Cellular Radiobiology*. New York: Cambridge University Press, 1979. This book successfully combines biology and radiobiology with simple math for a strong mechanism oriented approach.

ANDREWS, H. L. *Radiation Biophysics*. Englewood Cliffs, N. J.: Prentice-Hall, 1974. Very little biology but more physics and math for an encompassing view of physical interactions of radiation and the associated damaging effects. This text is recommended for the advanced reader.

ARENA, V. *Ionizing Radiation and Life*. St. Louis, Mo.: C. V. Mosby Co., 1971. A well-written, fairly simple text which assumes little or no background in biology and physics. This text is recommended for the beginning reader.

HALL, E. J. *Radiobiology for the Radiologist*, 2nd ed. New York: Harper & Row, 1978. A comprehensive text which assumes little math or physics preparation but requires a fair understanding of biology.

NOVIKOFF, A. B., AND E. HOLTZMAN, *Cells and Organelles*. New York: Holt, Rinehart, and Winston, 1976. One of the best, most readable texts on basic cell biology. This book should serve as a beginning point for all further study in radiobiology, since a strong background in cell biology is essential in radiobiology.

SUZIKI, D. T., AND A. J. F. GRIFFITHS, *An Introduction to Genetic Analysis*. San Francisco: W. H. Freeman and Co., 1976. A superb coverage of DNA structure, mitosis, mutation, and all other genetic information.

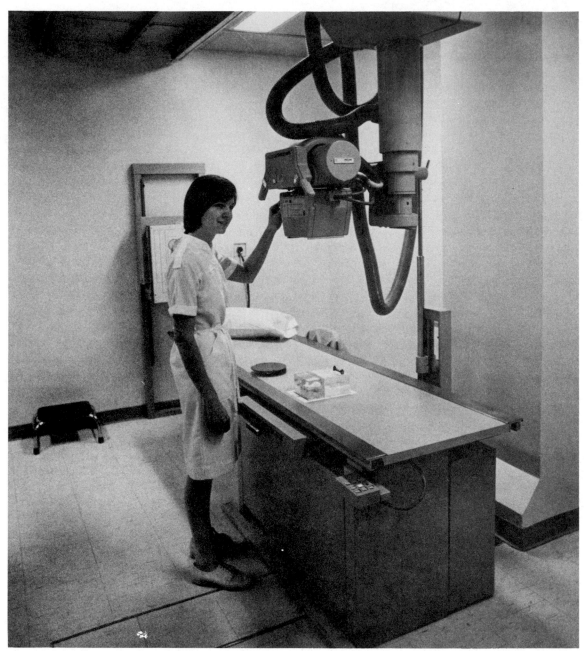

Radiation is a fact of life. In addition to the background radiation from natural sources, mankind has increased human exposure to radiation through exploitation of the earth's resources. The diagnostic use of X rays in medicine makes up the largest source of ionizing radiation exposure to the general public. Exposure to low-level radiation causes some increased incidence of cancer which is expressed years to decades after exposure.

13. Radiation and Public Health: *A Perspective*

Daryl E. Bohning, a physicist with long experience in biomedical and environmental research, presents a review of the natural and man-made sources of radioactivity in the environment. He shows that where we live and what we do strongly influence the amount of radiation we are exposed to.

LIFE AROSE AND MAN EVOLVED in the physical and chemical milieu created on the surface of the earth as it cooled and the atmosphere formed. For at least 100 million years,[1] life on earth has been exposed to a relatively constant background of low-level radiation from extraterrestrial and terrestrial sources determined by the composition of the atmosphere and the distribution of naturally radioactive elements in the earth's crust. Over the last 100 years, however, the ever-expanding appetite of modern society for energy and materials has begun to threaten the stability of this milieu with large-scale redistributions and recombinations of the elements. Mining brings into the human environment the heavy radioactive elements and toxic metals that had settled to the lower strata of the earth's crust before the earth cooled. The refinement and combustion of fossil fuels releases toxic and radioactive materials that are inhaled or ingested, and induces atmospheric changes that affect both our chemical environment and our exposure to radiation from extraterrestrial sources.

With the advent of the atomic age and the birth of the modern chemical industry—both products of World War II—mankind's ability to alter the environment increased dramatically. Today, just forty years later, modern technology is introducing synthetic chemicals and radionuclides into our environment at rates that may surpass our capacity to judge the consequences.

Effects of Radiation Exposure

Here we are concerned not with the massive radiation doses that might occur in an accident or from radioactive fallout, but with the imperceptible low levels of radiation exposure that arise from increased use of radiation and radioactive materials in everyday life. The effects of low-level radiation are not immediately apparent to human senses, yet the consequences may be disastrous to the individual or society. They

Daryl E. Bohning

Bohning served as a staff scientist in the Medical Department of the Brookhaven National Laboratory.

239

include cancer, genetic change (alteration of the genes), and radiation-induced birth defects.

Cancer   The incidence of cancer—the uncontrolled growth and proliferation of a group of cells—is increased by exposure to radiation. Exposure to radiation can induce cancer in nearly all the tissues of the body.

The biochemical causes of cancer and the steps in its development are unknown, but exposure of cell cultures to radiation can produce "transformed" cells. It is believed that the transformation of cultured cells corresponds to the induction of cancer in a living organism.

The immune system maintains the body's biochemical integrity by actively seeking out and removing or destroying foreign substances or organisms that have gained entry to the body. It is the body's first line of defense against transformed cells. Persons whose immune mechanisms are suppressed by drugs have increased risk of cancer.

The immune system is one of the body systems whose normal function is particularly sensitive to radiation; the blood lymphocyte count is a sensitive indicator of radiation exposure in humans. Nearly all lymphoid and bone-marrow cells responsible for rapid replacement of short-lived mature cells cease to divide after an individual is exposed to a large dose of whole-body irradiation. Leukemia (cancerous proliferation of white blood cells) is the first type of cancer to appear in an exposed population.

Inherited Genetic Defects   Mutations are inheritable alterations in the structure of the DNA in a germ cell and are almost always harmful. Such genetic defects can lay dormant, masked by dominant characteristics, to appear in future generations.

Birth Defects   Human abnormalities associated with irradiation of the fetus include: microcephaly, growth retardation, hydrocephaly, microphthalmia, coloboma, chorioretinitis, blindness, strabismus, nystagmus, mongolism, spina bifida, skull malformations, cleft palate, ear abnormalities, deformed hands, clubfeet, hypophalangism, and genital deformities. Microcephaly, particularly, is associated with exposure during early pregnancy. Atomic-bomb data for Hiroshima show that microcephaly was induced by fetal doses of less than ten rem received during the sensitive period and suggest its incidence was also increased for average fetal doses of as little as two rem.

Irradiation of a human fetus can damage the central nervous system, causing a range of neurophysiological and behavioral abnormalities, such as mental retardation and coordination defects. Some are immediately apparent, whereas others find expression later in the life of the individual. Data from primates indicate that readily measurable damage can be caused by doses well below ten rem of acute irradiation applied at sensitive stages.

Natural Background Radiation

Natural background radiation can be separated into that originating from extraterrestrial sources and that originating from the radionuclides, which have been present since the earth was formed, and their decay products. Exposure comes both as external whole-body doses from sources outside of the body and as internal doses from radionuclides that have been inhaled or ingested with water or foodstuffs. The average total dose received from all such sources is roughly 100 millirems (mrem) per year.

Extraterrestrial background radiation includes the high-energy photons, protons, electrons, and nuclear fragments—known as cosmic rays—that strike the earth from the sun and from sources in interstellar space, the cascade of secondary particles they create when they strike the atmosphere, and the small amount of radiation from elements in the atmosphere and soil that they activate. The dose from cosmic radia-

---

13-1 **EARLY CASUALTIES OF RADIATION**

Following Roentgen's discovery of X rays in 1895, physicists around the world began experimenting with this new kind of radiation. The medical potential was quickly exploited—X rays were used in 1896 to locate gunshot pellets in a man's hand. The early workers with X rays were quite casual in their use of the equipment, often exposing their hands to verify that the tube was operating properly. Elihu Thompson, American inventor and industrialist, and a designer of X-ray tubes, conducted ingenious experiments using his own finger as a subject to demonstrate that X rays cause injury, and that the biological effects occur some time after exposure.

During the next several years, doctors who worked extensively with X rays developed cancerous sores and cancer of the bone leading to amputations of fingers and hands. By 1900 there were 170 recorded cases of X-ray injury to people. By 1922 it was estimated that 100 radiologists had died as a result of radiation-induced cancer, including one Mr. Dally, who assisted Thomas Edison in experiments with X rays.

That radioactive material could be hazardous was also discovered through tragic experience. During World War I instrument dials painted with luminescent ma-terial containing radium salts were in great demand to facilitate night-time use. At the U.S. Radium Corporation in Orange, New Jersey, the dial painters would sharpen their brushes using their tongue and lips, swallowing tiny amounts of the radioactive material. One death occurred in 1922, and by 1931 eighteen deaths of former dial painters from various forms of cancer had been attributed to the ingestion of radioactive material.

About this time it became recognized that the unusually high incidence of lung cancer (thirty times the normal level) among mine workers in Czechoslovakia and Germany was probably a consequence of their contact with radioactive material associated with the mined ores. It was from the mines in which these workers toiled that Becquerel and the Curies had obtained pitchblende, the rich uranium ore for their early experiments. We now know that ores containing uranium and thorium emit the radioactive gas radon.

Marie Curie repeatedly exposed herself to radioactive substances, receiving skin burns and eventually dying of radiation-induced cancer. Her daughter, Irene, followed a similar path, choosing a scientific career and succumbing to radiation-induced leukemia.

---

tion gives a uniform whole-body exposure. It varies mainly with altitude because of the shielding provided by the atmosphere, though the earth's magnetic field affects it as well. The dose rate varies from 26 mrem per year at sea level to 107 mrem per year at an altitude of three kilometers, though it is less than 50 mrem per year for 99 percent of the population of the United States.[2] The population-weighted mean dose rate over the entire United States is 30 mrem per year.

Though fourteen radionuclides are produced in the earth's atmosphere and soil cover by cosmic radiation, atmospheric carbon-14 and

13-2　　　　　　　　　　**SOURCES OF RADIATION EXPOSURE**

Source and Exposed Population	Affected Body Tissue	Dose per Individual
Natural background radiation: world population		
Cosmic radiation	whole body	26–107 mrem per year
Internal radiation from natural radionuclides	whole body	25 mrem average per year
Terrestrial sources	whole body	15–140 mrem per year
Technologically enhanced natural radiation (TENR)		
Medical and dental use: patients		
Medical and dental X ray	bone	about 100 mrem average per year
	abdominal	about 70 mrem average per year
	lens of eye	up to 1,660 mrem per whole mouth examination
Radiotherapy	tumors in various organs	as high as 1,000s of rem per treatment
Coal-fired power plants (fly ash): nearby residents	lung	7–15 mrem per year
	bone	8–62 mrem per year
Phosphate rock		
Fertilizer: residents in farm areas	lung and bone	about 2,500 curies distributed in one year
Processing plants: nearby residents	lung	up to 85–740 mrem per year
	bone	up to 110–540 mrem per year
	kidney	up to 1,800 mrem per year
Construction materials (concrete, wallboard)	whole body	estimated at 80 mrem per year
Natural gas (cooking and unvented heaters): users	bronchial epithelium	6–22 mrem per year
Water supplies (release of radon): domestic use	stomach	250 mrem per year
	bronchial epithelium	800 mrem per year

Radiation exposure to persons in the United States from various sources. Accidental exposures are not included. The unit of dose is the rem (roentgen equivalent, mammal), which is a measure of the damage to human tissue by radiation. One mrem (millirem) is one one-thousandth of a rem.

tritium (H-3, the heaviest isotope of hydrogen) are the most important because they are in equilibrium throughout the biosphere and are incorporated directly into the DNA of living organisms. Only the radioactive carbon (C-14) presently causes any significant exposure—about 0.7 mrem per year—but both C-14 and H-3 are increasing as a result of nuclear explosions and contributions from the nuclear power industry. The radioisotopes beryllium-7 (Be-7) and sodium-22 (Na-22) produced by neutron-capture reactions in both atmosphere and soil cover also contribute, but the amounts are very small.

Terrestrial background radiation from primordial radionuclides and their decay products varies geographically with the local concentration

13-2   **SOURCES OF RADIATION EXPOSURE (continued)**

Source and Exposed Population	Affected Body Tissue	Dose per Individual
Consumer products: users		
Radioluminous wristwatch	gonads	1–3 mrem per year
Television receivers (X ray)	gonads	0.3–1 mrem per year
Cigarette smoking	bronchial epithelium	local dose as high as 8 rem per year
Commercial air travel (excess		
cosmic radiation): passengers	whole body	0.2 mrem per hour
Nuclear industry		
Uranium mines: nearby residents	lung	200 mrem per year
Reactors and materials plants (normal operation): nearby residents	lung	less than 10 mrem per year
Atmospheric weapons tests: world population	bone, gonads	4–5 mrem per year
Occupational exposure		
Uranium miners	lung	25 rem per year
Nuclear industry workers	whole body	25,000–42,000 rem spread over 93,000 workers in 1976
Nuclear submarine personnel	whole body	about 8,000 rem spread over 36,500 personnel in 1977
Airline crews	whole body	160 mrem per year
Medical X-ray personnel	whole body	320 mrem average in 1968
Dental X-ray personnel	whole body	50 mrem average; 5,200 mrem maximum in 1975

of naturally occurring radionuclides in the soil and the extent to which they leach into water supplies. In general, igneous rocks have more radioactivity than sedimentary rocks, though certain sedimentary rocks, especially shales and phosphate-bearing rocks, are highly radioactive. Metamorphic rocks have radionuclide concentrations representative of the sedimentary rocks from which they were formed.

Twenty-four naturally occurring radionuclides have been identified, though only potassium-40 (K-40), rubidium-87 (Rb-87), and the decay series of uranium (U-238) and thorium (Th-232) are believed to cause significant exposure. The activity concentration of the third naturally occurring radioactive series, U-235, is only 5 percent that of the U-238 series.

Potassium-40 is the main naturally occurring source of internal radiation, providing about 69 percent of the average whole-body dose of 25 mrem per year; rubidium-87 (Rb-87) and two radionuclides in the U-238 decay series, polonium-210 (Po-210) and radon-222 (Rn-222), provide most of the rest.

External irradiation from naturally occurring terrestrial sources, for the most part whole-body exposure to gamma rays, averages about 55 mrem per year—potassium-40 (K-40), the U-238 series, and the Th-232 series contribute 17, 13, and 25 mrem per year, respectively. Doses range from 15 to 35 mrem per year on the Atlantic and gulf coastal plains, 35 to 75 mrem per year in the northeastern, central, and far western portions of the country, and 75 to

140 mrem per year on the Colorado plateau. The population-weighted mean over the entire United States is 40 mrem per year.

Technologically Enhanced Natural Radiation

Many human activities, either directly or indirectly, increase human exposure to natural sources of radiation, even though they are not expressly designed to produce radiation. To distinguish these exposures from our common background exposures, Gesell and Pritchard coined the term "technologically enhanced natural radiation" (TENR).[3] Examples are medical irradiation, proximity to coal and oil-fired power plants, contact with phosphate products and byproducts, exposure to radon-222 (Rn-222) in natural gas and domestic water supplies, the use of construction materials incorporating high concentrations of radionuclides, and even air travel and the use of certain consumer products.

Medical Irradiation Diagnostic procedures in the medical profession are now recognized as the major source of public exposure to radiation; diagnostic radiology (X-rays) alone accounts for at least 90 percent of the total dose from manmade radiation, and at least 35 percent of the dose from all radiation sources. Though bone marrow doses range from about 10 mrem for a chest X-ray to over 1 rem for a barium swallow, the Environmental Protection Agency (EPA)[4] estimated that the average bone marrow dose rate from medical X-rays for the adult U.S. population was 83 mrem per year in 1964—77 percent from medical radiographic procedures (X-rays), 20 percent from fluoroscopic examinations, and 3 percent from dental examinations. By 1970 this had increased 23 percent to 103 mrem per year. Collective abdominal dose was estimated to be on the order of 15 million person-rem per year in the United States alone.

Though the doses from dental X-rays are usually considered to be small, the accompanying dose to the lens of the eye has been measured to be as high as 84 mrem for the two-film technique and 1.66 rem for the whole-mouth examination.[5] As with many other radiographic procedures, though improved films and equipment have tended to reduce exposures, this has usually been more than offset by the increased number of procedures done. Interestingly, there are only 11.2 annual dental X-ray visits per hundred people for those with only a grade-school education, jumping to 50.3 for people with thirteen or more years of education.

Except for thyroid scans, which give doses of 100,000 mrem, diagnostic nuclear medicine procedures using radiopharmaceuticals cause individual exposures of hundreds to thousands of mrem per administration. Because fewer people are involved, these contribute only about 20 percent of the total radiological dose. However, the use of radiopharmaceuticals increased five-fold from 1960 to 1970 and was predicted to increase another sevenfold between 1970 and 1980, to reach 3.3 million person-rem per year. About 90 percent of the reported radiopharmaceutical procedures involve five organ systems: specifically, 24.1, 20.3, 18.1, 16.5, 10.9, 3.2, and 2.5 percent of the procedures involve brain, liver, bone, lung, thyroid, kidney, and heart, respectively. The majority of the radiopharmaceuticals, 81 percent, incorporated technetium-99m (Tc-99m) as the labeling radioisotope; an additional 15 percent of the procedures used iodine-131 (I-131), xenon-133 (Xe-133), gallium-67 (Ga-67), and iodine-123, in that order. A pilot study conducted in 1975[6] indicated an average annual growth rate in the application of nuclear medicine procedures of 17 percent, and an increase in the average whole-body and gonad radiation doses for each radiopharmaceutical administration in 1975 compared with 1966.

Radiotherapy imposes the largest individual

radiation doses—in some cases, thousands of rem—to localized tumors. Though past abuses of such treatment are responsible for much of our epidemiological data on the effects of radiation, relatively small numbers of patients with very serious disease, usually cancer, are treated this way today. Hence, radiotherapy is not considered to be a significant source of public exposure to radiation. Nevertheless, the hazards as well as the benefits of its use should be considered carefully to avoid tragedies similar to those that occurred in the past.

In 1964, in an attempt to provide a standard for comparing and monitoring doses from medical procedures, the U.S. Bureau of Radiological Health introduced the "genetically significant dose" (GSD). However, the value of the GSD is limited because the gonads are not the only sensitive organ, are rarely the target organ, and genetic effects are now felt to be less important than somatic effects. The focus has shifted to the dose to target and/or sensitive organs. Unfortunately, this precludes any single measure of individual cumulative dose for general monitoring purposes and complicates comparisons of relative risks. In addition, dose estimates made in phantoms (dummy persons used to measure radiation doses) only approximate actual doses in living persons, and control of administered radiation varies widely, often being very crude. Finally, people to whom radiopharmaceuticals have been administered can be sources of exposure to others, especially family members, and it is almost impossible to estimate the public exposure and environmental contamination from radiopharmaceuticals released during the manufacturing process or from patients and medical facilities.

Industrial Products In 1977 the United States had 1,200 coal-fired electric power plants consuming 480 million metric tons of coal; 5 to 10 percent of this tonnage is left as ash, the highest percentage of any fuel. The atmospheric release of the gaseous and flue-stream-particulate (fly-ash) combustion products and the accumulation of slag (furnace bottom-ash) at sites where human exposures can occur are sources of TENR, in this case, 290 curies of U-238 and 250 curies of Th-232 along with their decay products, especially the alpha-emitters: lead-210 (Pb-210), and Th-232 and Th-228, respectively. Particulate emissions are of primary concern. Estimated doses to individuals living in the proximity of a typical coal-fired power plant range from 7 to 15 mrem per year for the lung, and 8 to 62 mrem per year to the bone, depending on plant siting.[7] Collective human exposure is on the order of 6,000 person-rad per year to the bone, and 2,000 person-rad per year to the lung.[8] The U.S. Department of Energy has estimated that by the year 2000, coal consumption will have more than doubled, and that as we shift to the low-heat, high-uranium-content Western coal, public exposure will increase further. Though stack-emitted radon is not an immediate problem because it is dispersed in the atmosphere, radon continues to emanate from collections of slag and fly-ash for thousands of years after the coal has been burned. Significantly, the TENR from a comparable oil-fired power plant is approximately 100 times less.

In 1973, 130 million tons of phosphate rock, containing high concentrations of U-238 series radionuclides, was mined in the United States.[9] In its conversion to marketable ore, half of which went into the production of phosphate fertilizers, 92 million tons of waste slime and sand was discarded; the slime and marketable ore have the highest concentrations of radionuclides. Though individual doses are generally very small, the widespread agricultural use of phosphate fertilizers exposes large numbers of people to U-238 and its decay products—through radioactive elements taken up by food crops or entering water supplies via runoff. In farming areas, individuals receive additional exposure from fertilizer in the soil and from the inhala-

13-3   THE RADIOACTIVE DAUGHTERS OF RADON

The heaviest of the 92 elements are generally radioactive with very long half-lives. Most are emitters of alpha particles which leave a short track of dense ionization as they decay in living tissue. Thus many of these elements pose a serious risk of cancer if ingested or inhaled. The decay of one heavy nuclide yields another nuclide, which is a little lighter and usually also radioactive. Four series of nuclides are defined by such chains of decay, and three of these series involve the naturally occurring nuclides thorium-232 (Th-232), uranium-235 (U-235), and uranium-238 (U-238). In each of these chains of decay there occurs an isotope of the heaviest noble gas—radon. These are of special concern because radon, being an inert gas, readily diffuses through soils and groundwater into our environment, and because the "radon daughters," the radioactive products of radon decay, are mostly alpha-emitters with short half-lives.

The radons of the Th-232 and U-235 series have half-lives so short that they usually transmute into nongaseous nuclides before escaping from the materials in which they are formed. But the U-238 radon, radon-222 (Rn-222), has a half-life of 3.8 days, and once it decays, a complex set of decay events follows in periods from minutes to years. The radioactive daughter nuclides that may be formed include:

Nuclide	Radiation	Half-life
Radon-222	alpha	3.8 days
Polonium-218	alpha	3.05 minutes
Lead-214	beta	26.8 minutes
Bismuth-214	alpha	19.7 minutes
Polonium-214	alpha	1.6×10^{-4} seconds
Polonium-210	alpha	138 days

Radon-222 reaches significant concentrations in human environments, especially in closed structures into which it has seeped from building materials or water supplies. Generated by almost every kind of mining waste, radon and its daughters are major contributors to indoor air pollution. Attached to airborne particles, the radon daughters are inhaled and deposited in the lung, resulting in massive local doses of radiation to the bronchial epithelium of building occupants. The U.S. Environmental Protection Agency has estimated that 10,000 more people would die each year of lung cancers due to inhalation of radon daughters if indoor air changes were reduced from one per hour to one per two hours.

tion of windblown particulate phosphate. Roughly 2,500 curies of U-238, Th-230, and radium-226 (Ra-226) were dispersed with the 4.7 million metric tons of phosphate fertilizer used in the United States in 1974, causing an estimated 1,500 person-rad of radiation dose to people.

The EPA[10] estimates that individuals living 700 meters from a model phosphoric acid plant receive doses as high as 85 mrem per year to the lung and 110 mrem per year to the bone, mostly from Rn-222 daughters. Doses from both particles and Rn-222 daughters for individuals living near an ore drying and grinding facility would be 54 mrem per year for lung and 79 mrem per year for bone. Dose estimates run as high as 1,800 mrem per year for kidney, 740 mrem per year for lung, and 540 mrem per year for bone for individuals living near elemental phosphorus plants.

A similar amount of potash fertilizer used in 1973 contained on the order of 3,200 curies of potassium-40, but because body uptake of potassium is homeostatically controlled and this is a small fraction of natural potassium-40, this is not considered to be a problem.

Construction materials incorporating radionuclide-rich wastes provide further human exposure from phosphorus and coal exploitation. By-product gypsum from the phosphate industry has been used in wallboard, and coal combustion fly-ash is used in making concrete. Estimates of individual average whole-body dose from fly-ash in concrete is 80 mrem per year but would be as high as 400 mrem per year if the Western coal with the highest uranium content is used.[11] Most of the dose comes from inhalation of accumulated radon daughters.

Doses to bronchial epithelium due to radon daughters from Rn-222 in natural gas burned in cooking ranges and unvented heaters are 6 to 9 mrem and 22 mrem per year, respectively.[12] Radon-222 in domestic water supplies can contribute even greater amounts. Regularly drinking water containing the recommended maximum permissible concentration of Rn-222, which is 2,000 picocuries per liter, would irradiate the stomach at the rate of 250 mrem per year; and Rn-222 released from the same water used domestically would give a dose of 800 mrem per year to the bronchial epithelium. In a sampling of U.S. water supplies in areas where radionuclides are relatively abundant, 25 percent exceeded the recommended maximum permissible concentration; in the Northeast the fraction is even higher—56 percent.

Though the doses are small, passengers of aircraft receive increased exposure to cosmic radiation because of the reduction in atmospheric shielding. On a subsonic flight at an average altitude of 9.47 km over U.S. latitudes, the dose rate is about 0.2 mrem/hour. At the altitudes flown by the supersonic Concorde, about 15 km, the passenger dose rate for similar latitudes would be about twice as high.

A large and growing number of consumer and industrial products incorporate radionuclides: (1) radioluminous products, (2) electronic and electrical devices, (3) antistatic devices, (4) smoke detectors, (5) ceramic, glassware, alloys, and other products containing uranium or thorium, and (6) other devices, including scientific instruments. However, judicious choice of nuclides and design improvements have significantly reduced hazards of early devices, and public exposure is not perceived to be a problem. The major contributors are radioluminous timepieces and television sets: 1 to 3 mrem per year to the gonads from a radioluminous wristwatch, 9 mrem per year wholebody from a radioluminous clock, and 0.3 and 1 mrem per year to the gonads for females and males, respectively, from a television set. Though these doses are small, because of the quantities produced and the numbers exposed, the use and disposal of such products should be monitored.

Surprisingly, cigarettes are the consumer product that causes the greatest exposures to TENR. Cigarette smoking causes uptake of lead (Pb-210) and polonium (Po-210), both volatile contaminants of tobacco. It has been estimated that areas of the bronchial epithelium of smokers' lungs receive doses as high as 8,000 mrem per year, 70 percent from the alpha emitter polonium-210.

Nuclear Industry

Nuclear industry, whether power or weapons related, depends on uranium mining and milling, fuel enrichment, and fuel processing; the materials must be transported between facilities, and wastes must be dealt with. At this level, they are one and the same industry, though exact fuel enrichment and processing specifications differ. The main difference with regard to public health effects is the way in which the radiation is released. For power production, the concern is over routine and accidental releases of even minute fractions of the billions of curies of activity contained within an operating reactor. In the case of weapons, the concern centers around public exposure in the case of accidental destruction of a device and the immediate and the long-term (fallout) irradiation resulting from the intentional detonation of a device, whatever the intent.

Public exposure from the several hundred uranium mines in the United States is small, but these mines employ about 5,000 men, who are all at extremely high risk of dying of lung cancer.[13] Some data indicate that uranium miners receive average annual lung exposures from radon daughters as high as 25 rems, five times higher than earlier estimates.[14]

Though it is estimated that individuals living at the boundary of a uranium mill would receive a lung dose of 2000 mrem per year just from inhaling routine effluents,[15] tailings (ore residues) around uranium milling facilities are the major problem. At present, there are 27 million tons of uranium mine tailings at twenty-four inactive sites, and another 113 million tons have accumulated at twenty-one active sites. It is estimated that there may be a billion tons of uranium waste tailings by the year 2000[16] which would become the dominant contributor to radiation exposure from the nuclear fuel cycle.

Gaseous diffusion technology is used to enrich the fuel from about 0.7 to about 4 percent for use in light-water reactors, to about 90 percent for use in high-temperature gas-cooled reactors, and up to 97 percent for weapons. There are three such enrichment facilities owned by the U.S. government and operated under contract with private industry. Though there is no evidence for significant routine release of activity, the material that would be released should containment fail is gaseous uranium fluoride at high temperature and under pressure.

In fuel fabrication, the uranium fluoride is converted to uranium dioxide powder, and it is then pelletized, sintered, and loaded into stainless steel or zircaloy tubing which is capped and welded into fuel rods. These completed fuel rods are assembled into the fuel element arrays installed in the reactor core. The work is done by the same four companies that sell nuclear power reactors. As is the case for the enrichment plants, routine releases are not felt to be a problem. The maximum lung dose to an individual at the plant boundary is only about 10 mrem per year.[17]

In a uranium-fueled reactor, only a few hundred curies of material, in the form of U-234, U-235, and U-238, is natural activity extracted from the earth; the vast majority, about 15 billion curies, is induced. This activity is usually well controlled, and so direct exposure is not significant except for reactor workers exposed during repairs, accidents, and decontamination procedures. Exposures to the general public come primarily from routine and accidental discharges of radionuclides, and proximity to spent fuel. In operation, such a plant discharges 5 billion curies of spent fuel each year, though most of the activity is in the form of short-lived isotopes. Even so, the spent fuel discharged each year retains a radioactivity of 100 million curies six months after its removal from the reactor.[18]

Three radionuclides are of significance from the standpoint of routine operation of nuclear power plants: tritium (H-3), carbon-14 (C-14), and krypton-85 (Kr-85)—all are difficult to remove from waste streams and confine. Iodine-131 (I-131) is also of concern but appears to be adequately controlled by current techniques. Typical amounts escaping yearly from a 1,000 megawatt light-water reactor power plant are:

tritium (H-3)	100 to 1,000 curies
krypton-85 and xenon-133	300 to 50,000 curies
iodine-128 and iodine-131	0.01 to 0.03 curies
carbon-14	8 curies

In 1981, there were seventy-five civilian nuclear power reactors operating in twenty-six states, having a combined electrical generating capacity of 57,000 megawatts, and almost seventy research reactors with capacities ranging up to 50 megawatts of thermal energy.

In the case of a major reactor accident, strontium-90 (Sr-90) with a half-life of twenty-eight years and cesium-137 (Cs-137) with a half-life of thirty years would have the most potential for public harm. The typical 1,000 megawatt light-water reactor contains 7.8 million curies of Sr-90 and 9.9 million curies of Cs-137.

There is some public exposure when materials such as fuel wastes are transported between facilities, but this is estimated at only three person-rem per year for each reactor. Those actually involved in the transport—approximately 200 people per reactor—receive doses of several hundred mrems per year. The real danger is of an accident. Though no releases from nuclear power shipments have been reported, there have been about 100 accidents over the past twenty-five years in which medical and industrial radiochemicals have been released.

Disposal of wastes from the nuclear power cycle, principally because of its long-lived constituents—cesium (Cs-137), strontium-90 (Sr-90), plutonium-238 (Pu-238), and plutonium-239—has become a major argument against nuclear power because there is no agreement on a long-term solution to the problem (see chapter 14). High-level waste, generated when the uranium and plutonium are extracted in fuel reprocessing, contains more than 90 percent of fission product and other actinide activity in the fuel. In 1978, there were about 75 million gallons and about 1,300 million curies of liquid sludge, salt cake, and other forms of high-level waste awaiting disposal at government facilities,[19] and this is growing at the rate of about 2.7 million gallons per year. There were also about 5,200 metric tons of spent fuel assemblies stored around the country, estimated to contain 2.5 to 3.0 billion curies of activity. Using projection of future nuclear generating capacity, it is estimated that there will be 89,000 metric tons of spent fuel assemblies by the year 2000.

High-level wastes are encapsulated and then disposed of on or under the seabed or in "stable" geological formations such as natural caverns or abandoned mines. In practice, containment vessels eventually leak, and natural water circulation in the ocean or in underground disposal sites could carry the materials away from their repositories and into the biosphere. At the Department of Energy Hanford facility at Richland, Washington, over 430,000 gallons of high-level wastes have leaked into the environment.

The tailings from uranium mills are one example of low-level solid waste. As was pointed out earlier, it is projected that there will be a billion tons of such nuclear wastes by the year 2000. Exposure to the radon daughters emanating from them can irradiate the lung at the rate of 14 rem per year. To prevent the wastes from being spread by the wind, they are often covered with water to form huge storage "ponds," but it has been reported that 30 percent of the ponded liquids seep from the pond into surface and ground water.[20]

The largest public dose associated with nuclear weapons and peaceful uses of nuclear devices is from the fallout of atmospheric nuclear tests conducted by the United States from 1945 to 1962 and by other countries during and since that time, and to a much lesser extent from U.S. underground testing from 1961 to the present.[21] Between 1945 and 1978, there have been about 905 nuclear explosions, 95 percent of them occurring between 1954 and 1962.[22] The total explosive yield of these tests was at least 366

13-4   HAZARDS OF PLUTONIUM

Experiments with animals show that plutonium is toxic: a fraction of a milligram causes lung cancer in beagle dogs. John Gofman, a physician at the University of California Division of Medical Physics, has extrapolated from the data on beagles to estimate the possible effects plutonium would have on humans. He argues that 5.2 micrograms of plutonium will cause one lung cancer, whether it is distributed among 100 people or 10; ingesting 0.52 micrograms of plutonium will be lethal to one out of 10 persons, whereas 0.052 micrograms will kill one person in 100. (In humans, the effects of cigarette smoking must be also considered since smokers are much more susceptible than others.) Dr. Gofman estimates that 116,000 lung cancers (a few percent of all lung cancers) have developed as a result of the 400 kilograms (880 pounds) of plutonium-239 (Pu-239) deposited on the United States as fallout from nuclear test explosions. Other experts believe the results of these calculations exaggerate the dangers.

In 1976, the U.S. Transuranium Registry in Richland, Washington, identified 5,800 workers whose jobs expose them to plutonium and other transuranics and is now following their medical histories. From autopsies performed on thirty of the workers who had died, Dr. Sidney M. Wolfe, of the Public Citizens Health Research Group, observed that the incidence of cancer or leukemia was almost twice that to be expected. Yet in all but one of these deaths, the persons retained less than the maximum permitted body burden of plutonium (40 nanocuries).

Twenty-five workers at the Rocky Flats weapons facility are known to have inhaled more than the maximum permissible lung burden of 0.016 microcuries at a plutonium fire on October 15, 1965. As of 1974, none of these individuals had developed lung cancer; however, the latent period is greater than the nine years between 1965 and 1974, and could be many decades.

In one case, a machinist working with plutonium retained less than 0.1 microgram of Pu-239 in a puncture wound of the hand. A physician removed a lesion at the site; the damage showed "similarity to known precancerous epidermal cytologic changes, [which] raised the question of the ultimate fate of such a lesion should it be allowed to exist without surgical intervention. . . ." The doctor judged the "cause and effect relationship [of the plutonium and the tissue changes] obvious."

Another case is that of Mr. Edward Gleason, who unloaded, rotated, and reloaded a shipping crate that contained a leaking container of plutonium-239 solution. He subsequently developed an extremely rare cancer which began in his palm and ultimately caused his death.

megatons (TNT equivalent). Of this figure, 72 megatons were from underground tests, so more than 294 megatons of detonations contributed fallout particles to the atmosphere. Some test explosions depended on fission using U-235 and Pu-239; others used fission and fusion—fusion of deuterium (H-2) and tritium (H-3), most of the tritium being supplied by fission from lithium-6. The fission component was 172 megatons; the fusion component, producing larger quantities of carbon-14 and tritium, was 122 megatons.

The major contributors to radiation from fallout are a number of short-lived isotopes, including iodine-131, and the long-lived isotopes—cesium-137, strontium-90, tritium, C-14, and various isotopes of plutonium; the largest dose is from Cs-137. Between 1945 and 1972 the amounts produced by weapons tests were:

cesium-137	27 megacuries
strontium-90	17 megacuries
tritium (H-3)	4500 megacuries
carbon-14	5.8 megacuries
plutonium-239	0.4 megacuries
krypton-85	3 megacuries
iron-55	50 megacuries
iodine-131	180 megacuries

Exposures from the short-lived isotopes cease after a few months, but the others persist in the environment, are inhaled and ingested, and irradiate people throughout their lives. Individual integrated doses to the sensitive bone-lining cells is estimated at 290 mrad; the dose to the lung is estimated to be 260 mrad. The BEIR-III report estimates the total whole-body dose from atmospheric weapons tests to be only 4 to 5 mrem per year. Such numbers may not adequately represent the hazards; for example, the inhalation of particles of alpha-emitting Pu-239, with a half-life of 24,390 years produce massive local doses to the lung.

The total annual whole-body dose to the U.S. population from global fallout has gradually increased since 1969 and is predicted to reach 1.6 million person-rem by the year 2000. However, this is only about 5 mrem per person and is not up to the level in 1963, just after the atmospheric test ban treaty. In spite of the fact that actual fallout deposition is decreasing, 92,000 curies of strontium-90 fell on the earth in 1975, thirteen years after major atmospheric testing ceased.

The United States has approximately 30,000 nuclear warheads with a combined explosive power of at least 3,500 megatons of TNT, more than ten times the 294 megatons exploded to date, and from which fallout still persists.

Public Health Effects of Radiation

Now that we understand some of the consequences of exposure to radiation and have gained some awareness of the pervasiveness of sources of exposure in our environment, how do we measure the ultimate impact of the uses and abuses of radiation on the health of our society?

Since it is believed that almost all of these consequences can arise naturally, as well as be induced by exposure to chemicals, what fraction is attributable to our exposure to radiation? In an attempt to determine this fraction, epidemiologists compare health data on groups of people who are similar except in their exposure to radiation and estimate the relative incidence of, say, lung cancer. By means of such studies, they attempt to construct a dose-response function giving the probability, for a given lung dose, of getting lung cancer; alternatively, if the lungs of one million people received a given dose, the number that would be expected to contract lung cancer as a result is estimated.

However, at the few hundred mrem level relevant to public exposure and of concern because of the large number of people involved, radiation-induced effects merge into a statistical sea of identical effects induced by other biologically malignant substances and influences. A study population large enough to give statistically significant results would require half the people in the United States and would include so many confounding factors that the study might still not be definitive.

Consequently, a function fitting the data points available at higher doses is extrapolated down to low dose levels. Unfortunately, several plausible functions fit the data points equally well yet have quite different behavior at low doses, with predictions differing by orders of magnitude. The still-contested consensus is that the function that best matches the points in the range over which data are available should be extrapolated linearly to zero. The BEIR-III committee, however, used a quadratic function

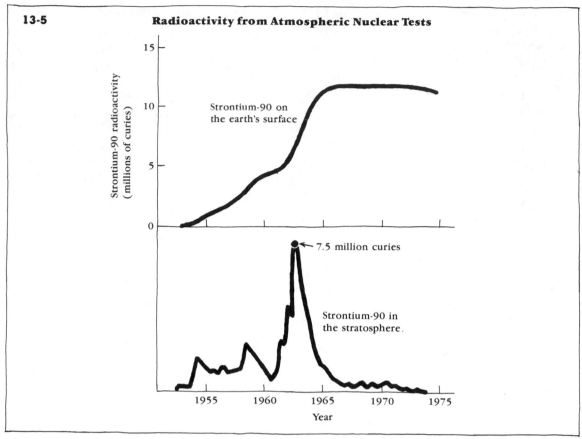

13-5

Radioactivity from Atmospheric Nuclear Tests

Although the testing of nuclear explosives in the atmosphere has remained far below the level it reached in 1962–63, the legacy of those years remains in the radioactive isotopes distributed evenly over the Northern Hemisphere. Much of the strontium-90 has left the atmosphere, but it remains in the topsoils of the earth—a source of radiation that will diminish by half only with the passing of each thirty years. Cesium-137 is present in slightly greater amounts and has a similar lifetime, but it is not as biologically damaging as strontium-90.

which gives lower estimates of cancer incidence, believing it was justified by available data and on theoretical grounds.

The principal data are from the Japanese citizens exposed in the atomic bomb attacks on Hiroshima and Nagasaki; medical patients, such as those with ankylosing spondilitis who were therapeutically exposed to radiation; and various occupationally exposed populations, such as radiologists, uranium miners, and the radium-dial painters. For the low to moderate doses (10 to 50 rads) critical for extrapolation to very low doses, however, estimates of effects rely almost entirely on the Hiroshima and Nagasaki bomb data.

The BEIR-III committee concluded that cancer was the major somatic effect of low doses of ionizing radiation. Though the natural incidence of cancer varies over several orders of magnitude, depending on the type and site of origin of the neoplasm, age, sex, and other factors, the major sites of solid cancers induced by whole-body irradiation are the breast in women, the thyroid, the lung, and some digestive organs.

With the exception of excess leukemia which has a latent period of two years and an expression period from two to thirty years after irradiation, and excess bone cancer from Rn-224 exposure which has a latent period of four years and an expression time from four to thirty years after irradiation, the excess cancer risk for virtually all other types of cancer arising from radiation exposure remains well beyond thirty years. Some types of cancers may not even appear until twenty or more years after exposure.

Because the major data set—the citizens of Hiroshima and Nagasaki—has been followed for only thirty-six years, many cancers are just beginning to appear, and lifetime incidence estimates require a projection of their future appearance. Two projection models are used: the absolute-risk model assumes that cancers will appear at a fixed rate during the expression period, and the relative-risk model assumes they will appear at a rate proportional to the "natural" appearance rate. In general, persons irradiated at higher ages have a greater risk of cancer than those irradiated at lower ages, or, at least, they develop cancer sooner, implying that some form of relative risk model should be used. R. Peto and co-workers feel that it is the rate at which somatic mutations are generated that determines both the rate of aging and the age-specific incidence of cancer![23]

The incidence of radiation-induced cancers is approximately the same in the two sexes except for breast cancer, which occurs almost exclusively in women, and thyroid cancer, which is three times more likely to occur in women. Based on the linear-quadratic dose-response function, the BEIR-III committee estimated that from a single whole-body absorbed dose of 10 rads, 766 to 2,255 people out of a million exposed would die of cancer. For continuous lifetime exposure to one rad per year, the estimates range from 4,751 to 11,970 deaths. The higher estimates in both cases are from the relative-risk projection. Normally, about 167,000 people in a population of a million will die of cancer.

Aware that even nonfatal cancers cause major psychological, social, and financial cost to the individual, E. P. Radford estimated the lifetime risk of developing cancer by adjusting BEIR-III estimates for the killing of transformed cells at high dose rates, and extrapolating linearly.[24] He found the risk per rad for a million persons exposed to be 260 to 880 excess cancers for men and 550 to 1620 for women, that is, roughly 1 in 1,000—approximately five times higher than the estimates of the BEIR-III committee. A lifetime of exposure at the rate of only 0.1 rad per year would result in 1,600 to 3,900 cases in males, and 3,100 to 18,500 in females.

Astoundingly, it has been discovered, about thirty-six years after the bombs exploded, that the exposures in both Japanese cities were almost entirely due to gamma irradiation rather than mixtures of neutrons and gamma rays as calculated earlier. Consequently, past quantitative estimates of dose-response are incorrect. The new dosimetry indicates that the risks of cancer mortality are two to three times higher than previously estimated, and the risk of cancer induction per rad more like two persons in a thousand. In addition, key data for estimating the biological effectiveness of neutrons relative to gamma rays have been nullified.

For susceptible individuals, these estimates must be increased further. Four human genotypes associated with the inherited diseases of ataxia telangiectasia, Fanconi's anemia, Bloom's syndrome, and one form of retinoblastoma are characterized by high risks of "spontaneous" cancer thought to be due to DNA repair deficiencies. Though a similar increase in the risk of cancer induction by radiation has not been demonstrated for these diseases, the first three are abnormally sensitive to radiation-induced chromosomal aberrations. Conversely, individuals with another genetic disorder, xeroderma pigmentosum, characterized by an inability to repair ultraviolet-light-induced DNA damage, do show an abnormally high rate of cancer induction.[25]

There are 736 known diseases and abnormalities, each caused by a single dominant mutation—and another 753 are suspected—affecting roughly 1 percent of people born.[26] Since genetic effects take generations for expression, and given the inadequate follow-up and uncertain exposure in the few cases involving humans, estimates of radiation-induced gene mutation are based almost entirely on animal studies.

In the first generation, BEIR-III estimates that one rem of parental exposure throughout the general population will result in an increase of 5 to 75 additional serious genetic disorders per million live-born offspring. Such an exposure of one rem received in each generation is estimated to result, at genetic equilibrium, in an increase of 60 to 1,100 serious genetic disorders per million live-born offspring, compared with the 100,000 from other causes. Though the number is small compared with that for other causes or for somatic effects, induced genetic disorders can be transmitted to many future generations, affecting many people besides the one exposed.

Resume

We know that exposure to radiation causes cancer. We know it causes genetic damage. We know that it causes structural and functional defects in the developing fetus. We suspect that it can cause physiological abnormalities.

Cancer-inducing effects can be discerned at lifetime exposure levels of only 0.5 to 5 rem per year, levels no higher than those now being received by hundreds of thousands of individuals occupationally. There is no guarantee that there are no detrimental effects from excess doses of as little as 100 mrem per year. They won't be recognized, since the effects could never be distinguished from identical ones induced by other influences.

In fact, as sources of radiation proliferate and exposure multiplies, epidemiological sensitivity to such effects may even decrease. Although there are other valid reasons to study human populations and their radiation exposure, epidemiological studies cannot be expected to determine the relationship(s) between low-level ionizing radiation exposure and its effects. This must come from a better understanding of the fundamental mechanisms by which the effects are produced. It is unlikely, however, that there is a threshold dose below which effects do not occur. If the radiation is sufficiently energetic to alter the DNA molecule, then radiation-induced effects can be expected.

It is argued that we are adding only small increments to existing exposures. But unlike the relatively uniform whole-body exposure from natural sources spread over the entire year, medical exposures and those from TENR are usually acute and localized, overwhelming DNA repair mechanisms. We are now incurring such additional exposure at the rate of over 20 million person-rem per year, and the amount is growing.

13-6   RADIATION PROTECTION STANDARDS

Major work on the development of radiation protection standards has been done by the International Commission on Radiological Protection (ICRP) and, in the United States, by the National Council on Radiation Protection and Measurements (NCRP). In the early days of radiology, the setting of limits on radiation dose was motivated by the need for safety in medical use of X rays; later it was driven by the needs of the nuclear industry and, more recently, by concern for public health and the human environment.

In 1953, the ICRP published the following definition of maximum permissible dose, which continues to express the basis for determining the amount of radioactivity that may be permitted in the human environment:

> The permissible dose for an individual is that dose, accumulated over a long period of time or resulting from a single exposure, which, in the light of present knowledge, carries a negligible probability of severe somatic or genetic injuries; furthermore, it is such a dose that any effects that ensue more frequently are limited to those of a minor nature that would not be considered unacceptable by the exposed individual and by competent medical authorities. Any severe somatic injuries (e.g., leukemia) which might result from exposure of individuals to the permissible dose would be limited to an exceedingly small fraction of the exposed group; effects such as shortening of life span, which might be expected to occur more frequently, would be very slight and would likely be hidden by normal biological variations. The permissible doses can therefore be expected to produce effects that could be detectable only by statistical methods applied to large groups.

The biological damage of concern is grave: it is the somatic injuries (cancers and leukemia)

Dose Limiting Recommendations (NCRP)

Group and Body Part Exposed	Exposure Limit (in rems)	Time Interval
Occupational Exposure (*limits for somatic injury*)		
Gonads, lens of eye, red bone marrow	5	Any one year
Skin	15	Any one year
Hands	75 (25)	Any one year (quarter)
Forearms	30 (10)	Any one year (quarter)
Whole body (accumulated exposure)	$(N - 18) \times 5$	Until age N years
Fetus (fertile women)	0.5	Gestation period
Public Exposure		
Whole body (limit for somatic injury)	0.17 rem	Each year, averaged over population
Gonads (limit for genetic injury)	0.17 rem	Each year, averaged over population

that show up many years after exposure, and the genetic injury (defective genes) expressed in future generations.

Primary radiation standards set the maximum radiation dose (measured in rems) that may be accumulated over a specified time period. The maximum permissible dose depends on age, and on whether it is the whole body or a part that is exposed. Also, limits are set separately for somatic damage (cancers) where the individual is of concern, and genetic damage, where the gene pool of the population is of concern.

The principal standardization effort has been to provide guidelines for limiting occupational exposure of workers in the nuclear industry. The limits are determined from the likelihood of somatic injury—the chance of individuals developing cancer. The standards recognize age as a factor in determining risk from radiation exposure: an older person will have less chance of developing cancer in his or her lifetime. Children are more sensitive than

Maximum Permissible Concentrations
for Occupational Exposure (ICRP)
(WORKING ENVIRONMENT—40-HOUR WORK WEEK)

Radionuclide	*Critical Body Organ*	*Maximum Body Burden (microcuries)*	*Maximum Concentration (microcuries per liter)*	
			In Water (soluble form)	*In Air*
Hydrogen-3 (tritium)	Body tissue	2,000	0.1	5×10^{-3}
Carbon-14	Fat	300	20.	4×10^{-3}
Krypton-85	Total body	----	----	1×10^{-2}
Strontium-90	Bone	4	0.004	3×10^{-7}
Iodine-131	Thyroid	0.7	0.06	9×10^{-6}
Cesium-137	Total body, liver, spleen, muscle	30	0.4	6×10^{-5}
Radon-222 (and daughters)	Lung	----	----	3×10^{-5}
Uranium-235	Lower large intestine, kidney, bone	0.03	0.8	5×10^{-7}
Plutonium-239	Bone	0.04	0.1	2×10^{-9}

Maximum Permissible Concentrations in Milk

Radionuclide	*Body Organ of Reference*	*Maximum Concentration (microcuries per liter)*
Strontium-90	Bone marrow	0.155
Iodine-131	Thyroid	0.084
Cesium-137	Whole body	2.4

adults, and the unborn fetus is very sensitive to radiation. The limit on exposure of the gonads to radiation is determined by considering genetic damage to the human population from propagation of defective genes.

The permissible doses for the general population are set far below those for occupational exposure. It is assumed that employment is voluntary and accepted with understanding of the risks involved. The assumption is that the standards should allow a risk of radiation injury comparable to risks of injury from other occupational hazards.

The source of radiation exposure may be outside or inside the body. The most important source of external exposure to the public is medical X rays under the control of physicians; yet medical X-ray exposure is exempted from limitation by the ICRP and the NCRP as being under the jurisdiction of the medical profession.

The control of internal exposure requires limiting absorption of radionuclides from the environment through water ingestion via food and drink, and by inhalation of air. Based on a "standard man" and knowledge of the retention and elimination of materials by the body, radiological researchers have derived maximum permissible concentrations for radionuclides in air and water, and limits on the amount present in the body, so that the accumulated dose will be within the primary standards for occupational exposure.

For the protection of the public, the U.S. Environmental Protection Agency administers standards limiting the concentration of radionuclides in foodstuffs. Milk, for example, is a food of great concern due to its consumption by nursing mothers, infants, and children.

Suggested Readings

The basic references on sources of low-level radiation and their public health aspects are the Report on Biological Effects of Ionizing Radiation of the National Research Council (BEIR-III), which is now in its third edition, and UNSCEAR, the report of the United Nations Committee on the Effects of Atomic Radiation.

"The Effects on Populations of Exposure to Low Levels of Ionizing Radiation." *Report of the Advisory Committee on the Biological Effects of Ionizing Radiations (BEIR-III).* Washington, D.C.: National Academy Press, 1980.

FABRIKANT, J. I. "The Effects on Populations of Exposure to Low Levels of Ionizing Radiation. Known Effects of Low Level Radiation Exposure." Proceedings of a conference, Health Implications of the Three Mile Island Accident. NIH Publication No. 80–2087. Bethesda: National Cancer Institute, 1980.

United Nations Scientific Committee on the Effects of Atomic Radiation. Report A/32/40. General Assembly Official Records. 32nd Sess. Suppl. No. 40. New York: United Nations, 1977.

A steel storage tank for high-level radioactive wastes under construction at the Hanford facility near Richland, Washington. The double-walled tank will be covered by a layer of concrete and seven feet of earth.

14. Radioactive Waste

Kai Lee surveys radioactive wastes, mainly in the United States, both by source and type, including a look at the implications of decommissioning nuclear facilities. The checkered history of waste storage and planning is also examined, in a search for institutional lessons relevant to handling the large and increasing volume of wastes contaminated with radioactive isotopes.

RADIOACTIVE WASTES—waste materials containing unstable isotopes—are produced in two basic ways. *Fission products* are the fragments of fissile nuclei split in nuclear reactions. They have half-lives measured in decades, and their radioactivity declines to innocuous levels in roughly 700 years. *Activation products* are formed when neutrons are absorbed by atomic nuclei; dense concentrations of neutrons are found within nuclear reactors and when nuclear weapons are detonated. Many activation products have short half-lives. The *actinide* elements form an important special case. This family of nuclei includes uranium and the *transuranic* (heavier than uranium) elements; the transuranics are all formed as activation products. Their half-lives are commonly long, and so materials contaminated with actinides require isolation from the biological environment for many thousands of years.

In principle the prudent management and disposal of radioactive wastes are not difficult. In practice, serious misjudgments have left us with potential and actual problems of pollution by nuclear wastes that will be costly to address and perhaps impossible to solve in a satisfactory way. The important task now is to make the best of an unfortunate legacy.

This chapter discusses radioactive waste management in the United States, the first nuclear weapons state and the largest user of nuclear power. Data on American inventories of radioactive waste are unusually complete, as is the documentation of policy making.[1] It is likely, however, that the United States is *not* responsible for the worst problems in the handling of radioactive wastes.[2]

Sources and Kinds of Radioactive Waste

Uranium Mill Tailings The mining of uranium is generally accompanied by milling, on-site beneficiation to concentrate uranium. Since uranium typically constitutes less than one part in 500 of the ore, milling operations produce large quantities of residues known as *mill tailings*—500 cubic meters per metric ton of re-

Kai Lee

Lee is an associate professor of environmental studies and political science at the University of Washington, Seattle.

14-1   CATEGORIES OF RADIOACTIVE WASTE

Radioactive wastes are conventionally divided into five categories, reflecting their origin in the mining, processing, and use of nuclear materials.

Mill Tailings   The mining and milling of uranium-bearing ores results in the production of sandy residues called mill tailings. The processed ore itself is destined to fuel reactors producing weapons material, electric power, or radioisotopes.

Spent Nuclear Fuel   Spent nuclear fuel has been irradiated in a nuclear power station and is not a waste in the normal sense. The fuel rods contain, in addition to radioactive fission products, substantial quantities of uranium and plutonium which could be utilized in reactors or in weapons after a chemical extraction process called reprocessing.

High-Level Waste   When it is done, reprocessing removes roughly 98 percent of the uranium and plutonium from either spent nuclear fuel rods or targets irradiated to produce nuclear materials for weapons. What remains is high-level waste, initially produced as an intensely radioactive liquid. United States policy calls for liquid high-level wastes to be converted into solid form to facilitate transportation and storage. The radioactivity in high-level waste generates considerable decay heat, complicating its storage and disposal.

Low-Level Waste   Low-level waste is contaminated material of widely varying hazard, originating from all uses of radioactive substances. The largest volumes come from power generation, and from industrial and medical uses. Though some of this material requires substantial shielding and special handling, most radioactive substances in low-level wastes are short-lived, with half-lives no longer than a few tens of years. Low-level waste contains little or no activity from actinide elements such as uranium or plutonium.

Transuranic Wastes   Materials contaminated with transuranic elements are called transuranic wastes. These wastes have low concentrations of radionuclides, and do not generate troublesome quantities of decay heat. Unlike low-level wastes, however, the transuranic contamination implies a long-lived radiation hazard from nuclei emitting alpha particles. Transuranic wastes, produced mostly in weapons-related activities and power generation, are defined as materials with transuranic activity of more than ten nanocuries per gram. This choice of definition reflects the limit of our ability to detect contamination by the transuranic elements.

covered uranium.[3] Both ore and tailings are only mildly radioactive, but the radioactivity is extremely long-lived. Uncontrolled tailings piles can release radioactive elements to the environment for centuries, with potentially serious cumulative health impacts. Tailings contain radium, which can contaminate water supplies, as well as radon, a heavy inert gas. Radon could

pose the most significant public health risk from routine nuclear operations.[4]

Historically, no effort was made to isolate tailings piles; tailings have entered watersheds and were used in the construction of residential and public buildings. The Uranium Mill Tailings Radiation Control Act of 1978 authorized the Department of Energy (DOE) to stabilize and con-

14-2   **SOURCES OF RADIOACTIVE WASTE**

Sources of Waste	Number of Facilities	Annual Output for a Single Model Facility		
		Form of Waste	Volume (cubic meters)	Radioactivity (curies)
Nuclear reactors	321	low-level	620	4,000
		spent fuel	35	11,000,000
Uranium enrichment plants	4	low-level	5,800	more than 350
Fuel fabrication facilities	21	low-level	1,255	negligible
Uranium mills	20	tailings	800,000	negligible
Reprocessing facilities	21	low-level	400	negligible
		high-level	456	900,000,000
		plutonium	310	5,000,000
		transuranic	2,520	175,000,000
Industrial and institutional users	20,000	—	—	—

The figures for annual output of wastes are for a typical large-scale facility. The numbers of facilities are listed for 1977 and include many research and experimental facilities of small capacity.

trol some inactive tailings piles, and established policies to regulate piles at active mines.[5]

There are 102 million cubic meters of tailings, approximately one-eighth at inactive sites. The accumulated volume of tailings is projected to quadruple to 333 million cubic meters by the year 2000.[6] This volume is large: one square mile in area by 425 feet in height—as tall as a nuclear power plant cooling tower.

Spent Nuclear Fuel   Virtually all fuel ever used in commercial nuclear reactors is still stored at the reactor sites; there were 6,700 metric tons of *spent nuclear fuel* at U.S. power plants at the end of 1980.[7] Spent fuel is intensely radioactive: five years after removal from the reactor core its activity level is 600,000 curies per metric ton.[8] The accumulated radioactivity in U.S. spent fuel is 10.4 billion curies. Radioactive decay from this quantity of fuel generates thirty-nine megawatts of heat.[9]

When the current generation of nuclear plants was designed, storage of spent fuel was planned for a period of six months, to permit intensely radioactive, short-lived nuclides to undergo decay. Fuel was then to be shipped to a reprocessing plant for recovery of uranium and plutonium for use in the fabrication of fresh fuel. With the halt in plans for reprocessing, nuclear fuel has been held at reactor storage pools. Management of spent fuel is complicated by the presence of uranium and plutonium. Reprocessing spent fuel to remove these elements produces copious amounts of transuranic wastes which must be permanently isolated.

By the mid-1980s, some reactors may run out of storage capacity.[10] Electric utility and government officials have discussed federal support for away-from-reactor storage, but the Reagan administration has not endorsed such a government role. Even if no more nuclear plants are ordered, the power stations already on line and under construction will increase the total quantity of spent fuel by an order of mag-

14-3 SPENT FUEL STORAGE POOL

Holding pool for spent nuclear fuel at the French reprocessing plant in La Hague. The water conducts decay heat away from the radioactive fuel and helps
shield personnel from its radiation. Similar pools exist
at most power reactor sites and presently hold nearly
all of the used fuel material from the world's commercial reactors.

nitude, to over 73,000 metric tons by the year
2000.[11] This no-growth scenario implies the
need for storage capacity equivalent to between
five and twelve storage facilities by the turn of
the century.[12]

High-Level Waste The inventory of *high-level
waste* is almost entirely derived from military
programs, having been produced in the manufacture of atomic weapons and in the fuel cycle
for naval reactors. The current inventory is siz-

able: 293,000 cubic meters at the end of 1980
(the volume of a cube sixty-six meters on a
side, or roughly a cubic city block). The radiological hazard of high-level waste is difficult to
express in terms that are readily grasped. A
committee of the National Academy of Sciences
characterized the high-level defense wastes at
Hanford, Washington, which account for three-
fifths of the high-level waste inventory, in this
way: The single most hazardous constituent of
high-level waste is strontium-90 (Sr-90), an element that resembles calcium chemically and
thus can be absorbed into bones. The Hanford
Reservation where the wastes are stored is located in the valley of the Columbia River,
whose annual flow of 100 billion cubic meters
of water makes it the second largest river in the
United States. To dilute the Sr-90 in the Hanford
wastes to levels acceptable for human consumption would require the annual flow of the Columbia for a thousand years.[13]

High-level waste is stored at four locations,
three of them federally owned. The wastes are
found in five forms. Three—liquid, salt cake, and
sludge—are stored in steel tanks; these account
for virtually all the *volume* of high-level waste.
At Hanford, the intensely radioactive elements

**14-4   NUCLEAR WASTES FROM
POWER REACTOR OPERATION**

Type of Waste	Quantity per Gigawatt-Year Operation	Decommissioning
Mill tailings	800,000	—
Spent fuel	44	—
High-level	3	—
Low-level	500	5
Transuranic	230	0.8
Airborne	2,500	—

Radioactive wastes created each year for each 1,000
megawatts (one gigawatt) of nuclear generating capacity. Quantities are in cubic meters except for airborne
waste, which is given in curies.

14-5   HIGH-LEVEL RADIOACTIVE WASTES IN THE UNITED STATES

Location and Form of Waste	Volume (cubic meters)	Specific Radioactivity (curies per cubic meter)
Hanford Reservation, Richland, Washington		
Liquid	39,000	887
Salt cake	95,000	17
Sludge	49,000	1,600
Strontium/cesium capsules	1.7	1,950,000
Idaho Chemical Processing Plant, Idaho Falls		
Liquid	9,340	1,820
Calcine	2,070	17,600
Nuclear Fuel Services, West Valley, New York		
Liquid	2,145	?
Sludge	47	?
Savannah River Plant, South Carolina		
Liquid	59,800	?
Salt cake	26,400	3,130
Sludge	10,500	40,900
Total	293,300	

These figures are for the end of 1980. The total radioactivity is 1,352 million curies with 52 percent at Savannah River, 41 percent at Richland, and the remainder divided between West Valley and Idaho Falls. At West Valley 457 kilograms of actinides in damaged spent fuel elements from a reactor at the Hanford Reservation are buried. This site, originally privately operated, is now owned by the state of New York.

Sr-90 and cesium-137 (Cs-137) have been partitioned from some of the high-level waste and are held as solids in capsules. High-level waste derived from the reprocessing of naval reactor fuel is stored at Idaho Falls, Idaho, as liquid or as calcine, a loose, granular material. The activity levels of high-level wastes vary significantly. Defense wastes in particular tend to be less radioactive than the liquids derived from reprocessing of commercial fuels, which will carry 100,000 curies per cubic meter.[14]

High-level wastes at Savannah River, South Carolina, and Hanford present serious challenges. Some storage tanks at both sites are operating well beyond their design lifetimes. Twenty of the 152 tanks at Hanford have leaked, with the loss of 450,000 gallons of waste into the soil.[15] Thus far, fortunately, the soil characteristics and low rainfall at the Hanford site appear to have immobilized the spilled radionuclides.

Because reprocessing of commercial nuclear fuels has been deferred, official projections for high-level waste consider only additions to the defense waste inventory. These amount to a 15 percent increase by the end of the century, reaching a total of 320,000 cubic meters by the year 2000. Studies are underway to plan for final disposal of defense wastes; current planning does not call for disposal to be accomplished until 2015, however.[16] As described below, work now in progress at two DOE facilities does offer hope that management of defense high-level wastes can be significantly improved.

Transuranic Nuclear Waste Materials contaminated with even small amounts of transuranic elements like plutonium can be dangerous for very long periods of time because the contaminants are both highly toxic and long-lived. In principle *transuranic wastes* should be isolated from the environment for thousands of years, as is proposed for high-level waste. The hazards of transuranic wastes were not reflected in public policy until 1970, however, when its definition as material containing more than 10 nanocuries of actinides per gram was proposed by the Atomic Energy Commission (AEC). In 1981 the AEC's successor, DOE, proposed to change this definition to 100 nanocuries per gram for the defense transuranic wastes, which it controls.

Transuranic wastes are stored at thirteen locations in the United States, eight at sites operated by the DOE. The eight DOE sites contain roughly 1,800 kilograms of transuranic elements. There are major gaps in our knowledge of waste inventories, however. To begin with, the testing of nuclear weapons at the Nevada Test Site has contaminated an undetermined quantity of subsurface rock and soil. Moreover, there are uncertainties deriving from earlier waste management practices. Before 1970, materials that later would have been classed as transuranic waste were treated as low-level waste. Liquids bearing transuranics were routinely disposed of in cribs—covered trenches from which liquid waste percolated into the soil. At the AEC locations where transuranic waste was disposed of, substantial volumes of subsurface soil and rock were contaminated: up to 9 million cubic meters of soil are affected, mostly at Hanford.[17] Similar practices prevailed at commercially-operated sites. Plutonium has apparently leaked into watercourses near the

Maxey Flats, Kentucky, repository, which was closed in 1977.[18]

Most transuranic wastes have been generated in military programs. In 1969 a bad fire at the AEC Rocky Flats, Colorado, facility contaminated a large quantity of material with plutonium and led the AEC to set the current definition of transuranic waste and to begin to package transuranic waste in retrievable form. The largest part of this retrievably-stored transuranic waste comes from the Rocky Flats fire and is now at Idaho Falls. Transuranic wastes are not now being emplaced at commercial facilities, but are being held, like spent fuel, at the locations where they are produced.[19]

Low-Level Waste The most diverse class of radioactive wastes also presents the most immediate problems of public policy. In contrast to the situation in high-level wastes, where interim storage has permitted deferral of issues, *low-level wastes* are normally held only briefly before disposal. Low-level waste is generated in many activities already under way: nuclear power generation, nuclear medicine and research, industrial uses of tracers and other radioactive materials, and military programs. Finding disposal sites for nongovernment low-level waste is an issue of near-term importance, as existing commercial sites face increased public controversy.

At the end of 1980, the accumulated volume of low-level waste was 2.29 million cubic meters. The estimated rate of generation of low-level waste in 1981 was 174,000 cubic meters per year. The largest contribution to this rate came from activities of DOE, mostly from military programs and the enrichment of uranium at federal facilities. The commercial nuclear fuel cycle accounted for 28 percent of the low-level waste, and industrial and institutional users accounted for 33 percent.[20]

Three commercial low-level waste sites are now open, in Nevada, South Carolina, and Washington state, with a licensed capacity of 4.6 mil-

14-6   TRANSURANIC AND LOW-LEVEL WASTES IN THE UNITED STATES

Location	Transuranic Wastes Buried as Solid Volume (cubic meters)	Transuranic Mass (kilograms)	Transuranic Wastes In Retrievable Storage Volume (cubic meters)	Transuranic Mass (kilograms)	Low-level Wastes Volume (cubic meters)
IDAHO					
Idaho Falls [DOE]	57,100	376	42,370	410	114,600
ILLINOIS					
Sheffield	86,700	13	(not known)		(included in transuranic)
KENTUCKY					
Maxey Flats	135,000	69	(not known)		(included in transuranic)
NEVADA					
Beatty	86,600	14	(not known)		(included in transuranic)
Nevada Test Site [DOE]	0		235	4	91,200
NEW MEXICO					
Los Alamos	11,500	13	4,366	81	163,600
NEW YORK					
West Valley	66,500	4	(not known)		(included in transuranic)
SOUTH CAROLINA					
Barnwell	0		0		324,000
Savannah River [DOE]	31,000	9	2,555	77	357,000
TENNESSEE					
Oak Ridge [DOE]	6,200	5	948	16	194,000
WASHINGTON					
Hanford	167,400	600	10,600	219	72,000
Richland	60,600	33	(not known)		(included in transuranic)

These figures are for the end of 1980. An additional 538,900 cubic meters of low-level wastes are stored at eight other Department of Energy (DOE) locations. A small quantity of commercial low-level waste—mostly from medical users—is stored at the Todd Shipyards in Galveston, Texas. Three sites are now closed to further disposal of wastes: West Valley in 1975, Maxey Flats at the end of 1977, and Sheffield in 1978. Substantial additional quantities of wastes at these closed sites are not reported.

14-7 DISPOSAL OF LOW-LEVEL RADIOACTIVE WASTE

Burial of low-level radioactive wastes in a shallow trench at the Maxey Flats site, Kentucky. This site is now closed.

lion cubic meters—enough to last until roughly the year 2000, according to current projections. Two of the six DOE low-level waste sites, at Oak Ridge and Savannah River, are projected to be filled by the 1990s, however.[21]

Low-level waste sites have experienced operational problems, such as those mentioned above in the discussion of transuranic wastes. At the Beatty, Nevada, site employees sold contaminated materials to local residents for use as tools and building materials.[22] Regulation and enforcement have been tightened recently. It is worth noting that much low-level waste poses only minor hazards.[23] Some low-level wastes from biomedical research contain organic chemicals that are carcinogenic or acutely toxic.

The Three Mile Island accident, in combination with unresolved tensions between state governments and the companies transporting and storing low-level waste, led to growing public controversy in the three states where commercial sites are operated. Nevada and Washington imposed temporary site closures in 1979.[24] Although all three sites are now open, storage fees have been increased and disposal rates have been limited. A citizen initiative banning out-of-state wastes was passed by a large majority in Washington in 1980. In June 1981, this initiative was declared unconstitutional by a federal district court judge, who ruled that it interfered with interstate commerce and that it trespassed upon an arena of public policy preempted by federal authority.

In 1980, Congress passed the Low-Level Radioactive Waste Policy Act, establishing a national policy framework for low-level waste. State governments are assigned primary responsibility for management of commercial low-level waste. States are also encouraged to form interstate compacts for regional repositories. Passed in the last-minute rush of a lame-duck Congress, the act was the only surviving remnant of attempts to frame a broad national policy for radioactive waste. Spurred by the Washington State initiative, three Pacific Northwest states have formed the first state compact; discussions are under way in the Southeast and the Northeast. Progress elsewhere is less certain.[25]

OPPOSITE:

The sites shown are the major locations in the United States used for the storage and disposal of nuclear radioactive wastes. In addition, high-level radioactive material is accumulating in the form of spent nuclear fuel rods at the seventy-five operating commercial power reactors scattered across the country. There are also locations where smaller amounts of low-level and transuranic wastes have been dumped. Many of these have been closed and are scheduled for cleanup over the next two decades. Wastes have also been stored at DOE sites where nuclear weapons are fabricated and weapon materials are processed.

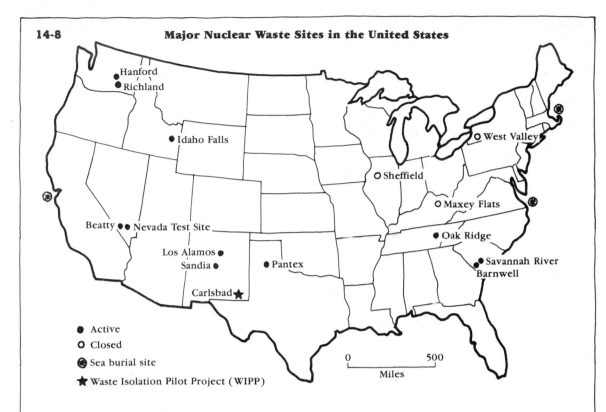

14-8   **Major Nuclear Waste Sites in the United States**

- ● Active
- ○ Closed
- ⊕ Sea burial site
- ★ Waste Isolation Pilot Project (WIPP)

Location		Low-Level	Transuranic	High-Level
Idaho	● Idaho Falls	✔	✔	✔
Illinois	○ Sheffield	✔	✔	
Kentucky	○ Maxey Flats	✔	✔	
Nevada	● Beatty	✔	✔	
	● Nevada Test Site	✔	✔	
New Mexico	● Los Alamos	✔	✔	
	● Sandia	✔		
New York	○ West Valley	✔	✔	✔
South Carolina	● Barnwell	✔	✔	
	● Savannah River	✔	✔	✔
Tennessee	● Oak Ridge	✔	✔	
Texas	● Pantex	✔	✔	
Washington	● Hanford	✔	✔	✔
	● Richland	✔	✔	
⊕ Sea burial sites (prior to 1970)		✔	✔	

One class of radioactive materials routinely released to the environment is radioactive gases. A typical light-water reactor releases 2,500 curies per year in this fashion. Much larger quantities of radioactive gases are contained in spent nuclear fuel—roughly 300,000 curies of krypton-85 alone for each gigawatt-year. Among the defense nuclear facilities, the Savannah River Plant stands out, with annual emissions of tritium of 400,000 curies, together with 560,000 curies of krypton-85.[26]

Decommissioning, Decontamination, and Accident Wastes

One category of wastes is worthy of special mention: those arising from the permanent closure of nuclear facilities, disposal of contaminated equipment, and cleanup of accidents. The materials to be disposed of are mostly low-level and transuranic wastes, but their form and levels of radioactivity are highly variable, ranging from relatively clean retired nuclear submarine hulls to the highly radioactive resins resulting from the decontamination of the Three Mile Island reactor. Experience is slender and planning for decontamination and decommissioning is still evolving.

Since 1960, fifty-five nuclear facilities, including thirty-three reactors, have been decommissioned.[27] These have been mainly small research reactors; there remains substantial uncertainty as to the magnitude of the job involved in cleaning up a major nuclear facility. Reviews by the Nuclear Regulatory Commission (NRC) and the DOE suggest that:[28]

1. The radiation hazard comes mainly from activation products. Cobalt-60 is the most dangerous to workers, but its relatively short half-life of 5.3 years means that waiting for several decades can lower occupational exposure considerably.

2. The principal occupational impacts of decommissioning would come in a serious attempt to *decontaminate* a nuclear facility; that is, going beyond removal of the most intensely radioactive pipes and vessels. Whether to run the risks of decontamination is thus a non-trivial question.

3. The largest contributions to radioactive waste come from the decommissioning of reprocessing plants and nuclear power stations, leading to the production of transuranic and low-level solid wastes.

4. The economic costs of decommissioning arise both from the need to handle radioactive equipment and from the difficulties of razing heavily reinforced concrete structures and moving thick-walled pressure vessels.

5. It may therefore be sensible to re-use a power plant site and even its structures, so as to minimize decommissioning costs and occupational impacts. If the site continues to be used, there is less need to assure that the decommissioned facility will present low risks to inadvertent intruders.

6. Designing nuclear facilities so as to reduce the costs of decommissioning and decontamination has been considered, but the ideas "have yet to reach the drawing board."[29]

Perhaps the most significant unknown is the cost of a full-scale cleanup. The General Accounting Office concluded that "the cost to decommission federally-owned nuclear facilities will run into billions of dollars."[30] This report cites a figure of $4 billion to clean up the Hanford Reservation, not taking into account the problems of the high-level waste there. Federal regulations require that an applicant for an operating license show it has funds to cover the estimated costs of "permanently shutting the facility down and maintaining it in a safe condition."[31] Until more experience is accumulated, however, the accuracy of these cost estimates and the adequacy of this rule will remain uncertain.

14-9   RADIOACTIVE WASTE MANAGEMENT PREHISTORY

Year	Events
1944	Single-walled mild steel storage tanks for high-level liquid waste built at Hanford. Wastes neutralized prior to storage.
1950	Savannah River plant authorized.
1953	Initial warning by U.S. Geological Survey that integrity of tanks at Hanford is doubtful.
1954	First wastes generated at Savannah River. Neutralized wastes stored in mild steel tanks set on steel "saucers"; tanks are isolated from environment by concrete vault.
1956	Purex process for reprocessing fuel elements from plutonium production reactors at Hanford is begun.
1958	First leak at Hanford, 55,000 gallons from a tank constructed in 1947.
	Du Pont suggests that high-level waste at Savannah River can be stored in bedrock under the plant; the shaft would traverse a large aquifer.
1959	Joint Committee on Atomic Energy holds hearing on radioactive waste and concludes that wastes do not pose an insuperable challenge.
1963	Nuclear Fuel Services obtains a construction permit for the West Valley reprocessing facility.
1965	In-tank solidification program initiated at Hanford, in order to guard against further leaks from single-walled tanks. Extraction of Sr and Cs from hot liquid wastes at Hanford is begun in 1968.
1966	West Valley begins reprocessing, using carbon-steel tanks for storage of neutralized waste.
1972	West Valley closes, after reprocessing 600 metric tons of fuel.
1973	Tank 106-T leaks at Hanford, releasing 115,000 gallons of high-level waste.

HISTORY

United States policy for radioactive waste may be divided into three overlapping phases. The first, running from 1943 to the mid-sixties, is "prehistoric": information on this period is still largely classified. It is clear, nonetheless, that wastes were generated and stored, but no comprehensive plan for the nuclear fuel cycle was either developed or thought necessary. As with an archeological record, one can discern fragments of "history"—from 1954 to the present—in the prehistoric. The history of radioactive waste is a trail of modest but genuine technological advance, combined with repeated institutional failures and political blunders. The result of "prehistory" and "history" has been a protracted, and thus far inconclusive, struggle for a coherent national policy for radioactive waste. This is the third evolutionary phase, beginning in the early seventies and not yet concluded.

Prehistory

The fact that radioactivity is dangerous was well known to those who designed and built the first nuclear devices. Radioactive materials were accordingly treated with respect from the beginnings of the nuclear era. But the obviously high costs of controlling *all* radioactive material involved in nuclear weapons manufacture and, later, power reactors influenced the thinking of the technical community and the quality of the practices instituted.

Large quantities of wastes were generated

without adequate means of coping with them over the long term. High-level wastes were stored, pending plans for final disposal; low-level wastes, including those containing long-lived actinides, were released to the environment, contaminating large quantities of soil; and the commercialization of nuclear power was vigorously pursued by the United States government without a sense of how vulnerable the nascent industry would be once confronted with controversy over wastes. "Because the AEC is an operating agency," a respected scientist wrote in 1965, "there has been a tendency to solve storage and disposal problems on an *ad hoc* basis."[32] By the time he wrote, much of the damage had been done.

The central problem is the waste generated in military programs, now stored as liquids, salt cake, and sludge at Hanford and Savannah River. A similar though much smaller quantity of wastes was created in the commercial reprocessing facility at West Valley, New York, and is stored in two tanks there.[33]

Plutonium—the basic ingredient of U.S. nuclear weapons—is manufactured by exposing uranium fuel rods to high neutron flux in a nuclear reactor. This process is similar to the one that takes place in a reactor used for electric power generation. After irradiation, the rods are chemically processed to extract plutonium. In chemical separation the fuel elements are dissolved in nitric acid; the intensely radioactive fission products remain in acid solution when processing is completed.

During World War II, production reactors at Hanford were used to manufacture plutonium for weapons, including the bomb dropped at Nagasaki. Liquid high-level wastes from chemical separation were neutralized and pumped into steel tanks as a temporary expedient. When the Savannah River plant was established in 1950 to manufacture special nuclear materials for thermonuclear weapons, the Hanford approach was adopted there too, with some improvements.

By 1963, when planning for the privately-owned West Valley facility was begun, problems with tank storage of neutralized liquid high-level wastes were well known within the military nuclear community. Indeed, liquid wastes were stored in acid form in stainless steel tanks at the Idaho Chemical Processing Plant designed in the early fifties in order to avoid some of these difficulties.[34] Yet in the commercial nuclear world, outside the curtain of national security, there was little inkling of trouble: in the belief that their choice was a cost-effective one, Nuclear Fuel Services chose to neutralize their wastes.

At each of the sites, some of the ordinary steel tanks leaked. Because of their large size, the tanks were built at the site by welding steel plates. The intense heating and rapid cooling produced localized stresses in the metal that left the steel susceptible to corrosion by nitrate salts in the neutralized wastes. Warnings that the integrity of the tanks at Hanford might be compromised came from the U.S. Geological Survey in 1953[35] and from the General Accounting Office in 1968.[36] By then the leaks had started, capped by the 115,000 gallon leak from Hanford tank 106-T in 1973.[37] Public confidence in the government's ability to contain radioactive wastes was understandably weakened.[38] (It should be noted that the lessons of storing high-level liquid wastes have been learned; storage tanks at the Barnwell, South Carolina, commercial reprocessing plant are designed to avoid the difficulties of the government tanks at the neighboring Savannah River Plant.)

By far the largest volume of "prehistoric" waste is low-level and transuranic waste, generated in a variety of activities ranging from weapons manufacture to medical research. Well into the seventies, low-level waste disposal was still in the dark ages. Sites were more garbage dumps than secure repositories, as suggested by the substantial quantities of long-lived actinides deposited in soil and waterways. "Disposal prac-

14-10   RADIOACTIVE WASTE MANAGEMENT HISTORY

Year	Events
1954	Atomic Energy Act passed, authorizing development of commercial nuclear power.
1955	Princeton meeting of National Academy of Sciences working group.
1957	Salt as a medium for geologic storage first proposed by National Academy.
1963	Calcination of acid wastes begun at Idaho Falls.
1966	Project Salt Vault demonstrates technical feasibility of storing high-level wastes in salt.
	National Academy panel endorses disposal in salt, but is critical of AEC practices at existing facilities.
1969	Rocky Flats, Colorado, fire contaminates structural material with transuranic elements. This large volume of transuranic wastes is shipped to Idaho Falls and put in retrievable storage.
1970	AEC proposes to use the Project Salt Vault site in Lyons, Kansas, as a permanent geological repository.
1971	South Carolina state legislature initiates a study opposing ultimate disposal of high-level waste in the state.
1972	Lyons, Kansas, repository site withdrawn in the face of social opposition and technical uncertainties.
	Retrievable surface storage facility (RSSF) announced by AEC.
	Studies of high-level waste disposal in the bedrock below Savannah River are shelved in the face of political criticism.
1974	A Waste Isolation Pilot Plant (WIPP) is announced; it is to be located in a bedded salt deposit in New Mexico.
1975	RSSF withdrawn in the face of controversy.
1976	Plans to proceed with reprocessing of commercial spent fuel are withdrawn during Presidential campaign.
1977	Federal intention to provide away-from-reactor storage of spent fuel is announced, together with the concept that the federal government will accept spent fuel in return for a one-time charge levied on utilities.
	Department of Energy is formed.
1978	Uranium Mill Tailings Radiation Control Act enacted. Nuclear Regulatory Commission reviews licensing of uranium mining and milling.
1979	Three Mile Island accident.
1981	Federal support for away-from-reactor storage is withdrawn by the Reagan Administration.

tices at Hanford and [Idaho Falls] are considered to be unsatisfactory," a member of the National Academy of Sciences concluded in 1967, "in that they do not ... provide assurance of safety over an adequate period of time."[39]

Technical Success . . .

Shrouded by secrecy, problems with wastes created in military programs could be deferred with little criticism. Once the decision was made in the Eisenhower administration to proceed with commercial development of atomic power, however, officials in the AEC began to search for a means to dispose of wastes from the peaceful atom. It has been an ironic and frustrating search, marked by technical advance and political defeat.

The AEC approached the National Academy of Sciences in 1955. The agency needed advice on radioactive wastes, one official said, since "it [the AEC] has at least temporarily relieved the industry of that particular combination of headaches." But cost was deemed important: "small as the total volume and weight are, the economic aspect is very large, and will become larger."[40]

In September 1955, geologist Harry Hess organized a two-day meeting at Princeton University, under National Academy sponsorship, to discuss the earth science ramifications of radioactive waste disposal. Geologic disposal would prove feasible, the scientists thought, though the chemical interactions between the waste and surrounding geologic media required more research. Momentarily—and apparently unconsciously—stepping beyond the bounds of their expertise, the Princeton group also said that safety, rather than cost, should be the governing consideration.[41] Most important, the Princeton conference led to a 1957 National Academy paper by William B. Heroy entitled "Disposal of Radioactive Waste in Salt Cavities."[42] In it, the Academy suggested that burial of waste in salt was a most promising avenue to study; it was influential advice.[43] Though it is not free of controversy, salt is now the best understood medium for waste disposal, in large measure because the AEC research program followed this suggestion.

The Academy has maintained a continuing relationship with the AEC and its successor agencies.[44] The National Academy suggested three elements of a systematic approach to radioactive waste management. The first was the choice of where to dispose of wastes. Academy scientists identified salt as a potentially suitable medium because it has the ability to heal fractures and to disperse the large quantities of heat emanated by fresh high-level waste. Porous media were thought to be suitable for low-level wastes, where decay heat was not a problem. This led to a line of developmental work at the Oak Ridge National Laboratory, where intermediate level wastes mixed with a cement grout have been injected into sedimentary formations lying under the laboratory site,[45] the only intentional irreversible disposal of non-low-level wastes now taking place in the United States.

Second, an Academy panel suggested in 1960 that it was important to locate chemical reprocessing facilities over geologic formations suitable for disposal of high-level waste.[46] The advice was ignored: the three reprocessing facilities subsequently built, at West Valley, Barnwell, and Morris, Illinois, have been located without regard to the suitability of the nearby geology for permanent containment of high-level wastes. Worse, two of the commercial low-level waste disposal sites, at Sheffield, Illinois, and at Maxey Flats, are located in geological settings now recognized as inappropriate.

Third, a National Academy panel introduced in 1975 the idea of a multiple barrier approach to waste disposal.[47] The point is *not* to rely on geology, the form in which the waste is encapsulated, or any other *single* barrier to contain the waste after disposal. Rather, the system of waste, waste form, and surrounding rock should be designed so that the strengths of one barrier compensate for weaknesses in another. As with its advice about salt as a medium of disposal, the Academy suggestion of a systems approach based on multiple barriers has now become conventional wisdom.

Not all technical progress came through outside experts, of course. In the sixties a plant to calcine liquid wastes was built at the Idaho National Engineering Laboratory. Calcining turns liquid acids into a dry powder by evaporating atomized fluids in a high-temperature chamber.

The high-level wastes at Idaho Falls are now the least problematic in the United States inventory; they are stored in steel bins, awaiting ultimate disposal.

. . . And Political Failure

By the late sixties, the AEC felt a growing sense of confidence. Project Salt Vault, a study done in an abandoned salt mine in Kansas using simulated wastes, suggested that salt was an appropriate geologic medium for disposing of high-level waste. Indeed, the research was so successful that AEC executives in Washington grew impatient with the "endless research."[48]

In May 1969, a fire at the AEC weapons plant at Rocky Flats contaminated a sizable quantity of material with plutonium. Now transuranic waste, this contaminated material was stored in drums at Idaho Falls.[49] The sheer volume of the Rocky Flats debris raised a public protest, however, and the AEC promised the Idaho congressional delegation that the transuranic waste would be removed within ten years. This was no more than the AEC wanted to do in any case: a policy for moving commercial high-level wastes to federal repositories within ten years was proposed in 1970 as Appendix F of 10 C.F.R. 50, the Code of Federal Regulations section of rules for commercial waste management.

So in June 1970, the AEC decided to proceed with a radioactive waste repository in Lyons, Kansas, where the salt research had been done. The downward spiral had begun.

Announcement that Lyons would become a nuclear repository aroused a public outcry, which might have been expected. But it was a knowledgeable protest. Kansas state geologist William Hambleton doubted the adequacy of AEC's geological models; perhaps more telling politically, he pointed out that solution mining of salt had been carried out close to the proposed site. This raised the danger of water intruding into the repository, carrying wastes back into the biosphere. The AEC had no coherent answer. Indeed, some of the Project Salt

Vault scientists agreed with the critics.[50] Before the end of 1971, work at Lyons was halted.[51]

Because deep geologic storage was too controversial, the AEC tried to defer ultimate disposal, by proposing a Retrievable Surface Storage Facility. This facility qualified as a major action affecting the environment, and, under the terms of the National Environmental Policy Act of 1969, the AEC had to file an environmental impact statement. The Natural Resources Defense Council, an environmental group, observed that retrievable storage avoided the problem of ultimate disposal. The Environmental Protection Agency and Department of the Interior agreed. The AEC retreated, and a generic environmental impact statement on waste management for the commercial fuel cycle was launched. This document, caught in the widening controversy, was not issued in final form until 1980, by the Department of Energy, AEC's successor twice removed.[52]

With permanent disposal and temporary storage both blocked, the AEC announced in 1974 that a Waste Isolation Pilot Project (WIPP) would be undertaken in the salt beds of southeastern New Mexico. WIPP would demonstrate the disposal of transuranic waste from Idaho Falls. The surrounding communities voiced no official opposition. By 1978, with pressures mounting to find a convincing solution for commercial high-level waste and spent fuel, the Department of Energy tried to expand WIPP into a test facility for spent fuel disposal too. This ignited opposition—ironically, from defense proponents who wanted to protect military wastes from the entanglements of commercial nuclear power—and WIPP was deferred by the Carter administration in 1980.[53]

What had happened? The repeated failures were part of both a larger pattern and a deeper failing. The late sixties brought a widespread disappointment in large-scale technologies—what antinuclear pamphleteer Amory Lovins has dubbed the "hard" path.[54] The intensity of opposition to nuclear power, the apotheosis of the

14-11   THE EMERGENCE OF NATIONAL PLANNING
IN RADIOACTIVE WASTE MANAGEMENT

Year	Events
1970	AEC proposes to require conversion of high-level liquid wastes to solid form five years after initial production, anticipating burial in federally owned geologic repositories.
1972	The AEC Division of Waste Management and Transportation is created; for the first time, waste management is administratively consolidated under a single budget. The following year, federal spending on waste management is expanded.
1974	AEC is replaced by the Nuclear Regulatory Commission and the Energy Research and Development Administration (ERDA).
1976	ERDA releases its "technical alternatives document," the first official survey of alternative means of ultimately disposing of high-level wastes.
1978	Interagency Review Group (IRG) if formed.
	Studies by various technical groups in and out of government begin to proliferate, including a critical review by the U.S. Geological Survey; a report by the American Physical Society; and the first of the informal dispute-settlement processes, the Keystone discussion group.
	NRC begins a systematic program to develop regulations for low-level waste. (A similar effort for transuranic wastes had bogged down in the mid-1970s.)
1979	After five years of litigation, the S-3 Table is adopted by the Nuclear Regulatory Commission, providing an official framework for analyzing the environmental effects of the nuclear fuel cycle.
	IRG final report is issued.
1980	Carter "comprehensive" policy announced, endorsing most of the conclusions of the IRG. Several geologic media are to be explored for repository sites, WIPP is deferred, and the intergovernmental State Planning Council is established.
1981	Reagan Administration rejects the Carter policy and the recommendations of the State Planning Council.
	Waste Isolation Pilot Plant program is revived.
	DOE is reorganized to separate civilian and military waste management programs.

hard path, caught the nuclear establishment by surprise. Accustomed to the close-knit world of military nuclear affairs, the AEC, its congressional patrons on the Joint Committee on Atomic Energy, and its utility and industrial clients all failed to appreciate the political energies that could be marshaled against them.

The gathering political storm broke with the California nuclear proposition of 1976. Proposing an effective moratorium on nuclear power plant construction until safe waste disposal methods could be demonstrated, the nuclear in-

itiative seemed certain to pass. It was defeated only after the state legislature acted, at the last minute, to put much of the initiative into state law. No nuclear plants have been authorized in California since 1976, in part because of the "moratorium" policy.

More broadly, the future of commercial nuclear power has been linked to the unsatisfactory state of affairs in radioactive waste.[55] The problems that nuclear technologists label "public acceptance" have acquired a self-reinforcing dynamic: nuclear power is unacceptable because the waste issue is unresolved; nuclear waste disposal nearby is unacceptable—the more so because the track record has been so poor; so public opposition to site-specific research on waste disposal has grown, hampering the development of a technically sound repository.[56] Thus the lingering problem of waste stymies nuclear power.

The Struggle for a National Policy

The deepening crisis of nuclear power paralleled the growing visibility of energy in general. In 1974 the AEC was supplanted by two agencies, the Energy Research and Development Administration (ERDA) and the Nuclear Regulatory Commission. Three years later, ERDA was merged with the Federal Energy Administration—the agency responsible for allocation of petroleum after the 1973 oil embargo—to form the cabinet-level Department of Energy (DOE) (see Chapter 3). Also in 1977 the Joint Committee on Atomic Energy was disbanded as part of a reorganization of congressional energy responsibilities. At the same time, government spending on nuclear waste was dramatically increased.[57] Spending on waste management increases, it seems, when nuclear power wanes.

By 1977 the governmental nuclear establishment, once a model bureaucratic and congressional fiefdom,[58] was reduced to being merely influential.

If waste was a millstone around the neck of nuclear power, there was also a dagger at its throat: nuclear proliferation. Plutonium is produced in nuclear reactors, as uranium is exposed to neutrons. The plutonium is held in spent fuel until it is reprocessed; afterwards it is readily separated, and, under the proper conditions, is suitable for the manufacture of atomic weapons. Nuclear power reactors, already in use in many nations, are projected to be even more widely used in the future, particularly in developing countries. Access to reprocessing, therefore, seemed to be a key point at which the proliferation of nuclear weapons material

could be controlled.[59] It seemed possible—if hardly certain—that independent action by the United States could affect the willingness of nations in unstable regions to press on with their plans to acquire reprocessing facilities. So the "back end" of the fuel cycle suddenly acquired momentous significance.[60]

Where radioactive waste was merely menacing, the link between proliferation and political action was immediate. In the 1976 campaign, President Gerald Ford backed away from a commitment to commercial fuel reprocessing. Early in 1977, successful candidate Jimmy Carter deferred reprocessing indefinitely and called for an International Nuclear Fuel Cycle Evaluation. The deferral of reprocessing halted the licensing of the Allied-General Nuclear Services plant in Barnwell, after much of the plant had been built. The policy shift also defined spent fuel as a form of nuclear waste—opening up the possibility of its disposal without reprocessing and the accompanying generation of radioactive wastes.

The change in policy led naturally to a fresh look at radioactive waste. A task force of the DOE was expanded in 1978 into the Interagency Review Group on nuclear waste management, a fourteen-agency study group that was directed to formulate a new policy for radioactive waste. The IRG marked a new phase in government policy toward radioactive waste, much as the Princeton meeting in 1955 marked a new phase of technical development. The effectiveness of the IRG, like that of the National Academy of Sciences, has been decidedly mixed. President Carter issued a policy directive in February 1980 accepting the principal recommendations of the IRG; yet Congress resisted codifying these policies in law.

In the Reagan administration's first detailed statement on nuclear waste policy,[61] most of the IRG strategy was implicitly spurned, together with the recommendations of the Carter-appointed State Planning Council.[62] Reprocessing of spent fuel was again endorsed. The administration remained internally divided, however, over whether government subsidies for reprocessing of commercial nuclear fuel were warranted. Separately, the Waste Isolation Pilot Plant in New Mexico, deferred amid controversy in early 1980, was revived, once again as a repository for defense transuranic wastes. Scheduled for operation in the late eighties, its estimated cost has risen to $4 billion.

The Carter IRG sought to steer a moderate course through the nuclear debate. Its analyses and recommendations sought to be neutral on whether nuclear energy would continue to grow. Beyond this, the IRG position advocated a technologically conservative approach, recognizing division within the scientific community and seeking to reassure a doubting public that safety was, in fact, uppermost in government planning. Thus, sites in several different geologic media would be systematically explored; and a multiple-barrier approach would be used to design the waste encapsulation and its host geologic medium. Since this would all take time, federally-sponsored storage of spent fuel would be provided, so that utilities would not be forced to shut down reactors for lack of storage space for spent fuel rods.

The IRG also advocated a conciliatory political stance, acknowledging that the most serious near-term issue was finding sites suitable for geologic repositories—an issue that rekindled states' rights for the first time since the civil rights era. The objective was to keep wastes Not In My Back Yard–NIMBY, the acronymists called it. The IRG recommended that the National Environmental Policy Act be scrupulously followed; an intergovernmental State Planning Council be empaneled to serve as a forum for state-federal discussions; and the federal approach to state and local governments be one of "consultation and concurrence," to encourage cooperation and to counter the fear that the federal government wanted to ram through a preselected site.[63]

Yet the IRG solutions, sensible as they were, were mainly procedural steps. The substance of decisions on repositories, disposal practices, safety regulations, and—most of all—the future of nuclear power all awaited further study. In a way, this was inevitable: the questions that were most urgent, politically, were also the least well understood technically. In particular, a troublesome institutional question remains: how can one assure *in advance* the safe operation of a whole new waste management industry?[64]

"The fundamental questions have endured for almost two decades," historian Richard Hewlett remarked in 1978, as the IRG began its work.[65] They endure still.

The Current State of the Art

Given the uncertainties of public policy, the clearest view of U.S. capabilities to deal with radioactive waste may be a technological one. [66] Work in the United States government emphasizes preliminary siting analyses and research, with an emphasis on developmental projects leading toward a geologic repository. These activities are directed by the Office of Nuclear Waste Management of the DOE.

A recent review of the technical literature summarizes the state of the art.[67] *Geologic repositories,* mined cavities in carefully selected rock formations, are clearly the principal alternative for permanent disposal.[68] Of the possible competitors reviewed in the mid-seventies,[69] the sub-seabed technology seems the most plausible alternative, and it will not be available for some time.[70] Salt has been most thoroughly studied, but no final decision has been made on the geological medium for the first repository. Salt remains technically controversial for three reasons: it is highly soluble, and thus vulnerable if water enters the formation; the mineral itself does not immobilize radioactive atoms, unlike some other candidate rocks; and salt is often found with oil and other valuable minerals, enhancing the likelihood of inadvertent intrusion into a repository. Basalt, granite, shale, and volcanic tuff are other media for geologic disposal being studied consistent with the technologically conservative approach recommended by the IRG.

Government researchers opine that satisfactory models exist to describe the processes of radionuclide transport, should a repository be breached. Uncertainties remain: neither the flow patterns of water carrying wastes through fractured rock, nor the chemical interactions among wastes, water, and rock have yet been modeled.[71] More generally, it is agreed that the detailed behavior of the rock surrounding a repository is likely to be difficult to analyze. Accordingly, painstaking *site-specific* field studies will be needed to confirm the suitability of any proposed repository.[72]

The basic design strategy will be the *multiple-barrier* concept described above: waste form, packaging material for the waste, and surrounding rock will be chosen so as to reinforce one another. If this approach is carried out, the predictive models give no indication that a mined geologic disposal system cannot isolate radioactive wastes safely.[73] Inadvertent breaching of the repository by future generations remains a significant issue. Regulations issued by the Nuclear Regulatory Commission on the near-surface disposal of *low-level* waste are designed to protect public health in the event of an accidental breaching of the burial ground after it has been decommissioned.

Three variations on the multiple-barrier approach, two developed in other nations, are worth mentioning. All attempt to compensate for the inherent uncertainties of any disposal method that relies upon geologic containment. An Australian group has designed an ultra-stable waste form that they call synthetic rock—a material that can hold radioactive wastes in a mineral matrix highly resistant to leaching.[74] A second concept has been developed in Sweden, where high-level waste and spent fuel are to be

kept in interim underground storage for forty years. After four decades the heat emanating from these wastes declines by half. This facilitates elaborate packaging in copper cylinders surrounded by bentonite clay, which absorbs ions if there should be a leak. This multiple-barrier waste package is highly resistant to radionuclide migration, even if the geologic surroundings are less than perfect.[75] Third, two geologists from the U.S. Geologic Survey have recently proposed selecting sites that can provide multiple *geologic* barriers. The idea is to choose a site, paying attention to both the formation where the waste is to be stored and its surrounding strata. In favorable cases, the water flow patterns can be predicted for layered strata. Thus, the means by which radioactivity can be transported back to the biosphere can be understood with confidence, and a location selected where leakage, were it to occur, would be slow enough to pose no danger.[76]

Official documents do not mention locations already contaminated by radioactive wastes, so as not to prejudice site selection. Yet it is doubtful that Hanford and the Nevada Test Site could ever be returned to wholly unrestricted use. These are accordingly "natural" candidates for repositories;[77] indeed, exploratory work on basalt is being done at Hanford, and granite and volcanic tuff are being studied at Nevada. Already-contaminated sites pose the most serious long-term environmental challenges.

Mill tailings could impose small annual public-health costs for tens of thousands of years. The tailings are so massive, however, that elimination of these potential health effects for thousands of years is of doubtful feasibility.

Two unresolved institutional issues are of fundamental importance. First, an arrangement to pay for long-run management and disposal of wastes has yet to be developed. Current policy assigns responsibility to the federal government to isolate long-lived wastes. Though there is widespread agreement that those who benefit

14-12 PROGRESS IN DEFENSE HIGH-LEVEL WASTES

High-level wastes from the military programs may turn out to be technologically tractable—but perhaps not at a politically affordable price. Since the Manhattan Project, radioactive wastes have been stored in steel tanks, some of which have leaked, symbolizing government ineptitude in waste management.

Very recently, however, engineering development at two Department of Energy laboratories has led to promising advances. At the Oak Ridge National Laboratory, six small storage tanks holding intermediate-level radioactive sludges are being cleaned out by using remote-controlled high-pressure water pumps. It is estimated that this cleanup will cost $4 million.

Developmental work has also been done at the Savannah River Plant, where there are twenty-four large high-level waste storage tanks now in service. It has been shown that water sluicing is capable of removing sludge from a twenty-year old tank with a record of leaks. The DOE has proposed to clean out its other tanks at Savannah River, converting the waste to glass cylinders intended for geologic disposal. This Defense Waste Processing Facility (DWPF) would cost more than $2 billion, and the project would take nearly a decade to complete. The first stage, costing $850 million, is projected for authorization by Congress in fiscal year 1983. Funding for the DWPF must be approved by the defense appropriations subcommittees of Congress. These bodies care most about future military capability. Their willingness to fund a cleanup project costing as much as an aircraft carrier cannot be assumed.

---

from the use of radioactivity should bear the costs of waste management, there is no payment required now. Instead, governmental appropriations fluctuate—buffeted by the nuclear controversy—programs are reorganized, and performance is at best uncertain. User fees, such as a surcharge on nuclear-generated electricity, and a dedicated trust fund for managing wastes from military programs are both needed.

Second, how to regulate waste management activities undertaken by the federal government remains a divisive and conceptually murky question. The Reagan administration proposes three geologic test and evaluation facilities, built by the DOE or its successor to study the engineering feasibility of high-level waste disposal. These would not be licensed by the NRC. Such an approach may lead to more rapid technical learning but retard the gathering of institutional experience, which remains the pacing factor.

More generally, the question remains of how to supervise the government waste management enterprise, in light of the track record. Proposals abound: self-regulation by the DOE; regulation by the NRC; oversight by state governments and others representing populations at risk; adjudication of claims by special-purpose tribunals; and review of management decisions by the President or by one or both houses of Congress. None seems clearly superior or even adequate to the two somewhat different tasks at hand—ensuring safety and distributing the remaining risks fairly.

CONCLUSION

Since few public policies wholly succeed, it is important to diagnose partial failures. To this end one can evaluate by using several independent criteria. Four dimensions of appraisal are suggested by Brewer: theoretical, technical, ethical, and practical.[78] The problematic circumstances of radioactive waste management can be usefully illuminated by considering these aspects of policy outcomes.

First, the *theories* on which the radioactive waste management program is based appear to be scientifically sound. Throughout the vexed history of nuclear waste fundamental science has not been a constraint—though it has not always been well used.[79]

The *technical* success of the practices implemented has been disappointing. While understandable in the historical context, the original decision to produce neutralized sludges at Hanford led to far more difficult problems later—problems that could have been foreseen. That they were neither foreseen nor avoided at Savannah River and West Valley must be counted a failure. The problems encountered in the management of low-level wastes similarly indicate a gap between actual and acceptable practice. This is not to deny that technological progress has been made, notably the development of the calcine process at Idaho, the multiple barrier design philosophy, and recent work on defense high-level wastes.

On the *ethical* dimension, the repeated deferral of decisions to spend what was necessary to remedy the problems created is a stark failure. Delay is hardly an uncommon attribute of human behavior, of course; yet the burden on future generations resulting from the poor stewardship of generations now living is one that weighs heavily.[80] The ethical shortcomings of past practices are clearest in the case of mill tailings. Their radon and actinides may cause disease and early death in generations that will have received no direct benefit from the production of nuclear power or weapons.

Finally, U.S. radioactive waste policy has failed miserably at the *pragmatic* level. The benefits of electric power from the atom—putting aside the arguable benefits of nuclear deterrence—once seemed unlimited. Indeed, they still bulk

large. But so do the debits of nuclear power. However intense and articulate the opposition to nuclear energy, the nuclear establishment, both governmental and industrial, has often been its own worst enemy, with shortsighted technical decisions and repeated frustrations in its attempts to win public acceptance.

This decline in passing from theory to practice is distressing but enlightening, for it serves as a reminder that the *technological* task of radioactive waste management and disposal is *not* daunting. Yet demonstrating this tractability in a publicly credible fashion—in the midst of a deeply divisive struggle over nuclear energy—remains a challenge of imposing dimensions. It is worth remembering that the wastes cannot be wished away. And their current conditions and locations are, in several instances, clearly unacceptable for the long term. This implies action: ethically, if not practically, it is hard to make a case for delay. Sadly, delay is the most likely outcome—especially since the current administration has acted thus far only to repudiate the progress eked out during the Carter years.

More generally, there is consensus among the technically knowledgeable—including many of those opposed to nuclear energy—that radioactive waste can *in principle* be disposed of with hazards that are small, even in a strongly risk-averse polity. And even ardent proponents of nuclear power admit that the management of radioactive waste *in practice* has been seriously flawed. But conflict reigns, and even to take the institutional view adopted here can be seen as a source of bias: which is the better indicator, technical analyses of the (low) risks of waste management, or historical appraisals of past (poor) performance? The record of radioactive waste management is one in which, for all the missteps, little demonstrable harm has been done. As for technical analyses, critics have successfully pointed out significant weaknesses, but they have not discovered any unrecognized potential for disaster. Meanwhile, the market demands electricity, and the electorate rejects nuclear disposal sites.

What is striking about these contrasts is that the strong views in the controversy go somewhat past one another. It is surely incorrect to *substitute* expert analysis for the will of the electorate, or *vice versa*. But for now, what is logically a complementary relationship between knowledge and action has become, sociologically, a competitive one. Radioactive waste is, in Clark's phrase, modern witchcraft.[81]

Perhaps the most troublesome fact we have learned about nuclear energy is that it takes imperfect human institutions to bring it into being and to sustain it. To err is inevitable, in nuclear power as in every other aspect of human life. The very *comprehensibility* of the errors made in the management of radioactive waste—and the political dilemmas that we face now—stand, therefore, as experiential estimates of what nuclear energy may mean.

Suggested Readings

COHEN, BERNARD. "The Disposal of Radioactive Wastes from Fission Reactors." *Scientific American*, July 1977.

COLGLAZIER, E. WILLIAM, ED. *The Politics of Nuclear Waste.* New York: Pergamon, 1981.

LIPSCHUTZ, RONNIE D. *Radioactive Waste: Politics, Technology and Risk (A Report of the Union of Concerned Scientists).* Cambridge, Mass.: Ballinger, 1980.

ROCHLIN, GENE I. *Plutonium, Power, and Politics.* Berkeley, Calif.: University of California Press, 1979.

U.S. Department of Energy, Assistant Secretary for Nuclear Energy, Nuclear Waste Management Program. *Spent Fuel and Radioactive Waste Inventories and Projections as of December 31, 1980.* DOE/NE-0017, September 1981.

WILLRICH, MASON, AND RICHARD K. LESTER. *Nuclear Waste Management.* New York: Free Press, 1975.

September 19, 1980, a Titan II missile silo at Damascus, Arkansas: An accidental puncture of its fuel tank released the liquid fuel into the missile silo. Later the fuel exploded, blowing off the heavy silo cover and throwing the nuclear warhead several hundred yards from the silo. It did not explode.

15. Nuclear Accidents

The devices and systems of human invention are universally liable to failures of mechanism and errors of human judgment. The era of nuclear energy has provided new kinds of consequences of human error or miscalculation: the disaster of an accidental nuclear explosion or massive release of radioactivity; accidental radiation injury; and the cumulative but invisible effects of small amounts of radioactivity unintentionally released into the environment. Here we illustrate the risks by reviewing actual incidents.

THE PUBLIC IS generally unaware of the frequency and seriousness of accidents involving nuclear materials, yet an appreciation of the likelihood and consequences of accidents is important in considering future development of nuclear power generation and the future deployment of nuclear weapons. A review of accidents is one way of assessing the risk of a major disaster occurring—detonation of a nuclear warhead, a major release of radioactivity from a nuclear reactor or fuel processing plant, or a dispersal of highly toxic, long-lived plutonium. Other concerns are occupational safety of workers exposed to radiation and the gradual increase of radioactivity in the environment. We must acknowledge the error-prone nature of human institutions and guide future policies with full awareness of the risks being taken.

Broken Arrows

Major incidents involving nuclear warheads where there is significant damage to the warhead or actual detonation of the high explosive trigger are called *broken arrows* by the U.S. Department of Defense. Public information about such incidents is certainly incomplete; the Defense Department normally withholds information unless it is forced to release it by public pressure or when it becomes obvious that not releasing information is more damaging to the government than making it public.

"Since the location of a nuclear weapon is classified information, it is Department of Defense policy normally neither to confirm nor deny the presence of nuclear weapons at any particular place."[1]

The unintended detonation of a nuclear explosive in a populated area would be a disaster of unprecedented proportion and warrants extraordinary measures of prevention. How close we may have come to such a catastrophe is not possible to know, but past events are cause for grave concern.

Titan II missiles are intercontinental ballistic

Charles Zimmermann
Jack Dennis

Zimmermann, an economist, has compiled information worldwide on the hazards that accompany the nuclear age. Dennis is editor of this book.

missiles that formed the entire U.S. land-based strategic missile force in the sixties. They are powered by liquid fuel (Aerozine 50), using nitrogen tetroxide as the oxidizing agent. Each missile is equipped with a nine-megaton thermonuclear warhead.

> Before dawn on September 19, 1980 a violent explosion rent the Titan II missile silo near Damascus, Arkansas. There was a tremendous wind blast and fireball. Large steel fragments flew into the sky as the force blew off the 740-ton silo cover. The silo and missile were destroyed—the nine-megaton nuclear warhead fell to the ground some 200 yards from the silo.

A fuel tank puncture the preceding evening began a tense night that ended in disaster:

> Eight maintenance men were pressurizing the oxidizer tank, a routine procedure. One man dropped a wrench socket at about 6:30 P.M. This particular socket had been dropped before because of its awkward size and weight. It had always landed on the workers' platform, but this time it fell onto a rubber mat between the platform and the missile. The mat was designed to catch falling objects, but it was not strong enough to support the weight of the socket, which fell about seventy feet, bounced off a mounting, and punched a three- to five-inch break in the metal skin of the fuel tank. The leaking fuel triggered an automatic safety system which sprayed water on the rocket to dissolve the fuel and carry it to a cavity below the missile. The system was not designed to handle fuel leaks as large as this one, however, and fuel vapors continued to enter the air in the missile silo. Another automatic safety system, a set of giant exhaust fans to drive vapors out of the silo, had been ordered to be disconnected only a few months earlier. The order was in response to a release of toxic gases at a Titan II silo in Kansas (April 1980) that posed a danger to local farmers.
> The violent explosion occurred shortly after a team of two airmen had been ordered to reenter the evacuated silo to determine whether the concentration of fuel vapors had subsided. One of the airmen was killed; his partner and twenty others were injured.[2]

One wonders about the possibility that a nuclear explosion might occur as a result of an accident of the sort that occurred at Damascus. Other events involving warheads accidentally dropped from airplanes or involved in crashes support the position that the safety devices and interlocks that prevent an unintended nuclear explosion are effective. Yet, since the weapons must explode in an actual conflict, it is certainly conceivable that the sequence of events required to set off an explosion could occur accidentally. Just how likely or improbable this is appears impossible to judge without access to classified information.

According to the Department of Defense, early nuclear weapons included a "capsule of nuclear materials" which was kept separate from the weapon itself (for safety purposes) "during most operations," presumably when weapons were being transported or stored. In the case of strategic bombers, it seems likely that the capsule would have to be in place in the weapon before takeoff in an "alert."[3] So long as the capsule is separate from the weapon, there is no possibility of detonating a nuclear explosion, although the high explosive charge required to trigger the weapon can be, and indeed has been, detonated accidentally. Furthermore, there is the serious possibility of hazardous plutonium contamination if the nuclear material were involved in explosion or fire. In later weapons designs the Defense Department does not include the separate capsule of nuclear materials, as it is believed that sufficiently improved redundant safety devices have been adopted.

To detonate a full-yield nuclear explosion, a sequence of events must occur with precise timing. It is extremely unlikely that the exact combination of events required would result from an airplane crash, explosion, or fire, although a prudent person cannot rule out the possibility. The more worrisome prospect is that some portion of the safety features would be bypassed through human error, misjudgment, sabotage, or terrorism—making an accidental nuclear explosion dangerously probable.

Following the Titan II silo explosion in Arkansas, the possibility of accidental detonation of the warhead was discussed publicly by Air Force Secretary Hans Mark:

"Mark told one reporter who asked whether the warhead on the Damascus Titan II was accidentally 'detonatable' that the reporter was 'close to the edge of classified data' and simply noted that 'it is extremely difficult to create a nuclear explosion.' Mark called the possibility of an accidental explosion 'extremely small' but, when asked whether it was possible for 'random explosions' to arm a warhead, answered, 'Yes.' "[4]

At this time, the Defense Department provided a news release describing twenty-seven "broken arrows" including five incidents not previously announced. An incident on January 24, 1961, near Goldsboro, North Carolina, is described by the DOD as follows:

"During a B-52 airborne alert mission structural failure of the right wing resulted in two weapons separating from the aircraft during aircraft breakup at 2,000–10,000 feet altitude. One bomb parachute deployed and the weapon received little impact damage. The other bomb fell free and broke apart upon impact. No explosion occurred. Five of the eight crew members survived. A portion of one weapon, containing uranium, could not be recovered despite excavation in waterlogged farmland to a depth of fifty feet. The Air Force subsequently purchased an easement requiring permission for anyone to dig there. There is no detectable radiation and no hazard in the area."[5]

A public debate ensued over how close this incident had come to being an accidental nuclear explosion. Dr. Ralph Lapp, former head of the nuclear physics branch of the Office of Naval Research, wrote in 1962 that only one switch prevented the explosion:

"The Defense Department has adopted complex devices and strict rules to prevent the accidental arming or firing of nuclear weapons. In this case

the 24-megaton warhead was equipped with six interlocking safety mechanisms, all of which had to be triggered in sequence to explode the bomb. When Air Force experts rushed to the North Carolina farm to examine the weapon after the accident, they found that five of the six interlocks had been set off by the fall! Only a single switch prevented the 24-megaton bomb from detonating and spreading fire and destruction over a wide area."[6]

After the Goldsboro accident, President John F. Kennedy initiated a review of mechanisms and procedures for nuclear weapon safety.[7] He even took steps to ensure that Soviet diplomats and scientists knew about U.S. safety concepts and were encouraged to see that similar safety measures were used in Soviet weapon systems.[8]

Another accident occurred at an "overseas base" on January 31, 1958:

"A B-47 with one weapon in strike configuration was making a simulated takeoff during an exercise alert.... The aircraft caught fire and burned for seven hours.... The high explosive did not detonate, but there was some contamination in the immediate area of the crash. After the wreckage and the asphalt beneath it were removed and the runway washed down, no contamination was detected."

It seems likely that "strike configuration" means that the capsule of nuclear materials was in place in the weapon at the time of the accident.

Several incidents have led to detonation of the high explosive trigger of a nuclear weapon, including one accidental drop of a weapon near Kirtland Air Force Base in New Mexico on May 27, 1957. But the two most serious accidents involving U.S. nuclear weapons took place outside the United States over Spain on January 17, 1966, and near Thule, Greenland, on January 21, 1968. In both cases the B-52 strategic bombers were flying airborne alert missions and are thought to have carried nuclear weapons in the 20 to 25 megaton range:

"The B-52 and the KC-135 collided during a routine high altitude air refueling operation. Both aircraft crashed near Palomares, Spain. Four of the eleven crewmembers survived. The B-52 carried four nuclear weapons. One was recovered on the ground, and one was recovered from the sea, on April 7, after extensive search and recovery efforts. Two of the weapons' high explosive materials exploded on impact with the ground, releasing some radioactive materials. Approximately 1400 tons of slightly contaminated soil and vegetation were removed to the United States for storage at an approved site. . . ."

"A B-52 from Plattsburgh AFB, New York, crashed and burned some seven miles southwest of the runway at Thule AB, Greenland, while approaching the base to land. Six of the seven crewmembers survived. The bomber carried four nuclear weapons, all of which were destroyed by fire. Some radioactive contamination occurred in the area of the crash, which was on the sea ice. Some 237,000 cubic feet of contaminated ice, snow, and water, with crash debris, were removed to an approved storage site in the United States over the course of a four-month operation. Although an unknown amount of radioactive contamination was dispersed by the crash, environmental sampling showed normal readings in the area after the cleanup was completed. Representatives of the Danish government monitored the cleanup operations."

Following the accidents at Palomares and Thule, the Defense Department discontinued the practice of keeping strategic bombers on "airborne alert"—in part because of the accidents and other costs, and partly because ICBMs had taken over their "more time-sensitive responsibilities." This explains why there have been no acknowledged broken arrows involving aircraft since 1968, although there have been many accidents involving aircraft capable of carrying nuclear weapons.

Silo explosions and aircraft crashes in populated areas are too noticeable to be denied by a government, but this is not as true for submarines, carrier aircraft, and much of the tactical nuclear armament.

"This near holocaust [Goldsboro] occurred on Jan. 24, 1961—four days after the inauguration of John

F. Kennedy. And as the new President soon learned, it was not an isolated affair. Since the end of World War II, Kennedy was told, there have been more than 60 accidents involving nuclear weapons—including two cases in which nuclear-tipped anti-aircraft missiles were actually launched by inadvertence."[9]

"In the mid-1960s an F-102 pilot fired a nuclear missile by accident against some North Vietnamese gunboats in Haiphong Bay. The error reportedly was caused by a crossed wire in the firing safety mechanism."[10]

"Premier Khrushchev is reliably reported to have told Vice-President Nixon about an erratic Soviet missile which was destroyed by a signal from the ground as it headed towards Alaska."[11]

In 1962 the United States conducted a series of high-altitude nuclear test explosions by launching Thor ICBMs to heights of from 30 to 500 miles above Johnston Island in the Pacific. In two attempts to carry out one of the test shots (June 4 and June 20), failure of the rocket made it necessary to abort the test and destroy the missile by signal from the ground.[12]

Accidents in Test Explosions

Nuclear weapons testing has had unfortunate consequences when unforeseen changes in the weather led to contamination of populated areas. The most severe U.S. accident of this type occurred in one of the first hydrogen bomb tests, the Bravo explosion of March 1, 1954, at Bikini Atoll:

"A total of over 7,000 square miles was contaminated to such an extent that avoidance of death or radiation injury would have depended upon evacuation of the area or taking protective measures. . . . At distances of 300 miles or more downwind, the number of deaths due to short-term radiation effects would have been negligible, although there would probably have been many cases of sickness resulting in temporary incapacity."[13]

The fallout on Rongelap Island "had the appearance of flour and salt" because it contained

15-1 CASTLE BRAVO THERMONUCLEAR TEST

March 1, 1954: This multimegaton thermonuclear test explosion unexpectedly exposed 23 Japanese fishermen, 239 natives of the Marshall Islands, and 28 American servicemen to radiation from fallout. One fisherman died as a consequence.

particles of coral reef pulverized by the bomb:

> "This phenomenon continued for approximately a 12-hour period by which time the palm leaf homes, cook houses, sheds, vegetation, and the inhabitants themselves had been blanketed with white material up to a depth of 0.5 in."[14]

Among sixty-four natives heavily exposed to radiation, 66 percent were nauseated for two days, 25 percent developed skin burns, and 10 percent vomited and had diarrhea.[15] Other victims of the Bravo test were the twenty-five-member crew of the Japanese fishing vessel *Lucky Dragon*. All twenty-five suffered radiation sickness from the effects of fallout, and one died seven months later.[16] After the Bravo test, the native population was evacuated from Bikini to prevent further injury and death.

Much controversy has surrounded the weapons tests carried out by the Atomic Energy Commission (AEC) at the Nevada Test Site (see Chapter 16). Many years after the progression of test series conducted between 1951 and the banning of atmospheric tests in 1963, it has been confirmed that thousands of deaths of sheep were caused by fallout from the testing program and that the excessively high incidence of leukemia and other forms of cancer in nearby populated areas was also a consequence of the tests:

> "The scientific evidence for the committee conclusion comes from former AEC official Harold Knapp, who put together a 450-page report on the sheep deaths in his spare time. Some 1,420 lambing ewes and 2,970 new lambs out of a sheep population of 11,710, died during the spring and summer of 1953. Although the AEC cites bad weather and lack of forage as a prime cause, Knapp says that the most likely explanation of the ewe deaths was eating radioactive grass, which led to irradiation of the gastrointestinal tract, and that new-

born lambs died from prenatal accumulation of radioactive iodine in their thyroid glands."[17]

It seems it was very difficult for the AEC to predict the path of the fallout cloud following a test explosion, and both livestock and the human population received high exposures without being aware of the hazards. The people of St. George, Utah, were hit with enough radioactivity that the AEC was specifically instructed to avoid sending nuclear clouds their way:

"It was the small Mormon towns, however, that were hit hardest by the fallout and which today are reporting the staggering cancer mortality rates. The town of St. George, Utah, which lies about 242 km east of Yucca Flats, has become known locally as Fallout City. On May 19, 1953, an unspecified accident with the detonation of a bomb called 'Harry' exposed St. George to more fallout than was ever to be measured in any other populated area.

"According to testimony of General Mahlon Gates, the current manager of the Yucca Flats site, Harry delivered a total dose of 6,000 millirems to St. George's population in one day...."[18]

The end of atmospheric testing did not end the danger of accidental exposure, for testing continued underground and some of the test shots have vented radioactive material into the atmosphere:

"This nuclear detonation [the Baneberry Shot] was conducted at the Nevada Test Site, at 0730 PST, on December 18, 1970, in a vertical hole 910 feet deep. The explosive yield of this test was less than twenty kilotons. All of the programmed operations proceeded normally until 3.5 minutes after the detonation when a release of radioactivity commenced from a fissure which opened up after the detonation at a distance of about 300 feet from the emplacement hole. This release continued over an extended period even after the commonly experienced surface collapse which occurred at 16.5 minutes after the detonation. This surface collapse was a normal and expected phenomenon. The effluent venting rate steadily decreased with time but visible vapor continued to emanate from

the fissure for twenty-four hours after the detonation. It is estimated that about 3,000,000 curies of radioactivity at R + 12 hours were released to the atmosphere.... The presence of the radioactive material was detected in environmental samples from central and northern Nevada and in most of the western United States."[19]

Plutonium

Plutonium is a most dangerous material. It can ignite spontaneously in air, and it is highly toxic to humans—a tiny amount of plutonium introduced into the bloodstream will deposit in the bone and is likely to cause leukemia. Plutonium dust in the lungs also poses a serious health hazard.

Plutonium was produced in natural nuclear reactors formed in uranium deposits early in earth's history, when fissionable U-235 accounted for a larger fraction of uranium than it does today.[20] Yet plutonium was not introduced into our human environment—the biosphere—in significant amounts until it was produced in the nuclear reactors of the Manhattan Project. It has since been given global distribution by the testing of nuclear weapons in the atmosphere because a fission explosion consumes only a portion of its fissionable material. Plutonium has contributed local contamination of the environment through a variety of accidents: whenever the explosive trigger of a nuclear weapon is set off without detonating a nuclear explosion, plutonium is distributed in dangerous concentrations in the immediate vicinity of the blast. The broken arrows at Palomares and Thule are examples.

The island of Runit was heavily contaminated in this way by a weapon test in 1958:

"In 1958, an 18-kiloton device exploded on Runit but failed to chain react, spreading plutonium all over the island. Officials decided the island could never be decontaminated and instead should be used as the burying ground for radioactive material and soil removed from other islands in the atoll."[21]

Reputedly, this test was made to prove the resistance of nuclear weapons to accidental nuclear detonation.

The U.S. Department of Energy operates a major plutonium works at Rocky Flats, Colorado, where parts for nuclear weapons are manufactured from the heavy, manmade metal. The plant, managed for some years by the Dow chemical company, was frequently criticized for being less than candid about environmental problems created by its operation. Major plutonium fires occurred in 1957 and 1969; and a large volume of contaminated material was shipped by train to a federal waste disposal site in Idaho following the 1969 fire.[22]

"In 1958, Dow Chemical took the plutonium contaminated oil used in the fabrication process and began storing it in steel drums in an open field. Leaks were discovered the following year.... Winds picked up the plutonium contaminated soil near the leaky drums and carried it south and east of the plant, toward Denver, Broomfield, and Golden. For ten years these leaks continued without the public's being informed."[23]

Plutonium-238 (Pu-238) is an alpha-emitter with a half-life of eighty-six years. The energy release rate of this material makes it useful as a power source for systems and equipment that must operate unattended in remote areas for long time periods. Power sources of this type have been used in space missions, including the Apollo 11 and 12 lunar expeditions. In April 1964 a U.S. satellite containing 900 grams of Pu-238 burned up on its premature reentry, dispersing the radioactive material throughout the Northern Hemisphere.[24]

In 1965 an India-U.S. intelligence team placed a device at an altitude of about 23,600 feet on the slopes of Nanda Devi for the purpose of monitoring Chinese nuclear weapons tests. The device used a power supply containing 3.8 pounds of Pu-238. It was lost in an avalanche and could not be found in three years of searching.[25]

Accidents in Nuclear Energy

The worst possible accident that could happen in a nuclear power plant is a reactor meltdown followed by release into the atmosphere of a substantial fraction of the fission products held in the reactor core. The possible danger from such an event is roughly the same as the fallout from a nuclear weapon detonated on the ground but without the blast and thermal effects of the nuclear bomb. An operating 1,000 megawatt power reactor holds roughly 3,000 kilograms of fission products. It is estimated that in an extremely serious reactor accident, including core meltdown and breach of the containment structure, 15 to 30 kilograms of radioactive fission products might be released—equivalent to the fission yield of a 300-kiloton to 500-kiloton nuclear weapon. However, a weapon detonation would produce much more of the short-lived radioactive material that can cause prompt fatalities.[26] In a serious reactor accident there would be more time for people to evacuate the fallout area—an area that would be uninhabitable and unusable for agriculture for many years. The melting of spent fuel rods or the overheating of high level nuclear wastes could also release large quantities of long-lived fission products, as would an explosion or fire involving these materials.

Before dawn on March 28, 1979, the power reactor of Unit 2 at the Three Mile Island nuclear power station shut down. The cause was loss of feed water supply to the steam generators, one of many contingencies engineers must anticipate in nuclear plant design. Yet, on this morning the succeeding events subjected a large population in Pennsylvania to the anguish and frustration of not knowing whether they would be forced to abandon their homes and neighborhoods by human acts in peacetime that were beyond their control.

Through a combination of confusing instrumentation, operator error, closed valves that should have been open, and a valve that failed to operate correctly, a minor problem transformed into a nightmarish "loss-of-coolant" event: The escape of

15-2   **NUCLEAR REACTOR SAFETY**

At Three Mile Island it was dramatically shown that the meltdown of a nuclear reactor and the consequent dispersal of large amounts of radioactive material are real possibilities. The experience at Harrisburg, and earlier incidents at Brown's Ferry and the Fermi Reactor in Detroit, have shown how large a role the difficult-to-quantify factors of human judgment and competence play in determining the likelihood of a major accident.

In 1974 the AEC sponsored a major study of safety issues for nuclear power plants. The study, directed by M.I.T. professor Norman Rasmussen, was undertaken "to reach meaningful conclusions about the risks of nuclear accidents using current technology. It is recognized that the present state of knowledge will probably not permit a complete analysis of low-probability accidents in nuclear plants with the precision that would be desirable...." The result was the Reactor Safety Study published in 1975, also known as WASH-1400 (its official report number), or the Rasmussen Report.

To assess the risk of a major reactor accident, one must know the probability that an accident will occur and estimate its probable consequences. The event of concern is a reactor meltdown leading to a massive release of radioactive material. Although one pathway for radioactive contamination is leakage into groundwater, the most significant public danger comes from the radioactive material that would be released to the atmosphere and distributed downwind. The consequences depend on the weather, topography of the land, population density, the success of any plans for evacuation, and on the volume and nature of material released. The Reactor Safety Study includes an estimate of the consequences of an "extremely serious reactor accident"—a massive release of radioactive material under the worst conditions of weather and population distribution to be expected for reactor sites in the United States. The most telling effect would be the 45,000 cancer fatalities to be expected during the 30-year period following the accident. Most of these would result from exposure during the first week of fallout.

Consequences of an Extremely Serious Reactor Accident

	Casualties	*Time Period*
Medical Consequences		
Radiation Sickness		
Prompt fatalities	3,300	1–6 weeks
Early illness	45,000	1–6 weeks
Long Term Effects		
Thyroid nodules	240,000	30 years
Cancer fatalities	45,000	10–40 years
Genetic defects	30,000	150 years
Economic Effects		
Loss Due to Contamination	$14 billion	
Decontamination Area	3,200 square miles	

How likely is it that a reactor will experience a fuel meltdown leading to a breach of the containment structure and a massive release of radioactivity? In the Reactor Safety Study this question is addressed by fault tree analysis, a method of estimating the probability of a combination of faults occurring in a complex engineering system. A conclusion of the study was that a core meltdown and breach of containment could be expected to take place once in each 20,000 years of reactor operation, or once every 200 years for a country with 100 operating nuclear plants. It is estimated that there would be one chance in 10,000 that the weather, population distribution, and the seriousness of the radiation release would combine to yield the "extremely serious reactor accident" described above.

The primary criticism of the Rasmussen Report concerns the difficulty of assigning specific probabilities to the simple faults and actions that may combine to cause a serious accident, when little relevant experience exists. A probability larger or smaller by orders of magnitude would express equally well the present state of knowledge. Of great concern are design errors, operator mistakes, deficiencies in operator training, inadequate or lax regulation. Responsible critics have concluded that the estimate of accident probability in the Reactor Safety Study could be high or low by a factor as large as 500. In addition, the analysis has been criticized for not considering unanticipated modes of failure.

The main argument of proponents of nuclear power is not that there is no risk, or that a disastrous meltdown is impossible, but rather that the expected damage to society from using nuclear power is worth the benefits to be gained.

water through a pressure relief valve continued until pressure in the reactor core was low enough that steam bubbles formed around the fuel elements. Circulation of water through the reactor core slowed to a trickle and was unable to carry away the decay heat of the shut down reactor. The temperature of the fuel elements rose from its normal 2,000 degrees Fahrenheit to as high as 4,000 degrees, causing the zircaloy cladding to react with the water—deforming and releasing hydrogen gas into the coolant. The rupture of fuel rods also released radioactive fission products—krypton, xenon, and iodine—into the coolant and subsequently into the atmosphere when overpressure in coolant tanks was vented. The possibility that a hydrogen bubble in the reactor core could explode caused a public scare which took some time to dispel once it was realized that the oxygen required to produce such an explosion could not possibly be present in the core.

The accident at Three Mile Island (TMI)[27] brought increased public attention to the safety problems of nuclear power reactors. Although no prompt deaths occurred at TMI, and the amount of radiation released was small, there was severe damage to the reactor core. Repairs on the damaged reactor core cannot begin until radioactive materials released from the overheated core are removed. Six months after the accident, close to a million curies of radioactive fission products remained in cooling water in the reactor and in various holding tanks at TMI. About 51,000 curies of the radioactive gas krypton-85 were still present in the atmosphere inside the containment structure. Cleanup of this radioactive contamination required careful planning and even the design and construction of new equipment for processing the cooling water and filtering the air. The first human entry into the reactor building to assess damage and contamination directly took place on July 23, 1980, sixteen months after the accident.[28] It was expected that as many as 2,000 truckloads of radioactive waste would be shipped from Three Mile Island during cleanup operations. It was estimated that the costs of removing hazardous materials, decontamination, and restarting the plant would amount to more than $1 billion.

Investigation of the TMI accident has revealed that although errors in plant design and equipment malfunction contributed to the accident, normal operation of the reactor would have been quickly restored if the operators had understood what was happening and followed well-known procedures. Thus the accident became serious only because of human failure—inadequate training of operators, poor supervision, and operating procedures that were inadequately stated or not followed. In addition, responsibility for alerting the public to the potential hazard was not clearly defined and communication between local, state, and federal agencies and the press was criticized.

Problems of overheating and fuel melting have arisen in all types of nuclear reactors. In each case the evidence shows a similar combination of equipment malfunction or failure, design defects, and human errors in plant operation.

The Enrico Fermi 1 reactor was the first commercial breeder power reactor constructed in the United States; it was designed to produce more plutonium fuel by conversion of uranium than the amount of uranium fuel consumed by fission to produce thermal energy. Construction of the Fermi reactor began in 1956 and operation commenced in 1963 as a demonstration of breeder technology by an AEC/industry development program.

> At 3:09 on the afternoon of October 5, 1965, radiation alarms in the reactor building announced a Class 1 radiation emergency. At the time of the alarm the reactor staff was raising the power level to test whether previously observed temperature anomalies would recur. It was discovered that portions of the reactor core had overheated due to obstruction of coolant flow in portions of the reactor core. The result was melting and deformation of fuel elements and the release of some

10,000 curies of radioactive fission products into the coolant. Three years after the fuel melting incident, the cause of the coolant obstruction was discovered—zirconium liners installed as an afterthought in the reactor design had torn loose and partially blocked the flow of coolant. Subsequently, analysis showed that the liners were unnecessary. Repairs were completed and full power operation of the reactor was achieved for the first time in October, 1970, seventeen years after the project started.[29]

The Fermi reactor was shut down permanently in 1972.

At Brown's Ferry, Alabama, two 1,100-megawatt water-cooled power reactors supply electricity to the Tennessee Valley Authority. On March 22, 1975, a small fire showed how poor design and lack of redundancy in a crucial part of the plant caused a control room nightmare and nearly led to a reactor meltdown.[30]

> With the two reactors operating at full power, two electricians were using sheets of polyurethane foam to stop air drafts in a wall opening for control and instrumentation cables to pass from the reactor control room above to the two reactor containment structures. During use of a candle flame to check whether the drafts had been stopped, the foam ignited and fire spread to the vinyl insulation on the cables. Attempts to put out the fire with carbon dioxide and dry chemical extinguishers failed. Twenty minutes after the fire began, operators in the control room began losing control and instrumentation of the two reactors. Ten minutes later the coolant pumps for Unit 1 lost power and the operator decided that the unit should be shut down. With the loss of control of the emergency core cooling system, and control and instrumentation of other equipment, there ensued a ten-hour struggle to find means of removing the heat of residual reactivity from the Unit 1 core so a fuel meltdown would not occur. The struggle ended when a makeshift arrangement was devised using a condensate pump to inject cooling water into the reactor.

The Saint Laurent reactor near Orleans, France, is a high temperature, gas-cooled power reactor

15-3 BROWN'S FERRY NUCLEAR POWER PLANT

In 1975 this large nuclear plant of the Tennessee Valley Authority was the site of a fire in electrical cables that disabled critical control systems. A fuel meltdown in one of the 1,065-megawatt reactors was narrowly avoided.

(HTGR) constructed by the French national electric power agency, Electricité de France. In this reactor design, fuel elements are replaced frequently, so a robot fuel-handling machine is built on top of the reactor structure to accomplish fuel replacement without shutting down the reactor. Construction of the power plant was completed in late 1968.

The reactor was being tested at about half power when a fuel melting incident occurred during a machine-controlled refueling operation. Because the refueling machine had been given incorrect instructions by an engineer and its human operator failed to heed warning signals, a graphite flow restrictor was mistakenly loaded into a fuel channel containing active fuel elements. The loss of coolant flow led to overheating and damage to some fifty kilograms of uranium fuel. After decontamination, repairs, and adoption of a fuel loading plan not requiring the graphite flow restrictors,

the reactor was expected to be in commercial operation by the end of 1970.[31]

Through 1981, the only reactor incident to have led to significant public hazard from radioactive contamination occurred in England in October 1957:

The Windscale Plant of the United Kingdom Atomic Energy Authority consists of a nuclear reactor fueled with magnox-clad uranium cartridges, moderated with graphite, and cooled by the flow of air. During a normal period of operation at low power, the temperature of the reactor was permitted to rise too rapidly, causing failure of the cladding of one or more fuel cartridges. The exposed fuel burned, releasing fission products to the atmosphere through a 405-foot tall stack. A cloud of Iodine-131 containing about 20,000 curies of radioactivity drifted southward from the plant, contaminating the countryside. The major hazard was the production of milk containing dangerous levels of radioactive iodine. Distribution of consumption of milk over an area of 200 square miles was banned for up to twenty-five days before the radio-iodine concentration fell to the arbitrarily chosen "safe" level of 0.1 microcuries per liter of milk. The farmers were compensated for loss of income by payments of 180,000 dollars.[32]

Experience with the operation of nuclear reactors and their safety arrangements points out the significance of human error—as expressed in design decisions, unwillingness to make needed changes when "the present mode of working seems satisfactory," as well as irresponsible management and inadequate training and operating procedures. This all combines to make one wonder whether expecting humans to operate such elaborate and hazardous systems is desirable, regardless of how safe they are in principle.

We know from the public record that in each significant reactor accident, a strange combination of events took place leading to the ultimate damage. In the case of nuclear weapons accidents we do not know the details to judge how close we have come to a major disaster and how far human errors have taken us along a path to calamity. However, the event in 1969 at the Oak Ridge Research Reactor showed that even a facility operated by the most knowledgeable and experienced team can run into trouble. In this case there were *seven* independent failures (equipment problems and human error), the absence of any one being sufficient to have prevented operation of the reactor without loss-of-coolant protection.[33]

At the Oak Ridge Research Reactor, protection against fuel melting from decay heat is provided by three battery-operated motors that drive the coolant pumps at a speed one-tenth of normal operating speed upon loss of power to the main pump motors. The reduced speed makes battery operation feasible, yet provides sufficient coolant flow to remove decay heat.

On November 19, 1969 the reactor was started up and operated for five hours without benefit of this emergency backup system, for, unknown to the operators, all three independent battery supplies were discharged. Investigation showed that the incident resulted from the same switch being operated in error in each of the three control panels for the backup system.

The scram system is the safety system designed to shut a reactor down quickly in case of failure of the normal operating mechanism for the control rods—the mechanism used to set the level of reactor power.

In 1970 the N Reactor of the Atomic Energy Commission's Hanford Works in Washington State was the largest commercial power reactor in operation. On September 30 in that year, a low coolant flow caused originally by a clogged pump strainer initiated a signal to scram the reactor. However, no safety rods moved to stop the chain reaction, even though each rod is driven by its own independent hydraulic mechanism. The cause is curious: each safety rod is held out of the reactor by a solenoid magnet so that the rod will operate if current to the solenoid is interrupted for any reason. The control circuit includes a group of four diodes that allows the rod to be held out of the reactor core for maintenance. It turns out that if the diodes for one rod are all shorted, and that rod is switched out of service, then reverse current through the diodes holds all other rods out in spite of the signal to scram. This is exactly what happened. Fortunately, a backup system consisting of neutron-absorbing balls that drop into the core from bins above the reactor brought about a normal shutdown of the reactor.[34]

Following a complicated incident at the Dresden power plant of the Commonwealth Edison Company of Chicago in June 1970, the author of a report on the accident wrote:

"It is unfortunate that procedural, mechanical, and control inadequacies can be recognized only upon the occurrence of some incident that puts them to a real test. The Dresden 2 installation, its procedures, and its operating staff have benefitted substantially, in the long run, from having suffered and recovered from this particular incident."[35]

Nuclear power reactors are not the only nuclear energy installations subject to nuclear accidents. Spills and other releases of radioactive

15-4   A POSSIBLE MAXIMUM NUCLEAR ACCIDENT

A reactor meltdown is not the worst kind of nuclear accident possible short of a weapon explosion. Some tanks of high-level nuclear wastes contain far more radioactive material than a reactor core. The heat generated by the radioactivity must be taken away or the tank could rupture, leading to a massive release of radioactive material. A similar event appears to have occurred in the 1957 Soviet accident at Kyshtym. The material quoted below is from a 1970 report of the Oak Ridge National Laboratory, where theoretical studies of such massive releases were performed at a time when commercial high-level wastes were expected to form a rapidly growing share of high-level wastes in the United States.

A maximum thoretical accident has been evaluated for the purpose of illustrating the worst possible consequences that could result from poor design and/or implementation of good practice. Since waste storage tanks are known to have the largest inventory of physiologically hazardous materials, we have assumed that a hydrogen-air explosion occurs in the vapor space of an acid waste tank containing a two-year accumulation of fission products.

. . . Assuming that the loss of purge air is undetected and that there is a source of ignition after twenty-four hours, the resultant explosion would . . . elevate the concrete roof and earth cover by several feet, and (we assume) rupture the coolant and off-gas piping in such a manner that complete loss of cooling would ensue, and the tank would be directly vented to the atmosphere.

. . . The consequences of a waste tank boildown may be found. . . . The doses thus obtained (more than 100,000 rems at 0.4 kilometers downwind) have little meaning other than to show why maximum theoretical accidents must be rendered incredible through the use of appropriate engineered safety features.

materials can and do occur in the mining and processing of uranium, in uranium enrichment, fuel fabrication plants, fuel reprocessing, nuclear waste processing, and in the transportation of nuclear materials.

The number of nuclear facilities makes it inevitable that mistakes, failures, and natural disasters will lead to unintended human exposures and releases of radioactive material into the environment. Releases of material are significant, not because they are an immediate lethal hazard but because long-lived radioactivity is added to the environment and contributes to a continuing, general, long-term increase in the risk of cancer and genetic defects which are suffered more by generations to come than by the present population.

A serious release occurred in 1979 when the dam of a uranium mill tailings pond failed; millions of gallons of uranium milling wastes were lost into a branch of the Little Colorado River, leaving a radiation hazard that will affect residents of the area for many centuries (see Chapter 20).

Another serious release occurred at the Hanford Reservation near Richland, Washington, when high-level liquid wastes were being transferred into a tank that, unknown to the operators, had a leak of about 100 gallons per hour. Some 115,000 gallons of liquid flowed into the earth and threatened to pollute groundwater near the Columbia River (see Chapter 14).

Accidents in transporting nuclear materials occur every so often. In a 1975 incident a con-

tainer of cobalt-60, an intensely radioactive isotope, was lost from a truck. A survey plane
flying the truck's 1,100-mile route at a 500-foot
altitude located the material in a ditch near St.
Joseph, Missouri.[36]

There have been few accidents in the United
States in commercial reprocessing or transportation of spent nuclear fuel because the reprocessing of this fuel to separate plutonium and
reusable uranium has been found to be uneconomical and to encourage proliferation of nuclear weapons. Not so in Europe:

> "A fire at a nuclear reprocessing plant has re-
> ignited controversy over France's nuclear energy
> program. Officials have been unable to determine
> the cause of the blaze that broke out last Tuesday
> in a silo housing nuclear wastes. The fire was ex-
> tinguished in a few hours and spread no further
> than the silo, but three employees were contami-
> nated by high-level radiation at the plant in La
> Hague, near Cherbourg."[37]

Large quantities of fission products are held in
the fuel rod storage pools at reactor sites and in
tanks of high-level nuclear wastes from processing nuclear materials for atomic weapons. These
concentrated holdings of highly radioactive materials pose the possibility of the ultimate nuclear tragedy—the explosion of a nuclear bomb
at a nuclear power reactor, a spent fuel storage
pool, or a high-level waste tank. The resulting
fallout radioactivity would be many times larger
than that due to the nuclear explosion by
itself.[38]

Industrial Nuclear Safety

The handling of nuclear materials must be
done with great care to avoid exposure of humans to radiation. A sure way to commit nuclear suicide is to assemble together sufficient
fissionable material to obtain a critical mass. The
resulting flux of neutrons and gamma rays will
deliver a lethal dose in a fraction of a second.
Such a *criticality accident* occurs when a critical mass is unintentionally assembled and harmful radiation exposure or equipment damage en-

sues.[39] The earliest criticality accidents occurred
at the Los Alamos Laboratory where experimen-
ters first worked with sufficient plutonium to
form a critical mass. In August 1945 and again
in May 1946 workers put together assemblies of
metallic plutonium and accidentally allowed
them to become supercritical. In both cases one
experimenter received a mortal dose and died
of radiation sickness within a month.

A criticality accident can also occur when the
fissionable material is in liquid form, as is typical
in a spent fuel reprocessing plant:

> At the Y-12 Chemical Processing Plant, Oak Ridge,
> Tennessee, workers were draining into a 55-gallon
> drum what they thought was only water used to
> check a piping arrangement for leaks. Because
> valves were not properly set process solution con-
> taining uranium-235 also flowed into the drum.
> The flow was such that for a brief time the drum
> held about 2.1 kilograms of U-235 in a geometry
> that was supercritical, yielding several brief power
> spikes amounting to some 10^{18} fissions. Eight per-
> sons received neutron and gamma-ray doses of as
> much as 461 rem.

When spills or exposures occur, elaborate and
expensive procedures are used to clean up the
resulting contamination. At the Hanford Reservation there are extensive facilities for decontamination of equipment that has seen service
in areas of high radioactivity or has received accidental exposure. There is also a new medical
center for handling persons accidentally exposed to radioactive materials. The planning for
this facility paid off when the first patient, victim of an explosion inside a special "glove box"
for working with plutonium and other actinides,
was brought in having inhaled a large dose of
americium-241.[40]

When Is an Incident an Accident?

In listing or counting "nuclear accidents,"
one must use some reasonable criterion for deciding which events to include. Even a careful
definition leaves doubt about what should be included and what should be left out. The "acci-

dents" surveyed here do not account for all undesirable or hazardous incidents involving death and injury from radiation or radioactive material. We have not included acts of war, terrorism, sabotage, the theft of nuclear weapons or nuclear material, the illegal dumping of nuclear waste, or the use of radioactive material to purposely cause injury or death.

We do not know how many accidents and serious exposures may have occurred that have not been reported for reasons of secrecy, and we do not know how much contamination of the environment by plutonium and other actinides may have occurred. We do know that at least several tons of uranium-235 and plutonium are unaccounted for in the inventories of the U.S. government.[41] A more difficult judgment is deciding what level of radiation exposure or contamination should be considered sufficiently hazardous to characterize an accident. Each government agency has its own criteria for reporting accidents and for classifying potentially hazardous incidents involving nuclear materials.[42]

Possibly the most bizarre kind of nuclear accident is an event like the fall of the Soviet Cosmos 954 satellite, powered by a nuclear reactor containing 100 pounds of enriched uranium. This satellite was designed to operate in a relatively low orbit and then rise to a higher orbit from which it would fall back into the atmosphere after 1,000 years.[43] Its fall was premature, and the satellite's reentry strewed nuclear reactor fragments and radioactive fission products over Canada in 1978. The "accident" was that it happened in 1978 rather than a thousand years later, and that the debris landed in Canada. The cleanup cost the Canadian and U.S. governments at least $15 million.[44]

Conclusion

Let us place the dangers of nuclear accidents in perspective with other risks faced by the human race. In global terms the leading causes of death have been disease, famine, and war, rather than catastrophic events. For example, in 1978 the death rates for children in developing countries aged one to five exceeded the comparable death rates in countries such as the United States by a wide margin—enough to create 12 to 13 million "excess deaths" per year.[45] Secondly, among catastrophes in history the largest death tolls have occurred in natural disasters such as earthquakes, floods, and volcanic eruptions, not accidents caused by human acts. The earthquake at Tangshan, China, on July 28, 1976, caused the death of at least half a million persons.[46] By contrast, very few man-made accidents in the twentieth century have claimed more than a thousand lives; the *Titanic* disaster, in which over fifteen hundred people perished, was exceptional.[47]

There has been only one nuclear accident that was truly a catastrophe; it occurred in the Soviet Union in 1957 or 1958 and appears to be the result of mishandling a large amount of high-level wastes from processing nuclear materials, probably for nuclear weapons manufacture. According to a Soviet scientist and emigré, "Tens of thousands of people were affected, hundreds dying, though the real figures have never been made public."[48] Despite the apparent severity of this Soviet disaster, information about the medical consequences is hard to find. An emigré who lived in the region made the following statement in 1977:

> "I went once to a hospital in Sverdlovsk for the removal of a wart, and one of my friends, a doctor, told me that the entire hospital was crammed with victims of the Kyshtym catastrophe. He said that all the hospitals in the entire area were crammed full, not only in Sverdlovsk but also in Chelyabinsk. These are huge hospitals with many hundreds of beds. The doctors all told me that the victims were suffering from radioactive contamination. It was a tremendous number of people, I believe, thousands. I was told that most of them died."[49]

It appears that a wide area of countryside has been heavily contaminated with long-lived iso-

15-5 TYPES AND FREQUENCIES OF NUCLEAR ACCIDENTS

Accident Type	Number and Period (region)	Hazard: Loss, Deaths, and Injuries
Major Radiation Accidents		
Criticality accidents	34 in 1945–65 (world)	Radiation deaths: 5 Blast deaths: 3 Persons receiving radiation injury: 36
Major external exposures	19 in 1954–79 (world)	Radiation deaths: 8 Radiation injury: 35
Major internal exposures	16 in 1955–77 (world)	Radiation deaths: 2 Dangerous exposures: 20
Local radiation burns	47 in 1948–79 (world)	Persons injured: 76
Military accidents		
Broken arrows	32 in 1950–80 (United States Forces)	Deaths from physical injury: 57 Instances of extensive plutonium contamination: 3 Detonation of high explosive of nuclear weapon by impact or fire: 9
Nuclear Explosions		
Atmospheric tests	hundreds 1946–80 (world)	Increased worldwide incidence of cancer and genetic defects
Bravo test	1 in 1954 (Marshall Islands)	Death from fallout: 1 Persons seriously exposed: 289
Vented underground tests	32 in 1958–70 (world)	Low-level radiation exposure

This listing counts only accidents for which definitive information is available, and most reports are from U.S. agencies. Thus the numbers of incidents and totals of damage must be regarded as lower limits on the world experience. In addition, there have been cases of deliberate harmful radiation exposure and in-

cidents of theft and sabotage. Secrecy has covered up some accidents; information about accidents in the Soviet Union and some other countries is hard to obtain. The single most serious nuclear accident was the Soviet accident at Kyshtym in 1957–58, which apparently resulted in many cases of radiation sickness.

topes of cesium and strontium and will be uninhabitable for decades.

With the exception of the Kyshtym disaster, immediate deaths and injuries from nuclear accidents have been rare. Why, then, should one study the record of actual nuclear accidents? There are three answers to this question. First, the record of accidents gives us a better understanding of the likelihood of nuclear catastrophe. Secondly, the health consequences of nuclear accidents are so long-term in nature that

the cumulative effect over hundreds of thousands of years will be much greater than any prompt effects. Thirdly, knowledge of accidents can influence the design and deployment of weapon systems to lessen the probability of accidental nuclear war.

Sources of Information

For the United States, an enormous amount of information about commercial reactors is pub-

15-5   TYPES AND FREQUENCIES OF NUCLEAR ACCIDENTS (continued)

Accident Type	Number and Period (region)	Hazard: Loss, Deaths, and Injuries
Nuclear Power Accidents		
Major reactor accidents	13 in 1952–80 (world)	Melting of reactor fuel; release of radioactive materials; enormous financial loss to reactor owner
Three Mile Island	1 in 1979 (Pennsylvania)	Cost of decontamination and rebuilding: more than $1 billion
Reactor shutdowns caused by unexpected incidents	87 in 1981 (United States)	Small releases of material; minor fires; malfunctions of operational and safety equipment
Release of Radioactive Material		
Major spills at plant sites	13 in 1959–74 (US AEC)	Total cost of lost material and decontamination: $1,012,000
Leaks in high-level waste storage tanks	20 in 1947–73 (United States)	Material lost: 1,150 cubic meters Radioactivity: 190,000 curies of cesium-137
Tritium gas releases from AEC facilities	17 in 1959–70 (US AEC)	Value of material lost: $712,000
Releases in material shipment	12 in 1959–75 (Reported by AEC)	Total cost of loss and cleanup: unknown
Miscellaneous		
Fires involving plutonium and other actinides	18 in 1951–75 (US AEC)	Average cost of loss and decontamination: $282,000
Major plutonium fire	1969 (Rocky Flats Plant)	Cost of decontamination and rebuilding: $45 million
Major accident in handling nuclear materials, Kyshtym	1957–58 (Soviet Union)	Widespread radioactive fallout; many radiation injuries

licly available. There is a tendency for opponents of nuclear power to take an interest in every minor malfunction at the reactor nearest their home, while losing sight of the importance of accidents that have taken place in other nuclear facilities. A fair amount of information is available on government-owned facilities through Environmental Impact Statements, budget hearings, and other government documents. Relatively little information is available on privately owned facilities that fabricate nuclear fuel, process spent fuel, or produce isotope thermal power sources such as those that convert the heat released by Pu-238 into electricity. Many aspects of the operation of plants handling plutonium or highly enriched uranium are kept secret for security reasons. Very little information is made public about facilities that produce nuclear reactors for military use but do not handle nuclear fuel, since they are not licensed by the Nuclear Regulatory Commission (NRC). Information about the handling of atomic weapons and operation of naval reactors is generally kept classified by the Defense Department.

Relatively little information is publicly available on nuclear safety experience in Communist countries and developing countries. Until 1976, the Central Intelligence Agency (CIA) withheld information on the Soviet Accident at Kyshtym,[50] so it is clear that the U.S. government may keep secret even the most serious accidents abroad.

Suggested Readings

The yearbooks of the Stockholm International Peace Research Institute *(SIPRI Yearbook)* are an important source of information on all aspects of nuclear weapons. In particular, the contributions by Milton Leitenberg to the yearbooks for 1969 and 1977 are the earliest summaries of nuclear accident experience in military operations. The book *Atomic Soldiers* by Howard Rosenberg gives an authoritative account of the human exposures to radiation from the weapons testing programs of the United States. The journal *Nuclear Safety* publishes reports and analyses of accidents and safety problems in nuclear reactors and nuclear chemical processing plants. This journal is especially valuable for accidents that occurred before the early seventies, when the nuclear safety debate gained widespread attention. The book *Nuclear Les-* *sons* is a provocative discussion of safety in nuclear power, and *No Nukes* lists fourteen serious accidents on pages 117–121.

CURTIS, RICHARD, AND ELIZABETH HOGAN. *Nuclear Lessons.* Harrisburg, Penn.: Stackpole Books, 1980.

GYORGY, ANNA, *No Nukes: Everyone's Guide to Nuclear Power.* Boston: South End Press, 1979.

Nuclear Safety. Oak Ridge, Tenn.: Oak Ridge National Laboratory.

ROSENBERG, HOWARD. *Atomic Soldiers.* Boston: Beacon, 1980.

SCHUBERT, JACK, AND RALPH E. LAPP. *Radiation: What It Is and How It Affects You.* New York: Viking, 1957.

Stockholm International Peace Research Institute (SIPRI). *World Armaments and Disarmament.* Stockholm: Almqvist and Wiskell, 1968/1969 through 1977; London: Taylor and Francis, since 1978.

WEBB, RICHARD E. *The Accident Hazards of Nuclear Power Plants.* Amherst, Mass.: University of Massachusetts Press, 1976.

Part Six

International Issues

July 1, 1946, Able Day at Bikini Atoll in the Marshall Islands, the first nuclear test in a time of peace.

16. Tests of Nuclear Explosives

The Partial Nuclear Test Ban Treaty of 1963 succeeded in limiting further contamination of the biosphere by radioactive fallout from atmospheric nuclear tests. Since it included no prohibition of underground tests, establishment of underground testing facilities by at least five nations, with increasing sophistication in computer modeling and design of new weapons and their components, has meant no slowing in the subsequent tempo of nuclear weapons development.

I remember one day when President Kennedy asked what happens to the radioactive fallout, and I told him it was washed out of the clouds by the rain and would be brought to earth by the rain. And he said, looking out the window, "You mean it's in the rain out there?" I said, "Yes." He looked out the window, very sad, and didn't say a word for several minutes....

Dr. Jerome Wiesner, science adviser to President Kennedy

RADIOACTIVE FALLOUT comes from nuclear explosions. A nuclear explosive test is an intentional detonation of a fission or fusion reaction that is permitted to spend itself, without control. Controlled reactions—in nuclear reactors and in fusion power research experiments—are not considered to be tests of nuclear explosives. Tests have been carried out by the United States, the Soviet Union, Great Britain, France, China, and India, and possibly by others.

The purposes of carrying out nuclear test explosions include testing subsystems of weapons, optimizing the design of new warheads, testing deliverable weapons, experimenting with ideas as in the first fusion test, testing the resistance of equipment to nuclear explosions, and testing equipment designed to detect nuclear explosions. Safety tests are conducted to determine the likelihood of accidental detonation of nuclear explosives.

Nuclear explosions have been considered useful for civil applications: digging canals, extracting minerals, recovery of oil and natural gas, construction of dams and reservoirs, and carrying out scientific experiments such as heavy element production. However, the potential for such peaceful nuclear explosions (PNEs) is thought to be limited, as perhaps hundreds of explosions would be required to carry out canal excavation or mineral extraction.[1] The United States has carried out at least thirty-eight PNEs, many amid public protest. (see Chapter 23).[2] The Soviet Union has set off many PNEs, and continues to do so, as indicated by the detection of recent nuclear explosions far from the usual weapons test sites.

Thérèse Dennis

Dennis received a physics degree from M.I.T. and has taught physics at the university level.

16-1   Nuclear Explosions Announced and Reported

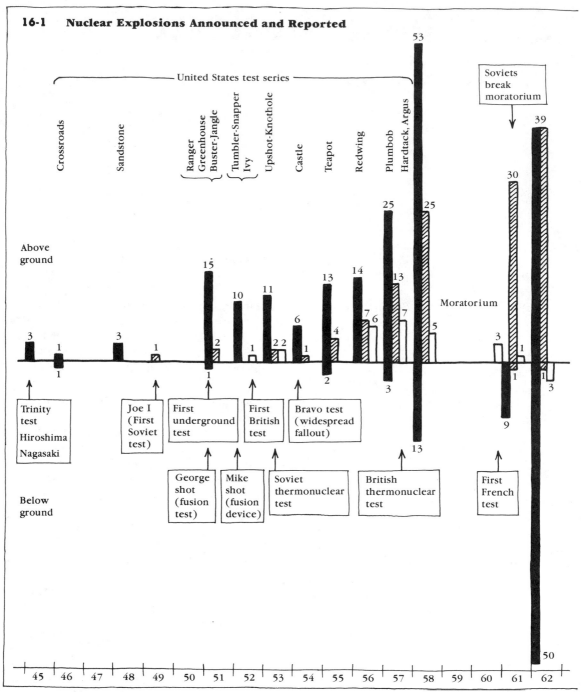

A presentation of the more than 1,200 nuclear explosions carried out by the world's nuclear powers through 1980. The main effect of the Partial Test Ban Treaty has been to drive almost all tests underground. The United States has announced twenty-four nuclear tests for nonweapons purposes, such as metallurgical

Underwater explosions

July 1946	US	Bikini
May 1955	US	E. Pacific
May 1958	US	Enewetak
June 1958	US	Enewetak
October 1961	USSR	Novaya Zemlya
May 1962	US	E. Pacific

Legend	Before test ban		After test ban	
	Above	Below	Above	Below
United States	193	119	0	369
Soviet Union	163	2	0	283
Other: Britain	21	2	0	10
France	4	1	41	48
China	0	0	22	4
India	0	0	0	1

In addition to the explosions recorded in the chart, the United States has reported 23 underground tests conducted between September 15, 1961, and August 20, 1963, and the Swedish Research Institute for National Defense has reported 30 Soviet tests at unspecified dates before 1959. These are included in the above totals.

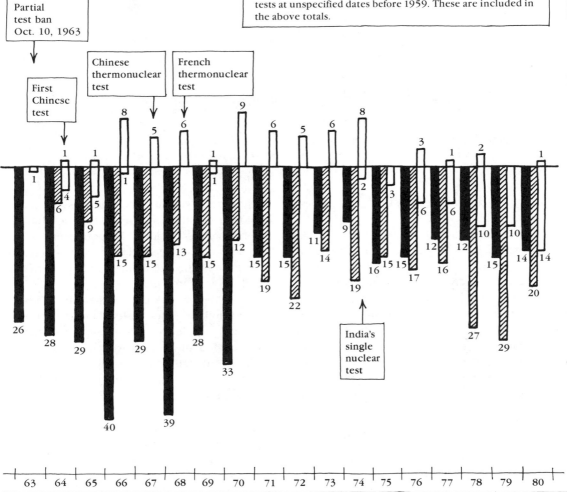

Partial test ban Oct. 10, 1963

First Chinese test

Chinese thermonuclear test

French thermonuclear test

India's single nuclear test

experiments, excavation, and stimulation of natural gas production. Many tests for similar purposes have been conducted by the Soviet Union, but only a few have been described. There have been only six underwater nuclear detonations.

16-2 EXCAVATION BY NUCLEAR EXPLOSION

July 6, 1962, the Sedan event: A 100-kiloton nuclear explosion 635 feet underground blew out 10 million tons of earth to form this crater 1,200 feet across. This experiment in nuclear excavation was carried out at the Nevada Test Site as part of the U.S. Plowshare program of nuclear explosions for peaceful purposes.

History of Testing

A successful nuclear explosion marks the entry of a nation into the nuclear club. The history of testing, therefore, tells how the ability to make nuclear weapons has spread to many nations. The increasing sophistication of weapons being tested is also part of the history. The nuclear club now includes at least six nations—the United States, the Soviet Union, Great Britain, France, China, and India. The United States and Britain collaborated in developing the first nuclear weapons. The Soviet Union, France, and China joined later, as did India. Of the six, only India has refrained from subsequent testing.

On July 16, 1945, Vannevar Bush, James Conant, J. Robert Oppenheimer, and many others witnessed the birth of the nuclear age. The sight of the first nuclear bomb test reminded Oppenheimer of Shiva, the Indian god of destruction. This first test, code-named Trinity, took place at Alamogordo, New Mexico, and was a trial of the implosion method of detonating a plutonium bomb; this test yielded the equivalent of nineteen kilotons of TNT.[3] The second nuclear explosion was the bomb dropped on Hiroshima, which was constructed of uranium-235 and used a simpler, gunlike mechanism. The Hiroshima bomb was not tested because there was so much confidence in its design. The Nagasaki bomb was a plutonium weapon of the design tested in the Trinity experiment.

Between 1945 and 1949, the period of U.S. nuclear monopoly, several series of test explosions were carried out. With the exception of one test thought to be an attempt to produce a fusion explosion, these were all tests of fission devices and weapons. In 1946, in peacetime, two nuclear bombs were tested in the Pacific island paradise of Bikini, part of the Marshall Islands. Shortly thereafter, the Atomic Energy Commission (AEC) was set up to monitor and conduct tests. The next series, Operation Sand-stone, comprised three shots exploded near Bi-kini on Enewetak Atoll, also part of the Marshall Islands. The distance of the Pacific test site from the United States mainland caused expense and logistic problems,[4] and in December 1950, a continental site was chosen—the Nevada Test Site—about sixty-five miles northwest of Las Ve-gas, where tests have been conducted ever since. Further testing has taken place at Enewe-tak, and also at Amchitka Island (in the Aleu-tians, off Alaska), in Colorado, and in Mississippi.

In 1949 the Soviet Union, as predicted by some scientists working on the U.S. atom bomb project, developed a bomb within five years after Trinity. The explosion was detected by ra-dioactive material picked up by a B-29 monitor-ing aircraft. A select committee of Oppenhei-mer, Bush, and Robert Bacher examined the evidence and decided that the Soviet Union had indeed exploded an atomic device. They named it Joe I, after Joseph Stalin.[5]

The Soviet success changed U.S. policy on weapons research. Prior to this time there were vocal supporters for the development of fusion weapons, but research in this area was not pushed by the government. After the Soviet test, efforts were increased, and the second labora-tory for nuclear weapons research was set up at Livermore, near the University of California at Berkeley.[6] Both fusion reaction research and the development of "tactical" small yield fission weapons were carried out between 1951 and 1952. The arms race had begun.

In 1951 President Harry S. Truman approved a series of tests, code-named Operation Ranger, using explosives ranging in yield from one kilo-ton to twenty-two kilotons. The noticeable ef-fects of this first series of tests carried out on the continental United States included broken windows in a store sixty-five miles away. Radio-activity appeared in New England snow shortly after the twenty-two kiloton test.[7] Enewetak At-oll hosted a four-shot series, Operation Green-house, in April and May of 1951. The test con-

16-3 ARMY TROOP EXERCISE AT THE NEVADA TEST SITE

November 1, 1951, Yucca Flats: Shot Dog of Operation Buster-Jangle. Army troops participate in Exercise De-sert Rock with a 21-kiloton nuclear detonation. Here many soldiers received unknown low-level radiation doses.

16-4   **THE PARTIAL TEST BAN TREATY**

Treaty Banning Nuclear Weapons in the Atmosphere, in Outer Space, and Under Water

Signed at Moscow August 5, 1963
Entered into force October 10, 1963

The Governments of the United States of America, the United Kingdom of Great Britain and Northern Ireland, and the Union of Soviet Socialist Republics, hereinafter referred to as the "Original Parties,"

Proclaiming as their principal aim the speediest possible achievement of an agreement on general and complete disarmament under strict international control in accordance with the objectives of the United Nations which would put an end to the armaments race and eliminate the incentive to the production and testing, of all kinds of weapons, including nuclear weapons,

Seeking to achieve the discontinuance of all test explosions of nuclear weapons for all time, determined to continue negotiations to this end, and desiring to put an end to the contamination of man's environment by radioactive substances,

Have agreed as follows:

Article I

1. Each of the Parties to this Treaty undertakes to prohibit, to prevent, and not to carry out any nuclear weapon test explosion, or any other nuclear explosion, at any place under its jurisdiction or control:

(a) in the atmosphere; beyond its limits, including outer space; or underwater, including territorial waters or high seas; or

(b) in any other environment if such explosion causes radioactive debris to be present outside the territorial limits of the State under whose jurisdiction or control such explosion is conducted. It is understood in this connection that the provisions of this subparagraph are without prejudice to the conclusion of a treaty resulting in the permanent banning of all nuclear test explosions, including all such explosions underground, the conclusion of which, as the Parties have stated in the Preamble to this Treaty, they seek to achieve.

2. Each of the Parties to this Treaty undertakes furthermore to refrain from causing, encouraging, or in any way participating in, the carrying out of any nuclear weapon test explosion, or any other nuclear explosion, anywhere which would take place in any of the environments described, or have the effect referred to, in paragraph 1 of this Article.

Article II

1. Any Party may propose amendments to this Treaty. The text of any proposed amendment shall be submitted to the Depositary Governments which shall circulate it to all Parties to this Treaty. Thereafter, if requested to do so by one-third or more of the Parties, the Depositary Governments shall convene a conference, to which they shall invite all of the Parties, to consider such amendment.

2. Any amendment to this Treaty must be approved by a majority of the votes of all the Parties to this Treaty, including the votes of all of the Original Parties. The amendment shall enter into

force for all Parties upon the deposit of instruments of ratification by a majority of all the Parties, including the instruments of ratification of all of the Original Parties.

Article III

1. This Treaty shall be open to all States for signature. Any State which does not sign this Treaty before its entry into force accordance with paragraph 3 of this Article may accede to it at any time.

2. This Treaty shall be subject to ratification by signatory States. Instruments of ratification and instruments of accession shall be deposited with the Governments of the Original Parties—the United States of America, the United Kingdom of Great Britain and Northern Ireland, and the Union of Soviet Socialist Republics—which are hereby designated the Depositary Governments.

3. This Treaty shall enter into force after its ratification by all the Original Parties and the deposit of their instruments of ratification.

4. For States whose instruments of ratification or accession are deposited subsequent to the entry into force of this Treaty, it shall enter into force on the date of the deposit of their instruments of ratification or accession.

5. The Depositary Governments shall promptly inform all signatory and acceding States of the date of each signature, the date of deposit of each instrument of ratification of an accession to this Treaty, the date of its entry into force, and the date of receipt of any requests for conferences or other notices.

6. This Treaty shall be registered by the Depositary Governments pursuant to Article 102 of the Charter of the United Nations.

Article IV

This Treaty shall be of unlimited duration.

Each Party shall in exercising its national sovereignty have the right to withdraw from the Treaty if it decides that extraordinary events, related to the subject matter of this Treaty, have jeopardized the supreme interests of its country. It shall give notice of such withdrawal to all other Parties to the Treaty three months in advance.

Article V

This Treaty, of which the English and Russian texts are equally authentic, shall be deposited in the archives of the Depositary Governments. Duly certified copies of this Treaty shall be transmitted by the Depositary Governments to the Governments of the signatory and acceding States.

IN WITNESS WHEREOF the undersigned, duly authorized, have signed this Treaty.

DONE in triplicate at the city of Moscow the fifth day of August, one thousand nine hundred and sixty-three.

For the Government of the United States of America	*For the Government of the United Kingdom of Great Britain and Northern Ireland*	*For the Government of the Union of Soviet Socialist Republics*
Dean Rusk		
	Alex Douglas-Home	A. Gromyko

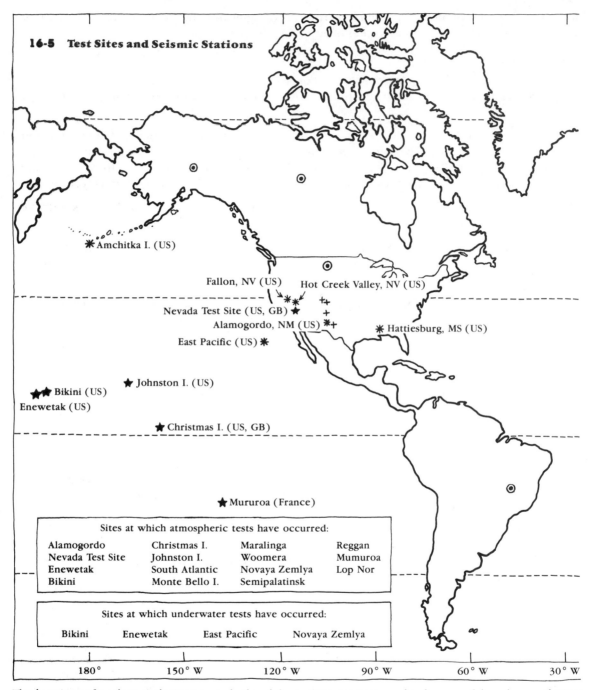

16-5 Test Sites and Seismic Stations

Amchitka I. (US)

Fallon, NV (US)   Hot Creek Valley, NV (US)

Nevada Test Site (US, GB)

Alamogordo, NM (US)

Hattiesburg, MS (US)

East Pacific (US)

Johnston I. (US)

Bikini (US)

Enewetak (US)

Christmas I. (US, GB)

Mururoa (France)

Sites at which atmospheric tests have occurred:

Alamogordo	Christmas I.	Maralinga	Reggan
Nevada Test Site	Johnston I.	Woomera	Mumuroa
Enewetak	South Atlantic	Novaya Zemlya	Lop Nor
Bikini	Monte Bello I.	Semipalatinsk	

Sites at which underwater tests have occurred:

Bikini	Enewetak	East Pacific	Novaya Zemlya

180°   150° W   120° W   90° W   60° W   30° W

The locations of nuclear explosions encircle the globe and include places within the Soviet Union but away from the usual weapon test sites, where the detona- tions are presumed to be peaceful nuclear explosions. The site indicated in South Africa was reportedly pre- pared for a nuclear test but was not used, perhaps be-

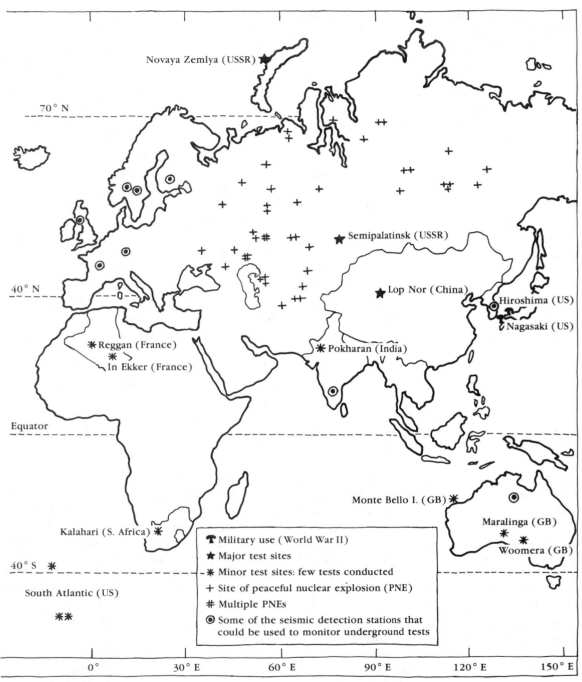

Novaya Zemlya (USSR)

70° N

Semipalatinsk (USSR)

Lop Nor (China)

Hiroshima (US)

40° N

Nagasaki (US)

Reggan (France)

In Ekker (France)

Pokharan (India)

Equator

Monte Bello I. (GB)

Maralinga (GB)

Kalahari (S. Africa)

Woomera (GB)

♆ Military use (World War II)

★ Major test sites

✳ Minor test sites: few tests conducted

40° S

＋ Site of peaceful nuclear explosion (PNE)

South Atlantic (US)

Multiple PNEs

◉ Some of the seismic detection stations that
could be used to monitor underground tests

0°   30° E   60° E   90° E   120° E   150° E

cause of international pressure. Also shown are some
of the more sensitive seismic detection stations used
to monitor underground tests. There are other networks of seismic stations in France and in the Soviet
Union.

ducted on May 8 was the first thermonuclear reaction on earth. Named George, this experiment was not a genuine hydrogen bomb, but rather a device exploded to further understanding of nuclear fusion reactions. Edward Teller and others at Los Alamos, including Stanislaus Ulam, used the results to devise designs for U.S. hydrogen bombs. This first fusion experiment, set off atop a tower, required cryogenic refrigeration equipment to maintain the density of the hydrogen isotopes needed for the reaction.[8]

Evaluation of fission weapons continued the following fall at the Nevada Test Site. Operation Buster-Jangle was a series of seven shots with yields ranging from one-tenth of a kiloton to thirty-one kilotons. The explosives were detonated from a tower, as airdrops (about 1,000 feet), as surface blasts, and from a crater. The most significant difference of Buster-Jangle from earlier test series was the presence of 5,000 U.S. soldiers, intentionally deployed in the vicinity of A-bomb explosions. Test explosions in April 1952, and in spring 1953, caused measurable radiation in Rochester and Troy, New York, respectively.

The second experiment in the development of a fusion weapon was the Mike event of Operation Ivy (November 1, 1952). This test was not yet a practical bomb, as it also required refrigeration equipment and weighed sixty-five tons. The Mike device yielded 10.4 megatons and dug a crater one mile long and 175 feet deep, obliterating Elugelab Island on which it was detonated.

The day before the Mike shot, Great Britain became a nuclear power by exploding a fission device installed in the frigate HMS Plym. This explosion, code-named Hurricane, was in the kiloton range and took place in the Monte Bello islands west of the Australian mainland.

On August 8, 1953, Stalin's successor Georgi Malenkov announced that the Soviets had produced a dry hydrogen bomb.[9] This bomb used lithium as a source of tritium and therefore did not require the bulky cryogenic equipment used in the U.S. tests. The United States reacted to the Soviet success by authorizing development of intercontinental ballistic missiles. These missiles were to be capable of striking within eight to ten miles of their aim point at intercontinental range. This was deemed sufficient by the military, since the huge yield of a thermonuclear warhead causes destruction over such a large area that the position inaccuracy of a ballistic missile was no longer considered inadequate.[10] Just such a weapon was tested in the Bravo explosion of Operation Castle on February 28, 1954, at Bikini.[11] This detonation was the first U.S. test of the three-stage, fission-fusion-fission bomb. Exploded at sea level, it yielded between fifteen and twenty-two megatons of energy; it contaminated the inhabitants of Ronegelap, Rongerik, and Uterik Islands, as well as the crew members of the *Lucky Dragon,* a Japanese fishing vessel located 120 miles distant from the test.[12]

Eighty percent of U.S. tests before 1956 were of fission devices, the rest thermonuclear. The large yield of the fusion weapons explains why these tests were conducted in the Pacific. The largest atmospheric explosion in the continental United States was the Hood test of the Plumbob series, which yielded seventy-four kilotons. The John shot, part of the same series, was the two-kiloton warhead of a Genie rocket launched and detonated from an F-89 Scorpion flying at 20,000 feet. The blast was experienced at ground zero by five volunteer officers as a demonstration that a nuclear air battle could take place without harming people on the ground.[13] The Soviet Union—according to Arnold Kramish, an Air Force specialist on Soviet atomic research—conducted an extensive series of tests in 1954, culminating in the test of a deliverable hydrogen bomb dropped from an aircraft on November 23, 1955.[14] He also notes that a series of tests was carried out by the Russians in 1956 to develop atomic warheads for tactical weapons. On March 31, 1958, Andrei Gromyko announced a Soviet decision to stop their own nuclear tests. He invited the West to do likewise, but at the end of April, the United States and Great Britain continued their tests, and on September 30, 1958, the Soviet Union resumed testing.[15]

The Banning of Atmospheric Tests

The testing was not without side effects; radioactive elements were being created and dispersed in the environment. Many citizens in the several testing nations wished to bring a halt to the test explosions. As early as 1954 Indian Prime Minister Nehru proposed a test ban in an address to the United Nations. Although many nations supported the idea, some assurance was needed that the nations signing a treaty would honor a test ban. Eventually, in July and August 1958, a group of experts from the United States, Great Britain, France, Canada, the Soviet Union, Czechoslovakia, Poland, and Romania met to discuss the feasibility of monitoring adherence to a test ban. Several methods of test detection were suggested, including collection of explosion debris, monitoring earth tremors (seismic activity), acoustic and hydroacoustic monitoring, detection of radio signals, and on-site inspection. The group concluded that between 160 and 170 land and sea based stations would serve to detect and identify nuclear explosions down to a yield of one to five kilotons.[16] Subsequently, the U.S. delegation raised the point that a nation might successfully decouple or muffle an underground explosion to avoid detection. As a result, work toward a test ban continued with the exclusion of underground tests.

While the basis for an international agreement to halt atmospheric testing was being worked out, U.S. and Soviet testing continued on the accelerated schedule that began in 1955. Then in November 1958, a moratorium on testing by the United States, the Soviet Union, and

Great Britain began. The moratorium was interrupted by the first French test in Reggan, Algeria, on February 13, 1960, a tower burst detonation of sixty to seventy kilotons. In 1961, after a U.S. high-altitude reconnaissance plane was shot down over Soviet territory, the Soviet Union broke the voluntary moratorium. Starting on September 1, more than thirty atmospheric tests were conducted in Siberia in sixty-five days, including a huge explosion of fifty-eight megatons. The United States resumed testing in September 1961 with a long series of underground detonations in Nevada—explosions about 2,000 feet below the surface in granite, alluvium, and tuff. The following spring, the United States resumed atmospheric testing in the Pacific with trials of submarine-launched missiles and an anti-submarine rocket (the ASROC) in the vicinity of Christmas Island, and a series of high-altitude explosions at Johnston Island. The Soviet Union carried out a second series of forty or more tests from July to December 1962.

Most of these tests were explosions above ground leading to further pollution of the atmosphere by radioactive particles. Dr. Linus Pauling led a collection of signatures of scientists on a petition to the United Nations for the cessation of nuclear weapons testing. The desire to prevent further pollution of the atmosphere, to restrict the proliferation of nuclear weapons, and to stop nuclear weapon testing resulted in the limited test ban treaty—officially known as the Treaty Banning Nuclear Weapons Tests in the Atmosphere, in Outer Space and Underwater, also called the Partial Test Ban Treaty.

The cessation of atmospheric testing in 1963 by the United States, the Soviet Union, and Great Britain had a decided effect upon the levels of strontium-90 (Sr-90) in the atmosphere. This material is particularly dangerous because it is chemically similar to calcium and concentrates in the bones, especially of children. There its radioactive decay increases exposure of the bone marrow to ionizing radiation, a known cause of leukemia, a cancer of the blood. Starting about 1971, the amount of strontium-90 in the environment began dropping gradually, though centuries must pass before its level will become insignificant.

The radioactive isotope carbon-14, present in the atmosphere in carbon dioxide, is a problem as well.[17] Carbon-14, with a half-life of 8,070 years, is produced at the rate of roughly sixteen pounds per megaton of nuclear explosion, whether fission or fusion; it results from nuclear reactions when neutrons react with nitrogen in the atmosphere. Dr. Pauling estimated that for every ten megatons of nuclear explosions, 15,000 children will be born with serious physical or mental defects. The dramatic decrease in concentration of strontium-90 in the atmosphere shows the success of the Partial Test Ban Treaty in reducing poisoning of the atmosphere by nuclear explosions.

Despite this concern, France continued to carry out atmospheric tests until 1965. The first French hydrogen bomb test occurred on September 24, 1968.[18] China had conducted atmospheric tests since 1963, including one in 1980, on October 16.[19] Fallout from these tests is not only local. Fallout from a Chinese test in September, 1976 was detected in Pennsylvania.[20] China's first thermonuclear test occurred on June 17, 1967. The single nuclear explosion carried out by India was an underground test on May 18, 1974.

Another goal of some supporters of the Partial Test Ban Treaty was a decrease in testing of nuclear explosives, but the treaty has not caused testing to cease but, rather, to move underground. Since 1976, the explosions carried out by the superpowers have been underground tests below or around the 150-kiloton yield level, in accordance with the U.S.-Soviet Threshold Test Ban Treaty, not formally in force.

Other nations may have conducted tests: evidence that initially indicated a nuclear test in the South Atlantic in September 1979 seemed, upon further analysis of signals, to be different from what would be expected of a nuclear explosion.[21]

Detection of Explosions

To avoid concern that clandestine testing might be performed by a signer of a test ban treaty, nations have developed surveillance systems for the detection of nuclear explosions. While some states may be reluctant to reveal the detection threshold of their monitoring systems, the effectiveness of some systems is well documented in the open literature. Detection of atmospheric explosions is done chiefly by observing acoustic (air-pressure) disturbances, by sensing the electromagnetic pulse (EMP), or by measurement of airborne radioactivity. Seismic monitoring is the principal method of detecting underground nuclear explosions, although other methods have been exploited.

Detection of a nuclear explosion from the resulting earth tremors requires the discrimination between an explosion and an earthquake as well as isolation of the seismic event from noise. Earthquake signals usually originate deeper in the earth, their source is less localized, and relatively more energy is in shear (transverse) waves than in the case of an explosion. Through the years, advances in the design and placement of seismometers have improved their sensitivity. Moreover, the signal components having frequencies around two Hertz have been found to provide the sharpest distinction between small, local earth tremors and a distant earthquake or nuclear detonation. Thus band-pass filtering of the seismic signal improves discrimination. Operating three or more seismometers and combining their signals improves discrimination against background signals unrelated to the seismic event of interest; this also provides the ability to reinforce signals from a particular direction. A seismic detection station using these techniques can detect seismic waves from nuclear explosions at distances as large as 10,000 km and can distinguish them from earthquake signals with a high degree of confidence.[22] Communication between stations of this sort enables combined analysis of signals, increasing discrimination.

In the sixties the U.S. Vela Uniform Project was devoted to development and construction of seismic detection stations for monitoring compliance with a comprehensive ban on nuclear tests. The World Wide Standard Stations Network, operated by the United States until 1968, was part of this project. The Standard Stations Network has been supplanted by a network of Seismological Research Observatories, established by the Defense Advanced Research Projects Agency (DARPA). Each station is equipped with specially designed broad-band borehole seismometers.[23] In 1977 at least eleven of these seismic observatories were operating. Many seismic stations have been established under the auspices of other nations, for example Sweden and Great Britain. A network of forty-seven of the existing stations in twenty-six countries would form a very sensitive watchdog for concealed weapon tests.[24] Nuclear explosions (called Vela tests) of announced yield and environment (granite, tuff, etc.) have been set off to aid in the calibration of seismic detection stations.

A nation wishing to avoid detection of an underground test could attempt to reduce seismic vibrations in several ways. An explosion in dry alluvium, a type of unconsolidated rock, produces vibrations one tenth the amplitude of vibrations resulting from an explosion in hard rock. However, a deep pocket of alluvium is required. Only one known site of this type exists in the United States: the Nevada Test Site, where a 600-meter depth of alluvium might conceal a test yield of about ten kilotons. Although dry alluvium exists in several areas of the Soviet Union, there may not be sufficient deposits in any one location to isolate tests. Another method of decoupling makes use of cavities in the earth such as holes or tunnels. The United States has tested in deep tunnels, and in holes close to the surface. Two nuclear explosions were detonated in a salt dome in Mississippi to ascertain the amount of decoupling available there.[25] To obtain decoupling of 100 requires salt formations of a thickness and homogeneity not found in the United States, so there is little possibility of achieving a fully decoupled explosion of yield greater than ten kilotons.

Dahlman and Israelson estimate that the Soviets might conduct perhaps three undetected explosions per year, of yields between three and five kilotons, near the Kuril Islands off the eastern coast of the Soviet Union, where natural tremors might mask the explosions' signals. Perhaps 0.3 such explosions per year would be undetected in the western United States.[26] Experts in seismology agree that the technical capacity exists to detect underground nuclear tests of a few kilotons or more. Dahlman and Israelson conclude that a single array station, which is a possible national means of detection, can locate a seismic event with an expected accuracy of about 300 kilometers.[27] This accuracy can be improved by using a network of stations. Dahlman and Israelson regard present detection capabilities as providing sufficient means of verification to support a comprehensive test ban treaty—a treaty that would ban all tests of nuclear explosives.[28]

A variety of other techniques exist for detecting nuclear explosions, including detection of either the immediately occurring ("prompt") or the delayed radiations: X rays, gamma rays, visible light, neutrons, and beta radiation, acoustic and hydroacoustic monitoring, sampling of debris, detection of the electromagnetic pulse (EMP), detection of the characteristic double flash, detection of ionospheric disturbances of various frequencies, and the scattering of sunlight from debris. Some of these means are used by earth satellites to detect nuclear explosions. A series of United States satellites, part of the Vela Uniform program, orbit the earth at 40,000 to 60,000 miles distance, beyond the Van Allen Radiation belts looking for nuclear bursts. Satellites with lower orbits have taken photographs of manmade objects, including the 390-meter crater formed in the Sedan explosion at the Nevada Test Site.[29] It is speculated that Soviet and U.S. satellite reconnaissance of South Africa once prevented a nuclear test by that state.[30] Satellites having low orbits, and satellites with orbits far beyond the 23,000-mile synchronous orbits are used.

Of the twelve nuclear explosion monitoring satellites that have been launched by the United States, three were operational in 1980. In 1980 it was reported that the United States was planning to install nuclear explosion detection sensors on board other satellites, including global positioning satellites and satellites of the NAVSTAR system. These sensors are part of the integrated Operational Nuclear Detection System.[31]

A Comprehensive Test Ban

The Report of the Secretary General to the United Nations points out that a comprehensive test ban treaty would have a "major arms limitation impact in that it would make it difficult, if not impossible, for the nuclear-weapons states parties to the treaty to develop new designs of nuclear weapons and would also place constraints on the modification of existing weapon designs."[32] Lacking the ability to test nuclear devices, nations would be less likely to rely upon their nuclear arsenals as a method of waging war.

A comprehensive test ban treaty, which would stop testing of nuclear explosives of all sizes in any environment, might redirect strategic and tactical war methodology away from nuclear explosives. Talks between the United States, the Soviet Union, and Great Britain on a comprehensive test ban convened in 1979.[33] After two years of negotiations, the three participants reported:

The negotiating parties have agreed that the treaty will require each party to prohibit, prevent and not to carry out any nuclear weapon test explosion at any place under its jurisdiction or control in any environment; and to refrain from causing,

encouraging, or in any way participating in the carrying out of any nuclear weapon test explosion anywhere.[34]

A moratorium on nuclear explosions for peaceful purposes has been made an element of the draft treaty, as have provisions for sharing of seismic data that could expose clandestine tests, and the establishment of international seismic data centers in agreed-upon locations. General procedures concerned with requests for on-site inspections have been negotiated. This is regarded as a significant achievement in resolving issues about verification of compliance with the treaty. There are still difficult issues, based on different interpretations of the intent or likely result of the treaty. Delegates of some nations have objected to the notion of a comprehensive test ban treaty. France and China, for example, take the position that a test bank is not disarmament, but maintenance of an imbalance of knowledge about nuclear weapons because it does not require any limitations or reductions of nuclear armament. A Swedish delegate to the test ban talks points out that it is not necessary for the United States and the Soviet Union, with their comparatively large stores of knowledge, to insist that all countries sign the treaty. A Soviet delegate states that that all countries must sign, else there will be detriment to the security of the signers. A U.S. delegate states that many options exist—for example, a limited duration agreement, not requiring universal participation, that would provide for review and extension. The tripartite report concludes much work is still to be done.

Suggested Readings

The yearbooks assembled by the Stockholm International Peace Research Institute (SIPRI) annually since 1969 contain much information on nuclear explosions. The exposure of American soldiers to nuclear weapons tests is covered by the Rosenberg book, *Atomic Soldiers*. The books *Brighter Than a Thousand Suns*, by Robert Jungk, and *Race to Oblivion*, by Herbert York, give very readable descriptions of the participants, and the tenor of the times during which the early tests were carried out. More information on the comprehensive test ban treaty can be found in the SIPRI yearbooks, and in the book by Dahlman and Israelson.

DAHLMAN, OLA, AND HANS ISRAELSON. *Monitoring Underground Nuclear Explosions*. Amsterdam: Elsevier, 1977.

GLASSTONE, SAMUEL. *The Effects of Nuclear Weapons*. Washington, D.C.: U.S. Government Printing Office, 1962.

JUNGK, ROBERT. *Brighter than a Thousand Suns*. New York: Harcourt, Brace and Co., 1958.

ROSENBERG, HOWARD L. *Atomic Soldiers*. Boston: Beacon Press, 1980.

Stockholm International Peace Research Institute (SIPRI). *World Armaments and Disarmament*. Stockholm: Almqvist and Wiskell, 1968/1969 through 1977; London: Taylor and Francis, since 1978.

YORK, HERBERT. *Race to Oblivion*. New York: Simon and Schuster, 1970.

President John F. Kennedy ratifying the Partial Test Ban Treaty in the treaty room of the White House, October 7, 1963—a high point in the history of arms control negotiations.

17. The Sorry History of Arms Control

International arms control negotiations may have produced some inhibitions in the growth of nuclear weapons stockpiles, as well as an effective treaty limiting the race in development and deployment of anti-ballistic missile systems. But the nuclear arms race between the superpowers has gone forward with vigor, with both sides now having achieved high overkill capacities. Nuclear weapons capabilities have spread to at least six nations; this number may double or triple in the next decade or two in the absence of a strengthened non-proliferation regime. New technological developments such as the Soviet SS-20 and the U.S. MX missile threaten to destabilize existing balances and become new barriers to nuclear arms control.

ON AUGUST 6, 1945, an American-made nuclear (atomic) bomb was dropped, without prior warning, on the Japanese city of Hiroshima. Already staggering under the merciless strategic mass-bombing of their cities with conventional high explosives, the Japanese government tried to extend and speed up its "feelers" on terms of surrender; but it was not fast enough, and on August 9 the city of Nagasaki was likewise obliterated. Two days later, the war in the Pacific was over.

The Hiroshima bomb was made of the uranium-235 isotope, separated from natural uranium by laborious, energy-consuming, and time-consuming processes. The Nagasaki blast (as well as the first man-made nuclear explosion in the New Mexico desert on July 16, 1945) used plutonium, a new element produced in nuclear reactors.[1] Once in operation, these reactors continued to turn out plutonium (and still continue today) at a rate sufficient to manufacture more than one new bomb per week. The military plan was to continue to drop these on Japan, as rapidly as they became available, until the Japanese cried "uncle"—or until there were no more targets left. Fortunately, the emperor's advisors took the decision out of the hands of their military and called off the holocaust before the first post-Nagasaki bomb was ready.

It did not take long for U.S. atomic bomb scientists (and their colleagues who had worked on other aspects of the war effort) to recover from the euphoria of having "won" the war. By the fall of 1945 they started to realize that they were in grave danger of losing the peace, by virtue of the imminent passage by the Congress of the May-Johnson Bill. This legislation—hastily submitted by the War Department (soon to become the Department of Defense—DOD), provided for the perpetuation into peacetime of the wartime Manhattan District and for its continuing control over *all* future aspects of nuclear

Feld is a physicist and veteran of the Manhattan Project and editor-in-chief of the *Bulletin of the Atomic Scientists*. He is also chairman of the executive committee of the Pugwash Conferences, the most enduring of international gatherings of scientists concerned with the impact of science on world affairs.

Bernard T. Feld

17-1   ARMS CONTROL AGREEMENTS SINCE WORLD WAR II

The countries signatory to a treaty are those officially represented at the negotiations and who sign the treaty approving its submission to governments for ratification or accession. Usually a treaty enters into force only when specified countries party to the treaty have delivered documents of accession or ratification to a specified depository government.

1959: Antarctic Treaty Provides that the Antarctic shall be used exclusively for peaceful purposes. No military bases, tests, maneuvers, or weapons storage. Signatories have automatic rights of inspection. Twelve signatories. Twenty-two accessions and ratifications, including all nations with claims in the Antarctic.

1963: United States-Soviet Union "Hot Line" Agreement Establishes a direct communications link between the two governments for use in emergencies. Agreements for improvements were signed in 1971 and 1975. A similar Soviet-British hot line was established in 1967.

1963: Partial Test Ban Treaty Prohibits nuclear explosions in atmosphere, oceans or space, or any other environment in which radioactive debris extends beyond territorial limits of testing state. 106 signatories. 108 accessions and ratifications, not including China (PRC), Cuba, France, Saudi Arabia (but including Israel, Pakistan, and South Africa).

1967: Outer Space Treaty Prohibits placing in orbit, or on the moon or other celestial bodies, of any weapons of mass destruction, and the use of the moon or any other celestial bodies for military purposes. Eighty-nine signatories. Seventy-six accessions and ratifications.

1967: Treaty of Tlatelolco This is the most extensive nuclear weapons restriction adopted to date. It not only makes Latin America a nuclear free zone, but also (in a protocol signed by all the nuclear

weapon states) establishes the principles of (a) non-intrusion by nuclear weapons states of nuclear weapons into the area, and (b) no-first-use by nuclear weapons state signatories of nuclear weapons against any Latin American adherents to the treaty. Twenty-five signatories. Twenty-two ratifications. Cuba is not a party to the treaty; Argentina has signed but not ratified it; Brazil and Chile have ratified but the treaty is not in force for these two countries due to reservations attached to their ratification.

1968: Nuclear Non-Proliferation Treaty Non-nuclear-weapon states agree neither to seek nor to acquire technology or materials for nuclear weapons production, while weapons states pledge not to transfer same to non-weapons states. Ninety-seven signatories. 115 accessions and ratifications. Approximately sixty non-nuclear weapons states have concluded agreements with the International Atomic Energy Agency (IAEA) for safeguard procedures on their peaceful nuclear programs. Parties to the treaty include Egypt, Iran, Iraq, Libya, Syria, but not Argentina, Brazil, Chile, Cuba, France, China (PRC), India, Israel, Pakistan, Saudi Arabia, South Africa, or Spain.

1971: Sea-Bed Treaty Prohibits emplacement of nuclear and other weapons of mass destruction on or under the ocean floor. Eighty-seven signatories. Sixty-six accessions and ratifications, including all the nuclear powers except France.

1971: United States-Soviet Union Nuclear Accidents Agreement Provides for immediate notification and exchange of information in case of accidental or unauthorized launching or detonation of a nuclear weapon. Specific application to possible incidents on the high seas concluded in 1972–73.

1972: Biological Weapons Convention Prohibits development, production and stockpiling of biological and toxin weapons and provides for the destruction of existing weapons. This is the most comprehensive disarmament agreement since the end of World War II. 111 signatories. Eighty-four accessions and ratifications, including almost all industrially developed nations.

1972: SALT I Interim Agreement Provides for a stand-still freeze in the deployment of new strategic nuclear weapons delivery systems, by the Soviet Union and the United States, but excluding certain systems, on each side, already in advanced development or in process of deployment.

1972: SALT I ABM Agreement Prohibits deployment of Antiballistic Missiles (ABM) by the United States and the Soviet Union, with two exceptions on each side—one for defense of the national capital, second for defense of a single ICBM site. Protocol of 1974 limits possible deployments to a single site in each country. This remains the high point of United States-Soviet arms control; the ABM treaty is scheduled for review in 1982.

1972–73: Standing Consultative Commission The United States and Soviet Union agree by "memorandum of understanding" to establish the Standing Consultative Commission for the adjudication of differences as to interpretation of and compliance with SALT agreements.

1974: Threshold Test Ban Treaty Limits underground tests of nuclear weapons to yields under 150 kilotons of TNT on a bilateral U.S.-Soviet basis. Never ratified, but still informally in force. This limitation was extended to "Peaceful Nuclear Explosions" (PNE) in 1976.

1977: Environmental Modification Treaty Prohibits military use of environmental modification techniques. Forty-eight signatories. Twenty-seven accessions and ratifications.

1979: SALT II Treaty Attempts to begin the long-promised process of reducing numbers of strategic weapons by setting strict limits on total numbers and on various sub-categories within these totals. The limits adopted required only very minor reductions, mainly in Soviet land-based ICBMs. SALT II was not ratified by the United States, and has, indeed, been repudiated by the Reagan administration, although neither side has as yet violated its provisions. SALT has been renamed START (Strategic Arms Reduction Talks) by the United States, which has agreed to resume negotiations during 1982.

energy development, peaceful as well as military.

This attempt by the military to retain control over the "project" roused immediate opposition among the scientists who had been primarily responsible for its success. Foremost among these were some of the refugee scientists—e.g., James Franck and Leo Szilard—who had originally been responsible for the project's initiation.

By dint of their hastily-assembled but effective amateur lobbying effort, the scientists managed to defeat the May-Johnson Bill and to substitute for it the McMahon Bill, which set up a civilian Atomic Energy Agency to control the American nuclear future. In the process, a number of local discussion and action groups were formed (in Chicago, Oak Ridge, and Los Alamos) which together with other local groups of wartime project alumni (in Berkeley, New York, Cambridge, and Rochester) formed the Washington-based Federation of Atomic Scientists, later to become today's Federation of American Scientists (FAS). In Chicago, Hyman H. Goldsmith and Eugene Rabinowitch started the *Bulletin of the Atomic Scientists*. It was first a connecting newsletter among the various groups, but has grown into a national journal aimed at bringing nuclear dangers under control.[2]

With the immediate task of thwarting military control over atomic energy accomplished, the atomic scientist movement soon turned its attention to the longer-term imperative of putting the nuclear genie back into the bottle—an objective that still eludes them thirty-five years later. The first need was for a program of broad public education to counter the militarily-inspired belief that the atomic bomb "secret" must be jealously and rigorously guarded. Today, the fallacies of this approach are universally understood, but this was far from the case in the late forties, when the myth of American technological invincibility was almost universally accepted, and spy-scares (Allan Nunn May, Claus Fuchs, Greenglass, the Rosenbergs) periodically whipped U.S. tabloids into a frenzy of security consciousness.

To counter the universal ignorance in the nuclear area, the FAS set up an education branch—the Committee on Atomic Education—and undertook a campaign to spread universal understanding of the following three basic truths of the nuclear age:

1. There is *no secret* of the atomic bomb: any technologically developed nation, with a reasonably advanced program in nuclear physics, chemistry, and metallurgy, is capable of repeating the American accomplishment sooner or later. For a technologically advanced country like the Soviet Union, given the knowledge that a bomb is possible (i.e., Hiroshima and Nagasaki), the time needed, assuming a vigorous effort, would be in the order of five years.

2. There is *no defense* possible against an adversary possessing nuclear weapons and the determination to use them.

3. *Therefore*, the only reliable guarantee against nuclear war in the future is strict *International Control* over all nuclear activities, peaceful as well as military.

There was, of course, strong resistance to these ideas by the "America-firsters" of the period. However, point one was soon vindicated by the first Soviet nuclear explosion in 1949 and, especially, by their simultaneous (with us) demonstration of a thermonuclear explosive capability in 1954. Point two has, of course, continued to rouse controversy and military opposition, despite its official recognition in the ABM-Ban Treaty of 1972. Point three is what arms control has been all about since the forties.

However, so successful was the scientists' educational campaign that the idea of an international control body, first spelled out in the Oppenheimer-Acheson-Lilienthal Report of 1949, became official U.S. policy throughout the fifties. Known as the Baruch plan (for Truman's official U.N. negotiator), it remained on the U.N. agenda, futilely discussed each year in the eternally optimistic Disarmament Commission of the United

Nations, until it was finally dropped in the late fifties, one of the less-noticed casualties of the McCarthy era.

It should be noted, however, in all honesty, that almost from its introduction, the Baruch plan served a political purpose of U.S. policy in the developing "cold war." It was the United States answer to the early and persistent Soviet campaign to "ban the bomb." Although in recent years the idea of "banning" or "outlawing" nuclear weapons has become widely (but by no means universally) accepted among many arms controllers (at least in the form of a no-first-use agreement) as representing an important first step toward the controlled elimination of nuclear weapons—analogous to the role of the Geneva Protocol of 1925 in eliminating biological and chemical weapons—the U.S. reception to the Soviet ban-the-bomb proposals of the late forties was decidely negative, even hostile. In a period when the United States either had a monopoly over nuclear weapons, or in any case an overwhelming advantage in their numbers and in the capability for their delivery on Soviet targets in a nuclear war, the proposal to ban the bomb was generally regarded either as a propaganda ploy or as an attempt by the wily Stalin to neutralize the main American obstacle to his expansionist tendencies by a purely declarative, unverifiable, and unenforceable measure that he would be sure to violate when he determined such violation to be in the Soviet interests.

Obviously, although similar arguments are now being resurrected by the current opponents of the no-first-use agreement, they have become largely irrelevant in the present situation of essential nuclear parity in an age of vast, mutual nuclear overkill capacity.

A number of circumstances conspired in the late fifties to completely change the strategic nuclear confrontation between the United States and the Soviet Union. First was Sputnik in 1957: not that this represented a sensational new breakthrough in rocket or missile technology. On the contrary, the United States already had

at the time a number of programs that were on the verge of being able to place a similar payload in earth orbit. But because of the habitual military propensity for secrecy (against whom?) this fact was not known to the American or European public. Hence, Sputnik came as a profound shock—as the first (and undeniable) demonstration that not only was the age of missiles upon us, but that this age would be irrevocably characterized by the *mutual* ability of both sides to inflict overwhelming destruction upon each other, irrespective of any prior offensive or defensive measures that might be undertaken by either of the antagonists. For better or worse, irreversibly, we were both henceforth in the unenviable situation of two scorpions in a bottle.[3]

The immediate reaction to Sputnik in the United States was one of apprehension—it came as a profound shock to discover that America was no longer "number one." However, this was soon followed by the realization that the missile age had brought a new stability to the now-traditional East-West rivalry. It would henceforth be completely irrational (and therefore, one hoped, impossible) for the military planners on either side to consider an attack on the other without facing the real prospect of a nuclear retaliation against its own population centers by intercontinental missiles, against which there was no effective defense. And so we were once again confronted with the three truths: no secret, no defense, therefore international control.

Thus the concept of deterrence soon emerged, mainly from a number of studies initiated by a group of Cambridge academics under the auspices of the American Academy of Arts and Sciences (e.g., the American Academy's Summer Study on Arms Control in 1958, which resulted in the 1959 special Arms Control issue of the Academy's journal *Daedalus*).[4]

Although the false impression of a "missile gap" was used to advantage in the 1960 presidential election of John F. Kennedy, there was no such phenomenon until one was created (in the U.S. favor) by the Kennedy DOD under Robert McNamara. (The "gap" is a constantly recurring U.S. phenomenon, periodically recreated by zealous defense analysts either for election-winning purposes or for purposes of raising the military budget. Thus, since the early fifties we have successively been through a bomber gap, missile gap, a civil defense gap, ABM gap, throw-weight gap, and now a counterforce gap, each time emerging with more weapons but militarily less secure, not to speak of the toll in misspent funds and fueled inflation. It is a tribute to the abiding gullibility of the American body politic that the same prophets of "gaposis"—the Nitzes, Rostows, and others—keep rising like the phoenix from the ashes of each such debacle to proclaim the next.) The thousand-odd Minuteman missile force, which was the McNamara answer to the 1960 missile gap, together with the Polaris submarine and B-52 bomber legs of the now-sacred triad of deterrents, is only now having its adequacy called into question.

But if the defense establishment saw in the new military technologies an opportunity for the United States to "get ahead" of the Soviet Union, the newly-emerging arms control intellectuals, recognizing the fleeting nature of advantages in a technologically driven arms race, saw in the new missiles an opportunity to halt the race, through the mutual establishment of secure, invulnerable minimum deterrent forces.[5] However, as in the tango, it takes two to forego racing; thus, the concept of a minimum deterrent requires a return to the negotiating table. Furthermore, negotiations on missiles, types and numbers require a common understanding of the technologies as well as the political aspects. This was completely lacking, at least on the official level.

Fortunately, since 1957, there had been in existence an unofficial exchange medium—the Pugwash Movement—which could be and was used to bridge the understanding gap. This movement was established in 1955, in response to an appeal by Bertrand Russell, Albert Einstein, and nine other distinguished scholars, for scientists from East and West to meet together to assess the growing dangers of nuclear war and to inform their colleagues and the leaders of their respective nations of the steps that needed to be taken to avert these dangers—the Pugwash Conferences on Science and World Affairs have been meeting annually since 1957. The Pugwash scientists first established their common language and understanding of the issues, and with the weight and prestige of their scientific distinctions, supported an international treaty banning the further testing of nuclear weapons; then the scientists turned their attention to the problems of ending the arms race in the accumulation of nuclear weapons and delivery systems.[6] It was another decade, however, before their governments were to follow their lead with the initiation of the Strategic Arms Limitation Talks (SALT) in 1969.

In the late fifties and sixties, the obstacles to arms control were, as always, political rather than intellectual or technical. When the nuclear test ban[7] was first broached in the late fifties and discussed in the earliest Pugwash Conferences, it was clear that the problems of verification of compliance (the needs, or lack thereof, of intrusive inspection) were being greatly exaggerated, mainly for political purposes by the opponents. With the exception of relatively small explosions (less than around 10,000 tons of high-explosive equivalent), all tests could be unequivocally identified by means unilaterally available to the interested parties, that is, "national" means. Even in the case of such "small" underground explosions of 10 kt or less, the chances of a country being able to undertake a significant series of these tests without detection were small. These chances could be reduced to a satisfactory low level by the provision of simple, unmanned detection stations (black boxes), controlled by one side, on the territory of the other, or by the provision of a small number of annual, mandatory on-site inspections, or some combination of the two. All this was well understood by the end of the fifties.

Furthermore, a very large public pressure, sparked by a campaign led by Linus Pauling, had been building up against the further radioactive pollution of the atmosphere by nuclear weapons tests.

However, although the cold war had ostensibly died with Stalin in 1953, its melody lingered on. The military hard-line pressures for further testing prevailed until 1963 when, in the immediate aftermath of the Cuban missile crisis, having faced nuclear war and been frightened by its grim aspect, John Kennedy and Nikita Khrushchev decided that it was important to demonstrate the future peaceful intentions of the antagonists. As a vehicle for this demonstration, they chose to complete the nuclear test ban negotiations and rapidly signed a test ban treaty.

Unfortunately, in the haste to conclude the agreement, there was no time to iron out the relatively small remaining differences on the verification of small underground tests, and they settled for a partial test ban treaty that prohibited nuclear weapons tests in the atmosphere, in the seas, and in outer space, but continued to permit testing under the ground. Since then, the time has not again been politically propitious for a comprehensive test ban treaty (CTBT), and the huge loophole of underground testing has been left open for ever-increasing development of new and more sophisticated models of devices whose only rational function is to assure that they will never be used. Thus, what was intended to be a symbol of the East-West commitment to eliminate their nuclear arms competition and reduce the lethality of their arsenals has been turned into an arms control disaster, albeit an ecological blessing. Today, almost two decades later, the failure to sign a comprehensive test ban treaty stands out as the major symbol of the hopelessly slow pace of East-West arms control.

Indeed, the failure to take advantage of the euphoria of the brief Kennedy-Khrushchev period of genuine détente will probably be recorded as one of history's great tragedies. With Kennedy's assassination, Khrushchev's fall from grace, and the reversal of the great Soviet-American thaw, deriving from America's involvement in Vietnam, the opportunity vanished.

Meanwhile, however, the Pugwash scientists and most of the U.S. arms control community were urging the need to find a negotiated means of controlling the growing race in the accumulation of nuclear weapons before it was completely out of hand. Finally, by the end of the sixties it had become clear, even to the most ardent hard-liners, that Soviet missile deployments were about to overtake those of the United States, if not in quality and variety then at least in numbers. At this point, the United States proposed to begin serious SALT negotiations and the Soviet Union, content at having achieved essential equality while U.S. military technology was pre-occupied with Vietnam, agreed to join. Hence, finally, in 1972, the SALT I Treaty was concluded.

The most important achievement of SALT I was the treaty prohibiting Anti-Ballistic Missile (ABM) deployments. This came just in time to halt an already dangerous, though fortunately not far advanced, race in the testing and deployment of various ABM technologies and the counter-deployment of offensive techniques capable of circumventing them either by stealth or by saturation. Because the Soviet Union had already deployed a primitive city-protecting system around Moscow, the so-called "Golash" system, and the United States a missile defense installation at Grand Falls, North Dakota, the original agreement permitted each side to deploy one of each type. This option was not used, however, and a 1974 protocol limits the two sides to no more than was deployed at the time.

The ABM ban is generally regarded as probably the most important and effective agreement arrived at to date,[8] because it has established the necessary physical and political conditions that have permitted the continued limitation, and even some reduction of offensive systems. Unfortunately, technology does not stand still, and new developments (mainly in intense directed energy beams—primarily laser improve-

17-2 THE SALT I AGREEMENTS

The following are official United States summaries of the two principal treaties concluded in 1972 by the United States and the Soviet Union in the Strategic Arms Limitation Talks (SALT).

Treaty Between the United States of America and the Union of Soviet Socialist Republics on the Limitation of Anti-Ballistic Missile Systems

Signed at Moscow on May 26, 1972
Entered into force on October 3, 1972

Summary

In the Treaty on the Limitation of Anti-Ballistic Missile Systems the United States and the Soviet Union agree that each may have only two ABM deployment areas, so restricted and so located that they cannot provide a nationwide ABM defense or become the basis for developing one. Each country thus leaves unchallenged the penetration capability of the other's retaliatory missile forces.

The treaty permits each side to have one limited ABM system to protect its capital and another to protect an ICBM launch area. The two sites defended must be at least 1,300 kilometers apart, to prevent the creation of any effective regional defense zone or the beginnings of a nationwide system. [The treaty was amended in 1974 to further restrict each party to a single ABM deployment area.]

Precise quantitative and qualitative limits are imposed on the ABM systems that may be deployed. At each site there may be no more than 100 interceptor missiles and 100 launchers. Agreement on the number and characteristics of radars to be permitted had required extensive and complex technical negotiations, and the provisions governing these important components of ABM systems are spelled out in very specific detail in the treaty and further clarified in the "Agreed Statements" accompanying it.

Both parties agreed to limit qualitative improvement of their ABM technology, e.g., not to develop, test, or deploy ABM launchers capable of launching more than one interceptor missile at a time or modify existing launchers to give them this capability, and systems for rapid reload of launchers are similarly barred. These provisions, the Agreed Statements clarify, also ban interceptor missiles with more than one independently guided warhead.

There had been some concern over the possibility that surface-to-air missiles (SAMs) intended for defense against aircraft might be improved, along with their supporting radars, to the point where they could effectively be used against ICBMs and SLBMs, and the treaty prohibits this. While further deployment of radars intended to give early warning of strategic ballistic missile attack is not prohibited, they must be located along the territorial boundaries of each country and oriented outward, so that they do not contribute to an effective ABM defense of points in the interior.

Further, to decrease the pressures of technological change and its unsettling impact on the strategic balance, both sides agree to prohibit development, testing, or deployment of sea-based, air-based, or space-based ABM systems and their components, along with mobile land-based ABM systems. Should future technology bring forth new ABM systems "based on other physical principles" than those employed in current systems, it was agreed that limiting such systems would be discussed, in accordance with the treaty's provisions for consultation and amendment.

The treaty also provides for a U.S.-Soviet Standing Consultative Commission to promote its objectives and implementation. The commission was established during the first negotiating session of SALT II, by a Memorandum of Understanding dated December 21, 1972. Since then both the United States and the Soviet Union have raised a number of questions in the Commission relating to each side's compliance with the SALT I agreements. In each case raised by the United States, the Soviet activity in question has either ceased or additional information has allayed U.S. concern.

Article XIV of the treaty calls for review of the treaty after 5 years after its entry into force, and at 5-year intervals thereafter. The first such review was conducted by the Standing Consultative Commission at its special session in the fall of 1977. At this session, the United States and the Soviet Union agreed that the treaty had operated effectively during its first 5 years, that it had continued to serve national security interests, and that it did not need to be amended at that time.

Interim Agreement Between the United States of America and the Union of Soviet Socialist Republics on Certain Measures With Respect to the Limitation of Strategic Offensive Arms

Signed at Moscow on May 26, 1972
Entered into force on October 3, 1972

Summary

As its title suggests, the "Interim Agreement Between the United States and the Union of Soviet Socialist Republics on Certain Measures With Respect to the Limitation of Offensive Arms" was limited in duration and scope. It was intended to remain in force for 5 years. (See preceding section on SALT.) Both countries undertook to continue negotiations for a more comprehensive agreement as soon as possible, and the scope and terms of any new agreement were not to be prejudiced by the provisions of the 1972 accord.

Thus the Interim Agreement was set essentially as a holding action, designed to complement the ABM Treaty by limiting competition in offensive strategic arms and to provide time for further negotiations. The agreement essentially freezes at existing levels the number of strategic ballistic missile launchers, operational or under construction, on each side, and permits an increase in SLBM launchers up to an agreed level for each party only with the dismantling or destruction of a corresponding number of older ICBM or SLBM launchers.

In view of the many asymmetries in the two countries' forces, imposing equivalent limitations required rather complex and precise provisions. At the date of signing, the United States had 1,054 operational land-based ICBMs, and none under construction; the Soviet Union had an estimated 1,618, operational and under construction. Launchers under construction could be completed. Neither side would start construction of additional fixed land-based ICBM launchers during the period of the agreement—this, in effect, also bars relocation of existing launchers. Launchers for light or older ICBMs cannot be converted into launchers for modern heavy ICBMs. This prevents the U.S.S.R. from replacing older missiles with missiles such as the SS-9, which in 1972 was the largest and most powerful missile in the Soviet inventory and a source of particular concern to the United States.

Within these limitations, modernization and replacement are permitted, but in the process of modernizing, the dimensions of silo launchers cannot be significantly increased.

Mobile ICBMs are not covered. The Soviet Union held that since neither side had such systems, a freeze should not apply to them; it also opposed banning them in a future comprehensive agreement. The United States held they should be banned because of the verification difficulties they presented. In a formal statement, the U.S. delegation declared that the United States would consider deployment of land-mobile ICBMs during the period of the agreement as inconsistent with its objectives.

Article III and the protocol limit launchers for submarine-launched ballistic missiles (SLBMs) and modern ballistic missile submarines. The United States is permitted to reach a ceiling of 710 SLBM launchers on 44 submarines, from its base level of 656 SLBM launchers on 41 ballistic missile submarines, by replacing 54 older ICBM launchers. The Soviet Union, beyond the level of 740 SLBM launchers on modern nuclear-powered submarines, may increase to 950. But these additional launchers are permitted only as replacements for older ICBM or SLBM launchers, which must be dismantled or destroyed under agreed procedures.

In a unilateral statement, the Soviet Union asserted that if U.S. NATO allies increased the number of their modern submarines, the Soviet Union would have a right to increase the number of its submarines correspondingly. The United States declared that it did not accept this claim.

ments) have permitted military planners to dream of possible ABM systems of very high putative efficiency, and therefore to question the value of the ABM ban.[9] Since this treaty comes up for mandatory review in 1982, there are already very strong pressures for its abdication—pressures which are likely to be resisted by the arms control community with all possible force.

For the rest, SALT I was essentially only a stand-still freeze in missile numbers, but it neither controlled types nor new missile technology; qualitative limitations were postponed to the next stages. Thus, while the Soviets were permitted to retain the slight advantages in numbers of land-based ICBMs and missile submarines that they possessed before the curtain was rung down in 1972, the United States was permitted to continue its conversion of single-warhead missiles to multiple, independently-targetable reentry vehicles (MIRV), a new approach with a U.S. technological edge over the Soviets.

It required no special genius to predict the instability of an attempted limitation in numbers that permitted the limitless multiplication of weapons through multiple warheads. Thus, this repetition of the limited test-ban blunder has had the inevitable outcome. By the time the SALT II negotiations have been able to arrive at some partial measures of qualitative constraints, some eight years after the conclusion of SALT I, the new race in counterforce (first-strike) systems is already too far under way to be seriously inhibited. Furthermore, new and essentially uncountable (and therefore unverifiable) deployments of weapons, such as cruise missiles, are rapidly being disseminated throughout the western alliance and will undoubtedly soon be followed by their eastern counterparts. When they appear, they will suddenly be recognized as destabilizing and become the targets of a new round of frenzied negotiations to "close the barn door."

In particular, because all SALT II does is impose quantitative (but not qualitative) limits on current deployments, such new developments are already undermining any remaining faith on the part of both the "hawks" and the "doves" in the SALT process. Furthermore, even the present weak limitations will expire in the absence of U.S. Senate ratification of SALT II, an act that now appears to be outside the realm of reasonable probability. However, SALT negotiations are scheduled to resume towards the end of 1982, although the Reagan administration prefers to symbolize its "new approach" to nuclear arms control by referring to the process as START (arms *reduction*, rather than limitation).

While both the United States and the Soviet Union are meanwhile adhering to the provisions of SALT II, it is difficult to believe that such behavior will continue to transcend the various political crises and confrontations that have marked the last decade. The future of SALT or START thus appears rather grim—not to speak of the prospects for any appreciable reduction of the present horrendous mutual overkill in the long-dreamed-of direction of a comprehensive disarmament treaty.[10]

The repetitious stupidity of this futile charade—the deployment of new technological advances followed by attempts to annul their damage via arms control measures—should have long since become evident to even the most obtuse observer. The unfortunate fact is that most people do not take arms control seriously because they believe neither in its proported efficacy nor in the consequences of its failure. It is, they believe, a meaningless game irrelevant to the real world. After all, they have seen it going on for over thirty years, with no serious effect on the course of events; at the same time, the dire predictions of the believers in arms control have not come to pass.

If the world has been able to blunder along for over thirty-five years, secure in its hope that the knowledge of the lethality of the nuclear arsenals will continue to inhibit national leaders from seriously considering their use, the great majority of people feel they have good reason to believe—when they give it any thought at all—that the system is good for another thirty-five years at least.

We can only pray that they are right.

Suggested Readings

The early concern of scientists over the use and spread of nuclear weapons and over establishing effective international control are reviewed in the account written by Alice Kimball Smith and in the documents collected by Weart and Szilard. The book by Herken is an account of U.S. attitudes and military planning during the first years of the cold war, and *Race to Oblivion* by York portrays the politics of distrust that drive the arms race. The space-age diplomacy that was initiated by the Soviet Sputnik and led to the Test Ban Treaty is recounted by participants in the drama—Killian as science advisor to President Eisenhower and Seaborg as chairman of the Atomic Energy Commission.

Reports on international negotiations toward arms control are to be found in the SIPRI *Yearbooks,* and background on the problems of arms limitation in the European Theater appears in the SIPRI volume, *Tactical Nuclear Weapons.* The volume edited by Epstein and Feld reports on the 1980 Pugwash conference devoted to the technology and politics of arms control.

EPSTEIN, WILLIAM, AND BERNARD T. FELD, EDS., *New Directions in Disarmament.* New York: Praeger, 1981.

HERKEN, GREGG. *The Winning Weapon: The Atomic Bomb in the Cold War, 1945–1950.* New York: Knopf, 1980.

KILLIAN, JAMES R., JR. *Sputnik, Scientists and Eisenhower.* Cambridge, Mass.: M.I.T. Press, 1977.

SEABORG, GLENN T. *Kennedy, Krushchev and the Test Ban.* Berkeley, Calif.: University of California Press, 1981.

SMITH, ALICE K. *A Peril and a Hope.* Chicago: University of Chicago Press, 1965; Cambridge, Mass.: M.I.T. Press, 1979.

Stockholm International Peace Research Institute (SIPRI). *Tactical Nuclear Weapons: European Perspectives.* London: Taylor and Francis, 1978.

SIPRI. *World Armaments and Disarmament.* London: Taylor and Francis. Yearbooks published annually.

WEART, SPENCER R., AND GERTRUD W. SZILARD, EDS. *Leo Szilard: His Version of the Facts.* Cambridge, Mass.: M.I.T. Press, 1978.

YORK, HERBERT F. *Race to Oblivion: A Participant's View of the Arms Race.* New York: Simon and Schuster, 1970.

The SALT II Treaty was signed by President Carter and First Secretary Brezhnev in Vienna on June 18, 1979, but it was never ratified by the U.S. Senate. Neverthe-less, in 1982 both parties were voluntarily observing the treaty provisions.

18. Prospects for International Arms Control

A major problem with the negotiations between the United States and the Soviet Union on the limitation and reduction of nuclear arms has come from the overwhelming tendency to "link" these negotiations to the ups and downs of relations between the superpowers. Very powerful arguments can be mustered for the overriding mutual interest of the two parties in reaching agreements that would on the one hand reduce the dangers of outbreak of nuclear war, and on the other hand limit the consequences of such a war if the prevention system should break down. Available evidence supports the contention that effective agreements with the current Soviet leaders on the reduction of nuclear weapons are possible. The major obstacle at the present time may lie in the ideological propensities of the Reagan administration.

WHAT BERNARD FELD has accurately called "the sorry history of arms control" is not the necessary result of intractable disagreement on substantive issues. Although the process of negotiation faces genuine difficulties arising from differences in national history, culture, negotiating style, and the past choices made on weapons systems, it is entirely possible to complete sound treaties limiting strategic arms and curbing their further development.

The stalling of the Strategic Arms Limitation Talks (SALT) is attributable to pressures of U.S. domestic politics and the linkage of arms control negotiations to the overall and fluctuating relationship between the United States and the Soviet Union. Unless we accept the argument that nuclear war is in some circumstances a rational choice, we should expect our political leaders to return to the bargaining table and get on with the tough business of concluding effective and verifiable arms control agreements.

Obstacles in Negotiation

There is nothing usual, or even natural, about a situation in which long-standing and even bitter rivals try to reach agreements by which each has a say about the quantity and quality of the other's arsenal of nuclear weapons. Moreover, important differences in culture, experience, and even the nature of the two languages add to the difficulties faced by U.S. and Soviet negotiating teams in making major progress in an area so basic to national security. The senior Soviet diplomats are not young; all were of a mature age and many held official positions during the years of the Stalin terror. This conditioning clearly puts a damper on any spontaneity or element of freewheeling in their negotiating style.

A number of commentators, including some who should know better, have ascribed the glacial pace of negotiations to a Soviet proclivity for setting forth a position, refusing to budge, and waiting to choose among a series of posi-

Paul C. Warnke

Warnke was director of the U.S. Arms Control and Disarmament Agency under President Jimmy Carter and a chief negotiator of the SALT II treaty.

tions put on the table by the U.S. negotiators. Former Secretary of State Henry Kissinger, in testifying on the SALT II treaty in the summer of 1979, drew a contrast between this purported Soviet negotiating stance and U.S. eagerness to get ahead with the job. This, he implied, gave the Soviets a negotiating edge and led to U.S. concessions.

This may have been Secretary Kissinger's experience. It was not mine. On the important issues of SALT II, including those involved in the agreement reached at Vladivostok with Leonid Brezhnev by Kissinger and President Gerald Ford in late 1974, it was the Soviet side that made the major concessions. But these changes are not achieved at the negotiating team level; they obviously require deliberations at the highest level in Moscow.

The Soviet negotiating style is characterized by a reluctance to depart at all from whatever formal position has been reached, by whatever the internal Soviet process may be, or even to discuss a possible alternative. Accordingly, surprising changes often occur without prior signal of any softening of a long-debated position. When bargaining parties find themselves at an impasse, this can often be broken by playing the "what if" game. Party "A" may, while disclaiming any authority to vary from his present position, ask Party "B" what he thinks his side might be willing to do if a particular change were to be approved by Party "A's" principals. This kind of negotiating approach sometimes proved possible with Ambassador Anatoliy Dobrynin or in talks between Foreign Minister Andrei Gromyko and Secretary of State Cyrus Vance. It was rarely if ever achieved with the Soviet SALT delegation in Geneva.

Another difficulty inherent in the SALT talks is the asymmetries in the respective strategic force structures of the United States and the Soviet Union. Different choices have been made and a different mix created. For example, the effort in SALT II to limit launchers of the so-called heavy missiles—the Soviet land-based SS-18

ICBMs—was doomed by the fact that the United States did not have and did not want ICBMs of that size and was unwilling to offer up concessions on weapons it did have. The limit on launchers of ICBMs with Multiple Independently-Targetable Reentry Vehicles (MIRVs) could not be as low as we wished because a much higher proportion of Soviet nuclear strategic resources was in launchers of land-based missiles, and the United States had technological superiority in MIRVed submarine-launched ballistic missiles. The U.S. negotiators always had to be conscious of the fact that domestic critics of SALT would seize upon instances in which the Soviets were allowed to retain a numerical advantage and would ignore the asymmetries where the United States has an appreciable edge.

Arrival at effective and enforceable arms control agreements is also handicapped by a deep discrepancy in underlying attitudes toward verification measures. The Soviet Union is a closed society, and its leadership shows every inclination to keep it that way. There is no Soviet parallel to the trade and popular press that make it virtually impossible to withhold information about the characteristics and deployment of new U.S. weapon systems. As a practical matter, therefore, the Soviets have verification means that we lack.

It should be noted, however, that our own national means of verification are more than adequate for policing compliance with the SALT II treaty and even more comprehensive quantitative and qualitative controls. Photoreconnaissance satellites enable us to tell how many and what kind of strategic nuclear vehicles the Soviet Union has. Moreover, the counting rules agreed upon by the two sides result in a "worst case" picture of the opposing force. For example, any launcher of a type that has ever contained or launched a missile of a type that has ever been MIRVed would count against the 1,200 limit specified in the treaty. Concern about verifiability is thus more a political than a practical problem.

18-1   WHAT ARE THE RUSSIANS UP TO?

Ever since the Russian rejection of the Baruch Plan, it has been an accepted tenet of arms control theory that no agreement is possible which requires verification procedures going beyond national means. History does not completely bear out this assumption: Khrushchev was willing to accept three mandatory annual on-site inspections to achieve a comprehensive nuclear test ban. Yet U.S. negotiators refused to settle for any number less than seven. More recently, the Soviets have expressed willingness to accept a form of verification via "challenge inspection," a limited form of international access, for verification of a chemical weapons ban. Nevertheless, there is a great reluctance on the part of Soviet leaders to throw open their country to free access by foreign agents, even if under international auspices.

Both the Soviet Union and the United States have developed reconnaissance satellites capable of essentially continuous observation of activities of the other side, with visual resolution and continuity that, for all intents and purposes, preclude the clandestine installation of any significant offensive military capability. This capability provides each side with effective national means that permit the verification of virtually all significant arms limitations, and even arms reduction agreements, and makes the issue of verification essentially irrelevant. No claim is made that every small addition or alteration of military potential will be detected. But, even with the pervasive penetration of both sides by conventional espionage activities left aside, the mutually accepted "open skies" policy and the ever-increasing technological capabilities of satellites ensure detection of any attempt by either superpower to secretly alter the status quo.

This situation may change by the end of this century if either or both sides deploy land- or sea-launched cruise missiles, because these would be easy to conceal. At present, the United States is starting to deploy air-launched cruise missiles, to be carried by verifiable numbers of B-52 aircraft.

Unlike the Soviet leadership, U.S. politicians have to contend with a vocal electorate that is all too ready to question whether those responsible for defense and foreign policy really know what they are doing. Those who have ventured to explain and support the SALT II treaty in public meetings usually have found that the major concern expressed is whether we are too credulous about Soviet adherence to the limitations. Confidence in our intelligence capabilities has not been at its peak in recent years. Whereas the Supreme Soviet has no authority to override the judgment of the politburo, our Constitution conditions treaty ratification on approval by two-thirds of the United States Senate.

Adding to these difficulties is the lack of congruity between the Russian and English languages. At times, what have appeared to be substantive differences have turned out to be a mere linguistic mismatch. For example, a negotiating problem in trying to arrive at a definition of strategic bombers was resolved when we found that our proposed provision was being converted into Russian by a word that meant "flying apparatuses" rather than airplanes. The Soviet delegation was apparently concerned that we might be planning to equip balloons and dirigibles with cruise missiles.

But despite the practical difficulties, U.S. and Soviet negotiators have been able to reach some useful agreements. The limited test ban treaty; the SALT I limits on Antiballistic Missiles (ABMs) and intercontinental missile launchers; and the SALT II treaty, signed but unratified, are conspicuous examples. The "sorry history of arms control" records a lack of political will rather than a bargaining impasse.

Salt as a Political Football

In U.S.-Soviet negotiations there are always the routine and expectable problems. Many of them could and do turn up in international bargaining about commercial sales, bilateral agreements on airplane landing rights, and diplomatic facilities.

From its genesis, however, the idea of strategic arms limitation has excited at least as much political resistance as it has political support. SALT as a political football has become even more attractive with the recent weakness of incumbent presidents facing tough reelection campaigns.

Had it not been for the unpopularity of his Vietnam policy, Lyndon Johnson very likely would have sought and secured another term as President in 1968. The appeal of his social programs and the sounder economy that would have existed, absent the enormous expense of the war, would in all probability have given him a strong mandate to obtain the strategic arms limitation agreement he so ardently desired. And it might well have brought it in time to prevent the MIRV deployment that now creates a growing counterforce capability and fears of first strike.

It is, I think, no coincidence that the SALT I agreements were completed and presented to the Congress at a time when President Richard Nixon was at the peak of his political power. In May 1972, he was still bathed in the glow of the historic breakthrough to China and the triumph of his visit there in what he called "the week that changed the world." In 1972, Nixon faced no perceptible opposition for the Republican nomination. "Watergate" was nothing more than

a hotel-office building complex. Despite the fact that the SALT I agreement on control of offensive arms froze ballistic missile launchers at levels that gave the Soviet Union a numerical advantage, congressional approval was overwhelming.

Neither President Ford nor President Jimmy Carter was ever in a remotely comparable position of strength. Shortly after President Ford's negotiating triumph at Vladivostok, where Mr. Brezhnev agreed to the U.S. position that excluded from SALT coverage our forward-based systems in Europe that could strike Soviet targets, he found himself in a hot campaign for the Republican nomination. The challenge of Governor Ronald Reagan and the attendant charge that President Ford and Secretary Kissinger were soft in dealing with the Soviet Union made completion of a SALT treaty and its presentation to the Senate an unacceptable political risk in 1975 and 1976.

Similarly in 1979 and 1980 it was clear that Democratic senators had little concern about the ability of President Carter to hand out political rewards or punishments. Republican senators could smell a victory and were little disposed tacitly to concede to President Carter a major diplomatic triumph. SALT was treated not on its merits but as a symbol of detente—which was seen more and more as a discredited policy.

The Concept of Linkage

The irrational but paramount question about SALT came to be whether or not we could trust the Soviets. SALT came to be regarded as a favor, and it became apparent that Americans wanted to do the Soviets no favors. However irrational and self-denying this attitude might be, it is one for which the Soviets must take a major share of the blame.

Soviet sponsorship of Cuban troops in Angola and the Horn of Africa led to an unacknowledged but nonetheless appreciable slowdown in the pace of SALT negotiations in the first half of 1978. These African adventures put an end to the U.S.-Soviet talks on stabilization of Indian Ocean forces and drained much of the enthusiasm for completion of the Comprehensive Test Ban Treaty being negotiated in Geneva by U.S., Soviet, and British teams. On our part, we certainly did not help move the SALT negotiations along by announcing our resumption of full diplomatic relations with the People's Republic of China and the forthcoming visit of Deng Xiao Ping just before a key meeting between Secretary Vance and Foreign Minister Gromyko in December 1978.

In June 1979, when President Carter and Mr. Brezhnev signed the SALT II treaty, the United States was again close to an election year, with influential Democratic senators already concerned that their own political fortunes would not be helped by President Carter's reelection campaign. Accordingly, although the opponents of the SALT II treaty failed to make a plausible case and it appeared that the treaty would be somewhat grudgingly accepted by the Senate in early summer, the silly flap about a Soviet brigade that had been in Cuba for well over a decade virtually spelled its doom. Its fate was sealed, at least for the time being, by the Soviet military intervention in Afghanistan.

During President Carter's years, the expressed policy was that the limitation of strategic nuclear arms should be pursued as a desirable goal regardless of the overall state of U.S.-Soviet relations. Although President Carter roundly condemned Soviet and Cuban interference in the affairs of African states, he stoutly denied press accounts that he desired to put SALT in the "deep freeze" until after the 1978 congressional elections. Secretary Vance repeatedly decried the policy of "linkage" whereby the presumed Soviet appetite for SALT could be used to influence Soviet international behavior.

To those who contend that strategic arms control negotiations should be suspended until, for example, Soviet forces get out of Afghanistan, SALT and detente have become virtually synonymous. This, it appears, is the unanimous position of the Reagan administration. In a speech to the Foreign Policy Association on July 14, 1981, the then Secretary of State Alexander Haig stated:

> A policy of pretending that there is no linkage promotes reverse linkage. It ends up saying that in order to preserve arms control, we have to tolerate Soviet aggression.

This, I believe, is a classic non sequitur. Because there is no logical linkage, we can oppose Soviet aggression and still recognize that limits on Soviet nuclear weapons serve our interests.

We should pursue the limitation of strategic arms and bring formal agreements into effect because, and only because, this improves our national security. The limitation of strategic nuclear arms is not only to our advantage but is essential to our survival. There is no other way to arrest the development of Soviet nuclear weapons of a kind and quantity that could challenge the survivability of our deterrent forces.

The Arms Race and "Rational Nuclear War"

Some officials in the administration of President Reagan, including the President himself and his chief arms negotiator, retired Army General Edward Rowny, have argued that a willingness of the United States to undertake an unrestricted nuclear arms race would discourage the Soviets because of their weaker economy and poorer technology and would thus bring about arms control by default. Informed observers of the Soviet society, including two of our most recent U.S. ambassadors, Malcolm Toon and Thomas Watson, see no such promise in this arms-race theory of arms control. Experts on the Soviet Union are persuaded that the Soviet leadership will impose whatever sacrifices by the Soviet people are necessary to prevent the United States from achieving the unrealistic goal of nuclear superiority.

But preoccupation with this goal is another underlying reason why the realistic goal of effective restrictions on nuclear weaponry continues to elude our grasp. While most Americans appear unwilling even to think about the effects of nuclear weapons, there are a number of pseudorealists who give increasing currency to the notion that a nuclear war can be fought and won and that we should busy ourselves with taking the steps to do just that.

The premise of SALT, indeed its underlying rationale, is that our strategic nuclear weapons can serve only one sane purpose: to prevent another country from using such weapons against us or our friends. Those who support control over strategic nuclear weapons recognize that they can have no utility for wider purposes of U.S. foreign policy.

SALT critics, on the other hand, refuse to accept this reasoning. Eugene Rostow, President Reagan's choice as head of the U.S. Arms Control and Disarmament Agency, has said that to negotiate an "agreement that would make a nuclear attack on the United States impossible, or at least unlikely" is to set a "totally inadequate standard." He told the Senate Foreign Relations Committee at his confirmation hearing that the "minimal goal of our nuclear arsenal and our minimal goal in arms limitation negotiations" includes the ability "to use military force in defense of our interests with comparative freedom." Presumably Rostow finds unexceptionable the argument of Colin Gray and Keith Payne:

If American nuclear power is to support U.S. foreign policy objectives, the United States must possess the ability to wage nuclear war rationally.[1]

Ever since the first primitive atomic bomb was invented, efforts have been made to find a way in which this vast new power could be usefully exploited by those who possess it. Initially, in the years when we had a nuclear monopoly, we were able to talk confidently about "massive retaliation." Other nations would have to be careful about challenging our interests because of our proclaimed willingness to blow them up if they ventured to do so. In those halcyon days, there were discussions of preemptive nuclear

strikes—against the Soviet Union, or even against China. And even after the Soviet Union developed its own nuclear weapons, there remained a residual affection for the idea that our threat to use our nuclear weapons could be employed rationally and successfully to promote our worldwide interests.

The growing realization that resorting to our strategic nuclear weapons against targets in the Soviet Union would only mean our own destruction from a Soviet retaliatory strike has dominated our strategic thinking since the sixties. But there have always been some U.S. theorists who have struggled to escape this straitjacket on our ability to exploit a nuclear military potential. And during the past couple of years there has been a strong upsurge in the view that a nuclear war may well have to be fought and that we should develop and optimize our nuclear weapons and our strategic doctrine so that we can fight, survive, and win such a war.

There are many current examples of a growing complacency about nuclear war. Herman Kahn, director of the Hudson Institute, is quoted as saying that those who view nuclear war as inherently suicidal are, in his term, "crazy." According to Kahn, "if 20 million Americans were killed there would be 200 million survivors." Former Secretary of State Alexander Haig, in his confirmation hearing, spoke of the "backdrop" of our nuclear strength: "[T]his backdrop serves to strengthen American diplomacy, to enable the American President to speak authoritatively," even at lower levels of tension. Secretary of Defense Caspar Weinberger, during his confirmation hearings, was asked whether he might have recommended the use of nuclear weapons in Vietnam. He replied: "Any time you get into a war the possibility that you will use every weapon available has to be left open." If we commit U.S. forces, he continued, "we owe it to them ... to be ready to utilize the strength that we have."

Misguided enthusiasm for the practical military utility of nuclear arms transcends partisan politics. Presidential Directive 59 was issued in the campaign heat of summer 1980 as a revision of our strategic nuclear doctrine. According to press accounts, some Carter administration officials described P.D. 59 as a major move away from reliance on deterrence alone and an effort to reshape our targeting policy so that we might take on the Soviet Union in a controlled and protracted exchange of strategic nuclear weapons—thus moving toward mutual destruction in neat, tidy stages. The so-called "Defense Guidance" leaked to the *New York Times* in the spring of 1982 topped this folly by announcing a Defense Department objective of creating nuclear forces that could prevail and compel the Soviet Union to sue for peace on terms favorable to the United States.

No one can say authoritatively just what would happen if the United States and the Soviet Union were to exchange even a few thousand of their nuclear warheads. What is known is that a multimegaton Soviet bomb would totally destroy New York City; the Soviets have between 100 and 200 of these bombs. Knowledgeable U.S. physicians have pointed out that our medical facilities would be unable to cope with the burn victims, even if any sizable fraction of the urban hospitals remained operational. The so-called counterforce attack, designed to eliminate our 1,052 land-based ICBMs, would require the launch of 2,000 to 3,000 Soviet warheads to stand even a theoretical chance of success.

The reemergence of the conceits of the early fifties that nuclear weapons are just another form of armament, to be employed rationally to advance our national interests, thus tragically confirms Albert Einstein's observation: "The unleashed power of the atom has changed everything—except our way of thinking."

Meaningful Agreements Are Possible

Unquestionably, the ability of SALT negotiators to produce arms-control agreements that make substantial cuts in existing nuclear weapons and prevent the development of even more destabilizing ones is seriously impeded by the persistence of the illusion that a diversified nuclear arsenal can serve a variety of military purposes and help achieve foreign policy goals.

Both supporters and opponents of the SALT process are wont to buttress their arguments by recalling the initial effort by the Carter administration, in March 1977, to get the Soviets to move well beyond the kind of SALT II treaty that had previously been under discussion. Pro-SALT commentators cite this as a misguided move that seriously set back the negotiating timetable. Those who have no faith in SALT use it to bolster their contention that the Soviets are not interested in serious controls that limit their own strategic weapons plans. I disagree with both positions.

The 1977 comprehensive package clearly surprised and upset the Soviets. Their rigid decision-making system perhaps was incapable of adjusting to the new approach even well enough to present a counterproposal. But just a few weeks later, in early May, the SALT negotiating teams met in Geneva and began to deal seriously with the remaining and major verification issues. In July 1977, discussions between Secretary Vance and Foreign Minister Gromyko produced at least the outline of a solution to most of the remaining problems, such as control over cruise missiles. SALT was due for far more serious setbacks, peripheral to the negotiations themselves.

Nor does this episode represent a fair test of possible Soviet responsiveness to large cuts on both sides. In the negotiations in 1977 and 1978, it became clear that completion of a treaty that would be recognizable as the outgrowth of the 1974 Vladivostok understanding was, for President Brezhnev, a political imperative. Senior Soviet officials, following the March 1977 meetings, explained to their U.S. counterparts that President Brezhnev had "spilled a lot of political blood at Vladivostok" and that he needed a treaty incorporating the points agreed to there to justify his action in overruling senior military advisors.

Some confirmation of the Soviet leader's concern for the form of the Vladivostok understanding came from subsequent negotiations about the numerical ceilings. The Vladivostok totals limited each country to 2,400 strategic nuclear delivery vehicles, of which 1,320 could be launchers of MIRVed missiles. The U.S. negotiators wanted lower figures. It was eventually agreed that the treaty would set forth the 2,400/1,320 totals but would further provide that the overall figure would be reduced to 2,250 by the end of 1981 and that only 1,200 of the 1,320 could be launchers of MIRVed missiles. The balance of 120 could be made up of strategic bombers equipped for cruise missiles—a system that the United States had under development but for which the Soviet Union then had no plans. The cosmetics of Vladivostok were preserved in the starting ceilings, and this seemed to suffice.

It is thus clear that negotiated controls over nuclear arms are achievable. The Soviets, because of their own national interest in survival, have demonstrated a willingness to compromise. What remains to be shown is a consistent American policy that accords nuclear arms control its proper role in protecting our national security.

The contention is frequently made that too much of our time and attention have been given to the effort to reach agreements constraining nuclear weapons. Officials of the Reagan administration have suggested that only a massive buildup of nuclear weaponry can induce the Soviets to bargain seriously. A panel convened by the Council on Foreign Relations issued a report on U.S.-Soviet relations in mid-1981. The panel stated its belief that "arms control has been the centerpiece of United States policy toward the Soviet Union, and that this was wrong." This is a curious distortion of the record. Strategic arms control has been virtually shelved while transient events in the fractious relations between the superpowers have often received disproportionate attention.

Indeed, reports of strategic papers prepared by the Department of Defense and the National Security Council suggest an approach toward U.S.-Soviet relations which would find no place for agreements on arms control, or anything else. The "Defense Guidance" referred to previously not only calls for nuclear superiority but proposes the development of weapons that would be "difficult for the Soviets to encounter, impose disproportionate costs, open up new areas of major military competition, and obsolesce previous Soviet instrument." Projected Defense Department expenditures for the next five years would be in the order of $1½ trillion.

At the same time, of course, negotiations on control of nuclear weapons have been resumed. But the presence within the administration of advocates of nuclear supremacy and of all-out economic, diplomatic, and even military confrontation with the Soviet Union justifies some skepticism about the zeal with which administration negotiators approach the bargaining table.

There is, I am sure, no chance that we can get the Soviet leadership to accept the cuts we propose in Soviet forces unless we are willing to accept constraints on U.S. systems that threaten the Soviet deterrent. The negotiating snag in the March 1977 comprehensive proposal was the request that the Soviet Union cut its heavy missiles and all other MIRVed ICBMs without commensurate reductions in areas where we have an edge.

The current U.S. START proposals, as publicly released, call for reductions in ICBM warheads to a level of 2,500 and a total ballistic missile warhead ceiling of 5,000. Again, the negotiability will depend upon our willingness to put on the table such proposed systems as the MX and the cruise missiles planned for deployment on general-purpose submarines.

In July 1979 the Joint Chiefs of Staff informed the Senate Foreign Relations Committee that "there are a number of restrictions in SALT II which operate primarily to our advantage ... the specific limits on the United States are quite nominal." If we really want the reductions that have been announced as our objective, we can try a lot harder than we have in the past and give more to get more.

What is most needed, if we are to free our negotiators to work for more significant reductions and controls, is a reevaluation of how our security may best be served. Continued adherence to the concept that strategic nuclear weaponry can somehow be molded into a flexible response force is fundamentally antithetical to effective nuclear arms control. The continued development of greater counterforce capability will do nothing to lessen the threat that greater Soviet accuracy poses for our own ICBMs. Nor will the ability to lob a nuclear warhead into the Kremlin from Western Europe, rather than from North Dakota or a ballistic missile submarine, add anything to our own ability to survive a nuclear war. As the nuclear arms competition continues, and fears of the other side's first-strike potential increase, "launch on warning" may loom as an inescapable strategy. Each side will feel a compulsion to draw its gun first, to follow the maxim "use them before you lose them."

The history of SALT is a history of lost opportunities. What it shows is a failure to order our priorities to deal with the gravest threat that humankind has ever faced.

It may be, however, that practical political considerations will provide the impetus for serious efforts at controlling nuclear weaponry. Certainly it is not cynicism to believe that the anti-nuclear weapons demonstrations in Western Europe have been largely responsible for the initiation of talks on control of so-called Intermediate Nuclear Forces (INF), the longer-range theater nuclear missiles. And the broad popular response throughout the United States to the proposition that we should seek a bilateral freeze on testing, production, and deployment of nuclear weapons can be credited for the

resumption of talks on reducing the intercontinental range systems, now rechristened as START.

After a period of apathy that is hard for me to understand, the American public has begun to show a recognition of the risk of nuclear holocaust and an awareness that it can use the power it possesses in our democracy to influence the course of U.S. strategic policy. Until very recently, more human energy and enthusiasm have been devoted to opposing nuclear power than supporting meaningful measures to pull back from the nuclear abyss.

What has now become a mass movement has already scored its successes. Administration officials, including President Reagan himself, have habitually referred to the SALT II treaty as "fatally flawed." But in his speech on Memorial Day 1982, President Reagan asserted that he would do nothing to undercut the treaty so long as the Soviet Union exercised comparable restraint. The 1982 edition of "Arms Control and Disarmament Agreements," published by the United States Arms Control and Disarmament Agency, notes: "Although Senate consent has not been given, both President Carter and President Reagan have declared that they would do nothing to jeopardize the treaty as long as the Soviet Union abided by it, and President Brezhnev has made a similar statement regarding Soviet intentions." So SALT II lives on, flaws and all, in part at least because of well-grounded concern about the political price of killing it off.

If further progress is to be made, however, some significant restructuring of the negotiations is required. Both the INF and the START talks deal with a single integrated problem: both deal with what must be considered as strategic nuclear weapons—weapons designed not for battlefield use but to destroy targets in the respective homelands of the adversaries. In the INF negotiations, the United States proposes to forgo deployment of 464 ground-launched cruise missiles and 108 Pershing II ballistic missiles in certain countries of Western Europe if the Soviet Union will dismantle its SS-20s and older medium-range ballistic missile systems that can strike NATO Europe but not the United States.

But air-launched cruise missiles are already subject to some controls in the SALT II treaty, and the proposed sea-launched cruise missiles must certainly be taken into account by the Soviet Union in considering American proposals for sharp reductions in Soviet ICBMs. Soviet aversion to ground-launched cruise missiles in Europe (which in the SALT II negotiations they often referred to as "German-launched cruise missiles") would give us useful bargaining leverage in securing reductions in the huge Soviet SS-18s that raise fears for survival of our own ICBM force.

The existence of these separate negotiations on an indivisible subject thus further complicates a process that is, at best, immensely difficult. But with serious, good faith purpose on both sides, the problems are not insolvable.

One possibility is the prompt completion of an interim agreement in the INF talks that would put off for two or three years deployment of U.S. ground-launched cruise missiles and Pershing IIs in exchange for the prompt elimination of a comparable number of Soviet medium-range ballistic warheads. Consideration of a permanent ban on U.S. nuclear missiles in Europe and reduction of the remaining Soviet SS-20s, SS-4s, and SS-5s could then take place in conjunction with restrictions and reductions in ICBMs, SLBMs, and strategic bombers.

The negotiations should also be expanded to deal with all the various elements that will make up a complete nuclear weapons freeze. These would include bans on any new ballistic missile systems and on missile flight tests. As agreement is reached on a particular element, it can be made effective—preferably as part of a formally ratified SALT treaty—without waiting for agreement on all other elements.

Concurrently, the United States should reconsider its announced decision to defer completion of a comprehensive ban on all testing of nuclear explosive devices. Because this does not involve any trade-off between specific weapons systems, the Comprehensive Test Ban talks should resume as a separate negotiation. The suggested concerns about verification of the signed but unratified "Threshold Test Ban Treaty" and "Peaceful Nuclear Explosions Treaty" are not adequate reasons for departing from the objective of ending nuclear weapons testing. A comprehensive test ban would not only be a major move toward a nuclear weapons freeze, but it would also be the most effective single step to block proliferation of nuclear weapons. A commitment on the part of the United States, the Soviet Union, and the United Kingdom to end nuclear weapons testing would bring the pressure of the world community to bear against additional countries contemplating entry into the nuclear weapons business.

The obstacles to nuclear arms control, therefore, are not procedural. Nor are there any substantive reasons why the goal of substantial qualitative controls and quantitative reductions cannot be achieved. What is required is a political decision that reducing nuclear weapons is a national goal and not just a rhetorical flourish. If we choose instead to try to regain nuclear superiority, to try to acquire the forces that can fight and win a nuclear war, then the "sorry history of arms control" may become the final chapter in the sorry history of humanity.

Suggested Readings

Understanding international negotiations involves appreciating the context—practical conditions and political pressures—under which both sides are operating. Some insight into the process may be had from the books listed below. The workings of the U.S. Arms Control and Disarmament Agency and its relations with the executive branch, the Congress, and the public are described in Clarke, *Politics of Arms Control.* The Jönsson book is an analysis of factors guiding the Soviet government in arms-control negotiations, based on the example of the Partial Test Ban Treaty. Soviet attitudes and policy in the SALT negotiations are interpreted in Samuel Payne, *The Soviet Union and SALT. Doubletalk* is the story of

18-2　　　　　　　　　　　　THE SALT II TREATY

The following is excerpted from the official United States summary of the SALT II treaty which, although signed, has not entered into force.

Treaty Between the United States of America and the Union of Soviet Socialist Republics on the Limitation of Strategic Offensive Arms

Signed at Vienna on June 18, 1979

The SALT II Treaty will provide for:

- an equal aggregate limit on the number of strategic nuclear delivery vehicles—ICBM and SLBM launchers, heavy bombers, and air-to-surface ballistic missiles (ASBMs). Initially, this ceiling will be 2,400. The ceiling will be lowered to 2,250 at the end of 1981;
- an equal aggregate limit of 1,320 on the total number of launchers of MIRVed ballistic missiles and heavy bombers with long-range cruise missiles;
- an equal aggregate limit of 1,200 on the total number of launchers of MIRVed ballistic missiles; and
- an equal aggregate limit of 820 on launchers of MIRVed ICBMs.

In addition to these numerical limits, the agreement includes:

- a ban on construction of additional fixed ICBM launchers, and on increases in the number of fixed heavy ICBM launchers;
- a ban on heavy mobile ICBM launchers, and on launchers of heavy SLBMs and ASBMs;
- a ban on flight-testing or deployment of new types of ICBMs, with an exception of one new type of light ICBM for each side;
- a ban on increasing the numbers of warheads on existing types of ICBMs, and a limit of 10 warheads on the one new type of ICBM permitted to each Party, a limit of 14 warheads on SLBMs, and 10 warheads on ASBMs. The number of long-range cruise missiles per heavy bomber is limited to an average of 28; and the number of long-range cruise missiles per heavy bomber of existing types is limited to 20;
- ceilings on the launch weight and throw weight of strategic ballistic missiles and a ban on the conversion of light ICBM launchers to launchers of heavy ICBMs;
- a ban on the Soviet SS-16 ICBM;
- a ban on rapid reload ICBM systems;
- a ban on certain new types of strategic offensive systems which are technologically feasible, but which have not yet been deployed. Such systems include long-range ballistic missiles on surface ships, and ballistic and cruise missile launchers on the seabeds;
- an agreed data base for systems included in various SALT-limited categories.

The Treaty also includes detailed definitions of limited systems, provisions to enhance verification, a ban on circumvention of the provisions of the agreement, and a provision outlining the duties of the SCC [Standing Consultative Commission] in connection with the SALT II Treaty. The duration of the Treaty will be through 1985.

Verification of the SALT II agreement will be by national technical means (NTM), including photo-reconnaissance satellites. The sides have agreed not to interfere with each other's national technical means of verification, and not to use deliberate concealment measures which impede verification by NTM of compliance with the provisions of the agreement. Because specific characteristics of some SALT-limited systems become apparent during the testing phase, monitoring of testing programs is an important aspect of SALT verification. Such monitoring may involve collection of electronic signals known as telemetry which are used during tests to transmit information about systems while they are being tested. Therefore, the sides have agreed not to engage in deliberate denial of telemetric information whenever such denial impedes verification of compliance with the provisions of the agreement.

In addition to these provisions of the agreement which directly address the question of verification, counting and distinguishability rules, as well as some constraints on specific systems, are incorporated into the agreement specifically for verification purposes.

To facilitate verification of the MIRV limits, the sides have agreed that once a missile has been tested with MIRVs, then all missiles of that type shall be considered to be equipped with MIRVs, even if that missile type has also been tested with a non-MIRV payload. Additionally, the sides have agreed that once a launcher contains or launches a MIRVed missile, than all launchers of that type shall be considered to be launchers of MIRVed missiles and would be included in the 1,320 limit. Similar counting rules have been adopted for cruise missiles and for heavy bombers.

A constraint included for verification purposes is a ban on production, testing, and deployment of the Soviet SS-16 ICBM. This missile appeared to share a number of components with the Soviet SS-20, an intermediate range ballistic missile (IRBM). As the Parties had agreed that land-based launchers of ballistic missiles which are not ICBMs should not be converted into launchers of ICBMs, the U.S. sought this ban on the SS-16 in order to prevent verification problems which might have arisen if the SS-16 program had gone forward, since in that case distinguishing between SS-16 and SS-20 deployments would have been very difficult.

Pursuant to a Memorandum of Understanding, the sides have exchanged data on the numbers of weapons in SALT-limited categories, and will maintain this agreed data base through regular updates at each session of the Standing Consultative Commission. Although the United States does not require (and does not rely upon) this data for verification purposes, maintenance of the agreed data base will ensure that both parties are applying the provisions of the Treaty in a consistent manner.

the SALT I negotiations by the chief U.S. negotiator, Gerard Smith.

Alva Myrdal's *The Game of Disarmament* is a thoughtful analysis of arms-control negotiations, and the Brennan book is an anthology of papers expressing a variety of outlooks on strategic arms-control principles and negotiations. Roger Fisher and William Ury discuss how to pursue successful bargaining in their *Getting to Yes.*

Two books expressing opposing views on arms control and the importance of "strategic superiority" are Lehman and Weiss, *Beyond the SALT II Failure,* and Alan Geyer, *The Idea of Disarmament!.* The book by Zagladin and Frolov gives a Russian view.

BRENNAN, DONALD G., ED. *Arms Control, Disarmament and National Security.* New York: Braziller, 1961.

CLARKE, DUNCAN L. *Politics of Arms Control.* New York: Free Press, 1979.

FISHER, ROGER, and WILLIAM URY. *Getting to Yes.* Boston: Houghton Mifflin, 1982.

GEYER, ALAN. *The Idea of Disarmament! Rethinking the Unthinkable.* Elgin, Ill.: The Brethen Press, 1982.

JÖNSSON, CHRISTER. *Soviet Bargaining Behavior: The Nuclear Test Ban Case.* New York: Columbia University Press, 1979.

LEHMAN, JOHN F., and SEYMOUR WEISS. *Beyond the SALT II Failure.* New York: Praeger, 1981.

MYRDAL, ALMA. *The Game of Disarmament.* New York, 1976.

PAYNE, SAMUEL B., JR. *The Soviet Union and SALT.* Cambridge, Mass.: MIT Press, 1980.

SMITH, GERARD. *Doubletalk: The Story of First Strategic Arms Limitation Talks.* New York: Doubleday, 1980.

ZAGLADIN, V. U., and I. T. FROLOV. *Modern Global Problems: Scientific and Social Aspects.* Moscow, 1981.

The French fuel reprocessing plant at La Hague—one of the most advanced facilities for recovering plutonium and reusable uranium from the spent fuel rods of nuclear power reactors. The operation of such plants by nonnuclear powers could allow them to build nuclear weapons.

19. Nuclear Weapons Proliferation

Nuclear weapons have spread to five countries, less proliferation than had been thought likely. But the factors that may promote further proliferation remain: widespread availability of nuclear materials and technology, and the security concerns of nations in confrontation with their neighbors. Limiting proliferation is a matter of controlling nuclear materials and facilities and reducing international tensions.

NUCLEAR PROLIFERATION is the increase in the arsenals of nuclear weapons available to the nuclear powers and the spread of these weapons to other countries. Five countries have produced and tested nuclear weapons: the United States, the Soviet Union, Great Britain, France, and China. Two more, Israel and South Africa, may have already developed nuclear warheads, and India has demonstrated the ability to do so.

Nuclear proliferation continues in the ever-growing arsenals of the major nuclear powers ("vertical" proliferation) and in the gradual spread to other countries of the ability to make nuclear weapons ("horizontal" proliferation). Although the overwhelming nuclear forces of the superpowers are of grave concern, we focus here on the prospect of a world with dozens of countries having possession of nuclear weapons.

The technology for producing and utilizing nuclear materials has become widely available through the development of commercial nuclear energy—as a substitute for the oil that is of increasing cost and limited supply, as an expression of national prestige, or as a hopeful means to quick entry into an industrial economy by a less developed country. The world's stock of plutonium in the spent fuel of nuclear power reactors increases each year by enough to build thousands of bombs, and the rate of accumulation is increasing as more nuclear plants go into operation throughout the world. Plant capacity for producing enriched uranium is gradually increasing, and cheaper and more efficient means for separating fissionable isotopes are being developed. These steps will place many more countries within reach of fabricating nuclear weapons.

The Nuclear Weapon Powers

Making the first atomic bomb was an enormous undertaking for the United States. Huge plants were built to implement untested processes and produce materials for a weapon that might well prove ineffective. Yet the motivation for the Manhattan Project is clear: German scientists knew the basic physics and work was

Jack Dennis

Dennis is a professor of computer science and engineering at M.I.T. and is editor of this volume.

going forward that might have yielded a German atomic bomb before the war's end. Once the war concluded in Europe, it was reasoned that the atom bomb could bring a quick end to the war with Japan. For the other nuclear powers, the path to a bomb has been much easier—for the most important secret of nuclear weapons was revealed by the Trinity test: a nuclear bomb can be built and has enormous destructive power.[1]

The Soviet government also knew that Germany had developed knowledge of nuclear physics and, as archrival for world power, was determined to match the achievements of the United States. In November 1947 Soviet Minister of Foreign Affairs V. M. Molotov declared that the secret of the atomic bomb had long been nonexistent; the Soviet Union detonated an atomic bomb in Siberia less than two years later.[2]

Great Britain's nuclear weapons program began even before British scientists joined in the U.S. Manhattan Project, but after the war Britain pursued an independent course leading to successful tests beginning in 1952. The effort was part of her struggle to maintain great-power status at a time when her vast colonial empire was shrinking.[3] Now, the British nuclear weapons program is again conducted in cooperation with the United States, and British warheads are deployed in U.S. missiles aboard British submarines.

The industrial countries of Europe, foreseeing the limits of coal and petroleum resources, became strong supporters of nuclear energy programs. But only France took the steps to apply this technology to a weapons program and determined to formulate its international policies independent of the United States and Western alliances.[4]

The Chinese nuclear weapons program began under Mao Tse-tung in 1954 and benefited from Chinese scientists educated in the United States. Soviet scientists, engineers, technicians, and military advisors participated in Chinese nuclear weapons research and development until 1960, but the Chinese were irked by Soviet reluctance to make available state-of-the-art expertise and equipment. The Chinese sought prestige and influence in international affairs appropriate to their numbers and a counterforce to Soviet— and U.S.—military strength.[5]

India exploited the sharing of nuclear technology by the United States and a reactor supplied by Canada to carry out her only test of a nuclear explosive in 1974. India's romance with nuclear technology dates from the forties. With the development of knowledgeable scientists, engineers, and technicians and a sophisticated nuclear industry, a weapons program became feasible and was debated at length within the Indian government. The decision to proceed with a test explosion was made in response to regional rivalries—the nuclear capability of China and potential developments in Pakistan—and in quest of prestige.

A country that is a "nuclear power" would be a country able to exert influence in international affairs because it is believed able to deliver a nuclear weapon in defense of its interests. By this definition, being a nuclear power is not synonymous with having detonated a nuclear explosive: it is debatable whether India should be regarded as a nuclear power. Although the single test explosion may have been a test of a nuclear warhead, the only delivery system available to India is a fleet of fighter-bomber aircraft of modest range, and India has publicly renounced any intention of producing nuclear weapons. Other nations, Israel and South Africa, are effectively nuclear powers on the basis of their suspected nuclear capability.

Nevertheless, the Treaty on Non-Proliferation of Nuclear Weapons has permanently distinguished five countries as "nuclear weapon states"—those countries that had exploded a nuclear device prior to January 1, 1967. The treaty gives these states special status by assigning asymmetric obligations to weapon and non-weapon states. By excluding India and any countries that may explode nuclear bombs in the future, a precedent has been set that establishes an unfortunate discrimination between the haves and the have-nots.

What It Takes to Make a Bomb

What does it take to make a nuclear bomb? One needs knowledge, technology, materials, the industrial and financial resources—and the motivation.

Knowledge and Technology The designer of a nuclear weapon must have knowledge of the physical processes and the properties of nuclear materials on which weapon designs are based. None of the fundamental knowledge is secret, and much of it is just as essential to competent work in nuclear energy as it is to weapons development. Through the worldwide exploitation of nuclear energy, much in response to the Eisenhower "Atoms for Peace" initiative, this fundamental knowledge is accessible to any country having a technically educated group and access to published scientific literature.

To build a fission bomb requires fissionable material, some means of producing a supercritical mass, and a means for initiating the chain reaction to ensure a detonation of high explosive yield. With these elements a crude weapon could be made—one relatively heavy for its explosive yield. Yet many details go into the design of a sophisticated nuclear weapon, leaving room for errors that would thwart attainment of an effective nuclear explosion. Even possessing engineering drawings would not suffice, for sophisticated technical support would be needed to duplicate materials and components. The superpowers have carried out extensive testing, experimentation, and modeling using large-scale computation to develop their lightweight and efficient warheads, and the results are not public information. A country desiring to build a sophisticated weapon system would have to acquire this knowledge—by espionage, or by repeating the work. Although it is generally conceded that any country with resources and competent physicists could develop a fission warhead, controls on nuclear materials make it unlikely that a subnational or terrorist group would be able to do so without knowledge of the host country.[6]

The building of a fusion weapon is a more demanding project. A source of tritium is necessary; creativity is needed to invent a workable configuration for directing the energy of a fission trigger to initiate fusion; and extensive computer modeling or test explosions are required to prove a design. Without proof by means of at least one test explosion, a country could never be sure that its bombs would explode. On the other hand, its adversaries would never know that the weapon possessed was not as powerful as a weapon of the claimed size could be.

Materials The only unusual material for a fission weapon is the fissionable uranium or plutonium. Other materials—conventional high explosives, electrical and electronic parts—although they must meet unusual and tight specifications, would be within the technical resources of any developed country. Something under 20 kilograms of uranium or roughly 10 kilograms of plutonium would suffice to make a fission bomb.[7] Weapons of advanced design would use less material; a crude bomb may require more.

Uranium-235 is obtained from natural uranium by an isotope separation process (see Chapter 20) that requires sophisticated technology. Yet every nuclear weapon state (not counting India) has developed uranium enrichment technology as a part of its nuclear weapons program. Any country that establishes a facility to enrich uranium fuel for power reactors could use the very same plant to produce highly enriched uranium for making nuclear weapons.

Plutonium is obtained by irradiation of uranium fuel in a nuclear reactor, followed by separation by a chemical process. Plutonium-239 produced in this way is accompanied by other plutonium isotopes, principally Pu-240. The degree of contamination is a function of the duration of irradiation. This presents problems to a weapon designer: plutonium-240 undergoes spontaneous fission with emission of neutrons. If the supercritical mass is not assembled quickly enough, these neutrons will cause premature initiation of the chain reaction. Even with plutonium-239 of relatively high purity, the Manhattan Project bomb designers concluded that the implosion trigger was necessary to prevent

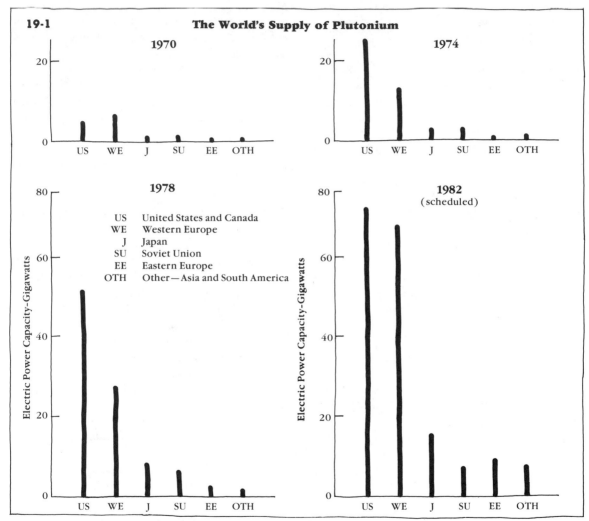

19-1   **The World's Supply of Plutonium**

1970

1974

1978

US	United States and Canada
WE	Western Europe
J	Japan
SU	Soviet Union
EE	Eastern Europe
OTH	Other—Asia and South America

1982 (scheduled)

These charts show the continuing growth in the production of plutonium by the world's operating nuclear power reactors. Each nuclear reactor that produces energy from the fission of uranium-235 creates about 200 kilograms of plutonium-239 for each gigawatt-year of full power operation. Assuming that reactors operate at an average of 65 percent of capacity and that 10 ki-

lograms of plutonium will suffice to build one nuclear weapon, each one-gigawatt nuclear plant will produce enough plutonium for thirteen bombs each year. In 1982 the nonnuclear powers were accumulating plutonium at the rate of 1,000 bombs per year and the rate was sharply increasing.

a premature chain reaction and a low-yield explosion caused by materials being blown apart before reacting.

It was once thought that this difficulty with plutonium would provide a means for denying governments the possibility of making weapons from spent nuclear fuel: fuel cycles and materials would be chosen so that the plutonium produced was sufficiently contaminated with Pu-240 or some other material that it could not be used to build weapons. Yet the International Nuclear Fuel Cycle Evaluation initiated by President Jimmy Carter concluded in 1980 without any recommendation that could permit efficient use of uranium in power reactors while making fissionable materials for weapons difficult to obtain.[8]

Heavy water—water containing the heavy hydrogen isotope deuterium—is a significant material in several ways. A reactor using heavy water as a neutron moderator (graphite will also do) can sustain a chain reaction in natural uranium fuel, providing means for producing plutonium and tritium without a source of enriched uranium. Deuterium obtained from heavy water is a more or less essential material for fusion bombs. Heavy water is produced by plants that separate out the tiny fraction of deuterium from the hydrogen in ordinary water.[9] In addition to U-235 and Pu-239, uranium-233 is fissile but is available only from conversion of thorium in nuclear reactors. Although there are substantial deposits of thorium in India, they have not so far been exploited, the extraction of thorium from deposits and its processing being more difficult than for uranium.

Motivation The motivation to acquire nuclear weapons is determined by attitudes, feelings, and political circumstances and cannot be treated so definitively. What group or institutions would aspire to possess nuclear weapons or to indulge in nuclear blackmail? Those of concern are countries, subnational political units, and terrorist groups.

For a country, the primary motivation is to respond to perceived threats to its national security. Generally the country does not wish ever to use its nuclear weapons. Instead, the desire is to achieve prestige in international affairs, to scare off potential aggressors, to use nuclear weapons as a bargaining tool, or to threaten and thereby obtain its wishes in international affairs. The route to possession of nuclear weapons is by their manufacture, employing domestic expertise, industrial and scientific resources, and critical materials. One source of fissionable material is the separation of plutonium from the spent fuel of nuclear power reactors. Other possibilities are the construction of a special production reactor for weapons-grade plutonium, by using uranium enrichment, or the theft or clandestine purchase of materials.[10]

A serious issue for a country is developing a credible delivery system. Before embarking on the development of nuclear weapons, a country would be expected to have a plan for how they might be used. Whether the plan involves aircraft, missiles, ships, or suitcases, the expense of posing a credible threat to the potential adversary must be accounted in the balance of gains and risks in deciding to pursue the nuclear path.

Building a nuclear bomb would almost certainly be beyond the technical expertise and resources of a subnational or terrorist group, unless the group had the complicity of the government of a host country. The needed resources and expertise are too varied and extensive; the materials are hazardous; there is risk of serious accident in working with near-critical assemblies; and the completed bomb may fail to work. The routes to possession would be outright theft or collusion.[11]

Sources of Fissile Material

The important fissionable materials for building nuclear bombs are uranium-235 and plutonium-239. Neither material is readily available from nature.

Uranium-235 is present as less than one per-

19-2   **World Nuclear Facilities**

Country	NPT signer	Research reactor	Power reactors		Enrichment plant	Reprocessing plant	Breeder reactors
			Operating	Under construction			
Argentina	X	1967	1	1		✓	
Australia	✓	1958					
Brazil	X	1956		3		✓	
Canada	✓	1945					
Chile	X	unknown					
Columbia	not ratified	1965					
China	X	?	?	?	★		
Cuba	X			1			
Egypt	✓	1961					
India	X	1956	3	5			
Indonesia	✓	1964					
Iran	✓	1967	project terminated				
Iraq	✓						
Israel	X	1960				?	

19-2			World Nuclear Facilities (continued)				
			Power reactors				
Country	NPT signer	Research reactor	Operating	Under construction	Enrichment plant	Reprocessing plant	Breeder reactors
Japan	✔	1960	23	9	★	★	★
Libya	✔						
Mexico	✔			2			
Pakistan	✗	1965	1			✔	
Philippines	✔	1963		1			
South Africa	✗	1965		2	✔		
South Korea	✔	1962	1	6			
Soviet Union	✔	1947(?)	32	15	★	★	★
Taiwan	✔	1961					
Thailand	✔	1962					
Turkey	✔	1962					
United States	✔	1942	70	88	★		
Uruguay	✔	unknown					
Venezuela	✔	1960					
Zaire	✔	1959					

The two maps here and on the following pages show the involvement of the countries of the world in nuclear technology. For many countries, establishing an operating research reactor—often provided by the United States—was the means of getting started in the field. A star indicates that the country has operated or is operating an enrichment, reprocessing, or breeder reactor facility on a commercial pilot-plant or production scale. A checkmark indicates experience with facilities on a smaller scale, or that a country has negotiated purchase of the technology from a foreign supplier. Few countries have the specialized facilities needed to enrich uranium or to separate plutonium from spent nuclear fuel, but the transfer of these technologies to more nonnuclear-weapon states is continuing.

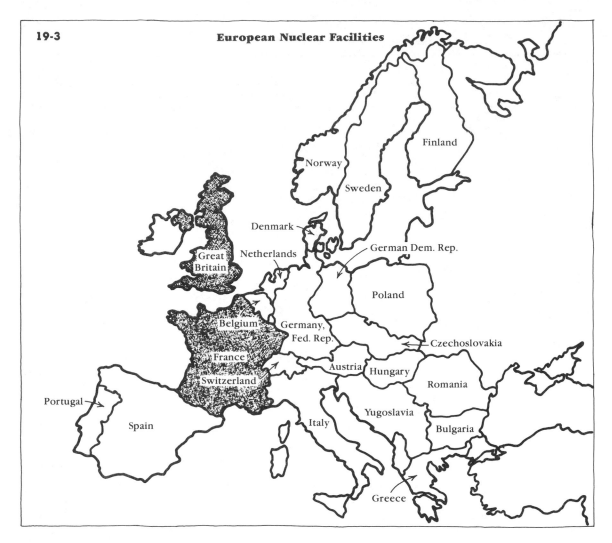

19-3   **European Nuclear Facilities**

cent of uranium metal in the compounds of natural uranium extracted by uranium mills. Only a few countries have uranium deposits that have been exploited to the extent that militarily significant quantities of uranium have been mined. In the Western world, the United States, Canada, and South Africa are the major sources; France, Niger, and Gabon supply most of the remainder. Australia has vast reserves of uranium deposits, and the Soviet Union and Warsaw Pact countries have sizable but unknown uranium resources.[12] For use in most power reactors, uranium is en-

riched so that its content of U-235 is about 3 percent. Since nuclear weapons require nearly pure U-235, the normal product of enrichment plants is not usable for weapons manufacture. Yet any technology for enrichment may be used to produce high-purity U-235 for weapons. The United States has the world's largest uranium enrichment capacity in its three gaseous diffusion plants; the Soviet Union has similar plants. In Europe, major plants are operating or under construction in Great Britain, France, the Netherlands, and West Germany. China operates a

19-3   **European Nuclear Facilities** (continued)

Country	NPT signer	Research reactor	Power reactors Operating	Power reactors Under construction	Enrichment plant	Reprocessing plant	Breeder reactors
Austria	✓	1960	project terminated				
Belgium	✓	1956	3	4		✓	
Bulgaria	✓	1961	2	2			
Czecholslovakia	✓	1957	2	6			
Denmark	✓	1957					
Finland	✓		3	1			
France	✗	1948	18	31	★	★	★
German Dem. Rep.	✓		5	4			
Germany, Fed. Rep.	✓	1958	14	10	✓	★	★
Great Britain	✓	1947	33	6	★	★	★
Greece	✓	1961					
Hungary	✓	1959		2			
Italy	✓	1965	4	2		✓	
Netherlands	✓	1959	2		★		
Norway	✓	1959	1				
Poland	✓	1958					
Portugal	✓	1961					
Romania	✓	1957					
Spain	✗	1960	3	7		✓	
Sweden	✓	1960	6	5			
Switzerlaı d	✓	1957	4	1			
Yugoslavia	✓	1958		1			

plant at Lanchow to support its weapons program. Canada and Japan are developing facilities
as well, but the enrichment plants operating in
South Africa and those under development in
Pakistan and Brazil are of greatest concern for
further proliferation.[13]

There is, naturally, a continuing search for
cheaper processes for uranium enrichment. A
centrifuge separation method has been developed in Europe, and in the United States and Japan, and a German invention (the Becker jet
nozzle process) is the basis for an enrichment
plant operating in South Africa. These processes
require less extensive physical plants than the
gaseous diffusion process.[14]

Plutonium is a manufactured element produced in nuclear reactors. Some reactors are
specifically designed to produce plutonium for
weapons, as are the American plants at the Hanford Reservation and Savannah River. Or the
plutonium can be obtained from the spent fuel
of commercial power reactors. Around the
world some 250 power reactors are now in operation, and each year adds a dozen or so more.
A typical 1,000-megawatt reactor produces
enough plutonium each year to make more than
ten nuclear bombs.[15]

To be available for the manufacture of weapons, plutonium in spent reactor fuel must be
separated by chemical processing. The facilities
that perform this work are called "reprocessing"
plants to distinguish them from the plants in
which fuel rods for reactors are fabricated.
Since the materials are highly radioactive, the
processing steps must be done in heavily shielded
chambers by remotely controlled equipment
that will become contaminated and therefore
difficult and hazardous to maintain. Interest in
reprocessing for the purposes of commercial
nuclear power is highest in Europe and Japan,
where there is concern about the availability
and cost of oil, and a desire to be less dependent on outside supplies of uranium. The use of
reprocessing plants and breeder reactors (which
produce more fissile material than they con-

sume) could reduce consumption of natural
uranium to a few percent of that required to
support the light-water reactors operating in the
United States. Pilot model and commercial reprocessing plants have been constructed in almost all Western European countries, India, and
Japan, and laboratory-scale facilities capable of
separating enough plutonium to make a bomb
may exist in many countries.[16] Breeder reactor
programs have been undertaken in at least eight
countries.[17]

Both the United States and the Soviet Union
are experimenting with schemes using lasers for
separating heavy isotopes. The process, if successful, would be usable not only for separating
U-235 from natural uranium but also for separating plutonium-239 from other plutonium isotopes, Pu-240 in particular. With this technology, it may be possible to produce high-grade
plutonium with a relatively small investment in
plant and equipment.

Besides the stock of plutonium being amassed
by the world's nuclear power industry, plutonium is being manufactured at sea in the nuclear power plants of more than 300 submarines, cruisers, and aircraft carriers of the U.S.
and Soviet nuclear navies. In the United States,
spent fuel from naval reactors is a source of
feedstock for the production reactors that manufacture plutonium and tritium for nuclear warheads (see Chapter 11).

The Beginnings of a Nonproliferation Regime

From the first awareness of nuclear energy at
the end of World War II, countries have been
concerned about "spreading the bomb." At first
the United States had a monopoly on the knowledge and resources for making atomic bombs.
Although it shared some information with Great
Britain, the United States guarded it carefully,
preferring to delay as long as possible the acquisition of nuclear arms by other countries, particularly the Soviet Union. After the war, cooperation on atomic energy with Great Britain and

19-4 ATOMS FOR PEACE

Excerpts from the address by President Dwight D. Eisenhower to the United Nations General Assembly, December 8, 1953

... I know that the American people share my deep belief that if a danger exists in the world it is a danger shared by all, and, equally, that if hope exists in the mind of one nation that hope should be shared by all. So my country's purpose is to help us move out of the dark chamber of horrors into the light—to find a way by which the minds of men, the hopes of men, the souls of men everywhere, can move forward toward peace and happiness and well-being. ...

Today the United States stockpile of atomic weapons, which, of course, increases daily, exceeds by many times the explosive equivalent of the total of all bombs and all shells that came from every plane and every gun in every theater of war in all of the years of World War II. ...

The Soviet Union has informed us that, over recent years, it has devoted extensive resources to atomic weapons. During this period, the Soviet Union has exploded a series of atomic devices, including at least one involving thermo-nuclear reactions.

If at one time the United States possessed what might have been called a monopoly of atomic power, that monopoly ceased to exist several years ago. Therefore, although our earlier start has permitted us to accumulate what is today a great quantitative advantage, the atomic realities of today comprehend two facts of even greater significance.

First, the knowledge now possessed by several nations will eventually be shared by others—possibly all others.

Second, even a vast superiority in numbers of weapons, and consequent capability of devastating retaliation, is no preventive, of itself, against the fearful material damage and toll of human lives that would be inflicted by surprise aggression.

The free world, at least dimly aware of these facts, has naturally embarked on a large program of warning and defense systems. That program will be accelerated and expanded.

But let no one think that the expenditure of vast sums for weapons and systems of defense can guarantee absolute safety for the cities and citizens of any nation. The awful arithmetic of the atomic bomb does not permit of any such easy solutions. Even against the most powerful defense, an aggressor in possession of the effective minimum number of atomic bombs for a surprise attack could probably place a sufficient number of his bombs on the chosen targets to cause hideous damage.

Should such an atomic attack be launched against the United States, our reactions would be swift and resolute. But for me to say that the defense capabilities of the United States are such that they could inflict terrible losses upon an aggressor—for me to say that the retaliation capabilities of the United States are so great that such an aggressor's land would be laid waste—all this, while fact, is not the true expression of the purpose and the hope of the United States.

To pause there would be to confirm the hopeless finality of a belief that two atomic colossi are doomed malevolently to eye each other indefinitely across a trembling world. To stop there would be to accept helplessly the probability of civilization destroyed, the annihilation of the irreplaceable heritage of mankind handed down to us from generation to generation, and the condemnation of mankind to begin all over again the age-old struggle upward from savagery toward decency and right and justice.

Surely no sane member of the human race could discover victory in such desolation. Could anyone wish his name to be coupled by history with such human degradation and destruction? . . .

I therefore make the following proposals:

The governments principally involved, to the extent permitted by elementary prudence, to begin now and continue to make joint contributions from their stockpiles of normal uranium and fissionable materials to an International Atomic Energy Agency. We would expect that such an agency would be set up under the aegis of the United Nations. . . .

The Atomic Energy Agency could be made responsible for the impounding, storage, and protection of the contributed fissionable and other materials. The ingenuity of our scientists will provide special safe conditions under which such a bank of fissionable material can be made essentially immune to surprise seizure.

The more important responsibility of this Atomic Energy Agency would be to devise methods whereby this fissionable material would be allocated to serve the peaceful pursuits of mankind. Experts would be mobilized to apply atomic energy to the needs of agriculture, medicine, and other peaceful activities. A special purpose would be to provide abundant electrical energy in the power-starved areas of the world. Thus the contributing powers would be dedicating some of their strength to serve the needs rather than the fears of mankind.

The United States would be more than willing—it would be proud to take up with others principally involved the development of plans whereby such peaceful use of atomic energy would be expedited.

Of those principally involved the Soviet Union must, of course, be one.

I would be prepared to submit to the Congress of the United States, and with every expectation of approval, any such plan that would—

First, encourage worldwide investigation into the most effective peacetime uses of fissionable material, and with the certainty that they had all the material needed for the conduct of all experiments that were appropriate;

Second, begin to diminish the potential destructive power of the world's atomic stockpiles;

Third, allow all peoples of all nations to see that, in this enlightened age, the great powers of the earth, both of the East and of the West, are interested in human aspirations first, rather than in building up the armaments of war;

Fourth, open up a new channel for peaceful discussion and initiate at least a new approach to the many difficult problems that must be solved in both private and public conversations, if the world is to shake off the inertia imposed by fear; and is to make positive progress toward peace.

Against the dark background of the atomic bomb, the United States does not wish merely to present strength, but also the desire and the hope for peace.

The coming months will be fraught with fateful decisions. In this Assembly; in the capitals and military headquarters of the world; in the hearts of men everywhere, be they governors or governed, may they be the decisions which will lead this world out of fear and into peace.

To the making of these fateful decisions, the United States pledges before you—and therefore before the world—its determination to help solve the fearful atomic dilemma, to devote its entire heart and mind to find the way by which the miraculous inventiveness of man shall not be dedicated to his death, but consecrated to his life.

Canada was terminated by the McMahon Act of 1946.[18] In that same year, prodded by scientists, U.S. Ambassador Bernard Baruch addressed the United Nations with a plan to develop nuclear energy under an independent international agency that would have authority over all nuclear production activities and would supervise the eventual destruction of all nuclear weapons. The plan failed to materialize; the U.S. government had not sincerely embraced the idea of international control, and the Soviets refused to agree to verification provisions deemed essential by the Western nations.[19] Similar proposals were to be discussed at length in a succession of United Nations bodies until it became apparent that no treaty requiring eventual elimination of nuclear weapons would have a chance of going into force.

Once the Soviet Union had demonstrated its nuclear expertise and the United States had exploded the first hydrogen bomb, the Eisenhower administration chose to lead the world in "Atoms for Peace." The hope was that by making nuclear technology and materials available to friendly and less developed countries, the United States could support a movement toward exploitation of nuclear energy that would be of mutual benefit to the Western Alliance, the less developed countries, and the United States, while somehow retaining control of the "dangerous technologies"—enrichment and reprocessing—that could be used to provide countries with nuclear weapons. In part this was an expression of U.S. guilt for having developed and tested the hydrogen bomb.[20] By offering uranium enrichment and nuclear fuel processing services, the United States would serve the cause of world peace, because other countries would forgo development of these technologies, opting to purchase fuel services from the United States—which would become the principal world source for enriched uranium and nuclear reactor technology.

The first Atoms for Peace conference assembled in Geneva in 1955 to formulate an international arrangement that would promote a broad expansion of atomic energy without undue risk of the diversion of plutonium into nuclear weapons. The International Atomic Energy Agency (IAEA) was formed in 1957 with its headquarters in Vienna.[21] The Baruch Plan had already laid down the essential methods of controlling the flow of nuclear materials and provided the pattern refined and adopted by the IAEA.

With this blessing from the international community, the United States embarked on a broad program of exporting nuclear technology to the world. Research reactors went into operation around 1960 in many countries using materials and technical assistance provided by U.S. companies: West Germany, Italy, Spain, Venezuela, Belgian Congo, Austria, and others, including Israel, Iran, South Africa, and Pakistan.[22] Great Britain, Canada, and France also participated in this dissemination of knowledge and resources by supplying reactors to Israel (France) and India (Canada), among others.

Many nations, including a large number of the less developed countries, realized with alarm that the spread of nuclear technology and nuclear reactors producing sizable quantities of plutonium would open the path to proliferation. The Irish delegation to the United Nations expressed this sentiment in a resolution calling for some collective action to prevent the wider dissemination of nuclear weapons. The United Nations General Assembly unanimously approved the resolution in 1960.

The Irish resolution contained the principle that was to become the basis for a landmark agreement: a commitment by the "powers producing such weapons" not to relinquish control over either the weapons or the information necessary to produce them, and a commitment by the "powers not possessing such weapons" to refrain from attempting to acquire them. In October 1961 the Soviet Union made known its willingness to conclude an agreement embodying such a two-way commitment.[23]

19-5 THE NONPROLIFERATION TREATY

The main provisions of the treaty are contained in the articles quoted below. For the treaty, the "nuclear-weapon states" are the United States, Great Britain, and the Soviet Union because France and China are not parties, and the treaty was negotiated before India exploded a nuclear device. The rules for ratification and the terms under which parties may withdraw from the agreement are stated in articles IX and X.

Treaty on the Non-Proliferation of Nuclear Weapons

Signed at London, Moscow, and Washington on July 1, 1968
Entered into force on March 5, 1970

Article I

Each nuclear-weapon State Party to the Treaty undertakes not to transfer to any recipient whatsoever nuclear weapons or other nuclear explosive devices or control over such weapons or explosive devices directly, or indirectly; and not in any way to assist, encourage, or induce any non-nuclear-weapon State to manufacture or otherwise acquire nuclear weapons or other nuclear explosive devices, or control over such weapons or explosive devices.

Article II

Each non-nuclear-weapon State Party to the Treaty undertakes not to receive the transfer from any transferor whatsoever of nuclear weapons or other nuclear explosive devices or of control over such weapons or explosive devices directly, or indirectly; not to manufacture or otherwise acquire nuclear weapons or other nuclear explosive devices; and not to seek or receive any assistance in the manufacture of nuclear weapons or other nuclear explosive devices.

Article III

1. Each non-nuclear-weapon State Party to the Treaty undertakes to accept safeguards, as set forth in an agreement to be negotiated and concluded with the International Atomic Energy Agency in accordance with the Statutes of the International Atomic Energy Agency and the Agency's safeguards system, for the exclusive purpose of verification of the fulfillment of its obligations assumed under this Treaty with a view to preventing diversion of nuclear energy from peaceful uses to nuclear weapons or other nuclear explosive devices. Procedures for the safeguards required by this article shall be followed with respect to source or special fissionable material whether it is being produced, processed or used in any principal nuclear facility or is outside any such facility. The safeguards required by this article shall be applied on all source or special fissionable material in all peaceful nuclear activities within the territory of such State, under its jurisdiction, or carried out under its control anywhere.

2. Each State Party to the Treaty undertakes not to provide: (a) source or special fissionable material, or (b) equipment or material especially designed or prepared for the processing, use or production of special fissionable material, to any non-nuclear-weapon State for peaceful purposes, unless the source or special fissionable material shall be subject to the safeguards required by this article.

3. The safeguards required by this article shall be implemented in a manner designed to comply with article IV of this Treaty, and to avoid hampering the economic or technological development of the Parties or international cooperation in the field of peaceful nuclear activities, including the international exchange of nuclear material and equipment for the processing, use or production of nuclear material for peaceful purposes in accordance with the provisions of this article....

4. Non-nuclear-weapon States Party to the Treaty shall conclude agreements with the International Atomic Energy Agency to meet the requirements of this article either individually or together with other States in accordance with the Statute of the International Atomic Energy Agency. Negotiation of such agreements shall commence within 180 days from the original entry into force of this Treaty. For States depositing their instruments of ratification or accession after the 180-day period, negotiation of such agreements shall commence not later than the date of such deposit. Such agreements shall enter into force not later than eighteen months after the date of initiation of negotiations.

Article IV

1. Nothing in this Treaty shall be interpreted as affecting the inalienable right of all the Parties to the Treaty to develop research, production and use of nuclear energy for peaceful purposes without discrimination and in conformity with articles I and II of this Treaty.

2. All the Parties to the Treaty undertake to facilitate, and have the right to participate in, the fullest possible exchange of equipment, materials and scientific and technological information for the peaceful uses of nuclear energy. Parties to the Treaty in a position to do so shall also cooperate in contributing alone or together with other States or international organizations to the further development of the applications of nuclear energy for peaceful purposes, especially in the territories of non-nuclear-weapon States Party to the Treaty, with due consideration for the needs of the developing areas of the world.

Article V

Each Party to the Treaty undertakes to take appropriate measures to ensure that, in accordance with this Treaty, under appropriate international observation and through appropriate international procedures, potential benefits from any peaceful applications of nuclear explosions will be made available to non-nuclear-weapon States Party to the Treaty on a nondiscriminatory basis and that the charge to such Parties for the explosive devices used will be as low as possible and exclude any charge for research and development. Non-nuclear-weapon States Party to the Treaty shall be able to obtain such benefits, pursuant to a special international agreement or agreements, through an appropriate international body with adequate representation of non-nuclear-weapon States. Negotiations on this subject shall commence as soon as possible after the Treaty enters into force. Non-nuclear-weapon States Party to the Treaty so desiring may also obtain such benefits pursuant to bilateral agreements.

There followed a decade of intensive diplomatic activity during which the Partial Test Ban Treaty was completed. Then in January 1964, President Lyndon Johnson indicated Western readiness to work out an agreement by placing before the United Nations a proposal that called for nondissemination and nonacquisition in the manner of the Irish resolution.[24] Other hurdles had to be dealt with before a treaty could be drafted: the United States desire for a Multilateral Force in Europe was unacceptable to the Russians, and the Europeans needed assurance that the conditions of an agreement would not remove them from competition in the booming nuclear power enterprise or interfere with arrangements already in place.[25] After the United States and Great Britain offered to place all their commercial nuclear facilities under international safeguards, the Treaty on the Non-Proliferation of Nuclear Weapons was drafted and signed, and it entered into force on March 5, 1970, upon formal ratification by the United States.

Agreements and Safeguards

The nonproliferation treaty assigns to the International Atomic Energy Agency (IAEA) the task of administering the conditions it imposes on international nuclear commerce. This is done through a system of safeguards which all nonweapon states signatory to the treaty are obliged to accept. Operators of nuclear facilities are required to maintain records of all nuclear materials processed, and inspectors verify the accuracy of the accounting and check for possible diversion of sensitive materials. The purpose of the safeguards is to inhibit countries from diverting nuclear materials for weapons use by providing for timely detection by the IAEA if diversion takes place.

Safeguards agreements required by the treaty have entered into force for all nonweapon signers of the treaty having significant nuclear activities—more than sixty-eight countries in 1982.[26] Of the nuclear weapon states, the United States and Great Britain have agreed to IAEA safeguards on all their commerical nuclear operations. France, though not a party to the treaty, is negotiating similar arrangements with the IAEA. Even India, also not a signer of the treaty, has accepted safeguards on most of its nuclear facilities.

The Soviet Union is a signer of the nonproliferation treaty, as are all the Warsaw Pact countries except Albania. Though the Soviet Union has not been willing to accept safeguards on its facilities, IAEA safeguards are in effect for all significant nuclear activities in Eastern Europe. The Soviet Union has been very reluctant to release nuclear technology to its satellite countries; all nuclear fuel material used in East Bloc reactors is supplied by the Soviet Union, and spent fuel is returned after use.[27]

In its goal of stemming the proliferation of nuclear weapons the treaty has two weaknesses: the nations not party to the treaty, and the provision in Article X allowing any party to withdraw if "extraordinary events, related to the subject matter of the Treaty, have jeopardized the supreme interests of its country."[28]

With respect to the nonsigners, an elaborate system of formal arrangements for nuclear materials and commerce exists outside the formal obligations of the nonproliferation treaty. France is a party to a number of joint nuclear energy ventures with other countries of Europe, and these projects are subject to conditions and safeguards imposed by the participants.[29] An influential institution is the group of fifteen nuclear supplier countries—Belgium, Canada, Czechoslovakia, France, the German Democratic Republic, the Federal Republic of Germany, Italy, Japan, the Netherlands, Poland, Sweden, Switzerland, Great Britain, the United States, and the Soviet Union—which began meeting in London in 1975. Assembled at the instigation of the United States, the so-called London Suppliers Club aims to make peaceful uses of nuclear energy widely available, while avoiding the spread of nuclear weapons by agreeing on uniform restrictions and conditions on the sale

19-6 UNSAFEGUARDED NUCLEAR FACILITIES

Country	Facility	Assisting Countries	First Year of Operation
Egypt	Inshas research reactor	Soviet Union (reactor)	1961
India	Apsara research reactor		1956
	Cirus research reactor	Canada (reactor) United States (heavy water)	1960
	Purnima research reactor		1972
	Trombay fuel fabrication plant		1960
	Hyderabad fuel fabrication plant		1974
	Trombay reprocessing plant		1964
	Tarapur reprocessing plant		1977
Israel	Dimona research reactor	France (reactor) Norway (heavy water)	1963
	Dimona reprocessing plant	France	
Pakistan	Chashma fuel fabrication plant	Belgium	1980
South Africa	Valindaba enrichment plant	West Germany	1975
Spain	Vandellos power reactor	France	1972

These facilities are not subject to the inspection and reporting requirements of the International Atomic Energy Agency or of equivalent bilateral agreements between user and supplier.

of nuclear materials and facilities.[30] Other agreements (a German sale of nuclear facilities to Brazil, for example) are bilateral arrangements between a supplier country and a user country that usually include conditions and verification provisions to help ensure that the materials and facilities provided are not used for other than peaceful purposes.

Through these independent mechanisms and those administered by the IAEA, safeguards are imposed on the nuclear commerce of most countries whether or not they are party to the nonproliferation treaty. Not surprisingly, the exceptions are Pakistan, Israel, India, and South Africa—nations of serious concern as possible next nuclear weapon states.

The effectiveness of these formal arrangements in preventing proliferation rests on the fact that few countries outside the nuclear weapon states have nuclear self-sufficiency. Canada, Australia, and South Africa are clearly exceptions, having both uranium ore and the industrial and scientific resources.

The IAEA inspections are intended to provide a timely warning if a country is discovered to be diverting nuclear materials. Whether the warning results from inspection or from a country's withdrawing from the treaty according to Article X, the time remaining before the country has a usable nuclear bomb could be very short—a few months or less to extract plutonium and assemble a bomb—if careful plans and preparations had been made.[31]

Toward the Plutonium Economy

Events in 1974 focused world attention, and more specifically U.S. attention, on the issues of nuclear proliferation. It was the time of the Iranian oil embargo, which had brought to the fore the fact that petroleum reserves would eventually run out. At that time nuclear energy programs were widely seen as an immediately desirable path toward reduced consumption of oil. Then in May 1974 India exploded a nuclear device. This caused a stir because some resources used in the Indian nuclear program had been supplied by Canada and the United States on the condition that they would be used solely for peaceful purposes.[32] These events brought forth the vision of a massive expansion of nuclear power and concern that existing international arrangements needed strengthening to forestall further proliferation.

In the United States, nuclear policy entered a period of great turmoil.[33] One outcome was a decision by the Ford administration to forgo the reprocessing of spent reactor fuel and discontinue the export of enrichment technology. This direction of policy was continued by President Carter, and the new policies were expressed in the Nuclear Non-Proliferation Act of 1978. This act provides that nonnuclear weapons nations wanting U.S. enrichment services, nuclear fuel, and equipment must agree to have international safeguards applied to all their peaceful nuclear activities and to grant the United States certain rights over spent reactor fuel. The act also provides that existing international agreements for cooperation be renegotiated to meet these requirements, a condition that demanded the breaking of contracts already in place.[34] In addition, the United States acted through the London Club to dissuade other suppliers from disseminating reprocessing technology.

These policies had the effect of promoting a desire for greater fuel cycle independence. West Germany and Japan have continued to pursue programs for reprocessing nuclear fuel and for the development of breeder reactors; France has become a leader in these technologies.

Yet there are hopeful signs. The further export of reprocessing and enrichment technology appears unlikely in the near future, and it may be possible to obtain agreement that all future nuclear exports be conditional on acceptance by nonnuclear weapons states of international safeguards on all their nuclear facilities.

Prospects

Potential for the proliferation of nuclear powers lies in the expansion of nuclear installations, research reactors, uranium isotope separation plants, nuclear fuel processing plants, and commercial reactors. Even though nuclear power is now seen as marginally economical in many countries, and few new orders are being placed, the number of large nuclear plants under construction is roughly equal to the number currently in operation; the amount of plutonium potentially available from spent fuel will rise steadily and at an increasing rate. In 1975 Albert Wohlstetter calculated that by 1985 about forty countries will have enough plutonium in the spent fuel of their nuclear power plants to make three or more bombs;[35] practically all of these countries will have enough for thirty weapons or more. Beyond 1985 the number of countries having spent fuel stocks will further increase as additional nuclear power plants are completed.

Yet the proliferation of nuclear powers has not been as great as had been thought likely. During the sixties and seventies many countries had the technological capacity and the industrial and material resources to build nuclear weapons but did not do so: Australia, Canada, West Germany, Japan, Italy, Sweden. In fact, most of these countries have publicly stated their intention not to acquire nuclear weapons. Why?

There are many good reasons. The responsibilities and pitfalls are great. A nuclear explosive is of little value without a practical delivery system against a foreseeable adversary. A country may believe it can rely for protection on its alliances with other powers. Countries realize that as they equip themselves with nuclear arms, the potential enemy may well respond in kind. Possessing nuclear weapons may very well lessen a nation's security instead of improving it. There is the obligation a nuclear power assumes to keep its weapons out of the hands of terrorists and revolutionaries. The motivation to possess nuclear weapons must be very strong to outweigh these factors, for nuclear weapons bring unprecedented responsibilities.

In 1966 Leonard Beaton named ten states that could become nuclear powers by 1985 and sixteen more nations that could join the club by

1995.[36] Some of these nations, such as Italy and Sweden, are not of present concern. They have the technical capability but little incentive to go nuclear. Once jealous of each other's aspirations for international standing and suspicious of the other's intentions, Argentina and Brazil are now cooperating in their nuclear energy activities, although time awaits their full support of the Tlatelolco treaty of 1967 which created a nuclear-weapons-free zone around Central and South America and the Caribbean countries.[37]

The countries of greatest concern are those facing regional adversaries of perhaps greater or even overwhelming military strength, whose alliances with major powers are of questionable value to their security and who have, or could have in the near future, the technological and economic resources to build nuclear weapons. The nations generally cited as being in these circumstances are Israel in confrontation with the Arab states, South Africa against its neighbors, Pakistan versus India, Taiwan and China, and South and North Korea.

Israel, with an unsafeguarded research reactor at Dimona and probably a small separation plant, has all the ingredients to make nuclear weapons. The government has even claimed its ability to produce nuclear weapons in a short time.[38] Certain Arab countries have become less likely to enter the nuclear club in the near future, for nuclear activities in Iran and Iraq have been set back by revolution, conflict, and the Israeli attack of June 1981 on Iraq's Osirak research reactor.[39] Other Arab countries—Saudi Arabia, Syria, Egypt—have some nuclear expertise and are possible future aspirants. It seems that Libya has tried persistently to barter for nuclear weapon technology throughout the seventies, including a reported attempt in 1971 to purchase bombs from the People's Republic of China.[40]

Having uranium enrichment facilities, plenty of ore, and an educated elite, South Africa is in a good position to use the threat of its potential nuclear capability as an element of its foreign policy. In 1977 satellite photographs reportedly disclosed test site preparations in the Kalahari Desert, but negotiations appear to have forestalled use of the site. Some neighboring countries have threatened retaliation in kind if South Africa were overtly to acquire nuclear weapons.[41]

India and Pakistan present a classic example of two countries in long-standing conflict over territory and power. Since the early seventies Pakistan has endeavored to develop facilities capable of producing fissionable materials for weapons. The Indian test explosion of 1974 only strengthened resolve in Pakistan to succeed. In turn, this has led India to consider reactivating its dormant program for nuclear arms.[42]

Both Taiwan and South Korea have carried on development programs for nuclear weapons as a hedge against possible loss of U.S. military support and security guarantees. For the present, these programs are dormant as a result of negotiations, assurances, and political pressure.[43]

The close geographic proximity of the adversaries in these situations implies that if the two sides possessed modern delivery systems—ballistic missiles—targeted at each other, the tensions of the confrontation would be enormous and probably unbearable. In consequence, the best strategy for such a nation may not be actually to possess nuclear weapons fully fabricated, ready for delivery. It seems better to use one's potential nuclear capability at the conference table—to limit the extent of conventional warfare, to bring the adversaries to the bargaining table, to increase their reluctance to carry out hostile acts, or perhaps to negotiate nuclear-weapons-free areas.

Conclusion

The main paths to reducing the likelihood of further proliferation of nuclear weapons are generally recognized: reduce the motivation of the nonnuclear powers to acquire these weapons by actions that decrease international tension and increase world security; and increase the cost of joining the nuclear club by international agreements and controls on the materials and technology necessary to build weapons.

Proliferation is a problem of the world as a whole; the resources and knowledge are so widespread that independent actions even by a major power can be effective only in special situations. Change for the better will come about through the collective actions of groups of nations. It is important to strengthen those institutions that permit the orderly development of international nuclear commerce within controls that limit access to materials usable in the fabrication of weapons: the nonproliferation treaty, the IAEA, and the intricate network of agreements that govern nuclear commerce between supplier firms and nonsigners of the nonproliferation treaty. It should be possible to reach agreement on applying IAEA safeguards to all nuclear commerce for all peaceful purposes. With persistent effort and sincere cooperation, the wisdom of international ownership of all facilities for uranium enrichment, spent fuel reprocessing, and plutonium storage should eventually prevail.

More important is work toward a world of reduced tensions among nations and toward international agreements that will lessen the appeal of possessing nuclear weapons as an approach to dealing with international conflict. The existing nuclear-weapons-free zone for Latin America should be supported and strengthened, and the establishment of additional zones should be encouraged. Work toward a comprehensive test ban treaty outlawing underground testing of nuclear explosives would make acquisition of credible nuclear weapons significantly more difficult. The attitude that nuclear weapons are practical battlefield armaments or would be useful in so-called limited war should be dispelled. Rather, universal agreements on no first use of nuclear weapons should be arranged. The nuclear powers should abandon any claim to status based on possession of nuclear weapons.

The United States has the opportunity to exercise leadership in pursuit of these goals, for the attitudes and policies of the United States still set an example for much of the world. Some significant steps would be to accept IAEA safeguards on all nuclear facilities, to ratify Protocol I of the Tlatelolco treaty, and to cut off manufacture of fissile materials for nuclear weapons. In addition, the postponement of reprocessing and recycling of plutonium for American power reactors should be continued because it will not be economical for many years.

The problem of nuclear weapons proliferation is a problem of strong isolated states in conflict with their neighbors. The principal reason these countries will abstain from nuclear weapons will be their perception that their security would not be heightened by the possession of such weapons. The world will not be free of the threat of nuclear destruction until nations recognize that working cooperatively to share the resources of the earth for human benefit is essential to survival—not until regional animosities are replaced by cooperation and respect. This is at best a distant prospect, but it is one worthy of our dedicated and ceaseless effort.

Suggested Readings

Many articles and books have been written on the subject of nuclear weapons proliferation. The book by Dunn is a thorough recent review, although somewhat alarmist in tone. A balanced review of the present political situation from an American perspective is the piece by Smith and Rathjens in *Foreign Affairs*. Another review with further information on the technical aspects of nuclear power and proliferation is Chapter 9 of *Nuclear Power Issues and Choices*. The possibility of nuclear terrorism is discussed in Chapter 10 of the same volume. The Lovinses' book expresses deep concern about the linkage of nuclear power with potential weapons development.

A good source for new developments in the nuclear fuel cycle, including plans for development of plutonium recyle and breeder reactor technologies, is the news pages of *Nuclear Engineering International*. The story of the vacillations in U.S. proliferation policy and attitudes about nuclear fuel services is told in Brenner's book.

The Stockholm Peace Research Institute (SIPRI) publishes yearbooks that often include data relating to nuclear weapons proliferation. The 1978 volume contains a review of international nuclear fuel cycle facilities and the agreements under which they are operated. The 1977 issue has a section on the London Suppliers Club. The 1981 edition includes discussion of the 1980 nonproliferation treaty review conference and the results of the International Nuclear Fuel Cycle Evaluation.

The circumstances of regional rivals and their likelihood of pursuing a nuclear weapons option are discussed in the books by Dunn and by Quester. Weissman and Krosney treat the Middle East situation in depth. Finally, the little paperback by Beaton, although published some years ago, is still a sound statement of the issues and chronicles the first decade of concerned reaction to the possible spread of nuclear weapons.

BEATON, LEONARD. *Must the Bomb Spread?* Harmondsworth, England: Penguin Books, 1966.

BRENNER, MICHAEL J. *Nuclear Power and Non-Proliferation.* Cambridge, England: Cambridge University Press, 1981.

DUNN, LEWIS A. *Controlling the Bomb: Nuclear Proliferation in the 1980's.* New Haven, Conn.: Yale University Press, 1982.

LOVINS, AMORY B., AND L. HUNTER LOVINS. *Energy/War: Breaking the Nuclear Link.* San Francisco: Friends of the Earth; New York: Harper and Row, 1981.

QUESTER, GEORGE H. *Nuclear Proliferation: Breaking the Chain.* Madison, Wis.: University of Wisconsin Press, 1981.

STOCKHOLM INTERNATIONAL PEACE RESEARCH INSTITUTE (SIPRI). *World Armaments and Disarmament.* Stockholm: Almqvist and Wiskell, 1968/1969 through 1977; London: Taylor and Francis, since 1978.

SMITH, GERARD, AND GEORGE RATHJENS. "Reassessing Nuclear Nonproliferation Policy." *Foreign Affairs,* Spring 1981, pp. 875–894.

WEISSMAN, S., AND H. KROSNEY. *The Islamic Bomb: The Nuclear Threat to Israel and the Middle East.* New York: Times Books, 1982.

Part Seven

Nuclear Energy

The uranium mine operated by Utah International in the Gas Hills of Wyoming.

20. Uranium: The Yellowcake Road

It all begins with yellowcake, the off-hand term of the industry for the bright, canary-yellow compound of uranium that makes up most of the crude concentrate shipped from the mills in the uranium-mining regions that grind and chemically treat newly dug uranium ore. As with many mineral resources, the story of uranium is one of boom and bust. The United States is the biggest producer, but also a big consumer, consuming roughly as much as it produces. The world trade is also vigorous. In the United States, in a long sequence of steps yellowcake passes through a variety of conversion and enrichment processes on the way to bombs and reactors. This chapter also outlines foreign developments, forecasts changes that may strongly affect worldwide uses of yellowcake, and treats the environmental questions raised by the large-scale mining of this radioactive substance.

URANIUM, the heaviest natural chemical element, was an exotic material at the dawn of the atomic age.[1] Discovered in 1789 and first obtained in pure form in 1841, it proved essential to the development of nuclear physics. A sample of uranium led to the discovery of radioactivity in 1896. The bombardment of uranium nuclei by neutrons late in 1938 resulted in the first recognized example of nuclear fission, and ever since, uranium has played a key role in the nuclear arms race and in the development of nuclear power.

In 1938, however, there were no significant commercial uses of uranium or its compounds. Its only industrial application in the United States was as a coloring agent for ceramics. The entire U.S. consumption of uranium and its compounds in 1938 was 168 tons. The bulk of this, 106 tons, came from the Belgian Congo, and 36 tons were imported from Canada. Only 26 tons were produced domestically—all from the Colorado plateau where the uranium compounds were obtained as by-products of the mining and refining of other minerals, notably vanadium.

Sources of Supply

Early in 1941, with the atomic bomb project already under way, the availability of uranium became a vital question. But obtaining an adequate supply did not prove difficult. Some 1,200 tons of 65 percent uranium ore had been shipped from the Congo to the United States in 1940 by the Belgian firm Union Minière, and this stockpile was warehoused on Staten Island. Another 100 tons of African uranium were stored in Canada, along with some 300 tons of Canadian origin. The Eldorado mines in the Canadian far north were expected to be able to produce 300 tons of oxides per year, and 500 tons might be obtained from Colorado. It was thought that these supplies would be adequate at least until the summer of 1944.

The uranium assets of the Manhattan Project were reviewed in August 1943, and it was confirmed that enough ore for expected wartime needs was available in the United States and Canada. Despite this favorable situation, General Leslie R. Groves was concerned for the long

John Lamperti

Lamperti is a professor of mathematics at Dartmouth College.

term. Groves told President Roosevelt that after the war the United States might face exhaustion of supplies in North America and therefore become dependent on shaky access to the world's major production center in the Belgian Congo.[2] It is noteworthy that as early as 1943 and 1944 the United States and Great Britain began moving to secure postwar access to supplies of a mineral that was needed, it might then have seemed, only as a wartime emergency resource.

Despite this foresight, the U.S. uranium-supply policy remained in an uncertain state at the end of the war. In the fall of 1947, John K. Gustafson was appointed the first director of raw materials for the Atomic Energy Commission (AEC). Gustafson was reportedly "shocked to discover" that the nation's atomic establishment was dependent on the production of uranium from "one mine deep in the Belgian Congo and another small source in the sub-Arctic regions of Canada."[3] He wanted to assure new sources, and he succeeded in finding them in South Africa and in North America. Both were to have far-reaching consequences.

Between 1953 and 1968 the United States imported some 43,000 tons of uranium oxide from South Africa.[4] This uranium was essential for building the huge U.S. stockpile of nuclear weapons, which by the early sixties already numbered tens of thousands. South African uranium was also critical for Great Britain's nuclear development. During the fifties, South Africa, with U.S. and British help, developed facilities to recover uranium from the wastes left by gold mining, opened new mines, and established a refining industry to turn ore into uranium concentrate. After 1968 the U.S. government no longer bought South African uranium, but today private companies are buying it—now for nuclear power rather than for weapons. Uranium export is expected to play an increasingly important role in South Africa's economy during the rest of this century.

The AEC also moved rapidly to develop a uranium mining and refining industry in the United States and then encouraged growth of the industry to assure ample supplies for the expanded weapons program. Between 1948 and 1955, the U.S. government carried out an extensive uranium exploration program. The AEC offered very favorable contracts to uranium producers: incentives included rapid amortization of investments, a bonus for discoveries, and a guaranteed market with established minimum prices. Until 1964, the government bought, at prices that it set, all domestic uranium ore as soon as it was mined. It was in this setting that the industry was born and developed.

The U.S. uranium industry grew rapidly under these conditions. According to the AEC, by 1955 the United States had become the world's largest miner of uranium ore. By 1957 annual production had reached 8,600 tons of uranium oxide (U_3O_8), a tenfold increase in only five years. Milling capability kept pace with mining, and in 1962, at the start of a new contract period, twenty-four ore-processing mills obtained contracts. In this year, purchases of U_3O_8 by the U.S. government totaled 28,690 tons, with the domestic mining industry accounting for 59 percent, Canada for 26 percent, and the rest coming from overseas, mostly from Africa.[5]

The AEC's uranium purchase program was planned to end in 1966, and by then ample supplies for the weapons program were indeed obtained. But it became evident in the early sixties that commercial nuclear power would not be ready to take up the slack in demand quickly enough to employ the U.S. mining and milling capability, and so government purchasing was stretched out until 1971 to protect the industry. Less concern was shown for foreign producers. The AEC's announcement in 1959 that it would halt new uranium purchases abroad was a particular blow to Canada, since sales of yellowcake to the United States had become its fourth largest export.[6]

In 1971 all AEC uranium buying ended, and the mining and milling industry became dependent on the commercial market. Between

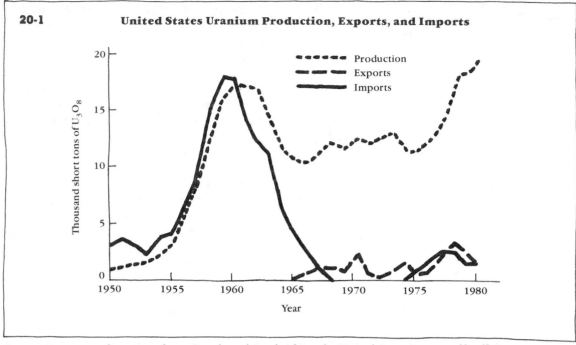

20-1   **United States Uranium Production, Exports, and Imports**

Once an importer of uranium from Canada and South Africa, the United States is now self-sufficient.

1947 and 1971 the U.S. government purchased 316,000 tons of uranium oxide. Fifty-five percent of this amount came from mines within the United States, which remained the largest uranium producer in the Western world. The quantity obtained was more than sufficient by any standard. At least 50,000 tons of the purchase was declared surplus by the AEC itself, and much of this has since been resold.[7]

Despite the end of government purchasing, there was an increasing demand for uranium in the mid-seventies due to the growth of nuclear power. The United States was (and is) the West's largest uranium consumer as well as the largest producer. Roughly 40 percent of the non-Communist world's nuclear electricity is generated in this country,[8] and the consumption of uranium will continue to increase as reactors under construction come on line. However, it is expected that domestic production will roughly match the demand, so that the United States, al-though it may well become a net importer, will play only a small role in the world trade.[9]

The seventies witnessed changes in world uranium prices at least as drastic as those of oil. The causes for the abrupt rise during the early seventies are said to include the impact of strengthened health, environmental, and safety regulations, as well as general inflation. A jump in demand was caused by a change in the form of U.S. contracts for uranium enrichment services, asking a long-term commitment with the customer responsible for the supply of feed material. The OPEC example since 1973 surely made a significant, if indirect, contribution.[10]

The most dramatic factor in the sudden jump in prices was the formation of a uranium-producers cartel in 1972. The organizers of the cartel included the governments of Canada, Australia, and South Africa, with the support of France. A number of the largest international corporations involved in uranium mining were

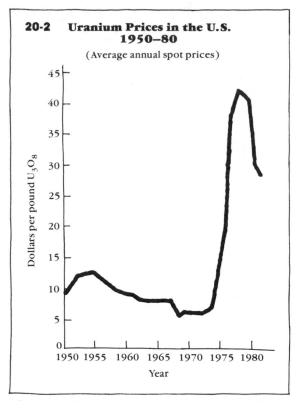

20-2   Uranium Prices in the U.S. 1950–80

(Average annual spot prices)

The price of uranium rose sharply when the 1973 oil embargo caused concern over future supplies of oil and a uranium producers' cartel was formed. Prices fell again as production facilities were expanded and projections of future energy demand were revised downward.

also members, including the Gulf Oil Company through its Canadian subsidiary. Gulf's board chairman testified in 1977 congressional hearings that the cartel had been "moderately successful" in raising uranium prices on the world market—possibly an overly modest assessment, since the increase was roughly sevenfold in three years.[11] A 1974 Gulf internal memo specifically acknowledged the OPEC parallel.

One of the largest vendors of nuclear power reactors, Westinghouse, was forced by the price jump to default on contracts totaling over a billion dollars with twenty-seven electrical utili-

ties, domestic and foreign. To promote its reactor sales, Westinghouse had promised to deliver uranium to its customers at pre-1973 low prices; in 1975 it faced huge losses if it did so. Litigation resulting from the defaults and a congressional investigation in 1977 have helped to expose, and possibly to restrain, the activities of the cartel, which is asserted to be no longer functioning.[12]

The high uranium prices of the mid-seventies did not last long. The nuclear power industry, and with it the demand for uranium, has grown much more slowly than was anticipated in almost all the predictions made before 1975. On the other hand, the temporary sellers' market encouraged major uranium producers, including Australia, Canada, Niger, South Africa, and Namibia, to expand their facilities. This resulted in falling prices and growing stockpiles, and the current buyers' market is expected to continue for some time. One recent study finds that "current conditions and trends are so favorable (at least to consumers) that there is little basis for worry about supply during the next 10 to 20 years. . . . and prices (in constant dollars) will be considerably below those of the past few years."[13]

Technology

The bulk of U.S. uranium is obtained by either open-pit or underground mining. These techniques for mining uranium ore do not differ in any essential way from other mining operations. Open-pit mines employ conventional earth-moving equipment such as diesel shovels, backhoes, bulldozers, front-end loaders, and large fleets of trucks to remove large bodies of ore located less than about 400 feet from the surface. The equipment and methods used in underground uranium mining vary with the size of the mining operation and the nature of the ore body, but again they resemble those used for other minerals. The deepest uranium mines in this country have shafts penetrating more than 3,000 feet below the surface.

A number of less well-known techniques account for a small but growing fraction of uranium production. One such process, solution mining or in-situ leaching, is done by injecting into the ore body a leaching solution which must flow through the mineralized zone and then be recovered, bringing with it some of the uranium. Injection and extraction wells are drilled into the ore body throughout the area to be mined, and the leaching solution, usually a dilute acid or a carbonate, is pumped into the ground. Uranium is then separated chemically from the fluid recovered through the extraction wells. Solution mining is now being done at depths of 300 to 600 feet; it works best when an impermeable layer of shale or mudstone lies beneath the ore body, thus containing the leaching solution. This form of mining is often inefficient in terms of the fraction of uranium recovered from the ore, but it can be economically attractive when the ore is of low grade.

Several related techniques can be used with mine tailings or in worked-out mines to recover some of the residual uranium, or applied directly to low-grade ore. In some mining areas the groundwater itself naturally leaches enough uranium to make treatment and recovery feasible. In "heap leaching," a sulfuric acid or other leach solution is allowed to percolate through a large pile of ore and is then treated chemically to remove the dissolved uranium. Finally, certain phosphate rocks, copper ores, and beryllium ores contain low-grade uranium, and a number of small operations have begun to recover uranium as a by-product from the production of phosphoric acid, copper, and beryllium.

The next stages in processing uranium ore are collectively known as "milling." In conventional mills, the uranium ore is first crushed and ground to a uniform consistency. The crushed ore is treated with an alkaline or (when the lime content of the ore is less than about 12 percent) an acid leach to dissolve the uranium. Decanting and filtering remove the solids, and a uranium compound can then be precipitated from the solution. Additional steps must be taken before the final precipitation in order to increase the uranium content of the solution, particularly when acid leaches are used; the most common of these processes are "ion-exchange purification" and "solvent extraction." After precipitation, the product is dried and packaged for shipping.

The output of a uranium mill is called "yellowcake" because of its appearance. Yellowcake is a compound of uranium oxide with either ammonium or sodium; its exact composition varies but it usually contains 80 to 85 percent U_3O_8. Additional chemical processing is necessary before nuclear reactor fuel can be produced. A high degree of purity must be achieved, since even small amounts of neutron-absorbing elements such as cadmium or boron can have a large effect on reactor performance. The refined product is usually converted into uranium tetrafluoride (UF_4, or "green salt"). From this stage, either uranium metal or the oxide UO_2 can be obtained, or the green salt can be converted into uranium hexafluoride (UF_6, or "hex") which is the starting point for the enrichment process.

Current State of the Industry

In 1979, the U.S. uranium industry had a record year which narrowly surpassed both 1978 (a previous record) and the earlier peak during 1960–61. An average of 46,000 tons of ore was processed each day, and almost 19,000 tons of uranium oxide were produced during the year. Compared with the previous year there was a 17 percent increase in the quantity of ore handled, but the average uranium content of the ore, about 0.11 percent, was 16 percent lower than that of the ore dug during 1978.

The bulk of the uranium produced, about 16,500 tons or nearly 90 percent, came from conventional mining. Sixty-two open-pit mines yielded over half the total output, and 300 underground mines shared the rest. The uranium content of the ore extracted from underground

20-3   **Uranium Mines and Mills in the United States**

The uranium reserves of the United States lie in the western plains and deserts and along the Texas gulf coast. The deposits are exploited by a cross section of U.S. mineral companies.

mines, at 0.14 percent, was substantially higher than the percentage for the open pits (less than 0.1 percent). The open-pit producing states are Wyoming, New Mexico, and Texas, in that order, while the underground mines are concentrated in New Mexico, Colorado, and Utah. In addition to the conventional mines, ten solution mines and eight by-product recovery and other nonconventional operations together yielded a total of 2,250 tons of concentrate. Most of the solution mining is in Texas, while phosphoric-acid by-product recovery operations are located in Louisiana and Florida.[14]

The output of the uranium mines was processed in 1979 by twenty-one mills. These mills operated close to their capacity during the year, and they recovered about 90 percent of the ura-

nium from the ore they handled. Most mills are located close to the major mining centers to minimize transportation of large quantities of ore.

Ownership of the uranium mining and milling industry is highly concentrated. Many of the nation's largest "energy" (oil) companies have become involved in uranium production, and a few of them have acquired dominant positions. A U.S. Senate study reported in 1977 that oil companies held almost half of the domestic uranium reserves estimated to be available at $30 per pound or less, and 72 percent of the more accessible reserves available at $15 to $20 per pound. Two companies control over half of the latter—Kerr-McGee with almost 33 percent and Gulf Oil with 18 percent. At the time of the

20-4 URANIUM MILL

Part of the uranium mill at Grants, New Mexico, operated by the Anaconda Copper Company. Here a salt of uranium is dissolved from ore and separated from the tailings.

study, Kerr-McGee also owned one-fourth of the total U.S. uranium milling capacity, and the top five companies in this field held two-thirds of the nation's total.[15] The opening of new mills has changed the picture somewhat, and Kerr-McGee's capacity of 7,000 tons per day now represents about one-seventh of the total. The top five companies, however, still account for 55 percent of all U.S. uranium milling capability.

Measuring "reserves" of charted but as yet unmined uranium ore is a difficult matter, and the estimation of potential "resources"—that is, discovered and undiscovered uranium deposits which do not now qualify as ore—is even more speculative and controversial. With this in mind, it is useful to know that the Department of Energy estimated in 1978 that about 920,000 tons of uranium oxide could be counted as proven reserves available at a "forward cost" not over $50 per pound, while there might be an additional 3.5 million tons of uranium in several categories of "resources."[16] This figure for proven reserves has, broadly speaking, been accepted by other authorities, but the estimate of resources has not. For example, in 1978 a study group of the National Academy of Sciences reported that its estimates were considerably lower, and it suggested that for prudent planning a figure of 1.8 million tons of uranium resources should be used.[17]

In view of the complexity of this question, we will not examine it here more completely. For perspective on the meaning of these estimates, however, it helps to note that the expected demand for natural (unenriched) uranium by a large (1,000 megawatt), modern nuclear power reactor of the "light-water" type, over its roughly thirty-year lifespan, is about 6,000 tons.[18] Thus the more-or-less accepted 920,000 tons of uranium reserves in the United States have the potential to fuel about 153 such reactors over their lifetimes. In other words, these reserves will just about provide the uranium that will be required by the nuclear power reactors now operating, plus those currently under construction or planned. Clearly, uranium supplies will extend considerably beyond this point, but they are not inexhaustible, and the limits are probably in sight.

Effects of Mining

Many of the environmental effects of uranium mining are fairly obvious. To establish an open-pit mine, the topsoil must be stripped away and the groundwater table lowered, a process that can devastate the local ecosystem. There is doubt whether strip-mined lands in dry areas can ever really be restored to acceptable condition for other uses. The direct effects of underground mining are less striking, but they can also be severe. Before shafts are drilled, the ore-carrying rock must be "dewatered" by pumping. This can cause a general lowering of the water table, and in arid regions nearby wells may become dry as a result. The water pumped from the mines generally cannot be used for agriculture or drinking because it is contaminated, and its disposal may itself cause a problem.

Solution mining poses problems of a different sort. To monitor the impact of a solution mine, wells are drilled around the area being leached as well as into formations above and below the ore body. Water samples are drawn from these monitoring wells and analyzed to determine whether the leaching chemicals have migrated from the mining zone. If this occurs, leaching should be discontinued until the problem can be corrected.

Restoration of a leached-out mining area is intended to remove the leach chemicals and soluble uranium from the groundwater. The process consists of pumping out contaminated water from the zone and may last from a few months to several years. Environmental monitoring and restoration have been described as "major items which contribute to solution mining costs."[19]

The direct effects of conventional mining of uranium, whether by open pits or underground mines, do not differ qualitatively from those of extracting other minerals. What is unique to the uranium industry is the radioactive nature of the materials involved. Uranium-bearing ores contain radium, which is a decay product of uranium-238 (U-238); radium decays into radon, a gas under normal conditions. Radon itself quickly undergoes alpha decay (its half-life is 3.8 days) and produces a sequence of "daughters" with even shorter half-lives which emit alpha, beta, and gamma rays. The greatest biological hazard in working with uranium ore comes from these daughter products, which can lodge in the lungs and expose nearby tissue to extensive damage, primarily from short-range alpha radiation.

During the years 1945 to 1971, but especially before 1960, some 6,000 underground uranium miners were exposed to significantly high levels of radioactive gases and dust in the mines. In 1973, a study of a subgroup of 4,200 of these miners indicated an excess of about 180 cases of lung cancer beyond the normal expectation. Thus for the whole group of miners the excess number of lung cancers must have been between 250 and 300 at that time. The ultimate number of excess lung-cancer deaths among the uranium miners is expected to be on the order of 1,000.[20]

These disastrous health effects were predictable, even in 1946, and avoidable. Elsewhere in the world, and particularly in Europe, many years of experience with mining radioactive minerals pointed clearly to the potential consequences. A miners' disease first known simply as the "bergkrankheit" (mountain sickness) was identified as lung cancer in 1879 and was later clearly linked to the breathing of dust and radon gas in the mines and the retention in the lungs of radon-daughter particles. The method of prevention—vigorous ventilation of the mine shafts—was also known, but this knowledge was not applied when the U.S. uranium mining industry was developed.

The danger to the health of uranium miners was recognized as early as 1949 by the Colorado Department of Health, which began studies in collaboration with the U.S. Public Health Service and others. In 1957, the Public Health Service published the results of radon-daughter surveys and predicted an excess lung-cancer mortality among the miners. Reports in the early sixties indicated that lung-cancer death rates among miners were five to ten times higher than normal, after correcting for contributing factors such as age and smoking habits. During the sixties, ventilation and other conditions were gradually improved in most of the mines, but it was not until 1971 that national health standards were finally put into effect to reduce the danger. And although these standards undoubtedly represent an advance in worker safety, many experts believe they still allow excessive occupational radiation exposure and recommend that the permitted levels be substantially reduced.[21]

Looking backward, it appears clear that the AEC did have the legal authority to regulate mining practices and to protect the health of the miners. The AEC based its inaction on a clause in the Atomic Energy Act of 1946 stating that "source material" was to be regulated by the commission only after its removal "from its place of deposit in nature." The AEC chose to understand this to mean removal of the ore from the mine, rather than from the ore body underground; this self-serving interpretation freed it from the responsibility to ensure safe working conditions in the mines. Economic considerations seem to explain the motives of both the

AEC and the industry: failing to provide adequate ventilation and other safe mining practices kept costs (to the companies) down and encouraged rapid expansion of the uranium industry.[22] Miners whose health was destroyed—or the surviving families of those who have died—have generally been unable to obtain compensation for their injuries, and the problem will persist for many years to come.

The Waste Problem: Front End

Radiation exposure from uranium ore is not limited to miners. The general population has also received substantial doses of radiation, both externally and internally, through pollution of air and water with radioactive waste materials and especially through the use of such materials in the construction of houses and other buildings. A member of the Nuclear Regulatory Commission stated in 1978 that "the extent of the radioactive releases from the so-called 'front-end' of the nuclear fuel cycle has been persistently underestimated in official reports until quite recently."[23]

When uranium ore is milled, almost all the mass of the ore remains at the mill site; most of it becomes a dry, sandlike waste called "tailings." Included in the tailings are nearly all the uranium decay products that the ore originally contained, especially the radium. The bulk of this material is accumulated in some thirty-five large mounds at active or inactive mill sites in the western states; it is estimated to total over 140 million tons, and about 17 million tons are being added annually. In addition to the solid tailings, mill operations produce liquid chemical wastes from the extraction process, plus semi-liquid waste materials called "slime." Before 1959 these materials were simply dumped into nearby rivers, where they often caused severe pollution and ecological damage. Today, they are usually retained by dams in storage ponds near the mills. Such "tailings ponds" have been the source of major accidents.

20-5 DISASTER AT CHURCH ROCK

On July 16, 1979, a tailings dam collapsed at the United Nuclear Corporation's uranium mill near Church Rock, New Mexico. The accident spilled almost 100 million gallons of acid and radioactive liquid milling wastes plus 1,100 tons of solid waste into the nearby Rio Puerco, a tributary of the Little Colorado River. Officials of the Nuclear Regulatory Commission have called the spill "the worst incident of radiation contamination in the history of the United States."

The Church Rock tailings dam was considered the best in the state, but there is evidence that it had been overloaded and improperly operated before the accident. Cleanup efforts by the company were delayed and desultory, and only a minute fraction of the radioactive material spilled from the pond was recovered.

High levels of both radioactive and acid contamination were soon measured many miles downstream from the broken dam. A few weeks after the accident, tests at a monitoring well near Gallup, New Mexico, showed that radioactivity and heavy-metal contamination had reached the groundwater at depths of thirty to forty feet below the surface. The New Mexico Environmental Improvement Division ordered the company to post signs along the river in three languages—English, Spanish, and Navajo—warning against use of the contaminated river water. However, as one Navajo farmer commented, "Our sheep don't read." The ultimate health costs of the accident, like those of other exposure of populations to large but diffused releases of radioactivity, will not be known reliably for a long time, if ever.

Even without considering accidents, the environmental impact of the waste from uranium milling has been severe, and the unavoidable problems have been compounded by neglect and mismanagement. The radium which remains with the tailings decays into radon gas and its daughter products. The radon diffuses easily from the tailings piles, and the radium compounds can be dissolved out of them. The piles themselves are gradually dispersed by wind and water. It was discovered as early as 1958 that there could be substantial airborne radioactivity near tailings piles, as well as significant gamma-ray levels at their surface. The AEC was slow to take notice of these dangers, however, and the public was not excluded from access to the tailings sites until 1969.[24]

The problem presented by uranium milling waste was multiplied by a remarkable error: for years mill tailings were used as a construction material not only for roads but also houses, public buildings, and even schools. The practice was noticed in 1966 by state health officials in Grand Junction, Colorado, where high levels of gamma radiation and radon daughters were found in certain buildings. It turned out that some 3,300 homes and other buildings in and around Grand Junction had tailings under or near their foundations. Tailings were even used as fill for children's sandboxes. Unfortunately the practice was not confined to Grand Junction, and there are thousands of buildings elsewhere in Colorado and in other western states that were built on a foundation of uranium mill tailings. In many of the affected buildings, long-term occupants will suffer a significantly increased risk of lung cancer.[25]

What must be done? The problem has at least

three facets: to render harmless the existing tailings mounds and ponds; to correct the radioactive buildings; and to prevent pollution from mining and milling operations in the future. Some progress is being made on the second and third of these points through stricter regulation of mining and milling and through removal of the tailings under some of the affected buildings in the Grand Junction area. These programs are being conducted by the Department of Energy in cooperation with the Environmental Protection Agency and with the Colorado Health Department. Studies on treatment of existing tailings mounds are also being made. It seems, however, that there is not yet sufficient agreement as to what should be done, and little action has been taken thus far.

Conversion and Enrichment

Natural uranium is a mixture of different isotopes. By far the largest part of it is the most stable isotope U-238 (99.3 percent), but there is also a small amount of the less stable U-235 (about 0.7 percent) as well as a trace of U-234. Soon after the demonstration of uranium fission in 1938, it was recognized that only the nuclei of U-235 were actually splitting. It was also soon realized that while a chain reaction might be achieved with natural uranium under favorable circumstances (as was first accomplished in December 1942), a uranium-fission bomb would require nearly pure U-235. For this reason one great task of the Manhattan Project was to separate these two isotopes on a large scale. Although a number of methods were possible in the laboratory, the small difference in the masses of U-235 and U-238 made the practical problem of separation very difficult.

The first large-scale separation of the uranium isotopes, a process which is called "enrichment," was done during 1944 by an electromagnetic method. Most of the U-235 in the bomb that destroyed Hiroshima was obtained in this way, using large machines called Calutrons which were set up in the Y-12 plant at Oak

Ridge, Tennessee. However, another enrichment plant at Oak Ridge, using the gas-diffusion method, also went into operation in 1944, and by mid-1945 the Calutrons were obsolete. Shortly after the end of the war, the Y-12 plant was converted to other uses.

Beginning in the late forties, and accelerating after the first Soviet nuclear explosion in August 1949, the uranium-enrichment facilities were greatly expanded. First the Oak Ridge plant was improved and enlarged. In November 1950 the AEC decided to build a second gas-diffusion plant at Paducah, Kentucky, and in the summer of 1952 plans were drawn for a third one in Portsmouth, Ohio. All three plants were in full operation by 1956.

The uranium-enrichment plants were originally constructed for the same purpose: to produce fissionable material for nuclear bombs. Over the years, however, an entirely adequate stockpile of enriched uranium for weapons was built up, and the purpose of enrichment shifted in large part to nuclear power. The needs of the navy for nuclear fuel and the beginning of the nuclear power industry took up the slack in the sixties, and since then the demand for low-enriched uranium (2 percent to 5 percent U-235) for nuclear power stations, both U.S. and foreign, has usually kept the three plants operating near full production.

Today, virtually all the yellowcake from the U.S. uranium industry is enriched to some extent before its use as fuel or in weapons. This requires that it first be purified and converted into uranium hexafluoride, which is a gas at very moderate temperatures. This conversion is done at two plants located in Sequoyah, Oklahoma, and Metropolis, Illinois; these plants are owned and operated by Kerr-McGee and by the Allied Chemical Company, respectively.

After the conversion stage, cylinders filled with the uranium hexafluoride are shipped to the enrichment plant at Paducah, Kentucky. Here all the uranium is normally enriched to just under 2 percent U-235. Some of this slightly

20-6   URANIUM-ENRICHMENT PROCESSES

The large gaseous diffusion plant at Portsmouth, Ohio.

Two isotopes of the same element, U-235 and U-238 for example, have nearly identical chemical properties and cannot be separated by chemical processes. Rather,

separation must depend on the slight differences in the masses of their nuclei. The most important processes are: gaseous diffusion, centrifuge, and the Becker nozzle process. Of these, gaseous diffusion is used in three United States plants and in several other countries, and accounts for most of the world's capacity for uranium enrichment.

Whether the plant uses the diffusion, centrifuge, or nozzle process, enriching uranium requires many stages. A gaseous diffusion plant will consist of a cascade of a thousand or more separate stages which handle the uranium in the form of uranium hexafluoride gas (UF_6). In each stage the UF_6 gas is pumped into one part of a converter, which a porous barrier divides into two chambers. The lighter molecules, those containing U-235, flow through the barrier slightly more readily than those

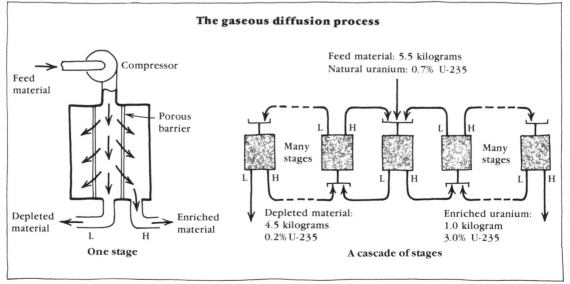

The gaseous diffusion process

In gaseous diffusion, uranium hexafluoride gas passes through many stages in which a porous barrier allows the lighter material containing uranium-235 to pass more readily.

containing U-239. Thus the stream flowing into the converter is divided into two streams, one slightly more enriched in U-235 and one slightly less enriched. The stream with higher enrichment is fed on to further enrichment by subsequent stages of the cascade. The stream with lower enrichment is recycled to an earlier stage where its enrichment matches that of the material there.

In the centrifuge process, UF_6 gas is whirled at high speed so the heavier material moves to the outside of the container. The centrifuge process appears to be more efficient than gaseous diffusion; in the United States, an experimental plant has been set at Oak Ridge, Tennessee, and a production facility is under construction at the Portsmouth, Ohio site. Similar plants have been built in Europe and elsewhere.

The Becker nozzle process injects the material to be separated into a small cavity where its momentum causes separation in the same manner as in the centrifuge. The process has been developed in Germany and is said to be the basis of the separation plants in South Africa.

The production capacity of an isotope separation plant is given in "separative work units" which measure the amount of material processed and the change in isotope enrichment achieved. Enormous amounts of energy are used in separation plants. In a gaseous diffusion plant the energy consumed in carrying out the separation is roughly one tenth the electrical energy produced when the enriched fuel is burned in a light water reactor.

A still unproven separation process that has considerable attraction makes use of laser beams. One way of distinguishing nuclei of two isotopes is through their resonances with light waves. Monochromatic light from a precisely tuned laser can ex-

Experimental gas centrifuges in a demonstration facility at Oak Ridge, Tennessee.

cite nuclei of one isotope without disturbing others. The excited nuclei may be induced to lose electrons and become ions which can then be separated easily from the neutral atoms. One application of laser separation is building small-scale plants that can efficiently enrich uranium for power reactors. Another application is to separate plutonium isotopes to obtain plutonium-239 less contaminated with other plutonium isotopes such as Pu-240 and Pu-241. A successful process would permit a reduction in the neutron radioactivity of stocks of nuclear weapons. It would also provide a simpler way to recover plutonium for nuclear weapons from spent commercial nuclear fuel. Authorization for such a plant is under discussion in the U.S. Congress.

enriched uranium then goes to Oak Ridge, Tennessee, for further enrichment to the degree needed for most nuclear power plants, between 2.5 percent and 5 percent. The rest is sent to the plant at Portsmouth, Ohio; there some of it is enriched to similar low levels, but a portion is used to obtain highly concentrated U-235 (85 to 97 percent) for navy propulsion, research reactor fuel, and weapons. The three gas-diffusion plants are owned by the U.S. government and are operated, under contract with the Department of Energy, by the nuclear division of Union Carbide Company (Oak Ridge and Paducah plants) and by Goodyear Atomic Company (Portsmouth plant). The combined staffs of the three plants total nearly 11,000 people.[26]

In the early seventies, further expansion of the U.S. uranium-enrichment capability was undertaken. The "cascade improvement program" and the "cascade uprating program" began in 1971 and 1974, respectively; when completed, they will add about 60 percent to the capability of the three gas-diffusion plants, while increasing their electricity consumption some 20 percent. These programs should be completed in the early eighties. In addition, a new plant now under construction near the Portsmouth site will add another third to the total U.S. enrichment capacity. This plant will use a gas centrifuge process rather than the diffusion method.

The main environmental impact of uranium enrichment lies in the enormous need of the gas-diffusion plants for electrical power to operate their compressors and coolers. The three U.S. plants required 6,065 megawatts for full operation before the uprating program; when the upgrading is completed the power consumption rate will have increased to about 7,380 megawatts.[27] These are very large requirements. The figure of 6,065 megawatts, for example, is roughly equal to the output of six large, modern nuclear power reactors all operating at full capacity. From another point of view, 6,065 megawatts equals about 2.4 percent of the average rate of electricity consumption by the entire

United States during 1978. In the late fifties, when overall electrical power consumption was smaller than it is today, the AEC at times used as much as 12 percent of the nation's total, mostly for enriching uranium.[28] The plants that supply the electricity for the enrichment facilities are fired by fossil fuel, mainly coal.

The slowdown of nuclear power development since the mid-seventies has naturally affected the uranium enrichment industry. During 1980 the three U.S. gas-diffusion plants operated at only about 40 percent capacity, consuming around 3,000 megawatt-years of electricity, 1,100 less than in 1979 and about 1 percent of total U.S. electrical use. The gas-diffusion plants continued to operate at a reduced level during 1981, and the construction schedule for the centrifuge plant has been delayed.[29] This plant is now expected to begin operation in 1989 at one-fourth of its planned total capacity; it can add additional capacity sequentially as demand requires.

Several other nations have uranium enrichment capabilities. All the acknowledged nuclear-weapons powers—the United States, the Soviet Union, England, France, and China—have operating gas-diffusion enrichment plants. The sizes of these plants vary widely: those of Britain and France are an order of magnitude smaller than the U.S. plants in capability, and China's is smaller still. There are also centrifuge enrichment plants in Great Britain and the Netherlands, and since 1975 South Africa has been operating a "pilot" operation with which it has probably prepared a small stockpile of material for fission bombs. The nuclear power industry of the West, however, is still about 95 percent dependent on the United States for enriched uranium fuel.[30]

The practical development of other enrichment technologies may radically change the picture. Gas centrifuge enrichment consumes far less electrical energy in operation than does gas diffusion, but centrifuge plants are presently more costly and difficult to construct. Although

20-7   NUCLEAR SOUTH AFRICA

The development of a uranium industry has had serious consequences within South Africa. In 1957, South Africa became one of the first U.S. partners in an "atoms for peace" agreement, a partnership that has been extended several times and continues today. Under this agreement a U.S. firm, Allis Chalmers, supplied South Africa with its first nuclear reactor in 1961, a large research reactor dubbed "Safari 1." Many South African scientists and engineers have studied or worked in the United States at government nuclear facilities as well as at universities. South Africa has developed a uranium enrichment capability with aid from West Germany, and a large nuclear power station is being built at Koeberg, near Capetown, by the French firm Framatome. (This firm is partly owned by Westinghouse and uses Westinghouse technology and designs under license.)

It is ironic that these developments were begun under the rubric of "atoms for peace," for today South Africa has almost certainly become a nuclear weapons power, the only one in its region. In August 1977, world pressure was applied to dissuade Pretoria from conducting nuclear weapons tests in the Kalahari desert; U.S. and Soviet satellite surveillance had revealed the preparation of the testing site. Again in September 1979, a U.S. satellite brought disturbing news, this time of a small atmospheric nuclear explosion in the South Atlantic. Some observers believe that this event was a South African weapons test, although no official confirmation of that inference has been forthcoming. Another mysterious flash resembling a nuclear explosion was reported in December 1980. Although these events remain ambiguous, there is no doubt that the government of South Africa does have the capability to produce nuclear fission weapons. There is also no doubt that nuclear cooperation with Pretoria, begun in order to secure the U.S. uranium supply, has been a major factor in making that possible.

the West German/South African "jet nozzle" process is cheaper to set up on a modest scale, it uses even more electricity than does gas diffusion. It seems possible that newer methods such as laser excitation may prove to be both more energy-efficient and cheaper to build. Such a development, desirable though it may appear, could contribute to the proliferation of nuclear weapons by making highly enriched uranium more readily available to any nation with a supply of natural uranium. Such a possibility—or probability—illustrates one of the many ways in which the development of nuclear power technology is inseparable from proliferation of the potential for making nuclear weapons.

Postscript: Further Along the Road

After enrichment, uranium destined to serve as fuel for light-water nuclear power reactors must be reconverted from the hexafluoride form to a solid oxide and then mechanically formed into pellets that can be packaged into fuel rods. (The "rods" are really tubes of a zirconium alloy, designed to resist high heat and neutron flux and to contain the radioactive fission products created during the reactor's operation.) The reconversion and fabrication operations are performed in seven commercially owned and operated plants located in different parts of the country. The four companies which sell nuclear power reactors—Westinghouse, General Electric, Combustion Engineering, and Babcock and Wilcox[31]—all own fuel fabrication facilities, as do Exxon Nuclear and General Atomic.

When the used fuel rods are removed from a power reactor, most of the uranium they contained is still there—virtually all the U-238 plus some unfissioned U-235. The rods (and the uranium) are then placed in a storage pool at the reactor site, where they remain until removed for reprocessing or for some form of disposal.

The smaller part of the uranium that was highly enriched at the Portsmouth plant, as well as some of the "depleted" uranium from which most of the U-235 has been removed, has a more varied future. This part of the story is continued in Chapter 11, which is devoted to the nuclear weapons industry.

Suggested Readings

A good reference on the early development of the nuclear energy is Frank Dawson, *Nuclear Power: Development and Management of a Technology*. Much information on the evolution of the nuclear industry may be found in the two-volume official history of the Atomic Energy Commission written by Richard Hewlett with Oscar Anderson and Francis Duncan. *Yellowcake: The International Uranium Cartel*, by June Taylor and Michael Yokell, focuses particularly on the consequences of the uranium producers' cartel, especially the Westinghouse defaults. The further evolution of the uranium industry in North America is traced in Dawson's *Nuclear Power*, Taylor and Yokell's *Yellowcake*, and Metzger's *The Atomic Establishment*.

Background on the technology of uranium mining and processing may be found in Don Clark, *State-of-the-Art: Uranium Mining, Milling, and Refining Industry*, and Walter Woodmansee's "Uranium." The problem of estimating "reserves" and "resources" of uranium is treated in Cheney's article in *American Scientist* and in Neff and Jacoby's article in *Technology Review*. The latter gives the most up-to-date analysis of uranium market conditions. Health and environmental problems associated with uranium mining

and milling are explained from various points of view in the chapter on radiation hazards by Hollocher and MacKenzie, the chapter on radiation-induced lung cancer among uranium miners by Schurgin and Hollocher, and in Metzger's *The Atomic Establishment*.

Nuclear developments in South Africa are analyzed in Cervanka and Rogers, *The Nuclear Axis,* and in the chapter by Ronald Walters on U.S. policy and nuclear proliferation in South Africa.

CERVANKA, Z., AND B. ROGERS. *The Nuclear Axis.* New York: Times Books, 1978.

CHENEY, ERIC S. "The Hunt for Giant Uranium Deposits," *American Scientist* 69 (1981), pp. 37–48.

CLARK, DON A. *State-of-the-Art: Uranium Mining, Milling, and Refining Industry.* Corvallis, Oregon: U.S. Environmental Protection Agency, June 1974.

DAWSON, FRANK G. *Nuclear Power: Development and Management of a Technology.* University of Washington Press, 1976.

HEWLETT, RICHARD G., AND OSCAR E. ANDERSON, JR. *The New World, 1939–1946.* Volume 1 of an official history of the United States Atomic Energy Commission. University Park, Penn.: Pennsylvania State University Press, 1962.

HEWLETT, RICHARD G. AND FRANCIS DUNCAN. *Atomic Shield, 1947–1952.* Volume 2 of an official history of the United States Atomic Energy Commission. University Park, Penn.: Pennsylvania State University Press, 1969.

HOLLOCHER, THOMAS C., AND JAMES J. MACKENZIE. "Radiation Hazards Associated with Uranium Mill Operations." Chapter 3 in *The Nuclear Fuel Cycle: A Survey of the Public Health, Environmental and National Security Effects of Nuclear Power.* Cambridge, Mass.: Union of Concerned Scientists, 1975.

METZGER, PETER H. *The Atomic Establishment.* New York, Simon and Schuster, 1972.

NEFF, THOMAS L., AND HENRY D. JACOBY. "World Uranium: Softening Markets and Rising Security." *Technology Review*, January 1981, pages 19–30.

SCHURGIN, ARELL S., AND THOMAS G. HOLLOCHER, "Radiation-Induced Lung Cancers Among Uranium Miners." Chapter 2 in *The Nuclear Fuel Cycle (see* Hollocher above).

TAYLOR, JUNE H., AND MICHAEL D. YOKELL. *Yellowcake: the International Uranium Cartel.* Pergamon Press, 1979.

WALTERS, RONALD W. "U.S. Policy and Nuclear Proliferation in South Africa." Chapter 9 in *U.S. Military Involvement in South Africa*. Boston: South End Press, 1978.

WOODMANSEE, WALTER C. "Uranium," in *Mineral Facts and Problems*. 1975 edition. Washington, D.C.: Bureau of Mines, U.S. Department of the Interior, 1976.

The Indian Point nuclear power plant is situated at Buchanan, New York, just 26 miles north of New York City. There are three reactors; units 2 and 3 have been operating successfully since the mid-seventies. The original unit 1 was permanently closed after ten years of operation because its safety deficiencies could not be corrected economically. The siting of plants near large cities is controversial, especially in this case because there is the possibility of earth shocks originating in the nearby Ramapo Fault.

21. Nuclear Power

Anthony Nero has written a guidebook on nuclear power reactors that surveys the principles and characteristics of the important types of nuclear power reactors. The most prevalent form of power reactor uses ordinary water to carry energy away from the fission reaction taking place in its core. But these reactors only consume a small fraction of the uranium fuel. The spent fuel can be processed chemically to recover fuel material, which can be recycled through the reactor. Since the spent fuel is highly radioactive, processing it is hazardous, expensive, and makes fissionable material more accessible to governments that might choose to make nuclear weapons.

COMMERCIAL NUCLEAR REACTORS have become a principal source of electrical energy in the United States and abroad. Because reactors depend directly on nuclear fission reactions, which leave a residue of highly radioactive materials, there is controversy over continued development of nuclear power. The radioactive products of nuclear reactors can contaminate the biosphere and harm people, and there is disagreement over the adequacy of measures taken to limit public exposure to radiation. In addition, the economic and social costs of nuclear power raise the question of whether commercial nuclear power is really competitive with other methods of generating electricity, with other forms of energy, or with the cost of using less energy. And since the basic materials of commercial nuclear power can be fashioned into nuclear weapons, nuclear power may have a critical effect on world stability.

These issues are not easily resolved. Mankind, and indeed the entire biosphere, has developed in a bath of natural background radiation that far exceeds the average exposure a person will suffer as a result of commercial nuclear power operations. However, some exposure to radioactivity from nuclear power operations is unavoidable, and large accidental releases of radioactivity from power reactors have occurred (see Chapter 15). Decisions concerning further development of nuclear power must balance the possible harm from these exposures against the advantages that nuclear power may offer and must be made in the light of equivalent cost/benefit comparisons for the alternatives to nuclear power, including the alternative of using less energy. The danger that widespread reliance on nuclear power may lead to wider access to nuclear weapons must also be considered.

Anthony Nero
Jack Dennis

Nero is a physicist at the Lawrence Berkeley Laboratory of the University of California. Dennis is editor of this book.

Power Reactors

In the United States the bulk of electrical power is generated using thermal energy—heat—to produce steam, which drives a turbine-generator system. In principle, even the sun may serve as the heat source for the steam supply system, but for the near future, fossil-fueled boilers and nuclear power reactors will be the heat source in large electrical-generating plants.

We may divide nuclear power reactors into two categories—*commercial* and *advanced.* Commercial reactors are those presently in service. Advanced reactors are those under development as potentially important to the future of nuclear power but not in widespread use. Two types of commercial power reactors account for nearly all plants in operation or under construction in the United States. These are the *pressurized water reactor* and the *boiling water reactor.* In either form of power reactor, nuclear energy is released in a core consisting of fissionable material held in assemblies of fuel rods. Water surrounds the core in a heavy steel reactor vessel and carries away the thermal energy of the nuclear reaction.

A nuclear *chain reaction* takes place in the reactor core, generating large amounts of thermal energy as well as intense radiation and a radioactive residue. To appreciate the issues and alternatives in nuclear plant design, we must understand the nature of nuclear fission and the maintenance and control of the chain reaction.

Chain Reaction

Fission is the splitting of the nucleus of a heavy atom following absorption of an extra neutron. A material whose atoms will split in this way is said to be *fissile.* The most common fissile material is uranium-235 (U-235), the lighter isotope of uranium which forms about 0.7 percent of the uranium in the earth's crust. One of the many possible fission reactions for a U-235 nucleus is described by the equation

$$\text{U-235} + n \rightarrow \text{La-144} + \text{Br-90} + 2n + (\text{energy})$$

This describes a typical nuclear fission event in which a U-235 nucleus absorbs one neutron and splits to yield two *fission fragments,* isotopes of lanthanum (La) and bromine (Br)—whose atomic numbers, 57 and 35, add up to 92, the atomic number of uranium. This fission event also yields two neutrons which can induce further fission events. The nuclear fragments, having many more neutrons than stable nuclei can have, quickly lose energy and transform with the successive emission of electrons:

$$\text{La-144} \rightarrow \cdots \rightarrow \text{Nd-144} + 3e + (\text{energy})$$
$$\text{Br-90} \rightarrow \cdots \rightarrow \text{Sr-90} + 3e + (\text{energy})$$

The products, neodymium (Nd) and strontium (Sr) in this illustration, may be stable or radioactive. Neodymium-144 is stable; strontium-90 is radioactive with a half-life of 28.1 years, posing a significant environmental hazard.

The fission of one uranium atom releases about 200 million electron volts of energy in the form of gamma rays and the energy of motion of neutrons and fission fragments. This energy, which is roughly 100 million times greater than the energy released in a chemical reaction of molecules, accounts for the fact that the complete fission of one pound of uranium would release roughly the same amount of energy as the combustion of 6,000 barrels of oil or 1,000 tons of high-quality coal.

A continuous *chain reaction* in fissile material is possible because a fission event yields one or more highly energetic neutrons which (under the right conditions) can cause further fission events. The chain is a series of fission reactions linked by neutrons, each neutron being generated by one fission event and inducing the next. In steady operation of a power reactor, it is only necessary that, on the average, one of the neutrons produced in each fission causes another fission. The number of neutrons in succeeding "generations" will then remain constant. This condition is called *criticality.*

Generally a fission produces two major fragments of almost but not quite equal mass. The

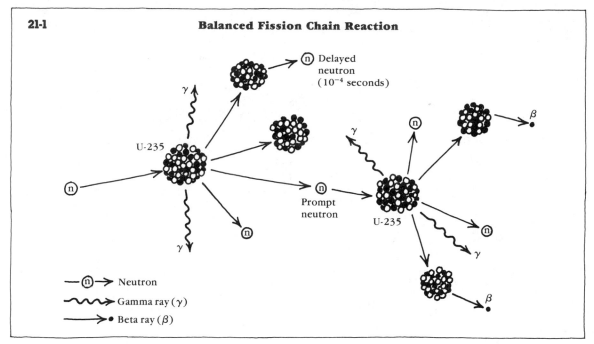

21-1   **Balanced Fission Chain Reaction**

In a power reactor the objective is to maintain a balanced chain reaction—one in which neutrons are being produced and consumed at the same rate. About half of the neutrons released in fission are required to sustain the reaction by splitting more uranium atoms. The excess neutrons are mostly absorbed into other materials present in the reactor core. It is possible to maintain the fragile balance by using neutron-absorbing control rods only because a small fraction of the neutrons from fission are released, not immediately, but a fraction of a millisecond after the fission event.

distribution of masses of fission fragments is found to have peaks in the vicinity of masses 95 and 140. The first group includes nuclei that yield radioactive isotopes of krypton and strontium; the second group yields radioactive iodine, xenon, and cesium. These substances are troublesome if released into the environment because their half-lives range from days to many years. Another radioactive product of fission is tritium, the mass 3 isotope of hydrogen, which has a half-life of 12.3 years. All these products of fission leave the reactor when spent fuel rods are replaced with fresh rods.

Since fission events often produce two or three neutrons, surplus neutrons are available and, in a balanced reaction, must disappear in a way that does not induce fission, either by absorption without fission in the fuel, by absorp-

tion in the reactor structure or coolant, or by leaving the reactor core. One of these possibilities is a nonfission reaction in which a heavy fuel nucleus absorbs a neutron and, instead of fissioning, transforms into a new nucleus of similar mass—thorium, protactinium, uranium, neptunium, plutonium, americium, or curium. These materials are members of the series of "rare earth" elements called the *actinides*. Many have long-lived radioactivity, but only thorium and uranium occur naturally. Among the actinides, plutonium-239 (Pu-239) and U-233 are fissile materials potentially important as fuel for power reactors. Operation of a nuclear reactor also induces radioactivity in the nonfuel materials used to construct the reactor core and in the coolant fluid, but these sources of radioactivity are relatively small.

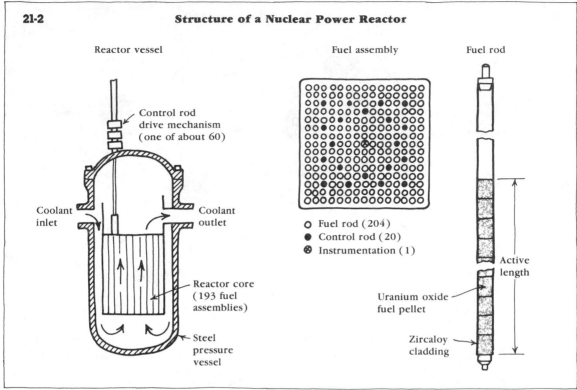

21-2   **Structure of a Nuclear Power Reactor**

Reactor vessel

Control rod
drive mechanism
(one of about 60)

Coolant
inlet

Coolant
outlet

Reactor core
(193 fuel
assemblies)

Steel
pressure
vessel

Fuel assembly

○ Fuel rod (204)
● Control rod (20)
⊗ Instrumentation (1)

Fuel rod

Active
length

Uranium oxide
fuel pellet

Zircaloy
cladding

The structure of a typical one-gigawatt (one-million-kilowatt) pressurized-water reactor showing the arrangement of its 39,372 fuel rods in 193 fuel assemblies. The fuel cladding must be designed for efficient transfer of heat from the fuel pellets to the coolant while keeping radioactive fission products sealed within the fuel rods.

The probability that a particular type of nuclear interaction occurs is expressed as a *cross-section* for that type of event and depends on the particle types involved and on their state of motion with respect to one another. For the fission of a uranium nucleus by a neutron, the cross-section is larger for slow neutrons than for highly energetic ones. Fission events produce fast neutrons which are much more likely to cause other fission events if they are slowed down. For this reason, most commercial power reactors include a material called a *moderator*. The moderator surrounds the fuel and absorbs energy from the neutrons to increase their chance of inducing fission of fuel nuclei. Most nuclear power plants in the United States use light-water reactors. The coolant is ordinary water, which also serves as the moderator. Other moderating materials in use include heavy water and carbon in the form of graphite.

Cooling and Heat Transfer

In a nuclear reactor, the energy released in fission is in part carried by fast neutrons and gamma rays, but most of the energy is the kinetic energy of recoiling fission fragments. Additional energy is subsequently released by the fission fragments in radioactive decay. Whatever form it takes, nearly all of the released energy is deposited in materials of the reactor: fission fragments are rapidly stopped by fuel rod materials, and their kinetic energy is converted to heat. The neutrons give up much of their energy in the moderator, but they have relatively little energy to begin with. The gamma rays are absorbed in reactor materials but also account for a relatively small portion of the energy released.

This thermal energy must be carried away for use in generating steam for operating a turbine. The fluid used to transfer heat away from the reactor core is called the *coolant* since removing heat also keeps the reactor core from overheat-

21-4   REACTOR FUEL LOADING
A bundle of fuel rods is lowered into the reactor core as part of the initial fuel loading of the Millstone 2 pressurized water plant in Waterford, Connecticut, August 1975. The plant began full-power operation for Northeast Utilities in 1976.

21-3   REACTOR PRESSURE VESSEL
Reactor pressure vessel being lowered into place at the Duke Power Company plant under construction in Clover, South Carolina. This is for one of two pressurized water reactors expected to start producing one million kilowatts apiece in 1986–87.

ing, possibly leading to its disintegration. In light-water reactors the coolant is ordinary water—H_2O. In one type of commercial reactor, the CANDU, the coolant is heavy water—D_2O—water in which the hydrogen atoms are replaced with deuterium, the mass 2 isotope of hydrogen. This is useful because heavy water does not capture, and therefore waste, as many neutrons as ordinary water. A gas, helium, is used as the coolant in the High Temperature Gas-Cooled Reactor (HTGR), and liquid sodium

21-5   **Flow Schemes for Light Water Nuclear Power Reactors**

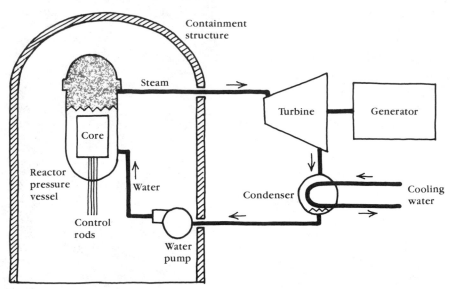

The Boiling Water Reactor (BWR)

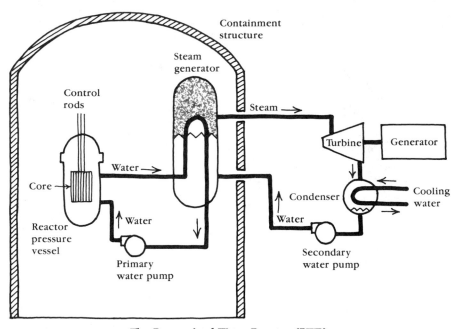

The Pressurized Water Reactor (PWR)

21-6   **CHARACTERISTICS OF LIGHT WATER REACTORS**

Reactor Type	Boiling Water (BWR)	Pressurized Water (PWR)
Manufacturer (representative)	General Electric	Westinghouse
Number in operation (United States)	26	48
Thermal power (megawatts)	3,579	3,411
Electrical output (megawatts)	1,220	1,100
Coolant, moderator	water/steam	water
Pressure in core (pounds per square inch)	1,040	2,250
Temperature at core outlet (degrees centigrade)	288	325
Coolant flow rate (kilograms per second)	13,000	17,000
Pressure vessel:	steel	steel
diameter (meters)	6.0	4.4
height (meters)	22	13
wall thickness (centimeters)	15.5	21.5
Active length of fuel elements (meters)	3.8	3.7
Number of fuel elements	46,376	39,372
Power density in core (kilowatts per liter)	54	98
Fuel material:	uranium oxide	uranium oxide
enrichment (percent uranium-235)	2.8	3.2
weight (kilograms)	155,000	98,000
Spent fuel:		
uranium-235 (percent)	0.8	0.9
plutonium (Pu-239, Pu-241) (percent)	0.6	0.6
Refueling	¼ per year	⅓ per year

serves as the coolant in the Liquid Metal Fast Breeder Reactor (LMFBR). Whatever the choice of coolant, heat from the reactor core produces steam in a separate heat exchanger called a *steam generator,* or boils water in the reactor core to produce steam directly.

When the thermal energy of steam is used to perform mechanical work, a fundamental principle of physics—the Second Law of Thermodynamics—limits the amount of heat that can be transformed into motion and thence into electricity. The remaining thermal energy is waste heat which must be disposed of into a body of water—a river, lake, or ocean—or into the atmosphere through large cooling towers. The re-

moval of waste heat from the steam cycle occurs at the condenser, where exhaust steam from the turbine reverts to liquid water before being returned to the reactor vessel or steam generator.

Reactivity Control

Keeping a nuclear reactor operating at a constant power level requires maintenance of a delicate balance between neutron production and absorption. Neutrons are produced predominantly by fission events which yield on average a bit more than two neutrons apiece. To maintain a constant power level, an average of one neutron per fission must induce another fission

OPPOSITE:

In the boiling-water reactor, the reactor core is immersed in water that boils at modest pressure, producing steam which is led outside the containment structure to the turbine. In a pressurized-water reactor,

water absorbs heat from the core and is led to a steam generator within the containment structure. The water in the primary loop is kept under high pressure so that boiling will not take place.

event. The remaining neutrons are accounted for by nonfission absorption in the fuel material, or absorption in the moderator or materials of the reactor structure.

Maintaining this balance of neutron production and absorption requires compensating for changing conditions in the reactor that affect the rates of neutron generation and absorption: as time passes, fissile material is consumed, reducing the rate at which neutrons cause fissions. Fission events and other reactions in the core produce materials that absorb neutrons, decreasing the supply of neutrons available to induce fission. For controlling the supply of free neutrons the reactor core includes *control rods* fabricated of a neutron-absorbing material such as boron or cadmium. Some control rods are used to adjust the power level in the reactor core; others are arranged to fall into place by gravity to shut down the chain reaction quickly in an emergency. Over the life of a fuel charge (one year or so), the reactivity of the fuel changes enough that the range of the control rods is not sufficient. For this reason, a second method of controlling reactivity is also used: boric acid, a neutron absorber, is added to the coolant to bring reactivity within the range of adjustment provided by the control rods.

It is truly remarkable that maintaining a balanced chain reaction is practically feasible. The fact that a critical mass of fissionable material can, in the form of an atomic bomb, support a chain reaction that completes in a fraction of a microsecond may lead us to wonder how it is at all possible to harness a chain reaction for practical energy production.

How quickly must the control rods be moved to maintain a balanced chain reaction? If all neutrons were to appear immediately at each fission event, control would be very difficult because the supply of neutrons in the reactor core could rise very dangerously in the time required to move the control rods. In reactors that use a moderator to absorb neutron energy, it takes about 10^{-4} seconds (one ten-thousandth

of a second) for a neutron released by one fission to induce a subsequent fission event. If there were an excess of just one neutron for each thousand free neutrons in the reactor, then in just one thousand generations of fissions the flux would be multiplied by 1.001 to the thousandth power, or 1.001^{1000}, which is 2.7, and this would occur in only one-tenth of one second. Thus moving the control rods quickly enough to maintain a balanced chain reaction would be difficult.

However, not all neutrons generated in the reactor appear immediately. Although most neutrons appear within about 10^{-17} second of the time of fission, about 0.5 percent of released neutrons come from the decay of fission fragments. This small number of "delayed" neutrons limits the change in neutron flux that may occur in a brief interval, and consequently the control rods can be used effectively to maintain a constant level of reactivity.

Fuel Cycles

The handling of nuclear fuels presents problems very different from the handling of coal and oil. The amounts of material are much smaller, but the spent fuel from a reactor is highly radioactive. Only a small portion of the fuel material is consumed in a power reactor, but some conversion of material from nonfissile to fissile takes place. Finally, the cost of the natural fuel material is only a small portion of the total cost of nuclear energy.

A fuel cycle is the path followed by the fuel material from mining through various processing and refinement operations, through the reactors that utilize the thermal energy of fission, to the disposal of the fuel material after its removal from the reactor. The simplest nuclear fuel cycle is the *once-through* cycle which describes present-day operation of light-water reactors. The uranium fuel used in light-water reactors must contain about 3 percent of fissionable U-235 to sustain a chain reaction economical for nuclear power generation.

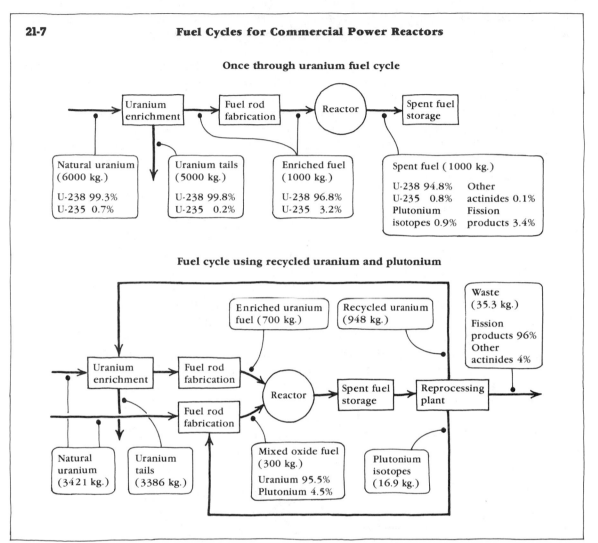

21-7 **Fuel Cycles for Commercial Power Reactors**

Once through uranium fuel cycle

Uranium enrichment → Fuel rod fabrication → Reactor → Spent fuel storage

Natural uranium (6000 kg.)

U-238 99.3%
U-235 0.7%

Uranium tails (5000 kg.)

U-238 99.8%
U-235 0.2%

Enriched fuel (1000 kg.)

U-238 96.8%
U-235 3.2%

Spent fuel (1000 kg.)

U-238 94.8%   Other
U-235 0.8%   actinides 0.1%
Plutonium   Fission
isotopes 0.9% products 3.4%

Fuel cycle using recycled uranium and plutonium

Enriched uranium fuel (700 kg.)

Recycled uranium (948 kg.)

Waste (35.3 kg.)

Fission products 96%
Other actinides 4%

Uranium enrichment → Fuel rod fabrication → Reactor → Spent fuel storage → Reprocessing plant

Fuel rod fabrication

Natural uranium (3421 kg.)

Uranium tails (3386 kg.)

Mixed oxide fuel (300 kg.)

Uranium 95.5%
Plutonium 4.5%

Plutonium isotopes (16.9 kg.)

The upper diagram shows the flow of uranium fuel material for nearly all U.S. power reactors. In this flow chart, less than one percent of the nuclear energy of natural uranium is released in the reactor. The remainder is in the uranium and plutonium held together with highly radioactive fission products in spent fuel rods. The lower diagram shows the mixed oxide fuel cycle in which fuel rods containing a mixture of uranium and plutonium are used, yielding a reduced use of natural uranium. The expense of reprocessing spent reactor fuel has discouraged use of this process. The use of breeder reactors would provide a much greater improvement in the utilization of uranium, but breeders are not economical given present uranium supplies.

Since natural uranium contains only about 0.7 percent U-235, it must be processed by *enrichment* to increase its portion of fissile U-235. Any scheme for uranium enrichment must separate the two uranium isotopes U-235 and U-238. Since these are not chemically different, no chemical process can work; the separation must be done on the basis of the small difference in the nuclear mass. Thus enrichment is a difficult and expensive process.

The principal schemes for enrichment involve passing uranium through a cascade of stages; each stage separates an incoming stream of material into two outgoing streams—one in which the fraction of material that is fissile U-235 is increased, and the other in which the fissile fraction is decreased. The principal scheme for enrichment is *gaseous diffusion* in which uranium in the form of uranium fluoride gas (UF_6) is pumped through a porous barrier. For this scheme one stage can improve the ratio of U-235 to U-238 by at best a theoretical factor of 1.0043, which is the square root of the ratio of molecular masses of the two species of uranium fluoride. To produce fuel from natural uranium that is sufficiently enriched for use in light-water reactors requires on the order of a thousand diffusion stages. (See Chapter 20, which tells more about separating uranium isotopes—where it is done, alternative processes, and how the enriched uranium is used.)

The enriched uranium is fabricated into fuel rods for installation in power reactors. After a year or more of reactor operation, the fuel composition has changed sufficiently that it is necessary to remove the spent fuel rod from the reactor. It then consists of about 94.4 percent U-238, 0.78 percent unconsumed fissile U-235, 1.8 percent fission products, many highly radioactive, and of great significance, 0.49 percent fissile Pu-239 created by conversion of U-238 through absorption of neutrons. Small quantities of other actinides including Pu-238, Pu-240, Pu-241, and Pu-242 are also produced.

Even though this spent fuel has been re-moved from the neutron flux of the reactor core, large amounts of thermal energy are still released from the radioactive decay of fission products. For this reason, fuel rods removed from power reactors are kept in storage pools filled with cooling water. At present most of this used fuel material is accumulating at reactor sites. Eventually it must be disposed of as radioactive nuclear waste, used in fabrication of recycled fuel materials for nuclear power plants, or perhaps used as a source of fissionable plutonium for making nuclear weapons.

Reprocessing and Advanced Reactors

Although U-235 is the only naturally occurring fuel for nuclear reactors, it is not the only fissile material important in nuclear power. There are three fissile nuclei useful in practical power reactors: U-235, U-233, and Pu-239.

The "manufactured" fissile materials U-233 and Pu-239 are the products of conversion reactions that take place in nuclear reactors:

U-238→ Pu-239:
    U-238 + n→ U-239 + γ
    (half-life of U-239: 23.5 minutes)
    U-239→ Np-239 + e
    (half-life of Np-239: 2.35 days)
    Np-239→ Pu-239 + e
Th-232→ U-233:
    Th-232 + n→ Th-233 + γ
    (half-life of Th-233: 22.1 minutes)
    Th-233→ Pa-233 + e
    (half-life of Pa-233: 27 days)
    Pa-233→ U-233 + e

In these reactions the starting material is said to be *fertile*. One of the fertile materials is thorium (Th), showing that thorium could become an important natural source of nuclear fuel.

A nuclear power reactor can be designed to be more or less efficient in the conversion of fuel material. Those specifically designed to provide fissile materials for use in other reactors are called *breeder reactors*. In Western Europe there is considerable interest in breeder reactors, and demonstration plants have been con-

21-8   BREEDER REACTORS

A nuclear breeder reactor can create at least as much nuclear fuel as it consumes, thereby reducing the dependence of nuclear power on secure resources of uranium. Breeder reactors are under commercial development in Europe and Japan, where the supply of uranium is low and uranium-enrichment facilities on the scale of the U.S. plants have not been built.

In a breeder reactor there is no moderator to slow down the high-energy neutrons released in fission of uranium or plutonium. Consequently, the core of uranium-235 (U-235) or plutonium-239 (Pu-239) fuel elements must be very compact to increase the probability of fission to the degree that a self-sustaining chain reaction can be maintained. Excess high-energy neutrons from the core irradiate a blanket of fertile U-238 rods and transmute some of the material into Pu-239 and other plutonium isotopes.

A fast-neutron breeder reactor has a very high power density in its core, perhaps five times as much as in typical power reactors. Liquid sodium is used as the coolant in most breeders because it

can carry away large amounts of heat from the small volume of material.

For a breeder to be useful, its irradiated fuel rods must be chemically processed to separate the converted plutonium for use in the reactor core, in other power reactors, or elsewhere.

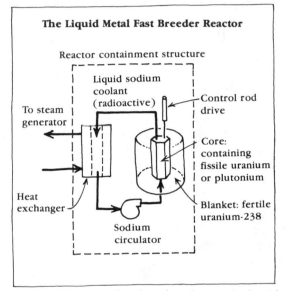

The Liquid Metal Fast Breeder Reactor

Configuration of fuel and coolant flow in the liquid metal fast breeder reactor (LMFBR).

structed in Britain and France. In the United States, debate continues over the wisdom of constructing the Clinch River breeder reactor. Since the envisioned rapid expansion of nuclear power in the United States has not taken place, it is not anticipated that breeder fuel will be required by the nuclear power industry until the next century. There is, of course, the argument that the United States must acquire experience in the design and operation of breeder reactors if it wishes to compete in the future market for these plants.

Use of the converted fuel requires chemical

processing of the fuel material to increase the concentration of fissile nuclei to the level required for economical use in power reactors. This operation is called *reprocessing* because it is done subsequent to irradiation of the fuel material in a reactor. At the reprocessing plant, the fuel rod is dissolved in acid and the chemical species separated from the solution. The separated plutonium is sent to a fuel-rod fabrication plant; the uranium can be returned to an enrichment plant to recover more U-235.

The reprocessing of nuclear fuel faces an uncertain future in the United States. Several plants have been built, but the challenge to make reprocessing economical and safe is hard to meet—primarily because the fuel material is highly radioactive and leads to high-level liquid wastes that are troublesome to dispose of (see Chapter 14). In 1977, President Jimmy Carter suspended reprocessing of nuclear fuel in the United States on the basis that the accompanying traffic in purified plutonium would increase the danger of nuclear weapons proliferation (see Chapter 19). Also, since enriched natural uranium is currently in plentiful supply, the operators of U.S. nuclear reactors have found the reprocessing of spent fuel to be uneconomical.

In consequence, spent fuel rods continue to accumulate in the storage pools at operating light-water reactor sites. These pools present an increasing problem as they are being utilized beyond their envisioned capacity, and there is as yet no accepted plan for disposal of their highly radioactive contents.

Safety Features

The designers of nuclear reactors must be concerned with limiting public exposure to radiation. The question of reactor safety may be divided in two parts: exposure of the public and the environment to radioactive materials from normal reactor operation, and the possibility of reactor accidents leading to large releases of radioactive material. There is in addition the occupational hazard to workers in nuclear energy facilities.

There is some contribution of radioactivity to the environment during normal operation of a nuclear power reactor. Some escape of radioactive materials, especially tritium (H-3), krypton, xenon, iodine, and carbon, is impossible to avoid. Reactor maintenance involves removing parts that have been exposed to intense radiation. Tools and clothing become exposed to radioactive contamination. Elaborate equipment and precautions are used to prevent general release of this material—even air circulated in the containment structure is filtered to remove ra-

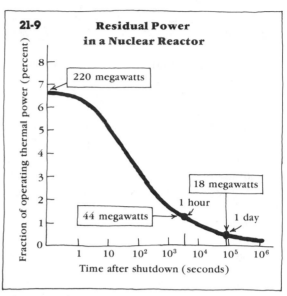

When a nuclear power reactor is shut down, release of heat in the core continues even though the chain reaction has stopped. Even after one day the power level in the core is equal to the electrical energy consumption of several thousand electric stoves.

dioactive material. When operated as intended by the designers, public exposure to radioactivity from nuclear power plants is well below the exposure from natural background radiation.

The most important safety concern is radiation exposure from a reactor accident that releases a large quantity of radioactive material. If the core of a nuclear reactor overheats to the extent that the melting point of the fuel cladding is approached, fuel rods may bend or expand enough to disturb the coolant flow pattern, exacerbating the difficulty of cooling. Actual disintegration of fuel rods would release large amounts of radioactivity into the cooling fluid.

The initial response in any emergency is to shut down the chain reaction. Whether a shutdown occurs during normal operation or in an emergency, the flow of coolant through the reactor core must continue. Although the fission reaction is stopped, the products of fission con-

21-10 NUCLEAR POWER CONTROL ROOM

The control room of the Robert Emmett Ginna nuclear power plant in New York on the south shore of Lake Ontario. The panels are filled with indicators to report conditions throughout the plant and contain the many switches and controls necessary to maintain safe operation.

tinue to generate heat through radioactive decay. Immediately after shutdown, the power level will still be about 7 percent of the level maintained before. This requires continued cooling of the core to prevent severe damage to the fuel from overheating. If some component of the reactor cooling system fails, shutting down the chain reaction is not sufficient. In the absence of cooling, portions of the core would melt, destroying the reactor and possibly leading to a disastrous release of radioactivity.

Since the consequences of failure are grave, components in the reactor cooling system are duplicated and have independent sources of power. Moreover, in light-water reactors there is an *emergency core cooling system* that is largely independent of the main coolant circuit. In addition to these safety features the reactor containment structure is designed to withstand the substantial overpressure that would occur with loss of primary coolant and to limit the escape of radioactive material. This redundancy and independence of subsystems is typical in nuclear reactor design and is particularly important in the shutdown and cooling systems. Even so, the safety of reactor designs is a matter of continuing dispute.

Power reactors are designed to limit radioactive releases and damage to the reactor system resulting from component failure, errors in operation, or outside causes such as an earthquake, airplane crash, or sabotage. Consideration of the possibility and probability of events leading to a serious accident is an intimate part of reactor design. Whether the risk of accident is worth the electrical energy produced is an issue facing the judgment of society.

Conclusion

While the importance of nuclear power as a future energy source in the United States is declining, the shrinking of fossil fuel reserves may

21-11   **Nuclear Power Reactors in the United States**

Operating	Under construction	Reactor type
● 26	○ 25	Boiling Water Reactor (BWR)
◼ 48	☐ 54	Pressurized Water Reactor (PWR)
▲ 1	—	High Temperature Gas-Cooled Reactor (HTGR)
—	☆ 1	Liquid Metal Fast Breeder Reactor (LMFBR)
75	80	

Alabama

Decatur ● ● ●
Dothan ◼ ◼
Scottsboro ☐ ☐

Arizona

Wintersburg ☐ ☐ ☐

Arkansas

ᴸope County ◼ ◼

California

Camp Pendleton ◼
Eureka ●

Sacramento County ◼
San Clemente ☐ ☐
San Luis Obispo ☐ ☐

Colorado

Platteville ▲

Connecticut

Haddam Neck ◼
Waterford ● ◼ ☐

Florida

Crystal River ◼
Florida City ◼ ◼

Fort Pierce ☐
Hutchinson's Island ◼

Georgia

Baxley ● ●
Waynesboro ☐ ☐

Illinois

Braidwood ☐ ☐
Byron ☐ ☐
Clinton ○ ○
Grundy County ● ● ●
Rock Island ● ●
Seneca ○ ○
Zion ◼ ◼

Indiana

Madison ☐ ☐
Westchester ○

Iowa

Cedar Rapids ●

Kansas

Burlington ☐

Louisiana

St. Francisville ○
Taft ☐

21-11   **Nuclear Power Reactors in the United States** (continued)

Maine
Wiscasset ■

Maryland
Lusby ■ ■

Massachusetts
Plymouth ●
Rowe ■

Michigan
Benton Harbor ■ ■
Charlevoix County ●
Covert Township ■
Midland □ □
Newport ○

Minnesota
Monticello ●
Red Wing ■ ■

Mississippi
Corinth □ □
Port Gibson ○ ○

Missouri
Fulton □ □

Nebraska
Nemaha County ●
Washington County ■

New Hampshire
Seabrook □ □

New Jersey
Forked River ●
Salem ■ ■ ○ ○

New York
Brookhaven ○
Buchanan ■ ■
Jamesport □ □
Ontario ■
Oswego ● ●
Scriba ○

North Carolina
Bonsal □ □ □ □
Brunswick County ● ●
Mount Holly ■ □

Ohio
Moscow ○
Ottawa County ■

Oregon
Columbia County ■

Pennsylvania
Berwick ○ ○
Middletown
  (Three Mile Island) ■ ■
Peach Bottom ● ●
Pottstown ○ ○
Shippingport ■ □

South Carolina
Cherokee County □ □ □
Clover □ □
Hartsville ■
Jenkinsville □
Oconee County ■ ■ ■

Tennessee
Daisy ■ ■
Hartsville ○ ○ ○ ○

Hawkins County ○ ○
Oak Ridge
  (Clinch River) ☆
Spring City □ □

Texas
Bay City □ □
Glen Rose □ □

Vermont
Vernon ●

Virginia
Louisa County ■ ■
Mineral □
Surry County ■ ■

Washington
Richland □ □ ○
Satsop □ □

Wisconsin
Genoa ●
Kewaunee ■
Manitowoc County ■ ■

Shown are the commercial nuclear power reactors in operation or under construction in the United States in 1981. In addition to these, about fourteen power reactors have been shut down; this includes the Enrico Fermi reactor in Detroit (a breeder reactor), which was shut down in 1972 following operational problems, one of which was a fuel-melting incident. Included in this list is the Three Mile Island site, where the well-known disaster led to the shutdown of both reactors, of which unit 2 had just attained full-power operation. Also shown is the Clinch River plant, a demonstration fast-breeder reactor under construction amid controversy over its economic justification.

eventually make nuclear energy more attractive again. Thus continued study of possible reactor types is warranted, with special attention to designs that offer inherent protection against major release of radioactivity.

Meanwhile, the study of nuclear fusion reactions as a source of electrical power has been receiving generous funding. The prospect of practical fusion power plants is very appealing: the primary fuel material, deuterium, is in plentiful supply if it can be economically separated from ocean waters; and there may be little chance that a fusion reactor will be subject to catastrophic failure leading to a massive release of radioactivity.

However, there are enormous difficulties to be overcome. A fusion power reactor would be based on the reactions:

$$D + D \rightarrow T + p + (energy)$$
$$D + D \rightarrow He\text{-}3 + n + (energy)$$

In the first, two deuterium (D) nuclei are converted to tritium (T), a proton, and energy; in the second, the product is helium (He), a neutron, and energy.

It is relatively easy for a neutron, being without electrical charge, to penetrate a nucleus and cause fission of a heavy atom. However, a fusion reaction requires that two nuclei combine in spite of their positive electrical charge which causes the nuclei to repel each other strongly. For a fusion event to occur, the interacting particles must have a large kinetic energy. At present, fusion is not very attractive as an energy source because the energy needed to establish conditions for fusion appears comparable to that released by the reactions. There is, however, some interest in using a fusion reaction as a source of high energy neutrons to drive fission reactions.

For the remainder of this century, water-cooled fission reactors will form the bulk of nuclear electrical-generating capacity in the United States and even abroad. However, use of advanced reactors and fuel reprocessing has been attractive in Western Europe where there is substantial dependence on nuclear energy. The importance of advanced reactors in the United States is not so clear since the choice of energy supplies is greater and the potential for increasing the efficiency of energy use is substantial.

The possibilities for more resource-efficient nuclear energy are many, including the use of reprocessed uranium and plutonium fuels in present light-water reactors and use of breeder reactors to improve utilization of uranium. Reliance on advanced nuclear reactors brings with it dependence on nuclear fuel-reprocessing facilities. This would increase public exposure to radioactive materials and open the possibility that relatively enriched fissile material could reach the hands of those who would make weapons. A decision to reprocess and recycle nuclear fuel is therefore not easy, although the choice has already been made in many countries.

Suggested Readings

The material of this chapter is drawn largely from Anthony Nero, *A Guidebook to Nuclear Reactors,* which includes a wealth of information on nuclear power reactors, fuel cycles, fuel processing, environmental hazards from radioactive emissions, and safety aspects of nuclear power. Annotated references to further source materials are included. Basic references on nuclear engineering include *Nuclear Reactor Engineering* by Glasstone and Sesonske, and *Introduction to Nuclear Engineering* by John LaMarsh. The LaMarsh book includes material on the biological effects of nuclear radiation and on radiation protection standards. Technical aspects of nuclear fuel cycles from the uranium mine through spent fuel reprocessing are treated in H. W. Graves, *Nuclear Fuel Management.* The pages of *Scientific American* often contain material of interest concerning nuclear energy, including an important article on breeder reactors ("Fast Breeder Reactors," Glenn T. Seaborg and J. L. Bloom) and an article on spent fuel reprocessing ("The Reprocessing of Nuclear Fuels," W. P. Bebbington). *Nuclear Power Issues and Choices,* by the Nuclear Energy Policy Study Group, and *Nuclear Lessons* by Richard Curtis and Elizabeth Hogan are books of analysis and opinion on the question of whether the need for energy justifies the risk to health and the environment brought about by exploiting nuclear power.

BEBBINGTON, W. P. "The Reprocessing of Nuclear Fuels." *Scientific American,* December 1976, p. 30.

CURTIS, RICHARD, AND ELIZABETH HOGAN. *Nuclear Lessons.* Harrisburg, Penn.: Stackpole Books, 1980.

GLASSTONE, S., AND A. SESONSKE. *Nuclear Reactor Engineering.* New York: Van Nostrand, Reinhold, 1963.

GRAVES, H. W. *Nuclear Fuel Management.* New York: J. Wiley, 1979.

LAMARSH, JOHN R. *Introduction to Nuclear Engineering.* Reading, Mass.: Addison-Wesley, 1975.

NERO, ANTHONY V., JR. *A Guidebook to Nuclear Reactors.* Berkeley, Calif.: University of California Press, 1979.

NUCLEAR ENERGY POLICY STUDY GROUP. *Nuclear Power Issues and Choices.* Cambridge, Mass.: Ballinger, 1977.

SEABORG, G. T. AND J. L. BLOOM. "Fast Breeder Reactors." *Scientific American,* November 1970, p. 13.

This solar home in western Tennessee embodies many ideas to achieve both passive solar heating in winter and summer cooling without powered air conditioning. The house maintains indoor temperature within 68 to 75 degrees throughout the year (1975) and is reported to be affordable by a middle-income family.

22. Energy Economics

Gordon Thompson is a consulting engineer and scientist who has worked for many years in the United States and Europe on energy, environmental, and international security problems. His discussion addresses controversies about the economic benefits of nuclear power—the original dream of low-cost energy, the sober realities of practice, and the economic rivalries between nuclear energy and energy from alternative sources, both traditional and novel.

UNTIL THE EARLY seventies, it was generally assumed in the United States and elsewhere that energy consumption would continue to rise indefinitely, in consort with gross national product (GNP). Many people also assumed that nuclear power would fulfill its earlier promise by providing, during the seventies and beyond, a significant and growing fraction of the energy supply.

Events of the last decade have confirmed the different view espoused by a minority of earlier analysts. Energy supply has been characterized by growing real costs, arising from resource limitations, technical difficulties, and the need to limit environmental damage. These higher real costs have played a major role not only in damping the growth of energy consumption but also in slowing total economic growth.

Nuclear fission power has exemplified the new trends. In its earlier days, this energy source was envisioned as cheap and benign. It was hoped that nuclear power would alleviate or remove the problems of scarcity, environmental pollution, and foreign dependence which, in various ways, characterize fossil fuel use. This vision has been only partially realized. Nuclear power is now widely perceived as dangerous. Its economics are increasingly unfavorable and, in consequence, many proposed or partially built plants have been cancelled.

The Evolution of Energy Consumption, Supply, and Cost

Total energy consumption in the United States showed a steady growth from 1950 to 1973, followed by a decline or slower growth from 1974 to 1980. The growth of U.S. electricity consumption was similarly inhibited after 1973. Despite the behavior of the later period, annual per capita consumption of all energy, for the entire period of 1950 to 1980, grew from 220 million British Thermal Units (BTU) to 350 million BTU (a 56 percent increase), whereas annual per capita electricity consumption grew

Gordon Thompson

Thompson is a staff scientist at the Union of Concerned Scientists.

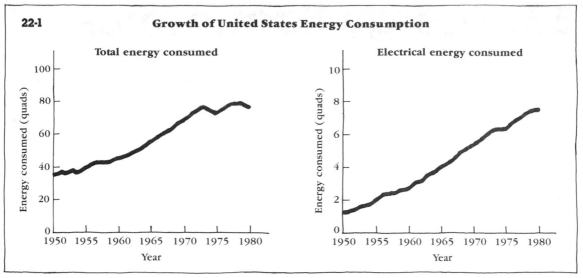

22-1   **Growth of United States Energy Consumption**

Total annual energy and electricity consumption in the United States, 1950–80. One quad is 10[15] British ther-mal units and is roughly the energy produced by one nuclear power plant operating for thirty-five years.

from 7.9 million BTU to 33.5 million BTU (a 320 percent increase).[1] (Note: one million BTU is equivalent to 293 kilowatt-hours.)

From 1950 to 1980, the residential and commercial share of total energy consumption rose from about 30 to 36 percent. Over the same period, the industrial share fell from 44 to 40 percent and the transportation share declined from about 27 to 24 percent. Residential and commercial electricity consumption markedly expanded its share of total electricity consumption, from 35 percent in 1950 to 56 percent in 1980.[2]

Rapid growth in per capita energy consumption, as experienced until the early seventies, was associated with declining real prices of fossil fuels and electricity. For example, the price of residential electricity, measured in constant 1975 dollars, fell from almost fifteen cents per kwhr in 1940 to about three cents per kwhr in 1970.[3] After 1973, the drop in demand growth was accompanied by increases in real energy prices. Total energy expenditures in the United

States rose from a minimum of about 8.5 percent of GNP, in the years prior to 1974, up to 15 percent in 1980. Electricity expenditures rose from a minimum of about 2.2 percent of GNP, prior to 1974, up to 3.7 percent in 1980.

Until the early seventies, net energy imports accounted for only a small fraction of GNP. However, these imports have become significant, accounting for 2.7 percent of GNP in 1980. Oil forms the bulk of energy imports, coal offsetting this in the net balance through a moderate export trade.

The sharp rises in fossil fuel prices and electricity prices after 1973 are frequently attributed to the cartel actions of the Organization of Petroleum Exporting Countries (OPEC). It should be noted, however, that OPEC's actions have been possible only because the real costs of employing new energy resources are now much greater than in previous decades. Resource limitations now demand greater capital and operating expenditures—for example, for enhanced recovery techniques in oil fields. Mitigation of

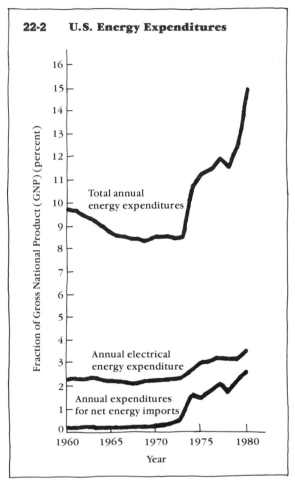

22-2   U.S. Energy Expenditures

These graphs show how imports of oil have satisfied U.S. demand not met by domestic supplies after world shortages drove up prices.

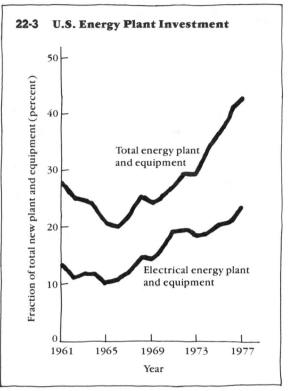

22-3   U.S. Energy Plant Investment

An increasing portion of expenditures for new plants and equipment in the United States is committed to facilities for energy supply.

environmental damage likewise requires greater expenditures, as in the scrubbing of the flue gases from coal-fired power plants. Investments in energy supply have therefore absorbed more of the available investment capital. The fraction of new plant and equipment expenditures in the United States committed to energy supply rose from a minimum of 20 percent in 1966 to 43 percent in 1977. A similar increase occurred in the electric utility portion of the energy indus-

try. Thus the real costs of employing new energy resources were rising even before 1973.

Nuclear power now accounts for some 11 percent of U.S. electric utility output, playing a role comparable to that of hydroelectric power. Coal provides for 51 percent of electric utility output. The share of total fossil fuel consumption now devoted to electricity generation is 26 percent, although the shares of coal and oil consumption devoted to this purpose are 78 percent and 8 percent, respectively.

Nuclear power made its first significant contribution to U.S. electric utility generation in 1960, showing rapid growth thereafter until 1978. Output from nuclear plants has declined slightly since 1978, reflecting shutdowns of re-

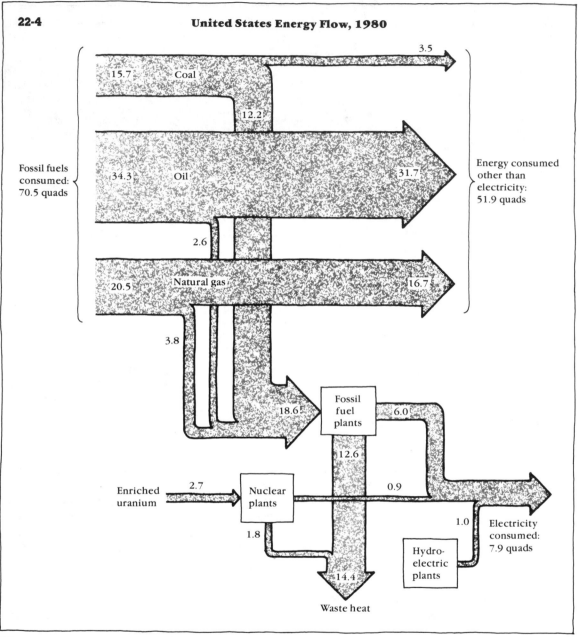

22-4   **United States Energy Flow, 1980**

The amounts are given in quads. About 0.1 quad of electricity was used to produce enriched uranium for the seventy-five nuclear plants in operation.

22-5 **Sources of Electrical Energy Production**

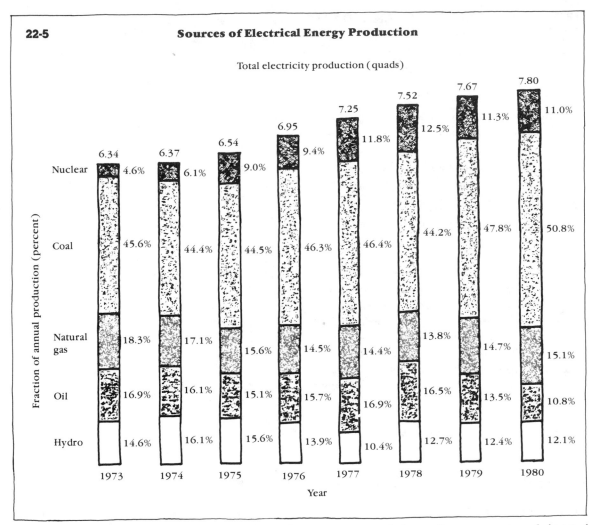

Total electricity production (quads)

Fraction of annual production (percent)

	1973	1974	1975	1976	1977	1978	1979	1980
Total	6.34	6.37	6.54	6.95	7.25	7.52	7.67	7.80
Nuclear	4.6%	6.1%	9.0%	9.4%	11.8%	12.5%	11.3%	11.0%
Coal	45.6%	44.4%	44.5%	46.3%	46.4%	44.2%	47.8%	50.8%
Natural gas	18.3%	17.1%	15.6%	14.5%	14.4%	13.8%	14.7%	15.1%
Oil	16.9%	16.1%	15.1%	15.7%	16.9%	16.5%	13.5%	10.8%
Hydro	14.6%	16.1%	15.6%	13.9%	10.4%	12.7%	12.4%	12.1%

Year

Nuclear power has more than doubled its share of electrical energy production from 1973 to 1980, whereas use of oil has shrunk. Coal is likely to have an important role in any future expansion of electrical energy production.

actors such as those at Three Mile Island (TMI). Coal-fired plants, however, have exhibited a steadily rising output, both to meet a slowly rising demand and to substitute for the rapidly declining output of oil-fired plants.

Recent stagnation in the output of nuclear plants has been accompanied by cancellation of many plants during their planning or construc- tion phases. During 1973 to 1980 the popula- tion of actual and potential plants fell from a peak of 236 units in 1975 to 172 units in 1980. Further cancellations occurred in 1981.

Trends in energy and electricity consump- tion, and in the role of nuclear power, have con- founded earlier projections by the nuclear power industry. For example, the U.S. Atomic

22-6   STATUS OF UNITED STATES NUCLEAR POWER PLANTS

Year	1973	1974	1975	1976	1977	1978	1979	1980
Reactors Licensed (by NRC) for Commercial Operation	40	53	56	62	67	71	71	75
Construction Permits (from NRC) Held	51	58	69	72	80	90	91	82
Construction Permits (from NRC) Pending	58	80	73	66	52	32	21	12
Reactor Units on Order but Construction Permit Not Applied For	48	28	19	16	13	9	3	3
Reactor Units Announced but Not Yet Ordered	20	16	19	19	9	4	0	0
Total Number of Existing or Potential Reactor Units	217	235	236	235	221	206	186	172

The decline in the number of construction permits held or pending reflects cancellation of nuclear plants by electric utility companies.

Energy Commission (AEC) published such a projection in 1974 to justify a breeder reactor program. This projection put 1980 total energy consumption at 94 quadrillion (10^{15}) BTU and electricity consumption at 10.2 quadrillion BTU. Actual 1980 consumptions of total energy and of electricity were 76 quadrillion BTU and 7.4 quadrillion BTU, respectively. More seriously, the AEC projected a continuing growth in all forms of energy consumption, including a doubling of U.S. oil consumption between the years 1975 and 2000. The AEC also projected that nuclear power would generate 28 percent of the nation's electricity in 1980 and 62 percent in the year 2000.[4] As mentioned above, nuclear plants actually provided 11 percent of electrical generation in 1980. It now appears that the projected energy and electricity consumptions were unrealistic. Nuclear power has not fulfilled the role projected for it by the AEC and others.

Costs of Electricity from Nuclear and Coal Plants

Utilities have turned from nuclear plants to coal plants largely for economic reasons. Study of generating costs reported for the year 1979 for nuclear and coal plants brought on line in the years 1970 to 1978 shows that newer nuclear plants tended to yield more expensive

power than newer coal plants. This ranking of generating costs is the reverse of that for plants brought on line in the early seventies. Oil plants produced relatively expensive electricity during this period (primarily due to high fuel cost), which explains their declining role.

The evidence suggests that the nuclear/coal cost trend will continue to move in favor of coal plants. Analysis by Charles Komanoff, using an extensive cost-data base, projects life-cycle generating costs (in constant 1979 dollars), for new plants completed in 1988, of 4.8 c/kwhr for nuclear plants and 3.9 c/kwhr for coal plants.[5] This projection assumes quite clean coal plants, as discussed below.

Electricity generated by coal plants has become more expensive, the increase in the capital cost component arising largely from the additional costs of effluent control. Technology for such control has become highly effective, however, so that new coal plants release less pollution than oil plants burning low-sulfur oil. A new coal plant on line in 1988 should be able to release less than 0.2 pounds of sulfur dioxide per million BTU of fuel burned, compared with 0.3 pound for an oil plant burning low-sulfur (0.3 percent) oil and the 3.8 pounds released by a typical new 1971 coal plant.[6]

The cost of electricity from a new 1988 coal

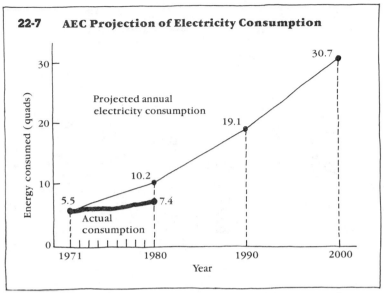

22-7   AEC Projection of Electricity Consumption

In 1974 the Atomic Energy Commission projected future U.S. electricity consumption up to the year 2000 and the role of nuclear power. The fraction of electrical energy projected to be produced by nuclear plants was 28 percent in 1980, 52 percent in 1990, and 62 percent in 2000. It is already evident that the projections were optimistic.

plant (cited above as 3.9 c/kwhr) assumes full use of such effluent control. In addition, it assumes escalation of coal cost (in real terms) at 2.3 percent per year (the 1974–79 rate).

The increased generating costs of nuclear plants arise largely from increased capital costs, the sources of which are not easily determined.[7] However, they are clearly linked to efforts to reduce the risk of accidents. Nuclear plants have been subject to numerous modifications both during and after construction, in large part mandated by the Nuclear Regulatory Commission (NRC). The TMI reactor accident of 1979 has motivated the NRC to demand additional modifications.

The New Perspective: Energy as a Supplier of Services

With the recent rise in energy prices has come a growing awareness that it is now more economical to invest in efficient techniques for using energy rather than in new sources of energy supply. This awareness is spreading rather slowly, however, perhaps because institutions and expertise have hitherto been focused mainly on energy-supply expansion.

The potential for saving both energy and money can be illustrated by the differing annual energy budgets of a new house under several options. Energy-conserving techniques such as thermal insulation and improved appliances can substantially reduce primary fuel use (including fuel for electricity production). Moreover, these techniques can lead to lower overall expenditures for energy (including operating, maintenance, and capital charges). It is important to note that no reduction in living standards is required to achieve these savings.

The overall capital requirements of different options can be illustrated by two examples:

1. Gas heat and hot water in a house built to the

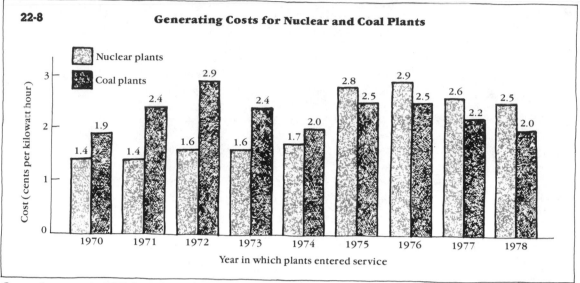

22-8 **Generating Costs for Nuclear and Coal Plants**

Generating costs in 1979 for U.S. nuclear and coal plants entering service from 1970 to 1978.

standards of the Farmers Home Administration (FHA), with conventional appliances

2. Gas heat and hot water in a thermally tight house, with more efficient appliances

The second (conservation) option yields an annual primary fuel use that is 44 percent of that for the first option (an annual saving of 120 million BTU). To achieve this decreased fuel use, a net increase in investment of $1,500 (constant 1976 dollars) in the house is required. At the same time, the second option permits a reduction in additional energy supply investments (for pipelines, powerplants, and so on) from $6,900 to $3,300 (constant 1976 dollars), yielding a net capital savings to the nation of $2,100 (constant 1976 dollars) per house.[8]

Investment in energy-efficient techniques is appropriate up to the point at which their marginal cost is equal to the cost of supplying energy. This concept can be illustrated by considering the potential nationwide energy savings if new electric appliances were made more effi-

cient. An energy saving of approximately 40 percent is achievable in this sector by the year 2000 for a cost at or below the 1980 average cost of residential electricity. Since the cost of electricity supply in the year 2000 is likely to be higher than in 1980, even further savings are likely to be available.

If all cost-effective investments in energy-efficient techniques were made, it would be possible to achieve further economic growth while primary energy requirements fall.[9] Indeed, pursuit of the most cost-effective energy investment strategy would enhance the prospects for economic growth.

Demand for electricity could fall if a minimum-cost energy strategy were pursued. Such a fall would have major implications for the electric utility industry, which has traditionally planned for annual load growth of about 7 percent, as experienced up to 1974. Although proposed generating plants with a total capacity of 155 gigawatts were canceled between 1974 and 1978, utilities may still be overbuilding. An annual demand growth of 2.5 percent, for example, would yield an unnecessarily large national reserve margin (generating capacity in excess of peak demand, expressed as a fraction of that demand) of 57 percent in 1988, if all scheduled generating capacity were completed. Cancellation of half of all scheduled capacity would still yield a comfortable 32 percent reserve margin in 1988.[10]

Other Generating Sources

As mentioned above, there would be no urgent need for new generating capacity if a cost-effective energy strategy were pursued. Nevertheless, some new capacity other than coal or nuclear plants might be a sound investment over the next one or two decades. In the longer term, an energy economy based on renewable energy sources (sun, wind, and so on) is feasible.[11] Transition to such an economy would require some use of renewable energy systems in the near term, to create an appropriate industrial base.

While fossil fuels continue to be used, it is possible to generate electricity from them more efficiently than at present. Some 18 percent of U.S. fossil fuel consumption is now wasted in electric plants, being discharged through cooling towers or into nearby bodies of water. This waste can be reduced through *cogeneration,* whereby waste heat from electrical generation is used for space heat or industrial process heat.

Industrial cogeneration is particularly interesting because there are many heat-consuming industries that operate continuously. These industries provide suitable sites for baseload cogeneration units. By the year 2000, the potential for generation from baseload industrial cogeneration units could equal that from 200 gigawatts of electric generating capacity in central stations, yielding an annual fuel saving of about 5 quadrillion BTU.[12]

In many instances, the electric output of an industrial cogeneration unit would be well in excess of the requirements of the host industry. Therefore, the economics of cogeneration are sensitive to the price a cogenerator can obtain for the sale of excess electricity. Under Section 210 of the Public Utilities Regulatory Policy Act of 1978, utilities are required to pay a price for this electricity that is equal to their own avoided generation cost. However, due to the excess generating capacity prevailing in much of the country, avoided costs are now high only in those regions that are heavily dependent on oil- or gas-fired central plants.

During a transition to a renewable-energy economy, certain cogeneration plants (such as those that burn low or medium BTU gas) could be adapted to biomass-derived fuels.

Renewable energy sources can be harnessed directly for electricity production, the leading techniques being hydropower, wind turbines, and photovoltaic cells.

Hydropower now provides an electric output comparable in amount to that of nuclear plants, and the technical potential for a substantial increase in hydro generation exists. However, only a small part of this potential is likely to be exploited because of the environmental impacts entailed. Expansion of generating capacity at existing dams is likely, with a trend toward use of hydro plants in periods of peak demand.[13]

Wind turbines may play a growing role in the near term, primarily to displace fuel used in conventional plants. Due to wind's intermittent nature, turbines at any given site cannot be relied upon to displace conventional generating capacity. If turbines at dispersed sites were interconnected, however, their combined output would become more reliable. In fact, the technical potential exists to provide most of the present U.S. electric consumption from a continental-scale interconnected array of wind turbines. Electricity could be supplied at a cost of the same order as the cost of power from new coal and nuclear plants.[14]

Photovoltaic cells also show promise in the near term, particularly if the U.S. Department of Energy's price goals are achieved. These goals call for a system capital cost of $1,600–$2,600 per peak kilowatt in 1986 and of $1,100–$1,800 per peak kilowatt in 1990 (costs in constant 1980 dollars). Attainment of such goals would place photovoltaic cells in a strong competitive position, initially for dispersed, and later for utility, application.[15]

It should be noted that the future of renewable energy technologies will be affected by national policies. The Reagan administration is widely viewed as hostile to renewable energy. The administration has proposed substantial budget cuts in solar (and conservation) programs, while pressing ahead with nuclear programs.

Unaccounted Costs

Present accounting ignores a number of environmental, social, and other costs associated with energy production. There is, however, a slow, often resisted, but perhaps inevitable trend to account for these costs. As mentioned previously, coal plants have exhibited increased capital costs largely because of requirements for pollution control.

For fossil fuels, one of the most serious unaccounted costs is the potential climatic perturbation arising from accumulation of carbon dioxide (CO_2) in the atmosphere.[16] For oil in particular, global security implications are also very important. However, this consideration has limited relevance to the generation of electricity since the use of oil is rapidly declining.

Nuclear power is accompanied by a unique set of costs. Serious reactor accidents could occur, potentially causing thousands of short-term and delayed deaths and billions of dollars in property damage.[17] The cost of insurance against such events is unknown because the probability of reactor accidents is extremely difficult, perhaps impossible, to determine. The commercial insurance sector has not addressed this question because the Price-Anderson Act of 1957 exempted the nuclear industry from liability exceeding $560 million.[18] Disposal of radioactive waste and the decommissioning of nuclear plants may prove more expensive than anticipated. Finally, diffusion of nuclear technology enhances the risk of nuclear weapons proliferation, although quantification of this increased risk is essentially impossible.

Renewable energy technologies are also accompanied by environmental and social costs. For example, hydroelectric power requires the flooding of river valleys, intensive biomass energy farming disrupts existing land uses, and wind power requires the construction of visually obtrusive wind turbines. Provided that renewable sources are not grossly exploited, however, their "unaccounted" costs do not seem of the same order as climatic change induced by carbon dioxide from fossil fuel combustion, nuclear weapons proliferation from plutonium in spent nuclear fuel, and the hazard of major reactor accidents.

Suggested Readings

The book by Ross and Williams provides a carefully documented analysis of past energy trends and potential energy futures. These authors conclude that economics and environmental concerns call for improved efficiency of energy use and increasing use of renewable energy sources. The Union of Concerned Scientists has sponsored a book edited by Kendall and Nadis that catalogs the problems associated with traditional energy policies and presents the technical case for preferring efficient use of renewable sources. Less technical than the other two books, the Harvard Business School study reaches similar conclusions. The authors argue that efficient use of energy and increasing roles for renewable sources are good business policies.

Ross, M. H., and R. H. Williams. *Our Energy: Regaining Control.* New York: McGraw-Hill, 1981.

Kendall, H. W., and S. J. Nadis, eds. *Energy Strategies: Toward a Solar Future,* report of the Union of Concerned Scientists. Cambridge, Mass.: Ballinger, 1980.

Stobaugh, R., and D. Yergin, eds. *Energy Future,* report of the Energy Project at the Harvard Business School. New York: Ballantine Books, 1979.

Part Eight

Action

June 12, 1982, New York City: Demonstrators march in protest against President Reagan's policy of attaining nuclear superiority before engaging in serious arms control negotiations.

23. The Future in Our Hands: Shaping Responsible Public Policy

Pamela Solo and Mike Jendrzejczyk are co-directors of a program concerned with the future of the Rocky Flats, Colorado, materials processing plant of the nuclear weapons industry. In the belief that public policy can be decisively influenced by an informed citizenry, they have collected a list of resources for those interested in organizing citizen groups: statements by political figures, religious leaders, labor officials; and information about national organizations actively concerned with nuclear policy in the United States. Brief chronologies of disarmament activities and public opposition to nuclear power are included.

BEFORE AND AFTER the first blinding flashes of nuclear fireballs over Japan in 1945, the development and stockpiling of nuclear weapons has been barely visible to the public. The United States tested the first deliverable fusion weapon in 1952; in the sixties, tens of thousands of U.S. nuclear warheads were stockpiled and deployed. Though the cold war and the quickening arms race have been common knowledge, few people knew of the vast industrial complex that produces the U.S. nuclear arsenal.

Despite public recognition of the destructiveness of nuclear war, the political climate in the United States has tolerated successively increased levels of nuclear armament. This is partly because of trust placed in nuclear weapons as unquestioned protectors of "national security" through deterrence of nuclear war. It is also partly because the apocalyptic danger that the weapons represent—so different from all past human experience—seems unreal and remote. The issues seem irrelevant to everyday life, but they are not. Each person on Earth carries a small amount of radiostrontium in their bones, and radioactive iodine in the thyroid, that would not be there but for the testing of nuclear weapons. Each person is affected by the large sums spent on these weapons and their delivery systems, whether they help foot the bill, experience a higher cost of living, or receive reduced U.S. aid.

Worldwide outrage in the late fifties over the effect of radioactive fallout brought about cessation of nuclear weapons testing in the atmosphere by the superpowers. In the late sixties, pressure from Americans concerned about the placement of nuclear-tipped missiles in their midst helped force the Pentagon to shelve plans for an ABM missile system. These two cases, in which aroused segments of the public success-

Pamela Solo
Mike Jendrzejczyk

Solo is on the staff of the American Friends Service Committee. Jendrzejczyk is on the staff of the Fellowship of Reconciliation.

fully limited the nuclear arms race in their own self-interest, demonstrate that nuclear policy can be influenced by the voters.

The Road Taken

Republican and Democratic administrations during the past three decades have voiced alarm about the unprecedented dangers of the arms race. Each has made nominal commitments to the absolute need to abolish nuclear weapons. The SALT I agreement is in force as is the partial test ban. President Carter set the goal of "zero nuclear weapons," but the goal has been abandoned.

Now under President Reagan, the United States proposes $1.6 trillion in military expenditures over the next five years, of which a substantial portion is allocated for nuclear weapons and delivery systems. It would take 2,740 years to spend this amount at the rate of $1 million per day. The economic costs of the arms race are largely born by lower-income and middle-in-

come Americans. The U.S. budget for fiscal year 1983 makes a massive shift of taxpayer dollars from social programs to military spending. Inflation is fueled by competition for the specialized talents demanded by sophisticated modern arms, and the U.S. position in the world marketplace is weakened.

The U.S. government has chosen a policy that threatens war over oil, rather than an energy program to achieve greater self-sufficiency through alternative energy sources and real conservation. Ultra right forces blatantly promote the following view, so accurately summarized by Penny Lernoux:

Once the permanence of world warfare is assumed, national security becomes the first priority of geopolitics. Individual rights are sacrificed to the power of the state, since only it can defend and develop the nation. Critics of government policy are considered traitors because in wartime opinions are weapons and everyone is a friend or foe. Civilian politicians having proved inept in

23-1   **THE PRICE OF STRATEGIC SUPERIORITY**

Weapon System	Units Planned	Unit Cost	Total Cost
		(millions of dollars)	
Trident Submarine	12	2,000	24,000
Long-range ballistic missile submarine			
Trident I	500	12	6,000
Long-range ballistic missile for Trident and Poseidon submarines			
Trident II		(not known)	
High-accuracy follow-on missile for Trident submarines			
ALCM	3,000	2	6,000
Air-launched cruise missile carried by B-52 and B-1 aircraft			
B-1	100	400	40,000
Supersonic strategic bomber aircraft			
MX	100	300	30,000
High-accuracy, multi-warhead intercontinental missile			

These figures indicate the impact of the strategic arms race on the U.S. economy. The MX and Trident II are high-accuracy missiles that would give the United States a counterforce or first-strike capability.

government, only the military can run the state and press the war against international communism.

An Agenda for Action

There is much to be done to stem this wave of militarism. We must question its purpose. Do we really feel so much in need of Middle East oil that we would risk our society to "protect our interests" in the Persian Gulf? Exactly how much armament is needed to discourage an invasion of Europe? Doesn't the missile race create more instability and less security?

The SALT I Treaty was a major step in international arms control. SALT II is a useful next step. However, negotiations and treaties only tend to manage the growth of the arms race. This is part of the rationale behind the freeze campaign, calling for an *immediate* freeze by the United States and the Soviet Union on testing, production, and deployment of new nuclear weapons and first-strike delivery systems, followed by negotiated reductions. Carefully drafted by Randall Forsberg, an arms control analyst, the "CALL TO HALT THE ARMS RACE" freeze proposal is not only a rallying cry, but a specific policy alternative. It has gained broad public support and endorsements from scientists, religious leaders, members of Congress, and former military and governmental figures.

It is also useful for citizens and arms control experts to call for independent U.S. initiatives towards a freeze and multilateral disarmament. Building visible and vocal support for such initiatives is crucial to the success of disarmament efforts in the 1980s. There is a wide range of initiatives that our government can take to build confidence and apply pressure on the other side to respond in kind. For example, the United States could put into place a cut-off in fissionable materials production; declare a moratorium on nuclear testing and resume negotiations towards a comprehensive test ban treaty; or cancel its plans to deploy the MX, cruise, and Pershing II missiles. Another possible initiative, proposed by George Kennan, Robert McNamara, and others, would involve a major change in U.S. policy: namely, renouncing the first use of nuclear weapons in any future conflict.

The U.S. government must be challenged for its actions done in the name of national security. Who defines "national security" in a democracy? Are there not other routes with a better prospect for bringing economic and physical security?

Let us recall the words of Albert Einstein that so aptly express the sentiments of many scientists who worked on the bomb:

> We must take the facts of atomic energy to the village square and from there a decision should be made about its future.

Suggested Readings

ALRIDGE, ROBERT. *The Counterforce Syndrome.* Washington, D.C. Institute for Policy Studies, 1980.

The Boston Study Group. *The Price of Defense.* New York: Times Books, 1980.

GYORGY, ANNA. *No Nukes: Everyone's Guide to Nuclear Power.* Boston: South End Press, 1979.

Makers of the Nuclear Holocaust. Denver: American Friends Service Committee, and Fellowship of Reconciliation, 1980.

THOMPSON, E. P., AND DAN SMITH. *Protest and Survive.* New York: Monthly Review Press, 1981.

WOLFE, ALAN. *The Rise and Fall of the Soviet Threat.* Washington, D.C.: Institute for Policy Studies, 1981.

©1981 Hal Aqua

THE FUTURE IN OUR HANDS
FREEZE THE ARMS RACE U.S.-U.S.S.R.

Proposal for a Mutual US-Soviet Nuclear-Weapon Freeze

To improve national and international security, the United States and the Soviet Union should stop the nuclear arms race. Specifically, they should adopt a mutual freeze on the testing, production and deployment of nuclear weapons and of missiles and new aircraft designed primarily to deliver nuclear weapons. This is an essential, verifiable first step toward lessening the risk of nuclear war and reducing the nuclear arsenals.

Over the next five years, the Federal Government plans the largest military buildup of our country's history. We will spend over one trillion dollars for the military and increase our stockpile of 30,000 nuclear warheads by another 9,000. New missile systems with "first-strike" capability may seduce the U.S. or the U.S.S.R. to risk nuclear war.

Military expansion will require financial and human resources causing higher inflation, fewer jobs and further industrial decline. Cuts in social and human service programs to fund this military expansionism only further undermine our country's strength.

It is time to say "enough is enough". The social, economic and environmental costs of preparing for nuclear war represent policy-making gone mad. It is up to us to press for some alternatives. The future is in our hands. Join in the call to the U.S. and Soviet Union to freeze the arms race.

A SAMPLING OF OPINIONS

Following are excerpts from the written or spoken opinions of prominent individuals in the fields of science, politics, labor, and religion. This sampling represents a broad range of opinion on the military and commercial applications of nuclear technology and reflects concern about contemporary problems such as the stability of the superpower arms race, the testing and deployment of nuclear weapons, the development of nuclear energy, and the disposal of radioactive waste.

Political Figures

Dixy Lee Ray
Governor (Washington State)

Why do I support nuclear power? First, in the question of cost, because it's cheaper; despite all the things that have happened to delay and therefore cause further increases in cost of construction of nuclear power plants ... I agree with Malcolm Forbes of *Forbes Magazine* that the greatest danger of nuclear power is not having enough of it.

Source: Governor Dixy Lee Ray's Speech to the Aikens Lecture Series, University of Vermont, April 13, 1980.

Pat Schroeder
Congresswoman (Colorado)

Once again we have succumbed to the anti-communist hysteria that has prevailed throughout the SALT debate.... By accepting an even more bloated military budget, we have fooled ourselves into believing that we are doing something for the defense of this Nation.... My conscience tells me that we have duped the American people into playing the "more for the military is better game" without telling them what some of the rules are. ... We have created a Soviet monster that we are going to overpower by spending more money for new weapons and more sophisticated technology.... What we have not dealt with is the U.S. monster that is going to overpower us with runaway inflation and increased unemployment.

Source: An Even More Bloated Military Budget, In the House of Representatives, Wednesday, November 28, 1979.

Richard Thornburgh
Governor (Pennsylvania)

I am impressed at how much so many are so sure in the debate that has developed over Three Mile Island, nuclear power and the American energy dilemma since those days of tension last spring.... It suggests that we be exceedingly cautious but not immobile in developing nuclear sources of energy, and exceedingly quick, but not reckless, in developing all of the others. ... We must shift our priorities dramatically toward the clean use of coal, the effective practice of conservation, the rapid development of domestic oil, and the wise use of wind, water, sunshine and other renewable energy sources.

Source: *New York Times*, March 27, 1980.

Morris K. Udall
Congressman (Arizona)

While I believe the nuclear technology has the potential to provide electricity with adverse side effects less than those associated with the available alternatives, I also believe several conditions must be met if this potential is to be achieved.... Reactors must be safe both in fact and in the public perception; nuclear power must be economic in comparison with the alternatives; people must be willing to accept nuclear facilities as neighbors; and there must be a technically and politically viable plan for dealing with nuclear wastes.... Congress should require that the NRC not issue operating licenses for new plants until the Commission certifies that the lessons learned from Three Mile Island have been incorporated into the plant's design, into its operating procedures and into its emergency plan.

Source: *Public Utilities Fortnightly*, June 19, 1980.

Mark O. Hatfield
Senator (Oregon)

SALT II fails to reverse the two most central dangers of the arms race: the increase in weapons and the qualitative improvements which increase the likelihood of using those weapons.... We must convert SALT II into an effective instrument for stopping the nuclear arms race.... For this reason I have introduced an amendment to the SALT II treaty which would mutually prohibit further testing, development, or deployment of any new strategic weapons system not already deployed.... It would prohibit deployment of any additional number of strategic arms beyond what each side possesses.... This moratorium amendment would freeze the strategic arms race ... it would represent a joint declaration that this race is not worth winning, and that we each passed long ago the threshold of sanity in our nuclear weapons competition.

Source: Testimony Before Foreign Relations Committee: SALT II September 18, 1979.

Benjamin L. Hooks
Executive Director
National Association for the Advancement of Colored People

All alternative energy sources should be developed and utilized. Nuclear power, including the breeder, must be vigorously pursued because it will be an essential part of the total fuel mix necessary to sustain an expanding economy.... We are fearful that an energy policy with an overriding concern for the protection of the environment may cause governmental policymakers in this area to lose sight of other more compelling economic and social objectives that are more important to black Americans.... We recognize that nuclear power does present certain problems. ... But we think these problems can be solved through dedicated efforts by government, the scientific community and industry working cooperatively together.... Notwithstanding the claims of opponents of this source of energy, the fact is that nuclear power will be required to meet our future needs for electricity.

Source: NAACP Statement of Policy on National Energy Plan; adopted on April 17, 1978.

John B. Anderson
Congressman (Illinois)

While hoping to preserve nuclear power as an option in the decade ahead, Anderson believes that its further expansion must be halted unless we can achieve and maintain adequate safeguards for the operation of reactors and the management of nuclear wastes.... Anderson believes that our best defense is a military that's lean and flexible.... Accordingly, he's opposed to such schemes as the B-1 bomber and the MX missile, which he feels will increase our military costs without adding to our security.

Source: Position Papers, National Unity Campaign for John Anderson.

Ralph Nader
(Consumer Advocate)

Nuclear power is a technology which involves health and economic risks of the most serious kind. One accident could cause more human destruction than any

civilian technological disaster in the history of mankind. It is an energy source which can be readily replaced, and for those reasons the best course of action would be to close down all existing nuclear power plants as soon as possible.[1] Even many of the advocates of nuclear power have peculiar qualifications to their support. For example, Alvin Weinberg believes in nuclear power, but he doesn't believe the utilities are competent enough to manage it. He believes in a nuclear park with a very strict technological authority—a nuclear priesthood, as he calls it. Edward Teller is a believer in nuclear power, but he thinks somehow it would be better if all the plants were built underground. Ralph Lapp is in favor of nuclear power but he thinks it would be better if plants were built further away from major metropolitan areas. Yet the utilities are still running these plants. The nuclear plants are not being built very far from metropolitan areas, and none of them are being built or are expected to be built underground.... For future generations, at least, we must bequeath a more rational trust. We must discipline ourselves to take care of our energy needs with conservation, with pollution control, with use of fossil fuels, and with rapid development of alternative forms of energy—bioconversion, solar, geothermal, and the rest. Under stress we can produce alternatives. Under stress engineers and scientists become very, very creative. Perhaps we can reorder our priorities and not leave a legacy of plutonium for future generations.[2]

Source: 1. Testimony before Subcommittee on Energy and the Environment, Committee on Interior and Insular Affairs, Hearings on the Price-Anderson Act, July 9, 1979
2. Reprinted from *New Engineer*, October 1975.

Mike McCormack
Congressman (Washington State)

It becomes more and more obvious that one of the greatest strokes of good fortune this nation has experienced is to have our nuclear industry as well advanced as we find it today, ready now to provide much of the energy this nation will need during the next 50 years. Nuclear energy is the cleanest, cheapest, most reliable energy source available, with the least environmental impact of any significant option. Each nuclear plant saves the equivalent of from 10 to 12 million barrels of oil a year. Thus it would require 6 to 7 million barrels of oil a day to produce the same electricity that these 221 plants will generate. This is the equivalent of all of the petroleum the United States imports today.... Just as with any other industry or any other energy technology, nuclear energy has some hazardous aspects, and we must assume that at some time in the future there will be an accident causing property damage, injuries, or even deaths—just as there has been in every other energy technology in this country on many occasions.... We have people who are refusing to face up to the realities, the hard economic, human realities of this day. For the balance of this century this nation must depend on coal and nuclear fission for its energy. This is the reality, and we can talk all we want to about solar energy or geothermal energy or fusion or anything else in an attempt to escape from this truth.

Souce: Reprinted from *New Engineer,* October 1975.

Vernon E. Jordan, Jr.

President
National Urban League

The world's total spending on armics and weapons of destruction comes to over $400 billion. That's nearly three times more than the income of the Third World's poor. Over half of that military bill is accounted for by the United States and Russia. Much of the rest is spent by poor nations, whose people often literally starve while their nation buys jets and tanks. Here at home, the arms race eats up tax dollars and forces cuts in programs needed by our own poor. No one benefits from this situation. The world seems on a road that can only lead to war and waste. It is clear that wild spending on arms and abject poverty are linked.... Critics are saying that the Russians are getting stronger while we're getting weaker. They are trotting out complex technical analyses of American and Russian military strength to support their case.... But the fact is both nations have more than enough firepower to blow each other off the face of the earth. That alone makes it necessary to maintain the momentum of arms limitation agreements and detente. It doesn't mean we've got to love the Russians or ignore their military power. But it does mean that there can be no alternative to talking with them, and to constructing a network of agreements in our mutual interest. So the debate over SALT should not degenerate into a revival of the Cold War. And rejection of SALT would do just that.... Unfortunately, the SALT debate has political side-effects. Senators and the Administration couple backing for SALT with beefing up our missile capabilities. We've already got enough missiles to blow up the world. Now we're

planning to spend over $30 billion on the MX missile, as well. That makes SALT an expensive proposition. Passing SALT should be followed by reconsideration of wasteful spending on weapons systems we don't need.[1]

We should be pragmatic and flexible. We should preserve the environment. Black people, the most urbanized group in the nation, have a stake in clean air and water too. We need jobs, but we also need to be healthy enough to hold those jobs, and that means adopting energy sources that will minimize pollution. And we need jobs, not only in the plants and factories of America, but at policy-making levels at the Department of Energy and environmental offices, where policies affecting our lives are set. Above all, we must remember that a national energy policy cannot be framed in a vacuum. So far, black people and low-income families have been allowed to participate by bearing the burden of energy prices. It is time now for those groups to participate in framing the policies as well, so that their interests, their concerns, and their needs may be honored.[2]

Source 1. News from National Urban League, June 17, 1979.
    2. Environmental Action, March 1978.

Scott M. Matheson

Governor (Utah)

In September of 1979, President Carter announced his proposal to deploy the MX Missile system, on the land, in horizontal multiple protective structures.... He also noted that the most likely site for deployment of the MX Missile system was in the Great Basin desert valleys of Utah and Nevada.... I believe the proposed system is fatally flawed for two very important reasons. First and most critical, it will be at least mid-1986 before the first ten MX Missiles are deployed in 230 shelters. Because the Soviet Union has so many warheads, this will result in only an insignificant increase in the survivability of our strategic land based missiles. Second, it is quite possible that the present MX deployment scheme will be obsolete before it is completed.... Because I believe in a strong national defense and because I am persuaded that Minuteman vulnerability is a real issue, I believe that we must seriously consider alternatives to the administration's proposal.... National security can be defined in many ways. It can be defined in terms of the number of nuclear devices which exist in our stockpiles. It can be measured in conventional weapons and the force readiness of the Army, Navy, Marine Corp and Air Force, an area where we are critically deficient and where any cost savings from MX could be usefully invested. . . . But national security can also be measured in terms which are critically important to the nation and to the state of Utah, such as energy independence and production of the strategic materials. The west in general and Utah specifically have been proposed as the target area not only for MX but for coal development, construction of large coal fired electrical generating plants such as IPP, the development of synthetic fuels from tar sands and oil shale, and the development of critically needed strategic materials. . . . Utah can and will play an important national security role. But I believe it should play that role primarily in terms of helping achieve energy independence—not as a location for the development of a strategic weapons system with such enormous impacts. This is a judgment which I have reached after long and serious soul searching.

Source: Statement made on the MX Missile, June 16, 1980.

Sam Nunn
Senator (Georgia)

I believe that nuclear energy will have to play an important role in our nation's energy future. . . . If America is to reduce our dangerous dependency on uncertain foreign sources of energy supply, alternate energy resources, including nuclear, must continue to be developed. . . . There are simply no risk-free energy sources. This is not to say that there are not certain serious risks involved in the development of nuclear power, and I will certainly support any reasonable efforts to minimize these as much as possible.

Source: Letter dated July 11, 1980.

Caspar W. Weinberger
Secretary of Defense
(Reagan Administration)

The President has determined that our defense budget must be increased if we are to preserve peace and freedom. Today, the budget is not sufficient for our strategic needs. It is clearly inadequate to support our widespread commitments in peacetime. . . . The perception of our inability to respond adequately and promptly has served to encourage Soviet and Soviet-inspired exploitation of areas of instability. . . . One of the most disturbing developments we confront is the continuing deterioration of the balance in intercontinental nuclear arms. We must make large investments in this area to deter the ultimate catastrophe. It is unacceptable to find ourselves today facing the prospect of Soviet strategic superiority and to watch the Soviet Union mass-producing both land-based missiles and a manned bomber fleet, while the U.S. has an open production line for neither. Our descent from a position of clear strategic superiority coincided with our strenuous attempt to bring the arms competition under control through negotiated agreements with the Soviet Union. . . . This Administration remains committed to equitable and verifiable arms control. But, our experience over the last two decades has demonstrated that we are not going to be able to limit the growth in Soviet strategic weapons unless we ourselves are fully prepared to compete.

Source: Statement delivered before the Senate Armed Services Committee on the Reagan administration's military budget proposals (FY 1981–82); excerpted from the *New York Times*, March 5, 1981.

George F. Kennan
Former U.S. Ambassador
to the Soviet Union
(Recipient of Albert Einstein
Peace Prize)

For over 30 years wise and far-seeing people have been warning us about the futility of any war fought with nuclear weapons and about the dangers involved in their cultivation. Some of the first of these voices were those of great scientists, including outstandingly that of Albert Einstein himself. . . . When one looks back today over the history of these warnings, one has the impression that something has now been lost of the sense of urgency, the hopes and the excitement that initially inspired them. . . . Over all these years the competition in the development of nuclear weaponry has proceeded steadily, relentlessly, without the faintest regard for all these warning voices. We have gone on piling weapon upon weapon, missile upon missile, new levels of destructiveness upon old ones. We have done this helplessly, almost involuntarily: like the victims of some sort of hypnotism, like men in a dream, like lemmings headed for the sea. . . . But we must remember that it has been we Americans who, at almost every step of the road, have taken the lead in the development of this sort of weaponry. . . . I can see no way out of this dilemma other than by a bold and sweeping departure—a departure that would cut surgically through the exaggerated anxieties, the self-engendered nightmares, and the sophisticated mathematics of destruction, in which we have all been entangled over these recent years, and would permit us to move, with courage and decision, to the heart of the problem. ... What I would like to see the President do, after due consultation with the Congress, would be to propose to the Soviet government an immediate across-the-boards reduction by 50 per cent of the nuclear arsenals now being maintained by the two superpowers—a reduction affecting in equal measure all forms of the weapon, strategic, medium range, and tactical, as well as all means of their delivery.... In the final week of his life, Albert Einstein signed the last of the collective appeals against the development of nuclear weapons that he was ever to sign.... I would like to quote one sentence from the final paragraph of that statement, not only because it was the last one Einstein ever signed, but because it sums up, I think, all that I have to say on the subject: "We appeal, as human beings to human beings: Remember your humanity, and forget the rest."

Source: Address in accepting the Albert Einstein Peace Prize on May 19, 1981 in Washington, D.C., excerpted from *Disarmament Times* (June 1981) reprint.

Scientists

Dr. Alvin M. Weinberg
Scientist
(Former Director of the Oak
Ridge National Laboratory)

If looked at objectively, in some ways the accident at Three Mile Island is the salvation of nuclear energy. ... The accident showed the possibility of a disaster to be more remote than was previously believed, but it also showed that there were likely to be more accidents and releases of low levels of radiation that people could learn to live with.

Source: *New York Times*, July 5, 1979.

George Wald
Scientist
(Professor Emeritus of Biology, Harvard University; Nobel Prize for Physiology and Medicine, 1967)

Nuclear power is life threatening in all its forms.... Expensive as it would be to shut down the 70 nuclear plants now licensed in the U.S., in the long run it will prove more expensive to keep them going. ... As long as they continue operating they will present dangers of malfunction and accident and will continue to accumulate radioactive wastes that no

one knows how to dispose of safely and that will remain dangerous for tens of thousands of years.... The most prudent and responsible procedure would be to shut them down now....[1] We live in a balance of terror. The United States and the Soviet Union together have already stockpiled nuclear weapons with the explosive force of ten tons of TNT for every man, woman and child on the earth.... My country at present is making three new hydrogen warheads per day. The Soviet Union keeps pace with us.... Getting rid of nuclear stockpiles would defuse the present threat of instant annihilation, it would gain us a little time.[2]

Source: 1. Dr. Wald on Nuclear Power.
       2. Excerpts from an address in Tokyo on August 2, 1974 at the 20th World Conference against Atomic and Hydrogen Bombs.

Dr. Edward A. Martell
Radiochemist
(National Center for Atmospheric
Research)

I hold strongly based convictions that nuclear energy is an unacceptable alternative due to the serious chronic health risks from the long-lived alpha emitting pollutants—plutonium, americium, and curium—with adverse effects on thousands of future generations of man. (sic)

Dr. Linus Pauling
Scientist (Nobel Prize for Chemistry, 1954)

I am opposed to the construction of any more nuclear fission power plants and I believe also that the existing ones should be taken out of commission as soon as circumstances—economic circumstances and circumstances about their safety and about the availability of energy permit it....[1] We deem it imperative that immediate action be taken to effect on international agreement to stop the testing of all nuclear weapons.... The great importance of the 1963 test-ban treaty lies in its significance as the first step toward disarmament. To indicate what other steps need to be taken, I shall quote some of the statements made by President Kennedy.... The goal of disarmament is no longer a dream. It is a practical matter of life or death. The risks inherent in disarmament pale in comparison to the risks inherent in an unlimited arms race.... Our new disarmament program includes... First, signing the test-ban treaty by all nations... Second, stopping production of fissionable materials and preventing their transfer to other nations...; Third, prohibiting the transfer of control over nuclear weapons to other nations; Fourth, keeping nuclear weapons from outer space; Fifth, gradually destroying existing nuclear weapons; and Sixth, halting the production of strategic nuclear delivery vehicles, and gradually destroying them.[2]

Source: 1. Address by Dr. Linus Pauling to Senate of the Tenth Legislature of the State of Hawaii on April 4, 1979.
2. Science and Peace, The Nobel Peace Prize Lecture.

Dr. Henry Kendall
Scientist (Department of Physics, MIT)

We believe that the key to a safer future lies in the control of strategic weapons technology. To protect the world from the disaster of a nuclear war the superpowers must halt the development of new weapons which frustrate attempts to curb the arms race.... We hereby recommend that (1) the United States announce that it will halt underground testing of nuclear explosives provided that the Soviet Union follows suit within a reasonable time, (2) the United States announce that it will not field test or deploy new strategic weapons, nuclear weapons systems, or missile defense systems for a period of 2 to 3 years provided the Soviet Union demonstrably does likewise.... The United States should take the initiative. The U.S. lead in new weapons technology in the nuclear era is a reflection of overall superiority in creating new technologies and sophisticated industries.... Under these circumstances, we cannot expect the USSR to take the initiative.[1] The Union of Concerned Scientists and other concerned citizens are not denying the energy potential that nuclear power could offer the U. S.... Our position simply recognizes that satisfactory safety precautions have to be taken before large-scale nuclear power production can be allowed.... The nuclear industry has failed so far to do this. A moratorium on the construction of new plants would allow an orderly assessment of the problems and the time to carry our research and development to decrease the risks.... The history of indifference, carelessness, poor engineering, near accidents and suppression of information to the public about nuclear safety problems demonstrates the need for considerable tightening of controls.[2]

Source: 1. Declaration on the Nuclear Arms Race, Union of Concerned Scientists.
2. The Nuclear Power Controversy, Union of Concerned Scientists.

Dr. Jerome B. Wiesner
Electrical Engineer (MIT)

How many people do you suppose think that Three Mile Island will be a major and positive learning experience for our nuclear industry and our nation?... These initiatives, plus a moderate increase in power from nuclear energy, should enable the U.S. to transit the next twenty years without major difficulties.... Fuel from shale will continue to be available for at least half a century, nuclear energy, in spite of its current problems, can remain a significant part of our energy system. Energy will doubtlessly continue to become more costly each year and have to be used more judiciously. As this happens, solar energy will become more attractive. Also, fusion energy should become available along the way. My technical intuition tells me that in the long run the world will obtain much of its energy from these two sources.... We desperately need to facilitate the most rapid development of domestic fossil fuel sources for the immediate future.

Source: Remarks, Energy Conference, USC, May 8, 1979.

John Kenneth Galbraith
(Harvard University)

I came to speak for all who wish to live—all who are concerned that, in some moment of accident, miscalculation, anger or sadness, all who inhabit this small globe will be destroyed, along with all that has been accomplished in the last five thousand years.... The resolution which I here urge is to show that we are still in control, that the decision to live is still ours. It offers a freeze on the development and deployment of weapons of mass destruction and their delivery systems with the prospect of prompt ensuing negotiations. It is a practical step. It is good politics. Americans have always shown that they have a will to live; no politicians have been more quickly discarded than those who have seemed to be casual about nuclear war.... We are not visionaries; the visionaries are those whose vision extends to the deaths of tens and hundreds of millions of our people.

Source: Speech before Democratic National Convention, New York City, August 13, 1980, in favor of minority platform plank.

Dr. Harold Agnew
Scientist
(Director, Lawrence Livermore Laboratories)

In looking ahead for the next five years, it is imperative that we maintain enough flexibility to respond rapidly to any presently unforeseen demands upon the nation's nuclear weapons program. The fact that

LASL's nonweapons work is so preponderantly nuclear in character permits an almost instantaneous response to any new weapons related initiatives....[1] I really don't know why people have not thought more on the use of these (deleted) weapons. It may be that people like to see tanks rolled over than just killing the occupants.[2]

Source: 1. H. M. Agnew, LASL Director writing in "Long Range Projections," March 1977.
2. Military Applications of Nuclear Technology, Hearings on Neutron Bomb, Subcommittee on Military Applications of the Joint Committee on Atomic Energy, April 16, 1973.

Religious Leaders

Rev. Billy Graham

The present arms race is a terrifying thing and it is almost impossible to overestimate its potential for disaster.... Is a nuclear holocaust inevitable if the arms race is not stopped? Frankly, the answer is almost certainly yes.... I know not everyone would agree with this, but I honestly wish we had never developed nuclear weapons.... We have nuclear weapons in horrifying quantities and the question is, what are we going to do about it? ...[1] If SALT II were the final treaty we would ever negotiate for arms limitation, then relatively little has been accomplished. But these things have to be taken one step at a time. SALT II should give way to SALT III. I wish we were working on SALT X right now! Total destruction of nuclear arms.[2]

Source: 1. Excerpted from Sojourners Magazine, August 1979.
2. Pamphlet, Fellowship of Reconciliation, "A Change of Heart."

Pope John Paul II

At Hiroshima, the facts speak for themselves, in a way that is dramatic, unforgettable and unique. In the face of an unforgettable tragedy, which touches us all as human beings, how can we fail to express our brotherhood and our deep sympathy at the frightful wound inflicted on the cities of Japan that bear the names of Hiroshima and Nagasaki? That wound affected the whole of the human family.... And then there arose the question that will never leave us again: Will this weapon, perfected and multiplied beyond measure, be used tomorrow? If so, would it not probably destroy the human family.... From now on, it is only through a conscious choice and through a deliberate policy that humanity can survive. The moral and political choice that faces us is that of putting all the resources of mind, science and culture at the service of peace and of the building up of a new society.... Our future on this planet, exposed as it is to nuclear annihilation, depends upon one single factor: humanity must make a moral about-face. At the present moment of history, there must be a general mobilization of all men and women of good will.... The moment is approaching when priorities will have to be redefined. For example, it has been estimated that about a half of the world's research workers are at present employed for military purposes. Can the human family morally go on much longer in this direction?

Source: An address by Pope John Paul II during visit to Hiroshima, February 25, 1981; excerpted from the Bulletin of the Atomic Scientists (April 1981).

Rabbi Isidor B. Hoffman
(Honorary Chairman of the Jewish Peace Fellowship)

At the present time acceptance of war as a means of settling disputes between nations requires the expenditure of vast funds on armaments, especially nuclear bombs and delivery systems. This diminishes the resources of substance and scientific attention necessary for the quantity and quality of life of hundreds of millions who need help with food, education and health.

Source: Written for Words of Conscience, March 1980.

Spencer Kimball
First Presidency of the Church
of Jesus Christ of Latter-Day Saints

We are dismayed by the growing tensions among the nations, and the unrestricted building of arsenals of war, including huge and threatening nuclear weaponry. Nuclear war, when unleashed on a scale for which the nations are preparing, spares no living thing within the perimeter of its initial destructive force, and sears and maims and kills wherever its pervasive cloud reaches. While recognizing the need for strength to repel any aggressor, we are enjoined by the word of God to "renounce war and proclaim peace." We call upon the heads of nations to sit down and reason together in good faith to resolve their differences. If men of good will can bring themselves to do so, they may save the world from a holocaust, the depth and breadth of which can scarcely be imagined.

Source: Christmas Message of the First Presidency, Mormon Church; reprinted in the Deseret News, week ending December 20, 1980.

We have received many inquiries concerning our feelings on the proposed basing of the MX missile system in Utah and Nevada. After assessing in great detail information recently available, and after the most careful and prayerful consideration we make the following statement.... First, by way of general observation we repeat our warnings against the terrifying arms race in which the nations of the earth are presently engaged.... Secondly, with reference to the presently proposed MX basing in Utah and Nevada, we are told that if this goes forward as planned, it will involve the construction of thousands of miles of heavy duty roads, with the building of some 4600 shelters in which will be hidden some 200 missiles, each armed with ten warheads. Each one of these ten nuclear warheads will have far greater destructive potential than did the bombs dropped on Hiroshima and Nagasaki.... Its planners state that the system is strictly defensive in concept, and that the chances are extremely remote that it will ever be actually employed. However, history indicates that men seldom created armaments that eventually were not put to use. We are most gravely concerned over the proposed concentration in a relatively restricted area of the West. Our feelings would be the same about concentration in any part of the nation.... Our fathers came to this western area to establish a base from which to carry the gospel of peace to the peoples of the earth. It is ironic, and a denial of the very essence of that gospel, that in this same general area there should be constructed a mammoth weapons system potentially capable of destroying much of civilization. With the most serious concern over the pressing moral question of possible nuclear conflict, we plead with our national leaders to marshal the genius of the nation to find viable alternatives which will secure at an earlier date and with fewer hazards the protection from possible enemy aggression which is our common concern.

Source: News Release, Church of Jesus Christ of Latter-Day Saints, First Presidency Statement on Basing of the MX Missile, May 5, 1981.

Bishop Thomas J. Gumbleton
(Archdiocese of Detroit)

I began to ponder the fact that SALT II would legitimate the destructive power of 615,000 Hiroshima bombs, the present American arsenal.... The arms race goes on. This is really the failure of SALT II. It is not the beginning of the reversal of the arms race. It is not the first step. The simple reason is that the arms race is no longer a matter of numbers, it is a race in technology and sophistication. It is a race to

increase the accuracy of these weapons.... In the view of many analysts, new arms agreements do not really limit arms competition, they only push it down different avenues. SALT II will be no different in this regard than any past agreement.... I would suggest the following as an outline of a carefully conceived effort to reverse the arms race. First, the religious community should pledge itself to undertake a massive effort of education and conscience formation. The second step the religious community can take is to promote a national effort to build a climate for conversion from an arms industry to exclusively peace production.... We must stop the arms race now and undertake this task with the greatest sense of urgency because the finish line in the arms race is not peace but holocaust.

Source: Article by Bishop Gumbleton, *Commonweal* magazine, January 1979.

Bishop Paul Moore, Jr.
(Episcopal Archdiocese of New York)

No way is known, or even imagined, by which to dispose of nuclear waste, already eating its cancerous way into the bowels of the earth.... Humanity does not have to have nuclear energy. It is ironic that if we had no armaments the fossil fuel saved thereby would go a long way toward making much further conservation unnecessary.... Nuclear arms, once let loose, can probably destroy us completely.

Source: Sermon for anniversary of Three Mile Island.

Marian McAvoy
(Sisters of Loretto)

The Loretto Community declares its commitment to an end to the production of nuclear weapons and nuclear energy. We are particularly committed to encouraging and assisting in the urgent work of educating ourselves and others to the perils of the continued proliferation of nuclear arms and power. Rooted as we are in our Judaeo-Christian heritage, we view our opposition to nuclear weapons and nuclear energy as an urgent moral imperative. We recognize that the burden of leadership in this regard falls not only on concerned persons throughout the world but especially on the community of faith. We realize that part of the struggle to disarm the world and create a clean, safe environment is to engage in a process of disarming ourselves of our sometimes violent and competitive behavior toward one another and toward our environment. Furthermore, we commit ourselves to press politically for the development of safe, alternative energy sources, especially renewable resources, to call for a moratorium on further development of nuclear power plants, to demand that our government take a moral stand on our use of energy as it affects future generations, and international relations, to support SALT II as a minimal step toward arms limitation, and to urge the U.S. government to work toward global disarmament.

Source: Nuclear Statement—General Assembly, August 1979.

Episcopal Church

The Archbishop of Canterbury in a speech in Washington said: "We have made a great advance in technology without a corresponding advance in moral sense. We are capable of unbinding the forces which lie at the heart of creation and destroying our civilization ... It is vital that we see modern weapons of war for what they are—evidence of madness." As Christians we recognize a demonic element in the complexity of our world, but we also affirm our belief in the good will and purpose and Providence of God for his whole creation. This requires us to work for a world characterized not by fear, but by mutual trust and justice.

"MANKIND IS CONFRONTED BY A CHOICE: WE MUST HALT THE ARMS RACE AND PROCEED TO DISARMAMENT, OR FACE ANNIHILATION." (Final document of the UNSSD)

Source: "Christian Attitudes to War in a Nuclear Age," statement of the Primates of the Anglican Communion, 1981.

Catholic Church

Any act of war aimed indiscriminately at the destruction of entire cities or of extensive areas along with their population is a crime against God and man himself. It merits unequivocal and unhesitating condemnation.

Whatever may be the case with the method of deterrence, men should be convinced that the arms race in which so many countries are engaged is not a safe way to preserve a steady peace.

Source: "The Constitution on the Church in the Modern World," document of the Second Vatican Council, 1965.

The right of legitimate defense is not a moral justification for unleashing every form of destruction. For example, acts of war deliberately directed against innocent noncombatants are gravely wrong, and no one may participate in such an act.

With respect to nuclear weapons, at least those with massive destructive capacity, the first imperative is to prevent their use. As possessors of a vast nuclear arsenal, we must also be aware that not only is it wrong to attack civilian populations but it is *also wrong to threaten to attack them as part of a strategy of deterrence*. We urge the continued development and implementation of policies which seek to bring these weapons more securely under control, progressively reduce their presence in the world, and ultimately remove them entirely.

Source: "To Live in Christ Jesus," pastoral statement of the National Council of Catholic Bishops, 1976.

Lutheran Church in America

It is clearly time for rethinking of the meaning of national security. In view of the overkill capacity now possessed by the superpowers, national security can no longer be defined in terms of either nuclear superiority or even nuclear stalemate. The common threat which such weapons hold for all mankind teaches that their continued development can only undermine security. It is now necessary both to create an international legal framework within which arms control can be brought about and to help nations perceive that their safety must be conceived in more than military terms.

A beginning has been made in the construction of the legal framework. This effort should be intensified, should include all weapons of mass destruction. In the meantime the United States should be encouraged to undertake such unilateral initiatives as may contribute to a climate more hospitable to the limitation of arms.

Source: "Social Statement on World Community," adopted in 1970.

Mennonites

Modern militarism, however, tempts the nation to assume the power of God. With their devastating arsenals of nuclear weapons nations today hold destructive power over every living cell on earth. Even without a war the arms race diverts resources from urgent needs, destroys community, and devastates the human spirit. In the United States the militaristic mood is evident in a renewed willingness to conscript young people, possibly women as well as men, for military service. In such times the church must give prophetic warning, calling its members and all people to trust God who is Sovereign, rather than the gods of war and military technology.

Source: Mennonite Church General Assembly statement on militarism and conscription, 1979.

National Council of Churches

As part of a people gripped by the anguish that their nation and the world are steadily moving toward war, it is time for the churches to cry "Enough." With the United States and the Soviet Union possessing destructive power which threatens God's creative work on earth, we who participate in the body of our incarnate Lord reject the blasphemy of nuclear destruction of those for whom Christ died. The Lordship of Christ demands that we turn anew to the task of creating a global human community in the spirit of Shalom. Recalling previous commitments to general and comprehensive disarmament made by the NCC and by the U.S. and Soviet governments, we call for a re-direction of national policy toward the achievement of that long-awaited goal.... Therefore, we urge the Governing Board of the NCC and the official bodies of our constituent communions to call upon the United States government to invite the government of the Soviet Union to negotiate a moratorium on their launchers. Such a nuclear weapons moratorium can be monitored by existing national means of verification. It would substantially arrest the present nuclear arms race. As an immediate first step toward such a moratorium, we call upon the United States government to stop all nuclear weapons tests, urging other nuclear powers to reciprocate in the hope that a complete comprehensive test ban treaty can be achieved. As a second step, we urge the United States to take additional initiative by stopping the production of all nuclear weapons and their launchers in the hope that the Soviet Union will reciprocate so that a negotiated moratorium may be achieved.

Source: National Council of Churches Disarmament Consultation, convened by Dr. Claire Randall, General Secretary, April 29, 1980.

United Church of Christ

NOW, THEREFORE, BE IT RESOLVED, the Thirteenth General Synod of the United Church of Christ affirms a commitment to nuclear disarmament through negotiation with all existing and developing nuclear powers, and communicates this commitment to the President of the United States of America, and the Secretaries of State and Defense, through the office of the President of the United Church of Christ; and BE IT FURTHER RESOLVED, that the United Church of Christ's President express to national leaders our forthright desire for nuclear disarmament even if this process must begin with unilateral initiative on the part of the United States.

Source: "Resolution: Broken Arrow," adopted by the 13th General Synod, 1981.

United Methodist Church

We believe that war is incompatible with the teachings and example of Christ. We therefore reject war as an instrument of national foreign policy and insist that the first moral duty of all nations is to resolve by peaceful means every dispute that arises between or among them; that human values must outweigh military claims as governments determine their priorities; that the militarization of society must be challenged and stopped; that the manufacture, sale and deployment of armaments must be reduced and controlled; and that the production, possession, or use of nuclear weapons be condemned.

Source: "Social Principles, The United Methodist Church," adopted by the General Conference, 1980.

Labor Representatives

Lance Compa
UE Washington Representative
United Electrical, Radio and Machine
Workers of America

Nowhere has there been greater disregard for the welfare of the American people than in the nuclear power industry.... The Karen Silkwood case, the nuclear waste disposal problem, the skyrocketing costs of nuclear plants and fuels and Three Mile Island have all badly damaged the credibility of the nuclear power industry and the U.S. government. The future of nuclear power plants is now seriously in doubt.... It is clear that, unless genuine steps are taken to deal with public concern over the safety and costs of nuclear power plants, few additional plants will ever be built and pressure will continue to grow to close down existing plants for keeps.... Recognizing the dangers of nuclear power, UE urges quick development of safe, clean, alternative power sources, so that generations yet to be born need not suffer from the greed for profits that permeates the nuclear power lobby.... After six years of negotiations, the U.S. and the Soviet Union have concluded the second Strategic Arms Limitation Treaty (SALT II) that puts a ceiling on nuclear weapons systems for both countries and prepares for continued negotiations for reductions in those armaments. The campaign for ratification of the treaty should be seen as the opportunity to develop a campaign to cut the arms budget which reached $126 billion this year and is scheduled to rise to $159 billion by 1982—further fueling the inflation machine that is destroying our living standards.... This 44th UE International Convention urges the ratification of the SALT II agreement. This Convention also urges the Congress and the Administration to reject new arms building programs as further endangering the peace of the world, especially the MX missile. This convention confirms its support for proposals to reduce the military budget through such means as the transfer amendments in Congress which would cut military expenditures and transfer to civilian projects the money saved, and to enact conversion legislation to save the jobs of workers who switch from military to civilian production.

Source: Resolutions and Reports Adopted by the 44th International Convention of the United Electrical, Radio and Machine Workers of America (UE), September 1979.

Frank Cowan
Assistant to the President
American Federation of State, County and Municipal Employees

Serious environmental and safety problems are associated with the use of coal and nuclear fuels.... Safety standards and environmental concerns should be made the primary concern with regard to the future use of nuclear power, including safety and particularly waste disposal.

Source: "Energy: Decontrol and Alternative Sources," adopted by AFSCME's International Executive Board, June 1979.

George W. Stone
President National Farmers Union

When nuclear wastes can be stored without being harmful to humanity and the environment, nuclear power should be given the same priority in resolving our energy shortage as hydroelectric, coal, solar, wind, methane, gasohol, alcohol, and geothermal.... We urge acceleration of development of fusion energy technology, which is relatively free of polluting effects.

Source: Policy statement adopted in 1980 National Farmers Union Convention.

United Mine Workers of America

The UMWA reaffirm its opposition to the use of nuclear power, until adequate safeguards against radiation poisoning are developed; until safe, permanent waste sites are devised; and until protection against catastrophic nuclear power plant accident is assured.

... There should be a moratorium on licensing of new nuclear plants until stronger safeguards are instituted.

Source: Report of the Compact/Legislative Committee, 48th consecutive constitutional convention, December 10–20, 1979.

International Woodworkers of America

The 30th International Convention of the International Woodworkers of America called for a slowing of nuclear plant construction.... There is still no safe system of storing nuclear wastes.... The accident at Three Mile Island points out the extreme health and safety hazards for both workers and communities.... The environmental and economic price of nuclear power continues to climb out of sight.... The 31st Convention of the International Woodworkers of America go on record in opposition to any new development of nuclear power.

Source: Nuclear Plant Construction Legislation, Resolution No.3.

William Winpisinger
President International Association of Machinists and Aerospace Workers

Whereas some 25,000 IAM members are involved directly in the production of radioactive materials, products of weaponry and countless others handle radioactive products in warehouses, shipping terminals and air cargo depots and an unknown number of IAM members service contaminated vehicles, craft, containers and equipment. ... Therefore, be it resolved: (1) that the IAM supports a moratorium on all nuclear plant construction; (2) that the IAM urges the federal government and the private and public power industries to commit resources, now directed toward nuclear development, to alternative sources of safe renewable energy, such as solar, biomass, low head hydro, and co-generation and to conversion of coal-fired generating plants; (3) that the federal government and the nuclear power industry spare no resources in determining what can safely be done to rid the nation of literally tons of radioactive waste poisons, which now threaten our people and the planet for generations to come; (4) that the federal government and the nuclear power industry immediately implement full scale inspections, for both design and operational flaws in all existing nuclear power plants, in order that the safety of workers and communities may be guaranteed, and where safety cannot be guaranteed, then operations be shut down.[1]

The only solution to the current balance of terror is for the U.S.A. and the Soviet Union to wind down the arms race together.... Military spending is by far the largest single expenditure from the federal government's general tax revenues and the largest contributor to the federal debt.... Yet, this inflationary spending creates fewer jobs than federal spending in the civilian economy. The MX missile, which would cost $30 to $70 billion, and undermine the SALT Treaty, will create only a few thousand jobs—an estimated 38,000 over the next eight years. Half of those will be in the engineer and professional ranks. ... Senate ratification of the SALT II will put a cap on the number of new nuclear weapons that can be produced in both the Soviet Union and the U.S.A. It will enable us to begin the long, tedious task of winding down the costly and inflationary arms race and transfer money and resources into secure and productive jobs in the civilian sector of our economy. ... President Carter has hampered the Treaty's chances of success by trying to buy votes from hardline foes— most of whom are right-wing and anti-labor with the MX folly, registration for the military draft, and appointing military men to head the Civilian Arms Control and Disarmament Agency.... But this issue is above politics. We must do all we can to gain Senate ratification.[2] Source: 1. Resolution for IAM Executive Council, July 1979. 2. Reprinted from *The Machinist*, 1979.

DISARMAMENT ACTIONS IN THE UNITED STATES, 1946–1982

Protests against nuclear armament and tests of nuclear weapons date from the first U.S. tests in the Pacific. With Senator Joseph McCarthy's Permanent Subcommittee on Investigations threatening to deny civil liberties to persons not supporting U.S. military policies, there were few protests in the United States in the early fifties. From 1963 until 1975, when U.S. military involvement in Indochina ended, the protests in the United States focussed on civil rights and the anti-Vietnam War effort.

Summer 1946	Times Square, New York, demonstration against first atomic bomb test at Bikini atoll, followed by similar protest at the Pentagon.
April 1–9, 1950	Holy Week, pacifists fast in Washington, D.C., to protest H-bomb, organized by Peacemakers and other groups.
Dec. 4, 1950	Eighty Protestant clergy in Buffalo, New York, issue statement condemning use of atom bomb.
Jan. 1951	Resolution protesting possible use of atom bomb sent to President Truman by sixty Methodist ministers in Michigan.
March 1, 1954	Fellowship of Reconciliation (FOR) issues protest and launches petition campaign against H-bomb tests in the South Pacific, urging President Eisenhower to immediately suspend all tests; by July 8,000 signatures collected.
April 1954	Associated Church Press urges United States to consult with other nations before conducting further H-bomb tests; call for disarmament efforts via United Nations Disarmament Commission.
July–Aug. 1954	Victims of fallout from H-Bomb tests in Micronesia petition United Nations.
Sept. 23, 1954	Aikichi Kuboyama dies in Tokyo, Japan, crew member of "Lucky Dragon" fishing boat caught in fallout; first victim of H-bomb tests; his death sparks protests in United States and Japan.
June 15, 1955	Catholic Worker, War Resisters League (WRL), FOR, Peacemakers organize protests against nationwide civil defense alert; 28 arrested in New York City for refusing to take shelter; similar demonstrations follow during drills in Philadelphia, Chicago, Boston, and other cities.
Aug. 6, 1957	Eleven members of Committee for Nonviolent Actions (CNVA) arrested at Nevada Test Site for crossing into prohibited area during atom bomb test.
1957–59	North California Committee against Nuclear Tests begin campaign focused on the Nevada Test Site, sit-ins at Lawrence Liver-

	more Laboratory, protests at Port Chicago Navy Munitions Base.
May 2, 1958	*Golden Rule,* CNVA ship sails from California to Honolulu into South Pacific nuclear test zone; crew arrested at Eniwetok.
June 1958	Second attempted sailing of *Golden Rule;* crew members arrested.
June 1958	Earle and Barbara Reynolds sail the *Phoenix* from Hiroshima, Japan, into bomb test areas.
Aug. 28, 1958	CNVA organizes demonstration to oppose construction of missile base at Cheyenne, Wyoming; five arrested.
1959	Omaha Action campaign, organized by CNVA, FOR to conduct vigils, organize public meetings and other protest action at Mead Missile Base near Omaha, Nebraska.
July 1, 1959	Fifteen pacifists arrested attempting to enter Mead Missile Base to protest construction of silos.
Dec. 1959	A. J. Muste, Bayard Rustin, William Sutherland join Africans attempting to enter French bomb test zone in Sahara Desert.
May 3, 1960	One thousand people participate in New York City protest organized by Civil Defense Protest Committee, picketing at Civil Defense Offices, public meetings.
Nov. 22, 1960	CNVA, Polaris Action campaign begins at nuclear submarine base in Groton, Connecticut.
1960–62	Polaris actions attempt to interfere with construction or launching of nuclear submarines.
Dec. 1, 1960	San Francisco to Moscow Walk for Peace begins; eleven pacifists leave San Francisco on 6,000 mile trek.
April 28, 1961	Citywide protests during the last civil defense drill to take place in New York City.
Oct. 3, 1961	American and European peace walkers arrive in Red Square, Moscow, conduct vigil urging unilateral disarmament.
May 1962	*Everyman I* protest ship leaves San Francisco for the Christmas Island nuclear test zone; crew arrested and imprisoned.
June 26, 1962	*Everyman II* sails from Honolulu into Johnson Island test zone where it remains for four days; ship seized and crew arrested.
Sept. 26, 1962	*Everyman III* sails from London to Leningrad, Moscow, denied entry and turned out to sea.
Spring 1962	CNVA organizes simultaneous walks beginning in New Hampshire, Chicago, and Nashville, Tennessee, culminating in Washington, D.C., with civil disobedience action at Pentagon.
May 1963	Quebec - Washington - Guantánamo Walk for Peace to protest Cuban missile crisis and existence of U.S. naval base in Cuba.
June 1963	Fourteen walkers arrested in Albany, Georgia, due to interracial makeup of the group; aborted attempt to sail the *Spirit of Freedom* from Miami to Cuba.
June 1974	Campaign is begun by the Colorado American Friends Service Committee (AFSC), to close and convert Rocky Flats nuclear weapons plant near Denver, Colorado.
June 1974	Campaign by the Colorado AFSC to close and convert Rocky Nuclear Weapons Plant near Denver, Colorado, begins.
July–Aug. 1975	Vigil on U.S. Capitol steps to protest first-strike nuclear policy, organized by CNVA of Baltimore and Washington, D.C.
July 4, 1975	Members of Pacific Life Community plant garden inside Bangor Naval Base, Bremerton, Washing-

	ton beginning campaign against proposed deployment of Trident nuclear submarine.
Nov. 1975	Members of Jonah House dig mock graves on White House lawn in symbolic protest of plan to use mines as civil defense shelters; similar actions follow elsewhere.
Jan. 30, 1976	Continental Walk for Disarmament and Social Justice begins cross-country trek in San Francisco with "feeder routes" from New Orleans, the Midwest, and Mountain States, sponsored by a coalition of peace and disarmament groups.
Jan. 1976	Safeguard antiballistic missile system near Grand Forks, North Dakota, shutdown following local and national opposition.
April 1976	Protest at Groton, Connecticut, Electric Boat shipyard at keel-laying of first Trident nuclear submarine.
July 13–16, 1976	National Nonviolent Training Workshop with Rocky Flats campaign, sponsored by AFSC and FOR, Denver, Colorado.
Oct. 3, 1976	Pacifists in United States and Canada begin fast urging both countries to renounce the first use of nuclear weapons.
Oct. 16, 1976	Continental Walk ends in Washington, D.C., with thousands rallying at the U.S. Capitol, the Pentagon, and the White House.
April 15, 1976	Demonstrations take place in 103 cities in thirty-five states to protest the B-1 bomber, as part of an ongoing campaign organized by Clergy and Laity Concerned (CALC) and AFSC.
April 1977	Campaign is launched to convert the Los Alamos and Lawrence Livermore nuclear weapons laboratories managed by the University of California.
May 1977	Local opposition in four states forces cancellation of Project Seafarer, underground communications system for nuclear submarine.
June 1977	FOR presents to the White House and Congress petition calling for U.S. unilateral disarmament initiatives with over 30,000 signatures.
June 1977	National Campaign to Stop the B-1 bomber, following presidential decision to cancel production, shifts focus to oppose cruise missile.
Aug. 6, 1977	Protests against neutron bomb take place at the White House and nationwide, organized by Women Strike for Peace and other groups.
Dec. 1977	12,000 scientists and engineers call on the United States to take unilateral actions to stop the arms race in a declaration published by the Union of Concerned Scientists.
Jan.–Feb. 1978	Thousands in Denmark, the Netherlands, Switzerland, and other countries sign petitions and appeals to the United States not to build and deploy the neutron bomb.
Feb. 1978	House of Representatives votes against B-1 strategic bomber, marking final victory in anti–B-1 campaign.
April 1978	Indefinite delay in production of neutron bomb announced.
April 29–30, 1978	Rocky Flats National Action at the nuclear weapons plant outside Denver, Colorado, as part of ongoing campaign to close and convert the facility, organized by AFSC, FOR, and a local coalition. Rally of over 6,000 and civil disobedience.
May 23 to June 28, 1978	United Nations Special Session on Disarmament.
May 27, 1978	International Religious Convocation for Human Survival, sponsored by Mobilization for Survival and religious groups.

	Rally for Disarmament in the Dag Hammarskjöld Plaza with more than 10,000.
June 12, 1978	Sit-in for Survival, at the U.S. Mission to the United Nations calling upon the United States to take steps toward disarmament; more than 300 arrested.
May–June 1978	Plowshare Coffee House and Discussion Center, sponsored by FOR during United Nations Special Session on Disarmament.
June 1978	Southern Baptist Convention approves resolution calling for multilateral arms control and shifts from military to nonmilitary spending in the United States.
July 4, 1978	WRL holds simultaneous demonstrations in Red Square in Moscow and at the White House, calling for U.S. and Soviet disarmament. Eleven persons arrested in Washington, D.C.
Aug. 6, 1978	Hiroshima Day protest actions around the country.
Sept. 1978	U.S. Air Force announces plans to deploy MX mobile missile system in the Midwest and Southwest; local and national peace and environmental groups begin campaign to oppose. A coalition of farmers with Nebraskans for Peace successfully persuades the air force not to base the system in that state.
Oct. 16–18, 1978	Protest at the annual convention of the Association of the U.S. Army weapons display, Washington, D.C., organized by SANE and other groups.
Dec. 4–5, 1978	Disarmament Convocation, attended by more than 600 people from around the country, at Riverside Church, New York.
Dec. 29, 1978	"Die-In" at Pentagon, forty people arrested protesting nuclear arms race, coordinated by Jonah House.
Feb. 1979	Vigil and shareholders actions at annual business meeting of Rockwell International Corporation in Dallas, Texas, challenging involvement in arms race and management of Rocky Flats nuclear weapons plant, coordinated by Interfaith Center on Corporate Responsibility, FOR, AFSC.
April 7, 1979	Vigil and demonstrations with 3,000 people to protest launching of first Trident submarine, *Ohio,* at Electric Boat shipyard, Connecticut, sponsored by Trident Conversion Campaign, 200 arrested.
April 28, 1979	Demonstration of 15,000 at Rocky Flats nuclear weapons plant, calling for its conversion and for U.S. initiatives toward disarmament; 284 arrested blocking entrances to the plant. Actions sponsored by AFSC, FOR, Rocky Flats Coalition, and Rocky Flats Truth Force.
June 12–24, 1979	Plowshare Discussion Center at World Council of Churches (WCC) Conference on Science and Technology at MIT; WCC resolution calling for moratorium on weapons passes.
Aug. 1979	Colorado Medical Society calls on the Department of Energy to establish a time-line to convert Rocky Flats nuclear weapons plant.
Aug. 6, 1979	Demonstrations commemorating Hiroshima and Nagasaki across the country, including Pittsburgh, Philadelphia, and Harrisburg, Pennsylvania; Berkeley, California; New York City; Denver, Colorado; Washington, D.C.
Oct. 14–16, 1979	Riverside Church, New York City, holds second Convocation to Reverse the Arms Race; more than 1,000 attend.
Oct. 24–31, 1979	United Nations World Disarmament Week—local actions calling for U.S. steps toward disarmament.

Oct. 28–29, 1979
Demonstrations calling for a nuclear moratorium; 500 block entrance at the Department of Energy. Religious services for nuclear victims, organized by Mobilization for Survival.

Oct. 28, 1979
Wall Street Action; thousands arrested in protest against corporate involvement in both nuclear weapons and nuclear power development.

Oct. 28, 1979
More than 2,500 participate in rally and march at Bangor, Washington, Trident submarine base; ninety arrested for civil disobedience. Organized by Live Without Trident and Ground Zero.

Nov.–Dec. 1979
Numerous peace groups begin campaign to oppose deployment of 600 new strategic missiles by the United States and NATO in Europe.

Christmas 1980
The Church of Jesus Christ of Latter-Day Saints (Mormon) issues a proclamation by "divine revelation" condemning the arms race on moral grounds and calling on individuals and national leaders to act "to save the world from a holocaust."

March 1980
Founding conference on nationwide campaign to call for a US/Soviet freeze on nuclear weapons draws over 300 people to Georgetown University, Washington, D.C.

April 14, 1981
Demonstration of 500 people in Rome, New York, opposes deployment of the first air-launched cruise missiles in the United States at nearby Griffiss Air Force Base.

April 25, 1981
Actions take place in sixty communities in the United States and Canada on the theme "Freeze the Arms Race," at nuclear weapons plants, corporate contractors, and military bases, sponsored by the Nuclear Weapons Facilities Task Force coordinated by the AFSC and FOR.

May 5, 1981
Mormon Church issues statement opposing MX missile.

Sept.–Nov. 1981
Nearly two million Europeans demonstrate in Paris, Brussels, London, Rome, Rumania, Amsterdam, and elsewhere in opposition to the arms race in Europe and plans to deploy US/NATO missiles. These actions help spark opposition in the United States.

Nov. 11, 1981
Over 100 campuses hold teach-ins on the arms race, sponsored by the Union of Concerned Scientists and other organizations. An ongoing campus network is formed to continue organizing and education.

Nov. 23–27, 1981
Representative of U.S. churches, peace groups, and members of government and scientific institutions present testimony at an International Public Hearing on Nuclear Weapons and Disarmament, Amsterdam, Holland, sponsored by the World Council on Churches.

Feb.–March, 1982
Over 300 town meetings in New England passed resolutions calling for a U.S./Soviet freeze following intense grass roots organizing. Over 166 members of Congress introduced a resolution calling for negotiation toward a freeze and reductions in nuclear weapons with endorsements from churches, scientists, former military and government officials. Through the spring and summer over two million signatures are collected on freeze petitions putting the issue on state and local ballots in the Nov. 1982 election.

April 18–25, 1982
"Ground Zero" observances take place in hundreds of communities to educate the public on the dangers of nuclear war.

June 1982
Demonstrations, religious convocation, vigils, and civil disobedi-

ence actions mark the Second U.N. Special Session on Disarmament, New York City.

June 12, 1982   Disarmament march and rally draws one million people to Central Park, New York City—the largest political protest action in U.S. history, sponsored by a coalition of peace, religious, labor, civil rights, and environmental groups.

Fellowship Magazine, 1950–79, Box 271, Nyack, New York.

Source: Helen M. Michalowski and Robert Cooney. *Power of the People, Active Nonviolence in the U.S.* (Culver City, CA: Peace Press, 1977).

ANTI-NUCLEAR POWER ACTIONS IN THE UNITED STATES, 1958–1981

The earliest actions expressing concern about the dangers of nuclear radioactivity were timid about addressing government military and nuclear policy. The cold war era and McCarthyism had an overwhelming influence on choices made in those years. The chronology of the nuclear power protest movement inevitably includes actions opposing nuclear weapons—the major critics of nuclear power came out of the U.S. weapons program due to suppression of their work on the effects of weapons tests.

April 1958   Scientists at Washington University in St. Louis formed Committee for Nuclear Information (CNI). CNI was formed in response to public fear of radiation from weapons tests. "They provided technical information but refrained from taking a position on U.S. policy." (Patterson)

Dec. 1958   Baby Tooth Survey launched by CNI looking for documentation of strontium-90. By 1966 they had gathered over 200,000 baby teeth, which made possible the first study of strontium-90 from fallout on children.

CNI also started a bulletin entitled *Nuclear Information,* which in the sixties became *Scientist and Citizen* and in 1969 *Environment.*

1959   Massachusetts Lower Cape Committee on Radiation Waste Disposal forced the Atomic Energy Commission (AEC) to stop dumping radiation waste into the Atlantic just twelve miles from Boston.

1960   Same group stopped attempts to build waste reprocessing center on Cape Cod.

1962   New York citizens stopped Con Ed from building a reactor in Queens.

1964   Northern California residents forced cancellation of reactor planned by PG&E. The reactor was to be built on top of an earthquake fault.

early 1960s   Pennsylvanians stopped "Project Ketch," a peaceful nuclear explosion (PNE) which would have used a twenty-four-kiloton bomb to create a storage cavern for natural gas.

1966   Citizens of Eugene, Oregon, voted to reverse their earlier choice to build a nuclear plant on Oregon's coast.

early 1960s   Dr. Ernest Sternglass, professor of radiation physics at University of Pittsburgh, increasingly concerned about health effects from weapons tests fallout: official AEC response to Sternglass's findings was "to deny validity, to cast doubts on his professional standing," and to try to stifle open discussion of his work.

1962   Dr. Harold Knapp of AEC's Division of Biology and Medicine completed a study on iodine-131 from its creation in weapons tests to its eventual placement in thyroids of children through milk.

1963   Knapp's report was made public, and Knapp resigned from AEC after ridicule and attempts to withhold his scientific findings. Dr. John Gofman's experience as a member of the AEC committee charged with "review" of the Knapp study led to his own conversion into one of the most outspoken critics of the AEC.

late 1960s   Scientists in Public Interest (SIPI) formed in New York City with other organizations affiliating, including CNI. SIPI later in 1973 began publishing *Environment*.

1969   A number of news stories appeared in major U.S. publications on the nuclear tests and Sternglass's research on infant mortality. *Esquire* advertised "The Death of All Children" in *New York Times* and *Washington Post* and also sent advance copies to every congressperson and senator.

1969   Dr. Art Tamplin was asked by AEC to critique Sternglass's findings. While he somewhat disagreed with Sternglass, he confirmed that as many as 4,000 children had been killed by fallout.

By the end of 1969, Sternglass, Gofman, and Tamplin all began looking into the health effects of the commercial nuclear industry. The experience and expertise of scientists studying the effects of the weapons program was now being applied to the civilian industry.

1969   The "Plowshare" program of the AEC set off its second PNE at Grand Junction, Colorado, codenamed Rulison. Demonstrators occupied the site and disrupted plans. The shot was eventually set off, and tritium and other radioisotopes were released into the environment.

1970s   The early seventies marked the beginning of legal interventions as a tactic with the focus on the commercial industry. The restrictions of the Atomic Energy Commission, the secrecy and self-regulation of all federal nuclear weapons activi-

ties meant that most actions gave emphasis to the commercial nuclear industry since challenges to it were more possible legally and politically. In addition, the resources and energies of organizations traditionally concerned with the weapons program, effects of fallout, etc., had become totally absorbed in trying to end the Indochina War.

early 1970s   The AEC held rule-making hearings on the emergency-core cooling system, largely brought about by Henry Kendall's efforts.

early 1970s   National Intervenors formed as a continuing coalition.

1972   Clean Environment Act citizen initiative appeared on California ballot losing 2 to 1.

1973   A second of over 40,000 PNE's planned for Colorado was detonated, called "Rio Blanco." Court interventions failed to stop Rio Blanco; however, a citizens ballot initiative brought a stunning end to Plowshare in Colorado in 1974.

Spring 1974   Sam Lovejoy toppled a 500-foot weather tower in Montague, Massachusetts.

June 1974   Environmental and peace groups formed a new alliance in Colorado to close and convert the Department of Energy's (DOE) nuclear weapons operation at Rocky Flats.

1974   Ralph Nader convened the first "Critical Mass" conference in Washington, D.C., with subsequent ones in 1975–78.

1975   The Sierra Club took a position against nuclear power after internal struggles resulting in David Brower leaving and founding Friends of the Earth.

1974   Massachusetts ballot initiative opposing reactors at Montague won 47.5 percent of the vote. Thirty-

	three percent of voters registered their willingness to shut down operating reactors in Rowe, Massachusetts, and Vernon, Vermont.
1976	Ballot initiatives appeared in California, Arizona, Oregon, Washington, Montana, Colorado, Ohio. All initiatives were defeated with heavy spending for publicity by the nuclear industries. A major evaluation of the initiative as a tactic began across the country.
1976	Economic issues began to be addressed by the anti–nuclear power movement. In St. Louis, Citizens for Reformed Electric Rates used the referendum to question the economic costs of nuclear power, winning a 2 to 1 margin to prevent utilities from charging utility consumers for the cost of new plant construction. At least one reactor was cancelled as a result. Other states have successfully prevented utilities from getting utility rate hikes in order to build nuclear reactors, including New Hampshire.
Feb. 1975	West German, French, and Swiss nuclear opponents overran a nuclear site at Wyhl, on the West German side of the Rhine River, sparking similar actions in the United States.
Aug. 1976	Occupiers marched onto the Seabrook, New Hampshire construction site.
April 1977	More than 2,000 Clamshell occupiers marched onto the Seabrook site. Occupations were also in the works at Diablo Canyon, California, and at Trojan, in Oregon.
	Through the efforts of the Environmentalists for Full Employment (EFFE), a new rapport began to develop between environmental groups and trade unions.
1977	EFFE coordinated the endorsement of the AFL-CIO's long-fought-

	for Labor Law Reform Act by more than two dozen leading environmentalists and groups.
1978	First Sun Day, to support solar energy.
1977–78	Clamshell Alliance supported striking coal miners.
1978	Major rallies of civil disobedience actions at the Barnwell-Savannah River weapons waste facility in South Carolina, and the Rocky Flats nuclear weapons plant in Colorado.
1978	Kern County, California, voters overwhelmingly rejected plans for a reactor in their community. This conservative county vote signaled a new tide of trouble for the nuclear power industry.
March 28, 1979	Accident at Three Mile Island (TMI) nuclear power plant near Harrisburg, Pennsylvania, stimulates national concern and debate; partial evacuation ordered of residents in the vicinity.
May 1979	Over 100,000 people rally in Washington, D.C., to call for the total shutdown of TMI and other power plants, sponsored by the May 6th Coalition, a diverse, national antinuclear grouping.
June 1979	Diablo rally of 30,000 with Gov. Jerry Brown speaking out publicly against a reactor in his own state.
Oct. 1979	Peace and environmental groups rally at DOE and Wall Street.
Sept. 1980	Antinuclear benefit concerts and a rally in New York City sponsored by Musicians United for Safe Energy (MUSE) draw tens of thousands.
March 1981	A march and rally in Harrisburg, Pennsylvania, on the second anniversary of the TMI accident sponsored by safe energy groups and national labor unions, cementing the alliance between them.

Fall 1980 to Spring 1981	Major environmental groups such as Friends of the Earth and the Sierra Club become involved in efforts to oppose the MX missile and join in other disarmament efforts.

Sources: Walter Patterson, *Nuclear Power* (1973). Anna Gyorgy, *No Nukes*, Boston: South End Press, 1979.

FILMS ABOUT NUCLEAR WAR

This list of 16-mm films available for rent or purchase is based on information from the Union of Concerned Scientists, the American Friends Service Committee, and the film review pages by John Dowling in *The Bulletin of the Atomic Scientists.* For a more complete listing of about 100 films see *Nuclear War Film List,* available for $2 from John Dowling, Physics Department, Mansfield State College, Mansfield, PA 16933. Videotape editions of many films are available from the same sources. Several slide shows are also available for rent or purchase.

Hiroshima: A Document of the Atomic Bombing

(28 minutes; black and white, some color)

An excellent documentary, including shots taking in Hiroshima in the weeks following the nuclear attack, interspersed with contemporary footage showing lingering medical and psychological effects. Gruesome, stark, and difficult to watch.

American Friends Service Committee
15 Rutherford Place
New York, NY 10003

Wilmington College Peace Resource Center
Pyle Center, Box 1183
Wilmington, OH 45177

Hiroshima/Nagasaki: August 1945

(16 minutes; black & white)

This excellent antiwar film describes the devastation and appalling agony wrought by nuclear war. It includes shots of the Hiroshima and Nagasaki bursts.

Museum of Modern Art
Circulating Film Program
11 West 53rd Street
New York, NY 10019

American Friends Service Committee
2161 Massachusetts Ave.
Cambridge, MA 02140

Wilmington College Peace Resource Center
Pyle Center, Box 1183
Wilmington, OH 45177

The Day After Trinity

(60 minutes)

Documentary film on J. Robert Oppenheimer and the development of the atomic bomb.

Pyramid Films
2801 Colorado Ave.
Santa Monica, CA 90404

Decision to Drop the Bomb

(82 minutes; black & white)

A review of the moral, military, and political issues surrounding the decision by President Truman to use the atomic bomb against Japan.

Films Incorporated
1144 Wilmette Ave.
Wilmette, IL 60091

The First Twenty-five Years

(28 minutes; color)

A documentary film presenting the recollections of Norris Bradbury of the first twenty-five years of the Los Alamos National Scientific Laboratory. It covers the development of fission and thermonuclear weapons and includes cameos of some scientists involved in the work.

U.S. Department of Energy
Technical Information Center
P.O. Box 62
Oak Ridge, TN 37830

The Atom Strikes

(31 minutes; black & white)

One of several U.S. Army training films available to the public, this films shows the bombing and devastation of Hiroshima and Nagasaki. A striking, cold account of nuclear effects on people and structures.

U.S. Army Training and Audio-Visual Center
Ft. Devens, MA 01433

Management of Mass Casualties

(24 minutes; black & white)

Another U.S. Army training film. This one discusses the mental breakdown of troops in nuclear war zones. Unrealistic—depicts infantry sergeants urging troops to take warm milk and a sedative and go back to battle.

U.S. Army Training and Audio-Visual Center
Ft. Devens, MA 01433

Fable Safe

(9 minutes; color)

An excellent animated satire that depicts the escalation of weapons development by the superpowers based on fear, misunderstanding, and misinterpretation of the other side's intentions.

Museum of Modern Art
Circulating Film Program
11 West 53rd Street
New York, NY 10019

The War Game

(49 minutes)

A realistic and gruesome depiction of a nuclear attack on England in some future time after diplomacy fails, nations are backed into corners, and bluffs are called. An outstanding and impressive film.

Films Incorporated
1144 Wilmette Ave.
Wilmette, IL 60091

Federation of American Scientists
307 Massachusetts Ave., NE
Washington, D.C. 20002

Armaments: The War Game

(24 minutes; color)

A powerful treatment of the full spectrum of the arms race, including possible future technologies, protest actions, and interviews of Donald Brennan of the Hudson Institute and Jerome Wiesner of M.I.T.

University of California Extension Media Center
223 Fulton Street
Berkeley, CA 94720

War Without Winners

(28 minutes; color)

The fears and hopes of experts, workers, students, and others, including Paul Warnke, former chief negotiator for SALT, and Dr. George Kistiakowsky, former scientific advisor to President Eisenhower, are expressed in interviews. The message is "There are no winners in nuclear war."

Films Incorporated
1144 Wilmette Ave.
Wilmette, IL 60091

American Friends Service Committee
2161 Massachusetts Ave.
Cambridge, MA 02140

Physicians for Social Responsibility
P.O. Box 144
Watertown, MA 02172

Nuclear Countdown

(28 minutes; color)

A documentary on the history of the arms race and the dangers of nuclear proliferation. This film discusses the successes, failures, and inadequacies of present arms control agreements and treaties.

Journal Films, Inc.
930 Pitner Ave.
Evanston, IL 60202

Paul Jacobs and the Nuclear Gang

(60 minutes)

Presents material on radiation, fallout, and the human costs of the arms race.

American Friends Service Committee
1660 Lafayette Street
Denver, CO 80218

Fellowship for Reconciliation
P.O. Box 271
Nyack, NY 10960

The Last Epidemic: Medical Consequences of Nuclear Weapons and Nuclear War

(36 minutes; color)

Presentation of a symposium of physicians, scientists, and military experts assessing the difficulties of providing medical aid to victims of nuclear attack.

Resource Center for Nonviolence
P.O. Box 2324
Santa Cruz, CA 96063

Eight Minutes to Midnight

(20 minutes)

A film portrait of Dr. Helen Caldicott, president of Physicians for Social Responsibility.

Direct Cinema, Ltd.
P.O. Box 69589
Los Angeles, CA 90069

Direct Cinema, Ltd. Library
P.O. Box 315
Franklin Lakes, NJ 07417

NATIONAL ORGANIZATIONS ACTIVE ON NUCLEAR ISSUES

The listing below of national organizations active in the United States on issues concerning nuclear weapons, arms control and disarmament, nuclear energy, conservation, and renewable energy resources is not exhaustive but indicates the broad cross-section of the U.S. population that is concerned. Most of these groups will provide literature, names of local or regional contacts, and further information upon request.

Organization	Activities
American Committee on East-West Accord 227 Massachusetts Ave., NE, Washington, DC 20002	*Corporate executives working for improved U.S.-Soviet relations through SALT agreements and trade*
American Friends Service Committee 1501 Cherry St., Philadelphia, PA 19102	*Education for a nuclear weapons freeze, programs to address the militarization of foreign policy and regional arms races, Quaker-supported*
Business Executives Move for New National Priorities 900 N. Howard St., Baltimore, MD 21201	*Active in promoting SALT, economic conversion of military to civilian industries, lobbies Congress against new nuclear weapons systems*
Center for Defense Information 122 Maryland Ave., NE, Washington, DC 20002	*Provides information and analysis on U.S. and Soviet military systems*
Center for Law and Social Policy 1751 N. St., NW, Washington, DC 20036	*Public interest law group, involved with MX legal challenges, main litigator in B-1 bomber case*
Center for Science in the Public Interest 1757 S St., NW, Washington, DC 20009	*Citizen action on energy issues*
Citizens' Energy Project 1413 K St., NW, Washington, DC 20005	*Nuclear opponents, offers publications primarily on energy issues*

Organization	Activities
Clergy and Laity Concerned 198 Broadway, New York, NY 10038	*Human Security Program has nuclear moratorium as goal, emphasis on corporate involvement in arms race*
Coalition for a New Foreign and Military Policy 120 Maryland Ave., NE, Washington, DC 20002	*Coalition of religious, peace, business, union, and other organizations involved in lobbying and education through Disarmament Working Group*
Committee for Nuclear Responsibility P.O. Box 332, Yachats, OR 97498	*Education on the hazards of nuclear power and alternative energy sources*
Common Cause 2030 M St., NW, Washington, DC 20036	*Citizens' lobby group concerned with government accountability*
Congress Watch 133 C St., SE, Washington, DC 20003	*Congressional lobby representing consumer interests, including development of alternative energy sources*
Conservation Foundation 1717 Massachusetts Ave., NW, Washington, DC 20036	*Research, education, and information organization concerned with environmental issues*
Council for A Livable World 11 Beacon St. Boston, MA 02108	*Sponsors educational programs and lobbies for alternative to current military policy. Supports senatorial candidates committed to disarmament.*
Council on Economic Priorities 84 Fifth Ave., New York, NY 10011	*Conversion Information Center provides research on military production, economic impact of military spending, and a quarterly listing of resources*
Critical Mass P.O. Box 1538, Washington, DC 20013	*Education and organizing on the problems of nuclear power, Nader-sponsored*

Disarm Education Fund
175 Fifth Ave.
New York, NY 10010

Provides information on the effects of military spending, counters right-wing groups with media campaign and information

Eastern Federation of Nuclear Energy Opponents and Safe Energy Proponents
317 Pennsylvania Ave., SE, Washington, DC 20003

Clearinghouse for East Coast groups involved in antinuclear energy work

Environmental Action
1346 Connecticut Ave., NW, Suite 731
Washington, DC 20036

Political lobby concerned with nuclear power issues

Environmental Action Foundation
724 Dupont Circle Bldg., Washington, DC 20036

Environmental research and resource organization

Environmental Action Reprint Service
2239 Colfax, Denver, CO 80206

Provides extensive information and publications on nuclear and other types of energy

Environmental Defense Fund
475 Park Ave. South, New York, NY 10016

Lawyers and scientists working to end degradation of the environment

Environmental Policy Center
317 Pennsylvania Ave., SE, Washington, DC 20003

Research organization on low-level radiation/ health effects, waste storage, and other issues

Federation of American Scientists
307 Mass. Ave. NE
Washington, DC 20002

Composed of 5,000 scientists and engineers, offers education on the arms race aimed at university and scientific audiences

Fellowship for Reconciliation
Box 271, Nyack, NY 10960

Pacifist, cosponsors with AFSC the Nuclear Weapons Facilities Project (see below), education and organizing in the religious community

Friends of the Earth
72 Jane St., New York, NY 10010
620 C St., SE, Washington, DC 20003
124 Spear St., San Francisco, CA 94105

International conservation organization, active against the MX missile, on nuclear transportation, and other issues

Gray Panthers
3635 Chestnut St., Philadelphia, PA 19104

Active against ageism and militarism

Great Decisions Program
345 East 46th St., New York, NY 10017

Student, senior citizens, and 4-H groups debating SALT and other foreign policy decisions

Green Mountain Post Films
P.O. Box 177, Montague, MA 01351

Produces and distributes films on nuclear power, antinuclear resistance, and the environment

Institute for Defense and Disarmament Studies
251 Harvard St.
Brookline, MA 02146

Publishes research on military/disarmament issues, clearinghouse for promotion of bilateral nuclear weapon freeze proposal developed by IDDS

Institute for Policy Studies
1901 Q St., NW, Washington, DC 20009

Research center on national security/foreign policy/arms trade issues, extensive publication program

Institute for World Order
777 U.N. Plaza, New York, NY 10017

Sponsors Operation Turning Point, educational project on the arms race

International Seminar on Training for Nonviolent Action
148 N. St., South Boston, MA 02127

North American branch of nonviolent training network for antinuclear activists and others

Media Access Project
1910 N St., NW, Washington, DC 20036

Public interest law firm

Mobilization for Survival
853 Broadway New York, NY 10003

Coalition of peace, environmental, and other groups challenging nuclear weapons and nuclear power through direct action and education

Northern California Alliance for Survival
944 Market St., San Francisco, CA 94102
Southern California Alliance for Survival
5539 West Pico Blvd., Los Angeles, CA 90019

West Coast coalitions of peace, environmental, and other groups involved in local organizing against nuclear weapons/energy

Movement for a New Society
4722 Baltimore Ave., Philadelphia, PA 19143

Works with local alliances in organizing and training for the antinuclear movement

NARMIC (National Action/Research on the Military Industrial Complex)
1501 Cherry St., Philadelphia, PA 19102

Resources on nuclear issues, particularly military contractors, sponsored by AFSC

National Association of Women Religious
1307 S. Wabash, Chicago, IL 60605

Religious women opposed to nuclear energy and the arms race

National Audubon Society
1511 K St., NW, Washington, DC 20005

Recently has become active against nuclear power

National Campaign to Stop MX
305 Massachusetts Ave., NE, Washington, DC 20002

Coordinates lobbying and educational efforts against the MX missile

National Committee for Radiation Victims
317 Pennsylvania Ave., SE, Washington, DC 20003

Resource/information center for persons exposed to radiation from weapons/energy production

National Council for a World Peace Tax Fund
2111 Florida Ave., NW, Washington, DC 20008

Advocate for conscientious objectors to military spending, encourages tax refusal

National Council of Churches of Christ
475 Riverside Dr., New York, NY 10027

Interdenominational, concerned with nuclear energy and arms proliferation

National Farmers Union
1012 14th St., NW, Washington, DC 20005

Actively promotes arms control, SALT, and reductions in weapons programs

National Intervenors
1757 S St., NW, Washington, DC 20009

Coalition of environmental and citizens' groups, clearinghouse for public interest opposition to nuclear power

National Wildlife Federation
1412 16th St., NE, Washington, DC 20036

Involved in anti-MX campaign on environmental grounds

Natural Resources Defense Council
1721 I St., NW, Washington, DC 20006
664 Hamilton Ave., Palo Alto, CA 94301
14 West 44th St., New York, NY 10036

Concerned about nuclear power and weapons proliferation, primary litigants against fast breeder reactor

NETWORK
806 Rhode Island Ave., NE, Washington, DC 20018

Lobbying group for religious orders

New American Movement
3244 N. Clark St., Chicago, IL 60657

Grass-roots political party involved in local organizing

Nuclear Information and Resource Service
1536 16th St., NW, Washington, DC 20036

Resource and coordination center for antinuclear, grass-roots movement

Nuclear Transportation Project/AFSC
92 Piedmont Ave., NE, Atlanta, GA 30303

Resource/coordination center for organizing against transport of nuclear wastes and weapons components

Nuclear Weapons Facilities Project
AFSC/1660 Lafayette St., Denver, CO 80218
FOR/Box 271, Nyack, NY 10960

Resource/coordination for organizing around weapons research, testing, production, and deployment sites including Rocky Flats (Denver) plant

Nuclear Weapons Freeze Campaign National Clearinghouse
4144 Lindell Blvd., Suite 201
St. Louis, MO 63108

A clearinghouse for broad-based grass-roots organizing for a US/Soviet freeze in nuclear weapons production

Packard Manse Media Project
Box 450, Stoughton, MA 02072

Produces and distributes slides and filmstrips on nuclear and military topics

Pax-Christi USA
3000 N. Mango, Chicago, IL 60634

Catholic group actively working on disarmament issues

People's Alliance
Box 998, Peter Stuyvesant Sta., New York, NY 10009

Coalition seeking to link minority/economic issues with disarmament

Physicians for Social Responsibility
P.O. Box 144, 56 N. Beacon St.
Watertown, MA 02177

Organization of physicians and other health professionals concerned about medical effects of nuclear weapons/energy, sponsors symposia

Progressive
408 W. Gorham, Madison, WI 53703

Monthly magazine restrained from publishing H-bomb article, gives extensive coverage of nuclear issues, sponsors educational Progressive Foundation

Promoting Enduring Peace
Box 103, Woodmont, CT 06460

Reprint service on arms issues, sponsors educational ads in major newspapers

Public Citizen
P.O. Box 19404, Washington, DC 20036

Supports the work of citizen advocates against nuclear power, Nader-sponsored

Public Interest Research Group
1346 Connecticut Ave., NW, Washington, DC 20036

Public interest law group concerned with environmental quality, Nader-sponsored

Resources for the Future
1755 Massachusetts Ave., NW, Washington, DC 20036

Research and education on use and development of natural resources, energy, and environmental quality

Riverside Disarmament Project
490 Riverside Dr.
New York, NY 10027

Based at Riverside Church, hosts annual conferences and provides resources for education and organizing in the religious community nationwide

SANE
514 C St., NE, Washington, DC 20002

Works with unions on economic peace conversion, coordinates organizing against MX missile

Sierra Club
530 Bush St., San Francisco, CA 94108

National conservation organization

Sojourners
1309 L St., NW, Washington, DC 20005

Monthly magazine, evangelical activists promoting education and organizing on arms and energy issues in churches

Supporters of Silkwood
317 Pennsylvania Ave., SE, Washington, DC 20003

Educational information related to the work of Karen Silkwood

Union of Concerned Scientists
1384 Massachusetts Ave., Cambridge, MA 02138

Coalition of scientists and other professionals concerned with nuclear safety and hazards, proliferation, active against MX missile and for SALT agreements

Unitarian Universalist Service Committee
100 Maryland Ave., NE, Washington, DC 20002

Member of Coalition for a New Foreign and Military Policy, Disarmament Working Group

United Church of Christ
110 Maryland Avenue, NE, Washington, D.C. 20002

Member of Coalition for a New Foreign and Military Policy, Disarmament Working Group

United Methodist Church/Women's Division
110 Maryland Ave., NE, Washington, DC 20002

Member of Coalition for a New Foreign and Military Policy, Disarmament Working Group

United Nations Association
300 East 42nd St., New York, NY 10017

Films, literature, and educational forums on alternatives to the arms race

War Resisters League
339 Lafayette St., New York, NY 10012

Nonviolent action against nuclear weapons/power, radical pacifist

WIN Magazine
326 Livingston, Brooklyn, NY 11217

Biweekly magazine, offers extensive coverage of antinuclear issues and activities

Women's International League for Peace and Freedom
1213 Race St., Philadelphia, PA 19107

Lobbying, public education, and nonviolent action against nuclear weapons/power

World Peacemakers
2852 Ontario Rd., NW, Washington, DC 20009

Religious group, reflection/action on disarmament

World Information Service on Energy
1536 Sixteenth Ave., NW, Washington, DC 20036

International research and reference source on nuclear industry and antinuclear movement

Worldwatch Institute
1776 Massachusetts Ave., NW, Washington, DC 20036

Research on global issues including energy, the environment, weapons proliferation

Part Nine

Background

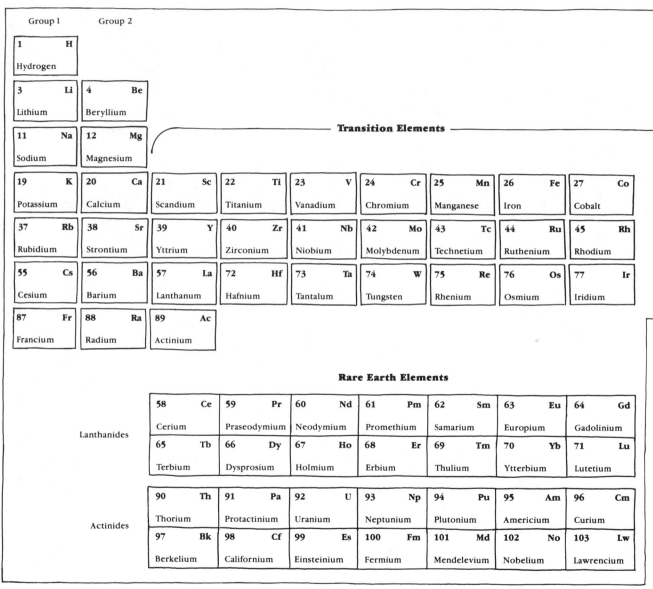

The periodic table is a list of the elements in order of increasing atomic number—the number of protons in an atom's nucleus. The columns of the table group together elements with similar chemical properties. The alkali metals appear in group 1. Likewise, the alkaline earths are in group 2, and the halogens appear in group 7. The two series of rare earth elements do not fit into the periodic pattern.

24. A Little Physics

	Group 3	Group 4	Group 5	Group 6	Group 7	Group 0
						2 He Helium
	5 B Boron	**6** C Carbon	**7** N Nitrogen	**8** O Oxygen	**9** F Fluorine	**10** Ne Neon
	13 Al Aluminum	**14** Si Silicon	**15** P Phosphorus	**16** S Sulfur	**17** Cl Chlorine	**18** Ar Argon
28 Ni Nickel	**29** Cu Copper	**30** Zn Zinc	**31** Ga Gallium	**32** Ge Germanium	**33** As Arsenic	**34** Se Selenium	**35** Br Bromine	**36** Kr Krypton
46 Pd Palladium	**47** Ag Silver	**48** Cd Cadmium	**49** In Indium	**50** Sn Tin	**51** Sb Antimony	**52** Te Tellurium	**53** I Iodine	**54** Xe Xenon
78 Pt Platinum	**79** Au Gold	**80** Hg Mercury	**81** Tl Thallium	**82** Pb Lead	**83** Bi Bismuth	**84** Po Polonium	**85** At Astatine	**86** Rn Radon

The intuition, discoveries, explanations, and in some cases arduous labors of the nineteenth- and twentieth-century physicists have made clear many facts about matter and energy. Understanding the basics of this hard-won knowledge is not difficult, and may help us to make informed decisions about the atomic and nuclear issues of our times.

Thérèse Dennis

Dennis received a physics degree from M.I.T. and has taught physics at the university level.

THIS CHAPTER EXPLORES at an elementary level some basic ideas underlying the physics of nuclear reactions and radiation—ideas about matter, the substances that make up the universe, and energy, the source of movement, warmth, and light.

Matter

The idea that matter was made up of tiny units that could not be further subdivided is often credited to Democritus, a Greek philosopher of the fifth century B.C. He called these units *atomos,* from which is derived the word we use today—atoms.

There exists more than one kind of atom, however. What the different atoms were like was just beginning to be understood in the 1800s. Experiments with gases made it possible to determine the relative weights of some of the atoms. Chemists were able to demonstrate that some substances, called compounds, were made up of more than one kind of element, in definite proportions. The smallest unit of a compound is called a molecule. Substances made of one kind of atom, such as carbon and iron, are called elements. Some elements take part in the forming of compounds—carbon dioxide, or iron oxide (rust), for example. A molecule of carbon dioxide consists of two oxygen atoms tightly bound to a single carbon. Several atoms of the same element may bind together as a molecule; for example, a molecule of oxygen gas has two oxygen atoms. Such a gas is called diatomic, in contrast to a monatomic gas which consists of single atoms.

The Periodic Table

How could this multiplicity of atoms, molecules, and their properties be understood? It was found possible to organize the elements into groups such that elements in the same group have similar properties. One such group is the noble gases: neon, argon, krypton, xenon, and radon. These have the common properties that they are monatomic gases at standard temperature and pressure, they do not readily form compounds, and their atoms pack in a similar way if they are frozen. The alkali metals also form a group. Lithium, sodium, potassium, rubidium, cesium, and francium are soft silvery metals in elemental state. They are very reactive, and are good conductors of heat and electricity.

It was discovered by Lothar Meyer in 1864, and independently by Dmitri Mendeleev in 1869, that if one lists the elements in the order of their relative weight, elements with similar properties do not fall together; rather they occur in the list at intervals with a certain pattern. Starting with fluorine, a halogen, we next find neon, a noble gas, then sodium, an alkali metal. Further on we encounter chlorine, another halogen, followed by a noble gas, argon, then potassium, an alkali metal again. The list may be broken into rows, such that elements with similar properties appear in the same column. The result is the periodic table. In the usual configuration of the periodic table, the noble gases appear in the last column, and the alkali metals appear in the first column. The second column contains the elements beryllium, magnesium, calcium, strontium, barium, and radium. These metals, called the alkaline earths, form similar compounds, so, for example, as calcium is one of the constituents of bone, strontium, or radium could take the place of calcium there.

The table displayed some of the similarities and differences among atoms and compounds, but it also showed some gaps. Enthusiastic searches began for the missing elements, and subsequently they have been found. One hole in the periodic table was filled in in 1937 by Emilio Segrè and Carlo Perrier, with technetium, the first element formed artificially by nuclear bombardment. Other elements not naturally occurring on earth (promethium and the transuranic elements—those with atomic number greater than that of uranium) have been created in the laboratory, leading to the periodic table as it stands today.

Atomic Structure

The table having been established, knowledge of chemical properties was organized, but still not explained. One important link in understanding the elements was provided by John Dalton, who measured relative weights of different atoms, and showed that the weights had a common factor. The counting numbers, multiplied by this factor, generated the known weights of the elements. This factor might be the weight of one unit; it is now called the *atomic mass unit* which is 1.6×10^{-27} kilograms.

At first the understanding of the periodic table was limited to a list of "magic numbers," telling when in the list to start a new row. The reasons behind this organization of the elements were not yet explained. Why should the properties of different elements, and therefore different atoms, repeat in this particular way? Why was carbon similar to silicon, rather than more like those atoms with closer atomic weights? The explanation of this requires some understanding of the atoms themselves. In Chapter 25 some history is related, including Rutherford's discovery of the particles given off by some atoms, which he called alpha particles (more about these later). By allowing alpha particles to strike a thin foil of metal, Rutherford found that many of the speeding particles came straight through, and did not hit anything—therefore, if the atoms are closely packed, they must contain mostly empty space. Moreover, some of those particles that were deflected bounced sharply back, showing that atoms have very tiny centers holding almost all the weight, surrounded by a volume which is virtually empty. Rutherford named the tiny, dense centers *nuclei*. The nucleus has a positive electric charge which is balanced by a negative charge held by electrons outside the nucleus.

On the scale of atoms, the laws of physics are manifest in ways unusual to our human scale, so great ingenuity is required to discover the secrets of nature. An early idea about the electrons is that they whirl in orbit about the nucleus, similar to the planets orbiting the sun. Because the electrons carry charge, this idea contradicts other known principles of physics. Nevertheless, Niels Bohr explained the structure of the periodic table with this model. In 1926 Max Born interpreted the equation of Erwin Schrödinger as describing the probability of an electron being in a given volume positioned around the nucleus. The probability depends upon the angle about and distance from the nucleus. In summary, there is a certain structured way in which electrons occupy the space around the nucleus. The volume taken up by the atom is partitioned into various shapes, called shells, which represent the most likely volumes in which the electrons may be found. The chemical properties of an element and the shape of molecules and crystals, even quartz and snowflakes, are determined by the arrangement of the electrons—the shape of the occupied shells. For example, alkali metal atoms, in their lowest energy state, have as their outermost occupied shell, a spherical volume occupied by a single electron.

The amount of charge in the nucleus was found to be proportional to the place the element had in the periodic table. Charge comes in discrete units, either equal or opposite to the charge carried by the electron. The nucleus of the first element has one unit of positive charge, that of the second element two, and so on. The term *atomic number* gives the number of positively charged units in the nucleus. The unit of charge is 1.6×10^{-19} coulombs, the amount of electricity carried by a single electron. The idea of atomic number is due to Henry G. J. Moseley, a British physicist who was killed in action during the English expedition to the Dardanelles.

The Nucleons

Nucleons are the particles that form the nuclei of atoms. Although both the atomic weight and the nuclear charge are a fundamental constant multiplied by a counting number, not every counting number corresponds to an atomic weight found in nature.

counting number

1	2	3	4	5	6	7	8	9	10	11	12

by atomic number

H	He	Li	Be	B	C	N	O	F	Ne	Na	Mg

by atomic weight

H	—	—	He	—	—	Li	—	Be	—	B	C

Some of the counting numbers of atomic mass units are not used, so that while hydrogen has one charge and one mass unit, carbon has six charges, but already has twelve mass units. There must be something else in the carbon nucleus to account for the extra mass units.

One hypothesis is that atomic nuclei are made up of two kinds of units—one, called a proton, that weighs one atomic mass unit and carries one unit of charge, and another, also weighing one atomic mass unit, but with no electric charge. These chargeless particles are the neutrons discovered by Chadwick in 1932; they are one of the kinds of particles that fly out of atoms when their nuclei break apart. Rutherford thought of this particle as a proton with an electron inside, which cancels its charge. It is the neutron's capability of splitting a nucleus and the consequent release of additional neutrons that make a nuclear chain reaction possible.

As all atoms are made up of some number of protons and neutrons, one would expect the mass of each element to be an integral multiple of the atomic mass unit. This would result in relative weights of elements being in simple proportion. For example, carbon with six protons and six neutrons would weigh twelve times the weight of hydrogen's single proton.

Why aren't the relative weights of the elements as found in nature in exact proportion? Each atom does have its mass approximately equal to the number of atomic mass units it contains. Dalton, however, was not weighing individual atoms. He weighed a great number all together, and not all the atoms were exactly alike. (Not so different as mixed nuts, but rather more like some oranges with seeds and some without.) Kinds of hydrogen exist with one proton and one neutron, and with one proton and two neutrons. The average weight of hydrogen depends upon how much of each kind is present. Each of these three nuclei is called hydrogen because all share the chemical properties of hydrogen.

The chemical properties of atoms come from the number of electrons, which exactly balances the number of protons in the nucleus. The number of neutrons in an atom, however, may vary without changing its chemistry. Atoms with the same number of protons are called isotopes, a name originated in 1913 by Frederick Soddy, who worked with Rutherford. Isotopes are distinguished from each other only by the number of neutrons; the three isotopes of hydrogen mentioned above are called hydrogen (H-1 or H), deuterium (H-2 or D), and tritium (H-3 or T).

Scientists experimenting with radioactive materials managed to separate isotopes in the laboratory before they were recognized for what they are. Once the concept of isotopes had been put forth, Joseph John (J. J.) Thomson carried out an experiment that clearly demonstrated the existence of two isotopes of the noble gas neon. Using the same sort of apparatus he had used to measure the charge to mass ratio of the electron, he showed that neon occurred with two different masses, neon-22 (with twelve neutrons) and neon-20 (ten neutrons).

Uranium-238 and uranium-235 are two of the uranium isotopes. The separation of U-235 from natural uranium is difficult and costly because isotopes are the same chemically, and differ only slightly in mass.

24-1 The Scale of Energy

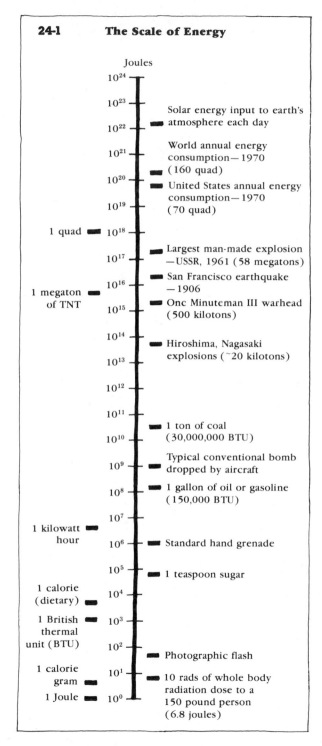

Joules

10^{24}

10^{23}

10^{22} — Solar energy input to earth's atmosphere each day

10^{21} World annual energy consumption—1970

10^{20} — (160 quad)
United States annual energy consumption—1970

10^{19} (70 quad)

1 quad — 10^{18}

10^{17} — Largest man-made explosion —USSR, 1961 (58 megatons)

10^{16} — San Francisco earthquake —1906

1 megaton — — One Minuteman III warhead
of TNT 10^{15} (500 kilotons)

10^{14} — Hiroshima, Nagasaki

10^{13} explosions (~20 kilotons)

10^{12}

10^{11}

— 1 ton of coal
10^{10} (30,000,000 BTU)

Typical conventional bomb
10^{9} — dropped by aircraft

— 1 gallon of oil or gasoline
10^{8} (150,000 BTU)

10^{7}

1 kilowatt —
hour 10^{6} — Standard hand grenade

10^{5} — 1 teaspoon sugar

1 calorie 10^{4}
(dietary) —

1 British — 10^{3}
thermal
unit (BTU) 10^{2} — Photographic flash

1 calorie 10^{1} — 10 rads of whole body
gram — radiation dose to a
1 Joule — 10^{0} 150 pound person
(6.8 joules)

Energy and Radiation

Energy is manifest in several forms. A flying baseball carries energy of motion—kinetic energy. If an object is heated, its constituent parts (atoms, molecules, or larger aggregates) move around, but not all in the same direction. We sense it not as motion of the object as a whole, but as a different form of energy we call heat.

Another form of energy is electromagnetic radiation, as in radio waves produced by the motion of electric charges in the antenna of a radio transmitter, or the thermal radiation from myriads of positively charged nuclei vibrating in a warm object. In radio broadcast waves, the vibrations have frequencies of about one million cycles per second. The unit, cycle per second, is named Hertz, in honor of Heinrich Hertz, who first demonstrated the existence of electromagnetic radiation—a phenomenon predicted by James Clerk Maxwell, who unified the theories of electricity and magnetism.

At frequencies millions of times higher than radio waves, electromagnetic radiation is perceived as heat. At even higher frequencies it is light. At these higher frequencies the dual nature of radiation becomes more evident. In some ways light behaves as waves; in other ways it behaves as if it consists of individual packets of energy called photons. Albert Einstein showed that the particle nature of light explained the photoelectric effect: current could be made to flow from a metal by a little bit of light at an energy above a threshold, whereas lots of light at a lesser energy was incapable of causing current. Arthur H. Compton also explained the change of energy and direction of light when interacting with electrons by means

The events of concern in this book span an enormous range of energy. The scale is marked off in joules, the energy unit used by scientists. It takes 4,185 joules to equal one dietary calorie, or 3.6 million joules to equal one kilowatt-hour. One quad, the unit in which global energy resources are often stated, is equal to about 252 megatons of nuclear explosive energy.

of the particle nature of light. There are expressions of the wave nature of light, as well. Light forms interference patterns similar to those made by ripples in the surface of a pond.

The energy carried by a photon is proportional to the frequency of the radiation it carries. The proportionality constant is named Planck's constant, in honor of Max Planck, who first proposed that energy might come in discrete units, called quanta.

Photons of energy higher than heat may dislodge electrons. The energy for this process corresponds to photons of visible light, and of the X rays familiar to us from medical procedures. Gamma rays, photons a million times more energetic than those of visible light, can be emitted from nuclei. For example, when a nucleus splits, energy released in the splitting is partly carried off by gamma rays, and partly in the kinetic energy of the fission fragments.

Binding Energy

Nuclei other than hydrogen nuclei have more than one proton very close together. Because particles of like charge tend to push each other away, an intervening force must be acting to hold the nucleus together. This is called the nuclear (or strong) force. The strong force is a short range force. Beyond a certain distance from the nucleus, the strength of nuclear force is insignificant. This means that, if enough energy were present to pry part of a nucleus a little distance away from the rest, then repulsion of like particles would take over, and the two pieces of nucleus would fly apart.

This happens in fission. Fission is the splitting apart of a nucleus, and it can be initiated by a neutron colliding with the nucleus. The amount

The energies encountered on the scale of atomic dimensions cover nine orders of magnitude from the energy in one quantum of light to the energy of the strongest cosmic rays. The erg, the physicist's unit of energy, has been called a "mosquito push-up." It takes 10 million ergs to equal one joule.

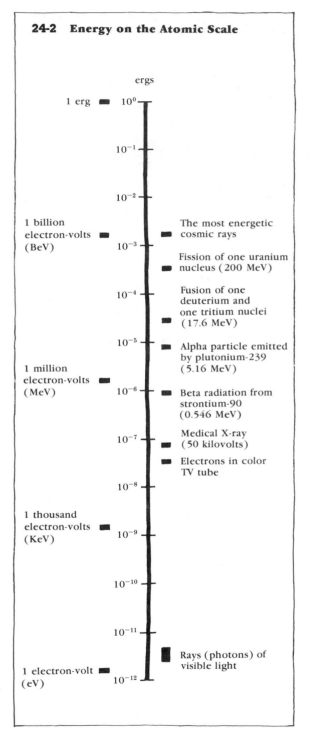

24-2   Energy on the Atomic Scale

ergs

1 erg — 10^0

10^{-1}

10^{-2}

1 billion electron-volts (BeV) — 10^{-3} — The most energetic cosmic rays

Fission of one uranium nucleus (200 MeV)

10^{-4} — Fusion of one deuterium and one tritium nuclei (17.6 MeV)

10^{-5} — Alpha particle emitted by plutonium-239 (5.16 MeV)

1 million electron-volts (MeV) — 10^{-6} — Beta radiation from strontium-90 (0.546 MeV)

10^{-7} — Medical X-ray (50 kilovolts)

Electrons in color TV tube

10^{-8}

1 thousand electron-volts (KeV) — 10^{-9}

10^{-10}

10^{-11}

Rays (photons) of visible light

1 electron-volt (eV) — 10^{-12}

of energy released in fission is closely related to the so-called *binding energy*.

The binding energy is different for different nuclei. Einstein's most famous formula, $E = mc^2$, is the one used to calculate this energy: E represents energy in ergs, m the mass in grams, and c the speed of light in centimeters per second. So, given a mass we can arrive at an energy, but what mass should we use? It was mentioned earlier that the weight (more correctly, the mass) of an atom was very close to the mass of the constituent neutrons and protons. The difference between this measured mass and the exact sum of the masses of the constituent parts is called the mass defect, and it is the amount of mass to use in the equation. It is different for different nuclei: light nuclei contain more energy per nucleon than do medium-weight atoms like iron or oxygen. Heavy elements also have more energy per nucleon than the middle ones. This implies that energy could be released if nucleons from the very light or heavy elements

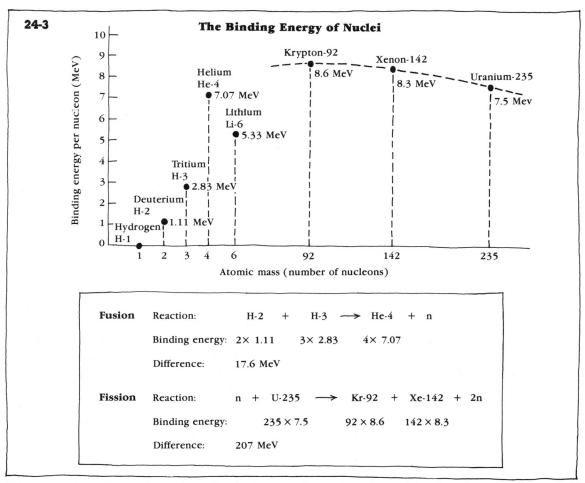

24-3

The Binding Energy of Nuclei

Fusion	Reaction:	H-2	+	H-3	$\longrightarrow$	He-4	+	n
	Binding energy:	2× 1.11		3× 2.83		4× 7.07		
	Difference:	17.6 MeV						
Fission	Reaction:	n	+	U-235	$\longrightarrow$	Kr-92	+	Xe-142	+	2n
	Binding energy:		235 × 7.5		92 × 8.6	142 × 8.3		
	Difference:	207 MeV						

When protons and neutrons are brought together to form an atomic nucleus, energy is released. This energy is called the *binding energy* of the nucleus. Nuclei near the ends of the periodic table have less binding energy per nucleon than those near the center; thus energy is available for release both in nuclear reactions in which light nuclei combine and in those in which heavy nuclei split.

24-4   **Nuclear Fission Reaction**

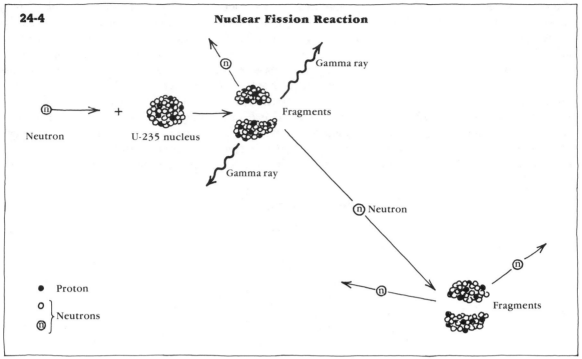

A neutron striking a uranium-235 (U-235) nucleus may cause it to split into two roughly equal fragments—yielding energy in gamma rays and in the motion of the fragments. Several neutrons are released that may go on to cause further fissions of U-235 nuclei. The fission fragments are themselves unstable and shoot off beta rays, gamma rays, and sometimes a neutron as they transmute into stable nuclides.

were used to assemble middle-weight elements instead.

Binding energy is released in the splitting of large nuclei, and the energy is high compared to the energy in a chemical reaction because the strong force is very large compared to the force involved in chemical bonds. It is an immense difference, and that is why pounds of plutonium produce as much energy as millions of tons of TNT.

Certain nuclei, called fissile, will split apart after absorbing a neutron. Upon absorbing an extra neutron, the nucleus becomes unstable and breaks into pieces. This breakage is called fission, in analogy to the fission of the amoeba, a single cell organism which reproduces by splitting. When an atom splits, two or three spare neutrons go flying off. These neutrons, having no charge, just keep going until they crash into other nuclei, which, if fissile, will probably break as well. Chain reactions are the result of this effect happening over and over.

It has been mentioned that heat is manifested in matter by the motion of atoms. If the temperature is high enough, as it is in stars, atoms will collide with each other with enough energy that the nuclei come close together. If they get close enough for the nuclear force to come into play, the nuclei may bind, forming a single larger nucleus, and release energy. This is the mechanism of energy release in the stars; solar energy comes from this nuclear reaction, called *fusion*. In a fusion weapon, deuterium and tritium—hydrogen with two and three nucleons,

24-5   Nuclear Fusion Reaction

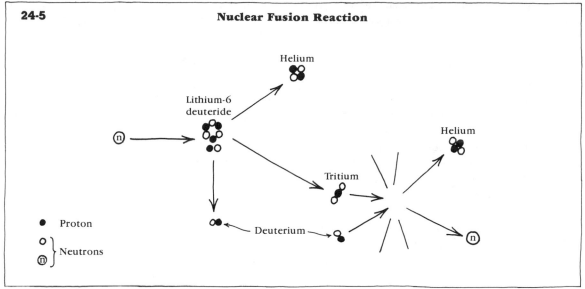

Lithium deuteride is a solid material made up of lithium and deuterium (heavy hydrogen). Molecules of this compound, which contain the light isotope lithium-6, can be used to supply tritium and deuterium for nuclear fusion. Upon absorbing a neutron, a lithium-6 nucleus will split into tritium and helium. Under conditions of very high temperature and pressure, the helium and deuterium nuclei will fuse together, releasing their nuclear energy.

respectively—collide to form helium. Helium contains less energy per nucleon than deuterium or tritium, and the excess energy is released in the explosion. The fusion process may also provide a source of energy for peaceful uses. Research on this comparatively clean nuclear energy source continues to progress.

Nuclear Radiation

Nuclei which do not have a satisfactory balance of protons and neutrons do not stay in the same configuration forever, so they are called unstable.

Unstable nuclei spontaneously emit radiations and decay toward a more stable configuration. A nucleus may just throw off neutrons, or it may convert a neutron into a proton. How can this happen? A neutron contains a proton and an electron bound together. If the electron is thrown out, the effect is to convert a neutron into a proton. In a slightly different process, a proton can be replaced by a neutron. In this transformation an electron with a positive charge, called a positron, is emitted. (This particle was predicted by P. A. M. Dirac, and later observed experimentally.) Both positrons and electrons are beta particles (rays), hence either of these two decay modes is called beta emission. Another chunk that gets thrown out (emitted) from unstable nuclei is made up of two protons plus two neutrons. This chunk is named an alpha particle, and is the same thing as the nucleus of a helium atom. When an atom decays by throwing out alpha particles from its nucleus, it is said to be an alpha emitter. If a nucleus emits alpha particles, beta particles, or neutrons, its identity must change. The rate at which particles are emitted is related to a quantity called half-life. The half-life is the amount of time it takes for one half of the atoms in a given amount of material to convert (transmute) into something else. The more stable a material is, the longer its half-life. A few elements exist naturally on earth that do not have a stable number of neutrons in their nuclei and so are slowly transmuting into more stable isotopes.

If an atom with ninety-two protons (uranium) emits an alpha-particle, it now has two fewer protons and is therefore a new element. The nuclear charge has become ninety, and the element has changed from uranium to thorium. The resulting thorium nucleus is not one with a stable number of neutrons either, and it also decays by alpha emission, leaving behind a radium atom. The radium emits an alpha and becomes radon, which becomes polonium; this is still an unstable combination, though, until the polonium atom throws out one last alpha-particle, leaving an isotope of lead which is stable. Each change of an atom's identity as it decays is called a transition. The decays may be by alpha-emission, which reduces the number of both protons and of neutrons by two, by positron emission, which leaves one fewer neutron and one more proton, or by electron emission, in which a neutron decays into a proton which stays in the nucleus and an electron which leaves it. It was not known at first that electron emissions were of the same particle as that which inhabits the outer, electron region of the atom, so another name, beta particle (or beta ray), was given to it.

The four types of radiation (alpha, beta, gamma, and neutron) are disruptive of the matter through which they pass; electrons are torn from atoms leaving behind charged atoms called ions which are chemically active. Alpha particles are easily stopped, but create a heavy track of ionization. The beta particles travel further, but are readily deflected through interactions with electrons bound to atoms. The gamma rays penetrate deeply and produce much ionization. Positrons are short lived; they recombine with electrons and shortly thereafter disappear, converting their combined mass into the energy of gamma rays. Neutrons don't interact much with charged particles, rather they crash into nuclei and displace them within their surroundings or transmute them into different elements.

The Chart of the Nuclides

The relationships among the isotopes are shown in a chart called the chart of the nuclides. The isotopes are entered in the chart with the row given by the atomic number of the element (the number of protons), and the column by the number of neutrons. When a radioactive nucleus emits a positron, an electron, a neutron, or an alpha particle it transmutes into some other nuclide, which has a different place in the chart. If an alpha particle is ejected, two protons and two neutrons leave the nucleus, and the new identity of the nucleus is found two columns left and two rows down. Electron emission accompanies the conversion of a neutron into a proton, so a nucleus, on emitting an electron, moves one column right and one row down. Positron emission corresponds to the reverse situation; the new nucleus has one more neutron and one fewer protons than before. Thus its position moves one column left and one row up.

The table starts with the single neutron, which decays into a proton and an electron. The next entry is for the element hydrogen. The most frequently found form of hydrogen, making up almost 100 percent of the hydrogen that exists, is that with a single proton nucleus. The natural occurrence of deuterium is about 0.014 percent. Deuterium, when bonded to oxygen to form water, increases the weight of the water molecule. Water so constructed is called heavy water, and is used as a neutron moderator in some nuclear reactors. The natural occurrence of tritium is extremely small, but tritium is manufactured for use in nuclear weapons, and in fusion power research.

The next isotopes in the chart are those of helium. By far the most common helium nucleus is He-4, composed of two protons and two neutrons. Helium also exists in two other isotopes, He-5,

24-6

Nuclides of the Light Elements

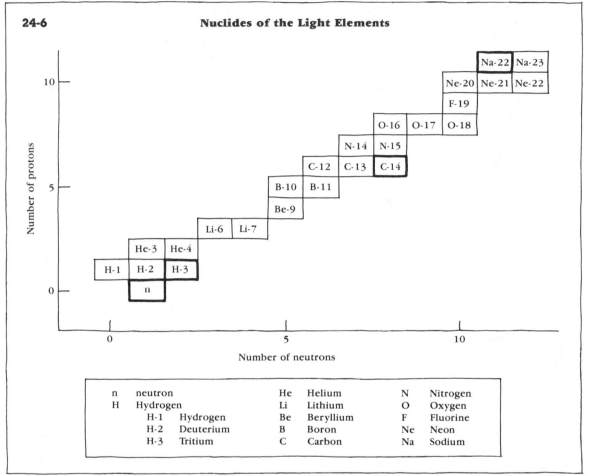

n	neutron	He	Helium	N	Nitrogen
H	Hydrogen	Li	Lithium	O	Oxygen
	H-1 Hydrogen	Be	Beryllium	F	Fluorine
	H-2 Deuterium	B	Boron	Ne	Neon
	H-3 Tritium	C	Carbon	Na	Sodium

All stable atomic nuclei have neutrons and protons in nearly the same ratio—hence, when arranged according to number of protons and number of neutrons, they lie on a diagonal swath. Those above or below the main sequence of nuclides are generally unstable. Among the eleven lightest elements, tritium (H-3) and carbon-14 emit beta particles to become helium-3 and nitrogen-14, respectively, and sodium-22 decays by positron emission to become neon-22. The free neutron itself is unstable and becomes hydrogen-1 (a proton) by beta emission in minutes.

having three neutrons, and He-6 with four.

Lithium is the next lightest element. It has four isotopes including one (Li-7) which also exists in an excited state. An excited state of a nucleus is one with more energy than the minimum required for that nucleus (called the ground state). The lightest of the lithium isotopes is Li-6, which is used in the fusion part of thermonuclear weapons. Li-6 deuteride (LiD) is a solid at atmospheric temperature and pressure, so does not require cryogenic equipment to provide the degree of aggregation required for fusion to occur. The first experiments with fusion didn't use LiD, so cooling equipment was necessary.

Another member of the chart is carbon-14,

which is radioactive with a half-life of 5,730 years. While living, a plant or animal exchanges carbon with its environment, and the fraction of radioactive carbon (C-14) in the organism is about the same as that in the carbon dioxide of the atmosphere. Following death, the fraction of C-14 the organism contains changes only by radioactive decay. Consequently, carbon-14 is useful for dating organic material.

Radioactive carbon is produced as a result of neutron capture by nitrogen in the atmosphere. The neutrons produced in the atmospheric testing of both fission and fusion weapons has introduced quantities of carbon-14 oxide, which is slowly dissolving into the oceans. That still in the atmosphere is inhaled by air-breathing creatures.

The elements of medium weight contain less energy per nucleon than do the light or heavy elements. Iron-55 (half-life 2.6 years) is produced by neutron irradiation of the structural material of a nuclear weapon. This nuclide is concentrated by fish, posing a hazard in the food chain. Cobalt-60 is produced by neutron irradiation of the cladding material of nuclear fuel rods. The radioactivity of this material prevents the disassembly of nuclear plants that have ceased operating until 100 years after cessation, if only personal local radiation shielding is to be used by disassembly workers. Krypton-85 is a noble gas which is occasionally released into the environment by operating nuclear reactors. It decays by beta emission, with a half-life of 9.4 years. Strontium-89 and Sr-90 have half-lives of 52.7 days and 28 years, respectively. These nuclides are present in spent nuclear fuel, and in radioactive fallout. Strontium-90 emits high energy beta rays, and is used to make small nuclear electric power sources.

Technetium-99m (half life sixty hours) is used in 81 percent of medical procedures involving radiopharmaceuticals. Tc-99, a component in nuclear waste, has a half-life of 210,000 years. It is a highly mobile material, and difficult to contain in the storage of nuclear waste. Ra-dioactive iodine, as I-129 and I-131, is produced in nuclear reactors. I-131 is a radiopharmaceutical. Iodine is concentrated in the thyroid, and there is much evidence of the production of nodules in the thyroids of people exposed to fallout. Use of iodine pills in the event of fallout is intended to saturate the thyroid with iodine so that no more would be taken up. Cesium is present in nuclear waste and radioactive fallout as several isotopes, of which Cs-137, with a half-life of thirty years, is the most important. A source of beta and gamma radiation, it is hazardous to muscle tissue, bone, and bone marrow.

Elements beyond the middle of the periodic table weight are generally unstable. An atom of one element decays into another which in turn decays, producing a path in the chart of the nuclides. The predominant mode of decay for the heaviest nuclei is by alpha emission which, as we have noted, transforms one nuclide onto another two rows down and two columns to the left in the chart. As four nucleons leave the nucleus in alpha emission, the atomic weight is reduced by four. At some points beta decay occurs, moving one position up and to the left; the atomic weight stays the same. It follows that all nuclides in the same series have atomic weights that differ by multiples of four. There are four separate series, and for each heavy nuclide one can identify the series to which it belongs by dividing its atomic weight by four and noting the remainder. For the thorium series, the remainder is zero. For example, plutonium-240 has 240 nucleons, four times sixty. It decays to U-236, four times fifty-nine. For both nuclides the remainder is zero, showing they are members of the thorium series. A remainder of one characterizes nuclides of the neptunium series, two, the uranium series, and three, the actinium series.

The diagonal track across the chart of the nuclides, which comes about by successive alpha emissions, is a characteristic of each series. Branches, parallel to the main line of descent, also exist.

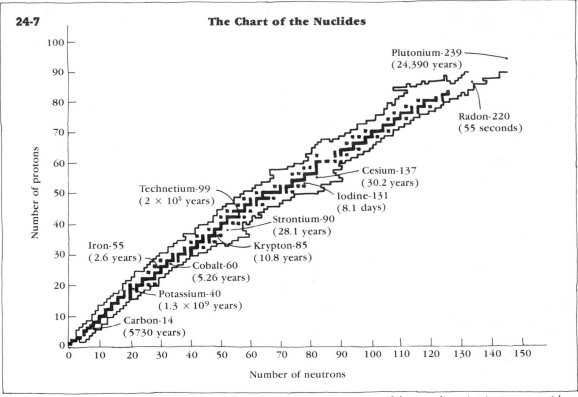

24-7

The Chart of the Nuclides

Plutonium-239
(24,390 years)

Radon-220
(55 seconds)

Cesium-137
(30.2 years)

Technetium-99
(2×10^5 years)

Iodine-131
(8.1 days)

Strontium-90
(28.1 years)

Iron-55
(2.6 years)

Krypton-85
(10.8 years)

Cobalt-60
(5.26 years)

Potassium-40
(1.3×10^9 years)

Carbon-14
(5730 years)

Number of protons

Number of neutrons

The stable isotopes of all the elements show as the black patterns in this chart. The boundary lines mark the extent of known unstable isotopes. A few of the more important of these radioactive isotopes are identified, and their half-lives are given.

Summary

This chapter just touches upon the ideas of physics underlying the phenomena of radioactivity and nuclear energy. It is written in the hope that physical concepts mentioned in other chapters will not seem arcane.

We have seen that the different nuclides are assemblages of neutrons and protons, and that some are stable but many are not, such as those formed as fission fragments. Energy may be released from the very heavy and very light elements, although controlling these processes, fission and fusion, is not easy nor is it without side effects.

The elements can be organized in the periodic table, which reflects chemical properties. The periodic table can be expanded by replacing each element with a list of its isotopes, yielding the chart of the nuclides.

The nuclides chart has been studied to find clues to nuclear structure. Many ideas exist, but the subject is not completely understood. Many more particles are known than those mentioned here, and fascinating research into the nature of elementary particles continues.

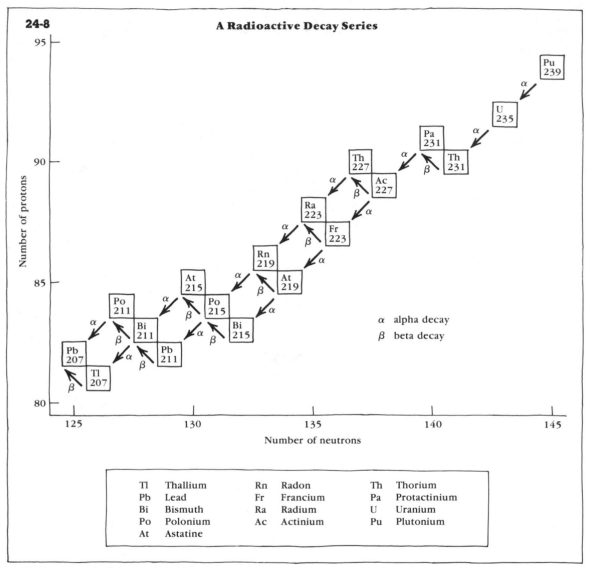

24-8

A Radioactive Decay Series

At the heavy end of the periodic table, only a few nuclides beyond lead are stable enough to be found in nature. Most decay by emitting an alpha particle, which takes away two protons and two neutrons. Thus plutonium-239 becomes uranium-235, to be followed by further changes—sometimes by beta emission—that yield the chain of transient nuclides shown, ending at the stable nuclide lead-207. There are three additional chains of nuclides having similar decay patterns.

Suggested Readings

Listed below is only a tiny sampling of the many available books about physics.

FEYNMANN, R. P., R. B. LEIGHTON, AND M. L. SANDS. *Feynman Lectures on Physics*. Reading, Mass.: Addison-Wesley, 1963.

FRENCH, A. P. *MIT Introductory Physics Series*. New York: W.W. Norton & Co., 1971.

SEGRE, EMILIO. *From X-Rays to Quarks: Modern Physicists and Their Discoveries*. San Francisco: W. H. Freeman and Co., 1980.

WEISSKOPF, VICTOR. *Knowledge and Wonder*. New York: Doubleday, 1962.

WEISSKOPF, VICTOR. *Physics in the Twentieth Century*. Cambridge: M.I.T. Press, 1972.

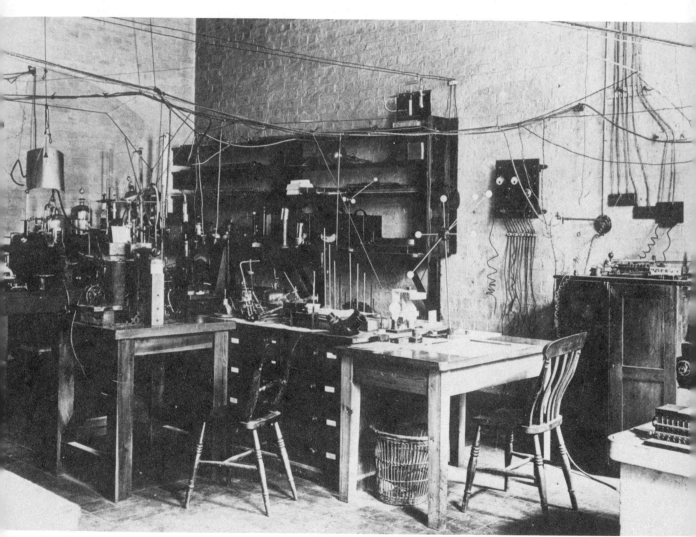

The laboratory of Ernest Rutherford at Cambridge University.

25. Unstable Atoms: 1896–1913

In these two chronological narratives, Alfred Romer surveys the pioneer times of and the scientists behind the birth of the nuclear age. Here one can read of the famous names, what they did, and how it added up: Becquerel and the Curies; Rutherford, Soddy, Hahn, and Geiger; Irène and Frédéric Joliet-Curie; and the Americans, from Boltwood to Lawrence and Urey. Here is the story of fission itself, of Otto Frisch and Lise Meitner, and of the anxious wartime beginnings of the large-scale release of nuclear energy, ending with the work of Fermi and the first chain reaction in Chicago in 1942 under Stagg Field stadium. On the way, Romer tells of isotopes and positrons, cyclotrons and cloud chambers, and how and where they came to be.

NUCLEAR PHYSICS BEGAN with uranium, an element named for a planet which, in turn, had been named for an ancient deity, the ancestor of the Olympian gods. In 1896, uranium was the heaviest of the seventy acknowledged elements. The story of nuclear physics, however, begins with X rays; and the story of X rays begins with the puzzle of the cathode rays.

From X Rays to Radium

The cathode rays first appeared with high-voltage discharges in glass bulbs from which most of the air had been pumped. Sometimes they showed as blue streamers, sometimes they were invisible; and where they touched the wall of the tube, they made it glow with a green or blue luminescence. They were either light rays or charged particles, depending on which of their contradictory properties one chose to ignore.

On New Year's Day in 1896, Wilhelm Conrad Röntgen of the University of Würzburg mailed a brief pamphlet to the leading physicists of Europe describing a new kind of radiation, an "X ray" which he had generated using cathode-ray tubes. These rays arose at the luminescent spot where the cathode rays played on the wall of the tube. The X rays themselves could excite luminescence; and they affected photographic plates and passed freely through opaque materials. In confirmation, Röntgen had included a few photographs made by the X rays. Most were merely curious, such as that of metal weights nested in their wooden box, but one was disconcerting. It showed the bones of a human hand, clearly delineated within the shadowy outline of living flesh.

Everyone had cathode-ray tubes and thus could produce X rays, and skeletal photographs appeared all over the world. However, it was the link with luminescence that caught the fancy of Henri Becquerel in Paris. He was familiar with phosphorescence—the glow excited in certain crystals by light—and he began to look for crystals in which this glow might be accompanied by penetrating rays. In February he

Alfred Romer

Romer is a physicist-historian who has published comprehensive studies of the discovery and development of radioactivity and the early growth of nuclear physics.

found one—potassium uranyl sulfate—which blackened photographic plates through opaque paper wrappings when it lay in the sunshine. Curiously, however, the same penetrating rays were emitted when the crystals lay in the dark; and they came indifferently from phosphorescent and nonphosphorescent compounds so long as they contained uranium. They came even from uranium metal, although, as Becquerel remarked, no other metal was known to be phosphorescent.

Meanwhile, in the first burst of excitement, another significant property of the X rays was independently discovered five times: by Röntgen, by Benoist and Hurmuzecu of Paris, by J. J. Thomson of Cambridge University, by Righi of Bologna, and by Bergman of St. Petersburg. X rays could make air a temporary conductor of electricity, an ability that Becquerel found to be shared by his rays from uranium.

Of the group, Thomson was best able to turn the discovery to a profit. He had long believed that gases conducted electricity by splitting their molecules into positive and negative ions. With X rays, he gained control of the process and was able to demonstrate their reality by experiments in which he formed ions, moved them about, or let them recombine into uncharged molecules.

Thomson soon shifted his interest to cathode rays, handing over the ionization studies to a postgraduate student from New Zealand, Ernest Rutherford. Both projects prospered. In particular, Thomson was able to resolve the contradictions in the cathode rays' behavior and demonstrate that they were streams of electrically charged particles. Widening his investigations, he found identical particles involved in other phenomena. Universally they carried negative charges, equal in magnitude to the charge associated with a single valence bond in electrochemistry. Unexpectedly, he found the particles were subatomic, no more than a thousandth as heavy as the atoms of hydrogen, and Thomson named them *corpuscles* because they seemed

like the basic stuff of matter. However, they are now called *electrons.*

In the summer of 1897, Becquerel lost interest in the uranium rays, but a newcomer, Marie Sklodowska Curie, presently began to study them. She gradually came to recognize what Becquerel had implicitly established—that the rays were an integral property of uranium—and this led her to an interesting discovery. She began with a borrowed disc of uranium metal, then switched to uranium oxide in the form of pitchblende, an ore of uranium. She detected the rays by the ionization they produced, a method that made quantitative comparisons possible, and she found that they came more profusely from the pitchblende than from the metal. This was odd, for the unmixed metal should have produced more radiation than the ore with its added oxygen. The reversal suggested the presence of some other emitter of rays in the ore. She searched vigorously among the known elements, and although she found one other ray-emitter, thorium, there was no thorium in her pitchblende. Whatever was there was something unknown.

With the help of her husband Pierre, Marie Curie set out to track it down. Element-hunting was no job for physicists, but the textbook chemistry they learned from Pierre's colleague Gustave Bémont was adequate. By the end of 1898 they had separated two ray-giving, or as they proposed to call them, *radioactive* substances from pitchblende. One substance accompanied bismuth, although it could be distinguished from it, and this they proposed to call *polonium* in honor of Marie's Poland, which no longer existed as a nation. The other substance accompanied barium, and its rays were so notably intense that they called it *radium.*

Radium and barium proved almost inseparable, but they could be nudged slightly apart by fractional crystallization. This gave promise that the radium might eventually be extracted from the mixture and established as a recognized element with a unique atomic weight and light-emission spectrum. In fact, such a spectrum had already begun to appear. Eugène Demarçay, a specialist in such matters, had detected one line that could not plausibly be assigned to any known element, and which grew stronger as the Curies' samples became more radioactive.

Decaying Radioactivity

In 1898, the story shifts from Paris to Montreal and from uranium and radium to thorium— a heavy element named for a pagan god and, like uranium, radioactive.

At Cambridge University, Rutherford was systematically working on ions and the various ionizing rays that produced them. The ionization that the rays produced from uranium proved precisely like that from the X radiation, but the rays themselves were a mixture of two kinds. One, which Rutherford called *alpha rays,* produced 95 percent of the ions but penetrated so weakly that they were stopped by a sheet of heavy paper. The other, which he called *beta rays*, although poor at ionizing, were about as penetrating as ordinary X rays.

In the fall of 1898, Rutherford was appointed Macdonald Professor of Physics at McGill University in Montreal, and there he involved another newcomer, R. B. Owens, professor of electrical engineering, in extending the same investigations to the rays from thorium. These rays proved to be very similar to the rays from uranium; the only novelty to emerge was that thorium oxide was curiously sensitive to drafts.

Working alone, Rutherford soon found that deliberate air currents could carry something away from thorium oxide: a subtle presence, which worked its way through paper wrappings and other filters and retained a power to ionize air, even after it had left the thorium. Rutherford called this presence an *emanation* but thought of it in quite material terms as a radioactive gas. Its radioactivity was transient, however—it tapered off gradually, halving itself over and over again as minutes passed, in what Rutherford described as a *geometric progression in*

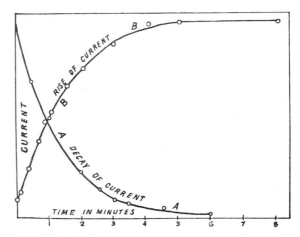

25-1 RADIOACTIVE DECAY IS EXPONENTIAL
Curves measured by Rutherford in radioactive decay experiments. Curve A shows the decay of activity of the "emanation" by one-half each minute. Curve B shows the rising activity in a box into which the emanation was allowed to diffuse; the activity gradually approaches a limiting value.

time. The more modern name for this phenomena is *exponential decay.*

Rutherford was prolific in devising experiments to test his understanding of what he saw. One of his experiments on the law of decay is worth notice because of the context in which he repeated it two years later. It concerned the growth of ionization in a space into which the emanation could diffuse steadily. The ionization must increase because of the radioactivity of the entering emanation, but at the same time, the radioactivity of the emanation present must continually decay. As mathematical analysis showed, the result would be an exponential approach to a final steady level at a rate that halved the gap in each succeeding minute.

In the course of these experiments, the walls of the ionization chamber developed a radioactivity of their own. Rutherford called it an *excited radioactivity*, but he soon convinced himself that it came from a material deposited on the walls. This radioactivity also was transient, with a halving time of eleven hours for its exponential decay. Although the new substance ultimately came from the thorium oxide, its source was the emanation, as Rutherford showed by a repetition of the growth experiment, collecting the active deposit in a chamber into which the emanation could diffuse.

These interpretations were not self-evident, as was apparent from a paper the Curies published while the second of Rutherford's two reports was still in proof. The Curies had observed a short-lived radioactivity on objects near the radium they were studying, which they attributed to some direct transfer of its energy rather than to a surface deposit; and they mentioned nothing to match Rutherford's emanation.

Of more evident importance, Marie Curie's principal work was beginning to show results. With the richest of her radium specimens, Demarçay measured the wavelengths of fifteen distinctive spectral lines. With another specimen, still a mixture of barium and radium chlorides, Curie determined an "atomic weight" that was higher than she got for barium alone. As was to be expected, radium was proving heavier than barium and was moving toward acceptance as an element.

Late in 1899, Sir William Crookes, a versatile chemist in London, undertook to extract his own radium from pitchblende. To monitor the process, he proposed photographic comparisons between his samples and a standard of pure uranium nitrate. Unfortunately, the purification by which he standardized his uranium nitrate also removed its radioactivity. Indeed, he soon found that, by appropriate chemistry, he could concentrate all the radioactivity of the uranium into a scanty precipitate that appeared to be mostly aluminum hydroxide tinted with iron. To the mysterious radioactive substance in the sample he gave the provisional name of *uranium X*.

By midsummer of 1900, Becquerel had accomplished something similar. He added barium chloride to a uranium solution and precipitated the barium as sulfate. Some radioactivity was al-

ways entrained in the precipitate, and although the separation was never complete, in one instance, by eighteen recyclings, he managed to reduce the activity of the uranium to one-sixth of its normal rate.

Radioactive Transmutation of Elements

In the fall of 1900, McGill University engaged a new instructor in chemistry, an Oxford graduate named Frederick Soddy. He was a rather combative person, and though there is no record of how the argument started, in March he was matched in formal debate with Rutherford before the McGill Physical Society. There Soddy defended the integrity of atoms, and Rutherford argued for the existence of electrons and the possibility that all matter was basically electrical. Within a year the two had become partners and were proposing the reality of the transmutation of elements.

What brought them together was Rutherford's perplexity over the radioactive emanations. He had acquired some German radium with which he verified that radium, like thorium, released a radioactive gas that in turn laid down a radioactive deposit. However, the relation between the emanations and the thorium and radium remained a puzzle. There were some indications that the solid preparations had simply trapped accumulations of gas; there were other indications that the gases were continually produced within them.

In the fall of 1901, Rutherford enlisted Soddy as a chemical partner. Soddy satisfied himself first that the emanation was produced directly by the thorium; then he sent it through ingenious chemical traps, none of which retained it. By this he established that the emanation was probably a member of Ramsay's new family of inert gases. Then just before Christmas, a chance precipitate indicated that neither the radioactivity nor the emanating power belonged to the thorium but, rather, to a separable *thorium X*.

Meanwhile Becquerel had become aware that in spite of his successful chemistry, inactive uranium could not really exist. Everyone who worked with it had always found it radioactive; hence the logical inference was that, however it might be impaired, uranium would eventually regain any activity it lost. In the laboratory, Becquerel's eighteen-month-old preparations justified his logic: the weakened uranium had returned to full strength and the precipitates were dead. He wrote to see whether Crookes might verify this discovery, and Crookes, rather by chance, passed the news to Montreal.

After a three-week holiday, Rutherford and Soddy received the news and found that, similarly, the radioactivity in their preparations had left the thorium X and returned to the thorium. They made a new separation, watched the separated fractions, and noted the behavior Rutherford had first discovered in his experiments on the emanation. Discounting some initial oddity, the activity of the thorium X decayed and that of the thorium returned by the two familiar exponential laws but with a new, characteristic halving period of four days.

The interpretation was straightforward: thorium must be steadily producing thorium X, and the radioactivity of the thorium X must be decaying. In what sense, however, were they to understand this "production"? Through sketchy but convincing exploration, Rutherford and Soddy determined that thorium X and thorium had well-defined and different chemical properties. In this respect the two substances behaved like different chemical elements. The "production" could be nothing less than an alchemical transmutation.

As chance would have it, Becquerel's theories about his radioactive transfers had disturbed the Curies, who preferred to think of radioactivity as a distinctive and inalterable property of the atoms of radium. In a vigorous and eloquent paper, they defended both their new element and their scientific philosophy, remarking that they had seen no evidence for the atomic transformations that Becquerel's notions implied.

This was hardly encouraging to Rutherford and Soddy, who proposed to advocate just such transformations. In their paper, they spoke only of "chemical changes" as they showed how thorium produced thorium X, thorium X produced the emanation, and the emanation laid down the active deposit. Only in their closing paragraphs did they argue that these changes had to be subatomic.

The immediate question was whether these new ideas would apply to other elements beyond thorium, and Soddy's first effort brought more answers than they expected. Soddy found himself unable to duplicate Crookes's separation of uranium X until he switched from ionization measurements to photographic registration. Then he realized that uranium must emit only alpha rays which could not penetrate the light-tight wrappings of the photographic plates, and that uranium X must emit only beta rays which did not ionize appreciably in his apparatus. This was the first hint that the two radiations might be independent. The beta rays were known to be electrons. It was assumed that the alpha rays were soft X rays which the beta-ray electrons excited by collisions within the radioactive preparations. A. G. Grier, a student of Rutherford, had tried to establish this assumed connection. With his special ionization chambers, Grier now confirmed Soddy's discovery and went on to show that a remnant radioactivity which Soddy had never been able to remove from thorium also consisted of alpha rays alone.

The discovery had interesting implications for Rutherford and Soddy's ideas about the transformation process. They had been supposing that the first step in a transmutation was the alteration of the atom's chemical nature. This alteration made available a certain stock of energy, and the transformed atom gradually radiated this energy away. Now they knew that alpha rays were being emitted by the unaltered primary elements, by both uranium and thorium.

It was apparent that the radiation did not follow the transmutation but accompanied it. The alpha rays from uranium and thorium marked the initial transformations in which uranium X and thorium X were produced. The activity of the thorium X marked the production of the emanation, that of the emanation, the production of the active deposit. The deposit was active because of still another transformation within it. The exponential law, by which these radioactivities decreased, no longer marked a decay of energy but, rather, the progress of the transformation. In fact, it corresponded to a well-known chemical law in which a single substance altered simply in proportion to its own quantity. Hence all radioactivities must decrease in time. If those of uranium and thorium seemed constant, it was only because their quantities were not perceptibly altered by the small fraction of them transforming.

This theory was based on decidedly limited knowledge, mostly derived from thorium and its derivatives; it had yet to be tested on uranium, polonium, and radium. Nevertheless, the theory of radioactive transmutations was already complete and competent to account for everything to which it would be applied in the future. It still lacked a description of how the atom changed its nature and how this involved the alpha and beta rays, but these things would come in time, as clarifications rather than alterations.

A few months later, on 21 July 1902, Marie Curie reported an atomic weight for radium. Three independent determinations gave values of 225.3, 225.8, and 224.0. These not only certified radium as an element but set it in the periodic table in the gap between bismuth and thorium, and below barium as its chemical behavior required.

Alpha Rays and Energy

Since the alpha rays were no longer a secondary effect, they were certainly worth investigating. Rutherford and Soddy had been speaking of atoms as "spontaneously breaking-up with evolution of energy." The beta-ray electrons could be fragments of a breakup. Perhaps the alpha rays were also particles carrying electric charges.

If so, they should swerve in crossing a magnetic field, and although Pierre Curie had reported that the nonpenetrating rays from radium did not do so this might only mean that their swerving was minute.

Rutherford managed to detect the swerve of the alpha-ray particles, but only after strenuous effort. He limited the paths of his rays to narrow corridors in which the least of curvings could be detected. He now had a rich supply of radium, but even so he needed a sensitive electroscope to observe the ionization from the scanty ribbons that passed through, and he had to dismantle Owens's biggest dynamo to get a magnet strong enough to deflect them. By that he knew that the alpha rays carried charges, and by half-capping the exits from the corridors, he determined the direction of their deflection and discovered that the charges were positive.

More information could be obtained if the rays could also be swerved in an electric field. This should have been possible with high voltages applied to alternating pairs of the metal barriers between the corridors, but unfortunately, the intense ionization that the alpha rays produced caused the plates to spark over before any considerable deflection occurred. However, from the slightest of indications, Rutherford made a guess and from it calculated a pair of numbers: the alpha-ray particles might have a charge-to-mass ratio of 6,000 (in the customary units of abcoulombs per gram) and travel at 2.5×10^9 centimeters per second.

From electrochemistry, the charge-to-mass ratio for a hydrogen ion was around 10,000; for electrons, it was nearer 10,000,000. The alpha rays were certainly particles with positive charges, quite likely the size of light atoms and moving at about one-twelfth the speed of light.

In his report on these experiments, Rutherford also named the *gamma rays*, which were first noticed by Paul Villard in Paris in 1900. Gamma rays were more penetrating than the beta rays, ionized even more weakly, and as Rutherford had already found, were emitted by

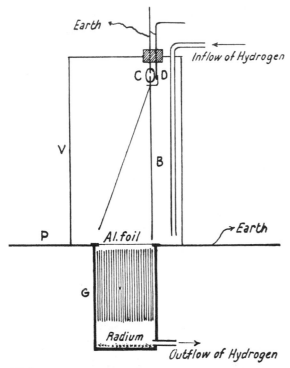

25-2 ALPHA RAYS ARE CHARGED PARTICLES

Rutherford and Soddy used this apparatus to demonstrate that alpha particles from radium carry an electrical charge. The alpha particles were made to travel upward through a set of narrow corridors (G) before passing through a thin sheet of aluminum foil to be detected by a sensitive electroscope (B). Placing the corridors between the poles of a strong magnet caused the alpha particles to curve into the walls and not be registered by the electroscope. A steady downward flow of hydrogen gas reduced interference with the measurement from radium emanation.

thorium and the two excited radioactivities as well as by radium.

The activities of Rutherford and Soddy during the following winter, with uranium X and the emanations of radium and thorium need not concern us. Soddy was offered a position in William Ramsay's laboratory in London, and in the spring of 1903 the two ended their partnership with a valedictory paper containing some energy calculations. It seemed likely that the swift

and heavy alpha particles were the chief carriers of energy, and one calculation set the total output of a gram of radium at a hundred million to a billion gram calories over its lifetime. Since hydrogen and oxygen released only 4,000 gram calories when burned to make a gram of water, it was evident that radioactive processes were altogether different from chemical reactions. Another calculation set the spending rate of radium at 15,000 gram calories per year.

Thus, on a geological time scale, the life of radium would be relatively short—no more than a few thousand years. Certainly radium was younger than the minerals from which it was extracted. The enormous total output must represent an internal energy of constitution of atoms. Aside from its radioactivity, there was nothing extraordinary about radium. It was reasonable to suppose that other elements held comparable stores which remained hidden only because their atoms were not transmuting. If this were so, Rutherford and Soddy suggested, the maintenance of the sun's energy need no longer be a problem.

Extravagant as these numbers seemed, they fell short of reality. The Curies had radium so concentrated that it kept itself warmer than its surroundings. With such a sample, during the same spring, Pierre Curie and Albert Laborde measured an energy output of 100 gram calories per hour per gram of radium. Pierre Curie was willing to entertain the idea of a transformation, which for radium would be very slow on any human scale of time, but he thought it still possible that the energy came through the radium from some outside source.

Curie and Laborde's value of energy output was about sixty times the rate Rutherford and Soddy had calculated. The discrepancy seems to have come from an accumulation of underestimates, but it worried Rutherford until he could make his own heat measurements on a new, large specimen of radium in the fall of 1903 and substantiate his assumption that the alpha particles carried the bulk of the energy.

25-3 RADIOACTIVE DECAY CHAINS

Radioactive decay chains, as proposed by Rutherford in 1903, with the substances named as they were at the time. The half-life of each substance is given. The emanation (EMAN.) is the substance we now know as radon.

Between 1894 and 1900, Ramsay had enlarged the periodic table with an entire family of inert gases. He had found argon first, in collaboration with Lord Rayleigh; then helium, already known by its spectrum to exist in the sun; then neon, krypton, and xenon. By the summer of 1903, with twenty milligrams of pure radium bromide—purchased from Friedrich Giesel, director of Buchler und Compagnie in Braunschweig—and Soddy's experience to draw on, Ramsay proposed to add a new member to the rare gas family by producing the spectrum of radium emanation. Together he and Soddy built

an apparatus of glass tubing, released the emanation within it, and excited the glow. What they saw was the spectrum of carbon dioxide, set free perhaps by the action of the alpha rays on their stopcock grease. They froze that out with liquid air, which also condensed the emanation—as Rutherford and Soddy had discovered in Montreal—and then they saw the spectrum of helium.

This was not unexpected. Rutherford and Soddy had twice pointed out that helium might be a product of radioactivity, since it was found occluded in minerals of uranium and thorium.

Nevertheless it was dramatic. The helium could have entered the apparatus only within the crystals of radium bromide. It was an inert gas; there was no way it could be drawn from the atmosphere by chemical combination. It could accumulate in the radium bromide only after its crystals had solidified from their last purifying solution. Here was direct and visible evidence of the formation of one established element by another.

For Rutherford, it undergirded his suspicion that the alpha particles might be helium atoms.

Identities and Kinships

By 1903 more than a dozen radioactive elements were known. Uranium and thorium had been discovered first. Others had been teased from uranium ores: polonium and radium by the Curies, actinium by André Debierne, emanium by Giesel, radio-lead by K. A. Hofmann, radio-tellurium by W. Marckwald. Still others appeared as transformation products, identified sometimes by their chemistry and sometimes only by the growth and decay of radiation. Among them they raised questions. Why did Giesel's polonium differ from Marie Curie's? Was emanium perhaps identical with actinium, or radio-tellurium with polonium? Were these puzzling substances related to radium or uranium? Was radium itself related to uranium?

Answers came as Rutherford studied the changes in radioactivity of the radium active deposit and deduced the succession of transformations through which its atoms ran. Each of the transforming substances had its distinctive half-value period, and a comparison of their half-value periods showed that radio-tellurium was identical with polonium and that both corresponded to the radium F in Rutherford's transformation chain. In a similar comparison, emanium was identical with actinium. The similarity of their rays suggested that radio-lead was Rutherford's radium D.

There was reason to suppose that the radium in minerals had once been uranium. Soddy tried, without success, to establish this by watching radium accumulate in a solution of purified uranium. However, a mathematical argument drawn from the exponential law which governed all radioactive transformations suggested a less direct method of deducing the connection. Two American chemists, Bertram B. Boltwood in New Haven and Herbert N. McCoy at the University of Chicago, applied such tests and verified that radium was descended from uranium. Soddy's failure to observe its growth was explained when, in 1908, Boltwood found a long-lived intermediate product which he named *ionium*.

Understanding thorium was not so easy. First, a *radiothorium* was discovered in Ramsay's laboratory by Otto Hahn in an extract from a new thorium mineral from Ceylon. The radiothorium released an emanation with a half-value period of one minute and somewhat resembled thorium in its chemical behavior, although it was far more radioactive. Ramsay was impressed and immediately secured Hahn a position in Emil Fischer's laboratory in Berlin, which Hahn thought prudent to defer until he had acquired a bit more experience with Rutherford in Montreal. Radiothorium proved to be the true parent of thorium X, but its relationship to thorium was not cleared until Hahn discovered a pair of intermediate products to which he gave names of *mesothorium 1* and *mesothorium 2*.

Even without these new substances, McCoy—now joined by W. H. Ross—and Boltwood had tied radiothorium to thorium by measurements like those with which they had connected radium to uranium. In addition, Boltwood pointed out that mesothorium 1 behaved chemically very much like thorium X and that radiothorium was remarkably like thorium. After strenuous efforts, McCoy and Ross reported that any chemical separation of radiothorium from thorium was "remarkably difficult if not impossible." Then in 1908, Boltwood found the chemistry of ionium curiously like that of both thorium and uranium X, and this was confirmed

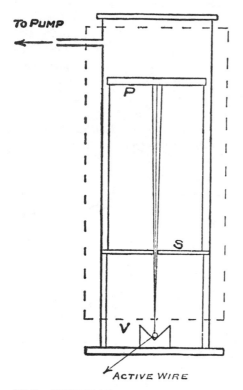

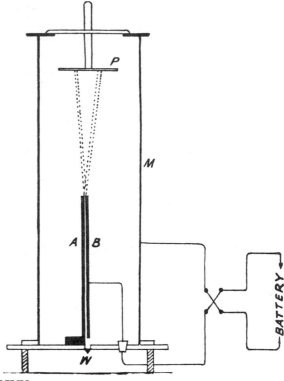

25-4 CHARGE-TO-MASS RATIO FOR ALPHA PARTICLES

Rutherford estimated the ratio of charge to mass for alpha particles by measuring their deflection in magnetic and electric fields. The apparatus for magnetic deflection is on the left; that for electric deflection, on the right. A ribbon of alpha particles from active deposits at V or W was formed by the slit (S) or by the narrow corridor between plates A and B, and allowed to impinge on a photographic plate (P). A magnet on the left, or the high-voltage battery on the right, created the fields to swerve the particles, shifting the position of their marks on the plates.

in 1909 by Bruno Keetman, a student of Marckwald's in Berlin. Experience with the rare earth elements had shown that at the upper end of the periodic table elements might resemble their neighbors closely. These new resemblances were close indeed, and more significant than anyone at the time could realize.

Alpha Particles and Nuclear Atom

In 1903, Rutherford bought thirty milligrams of Giesel's pure radium bromide, and by 1904 he was ready to employ it in alpha-particle experiments. The first job was to measure the total positive charge that the particles carried in order to estimate how many were being emitted. The experiment was complicated by some unexpected ionization but finally gave the number Rutherford wanted. From this number, if he supposed that each particle carried the electronic unit of charge, he could calculate that a gram of radium expelled 6.2×10^{10} alpha particles per second. This meant that an equal number of radium atoms were transmuting per second; thus the half-value period (or half-life) for radium was 1,280 years.

Next, Rutherford began deflection experiments to establish the charge-to-mass ratio. He could now use as a source of alpha particles a wire coated with radium C through exposure to the radium emanation. With photographic recording, he could improve his sensitivity by accumulating particle impacts over a long exposure and, at the same time, directly record the deflection of the arriving beam. The magnetic experiment was relatively easy, but an electric deflection required more ingenuity. When the experiments were finished in 1906, Rutherford calculated a speed of 2.06×10^9 centimeters per second and a charge-to-mass ratio of 5,070.

The result of Rutherford's experiments was somewhat ambiguous—the charge-to-mass ratio was half that for the hydrogen ion. If Rutherford supposed that, like hydrogen, the alpha particle carried a single electronic charge, then it must be twice as heavy. This would indicate that it was a hydrogen molecule or a half-atom of helium. If the alpha particle carried a double charge, it would be a helium atom. This was more likely and could be confirmed if the particles could be counted as they were emitted. Rutherford's electrometer was almost sensitive enough to respond to the trail of ions that a single alpha particle produced, but when he tried counting, the margin was too slender for certainty.

These same experiments showed an interesting side effect. When Rutherford slowed the particles by passing them through a slip of mica, his photographic image blurred at the edges. This meant that some particles were scattered slightly, swerved by a degree or two from their direct line of motion, yet even this trifling swerve required enormous forces, considering the brief time the particles took to cross the mica. Rutherford had no doubt that on their way the alpha particles had gone through atoms rather than between them. If the scattering could be studied in detail, it might reveal something about atomic structure.

In May 1907, Rutherford left Canada to succeed Arthur Schuster at the University of Manchester, England. A list of thirty "researches possible," which he drew up on the voyage, included both the counting and the scattering of alpha particles.

The counting proved more practical. Schuster had recruited a young Bavarian, Hans Geiger, as a research fellow, and Rutherford drew him into that work. The trick they needed was to multiply the slender set of ions that a single particle produced. In principle, this could be done by speeding up the ions electrically until they produced additional ions, in their turn. Ordinarily this led to a spark, but Rutherford knew of experiments in which the multiplication had been limited. From this beginning, Rutherford and Geiger refined details until they had a device that responded reliably to the particles they sent into it. Although Rutherford shortly abandoned it, twenty years later this invention, after being twice modified and improved, became the familiar Geiger counter that is now routinely used for measuring ionizing radiation.

Their direct count gave them half as many alpha particles as Rutherford had estimated in 1904. Thus, as they expected, each alpha particle carried a double electronic charge and was undoubtedly a helium atom. They also remeasured the total charge carried off and so could calculate the charge on an electron as 4.65×10^{10} statcoulombs. This was half again as large as the previously accepted value and a good deal more reliable.

Just at this time, in 1908, Erich Regener in Berlin was finishing an investigation of the scintillations discovered by Crookes. It was known that radium could excite a glow in phosphorescent zinc sulfide, and Crookes had found that under a microscope the glow divided into tiny sparks of twinkling light. Regener showed that each spark was produced by the impact of a single alpha particle, thus making it plausible that every alpha particle produced its separate spark. Rutherford and Geiger confirmed this, obtaining the same counts both electrically and by scintillations, and now had a means for studying scattering.

Meanwhile, Rutherford and Thomas Royds succeeded in directly proving that the alpha particles were helium. Otto Baumbach, the laboratory glassblower, had made them a small, slender glass tube that was completely gas-tight but so thin that an alpha particle could penetrate its walls. This tubelet fitted inside a larger tube arranged for spectroscopic excitation. Rutherford and Royds pumped radium emanation into the tubelet and watched while the spectrum of helium gradually appeared in the gas outside it; the helium could have made its way there only in the form of alpha particles shooting through the glass wall.

Rutherford had also asked Geiger to supervise an undergraduate project for a young man named Ernest Marsden, who was to look for a "diffuse reflection" of alpha particles from metal foils. To everyone's surprise, he found that some alpha particles swerved so sharply in the foil as to reemerge from the side by which they entered. This was quite incompatible with the measurements that Geiger was acquiring in his work on ordinary scattering, which was confined within angles of only a few degrees. It remained a mystery until the spring of 1911, when Rutherford began to remark that now he knew what an atom looked like.

It was plausibly an electrical force that swung the alpha particle, and it must have been a very intense force to cause the big deflections Marsden observed. For these deflections, the alpha particle must come very close to a concentrated charge at the atom's center. All the compensating charges that balanced the central charge and kept the atom neutral must be spread thinly where they would have little effect, occupying an outer region, thousands of times farther away.

Within such an atom the alpha particle would swing on a hyperbola, tightly or loosely curved as the particle was aimed closer to or farther

from the central charge. These central charges of the atoms were small targets which most particles would miss widely, suffering slight deflections. Only the few that came close would be turned sharply back. When Rutherford understood this, he saw how to predict what fraction of the alpha particles shot at a foil would be scattered through any specified angle. His prediction proved accurate under a quick test by Geiger and more precise and deliberate observations by Geiger and Marsden.

This was the nuclear atom. It accounted for alpha-particle scattering but seemed to have no other use, and outside Rutherford's own laboratory, the announcement was received with a vast silence.

Radioactive Elements and Isotopes

In 1910, both Marckwald and Soddy discovered that the chemistry of Hahn's mesothorium 1 was very similar to that of radium. This was no novelty to Marckwald, who already knew how much thorium, radiothorium, ionium, and uranium X resembled one another, but it surprised Soddy. For a half-dozen years Soddy had been laboring with recalcitrant solutions and precipitates, trying to establish links between uranium, uranium X, ionium, and radium, and he had obtained no clear-cut results. Then, as he continued his experiments, he saw more than a simple likeness—mesothorium 1 and radium appeared to be chemically identical.

Soddy knew how radical it was to propose identity for elements whose atomic weights were demonstrably different. He also saw that other "resemblances" might be identities and grouped the elements accordingly. Radiolead (210.4) and lead (207.1) formed one group. Thorium (232.4), ionium (230.5), and radiothorium (228.4) made up another. (His own unsatisfactory experience prompted him to exclude uranium X.) Mesothorium 1 (228.4), radium (226.4), and thorium X (224.4) occupied the third group.

Next, Soddy began a search of the radiochemical literature to see what was already known and sent one of his students, Alexander Fleck, into the laboratory to learn more. As he accumulated information, he noticed that the elements with known chemistry lay in the even-numbered columns of the periodic table, and that an element moved two spaces downward when it emitted an alpha particle in its transformation. By the summer of 1912, Fleck confirmed that uranium X belonged to the thorium group and had discovered that thorium B, the eleven-hour substance in the active deposit, had the chemistry of lead.

If all the members of an identical group could be packed into a single place, then there was room in the periodic table for the large number of radioactive elements. Early in 1913 three essays appeared which fit them in—one was written by Alexander Russell, who had worked with both Soddy and Rutherford; one by Kasimir Fajans, a young Pole who had also worked with Rutherford and was now a lecturer at Karlsruhe in Baden; the third was written by Soddy. They differed only in their treatment of the transmutations by which an atom passed from radium in the second column through the emanation (placed with the other noble gases in zeroth column), to polonium which lay back in the sixth. Russell created an imaginative bridge that took the active deposit outside the regular table; Fajans invented an unobserved transitional element; and Soddy, who had the advantage of Fleck's completed studies on uranium X, mesothorium 2, and the active deposits, found room for everything.

In the spring of 1912, Niels Bohr came to Rutherford's laboratory during a year of postdoctorate travel and stayed in Manchester until July, where he learned about the nuclear atom. Following his visit, he wrote three papers on atomic structure which appeared under Rutherford's sponsorship in the *Philosophical Magazine* during the summer and fall of 1913. (By now the atom's center had acquired the name of *nucleus*.) Bohr assumed that the nucleus contained most of the matter in the atom and that it had a positive charge. (Rutherford had been ambiguous, since charges of either sign would give the same scattering.) He set the amount of this charge in electronic units equal to the place-number of the element in the periodic table; that required, in neutral atoms, an equal number of negative electrons widely spread through their outer parts. The chemical properties of an atom and its spectrum would be established by these peripheral electrons. Its radioactivity, which had proved impervious to all outside influences, must belong to its nucleus. The sets of identical elements established by Soddy must have nuclei with the same charges (to establish the chemical identity) but different masses (to establish the differences in atomic weight).

Fajans and Soddy had both given rules for the displacement of an atom across the periodic table during its transformation. The emission of an alpha particle moved it two places downward; of a beta particle, one place upward. Bohr pointed out that this was to be expected. The loss of a positive alpha particle lowered the nuclear charge and, hence, the place-number by two units. The loss of a negative beta particle raised it by one.

Not long thereafter, Soddy introduced the name of *isotope* for these atomic varieties with identical chemistry and different weights. Soon it appeared that isotopes were not simply speculative. According to the displacement rules, the nonradioactive end-products from uranium and thorium should both be lead. The atomic weights of these lead isotopes could be calculated from the known weights of their predecessors by subtracting four units (the weight of helium) for each alpha particle expelled in the chain of transformations. This gave atomic weights of 206 for uranium lead and 208 for thorium lead in contrast to the standard value of 207.

These were differences that might be checked by ordinary chemistry from the atomic weight of the accumulated lead in radioactive minerals. Uranium could be found in relatively pure minerals, and both T. W. Richards at Harvard (working at Fajans's request) and Otto Hönigschmid in Prague determined values close to 206 for the lead from uranium. Later, with lead that Soddy supplied from a rare and exceptionally pure thorium mineral, Hönigschmid came close to 208. Richards went on to measure other properties and found no differences between ordinary lead and the light isotope from uranium.

It was an interesting question: Do isotopes exist only among radioactive atoms, or are there also isotopes among the stable atoms of lower atomic weight? The first, though tentative, answer appeared in 1913. Since 1906, Thomson at Cambridge had been working to identify the positive ions in the high-voltage discharge in gases at low pressures. He had hoped to find a carrier of positive electricity to complement the negative electron, but by 1911, when he had overcome his technical difficulties, his charge-to-mass ratios indicated that these were ions of the atoms and molecules in the gas. They were easy to identify and seemed to promise a simple method of chemical analysis. By the spring of 1913 he could show the presence of xenon, krypton, argon, and neon in the less volatile of two fractions of the residue from the slow evaporation of liquid air. In the more volatile fraction, he found argon, neon, and helium. The gases showed as curving traces and were arranged in order across a photographic plate; curiously, close to the trace for neon, with its atomic weight of 20, was a second, indicating a weight of 22. No gas of this weight was known, nor was there a place for one in the periodic table. After other tests by Thomson, it seemed plausible that these two sets of atoms must constitute one of Soddy's nonseparable pairs—two isotopes of neon. This suggestion was reinforced when F. W. Aston, also at Cambridge, managed to separate pure neon by diffusion through porous clay into two fractions of slightly different density.

Summary

By 1913, less than twenty years had passed since Becquerel had first glimpsed the black smudges on his photographic plates, and in this time there were remarkable changes in our understanding of the elements. Elements were no longer absolute, nor were atoms indivisible. Transmutation was no longer forbidden—it occurred continually. In fact, it was the rule that all the heaviest elements were in the process of transmuting. An atom that began as uranium or thorium repeatedly altered itself, sometimes after pauses of only seconds or minutes, sometimes after pauses of thousands of years.

Each of these alterations took place by a division, by the expulsion from the atom of a part of itself. In some cases what split off was a beta particle—an electron of almost inconsequential mass but a carrier of negative electricity. In other cases it was an alpha particle—a carrier of positive electricity and a body with an appreciable mass, because, as it was now clear, it was the nucleus of a helium atom.

This divisible atom had a structure in which electrical forces played a crucial part. In some strange way, the mass and the positive charge went together in the nucleus; the periphery was occupied only by negative electrons. Where they lay or how they traveled must be patterned in some way; the repetitions of the periodic table required this. One of the tasks of the future would be to find what the patterns were, for example, how the electron configuration of sodium might differ from that of aluminum.

The structure of the nucleus also needed exploration. This was where the transmutations occurred; it was also the seat of enormous energies that might some day explain the sun and the stars. So far, the energies and the changes that released them were beyond human control. Perhaps they might not remain so.

The pile in the squash court: photograph of a scale model of the first atomic pile, where Enrico Fermi produced the first laboratory chain reaction, December 2, 1942.

26. Toward Fission and Fusion: 1913–1942

EARLY IN 1902, Ernest Rutherford and Frederick Soddy recognized that radioactivity was a process of transmutation in which an atom spontaneously changed its chemical nature. This was a fascinating discovery, but it was not really alchemy. Radioactive atoms transmuted at their own rate, and the transmutation could not be stopped, started, or altered by human intervention. Then in 1919, Rutherford produced evidence that he could transmute atoms of nitrogen at will.

Splitting the Nucleus

The transmutation of nitrogen was an unforeseen consequence of Rutherford's curiosity about the structure of the nuclei of atoms. When he had first imagined the nucleus and worked out the path on which an alpha particle penetrated an atom, he had assumed for simplicity that both the alpha particle and the scattering nucleus were small featureless spheres of electric charge. Since Hans Geiger and Ernest Marsden's measurements had checked Rutherford's scattering formula, this was evidently a valid simplification. Perhaps the nuclei were really featureless; but it could also be that the alpha particle and the nucleus had remained relatively far apart in the experiments.

Closer collisions might reveal some sort of nuclear structure. This would require scattering studies with light elements of low nuclear charge. The alpha particles themselves were nuclei, they were certainly light, and probably compounded. Knowledge of how they scattered hydrogen and were scattered by it might reveal something of the way they were built. During the winter of 1913–14, C. G. Darwin worked out the mathematics, and Marsden, alone now that Geiger had returned to Germany, began the experiments.

In the simple circumstance of a head-on collision, the hydrogen nucleus would be knocked free of its circling electron and propelled forward, traveling four times as far as the alpha par-

Alfred Romer

Romer is a physicist-historian who has published comprehensive studies of the discovery and development of radioactivity and the early growth of nuclear physics.

ticle would have gone. When Marsden sent alpha particles into hydrogen gas, he could detect
the long-range hydrogen nuclei as sparklets on
a scintillation screen. To study scattering he
needed a well-defined target and thus prepared
one from a thin film of hydrogen-rich wax. Immediately there were difficulties: he saw hydrogen scintillations when the wax was present but
also saw them when it was removed. They
might easily have been dislodged from traces of
water (Manchester was notoriously damp), but
they persisted even when the apparatus was
baked out, and they remained a mystery when
Marsden left for a position in New Zealand in
1915.

During the war, Rutherford was drawn into
the pressing problem of submarine detection.
Nevertheless, he continued to work on hydrogen scattering and accumulated enough information to complete four papers by April 1919,
five months after the armistice. By this time, he
understood much more about the interaction of
alpha particles with hydrogen and with the
common atoms of the atmosphere. In particular,
he could show that Marsden's mysterious long-
range scintillators appeared only when there
was nitrogen in the apparatus; and consequently
in all experiments done in air. In a close encounter, an alpha particle could evidently dislodge a hydrogen nucleus from the nucleus of a
nitrogen atom.

Also in April, Rutherford was named Cavendish Professor of Experimental Physics at Cambridge University to succeed J. J. Thomson, who
was retiring to become Master of Trinity College.

F. W. Aston, who took over Thomson's posi-
tive-ray experiments, greatly improved their
precision. Ramsay had found the atomic weight
of neon to be 20.2, Thomson had assigned
weights of 20 and 22 to its two isotopes, and no
one could tell whether Ramsay's value represented an average for a mixture of the two isotopes or whether it should match Thomson's approximate value of 20. By 1919, Aston could
specify atomic weights to two places of deci-

26-1 WALTON, RUTHERFORD, COCKROFT
Ernest Rutherford (in the center), the great experimental physicist, with his colleagues E. T. S. Walton
and John Cockroft, who built early "atom smashers."

mals, and state with assurance that the values
for neon were 20.00 and 22.00. Using oxygen
and carbon dioxide, he found that both oxygen
and carbon were simple elements—each with a
single isotope—whose atomic weights were
16.00 and 12.00. However, chlorine, whose
atomic weight was given as 35.46, proved to be
another mixture of isotopes with whole-number
weights of 35.00 and 37.00. One of the curiosi-
ties of chemistry had been its systematic jumble
of whole-number and fractional atomic weights.
Here was a hint that perhaps other fractions also
represented isotopic mixtures and that all single
isotopes might have weights in whole numbers.

If this were so, then one might speculate that
all nuclei were built up from the nuclei of hydrogen, and Rutherford said as much in his
Bakerian Lecture of 1920. During the same
summer, at the British Association for the
Advancement of Science, he suggested that this
building unit might be called a *proton*. On both
occasions he spoke also of a neutral particle, or
neutron, which he imagined to be a proton and
an electron intimately bound together. The neutron, lacking any net charge, would not interact
with nearby electrons, and so, as Rutherford

pointed out, it should pass freely through matter.

Nuclear Disintegration and Atom Smashers

Rutherford, working with James Chadwick, extended his nitrogen experiments by bombarding other elements of low atomic number (that is, those with small nuclear charges). In their first attempt, they obtained protons from boron, fluorine, sodium, aluminum, and phosphorus. By 1924, with improved technique, they could add neon, magnesium, sulfur, chlorine, argon, and potassium to the list, which now included twelve of the seventeen elements immediately beyond helium.

At first it had seemed that the alpha particle might drag out a proton as it passed by the nucleus, but by the mid-twenties this appeared less likely. From some atoms, for example, the proton carried off more energy than the alpha particle brought in. Decisive evidence came from cloud-chamber experiments in 1925, which exploited a thirty-year-old discovery by C.T.R. Wilson that water vapor in chilled air condensed around ions. If the chilling were done delicately without creating air currents, the trail of ions along the path of a flying alpha particle or proton could be materialized and photographed as a line of water drops. At Cambridge, P.M.S. Blackett photographed the cloud-tracks of alpha particles in nitrogen. Several photographs showed an alpha particle coming in; the thinner trail of a proton going out; a short, thick track which marked the recoil of the bombarded nucleus—and nothing else. Evidently the nitrogen nucleus captured the alpha particle and then emitted the proton, leaving a new nucleus whose charge had increased by one unit and whose mass had grown by three. Thus nitrogen with a mass of 14 would become an isotope of oxygen with a mass of 17.

As Aston found ingenious means for putting more and more elements through his mass spectrograph, he became more and more convinced that all individual isotopes had whole-number

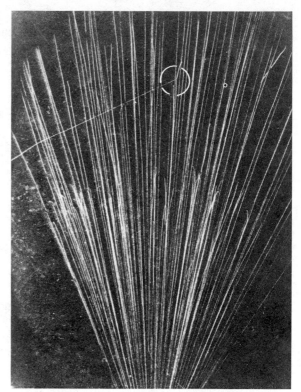

26-2 DISINTEGRATION OF NITROGEN

Photograph of the tracks of alpha particles in a Wilson cloud chamber. The circle picks out one of the occasional disintegrations of nitrogen, marked by the long, track of the proton downward to the left and the short recoil of the oxygen nucleus upward to the right.

masses, and that the fractional atomic weights of chemistry, as in the case of chlorine, were actually average values. The departures he found from this rule were only slight. Hydrogen was slightly overweight, some of the heavy elements were a trifle light. By 1927, after further improvements in precision, he discovered that these slight departures were general and systematic. If he used 16.00 for the mass of oxygen, as the chemists did, then the very lightest and the very heaviest elements had masses that were slightly greater than whole numbers; most of those in the middle had masses that were slightly less.

As Aston perceived, these differences in mass from whole numbers could reflect differences in the stability of the elements. The lowering of mass was a measure of the energy released in binding the components of the nuclei together. Aston phrased his argument in terms of Thomson's electrical theory of matter, later it would be based on Einstein's equivalence of mass and energy, the binding energy being calculated from the deficiency in mass by the equation $E = mc^2$.

The alpha particles were effective in producing transmutations, but they made an inflexible research tool. They were emitted with fixed energies, each characteristic of the transmutation stage it accompanied, and the energies available were limited by the small number of substances that furnished convenient sources. There was a real need for a high-voltage device that could produce copious streams of ultra-swift ions with controllable energies. Around 1930, various inventions of this kind were constructed.

The first device to come into operation was built at Cambridge by J. D. Cockroft and E.T.S. Walton. The high voltage was generated from a set of capacitors which were continuously charged and cascaded electronically. Whether such a scheme could produce energies equal to those of the alpha particles was an open question, but such energies might not be necessary. Using the new quantum mechanics, George Gamow was now predicting that nuclei might capture positive ions from relatively great distances. In 1930, Cockroft and Walton attained 280,000 volts. Early in 1932 they punctured a discharge tube at 710,000 volts, and by summer they were ionizing hydrogen to produce a reliable beam of protons. When the protons fell on a lithium target, alpha particles came off. Evidently a lithium nucleus with a charge of 3 and a mass of 7 was capturing a single proton and splitting neatly into a pair of helium nuclei. This could occur at any accelerating voltage between 125,000 and 500,000, and the effect was

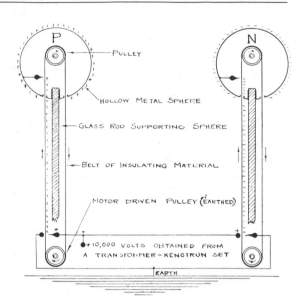

26-3   THE VAN DE GRAAFF GENERATOR

Van de Graaff's proposal of a machine for producing very high voltages for accelerating charged particles. The two insulating belts carry positive and negative electric charges, respectively, to the left and right metal spheres atop two columns. Practical machines of this type simplified the scheme to a single belt and column.

not limited to lithium. Under proton bombardment, alpha particles were emitted plentifully by boron and fluorine, certainly by calcium, potassium, nickel, iron, and cobalt, and possibly by nine other elements.

On the other side of the Atlantic, at Princeton University, Robert J. Van de Graaff conceived the simple notion of spraying electricity from pointed wires onto a conveyor belt of nonconducting silk and hauling it upward bodily to accumulate on an elevated sphere. In 1931, his second experimental model reached a potential of 1,500,000 volts, and he was thus encouraged to try for 10,000,000 volts with a giant machine to be built for the Massachusetts Institute of Technology.

Cockroft and Walton's electronic multiplier and Van de Graaff's conveyor belt produced ultrahigh voltages that were difficult to contain

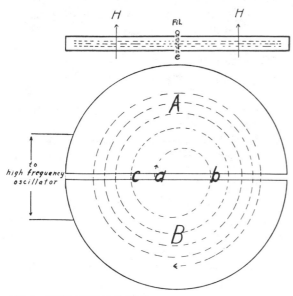

26-4 THE CYCLOTRON
Ernest Lawrence's cyclotron consisted of two hollow, D-shaped electrodes, A and B. An oscillating electric field would cause charged particles to accelerate in circular paths when the D's were placed between the poles of a strong magnet.

and formidably difficult to harness to discharge tubes. At the University of California in Berkeley, Ernest O. Lawrence realized that such problems could be avoided by accelerating ions through a long series of moderate shoves. It was well known that an ion that traveled directly across a magnetic field would swerve around the arc of a circle. Curiously the time it took an ion to complete a turn on its circle was independent of its speed: if it traveled faster, it swung wider, and the extra speed exactly compensated for the extra distance. Thus if an accelerating device could be established at some point in a magnetic field, the ions would return to it rhythmically for repeated accelerations. This was the machine that later acquired the name of *cyclotron*.

Beginning in 1930, Lawrence and M. Stanley Livingston developed the invention into a practical device, at first with a ten-centimeter mag-

net which gave the equivalent of 80,000 volts, then with a nine-inch magnet which reached 500,000 volts. They were working on their third model, with an eleven-inch magnet and 1,500,000-volt protons, when Cockroft and Walton announced the disintegration of lithium. This took Lawrence by surprise; he had expected to need higher energies, but with the help of colleagues from Yale, he was soon able to detect alpha particles.

These three machines were the *atom-smashers*, or more formally, the *particle accelerators* of the thirties; of the three, the Van de Graaff generator and the cyclotron proved the most useful. The first group to achieve transmutations with a Van de Graaff machine was headed by Merle Tuve at the Department of Terrestrial Magnetism of the Carnegie Institution of Washington in 1933. In 1935, R. G. Herb and his associates at the University of Wisconsin overcame some of the insulation problems by operating at increased air pressure inside a steel tank. At Berkeley, a new cyclotron with a twenty-seven-inch magnet was already under construction in 1933. By 1937, competing cyclotrons were operating at Cornell and at the Universities of Illinois, Michigan, and Rochester. These machines were used to accelerate every feasible ion for bombardment against every manageable target to discover what interactions took place and what isotopes were produced, with the eventual purpose of accumulating information about the structure of the nucleus.

Some Observed Oddities

In the twenties, our picture of matter was relatively simple. Negative electricity was carried exclusively by electrons; positive electricity was carried by protons, which were some 1,800 times heavier. The nuclei of atoms were assembled from protons and electrons—enough protons to make up the observed mass, enough electrons to bring the charge down to its proper value. Planetary electrons, enough to balance the nuclear charge, were distributed in a distinctive pattern through the outer region of each atom. An atom of aluminum was assumed to have twenty-seven protons and fourteen electrons in its nucleus, with thirteen planetary electrons outside. An atom of nitrogen had fourteen protons and seven electrons in its nucleus. This sum of twenty-one, however, was uncomfortable since there were compelling reasons, related to the statistical properties of large numbers of identical nuclei, for believing that the nitrogen nucleus contained an even number of particles. In 1932, all of this changed.

Part of the impetus came from Berlin where W. Bothe and his associates were producing disintegrations with the alpha particles from polonium. In 1930, together with H. Becker, Bothe observed a very penetrating radiation, coming from both beryllium and boron under alpha-particle bombardment, which they considered to be nuclear gamma rays excited by some mechanism like that which gave rise to the visible light emitted by the outer electrons.

In Paris, Irène Curie (the elder daughter of Pierre and Marie) and her husband Frédéric Joliot were trying to sort out the various weakly ionizing radiations that were reported to be emitted by polonium. Late in 1931 they found that they could obtain Bothe and Becker's penetrating radiation from lithium. They made their studies with absorbing screens, routinely using lead as an absorber of high atomic number, and, for low atomic number, either cellophane or paraffin. In January 1932 they observed that the rays from beryllium and boron were dislodging protons from their light absorbers, which were rich in hydrogen, and they suggested that these protons might be knocked out by collisions with the gamma rays.

This was possible, although unlikely. Chadwick in Cambridge realized that the penetrating "rays" might be Rutherford's neutrons. Like gamma rays, neutrons would ionize weakly, but unlike gamma rays, they would be effective in transferring momentum to light atoms. Chadwick's subsequent observations on the recoil

from these rays of the atoms of hydrogen, helium, lithium, beryllium, carbon, argon, and the two constituents of air, all bore out his identification. They were thoroughly consistent with the existence of a neutron whose mass was very close to that of the proton.

(As the idea of a neutron came presently to be accepted, nuclei were assumed to be built of protons and neutrons. On this assumption, a nitrogen nucleus, with seven protons and seven neutrons, had the necessary even number of constituent particles.)

Almost simultaneously, Harold C. Urey at Columbia announced the discovery of a hydrogen isotope with a mass of 2. F. G. Brickwedde had concentrated the heavy isotope for Urey by careful evaporation of liquid hydrogen at the Bureau of Standards in Washington; G. M. Murphy at Columbia detected it by a doubling of hydrogen's spectral lines. By the spring of 1933, G. N. Lewis of the University of California was concentrating the isotope more effectively by electrolysis. By July, the nuclei of the new isotope, called at first *deutons* and later *deuterons*, had been tried in the Berkeley cyclotron, and by September, in Rutherford's new discharge tube for the Cambridge voltage-multiplier. At the California Institute of Technology in Pasadena, with its million-volt transformer stack, C. C. Lauritsen and H. R. Crane had replaced their X-ray installation with an accelerator tube. By October, together with A. Soltan, they produced a deuteron beam that dislodged neutrons from beryllium and lithium targets.

Carl D. Anderson, also at the California Institute of Technology, had earlier produced evidence for a most contradictory object—a positive electron. He had been measuring the energy of the cosmic rays by observing electron tracks in a cloud chamber in a strong magnetic field. Most of the tracks crossed the cloud chamber from top to bottom and curved toward the left, as was to be expected for negative electrons moving downward. There were also similar tracks that curved to the right, which might have been made by negative electrons traveling up or positive particles going down. If they were made by positive ions, they were too thin for alpha-particle tracks and probably too thin for the tracks of protons. The more closely Anderson examined them, the more plausible it was to attribute the tracks to particles whose charge and mass were comparable with those of electrons. He tentatively suggested this in September 1932, and over the next six months, as he accumulated more tracks, he became increasingly certain.

In March 1933, Blackett and G. P. S. Occhialini at Cambridge, England, obtained other cloud-chamber pictures of cosmic ray tracks that showed positive electrons. In April, Irène Curie and Joliot observed symmetrical pairs of positive and negative electron tracks emerging together from a lead plate at the edge of a cloud chamber when it was exposed to the rays from beryllium bombarded by alpha particles.

In spite of the poetic suggestion that Orestes was the brother of Electra and so the new particle should be called the *oreston*, the name it finally acquired was *positron*.

Artificial Radioactivity

Curie and Joliot observed electron-positron pairs when they bombarded lead with the radiation from beryllium; however, when they switched to alpha-particle bombardment, they got only single positrons from aluminum and nothing at all from silver, lithium, or paraffin. Since they expected instant responses to the radiation, they activated their cloud chamber only during the bombardment of the target foil. Six months later, returning to these experiments at the beginning of 1934, they found that the positrons persisted even after the foil was removed from the alpha-particle source. In fact, the foil had become radioactive with an exponential decay and a half-value decay period (or *half-life*) of three minutes and fifteen seconds. Among the lighter elements, Curie and Joliot discovered

similar positron radioactivities from targets of boron (fourteen minutes) and magnesium (two minutes and thirty seconds), but not from those of eleven other elements.

It was a plausible guess that each of these substances captured an alpha particle, ejected a neutron, and so transformed itself into a radioactive species: isotopes of phosphorus from the aluminum, nitrogen from the boron, and silicon from the magnesium. The emission of a positron from each of these should leave stable isotopes of silicon, carbon, and aluminum already known to exist. The hypothesis was easy to test: one had only to irradiate a foil, dissolve it in acid, and analyze the solution chemically. When Curie and Joliot carried out the tests, they found radioactive phosphorus in the aluminum target and radioactive nitrogen in the boron.

This was an astonishing discovery which gave new capabilities to the accelerator laboratories. Up to then, a nuclear reaction could be monitored only by identifying the particles given off, but now it was possible to determine directly what new atomic species were formed. Within five months most of the light elements had been bombarded with protons in Cambridge, with deuterons and protons in Pasadena and Berkeley, and with alpha particles in Warsaw, London, and Berlin. Everywhere radioactivity appeared, half-lives were measured and even a few of the active isotopes were identified.

In Rome, Enrico Fermi recognized another implication of the new effect: if nuclei held together in spite of the mutual repulsion of the positively charged protons crammed into them, there must be very strong binding forces between the neutrons and the protons. To judge from the masses and charges of the known isotopes, a nucleus would be stable only if there was a proper balance in the number of its protons and neutrons. In the Curie-Joliot reactions, each new nucleus formed must have one proton too many. The emission of the positive electron was necessary to convert the extra proton to a neutron and restore stability.

The particles used thus far in nuclear transformations were all positively charged and would be deflected away from the positive nucleus. They needed high energies to drive them close enough for the nuclear binding forces to draw them inside. Neutrons, being uncharged and therefore not repelled, should be easy to introduce into nuclei. The instabilities they fostered should result in emission of negative electrons—the familiar beta particles—as extra neutrons were converted to protons.

Fermi and his co-workers, Franco Rasetti, Edoardo Amaldi, Emilio Segrè, and Oscar D'Agostino, carried out a grand survey of the known elements, starting with lithium and working systematically up the periodic table, bombarding each with neutrons from beryllium sealed into a glass tube with radium emanation. By April 1934, three months after Curie and Joliot's first announcement, they had come as far as barium (element 56), whose bombardment with neutrons resulted in thirteen measurable half-lives. By July they had tested everything feasible, sixty-four elements in all. As D'Agostino's chemistry showed, the capture of a neutron was sometimes followed by the expulsion of a proton, sometimes an alpha particle. With the heavy elements, however, the neutron was generally captured and retained. Since this produced no change in nuclear charge, the radioactive substance created was an isotope of the target element. In all these cases, the radioactive atom decayed by emitting a beta particle. Since the loss of a negative charge is equivalent to the gain of a positive charge, the atom moved one place up in the periodic table.

This discovery made the heaviest elements particularly interesting. From thorium, element 90, Fermi's group might expect neutron capture to give them element 91, about which little was known. From uranium they might get element 93, which no one had ever seen. When they tried these two, they found a surprising number of radioactivities, at least two from thorium and no less than five from uranium, all with different half-lives. One of the five was chosen for chemical tests, and it moved through the tests as element 93 might do.

This substance could be traced because it was itself a beta-emitter. If it was indeed element 93, then it was transmuting into element 94 which was equally unknown; however, the chemical evidence was suggestive rather than convincing. Within the research group, the two elements were referred to as *ausonium* and *hesperium*, but Fermi made no serious public claims for their identification. In any case, he had seen something else to investigate: the neutrons from beryllium came out at high speeds but could be slowed by collisions with hydrogen atoms (for example, by letting them pass through water), and these slow neutrons proved far more effective than the fast ones in promoting nuclear reactions. Fermi and his group undertook a systematic study of slow neutrons—their properties and how they were produced.

The Discovery of Fission

The work on the possible transuranic elements (elements with atomic numbers greater than that of uranium) moved from Rome to Paris and Berlin. In Paris, Irène Curie studied the action of neutrons on thorium, together with Hans von Halban, Jr. and Peter Preiswerk. In Berlin, the possibilities of using uranium and thorium for the production of new elements caught the interest of Otto Hahn, Lise Meitner, and Fritz Strassmann. Everything in this new field proved complicated: there were too many different radioactive products, too many overlapping half-lives, too many rapid decays. By 1937, the Berlin group could recognize nine substances with distinguishable half-lives which they sorted into three parallel series. Each began with a neutron capture by uranium and involved a succession of beta decays extending to elements 93, 95, and 97. However, those were reasonable rather than demonstrable interpretations and no one was yet willing to give these "elements" names.

In 1935, Hans Bethe decided to summarize

what was known of nuclear physics; with the collaboration of R. F. Bacher and Livingston, he compiled a monumental and extraordinarily useful work. With the detailed knowledge of that review, Bethe then undertook to study the problem of energy production in stars. Rutherford and Soddy had suggested thirty years before that the sun might be maintained by the internal energy of atoms, and Aston's isotope measurements showed how this energy might be realized. If four hydrogen atoms could be merged into a helium atom (or in nuclear terms, if four protons could be merged into an alpha particle), there would be a net decrease in mass and a consequent release in energy. In the interior of stars, at temperatures of millions of degrees, atoms should be stripped of their external electrons and driven close enough for nuclear reactions to occur.

Bethe calculated in detail what reactions were known to be possible and how rapidly they would occur. He found two sequences, each of which in the end assembled four protons into an alpha particle. With C. L. Critchfield in August 1938, he published a description of the first process, which began with a pair of protons colliding to form a deuteron and disposing of the excess charge by the emission of a positron. Collision with a third proton transformed the deuteron into a light isotope of helium, which through a chain of further reactions would acquire the fourth proton to become a stable alpha particle. For a star like our sun with an internal temperature of twenty million degrees, this chain should produce energy at very nearly the proper rate.

The second sequence, which Bethe published in March 1939, involved the mediation of carbon. By two successive collisions with protons and the emission of a single positron, a carbon nucleus could be transformed into the nucleus of nitrogen. When this had annexed another proton and emitted another positron, it would be a heavier isotope of nitrogen, and this in turn could react with the fourth proton to form an alpha particle and a carbon nucleus. Thus very

little carbon, by continual recycling, could bring about the steady merging of hydrogen into helium. A comparison of the two sequences showed that for lighter, cooler stars, up to about the mass and temperature of our sun, the proton-proton cycle should predominate; for heavier, hotter stars, the carbon-nitrogen cycle.

The process of "merging" has more recently acquired the name of *fusion*. As the stars bear witness, fusion is an excellent source of energy at the million-degree temperatures necessary to sustain it. Here on earth it can be produced momentarily and catastrophically in the hydrogen bomb. Whether it can be held under control and maintained steadily is still an open question.

By the early months of 1939, however, before Bethe's carbon-nitrogen paper appeared, nuclear energy was being made available from elements at the other end of the periodic table, where the reactions of uranium had been confusing Hahn and Strassmann, as they had confused Becquerel, Crookes, and Soddy before them. When uranium was bombarded with neutrons, many different half-lives could be detected, indicating the formation of many different substances, some of which could be linked into series of successive transformations. The difficulty was that there were three such series, each clearly independent of the other two, and all starting from uranium. It seemed necessary to believe that after a uranium nucleus had captured a neutron, it could transform itself in three different ways—each of which involved the emission of a beta particle, each of which had a different half-life, and each of which led to a different chain of transformations.

During 1937 and 1938, Irène Curie and Paul Savitch had concentrated their studies on still another product found in uranium that was bombarded by neutrons—a product that had a strong chemical resemblance to lanthanum. This was unexpected. The transuranic elements must lie above uranium in the periodic table and resemble those on its right-hand edge. However, lanthanum lay to the left.

Acting on this suggestion, Hahn and Strassmann changed the direction of their chemical analysis, and they soon found beta particles coming from something that resembled barium. This they identified with radium, which could certainly be produced if the uranium nucleus emitted a pair of alpha particles after it had captured its neutron. Then, just as they had previously found three kinds of uranium, all decaying with different half-lives, they now found four different radiums undergoing four different varieties of decay.

These conclusions were a straightforward interpretation of what Hahn and Strassmann had seen, and practically none of it was credible. The only thing reasonably certain was the chemistry, and this they undertook to confirm. They irradiated a new sample of uranium with neutrons, dissolved it, and added to the solution both barium and Hahn's old discovery, mesothorium 1, an isotope of radium which could be recognized by its characteristic beta rays. Then they carried out a classic radium-barium separation. To their astonishment, the beta rays from the irradiated uranium went with the barium, not with the mesothorium 1. The atoms that released them were barium, not radium.

It was December 1938. Hahn and Strassmann added this last-minute discovery to a paper already half-written and also reported it by letter to Meitner in Stockholm. She was enjoying a Christmas reunion with her nephew Otto Frisch, a physicist in Bohr's institute in Copenhagen. When he heard the news from Hahn and Strassmann, Frisch began to think about uranium in terms of Bohr's theory which considered the nucleus as a kind of liquid drop, held together against the electrical repulsion of its protons by short-range binding forces acting among all its particles. He realized that in the uranium nucleus the repulsion and the binding might be so closely balanced that the addition of an extra neutron could set up oscillations that would soon split the nucleus into two nearly equal parts.

As the nucleus split, there would be a tremendous release of energy. The two new nuclei, side by side and positively charged, would repel one another violently, and the energy supplied by this repulsion could be calculated. There would also be a loss of mass in the splitting. Uranium, an element at the end of the periodic table, had an atomic weight slightly greater than a whole number; the fragments would form elements in the middle whose weights would be slightly under. The difference in mass would appear as the energy released by the reaction, calculated according to $E = mc^2$. By either calculation, that energy came out the same.

Back in Copenhagen, at Bohr's urging, Frisch outlined a joint paper expounding these ideas, which he and Meitner then composed by long-distance telephone. For a name, he turned for help to William A. Arnold, an American biologist then in residence, and called the splitting *fission* after the familiar process of cell division.

Fission and the Chain Reaction

There were several ways of verifying that fission occurred. Hahn's chemical identification of fragments within the uranium sample would serve as one, now that the process had been identified. Since fission fragments would have more kinetic energy to dissipate than alpha or beta particles, they could also be recognized by the bursts of ionization they produced. This was the method Frisch chose in mid-January. In Paris, Joliot read Hahn and Strassmann's paper and, realizing what it implied, used the fission itself to segregate the fragments. He placed uranium on the outside of a brass cylinder and surrounded this with a cylinder of bakelite which soon became radioactive from the fission fragments projected across the gap. This radioactivity was precisely like that previously attributed to the transuranic elements. At the same time, Irène Curie and Savitch used Hahn's technique to establish that the lanthanum-like substance they had studied was actually an isotope of lanthanum and consequently another product of fission.

Meanwhile, Bohr had left for the United States, where he spread Frisch's news, first at Princeton and then at Columbia University in New York. Fermi also had crossed the Atlantic, a week earlier than Bohr, emigrating from Fascist Italy by way of Stockholm on the occasion of receiving the Nobel Prize, and he was now settling himself at Columbia. There was already a neutron group at Columbia, which on the evening of Bohr's visit instantly duplicated Frisch's experiment. The next day, Bohr and Fermi reported on fission in formal lectures at a conference on theoretical physics in Washington, and this led to additional repetitions of the experiment at the Carnegie Institution and at Johns Hopkins University.

The uranium nucleus contains far more neutrons than would be present in the stable isotopes of any fission fragments. Some of these excess neutrons would eventually convert to protons by emission of beta particles, but some might also be evaporated (shaken loose) immediately in the instant of fission. If this was so, and if some of the free neutrons could be captured in other uranium nuclei, then there was the possibility of a chain reaction. If, on the average, one free neutron from a dividing nucleus was caught and produced one fission in another, then the chain would proceed at a steady rate. If the number so caught averaged more than one, the rate of fission would increase; if it averaged less, the chain would die away. If a chain of fissions could be sustained at a high level, the industrial production of nuclear energy might be possible. If it could multiply rapidly, there was the possibility of a nuclear bomb.

All this was evident in the early months of 1939. It was also evident that war was very near, and this conjunction troubled a group of European-born physicists including Leo Szilard, Eugene Wigner, Edward Teller, and Fermi. They made efforts to inform the U.S. government of these possibilities and to institute a voluntary censorship among physicists against the publication of sensitive information, a censorship that was fully adopted a year later.

Many unanswered questions lay between the possibility of nuclear energy and its practical realization, whether under control in a reactor or violently discharged in a bomb. There was the business of the release of free neutrons: by midspring Joliot's group in Paris, and Szilard, W. Zinn, and Fermi's group at Columbia were finding evidence of neutrons accompanying the fission process.

There was the complex problem of obtaining enough absorption of the fission neutrons by other uranium nuclei. It was already known that fission could be produced by fast neutrons but occurred much more readily with very slow ones. It was also known from the earlier work of Meitner, Hahn, and Strassmann that there was an intermediate energy at which neutrons were preferentially captured to produce a heavier uranium isotope with a beta-particle radioactivity and a half-life of twenty-three minutes. In addition, Bohr was suggesting that the uranium that underwent fission with slow neutrons was not the abundant isotope with an atomic weight of 238 but a rare light isotope of weight 235; and this was confirmed by detailed calculations that Bohr made with John A. Wheeler of Princeton during the summer. Since there were 139 atoms of the heavy isotope for each atom of the lighter, the natural constitution of uranium seemed to provide a built-in bias against fast-neutron fission.

Szilard and Fermi perceived how this bias might be countered. The neutrons emitted in fission were fast but could be slowed by collisions with the atoms of light elements; hydrogen (in water), beryllium, or carbon. Of the three, carbon seemed the most promising. In addition, Fermi saw that the capture of the intermediate-energy neutrons could be minimized if the uranium was concentrated in carefully spaced lumps, surrounded and separated by the carbon *moderator*. With proper design, a neutron emitted in fission would clear the uranium in which it originated while it was still moving rapidly and would be sufficiently slowed before it reached an adjacent lump.

This process would reduce one source of "waste"—one route by which neutrons were removed from a possible fission chain. Neutrons would also be wasted if they reacted with remnant impurities in either the uranium or the carbon, as would those that escaped beyond the outer edges of the carbon and uranium pile. Whether enough excess neutrons would be emitted in the fission process and whether the wastage could be sufficiently reduced so that a sustained reaction would occur were questions that could only be answered by experiment.

The Pile in the Squash Court

Fermi's preliminary experiments were promising. Large-scale trials began in the spring of 1940 when money from the army and navy made it possible to purchase uranium oxide and graphite (as a convenient form of carbon) in quantity. The experiments continued at Columbia under Fermi's direction until the spring of 1942. Meanwhile, other discoveries were being made.

John Dunning, who had been working with neutrons at Columbia before Fermi arrived, persuaded A. O. Nier at the University of Minnesota and K. H. Kingdon and H. C. Pollock at the General Electric Research Laboratory to separate and collect observable samples of the two isotopes of uranium by prolonged operation of their mass spectrographs. While Fermi was building his uranium and graphite pile, tests on the isotope samples verified Bohr's prediction: slow neutrons produced fission in uranium-235, fast neutrons only in uranium-238. This suggested another way of promoting the fission chain—by separating the two isotopes in a giant mass spectrograph or increasing the concentration of U-235 by gas diffusion, as Aston had attempted with the isotopes of neon in 1913.

Early in 1939 in Berkeley, Edwin McMillan had tried to measure the range of the fission fragments by piling sheets of very thin absorb-

ers over a thin layer of uranium oxide which was activated by neutrons from the cyclotron. The fission fragments lodged in the absorbers where they could be detected by their radioactivity, but the paper on which the uranium oxide had been coated also showed a pair of residual radioactivities—one with a half-life of about twenty-five minutes, the other with a half-life of around two days. McMillan passed the material to Segrè (who had left Italy for California in 1938), and he identified the short-lived substance with the 23-minute isotope produced by neutron-capture (probably uranium-239). The longer-lived substance, whose half-life Segrè set at 2.3 days, had a curious chemistry, rather like that of a rare earth. This suggested that it was a fission product, although it was odd that it had remained with the uranium rather than recoiling into one of the absorbers.

The discrepancy was resolved in the late spring of 1940 when Philip Abelson returned from the Carnegie Institution in Washington for a visit to Berkeley where he had done his graduate study. Working with McMillan, he was able to show that the 2.3-day substance was the daughter of the 23-minute U-239, and since it was formed by a beta-particle emission, it must be element 93. A closer look revealed a chemistry more like that of uranium than of the rare earths. The rare earths made a curious sequence of elements, very similar but not identical in their chemistry, which seemed to be interpolated in the periodic table. Abelson suggested that uranium and this element 93 might stand at the beginning of another such sequence. Element 93 also had a beta-particle radioactivity and so was transmuted into element 94. McMillan and Abelson were unable to find any trace of radioactive emissions from this element, so they concluded that its half-life must be of the order of a million years. This was one of the last such papers to be published openly.

Louis Turner of Princeton, thinking in general terms about nuclear stability, had perceived that this isotope of element 94 also should undergo fission upon absorbing slow neutrons. Turner suggested that there might be enough neutrons in a nuclear reactor to convert U-238 into element 94 and sustain a continuing chain of fissions from both that element and U-235. Turner's paper on this question, submitted two days after McMillan and Abelson's was withheld from publication until the end of the war.

Thus the two genuine transuranic elements disappeared from view almost as soon as they were made known; years later they reappeared, having acquired the planetary names of neptunium (element 93) and plutonium (element 94). Secrecy, of course, did not mean loss of interest. The group at Berkeley continued to produce neptunium from uranium and to study the plutonium into which it decayed. Like U-235, plutonium did undergo fission with slow neutrons.

As more graphite and uranium oxide arrived, Fermi's experimental piles grew taller and taller. In the spring of 1942, with the country now at war, the piles were moved to the University of Chicago and remounted in a squash court under the west stands of Stagg Field. The possibility of the chain reaction was still limited by the loss of neutrons among the impurities of the constituents, but shortly the uranium oxide was being purified by the method Sir William Crookes had used in his discovery of uranium X, and improvements in the purity of graphite followed. By fall, high-purity uranium metal was becoming available.

The last impediment to a sustained chain reaction was the escape of neutrons from all the edges of the pile. The remedy for this was simple, to make the pile bigger. It is a well-known principle of geometry that large bodies have a smaller proportion of surface to bulk than small ones. From the beginning Fermi had calculated and recalculated what the critical size of the pile would be in order that the surface losses would no longer cut off the chain. By November 1942 it was evident that the critical size could be reached, and the construction of a re-

acting pile was begun. It was to be spherical (the geometric shape with the least surface for its bulk) and supported on a wooden cradle. It would be built with lumps of uranium oxide surrounded and separated by graphite moderator; uranium metal would be substituted as it became available. To control the reaction, strips of cadmium, which absorbs slow neutrons strongly, were nailed to wooden bars that could be inserted into slots left open in the pile. As fresh material arrived, it was put in place, and as the pile grew, the cadmium strips were withdrawn from time to time to monitor the multiplication of neutrons. By the end of November, it was clear that the critical size would be reached before the sphere was completed.

On December 2, everyone on the project, forty-three in all, gathered in the squash court to watch while the reactor was brought into operation. They stood there in the chill, expectant and a bit apprehensive while Fermi quietly and deliberately supervised the extraction of the last control rod. It was a familiar routine. The rod was pulled out a bit, the counter was read to assess the intensity of neutron flux, and Fermi calculated with his pocket slide rule how far the next withdrawal should go. This day the flux mounted higher and higher until Fermi could announce, "The pile has gone critical." There he permitted it to multiply for two or three endless minutes and at last allowed the control rod to be inserted.

Nuclear energy could be controlled. Its industrial future seemed assured. At the same time, another route to a nuclear bomb had become possible. With some redesign, a reactor could be built in which the surplus of neutrons, beyond those needed to maintain the fission chain, would be captured by atoms of U-238. The plutonium generated from the capture could be separated from the mass of uranium by chemical means. It was anyone's guess whether plutonium or U-235, obtained by isotope separation, might be ready sooner. That story is told in Chapter 1.

Suggested Readings

A few interesting books on the early history of radioactivity and nuclear physics are listed below. Eve Curie, daughter of Marie and Pierre Curie, tells the story of their discoveries. Several books document Lord Rutherford's life. His scientific work is carefully chronicled by Norman Feather, who worked under Rutherford's direction during the latter's last years at the Cavendish Laboratory. The official biography of Rutherford was completed in 1939 by Professor Eve of McGill University. Another book, edited by Afred Romer, contains more of the story of radioactivity and the puzzle of the isotopes. Charming personal episodes from the history of nuclear physics are told by Otto Frisch in *What Little I Remember*. The volume *Nuclear Physics in Retrospect,* edited by Roger Stuewer, is the proceedings of a 1977 symposium held to recall the major advances in physics that led to the discovery of fission. The life of Enrico Fermi is told by Emilio Segrè, who has also published *From X Rays to Quarks,* a popular history of some individuals and their contributions to modern physics.

CURIE, EVE. *Madame Curie.* Garden City, N. Y.: Doubleday, 1938.

FEATHER, N. *Lord Rutherford.* London: Blackie, 1940.

FRISCH, OTTO. *What Little I Remember.* Cambridge: Cambridge University Press, 1979.

ROMER, ALFRED, ed. *Radiochemistry and the Discovery of Isotopes.* New York: Dover Publications, 1970.

RUTHERFORD, ERNEST. *The Collected Papers of Lord Rutherford of Nelson,* 3 vol. London: Allen and Unwin, 1962–1965.

SEGRÈ, EMILIO. *Enrico Fermi, Physicist.* Chicago: University of Chicago Press, 1970.

SEGRÈ, EMILIO. *From X-Rays to Quarks: Modern Physicists and Their Discoveries.* San Francisco: Freeman, 1980.

STUEWER, ROGER. H., ed. *Nuclear Physics in Retrospect.* Minneapolis: University of Minnesota Press, 1979.

Notes and Credits

Abbreviations

ACDA	United States Arms Control and Disarmament Agency
AEC	United States Atomic Energy Commission
DOD	United States Department of Defense
DOE	United States Department of Energy
ERDA	United States Energy Resources and Development Administration
GPO	United States Government Printing Office
IAEA	International Atomic Energy Agency
IISS	International Institute for Strategic Studies
LANSL	Los Alamos National Scientific Laboratory
LLNSL	Lawrence Livermore National Scientific Laboratory
NASA	National Aeronautics and Space Administration
NAS	National Academy of Sciences
OTA	Office of Technology Assessment, United States Congress
SIPRI	Stockholm International Peace Research Institute

Frontispiece: Courtesy of Philip Morrison.

The Future Is Ours

Credits

Lead photograph: NASA.
Minutes to Midnight: Courtesy of *The Bulletin of the Atomic Scientists.*

Charlottesville

Note

Text condensed from OTA, *The Effects of Nuclear War* (Washington, D.C.: GPO, 1979), app. C, pp. 124–138.

Credit

Photographs by Jack Dennis.

Chapter 1
Manhattan Project

Notes

1. Spencer R. Weart and Gertrud Weiss Szilard, eds., *Leo Szilard: His Version of the Facts* (Cambridge, Mass.: MIT Press, 1978), p. 54.

2. Elting E. Morison, *Turmoil and Tradition* (Boston: Houghton Mifflin Co., 1960), p. 620.

3. Martin J. Sherwin, *A World Destroyed: The Atomic Bomb and the Grand Alliance* (New York: Alfred A. Knopf, 1975), p. 118.

4. J. Robert Oppenheimer, "Three Lectures on Niels Bohr and His Times; Part III: The Atomic Nucleus" (Pegram Lectures, Brookhaven National Laboratory, August 1963).

5. Richard G. Hewlett and Oscar E. Anderson, Jr., *The New World, 1939–1946* (University Park, Pa.: Pennsylvania State University Press, 1962), p. 329.

6. Quoted by Nat S. Finney, "How FDR Planned to Use the A-Bomb," *Look 14* (March 14, 1950): 24. *See also* Sherwin, *A World Destroyed*, p. 131 and note 40.

7. Weart and Szilard, *Leo Szilard*, pp. 205–207.

8. James Franck in conversation with the author, June 21, 1963.

9. Quoted in Alice Kimball Smith, *A Peril and a Hope: The Scientists' Movement in America, 1945–47* (Chicago: University of Chicago Press, 1965; paperback edition, Cambridge, Mass.: MIT Press, 1970), pp. 31–32.

10. Sherwin, *A World Destroyed*, pp. 202–210 and app. L, "Notes of the Interim Committee Meeting, May 31, 1945."

11. Sherwin, *A World Destroyed*, app. M, "Science Panel: Recommendations on the Immediate Use of Nuclear Weapons, June 16, 1945."

12. Weart and Szilard, *Leo Szilard*, pp. 211–212.

Credits

Lead photograph: LANSL.
1-1 The Einstein Letter: Reproduced from Weart and Szilard, *Leo Szilard*, pp. 94–95. The story of Sachs's meeting with Roosevelt is from Robert Jungk,

Brighter than a Thousand Suns (New York: Harcourt, Brace, 1958), pp. 110–111.

1-2 Fermi at the Blackboard: Philip M. Morse, *In at the Beginnings: A Physicist's Life* (Cambridge, Mass.: MIT Press, 1977), pp. 103–104. Photograph courtesy of Argonne National Laboratory.

1-3 General Groves: LANSL photograph.

1-4 The First Atomic Bomb: Prepared by Thérèse Dennis from material in Peter Goodchild, *J. Robert Oppenheimer: Shatterer of Worlds* (Boston: Houghton Mifflin, 1981), pp. 129–164. Photographs of tower, bomb, and cloud from LANSL; of Bush and Conant, from the MIT Museum and Historical Collections.

1-5 The First Nuclear Weapons: U.S. Air Force photographs.

1-6 Szilard Makes a Point: Photograph courtesy of Argonne National Laboratory.

1-7 The Franck Report: Smith, *A Peril and a Hope*, pp. 371–383.

Hiroshima and Nagasaki

Credits

Photograph of *Enola Gay* courtesy of Philip Morrison; Hiroshima Fire Truck and nuclear clouds over Hiroshima and Nagasaki by U.S. Air Force. The remaining photographs are from the slide series presented to the U.S. Arms Control and Disarmament Agency by the Hiroshima Peace Memorial Museum. The story of the Hiroshima survivor is from Robert Guillain, *I Saw Tokyo Burning* (New York: Doubleday, 1981), and is used here with the publisher's permission. The story originally appeared in *Atlantic Monthly*.

Chapter 2
The Superbomb

Notes

1. Edward Teller and Allen Brown, *The Legacy of Hiroshima* (Garden City, N.Y.: Doubleday, 1962), p. 37.

2. Edward Teller, "The Work of Many People," *Science* 121 (1955): 268.

3. Teller and Brown, *Legacy of Hiroshima*, p. 50.

4. AEC, *In the Matter of J. Robert Oppenheimer: Transcript of Hearing Before Personal Security Board and Texts of Principal Documents and Letters* (Cambridge, Mass.: MIT Press, 1971), p. 487.

5. Quoted in Herbert York, *The Advisors: Oppenheimer, Teller, and the Superbomb* (San Francisco: W. H. Freeman, 1976), p. 52; the full report is reproduced on pp. 150–159.

6. David Lilienthal, *The Atomic Energy Years,*

1945–1950, in *The Journals of David E. Lilienthal,* vol. 2 (New York: Harper & Row, 1964), pp. 587–590.

7. Strauss to Truman, November 25, 1949. This letter with an accompanying memorandum is reproduced in full in Lewis L. Strauss, *Men and Decisions* (Garden City, N.Y.: Doubleday, 1962), pp. 219–222.

8. McMahon to Truman, November 21, 1949. Quoted in Richard G. Hewlett and Francis Duncan, "Atomic Shield, 1947–1952," in *A History of the United States Atomic Energy Commission,* vol. 2 (University Park, Pa.: Pennsylvania State University Press, 1969), p. 394.

9. David Alan Rosenberg, "American Atomic Strategy and the Hydrogen Bomb Decision," *Journal of American History* 66 (1979): 86. The Military Liaison Committee and JCS statements appear on pp. 81–82.

10. *New York Times,* February 1, 1950, p. 1.

11. *New York Times,* February 1, 1950, p. 3.

12. J. Robert Oppenheimer, "Fateful Decision," *Bulletin of the Atomic Scientists* 6 (March 1950): 75. See also the April and May 1950 issues of the *Bulletin* and the series in *Scientific American* 182 (March 1950): 11–15; (April 1950): 18–23; and (May 1950): 11–15.

13. Teller, "Work of Many People," p. 272.

14. Teller and Brown, *Legacy of Hiroshima*, pp. 54–55.

15. SIPRI, *Tactical Nuclear Weapons: European Perspectives* (London: Taylor and Francis, 1978), p. 10.

Credits

Lead photograph: U.S. Air Force.

2-1 The McCarthy Era: Prepared by Elizabeth Cavicchi using the following materials: Senator Joe McCarthy, *McCarthyism: The Fight for America* (New York: Devin-Adair, 1952), p. 92; Walter and Miriam Schneir, *Invitation to an Inquest* (Garden City, N.Y.: Doubleday, 1965), pp. 53, 194, 247; John Wexley, *The Judgment of Julius and Ethel Rosenberg* (New York: Ballantine, 1977), pp. 117, 150, 369; Dwight D. Eisenhower, *Mandate for Change, 1953–56* (Garden City, N.Y.: Doubleday, 1963), p. 224.

2-2 "In the Matter of J. Robert Oppenheimer": Short accounts of the Oppenheimer security case are given in Herbert York, *The Advisors: Oppenheimer, Teller, and the Superbomb* (San Francisco: W. H. Freeman and Company, 1976), and in Corbin Allardice and Edward R. Trapnell, *The Atomic Energy Commission* (New York: Praeger, 1974). A slightly longer one is given in Nuel Pharr Davis, *Lawrence and Oppenheimer* (New York: Simon & Schuster, 1968), from which the Truman, Nichols, and Bush quotations are taken. These references also give guidance to many other sources.

2-3 The Superbomb Programs, 1949–55: Prepared by James Paradis from York, *The Advisors*, pp. 75–103.

Chapter 3
Government and the Atom
Notes

1. A sketch is given in Corbin Allardice and Edward R. Trapnell, *The Atomic Energy Commission* (New York: Praeger, 1974), pp. 25–32, and a thorough account may be found in Alice Kimball Smith, *A Peril and a Hope: The Scientists' Movement in America, 1945–47* (Chicago: University of Chicago Press, 1965); Cambridge, Mass.: MIT Press, 1970).

2. Between 1949 and 1951, shortly after leaving the AEC, Lilienthal published a series of articles in *Collier's* magazine arguing for a broad opening up of nuclear technology to private initiative and investment. In the issue of June 17, 1950, he wrote, "No Soviet industrial monopoly is more completely owned by the state than is the industrial atom in free-enterprise America. The government has today an iron-clad, airtight and all-embracing, legalized monopoly of this vast enterprise...." These articles foreshadowed many of the changes that came about after passage of the 1954 revision of the Atomic Energy Act.

3. Allardice and Trapnell, *Atomic Energy Commission*, p. 38.

4. Frank Dawson, *Nuclear Power: Development and Management of a Technology* (Seattle: University of Washington Press, 1976), p. 75.

5. A general explanation of the role of the Price-Anderson Act is given in Dawson, *Nuclear Power*, pp. 122–132. For an example of criticism by opponents of nuclear power, see Ralph Nader and John Abbotts, *The Menace of Atomic Energy* (New York: W. W. Norton, 1977), pp. 98–99 and 285–287.

6. As an example of this criticism, see H. Peter Metzger, *The Atomic Establishment* (New York: Simon & Schuster, 1972), especially chaps. 3 and 4.

7. Allardice and Trapnell, *Atomic Energy Commission*, p. 171.

8. For example, see Metzger's comments on the AEC's licensing process in *The Atomic Establishment*, pp. 249–253. Dawson discusses the AEC's regulatory side at some length and in particular describes the role of intervenors in licensing proceedings for three nuclear power stations in Dawson, *Nuclear Power*, chap. 6, especially pp. 191–203.

9. From *Report of the President's Commission on the Accident at Three Mile Island* (Washington, D.C.: GPO, October 1979), p. 51. The commissioner quoted was in office at the time the report was published.

10. *President's Commission ... Three Mile Island*, p. 56.

11. DOE, *DOE Research and Development and Field Facilities* (Washington, D.C., June 1979), p. I-3.

12. For example, see Robert Stobaugh and Daniel Yergin, eds., *Energy Future: Report of the Energy Project at the Harvard Business School* (New York: Random House, 1979).

13. A figure of $37 billion was recently obtained in a study performed by the DOE and reported in the *Wall Street Journal*, December 15, 1981, p. 8. More details of the study, entitled "Federal Subsidies to Nuclear Power: Reactor Design and the Fuel Cycle" and written by economist Joseph Bowering, can be found in an article by Richard Pollock in *Critical Mass Energy Journal*, January 1981, p. 5. Bowering's analysis was not published in its original form, however. The study was extensively revised early in 1981 after the Reagan administration took office, and many forms of support counted as subsidies in the initial version were excluded. The report as published gives $12.8 billion for the total government subsidy to nuclear power. It seems plausible to take this figure as a lower bound (*Critical Mass Energy Journal*, April 1981, p. 3).

14. Quoted in Richard Tybout, *Government Contracting in Atomic Energy* (Ann Arbor, Mich.: University of Michigan Press, 1956), p. 12.

15. Tybout, *Government Contracting*, p. vii.

16. President Reagan has stated a desire to see the DOE abolished. Commenting on this possibility, Daniel Yergin (see note 12) has written, "In some respects, its significance will not be so great. After all, more than a third of the Department of Energy's budget was earmarked for the nuclear weapons program, and obviously that effort will continue in another place. Funding for nuclear power will actually increase. The ax will fall, rather, on the conservation and renewable solar energy programs, eliminating them almost entirely" (*Boston Globe*, October 17, 1981, p. 11).

17. This exchange is well known and has been documented. For example, a study in 1976 by Common Cause, the citizens group, found that more than 50 percent of the 139 top employees of ERDA and more than 70 percent of the 429 senior personnel at the NRC had previously worked in private industry in the energy field. In the great majority of cases, these government employees had worked for companies being regulated by or holding contracts from ERDA or NRC. The Common Cause study is cited in Nader and Abbotts, *Menace of Atomic Energy*, pp. 277–278.

Credits

Lead photograph: Oak Ridge National Laboratory.
3-1 U.S. Government Nuclear Facilities: DOE, *Field Facilities.*
3-2 Nuclear Power: From Ship to Shore: Based on Richard G. Hewlett and Francis Duncan, *Nuclear Navy* (Chicago: University of Chicago Press, 1974).
3-3 Department of Energy Organization: DOE, *Field Facilities,* p. I-2.
3-4 Department of Energy Budget Estimates, 1982: *Nuclear News* (April 1981): 45–47.
3-5 Some Major U.S. Nuclear Contractors: Then (1965) and Now (1980): AEC, *Annual Report,* 1965; DOE, *Annual Report To Congress,* 1980. The 1965 AEC list does not include nonindustrial institutions. The University of California operates the Los Alamos, Lawrence Livermore, and Lawrence Berkeley Laboratories; the University of Chicago operates Argonne National Laboratory; and Associated Universities operates the Brookhaven National Laboratory. The role of the TVA and the Ohio Valley Electric Company is to supply electric power for the uranium enrichment plants, a function not included in the AEC list for 1965. The 1965 rank and dollar amounts given for Rockwell International are for a parent corporation, Atomics International.

Chapter 4
Blast, Heat, and Radiation

Notes

1. *Long-Term Worldwide Effects of Multiple Nuclear-Weapons Detonations* (Washington, D.C.: NAS, 1975), pp. 72–73.
2. *Nuclear Weapons,* Report of the Secretary-General of the United Nations (Brookline, Mass.: Autumn Press, 1981), p. 63.

Credits

Lead photograph: U.S. Defense Nuclear Agency.
4-2 The Radioactive Cloud of a Nuclear Explosion: S. Glasstone and P. J. Dolan, *The Effects of Nuclear Weapons,* 3rd ed. (Washington, D.C.: GPO, 1977), pp. 28–36.
4-3 Prompt Radiation from Nuclear Explosions: Glasstone and Dolan, *The Effects of Nuclear Weapons,* pp. 333–334.
4-4 Heat Damage from Nuclear Explosions: Glasstone and Dolan, *The Effects of Nuclear Weapons,* pp. 291, 309–311.
4-5 Skin Burns from Thermal Radiation: U.S. Defense Nuclear Agency.
4-6 Air Blast and Wind from Nuclear Explosions: Glasstone and Dolan, *The Effects of Nuclear Weapons,* pp. 82, 83, 114–115.

4-7 Weapon Effects on a Wood Frame House: Glasstone and Dolan, *The Effects of Nuclear Weapons,* paragraphs 5.55–5.62, 7.28. Photographs from the U.S. Defense Nuclear Agency.
4-8 Decay of Radioactivity from a One-Megaton Nuclear Explosion: Glasstone and Dolan, *The Effects of Nuclear Weapons,* pp. 392–393 and paragraph 9.159. Radioisotope half-lives from Robert C. Weast, *Handbook of Chemistry and Physics* (Cleveland: The Chemical Rubber Company, 1970), pp. B-245–B-541.
4-9 Radioactive Fallout from Nuclear Explosions: George E. Pugh and Robert J. Galiano, *An Analytic Model of Close-In Deposition of Fallout for Use in Operational-Type Studies,* WSEG Research Memorandum No. 10 (Washington, D.C.: The Pentagon, Weapon Systems Evaluation Group, October 15, 1959). Leo A. Schmidt, *A Study of Twenty-four Nationwide Fallout Patterns from Twelve Winds,* Paper P-1604 (Arlington, Va.: Institute for Defense Analysis, September 1981); Glasstone and Dolan, *The Effects of Nuclear Weapons,* pp. 400–401, 436–437.
4-10 Baker Day: Nuclear Explosions Go Underwater: Glasstone and Dolan, *The Effects of Nuclear Weapons,* pp. 244–247. Photograph from the U.S. Defense Nuclear Agency.

Chapter 5
Medical Effects of a Nuclear Attack

Notes

1. F. Barnaby, L. Kristofferson, H. Rodhe, J. Rotblat, and J. Prawitz, "Reference Scenario: How a Nuclear War Might Be Fought," *Ambio* 11:2–3 (1982): 94–99.
2. S. Glasstone and P. J. Dolan, *The Effects of Nuclear Weapons,* 3rd ed. (Washington, D.C.: GPO, 1977), pp. 541–559; E. Schildt, *Nuclear Explosion Casualties* (Springfield, Ill.: Charles E. Thomas, 1967), pp. 86–88.
3. Glasstone and Dolan, *The Effects of Nuclear Weapons,* pp. 552–558.
4. OTA, *The Effects of Nuclear War* (Washington, D.C.: GPO, 1979), p. 18.
5. Glasstone and Dolan, *The Effects of Nuclear Weapons,* p. 556.
6. A. W. Oughterson and S. Warren, eds., *Medical Effects of the Atomic Bomb in Japan* (New York: McGraw-Hill, 1956), cited in Schildt, *Nuclear Explosion Casualties,* p. 89.
7. OTA, *The Effects of Nuclear War,* pp. 16–17.
8. Schildt, *Nuclear Explosion Casualties,* pp. 90–91.
9. Glasstone and Dolan, *The Effects of Nuclear Weapons,* pp. 563–566.

10. Glasstone and Dolan, *The Effects of Nuclear Weapons,* pp. 561–562; Schildt, *Nuclear Explosion Casualties,* pp. 92–93; OTA, *The Effects of Nuclear War,* p. 21.

11. K. N. Lewis, "The Prompt and Delayed Effects of Nuclear War," *Scientific American* (July 1979): 35–47.

12. K. N. Lewis, "Prompt and Delayed Effects," pp. 40–41.

13. M. Caidin, *The Night That Hamburg Died* (New York: Ballantine, 1960), p. 158.

14. Glasstone and Dolan, *The Effects of Nuclear Weapons,* p. 325.

15. Glasstone and Dolan, *The Effects of Nuclear Weapons,* Figure 8.33b, p. 334, and Figure 8.64b, p. 347.

16. Patricia J. Lindop, "Medical Consequences of Radioactive Fallout," presented at the First Congress of the International Physicians for the Prevention of Nuclear War, Airlie House, Va., March 20–25, 1980, p. 10.

17. J. Smith and T. Smith, "Nuclear War: The Medical Facts, Medicine and the Bomb," *British Medical Journal* 283 (September 19, 1981): 774.

18. Patricia J. Lindop, "Medical Consequences," pp. 10–11.

19. Glasstone and Dolan, *The Effects of Nuclear Weapons,* p. 588.

20. OTA, *The Effects of Nuclear War,* p. 26.

21. J. W. Brooks et al., *Annals of Surgery* 136 (1952): 533–545.

22. Calculations in the following paragraphs are based on: *Urban Population Vulnerability* (Washington, D.C.: ACDA, August 1979); Glasstone and Dolan, *The Effects of Nuclear Weapons;* and OTA, *The Effects of Nuclear War.*

23. Glasstone and Dolan, *The Effects of Nuclear Weapons,* p. 573. See also F. R. Ervin et al., "Human and Ecologic Effects in Massachusetts of an Assumed Thermonuclear Attack on the United States," *New England Journal of Medicine* 266 (May 31, 1962).

24. These figures are adapted from *Urban Population Vulnerability* (Washington, D.C.: ACDA, August 1979).

25. V. W. Sidel, H. J. Geiger, and B. Lown, "The Physician's Role in the Post-Attack Period," *New England Journal of Medicine* 266 (May 31, 1962): 1137–1144; H. Johnston, L. D. Weiss, and T. Davis, *The Medical Effects of a Nuclear Attack on Albuquerque, New Mexico* (Albuquerque: University of New Mexico School of Medicine, August 1981), pp. 21–24; United States Congress, Senate Committee on Labor and Human Resources, Subcommittee on Health and Scientific Research, "Short- and Long-Term Health Effects on the Surviving Population of a Nuclear War," Hearing, 96th Cong. 2d sess. (Washington, D.C.: GPO, 1980); Z. B. Gerbarg and D. S. Greer, *Grappling with the Last Epidemic: The Medical Response to Nuclear War* (Providence, R.I.: Brown University, Section on Community Health, 1981).

26. C. M. Haaland, C. V. Chester, and E. P. Wigner, *Survival of the Relocated Population of the U.S. After a Nuclear Attack,* Report ORNL-5041, Defense Civil Preparedness Agency (Springfield, Va.: National Technical Information Service, 1976), p. 20-1.

27. H. L. Abrams, "Medical Problems of Survivors of Nuclear War: Infection and the Spread of Communicable Disease," *New England Journal of Medicine* 305:20 (November 12, 1981): 1226–1232.

28. Sidel, Geiger, Lown, "Physician's Role."

29. P. J. Lindop, "Medical Consequences," p. 12.

Credits

Lead photograph: Slide series from the Hiroshima Peace Memorial Museum.

5-1 Blast Effects on Detroit: OTA, *The Effects of Nuclear War,* pp. 29, 36.

5-2 Casualties from a One-Megaton Attack on Detroit: OTA, *The Effects of Nuclear War,* pp. 31–32.

5-3 Fallout Pattern from a 1 Megaton Surface Burst in Detroit: OTA, *The Effects of Nuclear War,* p. 25.

5-4 Influence of Duration of Exposure: National Council on Radiation Protection and Measurements, *Radiological Factors Affecting Decision-Making in a Nuclear Attack,* NCRP Report no. 42 (Washington, D.C., November 1974), p. 38.

5-5 Short-Term Effects of Acute Radiation Exposure: Glasstone and Dolan, *The Effects of Nuclear Weapons,* pp. 580–581.

5-6 Mortality from Whole-Body Radiation Exposure: Clarence C. Lushbaugh, "Human Radiation Tolerance," in C. A. Tobias and Paul Todd, eds., *Space Radiation Biology and Related Topics* (New York: Academic Press, 1974), p. 487.

5-7 Medical Resources for Treatment of Injury: Adapted from Gerbarg and Greer, *Grappling with the Last Epidemic.*

5-8 Effect of a Nuclear Attack on Medical Facilities: Philadelphia: Prepared by the Philadelphia Department of Health, Stuart C. Shapiro, M.D., Commissioner of Health.

5-9 Prompt Deaths and Injuries from a Nuclear Attack on U.S. Cities: Adapted from ACDA, *Urban Population Vulnerability.*

Chapter 6
Global Environment and the Social Fabric after Nuclear War

Notes

1. *Long-Term Worldwide Effects of Multiple Nuclear-Weapons Detonations* (Washington, D.C.: NAS, 1975), p. 38.

2. *Long-Term Worldwide Effects,* p. 165.

3. *Long-Term Worldwide Effects,* p. 168.

4. *Nuclear Weapons,* Report of the Secretary-General of the United Nations (Brookline, Mass.: Autumn Press, 1981), p. 91.

5. Arthur M. Katz, *Life After Nuclear War* (Cambridge, Mass.: Ballinger, 1982), chap. 7.

Credit

Lead photograph: Wide World.

Chapter 7
A Primer of Nuclear Warfare

Notes

1. See Chapter 10, this volume, and "General Principles of Nuclear Explosions," In Samuel Glasstone and Philip J. Dolan, *The Effects of Nuclear Weapons,* 3rd ed. (Washington, D.C.: GPO, 1977), chap. 1, pp. 1–25.

2. For a technical overview of nuclear weapons effects, see Chapter 4, this volume, and "Descriptions of Nuclear Explosions," in Glasstone and Dolan, *Effects of Nuclear Weapons,* chap. 2, pp. 26–79. More popular presentations are included in OTA, *The Effects of Nuclear War* (Washington, D.C.: GPO, 1979).

3. A good study of MIRV and defense policy making is Ted Greenwood, *Making the MIRV: A Study of Defense Decision Making* (Cambridge, Mass.: Ballinger, 1975).

4. See Chapter 4, this volume, and "Residual Nuclear Radiation and Fallout," in Glasstone and Dolan, *The Effects of Nuclear Weapons,* chap. 9, pp. 387–460.

5. Several hand calculators are available for figuring the bomb damage, probability of kill, and other such effects. See, for example, the Lovelace Biomedical and Environmental Research Institute, Inc., "Nuclear Bomb Effects Computer," rev. ed. (1977), available with *The Effects of Nuclear Weapons*; and General Electric, Electronic Systems Division, "Missile Effectiveness and CEP Calculator," Syracuse, N.Y.

6. See Chapter 16, this volume, for sources of information on nuclear test explosions.

7. For an overview and introduction to nuclear weapons and their delivery systems, see Norman Pol-

mar, *Strategic Weapons: An Introduction* (New York: Crane, Russak, 1975). Also, U.S. Air Force, "Strategic Air Command Information: The United States' Primary Nuclear Deterrent Force" (Omaha, Nebr.: Offutt Air Force Base, Directorate of Information).

8. For fuller discussion on basing modes, both land and sea, see Herbert Scoville, Jr., *MX: Prescription for Disaster* (Cambridge, Mass.: MIT Press, 1981); David Gold, Christopher Paine, and Gail Shields, *Misguided eXpenditure: An Analysis of the Proposed MX Missile System* (New York: Council on Economic Priorities, 1981); and OTA, *MX Missile Basing* (Washington, D.C.: GPO, 1981).

9. SIPRI, *Tactical Nuclear Weapons: European Perspectives* (London: Taylor & Francis, 1978). See also Robert Metzger and Paul Doty, "Arms Control Enters the Gray Area," *International Security* 3, no. 3 (Winter 1978/1979), pp. 17–52. For a discussion of how nuclear war might escalate from tactical war, see Nigel Calder, *Nuclear Nightmares: An Investigation into Possible Wars* (New York: Viking, 1979).

10. SIPRI, *Tactical and Strategic Antisubmarine Warfare* (Cambridge, Mass.: MIT Press, 1974).

11. See the latest *Annual Report* of the U.S. Department of Defense for budget accounting.

12. A good account of the early analysis in nuclear deterrence is Alain C. Enthoven and K. Wayne Smith, *How Much Is Enough? Shaping the Defense Program, 1961–1969* (New York: Harper & Row, 1971), especially chaps. 5–6, "Nuclear Strategy and Forces" and "Yardsticks of Sufficiency."

13. U.S. Senate, Committee on Foreign Relations, "Nuclear War Strategy," September 16, 1980. These are "sanitized" hearings based on classified sessions regarding Presidential Directive 59 and nuclear strategy.

14. For citations on "broken arrows," see Chapter 15, this volume.

15. OTA, *Effects of Nuclear War,* pp. 64–80.

16. See, for example, U.S. Congress, Congressional Budget Office, "Counterforce Issues for the U.S. Strategic Nuclear Forces" (Washington, D.C.: GPO, January 1978). Also, U.S. Congress, Congressional Budget Office, "Planning U.S. Strategic Nuclear Forces for the 1980s" (Washington, D.C.: GPO, June 1978).

17. *Long-Term Worldwide Effects of Multiple Nuclear-Weapons Detonations* (Washington, D.C.: NAS, 1975).

Credits

Lead photograph: U.S. Air Force.

7-1 Weapon Damage Equivalents: The Boston Study Group, *The Price of Defense* (New York: Times Books, 1979), p. 65.

7-2 Kill Probabilities Against Hard Targets: Calculated using *Missile Effectiveness and CEP Calculator,* General Electric Company.

7-3 Nuclear War Terms and Definitions: Joint Chiefs of Staff, *Dictionary of Military and Associated Terms* (Washington, D.C.: GPO, 1974).

7-4 Airborne Nuclear War: U.S. Air Force photographs.

7-5 The Titan Intercontinental Missile: Ronald T. Pretty, ed., *Jane's Weapon Systems, 1981–82* (London: Jane's Publishing Company, 1981), p. 15. Photographs: left, Wide World; right, U.S. Air Force.

7-6 Nuclear War Launched from the Sea: U.S. Navy photographs.

7-7 Nuclear War Under the Sea: U.S. Navy photographs.

7-8 Tactical Nuclear Weapons: Photographs of howitzer, Lance, and Pershing II: U.S. Army; Tomahawk: U.S. Navy; SRAMs: U.S. Air Force.

7-9 Growth of United States and Soviet Strategic Weapons: DOD, Annual Secretary of Defense reports; DOD, Annual Joint Chiefs of Staff reports; IISS, *The Military Balance* (London: Annual); Norman Polmar, *Strategic Weapons: An Introduction* (New York: Crane, Russak, 1975).

7-10 The Practice of MIRV: U.S. Air Force photographs.

7-11 "Limited" Attacks Against Oil Refineries: OTA, *Effects of Nuclear War,* pp. 64–80.

7-12 Fallout from an Attack on U.S. Strategic Forces: Drawn using data from OTA, *Effects of Nuclear War,* pp. 81–90.

7-13 Effects of a Major Nuclear War: OTA, *Effects of Nuclear War,* pp. 10, 113.

7-14 War with Tactical Nuclear Weapons: The Case of Europe: Adapted from *Nuclear Weapons,* Report of the Secretary-General of the United Nations (Brookline, Mass.: Autumn Press, 1981), pp. 76–82.

World Nuclear Arsenals

Credits

Data and outlines compiled from Ronald T. Pretty, ed., *Jane's Weapon Systems, 1981–82* (London: Jane's Publishing Company, 1981); John Moore, ed., *Jane's Fighting Ships, 1981–82* (London: Jane's Publishing Company, 1981); Edward L. Korb, ed., *The World's Missile Systems* (Pomona, Calif.: General Dynamics, April 1982). "World Nuclear Navies" is prepared from Moore, *Jane's Fighting Ships, 1981–82;* John E. Moore, ed., *Jane's Pocket Book of Submarine Development* (New York: Collier Books, 1976), p. 49. U.S. Navy photograph.

Chapter 8
The Control of Nuclear Warfare

Notes

1. See the *Annual Report* of the Department of Defense which includes a few pages on command, control, and communications (so-called C^3). A brief report of the U.S. Senate Committee on Armed Services also covers C^3 with regard to recent false alerts: *Recent False Alerts from the Nation's Missile Attack Warning System* (Washington, D.C.: GPO, October 1980). Some public information can also be obtained directly from the Strategic Air Command, Offutt Air Force Base, Omaha, Nebr. Several reports critical of the Worldwide Military Command and Control System are also available from the General Accounting Office (GAO); see, for example, the statement of Richard W. Gutmann, Director, GAO Logistics and Communications Division, before the U.S. House Committee on Armed Services, April 23, 1979.

2. DOD, *Annual Report,* Fiscal Year 1982 (Washington, D.C.: GPO, 1981), p. 120.

3. DOD, 1981 Press Release, "Narrative Summaries of Accidents Involving U.S. Nuclear Weapons, 1950–1980"; Center for Defense Information, "U.S. Nuclear Weapons Accidents: Danger in our Midst," *The Defense Monitor* 10:5 (1981).

4. See news accounts, such as those in the *New York Times,* for early August 1980. Of particular interest is an address by former Secretary of Defense Harold Brown at the Naval War College, Newport, R.I., August 20, 1980, available as News Release No. 344-80 from the Department of Defense. See also the Federation of American Scientists, "Command and Control: Use It or Lose It?" *F.A.S. Public Interest Report* 33:8 (October 1980).

Credits

Lead photograph: U.S. Air Force.

8-1 Ballistic Missile Warning and Attack Assessment Systems: *Aviation Week and Space Technology* (April 13, 1981): 68–70; U.S. Senate, Committee on Armed Services, *Recent False Alerts* (Washington, D.C.: GPO, October 1980). For a report on Soviet air defense, see Ronald T. Pretty, ed., *Jane's Weapon Systems, 1981–82* (London: Jane's Publishing Company, 1981), pp. 229, 231–235.

8-2 Strategic Air Defense Systems: *Aviation Week and Space Technology* (April 13, 1981): 68–70.

8-3 AWACS Surveillance Aircraft: U.S. Air Force photograph.

8-4 Selected False Nuclear Alerts: U.S. Senate, Armed Services, *Recent False Alerts.*

Chapter 9
Future Technologies for Nuclear War-Fighting

Notes

1. Norman Polmar, *Strategic Weapons: An Introduction* (New York: Crane, Russak, 1975), p. 4.

2. See U.S. Air Force, "Strategic Air Command Information: The United States' Primary Nuclear Deterrent Force" (Omaha, Nebr.: Offutt Air Force Base, Directorate of Information), p. 56, on the "Short Range Attack Missile."

3. Accuracy estimates vary according to different unclassified sources. See, for example, U.S. Congress, Congressional Budget Office, *Counterforce Issues for the U.S. Strategic Nuclear Forces* (Washington, D.C.: GPO, January 1978), especially pp. 16–19. See also Robert C. Aldridge, *The Counterforce Syndrome: A Guide to U.S. Nuclear Weapons and Strategic Doctrine* (Washington, D.C.: Institute for Policy Studies, 1978).

4. For a discussion of neutron radiation, see chap. 8, "Initial Nuclear Radiation," in S. Glasstone and P. J. Dolan, *The Effects of Nuclear Weapons,* 3rd ed. (Washington, D.C.: GPO, 1977). The debate over neutron warheads is a volatile one; see, for example, Herbert Scoville, Jr., "The Neutron Bomb Makes Politics, Not War," *New York Times,* August 26, 1981, and Caspar W. Weinberger, "Why Neutron Weapons, Why Now," *Washington Post,* August 11, 1981.

5. Herbert Scoville, Jr., *MX: Prescription for Disaster* (Cambridge, Mass.: MIT Press, 1981); David Gold, Christopher Paine, and Gail Shields, *Misguided eXpenditure: An Analysis of the Proposed MX Missile System* (New York: Council on Economic Priorities, 1981); and OTA, *MX Missile Basing* (Washington, D.C.: GPO, 1981).

6. See the discussion of submarine basing in *MX Missile Basing.* For a more technical analysis of the small submarine system, see DOD, *An Evaluation of the Shallow Underwater Missile (SUM) Concept,* special report, April 9, 1980; System Planning Corporation, *An Assessment of Small Submarines and Encapsulation of Ballistic Missiles—Phase I,* unclassified report for the Deputy Under Secretary of Defense for Research and Engineering, May 1980. See also Sidney Drell, "SUM," *Arms Control Today* 9:8 (September 1979).

7. Background on the past debate over antiballistic missiles is available in Jerome B. Wiesner et al., *ABM: An Evaluation of the Decision to Deploy an Antiballistic Missile System* (New York: Signet, 1969); see also B. Alexander, "The Performance of Anti-Ballistic-Missile Systems," in B. T. Feld et al., eds., *Impact of New Technologies on the Arms Race* (Cambridge,

Mass.: MIT Press, 1971). Much information is available on current research in ballistic missile defense in Senate and House hearings.

8. Kosta Tsipis, "Laser Weapons," *Scientific American* 245:6 (December 1981): 51–57.

9. The text and overview of both bilateral and multilateral treaties are found in ACDA, *Arms Control and Disarmament Agreements: Texts and Histories of Negotiations,* 1980 ed. (Washington, D.C.: GPO, 1980).

10. Information on antisatellite weaponry can be found in Harvey Brooks, "Notes on Some Issues on Technology and National Defense," *Daedalus* (Winter 1981): 129–136; Raymond L. Garthoff, "Banning the Bomb in Outer Space," *International Security* 5:3 (Winter 1980/81): 25–40; *Strategic Survey, 1976* (London: IISS, 1977), pp. 26–30, and *Strategic Survey, 1978,* pp. 23–28. For an optimistic view on ASAT weapons, see "Particle Beams, Laser Weapons," *Aviation Week and Space Technology* (July 28, 1980): 32–66 and (August 4, 1980): 44–68.

11. Joel S. Wit provides a good introduction to ASW in "Advances in Antisubmarine Warfare," *Scientific American* 244:2 (February 1981): 31–41. See also SIPRI, *Tactical and Strategic Antisubmarine Warfare* (Cambridge, Mass.: MIT Press, 1974).

12. An interesting budget analysis, in guns-butter terms, is Gold, Paine, and Shields, *Misguided eXpenditure.* The difficulty of estimating weapons costs is shown in U.S. Congress, House Committee on Government Operations, *Inaccuracy of Department of Defense Weapons Acquisition Cost Estimates* (Washington, D.C.: GPO, June 25–26, 1979).

13. Multiple volumes on the environmental impact of the proposed MX basing schemes are available from the U.S. Air Force. See, for example, *MX: Deployment Area Selection and Land Withdrawal/Acquisition DEIS* (San Bernardino, Calif.: Norton Air Force Base, December 1980).

Credits

Lead photograph: U.S. Navy.

9-1 Old and New Nuclear Weapons: Norman Polmar, *Strategic Weapons;* Ronald T. Pretty, ed., *Jane's Weapon Systems, 1981–82* (London: Jane's Publishing Company, 1981); Edward L. Korb, ed., *The World's Missile Systems* (Pomona, Calif.: General Dynamics, April 1982).

9-2 Nuclear Weapon Destructiveness: Author's calculations.

9-3 Nuclear Weapon Accuracy: Author's calculations.

9-4 Prime Counterforce Targets: "The New Nuclear Strategy: Battle of the Dead?" *The Defense Monitor* V:5 (July 1976): 3; *Aviation Week and Space Technology* (September 22, 1980): 15.

9-5 A New Generation of Strategic Aircraft: U.S. Air Force photograph.

9-6 Ballistic Missile Defense: Evolving Technology: Chayes and Wiesner, *ABM: An Evaluation;* ACDA, *Arms Control and Disarmament Agreements* (Washington, D.C.: GPO, 1980); *Aviation Week and Space Technology* (January 11, 1982): 20–21.

9-7 Space Shuttle, a Military Program?: NASA photograph.

9-8 The MX Missile: Pretty, *Jane's Weapon Systems, 1981–82,* pp. 13–15; Scoville, *MX: Prescription for Disaster.* U.S. Air Force photograph.

Chapter 10
The Physics of Nuclear Weapons

Credits

Lead photograph: Courtesy of Dr. Harold Edgerton, MIT Strobe Laboratory.

10-1 Fireball—Later Stage: LANSL photograph.

10-2 Test Explosion at Bikini: U.S. Air Force photograph.

10-4 The Materials of Nuclear Destruction: The photographs of U-235 and Pu-239 are from the slide show *The H-Bomb Secret* by Howard Morland; that from the Y-12 plant was supplied by the Union Carbide Corporation.

10-5 How Nuclear Weapons Work: *Encyclopedia Americana* (Danbury, Conn.: Grolier, 1981), the articles by Edward Teller on "Hydrogen Bomb" in vol. 14, pp. 654–656, and by John S. Foster, Jr., on "Nuclear Weapons" in vol. 20, pp. 518–528. S. Glasstone and P. J. Dolan, *The Effects of Nuclear Weapons* (Washington, D.C.: GPO, 1977), pp. 12–22.

Chapter 11
Nuclear Weapons Manufacture

Notes

1. No official figure for the number of U.S. nuclear weapons has been published, but the estimate of about thirty thousand is widely used. See, for example, *The Defense Monitor,* February 1975.

2. "A complete one-megaton bomb ... would fit under your bed," according to Howard Morland's article in *The Progressive* Magazine (November 1979). The article is reprinted in Howard Morland, *The Secret That Exploded* (New York: Random House, 1981), pp. 239–271. See also pp. 51 and 69 for interesting comments on the sizes of nuclear weapons.

3. For an interview of Dr. Carl Walske, president of

the Atomic Industrial Forum, see Sheldon Novick, *The Electric War* (San Francisco: Sierra Club Books, 1976), p. 32. See also H. Peter Metzger, *The Atomic Establishment* (New York: Simon & Schuster, 1972), p. 64, for quote of Herbert York.

4. For the fire and cost estimates, see Metzger, *Atomic Establishment,* pp. 147–150 and 288–289; see also Roger Rapoport, *The Great American Bomb Machine* (New York: Ballantine Books, 1971). For current concerns see Peter Ognibene, "Living with the Bomb," *Saturday Review* (June 24, 1978): 8–12.

5. Reports of plans to expand the production of plutonium and other bomb materials were published in *Science* (January 9, 1981): 146–147 and (October 16, 1981): 308–309.

6. Bendix Corporation, 1978 Annual Report.

7. DOE, *DOE Research and Development and Field Facilities* (Washington, D.C., June 1979), p. V-39.

8. DOE, *Field Facilities,* p. V-41.

9. Current plans to step up the production of nuclear weapons materials include restarting one of these reactors (see note 5).

10. DOE, *Field Facilities,* p. V-18.

11. DOE, *Field Facilities,* p. V-24.

12. See Thomas C. Hollocher, "Storage and Disposal of High Level Radioactive Wastes," in *The Nuclear Fuel Cycle,* Union of Concerned Scientists (Cambridge, Mass.: MIT Press, 1977), pp. 219–275; pp. 238–244 and 267–269 are especially relevant.

13. See note 5.

14. DOE, *Field Facilities,* p. IV-120.

15. Operating nuclear weapons laboratories is an unusual function for a university, and many people have considered it to be an undesirable one. In recent years, national peace organizations have been working not merely for the operation of the laboratories under other auspices but for their conversion from weapons development to constructive activities.

16. For the origin of the Shippingport Station and a detailed history of naval nuclear propulsion, see Richard Hewlett and Francis Duncan, *Nuclear Navy* (Chicago: University of Chicago Press, 1974).

17. General Electric's Department of Defense contracts for fiscal year 1980 totaled more than $2.2 billion, making it the fifth-largest military contractor in that year; it ranked fourth in 1979 and again fifth in 1978. In 1980, Rockwell, Bendix, and AT&T ranked fourteenth, thirty-ninth, and twenty-first, respectively. Westinghouse Electric Company also ranks high on the Department of Defense's contractor list at fifteenth. See *Aviation Week and Space Technology* (April 27, 1981).

18. See, for example, Norman Solomon, "The

Atom-Weapons Lobby Is Gaining," *The Nation* (October 11, 1980): 334–338.

19. George Kennan, "Cease This Madness," *The Atlantic Monthly* (January 1981): 25–28.

Credits

Lead photograph: DOE.

11-1 Principal Plants of the U.S. Nuclear Weapons Industry: Compiled from DOE, *Field Facilities.*

11-2 Nuclear Weapons Employment and Budget: DOE, *Field Facilities,* pp. IV-68, 73, 77, 111, 116; V-29, 32, 35, 43.

11-3 Workman Using Glove Box: Photograph courtesy of Brookhaven National Laboratory.

11-4 Production Reactor—Savannah River: DOE photograph.

11-5 Lawrence Livermore National Laboratory: LLNSL photograph.

Chapter 12
Biological Effects of Ionizing Radiation

Notes

1. V. P. Bond, T. M. Fliedner, and J. O. Archambeau, *Mammalian Radiation Lethality* (New York: Academic Press, 1965).

2. P. C. Hanawalt, "Repair of Genetic Material in Living Cells," *Endeavor* 31 (1972): 83–87.

Credits

Lead photograph: Courtesy of Dr. Anthony V. Carrano at LLNSL.

12-1 Penetration of Radiation in Air and Tissue: See, for example, Hugh F. Henry, *Fundamentals of Radiation Protection* (New York: John Wiley, 1969), pp. 70–81.

12-3 Curies, Roentgens, Rads, and Rems: John R. LaMarsh, *Introduction to Nuclear Engineering* (Reading, Mass.: Addison-Wesley, 1975), pp. 369–374. Henry, *Fundamentals of Radiation Protection,* pp. 81–93.

12-4 Acute Radiation Syndromes in Humans: Bond, Fliedner, and Archambeau, *Mammalian Radiation Lethality.*

12-5 The Bone Marrow Syndrome: The graphs of blood changes are adapted from G. H. Andrews, B. W. Sitterson, A. L. Kretchman, and M. Brucer, "Criticality Accident at the Y-12 Plant," *Diagnosis and Treatment of Acute Radiation Injury* (Geneva: World Health Organization, 1961), pp. 27–48. Republished in Herman Cember, *Introduction to Health Physics* (Oxford: Pergamon, 1969), p. 182.

12-6 The Gastrointestinal Syndrome: Scanning electron micrograph provided by Dr. K. E. Carr of the

University of Glasgow, Department of Anatomy. Drawing: Author's sketch.

12-7 Genetic Damage from Radiation: Photograph from the Hiroshima slide series provided by the U.S. Arms Control and Disarmament Agency.

Chapter 13
Radiation and Public Health

Notes

1. D. T. Oakley, *Natural Radiation Exposure in the United States,* Report ORP/SID 72-1 (Washington, D.C.: U.S. Environmental Protection Agency, June 1972).

2. *The Effects on Populations of Exposure to Low Levels of Ionizing Radiation: 1980,* Report of the Advisory Committee on the Biological Effects of Ionizing Radiation (BEIR-III) (Washington, D.C.: NAS, 1980).

3. T. F. Gesell and H. M. Pritchard, "The Technologically Enhanced Natural Radiation Environment," *Health Physics* 28:4 (1975): 361–366.

4. A. W. Klement, Jr., et al., *Estimates of Ionizing Radiation Doses in the United States, 1960–2000,* Report ORP/CSD 72-1 (Washington, D.C.: U.S. Environmental Protection Agency, 1972).

5. R. W. Alcox, "A Dosimetry Study of Dental Exposures from Intraoral Radiography," in *Health Physics in the Healing Arts,* Report DHEW (FDA) 73-8029, U.S. Department of Health, Education, and Welfare (San Juan, P.R.: Health Physics Society, December 1972), pp. 107–114.

6. A. B. McIntyre, D. R. Hamilton, and R. C. Grant, *A Pilot Study of Nuclear Medicine Reporting through the Medically Oriented Data System,* Report FDA 76-8045 (Rockville, Md.: Radiological Health, June 1976).

7. Office of Radiation Programs, *Radiological Impact Caused by Emissions of Radionuclides into Air in the United States,* Report EPA 520/7-79-006 (Washington, D.C.: U.S. Environmental Protection Agency, August 1979).

8. United Nations Scientific Committee on the Effects of Atomic Radiation (UNSCEAR), Report A/32/40, General Assembly (New York: United Nations, 1977).

9. UNSCEAR, 1977.

10. Office of Radiation Programs, *Radiological Impact.*

11. K. L. Feldman, ed., *Radiological Quality of the Environment in the United States,* Report EPA 520/1-77-009, Office of Radiation Programs (Washington, D.C.: U.S. Environmental Protection Agency, September 1977).

12. *Radiation Exposure from Consumer Products*

and *Miscellaneous Sources,* Report no. 56 (Washington, D.C.: National Council on Radiation Protection and Measurements, 1977).

13. V. Archer, J. Wagoner, and F. Lundin, "Lung Cancer Among Uranium Miners in the United States," *Health Physics* 25 (1973): 351–371.

14. U.S. Mining Enforcement and Safety Administration, *Administration of the Federal Metallic and Non-Metallic Mine Safety Act (PL89-577),* Annual Report to Congress of Secretary of Interior (Washington, D.C.: GPO, 1976).

15. Feldman, *Radiological Quality of the Environment.*

16. A. V. Nero, Jr., *A Guidebook to Nuclear Reactors* (Berkeley, Calif.: University of California Press, 1979), pp. 36–37.

17. Feldman, *Radiological Quality of the Environment.*

18. Nero, *Guidebook to Nuclear Reactors,* pp. 36–37.

19. D. Majumdar and J. P. Indusi, *Inventory of High Level and Transuranic Wastes in the United States,* Report BNL-NUREG-27817R (February 1981). Informal report, limited distribution, prepared by Nuclear Waste Management Division, Department of Nuclear Energy, Brookhaven National Laboratory, Upton, N.Y.

20. Feldman, *Radiological Quality of the Environment.*

21. F. P. Libassi (chairman), "Summary of Work Group Reports of the Interagency Task Force on Ionizing Radiation," Department of Health, Education, and Welfare (Draft, February 27, 1979).

22. M. Eisenbud, "The Status of Radioactive Waste Management: Needs for Reassessment," *Health Physics* 40 (1981): 429–437.

23. R. Peto et al., "Cancer and Aging in Mice and Men," *Brit. J. Cancer* 36 (1975): 411–426.

24. E. P. Radford, "Human Health Effects of Low Doses of Ionizing Radiation: The BEIR-III Controversy," *Radiation Research* 84 (1980): 369–394.

25. R. B. Setlow, "Repair Deficient Human Disorders and Cancer," *Nature* 271 (1978): 1713–1717.

26. V. A. McKusick, *Mendelian Influence in Man: Catalogs in Autosomal Dominant, Autosomal Recessive, and X-linked Phenotypes,* 5th ed. (Baltimore: The Johns Hopkins Press, 1978).

Credits

Lead photograph: Margaret Woodruff, courtesy of MIT Medical Department.

13-1 Early Casualties of Radiation: Jack Schubert and Ralph E. Lapp, *Radiation: What It Is and How It Affects You* (New York: Viking Press, 1957), chap. 2, Hugh F. Henry, *Fundamentals of Radiation Protection* (New York: John Wiley and Sons, 1969),

pp. 3–6; John R. LaMarsh, *Introduction to Nuclear Engineering* (Reading, Mass.: Addison-Wesley, 1975), pp. 367–369.

13-2 Sources of Radiation Exposure: *The Effects on Populations of Exposure to Low Levels of Ionizing Radiation: 1980,* Report of the Advisory Committee on the Biological Effects of Ionizing Radiation (BEIR-III) (Washington, D.C.: NAS, 1980), pp. 56–57, 60–61, 64, 66–67, and other sources.

13-3 The Radioactive Daughters of Radon: Committee on Indoor Pollutants, Board on Toxicology and Environmental Health Hazards, Assembly of Life Sciences, *Indoor Pollutants* (Washington, D.C.: National Academy Press, 1981).

13-4 Hazards of Plutonium: Prepared by Thérèse Dennis based on the following material: W. J. Bair and R. C. Thompson, "Plutonium: Biomedical Research," *Science* 183 (February 22, 1974): 715; J. T. Edsall, "Toxicity of Plutonium and Some Other Actinides," *The Bulletin of the Atomic Scientists* (September 1976): 27.

13-5 Radioactivity from Atmospheric Nuclear Tests: S. Glasstone and P. J. Dolan, *The Effects of Nuclear Weapons* (Washington, D.C.: GPO, 1977), p. 449.

13-6 Radiation Protection Standards: Prepared by Jack Dennis using the following: The International Commission on Radiological Protection, *Report of Committee II on Permissible Dose for Internal Radiation* (New York: Pergamon, 1959); U.S. National Council on Radiation Protection and Measurements, *Basic Radiation Protection Criteria* (Washington, D.C., 1971); U.S. Code of Federal Regulations, Title 10, Part 20, Radiation Protection Standards; Committee on Food Protection, Food and Nutrition Board, *Radionuclides in Food* (Washington, D.C.: National Academy of Sciences, 1973).

Chapter 14
Radioactive Waste

Notes

1. Other nations' and international programs are described in David A. Deese, *Nuclear Power and Radioactive Waste: A Sub-seabed Disposal Option?* (Lexington, Mass.: Lexington Books, 1978); *Decommissioning of Nuclear Facilities,* Proceedings of a Symposium (Vienna: IAEA, 1979); *Assessment of National Systems for Obtaining Local Acceptance of Waste Management Siting and Routing Activities (Belgium, Canada, Federal Republic of Germany, France, Japan, Sweden, Switzerland, United Kingdom),* Report IEAL-58, prepared for the U.S. Department of Energy by International Energy Associates Limited, July 1980; Dieter K. Richter, "National and

International Activities in the Field of Underground Disposal of Radioactive Wastes," *IAEA Bulletin* 20:4 (August 1978): 30–41; Gene I. Rochlin, *Plutonium, Power, and Politics* (Berkeley, Calif.: University of California Press, 1979).

2. For a discussion of the mysterious Soviet accident in the Ural Mountains in the late 1950s, see John R. Trabalka, L. Dean Eyman, and Stanley I. Auerbach, "Analysis of the 1957–1958 Soviet Nuclear Accident," *Science* 209 (1980): 345–353.

3. DOE, Oak Ridge Operations Office, *Spent Fuel and Waste Inventories and Projections,* ORO-778, August 1980, p. 59.

4. Helene Linker, Roger Beers, and Terry Lash, "Radioactive Waste: Gaps in the Regulatory System," *Denver Law Journal* 56 (1979): 4; William Ramsay, *Unpaid Costs of Electrical Energy* (Baltimore: Johns Hopkins University Press, 1979), pp. 36–40.

5. U.S. Nuclear Regulatory Commission, *Final Generic Environmental Impact Statement on Uranium Milling, Project M-25,* Report NUREG-0706, September 1980.

6. DOE, Assistant Secretary for Nuclear Energy, Nuclear Waste Management Program, *Spent Fuel and Radioactive Waste Inventories and Projections as of December 31, 1980,* Report DOE/NE-0017, September 1981, pp. 34, 113, 114.

7. DOE, *Spent Fuel and Radioactive Waste Inventories,* September 1981, p. 9.

8. Ronnie D. Lipschutz, *Radioactive Waste: Politics, Technology, and Risk,* Report of the Union of Concerned Scientists (Cambridge, Mass.: Ballinger, 1980), p. 43.

9. DOE, *Spent Fuel and Radioactive Waste Inventories,* September 1981, p. 9.

10. A. Ghovanlou, L. Ettlinger, A. Deagazio, and N. Lord, *Analysis of Nuclear Waste Disposal and Strategies for Facilities Deployment,* Report MTR-80W88, (McLean, Va.: Mitre, Metrek Division, April 1980), p. 5-13.

11. Ghovanlou et al., p. 4-12.

12. Ghovanlou et al., p. E-13.

13. Committee on Radioactive Waste Management, Panel on Hanford Wastes, *Radioactive Wastes at the Hanford Reservation, a Technical Review* (Washington, D.C.: NAS, 1978), p. 9.

14. Hartmut Krugmann and Frank von Hippel, "Radioactive Wastes: A Comparison of U.S. Military and Civilian Inventories," *Science* 187 (1977): 883–885.

15. Committee on Radioactive Waste Management, Panel on Hanford Wastes, *Radioactive Wastes at the Hanford Reservation,* p. 9.

16. DOE, *Spent Fuel and Waste Inventories and Projections,* August 1980, pp. 16–17.

17. DOE, *Spent Fuel and Radioactive Waste Inventories,* September 1981, p. 21.

18. Lipschutz et al., pp. 132–134.

19. DOE, *Spent Fuel and Radioactive Waste Inventories,* September 1981, p. 62.

20. Ibid., pp. 29, 85–87.

21. Ibid., p. 89.

22. Lipschutz et al., p. 134.

23. Merril Eisenbud, "Radioactive Wastes from Biomedical Institutions," *Science* 107 (1980): 1299.

24. Eliot Marshall, "Governor Ray Relents, Opens Waste Site," *Science* 206 (1979): 1165; Eliot Marshall, "Radioactive Waste Backup Threatens Research," *Science* 206 (1979): 431–433; Jan Stucker, "Suddenly Nuclear Energy Is Not the Undisputed Answer," *Columbia, S.C., Record,* three-part series, April 11, 1979, p. 1-8; April 12, p. 2-8; April 23, p. 1-8.

25. See EG&G Idaho, *Managing Low Level Radioactive Waste, A Proposed Approach,* Report LLWMP–1, August 1980; Dialogue Group on Low-Level Radioactive Waste Management, *Striking a Balance: Toward a National Policy for Managing Low-Level Radioactive Waste* (Washington, D.C.: Conservation Foundation, 1981); Frederic A. Morris, "Role of the States in Low-Level Waste Management," *Nuclear News* (May 1981): 53–56.

26. DOE, *Spent Fuel and Radioactive Waste Inventories,* September 1981, pp. 119, 120.

27. William P. Bishop and Frank J. Miraglia, Jr., eds. *Environmental Survey of the Reprocessing and Waste Management Portions of the LWR Fuel Cycle,* Report NUREG-0116, U.S. Nuclear Regulatory Commission, Office of Nuclear Material Safety and Safeguards, October 1976, p. 4-129.

28. Ibid., p. 4-133; Nuclear Energy Services, *Decommissioning Handbook,* Report DOE/EV/10128-1, prepared for DOE, November 1980, pp. 1-2, 2-6.

29. Nuclear Energy Services, *Decommissioning Handbook,* p. 1-2.

30. Comptroller General of the United States, *Cleaning Up the Waste—Proposals for Organization and Siting,* Report EMD-79-77, U.S. General Accounting Office, June 21, 1979.

31. Code of Federal Regulations, vol. 10, sec. 50.33(f). See also Luther J. Carter, "Nuclear Wastes: The Science of Geologic Disposal Seen as Weak," *Science* 200 (1978): 1135–1137.

32. Abel Wolman, letter to Frederic Seitz, August 11, 1965, Archives of the NAS, Washington, D.C.

33. Richard K. Lester and David J. Rose, "The Nuclear Wastes at West Valley, New York," *Technology Review* (May 1977): 20–29.

34. John O. Blomeke, Interview, Oak Ridge National Laboratory, Tenn., April 1981.

35. Robert Gillette, "Radiation Spill at Hanford: The Anatomy of an Accident," *Science* 181 (1973): 728–730.

36. Richard Hewlett, "Federal Policy for the Disposal of Highly Radioactive Wastes from Commercial Nuclear Power Plants: An Historical Analysis," unpublished paper, DOE, Executive Secretariat, March 9, 1978, p. 11.

37. Gillette, "Radiation Spill at Hanford."

38. Hewlett, "Federal Policy," p. 25.

39. J. Hoover Mackin, letter to Dr. Frederick Seitz, June 14, 1967, Archives of the NAS, Washington, D.C., p. 4.

40. Committee on Geologic Aspects of Radioactive Waste Disposal, *Minutes of January 7, 1955 Meeting,* Archives of the NAS, Washington, D.C., p. 2.

41. Committee on Geologic Aspects of Radioactive Waste Disposal, *Minutes of September 11, 1955 Meeting,* Archives of the NAS, Washington, D.C.

42. Committee on Radioactive Waste Disposal, Division of Earth Sciences, *Interim Storage of Solidified High-Level Radioactive Wastes* (Washington, D.C.: NAS, April 1957), app. F.

43. Frank L. Parker, Interview, Vanderbilt University, Nashville, Tenn., April 1981.

44. For a critical appraisal, see Philip Boffey, *The Brain Bank of America* (New York: McGraw-Hill, 1975), chap. 5.

45. H. O. Weeren, "Waste Disposal by Shale Fracturing at Oak Ridge National Laboratory," in *Underground Disposal of Radioactive Wastes,* Report IAEA-SM-243/42 (Vienna: IAEA, 1980), pp. 171–176.

46. Committee on Geologic Aspects of Radioactive Waste Disposal, *Minutes of March 26, 1960 Meeting,* Archives of the NAS, Washington, D.C., p. 5.

47. Committee on Radioactive Waste Management, Panel on Engineered Storage, *Interim Storage of Solidified High-Level Radioactive Wastes* (Washington, D.C.: NAS, 1975).

48. G. Edwin Brown, Jr., "Nuclear Waste Disposal Policy: A Case History of Change and Uncertainty," unpublished paper, Atomic Industrial Forum, January 31, 1979, p. 6.

49. Lamm-Wirth Task Force on Rocky Flats, preliminary report, February 1975.

50. Parker interview, April 1981.

51. Randall F. Smith, *Strategies for Siting Nuclear Waste Repositories,* unpublished doctoral dissertation, Harvard University, 1981, chap. 6.

52. DOE, *Management of Commercially Generated Radioactive Waste,* Report DOE/EIS-0046, 1980.

53. Smith, *Strategies for Siting,* chap. 6.

54. Amory B. Lovins, "Energy Strategy: The Road Not Taken?" *Foreign Affairs* 55 (1976): 65–96.

55. Barbara D. Melber, Stanley M. Nealey, Joy Hammersla, and William L. Rankin, *Nuclear Power and the Public: Analysis of Collected Survey Research,* Report PNL-2430 (Seattle: Battelle Human Affairs Research Centers, November 1977), pp. vii–ix.

56. Smith, *Strategies for Siting,* chap. 6.

57. Hewlett, "Federal Policy," p. 36.

58. Harold P. Green and Alan Rosenthal, *Government of the Atom* (New York: Atherton, 1963).

59. Nuclear Energy Policy Study Group, *Nuclear Power Issues and Choices* (Cambridge, Mass.: Ballinger, 1977), chap. 9.

60. See Chapter 19, this volume, and David J. Rose and Richard K. Lester, "Nuclear Power, Nuclear Weapons, and International Stability," *Scientific American* (April 1978).

61. Kenneth Davis, "Statement before the Subcommittee on Energy and the Environment," U.S. House of Representatives, July 9, 1981.

62. State Planning Council on Radioactive Waste Management, Sixth Meeting Docket Book, June 8, 1981.

63. Hewlett, "Federal Policy"; Office of the White House Press Secretary, "Fact Sheet: The President's Program on Radioactive Waste Management," February 12, 1980. See also Kai N. Lee, "A Federalist Strategy for Nuclear Waste Management," *Science* 208 (1980): 679–684; Gene I. Rochlin, "Irreversibility and Multiplicity," *Science* 195 (1977): 23–31.

64. Todd R. LaPorte, "Nuclear Waste: Increasing Scale and Sociopolitical Impacts" *Science* 201 (1978): 22–28.

65. Hewlett, "Federal Policy," p. 1.

66. E. William Colglazier, ed., *The Politics of Nuclear Waste* (New York: Pergamon, 1981); Randall F. Smith and Frederic A. Morris, "The Regulatory and Political Framework for High-Level Radioactive Waste Management," *Underground Space,* to appear.

67. Cyrus Klingsberg and James Duguid, *Status of Technology for Isolating High-Level Radioactive Wastes in Geologic Repositories,* Report DOE/TIC 11207 (draft), DOE, Office of Nuclear Waste Isolation, October 1980.

68. DOE, *Management of Commercially Generated Radioactive Waste.*

69. ERDA, *Alternatives for Managing Wastes from Reactors and Post-Fission Operations in the LWR Fuel Cycle,* Report ERDA 76-43, 1976.

70. See W. P. Bishop and C. D. Hollister, "Seabed Disposal—Where to Look," *Nuclear Technology* 24 (1974): 425–443; Deese, "Sub-seabed Disposal Program Plan," in *Nuclear Power and Radioactive Waste,* Report SAND80-007/I, Sandia Laboratories, January 1980.

71. See Luther J. Carter, "Nuclear Wastes: The Science of Geologic Disposal Seen as Weak," *Science* 200 (1978): 1135–1137; G. deMarsily, E. Ledoux, A. Barbreau, and J. Margat, "Nuclear Waste Disposal: Can the Geologist Guarantee Isolation?" *Science* 197 (1977): 519–527; Klingsberg and Duguid, *Status of Technology.*

72. P. A. Witherspoon, N. G. W. Cook, and J. E. Gale, "Geologic Storage of Radioactive Waste: Field Studies in Sweden," *Science* 211 (1981): 894–900.

73. Klingsberg and Duguid, "Status of Technology," p. 6.

74. A. E. Ringwood, S. E. Kesson, N. G. Ware, W. Hibberson, and A. Major, "Immobilization of High-Level Reactor Wastes in SYNROC," *Nature* 278 (March 15, 1979): 219–223.

75. Committee on Radioactive Waste Management, Subcommittee for Review of the KBS-II Plan, *A Review of the Swedish KBS-II Plan for Disposal of Spent Nuclear Fuel* (Washington, D.C.: NAS, 1980).

76. J. D. Bredehoeft and T. Maini, "Strategy for Radioactive Waste Disposal in Crystalline Rocks," *Science* 213 (1981): 293–296.

77. Comptroller General of the United States, *The Nation's Nuclear Waste—Proposals for Organization and Siting,* Report EMD-79-77, General Accounting Office, June 21, 1979.

78. Garry D. Brewer, *Politicians, Bureaucrats and the Consultant* (New York: Basic Books, 1973).

79. J. D. Bredehoeft, A. W. England, D. B. Stewart, N. J. Trask, and I. J. Winograd, *Geologic Disposal of High-Level Radioactive Wastes—Earth-Science Perspectives,* Circular 779, U.S. Geological Survey, 1978; Interagency Review Group, *Subgroup Report on Alternative Technology Strategies for the Isolation of Nuclear Waste,* Report TID-28818, October 1978, app. A.

80. W. P. Bishop, I. R. Hoos, N. Hilberry, D. S. Metlay, and R. A. Watson, *Essays on Issues Relevant to the Regulation of Radioactive Waste Management,* Report NUREG-0412, Division of the Fuel Cycle and Material Safety, U.S. Nuclear Regulatory Commission, May 1978; Robert E. Goodin, "Uncertainty as an Excuse for Cheating our Children: The Case of Nuclear Wastes," *Policy Sciences* 10 (1978): 25–43.

81. William C. Clark, "Witches, Floods, and Wonder Drugs: Historical Perspectives on Risk Management," in Richard C. Schwing and Walter A. Albers, Jr., eds., *Societal Risk Assessment* (New York: Plenum, 1980).

Credits

Lead photograph: DOE.
14-2 Sources of Radioactive Waste: Data on number of facilities are from Comptroller General of the United States, *Cleaning Up the Remains of Nuclear Facilities,* U.S. General Accounting Office, 1977, p. 3-7. Quantities of wastes from Bishop and Miraglia, *Environmental Survey.* Quantities of tailings from DOE, *Spent Fuel and Radioactive Waste Inventories,* September 1981, pp. 110, 114.

14-3 Spent Fuel Storage Pool: Photograph provided by the French Embassy, Washington, D.C.

14-4 Nuclear Wastes from Power Reactor Operation: Figures from DOE, Assistant Secretary for Defense programs, Office of Nuclear Waste Management and Fuel Cycle Programs, *Defense Waste Processing Facility, Savannah River Plant, Aiken, South Carolina, Draft Environmental Impact Statement,* Report DOE/EIS-0082D, September 1981: mill tailings, p. 61; high-level and low-level, p. 37; airborne, p. 120. For spent fuel: Ronnie D. Lipschutz, *Radioactive Waste: Politics, Technology and Risk* (Cambridge, Mass.: Ballinger, 1980), p. 32; this amounts to thirty metric tons of fuel. Decommissioning: Gene I. Rochlin, *Plutonium, Power and Politics* (Berkeley, Calif.: University of California Press, 1979), p. 92.

14-5 High-Level Radioactive Wastes in the United States: Waste volumes and specific activities for December 31, 1980, are reported in DOE, *Savannah River Plant, Draft Environmental Impact Statement,* September 1981, pp. 51, 154, 160, 167, 173. The damaged fuel elements buried at West Valley are described in DOE, *Western New York Nuclear Service Center Study,* companion volume, Report TID-28905-2, November 1978.

14-6 Transuranic and Low-Level Wastes in the United States: Waste volumes and specific activities are reported in DOE, *Spent Fuel and Radioactive Waste Inventories and Projections as of December 31, 1980,* September 1981, pp. 57–93.

14-7 Disposal of Low-Level Radioactive Waste: Photograph by Ron Garrison, Lexington, Kentucky, *Herald-Leader.*

Chapter 15
Nuclear Accidents

Notes

1. "Narrative Summaries of Accidents Involving U.S. Nuclear Weapons, 1950–1980," DOD news release, 1981.

2. The source material is newspaper reports: John Noble Wilford, "The Perilous World of the Missile Man," *New York Times,* September 22, 1980; Walter Pincus, "Air Force Missile Blast Survivors Wonder If Buddy Died in Vain," *Washington Post,* October 22, 1980, p. A-16; and Pincus, "Titan II Blast: A Long

String of Mistakes," *Washington Post,* September 25, 1980, p. A-14.

3. DOD news release, 1981.

4. James Scudder, "Military to Allow Exceptions to Its Nuclear Arms Silence," *Arkansas Gazette,* October 11, 1980, p. 10.

5. DOD news release, 1981. The four descriptions of accidents involving strategic bombers are quoted from this undated document. Further details of these incidents have been gathered and assembled in Center for Defense Information, "U.S. Nuclear Weapons Accidents: Danger in Our Midst," *The Defense Monitor* 10:5 (1981). See also Gary Hanauer, "The Story Behind the Pentagon's Broken Arrows," *Mother Jones* (April 1981): 23.

6. Ralph E. Lapp, *Kill and Overkill* (New York: Basic Books, 1962), p. 127.

7. Ralph E. Lapp, *The Weapons Culture* (New York: W. W. Norton, 1968).

8. Edward Klein and Robert Littel, "Shh! Let's Tell the Russians," *Newsweek* (May 5, 1969): 46–47.

9. *Newsweek* (May 5, 1969): 46–47.

10. Jack Anderson and Les Whitten, "Risk of Nuclear War in Korea Hinted," *Washington Post,* June 20, 1975, p. D-19.

11. V. B. Phelps et al., *Accidental War: Some Dangers in the 1960's,* Mershon National Security Program Research Paper RP-6 (Columbus, Ohio: Ohio State University, June 28, 1960).

12. *New York Times,* June 5, 1962, p. 1, and June 21, 1962, p. 1.

13. Samuel Glasstone, ed., *The Effects of Nuclear Weapons,* 2d ed. (Washington, D.C.: GPO, 1962), p. 461.

14. John R. Horan and L. J. Cunningham, "Decontamination after Widespread Release to the Environment," in J. A. Ayres, ed., *Decontamination of Nuclear Reactors and Equipment* (New York: Ronald Press, 1970), p. 747.

15. Ibid., pp. 747–749.

16. Howard Rosenberg, *Atomic Soldiers* (Boston: Beacon Press, 1980), p. 131; Karl F. Hubner and Shirly A. Fry, *The Medical Basis for Radiation Accident Preparedness* (New York: Elsevier/North Holland, 1980), p. 33.

17. Constance Holden, "House Report Nails AEC for Sheep Deaths," *Science* (September 5, 1980): 1097.

18. *New Scientist,* November 1, 1979.

19. Robert E. Allen, *Summary Information on Accidental Releases of Radioactive Effluent to the Atmosphere from Underground Nuclear Detonations Designed for Containment,* Report WASH-1183 (Washington, D.C.: GPO, June 1971), p. 27.

20. George A. Cowan, "A Natural Fission Reactor,"

Scientific American 235:1 (July 1976): 36–47.

21. Walter Pincus, "Pacific Experience Shows Difficulty of Cleaning Up Radiation," *Washington Post,* April 18, 1978, p. A-2.

22. According to one newspaper report, cleanup plans called for "hundreds of railroad cars" carrying "an estimated 330,000 cubic feet of contaminated waste to be buried below ground" in Idaho: Lawrence E. Davies, "Fire Cleanup Keeps Plutonium Plant Busy," *New York Times,* June 27, 1969, cited in H. Peter Metzger, *The Atomic Establishment* (New York: Simon & Schuster, 1972), p. 150.

23. Peter Ognibene, "Living with the Bomb: How 'Safe' is Nuclear Pollution?" *Saturday Review* (June 24, 1978): 8–12.

24. B. Shleien, *Health Physics* 18 (1970): 267.

25. "Himalayan Spy Device Said to Pose No Radiation Risk," *Science* 204 (1979): 1180.

26. The Boston Study Group, *The Price of Defense* (New York: Times Books, 1979), p. 69.

27. *Staff Reports to the President's Commission on the Accident at Three Mile Island,* vol. 1 (Washington, D.C.: GPO, October 1979).

28. John C. DeVine, "A Progress Report: Cleaning up TMI," *IEEE Spectrum* 18:3 (March 1981): 44.

29. R. L. Scott, Jr., "Fuel-Melting Incident at the Fermi Reactor on October 5, 1966," *Nuclear Safety* 12:2 (March-April 1971).

30. Peter Gwynne and James Bishop, Jr., "Incident at Brown's Ferry," *Newsweek* (October 27, 1975): 51–52.

31. B. L. Corbett, "Fuel Meltdown at St. Laurent I," *Nuclear Safety* 12:1 (January-February 1971).

32. "Accident at Windscale No. 1 Pile on 10th October, 1957," Cmnd. 302, Her Majesty's Stationery Office, London, November 1957; Horan and Cunningham, "Decontamination," pp. 745–746.

33. E. P. Epler, "The ORR Emergency Cooling Failure," *Nuclear Safety* 11:4 (July-August 1970).

34. George R. Gallagher, "Failure of N Reactor Primary Scram System," *Nuclear Safety* 12:6 (November-December 1971).

35. C. D. Cagle, "Dresden 2 Incident of June 5, 1970," *Nuclear Safety* 12:5 (September-October 1971).

36. W. L. Smalley, "The ERDA Radiological Assistance Program," *Nuclear Safety* 15:5 (September-October 1974).

37. *International Herald Tribune,* January 13, 1981.

38. Steve Fetter and Kosta Tsipis, *Catastrophic Nuclear Radiation Releases,* Program in Science and Technology for International Security, Report No. 5 (Cambridge, Mass.: MIT Department of Physics, 1980), pp. 27–34.

39. William R. Stratton, *A Review of Criticality Ac-*

cidents, Report LA-3611, LANSL, 1967. The accidents mentioned in the text are described in detail in this report.

40. Matt Clark and Peter S. Greenberg, "Riddled by Isotopes," *Newsweek* (March 31, 1977): 49.

41. David Burnham, "8,000 Pounds of Atom Materials Unaccounted for by Plants in U.S.," *New York Times*, August 5, 1977, p. 1.

42. In 1965, 1968, 1971, and 1975, the U.S. government published reports on "Operational Accidents and Radiation Exposure Experience Within the United States Atomic Energy Commission." These publications list events called "radiation exposures and industrial accidents" and implicitly set a level of radiation exposure considered to be unsafe. Official definitions of terms such as "nuclear accident" and "nuclear incident" have been given by the U.S. Army, Navy, and Air Force and are published in *World Armaments and Disarmament: SIPRI Yearbook 1977* (London: Taylor and Francis), pp. 83–85. The Navy definition of "nuclear accident" includes "radioactive contamination" and "public hazard, actual or implied"; these phrases could be used to describe minor incidents. A literal interpretation would classify the mere existence of nuclear weapons as a public hazard. In 1961, the Air Force defined a "nuclear accident" to include "an occurrence from any cause leading to radioactive contamination of sufficient magnitude to affect the community adversely." The Price-Anderson amendment to the Atomic Energy Act (United States Code, vol. 42, sec. 2210) placed a ceiling on third-party liability claims. It does not use the word "accident"; instead it uses the term "substantial nuclear incident." In writing regulations to carry out the amendment, the Atomic Energy Commission, faced with the question of when to waive immunity from public liability, invented the term "Extraordinary Nuclear Occurrence" (ENO). The Nuclear Regulatory Commission staff found that the accident at Three Mile Island was not an ENO because very little radiation exposure resulted from it (*Energy Daily*, January 8, 1980, pp. 3–4).

43. Milton Leitenberg, "Don't Look Now But...," *Commonwealth* 105:18 (September 15, 1978): 586.

44. *Science* 203 (1979): 1179.

45. Davidson Gwatkin and James Grant, Report to the Overseas Development Council, May 1978, cited in Charles Zimmermann and Milton Leitenberg, "Hiroshima Lives On," *Mazingira* 9 (Elmsford, N.Y.: Pergamon Press, 1979), p. 64.

46. Andrew H. Malcolm, "Chinese Disclose That 1976 Quake Was Deadliest in Four Centuries," *New York Times*, June 2, 1977, p. A-16.

47. Editors of *Encyclopaedia Britannica*, *Catastrophe! When Man Loses Control* (New York: Bantam Books, 1979), p. 168.

48. Zhores Medvedev, "Two Decades of Dissidence," *New Scientist* (November 4, 1976): 265. See also John R. Trabalka, L. Dean Eyman, and Stanley I. Auerbach, "Analysis of the 1957–1958 Soviet Nuclear Accident," *Science* 209 (1980): 345–353.

49. Medvedev, *Nuclear Disaster in the Urals* (New York: W. W. Norton, 1979), p. 166.

50. Ibid., pp. 3–18, 129–141, 181–198.

Credits

Lead photograph: Associated Press photograph provided by Wide World Photos.

15-1 Castle Bravo Thermonuclear Test: Hubner and Fry, *Radiation Accident Preparedness*, p. 33. DOE photograph.

15-2 Nuclear Reactor Safety: Prepared from U.S. Nuclear Regulatory Commission, *Reactor Safety Study: An Assessment of Accident Risks in U.S. Commercial Nuclear Power Plants*, Report WASH-1400 (NUREG-75/014), October 1975. See also The Nuclear Energy Policy Study Group, *Nuclear Power Issues and Choices* (Cambridge, Mass.: Ballinger, 1977), pp. 213–242; *Staff Reports to the President's Commission on the Accident at Three Mile Island*, vol. 1.

15-3 Brown's Ferry Nuclear Power Plant: DOE photograph.

15-4 A Possible Maximum Nuclear Accident: Oak Ridge National Laboratory, *Siting of Fuel Reprocessing Plants and Waste Management Facilities*, ORNL-4451 (Oak Ridge, Tenn.: ORNL, July 1970), pp. 8-92, 8-96.

15-5 Types and Frequencies of Nuclear Accidents: Criticality accidents: Stratton, *A Review of Criticality Accidents*. Data on radiation accidents: Hubner and Fry, *Radiation Accident Preparedness*, pp. 6–10. Broken arrows: DOD news release, 1981; "U.S. Nuclear Weapons Accidents," *The Defense Monitor* 10:5; Hanauer, "The Story Behind the Pentagon's Broken Arrows." For publications listing nuclear explosions, see sources listed for Chapter 16. Radiation exposures from the Bravo test are reviewed in T. Kumatori et al., "Follow-up Studies over a 25-Year Period on the Japanese Fishermen Exposed to Radioactive Fallout in 1954," and R. A. Conard, "The 1954 Bikini Atoll Incident: An Update of the Findings in the Marshallese People," in Hubner and Fry, *Radiation Accident Preparedness*, pp. 33–54, 55–58. Vented underground tests: Robert E. Allen, *Summary Information on Accidental Releases of Radioactive Effluent to the Atmosphere from Underground Nuclear Detonations Designed for Containment*, Report

WASH-1183 (Washington, D.C.: GPO, June 1971), p. 27. Major reactor accidents: Anna Gyorgy, *No Nukes: Everyone's Guide to Nuclear Power* (Boston: South End Press, 1979), pp. 117–121. Minor reportable incidents: "Events Resulting in Reactor Shutdown and Their Causes," *Nuclear Safety,* issues for May/June 1981 through July/August 1982. Releases of radioactive material and tritium gas, fires involving actinides: AEC, Division of Operational Safety, *Operational Accidents and Radiation Exposure Experience within the United States Atomic Energy Commission,* Report WASH-1192 (Washington, D.C., 1975); William L. Lennemann, "Management of Radioactive Aqueous Wastes from AEC Fuel-Reprocessing Operations," *Nuclear Safety* 14:5 (September-October 1973): 493.

Chapter 16
Tests of Nuclear Explosives

Notes

1. *SIPRI YEARBOOK 1972, World Armaments and Disarmament* (Stockholm: Almqvist and Wiksell, 1972), p. 425.

2. Ola Dahlman and Hans Israelson, *Monitoring Underground Nuclear Explosions* (Amsterdam: Elsevier, 1977), p. 295.

3. Alice K. Smith, *A Peril and a Hope: the Scientists' Movement in America, 1945–47* (Cambridge, Mass.: MIT Press, 1970); *Arms Control: Readings from Scientific American* (San Francisco: W. H. Freeman, 1973), p. 49.

4. "What It Does and Why," Department of Energy's Nevada Operations Office.

5. Robert Jungk, *Brighter than a Thousand Suns* (New York: Harcourt, Brace, 1958), p. 264.

6. *Arms Control,* p. 40.

7. Howard L. Rosenberg, *Atomic Soldiers* (Boston: Beacon Press, 1980), p. 34.

8. Jungk, *Brighter than a Thousand Suns,* p. 294; Herbert York, *Race to Oblivion* (New York: Simon & Schuster, 1970), pp. 39–46.

9. Jungk, *Brighter than a Thousand Suns,* p. 302.

10. Ibid., p. 308.

11. York, *Race to Oblivion,* pp. 39–46.

12. Jungk, *Brighter than a Thousand Suns,* p. 310.

13. Rosenberg, *Atomic Soldiers,* pp. 88–90.

14. Arnold Kramish, *Atomic Energy in the Soviet Union* (Stanford, Calif.: Stanford University Press, 1959).

15. *SIPRI Yearbook 1972,* p. 391.

16. Dahlman and Israelson, *Monitoring,* p. 2.

17. Linus Pauling, *No More War* (New York: Dodd, Mead, 1958), pp. 73–75.

18. *SIPRI Yearbook 1968/69,* p. 384.

19. *Strategic Survey 1976* (London: IISS); *SIPRI Yearbook 1981,* p. 381.

20. *Strategic Survey 1976,* p. 120.

21. Philip Klass, *Aviation Week and Space Technology* (August 11, 1980): 67–72.

22. Dahlman and Israelson, *Monitoring,* p. 7.

23. *SIPRI Yearbook 1978,* p. 339.

24. Dahlman and Israelson, *Monitoring,* p. 346.

25. "What It Does and Why," Department of Energy's Nevada Operations Office.

26. Dahlman and Israelson, *Monitoring,* p. 320.

27. Ibid., p. 175.

28. Ibid., p. 189.

29. Ibid., p. 332.

30. *SIPRI Yearbook 1978,* pp. 73–82.

31. *SIPRI Yearbook 1980,* p. 198; *SIPRI Yearbook 1981,* p. 130.

32. *Nuclear Weapons,* Report of the Secretary-General of the United Nations (Brookline, Mass.: Autumn Press, 1981).

33. *Strategic Survey 1979,* p. 139.

34. The source cited by SIPRI is Committee on Disarmament document CCD/130, July 30, 1980.

Credits

Lead photograph: U.S. Air Force.

16-1 Nuclear Explosions Announced and Reported: *SIPRI Yearbook,* editions for 1979, 1980, and 1981; Glasstone, *The Effects of Nuclear Weapons,* 1964 printing, pp. 672–681b (nuclear detonations 1945–1963); Dahlman and Israelson, *Monitoring,* pp. 387–405 (explosions 1963–1976); pp. 296–299 (U.S. and Soviet peaceful explosions). Also helpful is DOE, *Announced United States Nuclear Tests, July 1945 through December 1980,* NVO–209 (Rev. 1) (Washington, D.C., January 1981).

16-2 Excavation by Nuclear Explosion: Photograph provided by U.S. Defense Nuclear Agency.

16-3 Army Troop Exercise at the Nevada Test Site: U.S. Army photograph.

16-4 The Partial Test Ban Treaty: ACDA, *Arms Control and Disarmament Agreements,* 1980, pp. 41–43.

16-5 Test Sites and Seismic Stations: *SIPRI Yearbook 1968–69,* p. 244, and editions for 1979, 1980, and 1981; Samuel Glasstone, *The Effects of Nuclear Weapons,* 2d ed. (Washington, D.C.: GPO, 1962), 1964 printing, pp. 671, 672–681b; Dahlman and Israelson, *Monitoring,* pp. 387–405 (explosions 1963–1976); pp. 296–299 (U.S. and Soviet peaceful explosions).

Chapter 17
The Sorry History of Arms Control

Notes

1. Henry D. Smyth, *Atomic Energy for Military Purposes* (Princeton, N.J.: Princeton University Press, 1945).

2. Alice Kimball Smith, *A Peril and a Hope* (Chicago: University of Chicago Press, 1965; also Cambridge, Mass.: MIT Press, 1970).

3. George B. Kistiakowsky, *A Scientist at the White House* (Cambridge, Mass.: Harvard University Press, 1976).

4. Donald G. Brennan, ed., *Arms Control, Disarmament and National Security* (New York: Braziller, 1961).

5. D. H. Frisch, ed., *Arms Reduction* (Twentieth Century Fund, 1961).

6. J. Rotblat, *Scientists in the Quest for Peace* (Cambridge, Mass.: MIT Press, 1972).

7. See, for example, *World Armaments and Disarmament: SIPRI Yearbook 1978,* chap. 11.

8. Herbert F. York, *Race to Oblivion: A Participant's View of the Arms Race* (New York: Simon & Schuster, 1970).

9. Bernard T. Feld, T. Greenwood, George W. Rathjens, and S. Weinberg, eds., *Impact of New Technologies on the Arms Race* (Cambridge, Mass.: MIT Press, 1971).

10. William Epstein and Bernard T. Feld, eds., *New Directions in Disarmament* (New York: Praeger, 1981).

Credits

Lead photograph: Associated Press photograph provided by Wide World Photos.

17-1 Arms Control Agreements Since World War II: ACDA, *Arms Control and Disarmament Agreements* (Washington, D.C.: GPO, 1980).

17-2 The SALT I Agreements: ACDA, *Arms Control and Disarmament Agreements,* 1980, pp. 139–142, 150–152.

Chapter 18
Prospects for International Arms Control

Note

1. Colin Gray and Keith Payne, "Victory Is Possible," *Foreign Policy* 39 (Summer 1980): 14–27.

Credits

Lead photograph: Courtesy of ACDA.

18-1 What Are the Russians Up To?: Written by Bernard T. Feld.

18-2 The SALT II Treaty: ACDA, *Arms Control and Disarmament Agreements,* 1980, pp. 201–238.

Chapter 19
Nuclear Weapons Proliferation

Notes

1. Three chronicles of the United States atomic bomb program are Henry D. Smyth, *Atomic Energy for Military Purposes* (Princeton, N.J.: Princeton University Press, 1945); Robert Jungk, *Brighter than a Thousand Suns* (New York: Harcourt, Brace, 1958); and Alice K. Smith, *A Peril and a Hope* (Cambridge, Mass.: MIT Press, 1970).

2. Arnold Kramish, *Atomic Energy in the Soviet Union* (Stanford, Calif.: Stanford University Press, 1959).

3. Margaret Gowing, *Independence and Deterrence: Britain and Atomic Energy, 1945–1952* (London: Macmillan, 1974); R. N. Rosecrance, *The Dispersion of Nuclear Weapons* (New York: Columbia University Press, 1964), chaps. 2–6.

4. Lawrence Scheinman, *Atomic Energy Policy in France under the Fourth Republic* (Princeton, N.J.: Princeton University Press, 1965); Ciro Zoppo, "France as a Nuclear Power," in R. N. Rosecrance, *The Dispersion of Nuclear Weapons* (New York: Columbia University Press, 1964), chap. 7.

5. William L. Ryan and Sam Summerlin, *The China Cloud* (Boston: Little, Brown, 1968); Alice Langley Haeih, "Communist China and Nuclear Force," in Rosecrance, *The Dispersion of Nuclear Weapons,* chap. 8.

6. Nuclear Energy Policy Study Group, *Nuclear Power Issues and Choices* (Cambridge, Mass.: Ballinger, 1977), pp. 305–306; Albert Wohlstetter et al., *Moving toward Life in a Nuclear Armed Crowd* (Los Angeles: Pan Heuristics, 1976), pp. 25–26.

7. Wohlstetter, *Moving toward Life,* p. 26; *Nuclear Power Issues and Choices,* p. 285; Leonard Beaton, *Must the Bomb Spread?* (Harmondsworth, England: Penguin Books, 1966), p. 38; John S. Foster, Jr., "Nuclear Weapons," in *Encyclopedia Americana* (Danbury, Conn.: Grolier, 1981) vol. 20, p. 521.

8. "Denaturing is no longer considered effective": Leonard Beaton, *Must the Bomb Spread?,* p. 98, quoting Arnold Kramish, *The Peaceful Atom in Foreign Policy* (New York: Harper & Row, 1963), p. 25. See also the early technical discussion in Arnold Kramish, "The Emergent Genie," in Rosecrance, *The Dispersion of Nuclear Weapons,* chap. 11. The report of the International Fuel Cycle Evaluation was published in Vienna by the IAEA, February 1980.

9. Heavy-water plants have been built in at least eight countries; see *World Armaments and Disarmament: SIPRI Yearbook 1978* (London: Taylor and Francis, 1978), pp. 315–316.

10. Mohammed Heikal, *The Road to Ramadon*

(New York: Ballantine Books, 1975), pp. 70–71, cited in Lewis A. Dunn, *Controlling the Bomb: Nuclear Proliferation in the 1980's* (New Haven, Conn.: Yale University Press, 1982), p. 15.

11. *Nuclear Power Issues and Choices,* chap. 10; Theodore Taylor and Mason Willrich, *Nuclear Theft: Risks and Safeguards* (Cambridge, Mass.: Ballinger, 1974).

12. *Nuclear Power Issues and Choices,* chap. 2, in particular table 2-3 on p. 81.

13. *Nuclear Engineering International* occasionally publishes a chart of the "World Nuclear Fuel Cycle" that lists known operating and planned nuclear fuel cycle facilities: mines, enrichment plants, fuel processing and reprocessing plants. The most recent chart appeared in the November 1979 issue. Wohlstetter, *Moving toward Life,* lists enrichment plants on p. 267; *SIPRI Yearbook 1978* has a list on p. 30.

14. Harvey W. Graves, Jr., *Nuclear Fuel Management* (New York: John Wiley, 1979), pp. 28–33; Colin Norman, "Weapon Builders Eye Civilian Reactor Fuel," *Science* 214 (October 1981): 307–308.

15. *Nuclear Power Issues and Choices,* p. 285.

16. *Nuclear Engineering International* (November 1979), pp. 49–50; Wohlstetter, *Moving toward Life,* pp. 265–266; *SIPRI Yearbook 1978,* pp. 17, 18–19; *SIPRI Yearbook 1980,* p. 321.

17. *SIPRI Yearbook 1978,* pp. 17, 21–25; *SIPRI Yearbook 1980,* p. 328; *Nuclear Engineering International,* July 1981 supplement, pp. 34–35.

18. Margaret Gowing, *Independence and Deterrence: Britain and Atomic Energy, 1945–1952* (London: Macmillan, 1974), pp. 105–108.

19. ACDA, *Arms Control and Disarmament Agreements* (Washington, D.C.: GPO, 1980), pp. 5–6; Smith, *A Peril and a Hope,* chap. 11.

20. Beaton, *Must the Bomb Spread?,* pp. 87–90: Michael J. Brenner, *Nuclear Power and Non-Proliferation* (Cambridge, England: Cambridge University Press, 1981), p. 79.

21. Beaton, *Must the Bomb Spread?,* pp. 34–35.

22. Beaton gives a table on pp. 91–92 of *Must the Bomb Spread?* and lists others on p. 89. See also Wohlstetter, *Moving toward Life,* pp. 257–261; *Directory of Nuclear Reactors, Volume II: Research, Test and Experimental Reactors* (Vienna: IAEA, 1959).

23. Beaton, *Must the Bomb Spread?,* pp. 104–105.

24. ACDA, *Arms Control and Disarmament Agreements,* p. 83.

25. Ibid., pp. 85–87.

26. Ibid., p. 88: "Safeguards agreements required by the NPT have entered into force for 68 countries. For 44 nonnuclear-weapon states party to the treaty, the relevant safeguards agreements have not yet entered into force; however, none of these states has significant nuclear activities."

27. *SIPRI Yearbook 1978,* p. 29: "The Soviet Union has always strictly controlled the utilization of nuclear energy within Eastern Europe. It takes complete responsibility for supplying manufactured fuel to other members of the Warsaw Treaty Organization (WTO), and the irradiated fuel is returned; fuel cycle facilities do not exist on the territory of other WTO countries."

28. ACDA, *Arms Control and Disarmament Agreements,* p. 93.

29. A listing of bilateral agreements between supplier and user countries is given in *SIPRI Yearbook 1977,* pp. 40–41; *SIPRI Yearbook 1978* gives sponsorship of enrichment, reprocessing, and breeder projects, which are in many cases operated under international agreements.

30. *SIPRI Yearbook 1981,* pp. 315–316; *SIPRI Yearbook 1978,* pp. 488–489.

31. See Wohlstetter, *Moving toward Life,* chap. 1, for an extensive analysis of the factors affecting warning time.

32. Beaton, *Must the Bomb Spread?,* pp. 71–77, gives a brief early history of the Indian nuclear program.

33. Brenner, *Nuclear Power and Non-Proliferation,* chap. 2.

34. Gerard Smith and George Rathjens, "Reassessing Nuclear Nonproliferation Policy," *Foreign Affairs* (Spring 1981): 875–894, cite two articles on the 1978 Act: Frederick Williams, "The United States and Nonproliferation," *International Security* (Fall 1978), and Ronald Bettauer, "The Nuclear Nonproliferation Act of 1978," *Law and Policy in International Business* (1978): 1105–1180.

35. Wohlstetter, *Moving toward Life,* p. 143.

36. Beaton, *Must the Bomb Spread?,* pp. 80–81.

37. John R. Redick, "The Tlatelolco Regime and Nonproliferation," in George H. Quester, *Nuclear Proliferation: Breaking the Chain* (Madison, Wis.: University of Wisconsin Press, 1981), pp. 103–113; Dunn, *Controlling the Bomb,* pp. 131–132.

38. Dunn, *Controlling the Bomb,* p. 49.

39. Ibid., pp. 48–53.

40. Ibid., p. 51.

41. Ibid., pp. 53–56.

42. Ibid., pp. 44–48.

43. Dunn, *Controlling the Bomb,* pp. 56–59.

Credits

Lead photograph: Courtesy of the French Embassy, Washington, D.C.

19-1 The World's Supply of Plutonium: Computed from power reactor listing in *Nuclear Engi-*

neering International, July Supplement, 1981. See also *Nuclear Power Issues and Choices,* pp. 279, 284–285.

19-2 World Nuclear Facilities and **19-3 European Nuclear Facilities:** Signers of the NPT: *SIPRI Yearbook 1981,* p. 303. First nuclear research reactors: Wohlstetter, *Moving toward Life,* pp. 257–261. Power reactors: *SIPRI Yearbook 1981,* p. 315. Breeder reactors: *Nuclear Engineering International,* July Supplement, 1981, p. 34. Enrichment and reprocessing facilities: Wohlstetter, *Moving toward Life,* pp. 265–267; "World Nuclear Fuel Cycle," *Nuclear Engineering International,* November 1979; Albert Carnesale, "Nuclear Power and Nuclear Proliferation," in Albert Carnesale et al., *Options for U.S. Energy Policy* (San Francisco: Institute for Contemporary Studies, 1977), p. 66. See also news stories in *Nuclear Engineering International.*

19-4 Atoms for Peace: Brenner, *Nuclear Power and Non-Proliferation,* pp. 252–258.

19-5 The Nonproliferation Treaty: ACDA, *Arms Control and Disarmament Agreements,* pp. 90–94.

19-6 Unsafeguarded Nuclear Facilities: *SIPRI Yearbook 1981,* p. 310.

Chapter 20
Uranium

Notes

1. More precisely, uranium *was* the last element in the table until the addition of the laboratory-made transuranium elements, beginning with neptunium and plutonium (elements 93 and 94) in 1940.

2. Richard G. Hewlett and Oscar E. Anderson, Jr., *The New World, 1939–1945,* vol. 1 of an official history of the United States Atomic Energy Commission (University Park, Pa.: Pennsylvania State University Press, 1962), p. 285.

3. Richard G. Hewlett and Francis Duncan, *Atomic Shield, 1947–1952,* vol. 2. of an official history of the United States Atomic Energy Commission (University Park, Pa.: Pennsylvania State University Press, 1969), p. 147.

4. Ronald W. Walters, "U.S. Policy and Nuclear Proliferation in South Africa," in *U.S. Military Involvement in South Africa* (Boston: South End Press, 1978), chap. 9, pp. 187–188.

5. Frank G. Dawson, *Nuclear Power: Development and Management of a Technology* (Seattle: University of Washington Press, 1976), p. 162. These data are taken from several annual reports of the Atomic Energy Commission.

6. June H. Taylor and Michael D. Yokell, *Yellowcake: The International Uranium Cartel* (New York: Pergamon Press, 1979), p. 33.

7. Dawson, *Nuclear Power,* p. 163.

8. In 1980, U.S. nuclear power plants generated 251 billion kilowatt-hours of electricity, while those of seventeen other noncommunist nations generated about 353 billion; thus U.S. nuclear production was 41.6 percent of the total. The figures are from the Energy Information Administration's 1980 Annual Report to Congress, vol. 2, p. 173.

9. Thomas L. Neff and Henry D. Jacoby, "World Uranium: Softening Markets and Rising Security," *Technology Review* (January 1981): 19–30.

10. Taylor and Yokell, *Yellowcake,* chap. 8. See also Hugh C. McIntyre, *Uranium, Nuclear Power, and Canada-U.S. Energy Relations* (Montreal and Washington: Canadian-American Committee, 1978), pp. 16–17.

11. *New York Times,* June 17, 1977, p. 1.

12. Taylor and Yokell, *Yellowcake,* p. 214.

13. Neff and Jacoby, "World Uranium," p. 20.

14. The figures on uranium production are taken from papers by J. Fred Facer given at the uranium industry seminars held by the Grand Junction, Colo., DOE office. The papers were entitled "Trends in Uranium Production" and "Uranium Production" and were presented at the seminars held in October 1978 and October 1979, respectively. A preliminary report from the DOE indicates that total production increased substantially in 1980, reaching a new record level at around 21,000 tons.

15. *Petroleum Industry Involvement in Alternative Sources of Energy,* prepared for the Committee on Energy and Natural Resources, U.S. Senate, September 1977, pp. 8–9.

16. See the papers by Robert J. Meehan and Donald L. Hetland in the uranium industry seminar held by the Grand Junction, Colo., DOE office in 1979. A table summarizing reserve and resource estimates by the DOE is given on p. 154. "Forward costs" resemble marginal costs and do not represent prices.

17. The NAS study is entitled "Problems of the U.S. Uranium Resources and Supply to the Year 2010." It is the report of the Uranium Resources subpanel to the Committee on Nuclear and Alternative Energy Sources (CONAES) of the NAS, issued in 1978.

18. Estimates both slightly lower and much higher than 6,000 tons have been published. The figure of 6,000 tons is obtained as follows: A large reactor requires about 100 tons of enriched uranium as fuel, and one-third of this is replaced each year. Thus during thirty years of operation, some 1,000 tons of uranium fuel are used. At least six tons of natural uranium at 0.7 percent U-235 are needed in order to obtain one ton of uranium enriched to 3 percent U-235, assuming that 0.2 percent is the U-235 content of the "tails" discarded after enrichment. Thus

the total requirement of the reactor will be at least $6 \times 1,000$ tons. When allowances are made for losses during processing of the uranium, it seems likely that this estimate errs on the low side.

19. J. Fred Facer, paper given at the uranium industry seminar in Grand Junction, Colo., October 1979, p. 196.

20. Arell S. Schurgin and Thomas G. Hollocher, "Radiation-Induced Lung Cancers Among Uranium Miners," in *The Nuclear Fuel Cycle* (Cambridge, Mass.: Union of Concerned Scientists, 1975), chap. 2, p. 9.

21. Ibid., pp. 11, 30–31.

22. H. Peter Metzger, *The Atomic Establishment* (New York: Simon & Schuster, 1972), chap. 4, especially sec. 3–6 and 14.

23. The quote is from NRC Commissioner Victor Gilinsky. See U.S. House of Representatives, *Uranium Mill Tailings Control Act of 1978,* hearings before the Committee on Interstate and Foreign Commerce, Subcommittee on Energy and Power, June 19, 20, and August 2, 1978, p. 228. In his statement Gilinsky makes an unusual acknowledgment of the role of citizens' "public interest groups" in bringing the problem to light.

24. Metzger, *The Atomic Establishment,* p. 168.

25. Ibid., pp. 171–194.

26. DOE, *DOE Research and Development and Field Facilities* (Washington, D.C., 1979), pp. V-5–V-10.

27. DOE, *United States Gaseous Diffusion Program for Uranium Enrichment* (Washington, D.C., 1978), p. 12.

28. Ralph Lapp, *The Weapons Culture* (New York: W. W. Norton, 1968), p. 84.

29. DOE, *Annual Report to Congress,* January 1981, vol. 1, p. 9-4.

30. Taylor and Yokell, *Yellowcake,* p. 15.

31. In 1977, Babcock and Wilcox was taken over by the J. Ray McDermott Company after a spectacular and controversial stock market battle. See, for example, Anna Gyorgy et al., *No Nukes: Everyone's Guide to Nuclear Power* (Boston: South End Press, 1979), pp. 156–157, and the references cited there.

Credits

Lead photograph: DOE.

20-1 United States Uranium Production, Exports, and Imports: DOE, Energy Information Administration, *1980 Annual Report to Congress,* vol. 2, p. 180.

20-2 Uranium Prices in the U.S., 1950–80: Hugh C. McIntyre, *Uranium, Nuclear Power and Canada-U.S. Energy Relations* (Montreal and Wash-

ington, D.C.: Canadian-American Committee, 1978), p. 14; the graph has been updated from trade journals.

20-3 Uranium Mines and Mills in the United States: J. Fred Facer, *Trends in Uranium Production,* 1978, and *Uranium Production,* 1979.

20-4 Uranium Mill: DOE photograph.

20-5 Disaster at Church Rock: See Mark Pinksy, "New Mexico Spill Ruins a River," *Critical Mass Journal* (December 1979); Allan Richards, "Disaster at Church Rock: The Untold Story, *Sierra* (November/December 1980): 30.

20-6 Uranium-Enrichment Processes: Prepared by Jack Dennis using Harvey W. Graves, Jr., *Nuclear Fuel Management* (New York: John Wiley, 1979), pp. 28–33; Colin Norman, "Weapon Builders Eye Civilian Reactor Fuel," *Science* 214 (October 1981): 307–308. Photographs provided by DOE.

20-7 Nuclear South Africa: For a discussion of the 1977 aborted weapons tests see Walters, "U.S. Policy and Nuclear Proliferation in South Africa," pp. 172–176. The presumed 1979 test was described in *Science* (November 30, 1979): 1051–1052, in a brief report that stresses ambiguities in the evidence; a later and fuller account is given by Dan Smith in *South Africa's Nuclear Capability* (London: World Campaign Against Military and Nuclear Collaboration with South Africa, 1980), pp. 9–11. The possible nuclear explosion detected in December 1980 took place on the 16th. On February 19, 1981, the Johannesburg *Star* reported that U.S. officials "strongly" suspected South Africa was carrying out a full-scale nuclear testing program, and an official denial was issued from Pretoria. Also on February 19, 1981, a story by Walter Sullivan in the *New York Times* announced a Defense Department conclusion that the December 1980 flash was not a nuclear explosion, while the department reaffirmed its earlier conclusion that the September 1979 event *was* a nuclear test.

Chapter 21
Nuclear Power

Credits

Lead photograph: Courtesy of the U.S. Nuclear Regulatory Commission.

21-2 Structure of a Nuclear Power Reactor: Anthony V. Nero, *A Guidebook to Nuclear Reactors* (Berkeley, Calif.: University of California Press, 1979), pp. 79, 82; Graves, *Nuclear Fuel Management,* pp. 19–20.

21-3 Reactor Pressure Vessel: Duke Power Company photograph.

21-4 Reactor Fuel Loading: Northeast Utilities photograph.

21-5 Flow Schemes for Light Water Nuclear Power Reactors: Drawn after the Nuclear Energy Policy Study Group, *Nuclear Power Issues and Choices* (Cambridge, Mass.: Ballinger, 1977), pp. 394–395.

21-6 Characteristics of Light Water Reactors: Nero, *A Guidebook,* pp. 81, 97. Harvey W. Graves, Jr., *Nuclear Fuel Management* (New York: John Wiley, 1979), app. C.

21-7 Fuel Cycles for Commercial Power Reactors: Graves, *Nuclear Fuel Management,* pp. 24–27. Quantities calculated from Carl M. Malbrain, Richard K. Lester, and John M. Deutch, *Analytical Approximations for the Long-Term Decay Behavior of Spent Fuel and High-Level Waste,* Working Paper MIT-EL 81-022WP (Cambridge, Mass.: MIT Energy Laboratory, May 1981).

21-8 Breeder Reactors: Two survey articles on breeder reactors have appeared in the pages of *Scientific American:* Glenn T. Seaborg and Justin L. Bloom, "Fast Breeder Reactors," *Scientific American* 223:5 (November 1970): 13–21; Alvin M. Weinberg, "Breeder Reactors," *Scientific American* 202:1 (January 1960): 82–94. Other data for this box are from Graves, *Nuclear Fuel Management,* chap. 13 and app. C.

21-9 Residual Power in a Nuclear Reactor: Graves, *Nuclear Fuel Management,* p. 36.

21-10 Nuclear Power Control Room: Photograph by Rochester Gas and Electric Company.

21-11 Nuclear Power Reactors in the United States: *Nuclear Safety* 20 (November-December 1981): 798–801; *Nuclear Engineering International,* July Supplement, 1981, pp. 28–33; Anna Gyorgy, *No Nukes* (Boston: South End Press, 1979), pp. 391–458.

Chapter 22
Energy Economics

Notes

1. The U.S. population in 1950 was 152 million (*Statistical Abstract of the U.S.: 1976,* U.S. Department of Commerce), and in 1980 it was 221 million (*New York Times,* May, 26, 1981).

2. Energy Information Administration, *1980 Annual Report to Congress* (Washington, D.C.: DOE, April 1981).

3. M. H. Ross and R. H. Williams, *Our Energy: Regaining Control* (New York: McGraw-Hill, 1981), Fig. 2.4.

4. AEC, *Environmental Statement: Liquid Metal Fast Breeder Reactor Program,* WASH-1535 (Washington, D.C.: GPO, December 1974).

5. Charles Komanoff, *Power Plant Cost Escalation:*

Nuclear and Coal Capital Costs, Regulation, and Economics (New York: Komanoff Energy Associates, 1981), p. 281.

6. Ibid., chap. 7.

7. Ibid., p. 36. Komanoff's projected costs for new 1988 plants have the following components:

Life-Cycle Generating Costs (1979 cents per kWhr)	*Nuclear*	*Coal*
Capital cost fixed charges	2.86	1.34
Decommissioning fixed charges	0.21	
Fuel	1.09	1.96
Operating and maintenance	0.62	0.62
Total	4.78	3.92

8. Ross and Williams, *Our Energy,* chap. 8.

9. *Building a Sustainable Future,* report prepared by the Solar Energy Research Institute, Committee Print, Committee on Energy and Commerce, U.S. House of Representatives, April 1981.

10. *Electric Powerplant Cancellations and Delays,* Report to the U.S. Congress by the Comptroller General, December 1980.

11. H. W. Kendall and S. J. Nadis, eds., *Energy Strategies: Toward a Solar Future,* Union of Concerned Scientists (Cambridge, Mass.: Ballinger, 1980).

12. R. H. Williams, "Industrial Cogeneration," *Annual Review of Energy* (1978): 313–356.

13. G. R. Thompson, *Hydroelectric Power in the USA: Evolving to Meet New Needs,* Report PU/CEES 115, Center for Energy and Environmental Studies (Princeton, N.J.: Princeton University, June 1981).

14. G. R. Thompson, *The Prospects for Wind and Wave Power in North America,* Report PU/CEES 117, Center for Energy and Environmental Studies (Princeton, N.J.: Princeton University, June 1981).

15. D. Redfield, *Photovoltaics: An Overview,* Report of RCA Laboratories (Princeton, N.J., 1980).

16. J. Hansen et al., "Climate Impact of Increasing Atmospheric Carbon Dioxide," *Science* 213 (August 28, 1981): 957–966.

17. R. B. Hubbard and G. C. Minor, eds., *The Risks of Nuclear Power Reactors* (Cambridge, Mass.: Union of Concerned Scientists, 1977).

18. K. Kehoe, *Unavailable at Any Price* (Washington, D.C.: U.S. Environmental Policy Center, 1980).

Credits

Lead photograph: Lee Porter Butler, Architect, San Francisco.

22-1 Growth of United States Energy Consumption: DOE, Energy Information Administration,

1980 Annual Report to Congress, vol. 2 (Washington, D.C., April 1981).

22-2 U.S. Energy Expenditures: Robert Williams, Center for Energy and Environmental Studies, Princeton University, March 1981.

22-3 U.S. Energy Plant Investment: M. H. Ross and R. H. Williams, *Our Energy,* p. 45.

22-4 United States Energy Flow, 1980: Data from *Monthly Energy Review* (Washington, D.C.: DOE, April 1981).

22-5 Sources of Electrical Energy Production: DOE, *Monthly Energy Review,* March 1981.

22-6 Status of United States Nuclear Power Plants: DOE, *Monthly Energy Review,* April 1981.

22-7 AEC Projection of Electricity Consumption: Data from AEC, *Proposed Final Environmental Statement: Liquid Metal Fast Breeder Reactor Program,* December 1974.

22-8 Generating Costs for Nuclear and Coal Plants: Data from *AIF 1979 Economic Survey* (Washington, D.C.: Atomic Industrial Forum, February 1981).

Chapter 23
The Future in Our Hands

Credits

Lead photograph: L. M. Jendrzejczyk.

23-1 The Price of Strategic Superiority: Ronald T. Pretty, ed., *Jane's Weapon Systems, 1981–82* (London: Jane's Publishing Company, 1981); U.S. Congress, *Fiscal Year 1982 Arms Control Impact Statements* (Washington, D.C.: February 1981); DOD, *Annual Reports.*

Chapter 24
A Little Physics

Credits

Lead drawing: Robert C. Weast, *Handbook of Chemistry and Physics* (Cleveland: The Chemical Rubber Company, 1970), back coverleaf.

24-1 The Scale of Energy: The Boston Study Group, *The Price of Defense* (New York: Times Books, 1979), p. 64; S. Glasstone and J. Dolan, *The Effects of Nuclear Weapons* (Washington, D.C.: GPO, 1977), p. 13; S. S. Penner, *Nuclear Energy and Energy Policies* (Reading, Mass.: Addison-Wesley, 1976), p. xxxi.

24-3 The Binding Energy of Nuclei: Robley D. Evans, *The Atomic Nucleus* (New York: McGraw-Hill, 1955), p. 299.

24-7 The Chart of the Nuclides: Robert C. Weast, *Handbook of Chemistry and Physics,* 1970, pp. B-245–B-541.

Chapter 25
Unstable Atoms

Credits

Lead photograph: Science Museum, London.

25-5, 25-9, 25-7, 25-6, and **25-8:** Reproduced from *The Collected Papers of Lord Rutherford of Nelson,* vol. 1 (London: Allen and Unwin, 1962), pp. 62, 224, 551, 805, and 883.

Chapter 26
Toward Fission and Fusion

Credits

Lead photograph: Courtesy of Argonne National Laboratory.

26-1 Walton, Rutherford, Cockroft: Photograph courtesy of Argonne National Laboratory.

26-2 Disintegration of Nitrogen: Photograph due to P. M. S. Blackett, from the Science Museum, London.

26-3 The Van de Graaff Generator: Reproduced from R. J. Van de Graaff, K. T. Compton, and L. C. Van Atta, *Physical Review* 43 (1933): 152.

26-4 The Cyclotron: Reproduced from E. O. Lawrence and M. S. Livingston, *Physical Review* 40 (1932): 23.

Index

Cancer, 122, 223, 225, 228, 229,
    235, 238, 240, 241, 246,
    248, 250, 255–56, 287,
    288, 290, 295
    following accidental exposure
      to toxic material, 250
    following nuclear attack, inci-
      dence of, 12, 17, 104,
      105, 109, 115, 120, 121,
      124, 154, 156
    following nuclear reactor acci-
      dent, 290
    leukemia, *see* Leukemia
    studies of radiation exposure
      and incidence of, 251–54
    uranium mining and, 376–77
CANDU nuclear reactor, 391
Carbon, 398, 460, 482, 486, 487,
    489, 491, 492
Carbon dioxide, 103, 414, 472,
    482
Carbon-14, 241–42, 248–49,
    250, 251, 314, 459–60
Carbon-14 oxide, 460
Carnegie, Andrew, 4
Carnegie Endowment for Peace,
    4
Carnegie Institute, 24, 491, 492
    Department of Terrestrial Mag-
      netism, 485
Carribean region, 320, 363, 364
Carter, Jimmy, 75, 185, 190,
    275, 276, 349, 362, 398,
    418
    SALT II Treaty and, 330, 334,
      335, 337, 339
Carter administration, 273, 279,
    337
Cataracts, 233
Catherine the Great, 4
Cathode-ray tubes, 465, 466
Catholic Church, 429
CB radio, 12
Center for Defense Information,
    442
Center for Law and Social Policy,
    442
Central America, 320, 363, 364
Central Intelligence Agency
    (CIA), 299–300
Central nervous system, 105,
    228, 229, 232
Centrifuge process for uranium
    enrichment, 380, 381, 382

CEP, *see* Circular Error Probable
Cesium, 297–98, 389
Cesium-137, 109, 124, 249, 251,
    263, 460
Chadwick, James, 452, 483, 486
Chain reaction, nuclear, 21, 22,
    23, 197, 202, 349, 379,
    388–90, 394, 452, 456,
    480, 490–93
    Fermi and, 24, 26, 480,
      491–93
Charles II, King of England, 2
"Charlottesville: a Fictional Ac-
    count," 10–17
Chart of the nuclides, 458–60
Cherokee nuclear test, 197
China, 40, 41, 121, 154, 334,
    335, 363
    detection of testing by, 289
    nuclear explosions by, 305
    as nuclear power, 8, 158, 160,
      164, 165, 181, 187, 306,
      316, 345, 346
    nuclear test site, 311
    testing of nuclear explosives
      by, 303, 306, 314
    uranium enrichment plant in,
      350, 352–54
Chlorine, 482, 483
Chorioretinitis, 240
Christmas Island, 310, 313
Chromosomes, damage to, *see*
    Genetic damage
Church Rock, New Mexico, 378
Churchill, Winston, 6, 34–35, 41
CIA, *see* Central Intelligence
    Agency
Cigarette smoking, 247, 250
Circular Error Probable (CEP),
    132, 183
Circulatory system, 100
Cities:
    Ballistic Missile Defense for, 187
    effect of nuclear explosion on,
      93–96, 131–32
    casualties, estimated, 112
    Detroit, 101, 103, 105
    hospital resources, 113–14
    medical implications, 100,
      102–103, 104, 108,
      110–12
    Philadelphia, 110–11
    social consequences,
      124–25

siting of nuclear power plants
    near, 386
Citizens' Energy Project, 442
Civil targets, 131–32
    Ballistic Missile Defense for,
      187
Clark, William C., 280
Clayton, William L., 37
Cleft palate, 240
Clergy and Laity Concerned, 442
Climatic effects of nuclear war,
    121, 122
Clinch River breeder reactor,
    397, 401
Clinton Laboratories, Oak Ridge,
    27, 28, 40–41
Cloots, Baron de, 2
Cloud chamber experiments,
    483, 486–87
Cloud of a nuclear explosion, *see*
    Mushroom cloud
Clubfeet, 240
Coal, 245, 407, 409, 410–11,
    412, 414
    see also Fossil fuels
Coalition for a New Foreign and
    Military Policy, 442
Cobalt, 484
Cobalt-60, 268, 296, 460
Cobra Dane radar, 172
Cockroft, John, 482, 484–85
Cogeneration, 413
Cold war, 6–7, 323
Coloboma, 240
Colombia River, 295
Colorado, 307, 369, 373, 374,
    378–79
Colorado Department of Health,
    377, 379
Columbia space shuttle, 189
Columbia University, 21, 23, 24,
    25, 486, 491, 492
Coma, 232
Combustion Engineering Com-
    pany, 384
Commager, Henry Steele, 1–7
Committee on Atomic Energy,
    Federation of American
    Scientists, 322
Committee on Postwar Policy,
    33
Commonwealth Edison Com-
    pany, 294
Common Cause, 442

Polonium, 458, 466, 470, 473, 477, 486
Polonium-210, 243, 246, 247
Polonium-214, 246
Polonium-218, 246
Portsmouth, Ohio uranium enrichment plant, 208, 379, 380, 381, 382, 384
Poseidon missiles, 139, 147, 180
Poseidon submarine, 186
Positron, 224, 457, 458, 459, 486–87, 489
Potassium, 483, 484
Potassium-40, 243, 247
Potsdam conference, 40, 41–42
Pounds per square inch (psi), 89, 101
Precipitation, *see* Weather conditions
Preemptive strike, *see* First strike
Preiswerk, Peter, 488
Presidential Directive 58 (P.D. 58), 178
Presidential Directive 59 (P.D. 59), 149–50, 178, 337, 338
President of the United States, 174–75, 278
Price-Anderson Act, 72, 414
Priestley, Joseph, 2
Princeton University, 21, 23, 25, 57, 61, 202, 484, 491
conference on radioactive waste disposal, 272
Project Matterhorn-B, 57
Progressive, 445
Project Salt Vault, 273
Project Vista, 64
Proliferation of nuclear weapons, 189, 340, 344–65, 383, 414
agreements and safeguards, 360–61, 364
beginning of a nonproliferation regime, 354–60
conclusion, 363–64
defined, 135, 345
Eisenhower "Atoms for Peace" speech, 70, 347, 355–56, 357
elements necessary to make a bomb, 347–49
knowledge and technology, 347

materials, 347–49
motivation, 349
horizontal, 135, 345
"nuclear power," definition of, 346–47
overview of countries with nuclear technology, 350–53
prospects for, 362–63
reprocessing facilities and, 275, 344, 351, 354, 361–62, 364
sources of fissile material, 349–54
spent fuel from nuclear reactors and, 344, 347–49, 351, 354, 362, 387, 398, 414
vertical, 135
worldwide nuclear facilities, 350–53
see also Nuclear arms control talks and treaties; nuclear arms race
Promethium, 450
Promoting Enduring Peace, 445
"Prospectus on Nucleonics," 33, 34, 36, 40
Protactinium, 389
Protest actions in U.S., chronology of:
anti-nuclear power, 437–40
disarmament, 432–37
Protons, 199, 448, 452, 454, 457, 458, 459, 482–89 *passim*
Psi, *see* Pounds per square inch
Public Citizen, 445
Public Citizens Health Research Group, 250
Public health perspective on radiation, *see* Radiation, ionizing, public health and
Public Interest Research Group, 445
Public policy, shaping responsible, 416–46
anti-nuclear power actions in the U.S., 437–40
disarmament actions in the U.S., 432–37
films about nuclear war, 440–42
national organizations active on nuclear issues, 442–46

sampling of opinions, 421–32
Public Utilities Regulatory Power Act of 1978, 413
Pugwash Conferences on Science and World Affairs, 324
Pugwash Movement, 324, 325
Pyramid Films, 440

Quads (energy unit), 453
Quanta, 454
Quesada, General Elwood R., 64

Rabi, Isidor I., 54, 58
Rabinowitch, Eugene, 33, 36, 39, 40, 54, 322
Radar:
for control of nuclear weapons, 170, 172–77
in ballistic missile defense, 187
Radford, E. P., 253
Radiation, ionizing, 11–12, 13–15, 17, 72, 85–86, 100, 130, 131, 132, 204, 222–36, 307
biological effects, 222–26, 230–31, 233, 234–35, 239–40, 241, 251–54
dental use, 242
discoveries about, 241, 464–78, 486–88
alpha particles and the nuclear atoms, 474–76, 487
alpha rays and energy, 470–73
radioactive elements and isotopes, 476–78, 487
summary, 478
measurement of, 227–28
medical effects of, 12, 15, 17, 86, 92–93, 100, 103–109, 114, 154, 155, 156, 226–34, 239–40, 251–54
cancer, *see* Cancer
early victims of radiation injury, 241
genetic damage, 84, 105, 121, 154, 223, 226, 228, 234–35, 240, 254, 256, 257
radiation sickness, *see* Radiation sickness
on unborn children, 121, 228, 232, 240, 257